DOMESDAY BOOK

Suffolk

History from the Sources

DOMESDAY BOOK

A Survey of the Counties of England

LIBER   DE   WINTONIA

Compiled by direction of

KING   WILLIAM   I

Winchester
1086

DOMESDAY BOOK

general editor

JOHN MORRIS

34

Suffolk

edited by

Alex Rumble

from a draft translation prepared by
Marian Hepplestone, Barbara Hodge, Margaret Jones,
Judy Plaister, Catherine Coutts, Faith Bowers and Elizabeth Teague

(Part Two)

PHILLIMORE
Chichester
1986

1986
Published by
PHILLIMORE & CO. LTD.
London and Chichester
Head Office: Shopwyke Hall,
Chichester, Sussex, England

ISBN 0 85033 480 2 (case)
ISBN 0 85033 481 0 (limp)

*Printed in Great Britain by
Titus Wilson & Son Ltd.,
Kendal*

SUFFOLK

(Part One)
Introduction

The Domesday Survey of Suffolk
(to Landholder XV, Archbishop Lanfranc)

(Part Two)

The Domesday Survey of Suffolk
(Landholder XVI, the Bishop of Bayeux to Holdings Elsewhere)
Bibliography and Abbreviations
Notes
Appendices
Index of Persons
Index of Places
Maps and Map Keys
Systems of Reference
Technical Terms

TRÆ baiocenſis epi . Riſebruge . H̃ In hauer hella . I . liƀ hõ . xx . IIII.
ac̄ . 7 dim̃ . car̃ . & ual& . III . ſol . ħ ten̄ . Tihell͗ de epõ . ſuus antec͗ . t . r . e.
c̄m̃d . ſc̄s . eadm̃ . vi . forisfactuͬas.

/ . H̃ . DE CARLEFORDA . In ſekeforda ten̄ Aluric͗ fil͗ Wluiet
com̃d heroldi . t . r . e . II . car̃ tr̃æ . ꝑ . man̄ . Sẽp . IIII . uilli . Tc̄ . xiii . borɗ.
m̊ . xv . Sẽp in dn̄io . II . car̃ tc̄ia poteſt fieri . & . hom̄ . III . car̃ . x . ac̄ ꝑti.
. I . molin̄ . Tc̄ . I . runc̄ . m̊ . n̄ . 7 . IIII . an̄ . Tc̄ . xxx . porc͗ . m̊ . n̄ . Tc̄ . c . ous̄.
m̊ . xxx . vi . Tc̄ ual . IIII . liƀ . m̊ . xL . ſol . 7 ħt in long͗ . vi . qr̄ . & vi . in lat͗.
7 de gelt͗ . vii . ɗ . & oƀl . In eaɗ . IIII . liƀi hões com̃d eiɗē . Alurici . de.
viii . ac̄ . I . ac̄ ꝑti . 7 dim̃ . car̃ . 7 ual . xvi . ɗ . ħ ten̄ . R . bigot . de epõ
In paruo belinges . ten̄ idē Aluric͗ . t . r . e . L . ac̄ . ꝑ . man̄ . 7 . II . borɗ.
Tc̄ . I . car̃ . m̊ dim̃ . III . ac̄ ꝑti . Tc̄ . I . mol͗ . m̊ . n̄ . Tc̄ ual . xx . ſol . m̊ . x.

RISBRIDGE Hundred
1 In HAVERHILL 1 free man; 24 acres. ½ plough.
   Value 3s.
      Tihel holds this from the Bishop. His predecessor before 1066
   (had) the patronage, St. Edmund's (had) the 6 forfeitures.

Hundred of CARLFORD
2 In SECKFORD Aelfric son of Wulfgeat, under the patronage of Harold
   before 1066, held 2 carucates of land as a manor.
      Always 4 villagers. Then 13 smallholders, now 15.
      Always 2 ploughs in lordship; a third possible. 3 men's ploughs.
      Meadow, 10 acres; 1 mill. Then 1 cob, now none; 4 cattle; then
         30 pigs, now none; then 100 sheep, now 36.
   Value then £4; now 40s.
      It has 6 furlongs in length and 6 in width; 7½d in tax.
   In the same (Seckford) 4 free men under the patronage of the same
   Aelfric, with 8 acres.
      Meadow, 1 acre.
      ½ plough.
   Value 16d.
      R(oger) Bigot holds this from the Bishop.

3 In LITTLE BEALINGS Aelfric also held 50 acres as a manor before 1066.
      2 smallholders.
      Then 1 plough, now ½.
      Meadow, 3 acres; then 1 mill, now none.
   Value then 20s; now 10[s].

In ead̄ ten̄ Beor̊ lib̄ hō.t.r.e.l.ac̄.p̄.man̄.7.iii.ac̄ p̄ti.7 tc̄ ual & sc̄p
viii.fot.hāc emit ipfe beorn̊ lib̄ hō ab abbate.eo cūn̄tione qđ p̊ mor-
tē fuā rediret ad æcctiā.scæ Ældred teftante hund.h̄ ten̄.Ro.bigot.
de ep̄o.7 W.de more de eo.h̄ tria maneria ten̄.R.coms.die q̊ fe forifecit.
| 7 Ilari⁹ de eo.

H̃. DE WILEFORD.In Wikhā.R.bigot.1.lib̄u hŏem cō

mdat̄.S̃.e.xxv.ac̄.7 fub eo.iiii.lib̄ hŏes.vii.ac̄.Tc̄.1.car̊.m̊ dimiđ.
ii.ac̄ p̄ti.7 ual.v.fot.h̄ ten̄.Radulfus.de fauenie.de.Ro bigot.de
feudo ep̄i.In debeis.xv.ac̄.& ꝑtinent ad cerfella.In eadē.lib̄u hŏem
de dim̊.ac̄.

⌈ H̃.DE LOSA.In cerresfella.xiiii.lib̄i hŏes.1.car̊ træ̊..tc̄n̄.Ro.
bigot.7 Radulfus de faugno ten̄ de eo.7 xiii.ac̄.Tc̄.v car̊.m̊.iii.
.1.ac̄ p̄ti.tres ex iftis.7.1.dim̊ fuer̊.com̊d.scē eldrede.7 edrici.de lefſe-
fella.W.mal&.fuit faifit die fui obitus.7 alii.com̊d abbis tantū.tc̄
ual.lx.fot.m̊ fimilit̄.In ead̄.ii.foc̊ mans.scē eldrede.vii.ac̄ in eodē p̄tio ſt.
In ead̄.1.lib̄u hŏem.marculf.com̊d.Edrici.de leſſefella.Wiitm mal&⁹
fuit faifitus die q̊ obiit.1.borđ.Tc̄.1.car̊.1.ac̄ p̄ti.7 fub eo.iiii.lib̄i hŏes
iiii.ac̄.Tc̄ ual.x.fot.m̊.v.7 ht̄.viii.qr̄.in long.7.vi.in lat.xi.d.de ḡ.
⌈ alii ibi ten̄et.

7 In CRETINGHAM Ralph also holds 1 free man, Balki, under the patronage of Aethelstan; 24 acres of land.
> Meadow, 1 acre.
> Then ½ plough, now the same.

In the same (Cretingham) 1 free man under the patronage of the same man; 38½ acres.
> 1 smallholder.
> Meadow, 2 acres.
> 1 plough.

Value then 12s; now the same.

8 In KENTON 5 free men; 4 were under the patronage of St. E(theldreda's), and Saxi, R(alph) of Savenay's predecessor, (had patronage) over one; 30 acres of land. Always 1 plough.
Value then 10s; now 6s.
> Now R(alph) of Savenay holds (this) from Ro(ger) Bigot.

BABERGH Two Hundreds

9 In ELEIGH 3 free men under the jurisdiction and patronage of Earl Algar. Now Tihel of Helléan holds (them) from the Bishop. They have 30 acres. Then 1 plough, now ½.
> Meadow, ½ acre.

Value 5s.

10 Aelfeva mother of Earl Morcar held BRANDESTON as a manor before 1066; 3 carucates of land.

374 a

> 5 villagers; 6 smallholders; 5 slaves.
> Always 2 ploughs in lordship. Then and later 2 men's ploughs, now 1.
> Meadow, 4 acres; woodland at 10 pigs. Always 2 horses at the hall. Then 5 cattle, now 3; then 20 pigs, now 23; then 100 sheep, now 120.

In the same (Brandeston) 3 free men under the patronage and full jurisdiction of Aelfeva, but they could sell without permission; 24 acres of land.

Value always £5.
> It has 1 league in length and 3 furlongs in width; 6d in tax. Ralph of Courbépine holds this manor from the Bishop.

STOW Hundred

11 In CREETING (St. Peter) Aelfric son of Brown, 1 free man under the patronage only of Withgar before 1066; held 1 carucate of land in the King's jurisdiction. Now William of Bouville holds (it) from the Bishop.

Sep.v.bord.7.1.feru.Sep.1.car in dnio.&.d.car hoium.7 ítia pars molin.&.IIII.ac pti.&.IIII.an.7 VIII.porc.Tc.VIII.ous.m.xx.Sep ual xx.fot.ht.1.lg.in long & dim in lat.& de gelto.xxx.den.Sz plur ibi ten. & ibi.v.libi hoes eide alurici.com tant de xVIII.ac.& dim.car & fuer libati cu man.& ual.II.fot.Rex & com foca 7 faca.

⨍In newetona ten.II.libi hoes Alfi comdatione tantu Lxxx.ac.fræ. in foc regis & com.m ten Ro.bigot de epo fub Rog Wareng.Tc.II. bord.P 7 m.I.Tc.I car 7 dim in dnio.p nult.m.I.7.III.ac pti.& m.II.an.&.vi.porc.& xL.ous.Sexta pars æcctiæ.x.ac.libæ træ Tc ual.xxx.fot.p.xx.fot.m.xL.fot.

⨍In Rodeha.I.lib ho.faxonis.fub sca aldreda.comd.T.R.e.x.ac in foc h Sep dim car.Roger bigot ten de epo.7 fub eo.Rad de fauiniaco.7 ual.II.fot.

⨍BofemeRA.H.In Crofelda ten Wdebrun.lib ho cmdat Edrico anteceffori Robti mal&.xx.ac.p man.Tc 7 p.I.car.m.nichil. &.I.ac pti.Tc 7 p ual.v.fot.m.III.Rog bigot de epo ten.

374 b

In ead.v.libi hoes.xL.ac.Tc 7 p.II.car.modo nult.I.ac pti.h ten& Ro. bigot.Tc ual.xvi.fot.m xx.fot.

Always 5 smallholders; 1 slave.

Always 1 plough in lordship; ½ men's plough.

The third part of a mill; meadow, 4 acres. 4 cattle, 8 pigs; then 8 sheep, now 20.

Value always 20s.

It has 1 league in length and ½ in width; 30d in tax. But several hold there.

There also 5 free men of the same Aelfric under patronage only, with 18 acres. ½ plough. They were delivered with the manor.

Value 2s.

The King and the Earl (have) full jurisdiction.

12 In (Old) NEWTON 2 free men of Alsi's, under patronage only, held 80 acres of land; in the jurisdiction of the King and the Earl. Now Roger Bigot holds (it) from the Bishop; Warengar [holds it] under Roger.

Then 2 smallholders, later and now 1.

Then 1½ ploughs in lordship, later none, now 1.

Meadow, 3 acres. Now 2 cattle, 6 pigs, 40 sheep.

The sixth part of a church, 10 acres of free land.

Value then 30s; later 20s; now 40s.

13 In *RODEHAM* 1 free man of Saxi's, under the patronage of St. Etheldreda's before 1066; 10 acres; in the jurisdiction of the Hundred. Always ½ plough.

Roger Bigot holds (it) from the Bishop; under him, Ralph of Savenay.

Value 2s.

BOSMERE Hundred

14 In CROWFIELD Woodbrown, a free man under the patronage of Edric, Robert Malet's predecessor, held 20 acres of land as a manor. Then and later 1 plough, now nothing.

Meadow, 1 acre.

Value then and later 5s; now 3[s].

Roger Bigot holds (this) from the Bishop.

In the same (Crowfield) 5 free men; 40 acres. Then and later 2 ploughs, now none.   374 b

Meadow, 1 acre.

Ro(ger) Bigot holds this.

Value then 16s; now 20s.

In ſtanhā . i . lib hō . Lewin . cmdat . Edrico de laxefella xx . ac . p man
t . r . e . & . ii . bord . Sep . i . car . & . ii . ac pti . & . ii . Æcclie de . iii . ac . Tc
ual . v . ſol . & . iiii . d . m . x . ſol 7 viii . d . & . Ro . bigot ten de epo . Rex .
: ex hoc fuit . Rob malet ꝗ paſ ɛ' die ſui obit . 9
7 . c . ſoca : In Eadē . i . lib hō . Aluric . xx . ac . & . ii . bord . 7 . i . ac pti .
Tc . iiii . ſol . m . ual . viii . ſol . hic erat comdat . ante ceſſori . Ricardi . filii
Comitis . G . Rex . 7 ſoca . In ead . ii . libi hoes . ii . ac . & . ual . vi . d .
In ead ten Leuuric . i . lib hō . x . ac . comdat Leuuino . Tc dim car ;
Tc ual . iii . ſol . m . ii . In ead . xi . libi hoes . lii . ac 7 . x . ex h fuer co
mdati Leuino comdato ante ceſſori . Robti malet . & xi .
nōe Sperun fuit comdat burcardo tēpore regis . e . 7 ht ex eadē
. viii . ac
tra . Tc . iiii . car . poſt & m . ii . & . ii . ac pti . Tc ual . xx . ſol . m . xxx .
ht . i . lg in long . 7 vi . qr 7 dim . in lat . 7 xx . d . de gl . Alii ibi tenent .
Rex . & . c . ſoca . In Vledana . i . lib hō . Aluric comdt Saxo . xvi . ac .
ſemp . i . car . Tc . i . bord . m . null . Hc Aluricū calupniatur . Ro .
de ramis tenuiſſe ſuo feudo pqua fuiſſent libati epo Tc . ſilua . de . xx .
iiii . porc . 7 viii . por . 7 xxii . ous . & . iii . cap . Tc ual . x . ſol . m . viii . ſol .
In ead . vi . libi hoes . l . ii . ac . De uno & dimidio ex his ſcilic . Leuuino .
7 Thurmero . habuit Abb ſci eadmundi . cmdt . t . r . e . 7 ꝗda nōe
brictuolt . fuit comdat Edrico antec mal . Tc int tot . ii . car
& dim . m . ii . Tc ual . xx . ſol . 7 m . Rog bigot ten de epo . & Gar
de illo .

15 In STONHAM 1 free man, Leofwin, under the patronage of Edric of Laxfield; 20 acres of land as a manor before 1066.

2 smallholders.

Always 1 plough. Meadow, 2 acres.

2 churches with 3 acres.

Value then 5s 4d; now 10s 8d.

Ro(ger) Bigot holds (this) from the Bishop. The King and the Earl (have) the jurisdiction. Robert Malet was [in possession of] this, and his father on the day of his death.

In the same (Stonham) 1 free man, Aelfric; 20 acres.

2 smallholders.

Meadow, 1 acre.

Value then 4s; now 8s.

This (free man) was under the patronage of the predecessor of Richard son of Count Gilbert. The King and [the Earl] (have) the jurisdiction.

In the same (Stonham) 2 free men; 2 acres.

Value 6d.

In the same (Stonham) Leofric, 1 free man under the patronage of Leofwin, held 10 acres. Then ½ plough.

Value then 3s; now 2[s].

In the same (Stonham) 11 free men; 52 acres. 10 of these (free men) were under the patronage of Leofwin (who was) under the patronage of Robert Malet's predecessor. The eleventh, Sperun by name, was under the patronage of Burghard before 1066; he had 8 acres of this land. Then 4 ploughs, later and now 2.

Meadow, 2 acres.

Value then 20s; now 30[s].

It has 1 league in length and 6½ furlongs in width; 20d in tax. Others hold there. The King and the Earl (have) the jurisdiction.

16 In 'OLDEN' 1 free man, Aelfric, under the patronage of Saxi; 16 acres. Always 1 plough.

Then 1 smallholder, now none.

Ro(ger) of Rames claims that he held this Aelfric in his Holding after (the men) were delivered to the Bishop.

Woodland then at 20 pigs. 8 pigs, 22 sheep, 3 goats.

Value then 10s; now 8s.

In the same ('Olden') 6 free men; 52 acres. Over one and a half of these, that is Leofwin and Thormar, the Abbot of St. Edmund's had patronage before 1066; one, Brictwold by name, was under the patronage of Edric, Malet's predecessor. Then between them all 2½ ploughs, now 2.

Value then and now 20s.

Roger Bigot holds (this) from the Bishop; War(engar) [holds it] from him.

⁊In Cratingis . teñ Ofgot liƀ hõ treginta ac̃ . t . r . e . ꝑ mañ.
sep . i . borð . 7 . i . car̃ . viii . porc̃ . 7 ɪx . oũs . 7 . i . ac̃ p̃ti . sep ual . xii . fol.

375 a

⁊ Rog̃ bigot teñ de ep̃o . 7 Gar̃ . de illo . Rex 7 C . de toto foca̅.

In Burgeftala . i . liƀ hõ . t . r . e . Aiƀnus teñ . xiiii . ac̃ . Ecclia . xxvi . ac̃

Sep dim̃ car̃ . & . i . ac̃ p̃ti . Tc̃ ual . x . fol . m̃ viii . & . iiii . ð.

In ead̃ liƀ hõ . reg̃ . e . Ailric̃ . xiiii . ac̃ . 7 dim̃ car̃ . 7 . i . ac̃ p̃ti . Tc̃ ual

v . fol . & . iiii . ð . m̃ . iiii . fol . In ead̃ Vlui liƀ hõ reg̃ . ii . ac̃ . & tc̃

ual . v . ð . m̃ . vi . lit . vi:i . qr̃ in lõ . & . i . qr̃ 7 d in lat̃ . & vi . ð . 7 oboł

de gelto . Rex 7 . c . foca̅.

In PAchetuna . iii libi . hões . reg̃ . e . xxiiii . ac̃ . femp . i . car̃ . & . i . ac̃ p̃ti.

Tc̃ ual & . viii . fol . & m̃ fimilit̃ . In ead̃ . i . liƀ hõ . reg̃ . e . 7 dim̃ . v . ac̃ & dim̃.

& ual & xii . ð . ⁊In Codeham . i . liƀ hõ . nõe Almar cõmð Abƀi de heli

lx . ac̃ trǣ ꝑ mañ . Tc̃ . ii . car̃ . m̃ . i . 7 dim̃ . 7 . i . borð . Tc̃ filua de . x . porc̃ . m̃.

ii . Semp ual . xxx . fol . Ecclia de . iii . ac̃ & ual . vi . ð.

In ead̃ . ii . libi hões Aluric̃ 7 Vluric̃ . lx . ac̃ . ꝑ . ii . mañ . 7 . i . uilt̃ . 7 . ii.

borð . 7 . ii . car̃ . 7 xl . oũs . 7 . ii . añ . & . iiii . ac̃ p̃ti . Tc̃ filua xxx . porc̃.

17 In CREETING Osgot, a free man, held 30 acres before 1066 as a manor.
Always 1 smallholder;
1 plough;
8 pigs, 9 sheep. Meadow, 1 acre.
Value always 12s.
Roger Bigot holds (this) from the Bishop; War(engar) [holds it]   375 a
from him.
The King and the Earl (have) jurisdiction over the whole.

18 In BURSTALL 1 free man, Ailbern, held 14 acres before 1066.
A church, 26 acres.
Always ½ plough. Meadow, 1 acre.
Value then 10s; now 8[s] 4d.
In the same (Burstall) a free man of King Edward's, Aethelric; 14
acres. ½ plough.
Meadow, 1 acre.
Value then 5s 4d; now 4s.
In the same (Burstall) Wulfwy, a free man of the King's; 2 acres.
Value then 5d; now 6[d].
It has 8 furlongs in length and 1½ in width; 6½d in tax. The King
and the Earl (have) the jurisdiction.

19 In *PACHETUNA* 3 free men of King Edward's; 24 acres. Always 1
plough.
Meadow, 1 acre.
Value then 8s; now the same.
In the same (*Pachetuna*) 1 free man and a half of King Edward's;
5½ acres.
Value 12d.

20 In CODDENHAM 1 free man, Aelmer by name, under the patronage of
the Abbot of Ely; 60 acres of land as a manor. Then 2 ploughs,
now 1½.
1 smallholder.
Then woodland at 10 pigs, now at 2.
Value always 30s.
A church with 3 acres; value 6d.
In the same (Coddenham) 2 free men, Aelfric and Wulfric; 60 acres
as 2 manors.
1 villager; 2 smallholders.
2 ploughs.
40 sheep, 2 cattle. Meadow, 4 acres; woodland then at 30 pigs,

m̃.xi.Tc̃ ual xxx.fol.m̃.xl.Abbas de eli habuit c̃om̃d.In eadẽ
ii.libi.hões Aluricus.& Wiſtricus.ii.ac̃.&.ual xii.d.Ecclia.i.ac̃.7.
ual.ii.d Rex.7.c.de toto.focã./ In ead heroldus lib hõ in foca 7 in
comendatione abbis de heli.xϝx.ac̃.⁊p man.t.r.e.femp.ii.bord.&.
.i.car.&.ii.ac̃ p̃ti.filu.x.porc.7 ual.x.fol: In eadẽ.iii.libi hões
vii.ac̃ & dim̃.7 dim̃.car.& ual.ii.fol.Rex.&.c.foc̃.In ead Leueua
liba femina.t.r.e.x.ac̃.& dim̃.car.&.iii.bord.7.i.ac̃ p̃ti.& ual.iiii.fol.
In ead xv.libi hões lxxx.ac̃.i.min.Ex hiſtis fuer.vi.c̃m̃d faxo ante c̃
.Ra.piperclli.Tc̃ & p̃.ϝ.car.m̃.i.filu.x.porc.ii.ac̃ p̃ti.Tc̃ & p̃ ual.xxx.
fol m̃ xx.Rex 7.c.focã.

375 b

In Vledana.viii.libi hões.xl.ac̃.Ex h̃.fuere.iiii.c̃om̃dti Saxo
ante ceſſori.Ra.pip̃.hñts.xx.v.ac̃.Tc̃ int̃ tot̃.ii.car̃.m̃.i.7.i.ac̃
& dim̃ p̃ti.7.i.runc̃.Tc̃.vi.an̄.m̃.vii.Tc̃ xx.viii.oũs 7 m̃ xvii.oũs.
m̃.xx.cap̃.Tc̃.v.porc̃.m̃.xix.| Tc̃ ual xx.fol.m̃ xxi.R.&.c.foc̃.
In Stanham tenuit Vluric̃ lib hõ.lx.ac̃.⁊p man in c̃om̃d Abbis
de eli Tc̃.iiii.bord.m̃:iii.Tc̃.ii.car in dñio.m̃.i.Tc̃.i.car hom̃.m̃
d.7.iii.ac̃ p̃ti.Ecclia.de.vii.ac̃ & d.7 ual.xv.d.Tc̃ ual.xl.fol.m̃.xx.

: Ecclia de.vii.ac̃.val.iiii.d.
:+Ecclia de.vii.ac̃ 7 dim̃.7 ual.xv.d.

375 a, b

now at 11.
Value then 30s; now 40[s].
    The Abbot of Ely had the patronage.
In the same (Coddenham) 2 free men, Aelfric and Wihtric; 2 acres.
Value 12d.
    A church, 1 acre; value 2d.
    The King and the Earl (have) jurisdiction over the whole.
In the same (Coddenham) Harold, a free man in the jurisdiction and
patronage of the Abbot of Ely; 30 acres as a manor before 1066.
    Always 2 smallholders;
    1 plough.
    Meadow, 2 acres; woodland, 10 pigs.
Value 10s.
2 acres belonging to the church; value 4d.
In the same (Coddenham) 3 free men; 7½ acres. ½ plough.
Value 2s.
    The King and the Earl (have) the jurisdiction.
In the same (Coddenham) Leofeva, a free woman, before 1066; 10
acres. ½ plough.
    3 smallholders.
    Meadow, 1 acre.
Value 4s.
In the same (Coddenham) 15 free men; 80 acres less 1. Of these, 6
(free men) were under the patronage of Saxi, Ranulf Peverel's
predecessor. Then and later 5 ploughs, now 1.
    Woodland, 10 pigs; meadow, 2 acres.
Value then and later 30s; now 20[s].
    The King and the Earl (have) the jurisdiction.

21 In 'OLDEN' 8 free men; 40 acres. Of these (free men), 4 who had 25   375 b
acres were under the patronage of Saxi, Ranulf Peverel's
predecessor. Then in total 2 ploughs, now 1.
    Meadow, 1½ acres. 1 cob; then 6 cattle, now 7; then 28 sheep,
        now 17 sheep; now 20 goats; then 5 pigs, now 19.
    A church with 7½ acres; value 15d.
Value then 20s; now 21[s].
    The King and the Earl (have) the jurisdiction.

22 In STONHAM Wulfric, a free man, under the patronage of the Abbot
of Ely, held 60 acres as a manor.
    Then 4 smallholders, now 3.
    Then 2 ploughs in lordship, now 1; then 1 men's plough, now ½.
        Meadow, 3 acres.
    A church with 7½ acres; value 15d.
Value then 40s; now 20[s].

In eadē Aluoſ pbr . 7 Gōduͥ libͥ hões cōmdati Saxo ante . c . Ra.
piⱛ . xl . ac . ⱛ . ii . man . t : r . e . ſep . iii . bord . Tc 7 ⱛ . ii . caⷬ in dnio.
ſep dim caⷬ hoiū . 7 . i . ac & dim ⱛti . Eccłia de . ii . ac . & . ual
iiii . đ . Tc ual . xxx ; ſoł . m . xii . In eadē . xxvi . libͥ hões . cōmdati
Saxo ⱛt un . nōe Wichinḡ cxl . ii . ac . Tc . vii . caⷬ ; m . v . 7 . i . ac
& dim ⱛti . Tc ual . iiii . liƀ . m . xl . ſoł . 7 iiii . đ .
In ead . i . liƀ . hō . iii . ac . 7 ual . x . đ

/ In hamingeſtuna . ii . libͥ hões cōmdati . Saxo antec . piⱛ . x . ac
& ual . xx . viii . đ . hoc tot ten& Radulfus de ſauigni de . R . bigot
& . Ro . de eⱛo . Rex 7 . c . ſoca de toto.

/ In ead . ii . libͥ hões Brunnuin . & Godric . iii . ac . & ual . vi . đ . Id
Roḡ ten . R . 7 . c . ſoca

/ In Scarueſtuna . iii . libͥ . hões . Leuuin . Leuuric Edric . iiii.
ac . 7 . ii . bou . 7 ual . x . đ . Rađ . de ſauigni . ten de Roger

/ CLAINDVNE . H . In helmingehā tenuit . Durandus
liƀ hō cmdat . Edrico de laxefelda . antec . lxxx ac ⱛ man
T . r . e . ſep . i . uiłłi . & . ii . bord . Tc . ii . caⷬ in dnio . P . i . m . nułła ;

376 a

ſep . i . caⷬ houm . & . ii . ac ⱛti . Tc ual . xxx . ſoł . m . xx .
/ In Hmingeham ten . Balchi Cōmdat Aiſtan xl . ac . ⱛ man.
ſemⱛ . iiii . bord . & . i . caⷬ in dnio . & . i . ac ⱛti . & . i . runc . Tc . iiii.
an . m . ii . Tc . xxx . porc . m . xx . vii . Tc . xl . ou . m . xxiiii . 7 ual . x . ſoł .

In the same (Stonham) Alwold the priest and Godwy, free men under the patronage of Saxi, Ranulf Peverel's predecessor; 40 acres as 2 manors before 1066.

Always 3 smallholders.

Then and later 2 ploughs in lordship; always ½ men's plough. Meadow, 1½ acres.

A church with 2 acres; value 4d.

Value then 30s; now 12[s].

In the same (Stonham) 26 free men under the patronage of Saxi, except for one, Viking by name; 142 acres. Then 7 ploughs, now 5. Meadow, 1½ acres.

Value then £4; now 40s 4d.

In the same (Stonham) 1 free man; 3 acres. Value 10d.

23 In HEMINGSTONE 2 free men under the patronage of Saxi, Ranulf Peverel's predecessor; 10 acres.

Value 28d.

Ralph of Savenay holds the whole of this from R(oger) Bigot; Ro(ger) [holds it] from the Bishop.

The King and the Earl (have) jurisdiction over the whole.

In the same (Hemingstone) 2 free men, Brunwin and Godric; 3 acres. Value 6d.

Roger also holds (this).

The King and the Earl (have) the jurisdiction.

24 In SHARPSTONE 3 free men, Leofwin, Leofric, and Edric; 4 acres. 2 oxen.

Value 10d.

Ralph of Savenay holds (this) from Roger.

CLAYDON Hundred

25 In HELMINGHAM Durand, a free man under the patronage of Edric of Laxfield, Malet's predecessor, held 80 acres as manor before 1066.

Always 1 villager; 2 smallholders.

Then 2 ploughs in lordship, later 1, now none; always 1 men's plough. Meadow, 2 acres.   376 a

Value then 30s; now 20[s].

26 In HELMINGHAM Balki, under the patronage of Aethelstan, held 40 acres as a manor.

Always 4 smallholders;

1 plough in lordship;

Meadow, 1 acre. 1 cob; then 4 cattle, now 2; then 30 pigs, now 27; then 40 sheep, now 24.

Value 10s.

In ead lib hō Wichinc cōmdat . Burcardo . xxx . ac ꝑ . man . t . r . e.

sēp . 1 . car . & . 1 . ac p̄ti . filu de . 1111 . porc . & tc ual . v1 . fol . m̄ x111 . fol 7 . 1111 . d

In ead lib hō . reg . e . Ailricus xxv . ac . & . 1 . bord . Tc & p̄ . 1 . car . modo

dim̄ . Tc ual . L . d . & fuit ad firmā ꝑ . x . fol . m̄ ual . 1111 . fol . In ead

lib hō . Blacheman . dimidi cōmdat cuidā cōmdato . Edrici antec

mal& . & dimidi cōmdat . faxo xx1111 . ac ꝑ man . sēp . 1 . car . Tc

ual . v . fol . 7 fuit ad firm̄ . ꝑ . xv . fol . m̄ ual . v111 . fol.

In ead Godric lib hō . dimid cōmd cuidā cōmdato Edrici . ante

ceffori mal& . 7 dim̄ . faxo . xx . ac . ꝑ man . & . 1 . bord . & . 1 . car &

q̄rta pars æcclæ . 1 . ac & dim̄ libæ tr̄æ . Tc ual . v1 . fol . & . 1111 . d . 7

fuit ad firmā ꝑ x1111 . fol . m̄ ual x . fol . In ead lib hō Leue

ftan . cōmdat cuidā cōmdato . edrici . xx . ac . ꝑ . man . sēp . 1 . car

& q̄rta pars æcclia libæ tr̄æ . Tc ual . v1 . fol . & fuit ad firmā ꝑ.

x1111 . fol . m̄ ual . x . fol . In ead x1 . libi hoēs . Lxx1 . ac De duob;

7 dimidio ex his habuit fup̄dict faxo anteceffor . Ra piperelli.

cōmdation . 7 . 1 . Dimid fuit cōmdat cuidā cōmdato Ædrici

ante ceffori . R . malet . Int eos habeb . tc . 11 . car . m̄ . 111 . & . 11 . ac

p̄ti . 7 dim æcclia . 111 . ac . Tc ual . xx . fol . m̄ xx . Rex 7 cōms de

In Efcaruestuna . xxv11 . libi hōes in foca 7 cōmdtoe / toto foca.

Abbis de eli . 1 . car tr̄æ . Tc 7 p̄ . 1111 . car . & . m̄ 111 . & . 11 . ac p̄ti,

. . . . sēp ual xL . fol ;

In the same (Helmingham) Viking, a free man under the patronage of Burghard; 30 acres as a manor before 1066. Always 1 plough.

Meadow, 1 acre; woodland at 4 pigs.

Value then 6s; now 13s 4d.

In the same (Helmingham) a free man of King Edward's, Aethelric; 25 acres.

1 smallholder.

Then and later 1 plough, now ½.

Value then 50d; it was at a revenue for 10s; value now 4s.

In the same (Helmingham) a free man, Blackman, half under the patronage of someone under the patronage of Edric, Malet's predecessor, and a half under the patronage of Saxi; 24 acres as a manor. Always 1 plough.

Value then 5s; it was at a revenue for 15s; value now 8s.

In the same (Helmingham) Godric, a free man half under the patronage of someone under the patronage of Edric, Malet's predecessor, and half (under the patronage) of Saxi; 20 acres as a manor.

1 smallholder.

1 plough.

The fourth part of a church, 1½ acres of free land.

Value then 6s 4d; it was at a revenue for 14s; value now 10s.

In the same (Helmingham) a free man, Leofstan, under the patronage of someone under the patronage of Edric; 20 acres as a manor. Always 1 plough.

The fourth part of a church, ... of free land.

Value then 6s; it was at a revenue for 14s; value now 10s.

In the same (Helmingham) 11 free men; 71 acres. Over two and a half of these (free men) the above-mentioned **Saxi**, Ranulf Peverel's predecessor, had patronage; and 1 half (free man) was under the patronage of someone under the patronage of Edric, R(obert) Malet's predecessor. Between them, they had then 2 ploughs, now 3.

Meadow, 2 acres.

½ church, 3 acres.

Value then 20s; now 20[s].

The King and the Earl (have) jurisdiction over the whole.

27 In SHARPSTONE 27 free men in the jurisdiction and patronage of the Abbot of Ely; 1 carucate of land. Then and later 4 ploughs, now 3.

Meadow, 2 acres; ...

Value always 40s.

⌐In depƀeham Godui . ı . liƀ hō cōm̄dat̄ ſaxo . xL . ac̄ ℈p man̄ . ſēp . ıı.

bord 7 . ı . car̄ . & . ı . ac̄ p̃ti . & q̃rta pars ecclíæ . ſc̄e mariæ . de . x . ac̄ . & ual

xx . ſoł . Sc̄a Adeldreda . ſoc̄a . 7 . ııı . part ecclíæ ſc̄i andreæ . ı . ac̄ . 7 . d̄ . 7 . ıııı pa

⌐In Vlueſtuna . xv . ac̄ . t . r . e . Idē Godui᷉ 7 jn Asfelda . vııı . ac̄ . ſēp . ııı.

bord . 7 . ı . car̄ . In eadē . ı . liƀ hō . Goda . Com̄dat̄ . cuidā cōm̄dato . Edri-

ci ante cefforis Roƀti malet xv . ac̄ . tc̄ . ı . car̄ . m̄ dim̄ 7 . ı . ac̄ p̃ti . H̄ tria

ſt̄ ℈p . uno manerio . m̄ . ıııı . an̄ . in dn̄io . 7 . x . porc̄ . 7 xxx . oūs . 7 . xıı . cap̄.

ſēp ual xx . ıı . ſoł . Soca Aƀƀis.

⌐In Vlueſtuna . Aluin̄ pƀr liƀ hō . 7 ſexta pars cōm̄dationis ſuæ

erat cuidā cōm̄dato . antecefforis mal& & quinq̃ partes ſaxo . ante

ceffori pip̄ . xxxx ac̄ . ℈p man̄ . ſēp . ı . uiłł . & . ı . pƀr . & . ıı . bord . & . ıı . ac̄

p̃ti . & . ı . car̄ in dn̄io Tc̄ 7 p̄ ual . xx . ſoł . m̄ . x . Soc̄ aƀƀis De quarta

parte iſti̯ t̄ræ erat faifitus . Viłłm̄ malet . . & de pƀro q̄ in ea manebat

die ſui obitus . In ead Aluricus pƀr liƀ hō ℈p man̄ . xxx . ac̄ . in ſoca &

cōm̄datiōe aƀƀis . Tc̄ . ı . car̄ . Tc̄ ual . x . ſoł . m̄ . v.

In ead . ıı . liƀi . hōcs . Cōm̄dati Saxo . Edric̄ 7 Alnod . xL . ac̄ . & . ı . bord

ſēp . ı . car̄ . m̄ . ıı . uac̄ . 7 xıı . porc̄ . 7 xx . oūs . 7 ual xx . ſoł.

28 In DEBENHAM Godwy, 1 free man under the patronage of Saxi;
40 acres as a manor.
    Always 2 smallholders;
    1 plough. Meadow, 1 acre.
    The fourth part of a church of St. Mary, with 10 acres.
Value 20s.
    St. Etheldreda's (has) the jurisdiction.
    3 parts of a church of St. Andrew, 1½ acres. The fourth part of
a church of St. Mary, 10 acres.

29 In ULVERSTON the same Godwy; 15 acres before 1066; and in
ASHFIELD 8 acres.
    Always 3 smallholders;
    1 plough.
In the same (Ulverston) 1 free man, Goda, under the patronage of
someone under the patronage of Edric, Robert Malet's predecessor;
15 acres. Then 1 plough, now ½.
    Meadow, 1 acre.
    These three are [held] as one manor.
    Now 4 cattle in lordship, 10 pigs, 30 sheep, 12 goats.
Value always 22s.
    The jurisdiction (is) the Abbot's.

30 In ULVERSTON Alwin the priest, a free man the sixth part of whom
was under the patronage of someone under the patronage of Malet's
predecessor and five parts (were under the patronage) of Saxi,
Ranulf Peverel's predecessor; 40 acres as a manor.
    Always 1 villager; 1 priest; 2 smallholders.
    Meadow, 2 acres.
    1 plough in lordship.
Value then and later 20s; now 10[s].
    The jurisdiction (is) the Abbot's.
    William Malet was in possession of a fourth part of this land, and
of the priest who dwelt on it, on the day of his death.
In the same (Ulverston) Aelfric the priest, a free man in the
jurisdiction and patronage of the Abbot; 30 acres as a manor. Then
1 plough.
Value then 10s; now 5[s].
In the same (Ulverston) 2 free men under Saxi's patronage, Edric
and Alnoth; 40 acres.
    1 smallholder.
    Always 1 plough. Now 2 cows, 12 pigs, 20 sheep.
Value 20s.

In ead Thure lib hō.xl.ac̄.p̄ man.&.ii.borđ.&.i.car.Tc̄ ſilua.viii.
porc̄.m̄.iiii.7 ual.xx.ſot.Soca 7 c̄omdatio abbis.

In ead Leuuin cilt lib hō.t.r.e.in ſoca 7 comendatione abbis.xl.
ac̄.p̄ man.&.ii.uitt.in alio hundret.Tc̄.i.car.7.i.ac̄ p̄ti.ſilu.xii.
porc̄.Tc̄ ual.xx.ſot m̄.xv.h̄ tot ten Roḡ bigot de ep̄o.7 Rađ
de ſauigni.de illo.   / ✗ & ual&.iiii.đ.

/ In depham.i.lib hō.Ailric̄ c̄omdat̄ ſaxo in ſoca abbis dim̄ ac̄ ✗

377 a

/ In manc wic.W de brun lib hō.in ſoca & c̄omdatione abbis.xxvii.
ac̄.ſēp.i.car.7.iii.borđ.7 dim̄ ac̄ p̄ti.Tc̄ ual.x.ſot.m̄.vi.
/ In Wineſtuna.xx.i.libi.hōes.i.car trǣ.7.ii.ac̄ iſti trǣ fuer̄ de dn̄io
ſaxi.t.r.e.ante ceſſoris.Ran.pip̄.in depbenhā.un̄ ex his.fuit c̄o
m̄dat ſc̄o eadmund.cū.xii.ac̄.7 fuit inde ſaiſitus donec Rađ forisfec̄.
ſēp.v.car.&.iiii.ac̄ & đ p̄ti.Tc̄ ual xl.ſot.m̄ xl.v.Ex.viii.habuit
Saxo c̄om̄d & abbas de cti de aliis.7 ſocā 7 c̄omdatiōe p̄t de duob₇
ſciti.Alwino 7 Leuino.c̄om̄datis cuidā c̄om̄dato.Edrici an̄ malet.

376 b, 377 a

In the same (Ulverston) Thuri, a free man; 40 acres as a manor.
  2 smallholders.
  1 plough. Woodland then 8 pigs, now 4.
Value 20s.
  The jurisdiction and patronage (are) the Abbot's.
In the same (Ulverston) Young Leofwin, a free man before 1066 in
the jurisdiction and patronage of the Abbot; 40 acres as a manor.
  2 villagers in another Hundred.
  Then 1 plough.
  Meadow, 1 acre; woodland, 12 pigs.
Value then 20s; now 15[s].
  Roger Bigot holds the whole of this from the Bishop; Ralph of
Savenay [holds it] from him.

31 In DEBENHAM 1 free man, Aethelric, under the patronage of Saxi,
in the jurisdiction of the Abbot; ½ acre.
Value 4d.

32 In *MANEWIC* Woodbrown, a free man in the jurisdiction and patronage   377 a
of the Abbot; 27 acres. Always 1 plough.
  3 smallholders.
  Meadow, ½ acre.
Value then 10s; now 6[s].

33 In WINSTON 21 free men; 1 carucate of land. Before 1066, 2 acres of
that land were in the lordship of Saxi, Ranulf Peverel's predecessor,
in Debenham. One of these (free) men, with 12 acres, was under the
patronage of St. Edmund's and was in possession of it until (Earl)
Ralph forfeited. Always 5 ploughs.
  Meadow, 4½ acres.
Value then 40s; now 45[s].
  Saxi had patronage over 8 (free men) and the Abbot of Ely had
jurisdiction and patronage over the others, except for 2, that is
Alwin and Leofwin, (who were) under the patronage of someone
under the patronage of Edric, Malet's predecessor.

In Asfelda Suarin p̄br lib hō in ſoca & cōmd abbis . xxx ac̄ . ſemp . ii.
borđ . & . i . car̄ . 7 ual . x . ſol . Ex hoc p̄bro erat ſaiſitus Galī dedol
qdo foriſfecit ſuā trā . 7 cōms hugo poſtea ſic̄ hundret teſtatur.
Et normannus dicit qđ rex miſit ei . unū breuē ut ſaiſiret Radul —
fū de ſauigni ex oib; libis hominib; ex qb; Hubtus de portu ſaiſierat
ep̄m . & idō Normannus ſaiſiuit Radulfū ex h̄ p̄bro ſ7 tm̄ neſcit
ſi ubtus pus ſaiſierat ep̄m de illo . & h̄c inueneī barones regis in
pace inī Rogum bigot 7 hugonē comite . qdo ueneī in comitatū
& ita erit in pace donec ſit derationatus.

⌐ SANFORT . H̄ & dim̄ . In Burgheſtala . iii . libi hōes . xxx.
vii . ac̄ . Godinc . Vlmar . Aluiet . Vn̄ Cōmdatus . Guert . 7 alī . Alurico,
7 īci Salpo . Tc̄ . i . car̄ . m̄ . dim̄ . 7 . iiii . ac̄ p̄ti . 7 ual viii . ſol . Soca
in bcolt . In Ead̄ Goduuin lib hō . Stigandi . xxx . ac̄ . p man̄.
Tc̄ 7 p̄ . i . car̄ . 7 . i . molin̄ m̄ d . & ual . vii . ſol . Saca in bcolt . p̄t
de domo ſua . & . de . iii . ac̄ . In ead̄ . iii . libi hōes . xviii . ac̄ . Vluiet.
Brungar . Blacſune . ſēp dim̄ . car̄ . 7 ual . iiii . ſol . h̄ tenet de ep̄o . Ro.
⌐ bigot . 7 Ra de ſauigni de illo.

⌐ SANFORT . H̄ . 7 dim̄ . In Wenham . Algar lib hō . xx . iiii
ac̄ . p man̄ . t . r . e . & ual . iiii . ſol . Soca in bcolt . In ead̄ . iiii . libi hōes
Briftuolt . Oſgot Ledmer . Godricus hn̄ts . l . ac̄ . & . vi . borđ . &
ual x . ſol Soc̄ in bercolt;

34 In ASHFIELD Snaring the priest, a free man in the jurisdiction and patronage of the Abbot; 30 acres.
> Always 2 smallholders.
> 1 plough.
> Value 10s.
> Walter of Dol was in possession of this priest when he forfeited his land, and afterwards Earl Hugh (was in possession), as the Hundred testifies. And Norman says that the King sent him a writ (stating) that he should put Ralph of Savenay in possession of all the free men of whom Hubert of Port had put the Bishop in possession. And so Norman put Ralph in possession of that priest; but however he does not know whether Hubert had first put the Bishop in possession of him. And the King's Barons kept the peace on this between Roger Bigot and Earl Hugh when they came into the County; and so it shall be at peace until there is a judgement.

SAMFORD Hundred and a Half
35 In BURSTALL 3 free men; Goding, Wulfmer (and) Alfgeat, one under the patronage of Gyrth, another (under that) of Aelfric, and the third (under that) of Scalpi; 37 acres. Then 1 plough, now ½.
> Meadow, 4 acres.
> Value 8s.
> The jurisdiction (is) in (East) Bergholt.
In the same (Burstall) Godwin, a free man of Stigand's; 30 acres as a manor. Then and later 1 plough and 1 mill, now ½.
> Value 7s.
> The jurisdiction (is) in (East) Bergholt, except over his house and 3 acres.
In the same (Burstall) 3 free men, Wulfgeat, Brungar, and Blackson; 18 acres. Always ½ plough;
> Value 4s.
> Ro(ger) Bigot holds this from the Bishop; Ra(lph) of Savenay [holds it] from him.

SAMFORD Hundred and a Half   377 b
36 In WENHAM Algar, a free man; 24 acres as a manor before 1066.
> Value 4s.
> The jurisdiction (is) in (East) Bergholt.
In the same (Wenham) 4 free men, Brictwold, Osgot, Ledmer (and) Godric, who have 50 acres.
> 6 smallholders.
> Value 10s.
> The jurisdiction (is) in (East) Bergholt.

ꝟIn Reinduna teñ . Ednod liƀ hō . ı . caꞃ tꞃe . & . c . aꞓ . ᵽ man.

femp . ııı . uiłł . 7 vı . borđ . & . ı . caꞃ . & dim . in đño . ſep . ı . caꞃ hoiũm,

& . ıııı . aꞓ ᵽti . ſilua x . porꞓ . Quinta pars æccłiæ . de . v . aꞓ . Tꞓ

uał . ııı . liƀ . m̃ . ıııı . liƀ . ſed fuit ad firmā . ᵽ . vı . liƀ . Soca . in ƀ

colt hoc teñ . Ro . bigot de eᵽo.

ꝟ*CLAINDVNE* . *H̃* . In Vlueſtuna . ıı . liƀı hoꝫs . Aluricus 7

Leuuinus . iſte fuit cõmdᷓtus cuidᷓ cõmdato edrici anteceſſorᷓes

malet . 7 Aluricus cõmdᷓt Wiſgaro . xxx . aꞓ . 7 . ıı . borđ . Tꞓ

ıı . caꞃ . P̃ . nichil . m̃ dim̃ . & . ıı . aꞓ ᵽti . Tꞓ uał . x . ſoł . Ꝏ . vııı . Roᷚg

ten& de eᵽo . 7 garenᷚg de illo . Soꞓ aƀƀis . In eᷓđ dimiđ liƀ homo

ıı . aꞓ . 7 ſt̃ in eođ ᵽtio.

In petehaga . Siwardus liƀ hō . t . r . e . v . aꞓ . 7 uał . ıı . ſoł . ſoca aƀƀis

Idē Gaꞃ . ꝟ*SANFORT* . *H̃* . Eꞇ ᴅɪᴍ̃.

Wenham tenuit . Tuneman . cõm̃ heroldi . T . r . e . : reᷚg . e . ı.

caꞃ tꞃæ . ᵽ man . Tꞓ 7 vıı . uiłł . m̃ . ıı . Tꞓ . ııı . borđ . m̃ . xvıı . Tꞓ . ıı

ꝼeruꞋ . modo . ı . ſep . ıı . caꞃ in đñio . Tꞓ . v . caꞃ . hoûm . P̃ 7 m̃ . ıı . vı aꞓ

ᵽti . Silua . vııı . porꞓ . Eccłiæ . vı . aꞓ . Tꞓ . ı . runꞓ . m̃ . ıı . Tꞓ . ıııı . añ.

Tꞓ xx . ıııı . porꞓ . m̃ . xʟ . Tꞓ . ʟx . oũs . m̃ ʟxx . Tꞓ uał . ʟx . ſoł . 7 m̃

ſimiłꞇ . Roᷚg . bigot de eᵽo . ħt vı . qꞃ in longᷓ . 7 . ıı . qꞃ & dim̃

 in lᷓt . 7 . ıııı . d . In eᷓđ . teñ Vluriꞓ liƀ hō . xʟ . aꞓ . ᵽ mañ . t . r . e.

378 a

Tꞓ . ı . caꞃ . tꞓ uał . v . ſoł . m̃ . vı . Haroldus ſocᷓ Idē . Roᷚg . de eᵽo.

37 In RAYDON Ednoth, a free man, held 1 carucate of land and 100 acres
as a manor.
Always 3 villagers; 6 smallholders;
1½ ploughs in lordship. Always 1 men's plough.
Meadow, 4 acres; woodland, 10 pigs.
The fifth part of a church with 5 acres.
Value then £3; now [£] 4; but it was at a revenue for £6.
The jurisdiction (is) in (East) Bergholt.
Ro(ger) Bigot holds this from the Bishop.

CLAYDON Hundred
38 In ULVERSTON 2 free men, Aelfric and Leofwin, the latter was under
the patronage of someone under the patronage of Edric, Malet's
predecessor, and Aelfric (was) under the patronage of Withgar;
30 acres.
2 smallholders.
Then 2 ploughs, later nothing, now ½. Meadow, 2 acres.
Value then 10s; now 8[s].
Roger holds (this) from the Bishop; Warengar [holds it] from him.
The jurisdiction (is) the Abbot's.
In the same (Ulverston) a half free man; 2 acres.
They are in the same assessment.

39 In PETTAUGH Siward a free man before 1066; 5 acres.
Value 2s.
The jurisdiction (is) the Abbot's.
Warengar also [holds this].

SAMFORD Hundred and a Half
40 Tuneman, a thane of King Edward's and under the patronage of
Harold, held WENHAM before 1066; 1 carucate of land as a manor.
Then 7 villagers, now 2; then 3 smallholders, now 17; then
2 slaves, now 1.
The fourth part of a church.
Always 2 ploughs in lordship. Then 5 men's ploughs, later and
now 2.
Meadow, 6 acres; woodland, 8 pigs.
6 acres belonging to the church.
Then 1 cob, now 2; then 4 cattle; then 24 pigs, now 40; then
60 sheep, now 70.
Value then 60s; now the same.
Roger Bigot [holds this] from the Bishop.
It has 6 furlongs in length and 2½ furlongs in width; 4d [in tax].
In the same (Wenham) Wulfric, a free man, held 40 acres as a manor
before 1066. Then 1 plough.
378 a
Value then 5s; now 6[s].
Harold (had) the jurisdiction.
Roger also holds (this) from the Bishop.

Reindune tenuit. Eduí liƀ hõ . t . r . e . ɪ . car̃ trǣ . ꝓ mañ . femꝑ ɪɪɪɪ .
bord . & . ɪ . car̃ . v̠ . ac̃ p̃ti . & . ɪ . moliñ . Qñta pars æccłiæ . v . ac̃ . Tc̃ uał
xxx . foł . 7 m̃ fimiłi͠t . fed fuit ad firm̃ā . ꝓ ʟx . foł . ħt . ɪ . lg̃ in long̃
in long̃ . & . vɪɪɪ . q̃r in lat̃ . 7 xxx ƌ . de gł . alii ibi teñ .
In ead . teñ . liƀ hõ Aluuiñ . ʟx . ac̃ . ꝓ . mañ . Tc̃ . ɪ . bord . fc̃p . ɪ . car̃ &
ɪɪɪɪ . ac̃ p̃ti . Quinta pars æccłiæ . v . ac̃ . m̃ . ɪɪɪɪ . añ . 7 xɪɪɪ . porc̃ .
& xxx . vɪ . ous̃ . Tc̃ uał xx . foł . modo . xv . In ead liƀ hõ Smeri
xxx . ac̃ . ꝓ mañ . t̠ . r . e . c̃omdat̃ Alurico capiñ antec̃ . Eudonis
dapiferi . fc̃p . ɪ . bord . Tc̃ dim̃ car̃ . ɪɪ . ac̃ p̃ti . 7 uał . v . foł . In ea
★ ƌ . liƀ hõ Vluuiñ xxx . ac̃ . fc̃p . ɪ . bord . 7 tc̃ dim̃ . car̃ . m̃ . ɪɪ . bou͠ .
7 ɪɪ . ac̃ p̃ti . 7 uał . v . foł . In ead liƀ hõ Aluric̃ xxx . ac̃ . ꝓ mañ . fc̃p
dim̃ car̃ . & . ɪɪ . ac̃ p̃ti . 7 tc̃ uał . v . foł . m̃ . x . Soca in Bercolt .
In Reindune . ɪ . liƀ hõ . Aluricus . v . ac̃ . & c̃ in p̃tio de reinduna
In belefteda . tenuit Aluricus liƀ hõ . xxx . ac̃ . ꝓ mañ . 7 . ɪɪ . bord .
Tc̃ . ɪ . car̃ . & uał . v . foł .
In Branthã . ɪɪɪ . libi hões . Brun . Siricus . Godeftañ 7 in Belenei
. ɪ . liƀ hõ Burcheric . 7 in hechã . ɪ . liƀ hõ . Edricus ħnts ʟx . ac̃ . &
. ɪ . bord . & tc̃ . ɪɪ . car̃ . m̃ . ɪ . Tc̃ uał . x . foł . m̃ . xɪɪɪɪ .

41 Edwy, a free man, held RAYDON before 1066; 1 carucate of land as
a manor.
　Always 4 smallholders;
　1 plough.
　Meadow, 5 acres; 1 mill.
　The fifth part of a church, 5 acres.
Value then 30s; now the same; but it was at a revenue for 60s.
　It has 1 league in length and 8 furlongs in width; 30d in tax.
Others hold there.
In the same (Raydon) a free man, Alwin, held 60 acres as a manor.
　Then 1 smallholder.
　Always 1 plough. Meadow, 4 acres.
　The fifth part of a church, 5 acres.
　Now 4 cattle, 13 pigs, 36 sheep.
Value then 20s; now 15[s].
In the same (Raydon) a free man, Smeri, under the patronage of
Aelfric Kemp, Eudo the Steward's predecessor; 30 acres as a manor
before 1066.
　Always 1 smallholder.
　Then ½ plough. Meadow, 2 acres.
Value 5s.
In the same (Raydon)[1] free man, Wulfwin; 30 acres.
　Always 1 smallholder.
　Then ½ plough, now 2 oxen. Meadow, 2 acres.
Value 5s.
In the same (Raydon) a free man, Aelfric; 30 acres as a manor.
Always ½ plough.
　Meadow, 2 acres.
Value then 5s; now 10[s].
　The jurisdiction (is) in (East) Bergholt.
In RAYDON 1 free man, Aelfric; 5 acres.
It is in the assessment of Raydon.

42 In BELSTEAD Aelfric, a free man, held 30 acres as a manor.
　2 smallholders.
　Then 1 plough.
Value 5s.

43 In BRANTHAM 3 free men, Brown, Siric, and Godstan; in *BELENEI*
1 free man, Burgric; in HIGHAM 1 free man, Edric; these have 60
acres.
　1 smallholder.
　Then 2 ploughs, now 1.
Value then 10s; now 14[s].

In Boituna ten̄ Goduin lib hō . t . r . e . lx . ac̄ ꝑ man̄ . iii . uill
& i . car in dn̄io . 7 . i . car hoium . filua . x . porc̄ . Q̄rta pars
æccliæ . vi . ac̄ . 7 ual xx . fol.

Alfildeftunā . ten̄ . Alnold . lib hō . t . r . e . ii . car træ . ꝑ man̄ .
Tc̄ . i . bord . m̄ . v . Tc̄ . ii . car in dn̄io . m̄ . i . 7 . i . ac̄ 7 dim̄ p̄ti . sc̄p . i . molin .

378 b

7 ual xx . v . fol . h̄t . vi . q̄r in long . 7 . iii . in lat̄ . 7 . ii . đ 7 obł de gelt .
In tatituna ten̄ . Turgot lib hō lx . ac̄ . ꝑ man̄ . tc̄ . i . car . 7 . i . ac̄ 7 dim̄
p̄ti . Tc̄ ual . x . fol . m̄ . iiii . Totū ten̄ Ro . bigot de ep̄o . 7 de tota ē foca
in bercolt.

In Gȳpefwiz . i . domū de dim̄ ac̄ . 7 In toft . Edui lib hō . ii . ac̄ &
dim̄ 7 ual vi . đ . Ro . bigot . Soca in b̄colt.

Hertefmara . H̄ . In efpala . xx . ac̄ . ten̄ . Leueua comm̄data abb̄i
de eli 7 in foca ei 7 ual . iiii . fol . h̄ ten& Ro . bigot 7 Rad de fauigni
de Roḡrio . In ead . xii . ac̄ de dn̄io . de dephenhā . & . v . bord . 7 in eod̄
pretio.

.XVII. Tra Sc̄i Benedicti de Ramefeia . Duo Hund̄ de babenb̄ga. ★
Laweffelam tenuit Sc̄s benedict t . r . e . ꝑ Man̄ . viii . car træ c̄ foca.

378 a, b

44 In BOYNTON Godwin, a free man, held 60 acres as a manor before
1066.
    3 villagers.
    1 plough in lordship; 1 men's plough. Woodland, 10 pigs.
    The fourth part of a church, 6 acres.
Value 20s.

45 Alwold, a free man, held *ALFILDESTUNA* before 1066; 2 carucates
of land as a manor.
    Then 1 smallholder, now 5.
    Then 2 ploughs in lordship, now 1.
    Meadow, 1½ acres; always 1 mill.
Value 25s.
    It has 6 furlongs in length and 3 in width; 2½d in tax.

378 b

46 In TATTINGSTONE Thurgot, a free man, held 60 acres as a manor.
Then 1 plough.
    Meadow, 1½ acres.
Value then 10s; now 4[s].
    Ro(ger) Bigot holds the whole from the Bishop.
Jurisdiction over the whole is in (East) Bergholt.

47 In IPSWICH 1 house with ½ acre. In *TOFT* Edwy, a free man; 2½ acres.
Value 6d.
    Ro(ger) Bigot [holds this].
The jurisdiction (is) in (East) Bergholt.

HARTISMERE Hundred
48 In ASPALL Leofeva, under the patronage of the Abbot of Ely and in
his jurisdiction, held 20 acres.
Value 4s.
    Roger Bigot holds this; Ralph of Savenay [holds it] from Roger.
In the same Aspall 12 acres of the lordship of Debenham.
    5 smallholders.
(It is) in the same assessment.

17   **LAND OF ST. BENEDICT'S OF RAMSEY**

The Two Hundreds of BABERGH
1 St. Benedict's held LAWSHALL before 1066 as a manor; 8 carucates
of land with the jurisdiction.

Tc̄.xiiii.uitt.m̄.xvi.Tc̄.xii.borđ.m̄.x.Tc̄.iiii.ser̄.m̄.v.Tc̄.ii.car̄ iñ
dñio.m̄.iii.Sēp.x.car̄ hom̄.viii.ac̄ p̄ti.Sēp.i.runc̄.M̄.x.anim̄.7
.xxx.porc̄.c.ou̅.7.xii.cap̄.Ecclia.xxx.ac̄ libæ t̄ræ.Tc̄ ual.viii.lib̄
m̄.xii.ħt.i.leug in lonḡ.7 dim̄ in lat̄.7 de gelto.xv.đ.

FTRÆ WiLL̄mi.EP̄I DE TETFORT. *BISCOP̄ES.II.* .XVIII

Hoxanā tenuit Ailmarus ep̄s.t.r.e.p̄.mañ.ix car̄.t̄ræ.Tc̄ xl.uitt
m̄.xx.Tc̄ xv.borđ.m̄.L.i.Tc̄.iiii.serui;sēp.iii.car̄ in dāio.Tc̄.xl.car̄ hou̅
m̄.xx.ii.& dim̄.7 xl ac̄ p̄ti.Silua.de.ccl.porc̄.Semp.ii.molin̄.&
.ii.runc̄.& xii.añ.7 lxxx.porc̄.7 xvii.ou̅s.& xl.cap̄.In ħ manerio
erat unū mercatū.t.r.e.7 p̄q̄.Wittmus rex aduēn;& sedebat in
sabbato.& W.malet fecit suū castellū ad eiam 7 eadē die q̄ erat
mercatū in manerio ep̄i.W.malet fecit aliū mercatū in suo castcllo
& ex hoc ita peioratū ē mercatū ep̄i:̄ ut paru ualeat.& m̄ sedet die
ueneris.Mercatū aut de heia sedet die sabbati.m̄ teñ.Rob̄.de dono.reḡs
FIn ħ mañ.ē æcclia sedes episcopatus de sudfolc.t.r̄.ē.Tc̄ ual ħ mañ
xxviii.lib̄.m̄.xx.sed erfasto reddidit.xxx.lib̄.ħt.i.lḡ in lō.7 viii.
q̄r in lat̄ 7 xxii.đ.& obol.de gt.In Wcibrada.i.soc̄.ii.ac̄.7 ual.x.đ.
FIn Wilebi.i.soc̄.xl.ac̄.7.i.borđ.7.i.car̄.7.ii.ac̄ p̄ti.silu̅ xx.porc̄.Tc̄ ua̅
x.sot.modo.viii.sot.

Then 14 villagers, now 16; then 12 smallholders, now 10; then
4 slaves, now 5.
Then 2 ploughs in lordship, now 3; always 10 men's ploughs.
Meadow, 8 acres. Always 1 cob. Now 10 cattle, 30 pigs, 100
sheep, 12 goats.
A church, 30 acres of free land.
Value then £8; now [£] 12.
It has 1 league in length and ½ in width; 15d in tax.

18   LANDS OF WILLIAM, BISHOP OF THETFORD   379 a

BISHOP'S Hundred
1 Bishop Aelmer held HOXNE as a manor before 1066; 9 carucates of
land.
Then 40 villagers, now 20; then 15 smallholders, now 51; then
4 slaves.
Always 3 ploughs in lordship. Then 40 men's ploughs, now 22½.
Meadow, 40 acres; woodland at 250 pigs. Always 2 mills; 2 cobs,
12 cattle, 80 pigs, 17 sheep, 40 goats.
In this manor there was a market before 1066 and after King
William came, and it took place on Saturdays. W(illiam) Malet made
his castle at Eye and, on the same day that there was a market on
the Bishop's manor, W(illiam) Malet established another market in
his castle. Because of this, the Bishop's market declined so that it is
worth little; and now it takes place on Fridays. However, the market
at Eye takes place on Saturdays; Robert (Malet) now holds (it) by
the King's gift.
In this manor is a church, the episcopal see of Suffolk before 1066.
Value of this manor then £28; now [£] 20; but it paid £30 to Erfast.
It has 1 league in length and 8 furlongs in width; 22½d in tax.

2 In WEYBREAD 1 Freeman; 2 acres.
Value 10d.

3 In WILBY 1 Freeman; 40 acres.
1 smallholder.
1 plough.
Meadow, 2 acres; woodland, 20 pigs.
Value then 10s; now 8s.

HVmbresfelda . teñ Ælmer eṗs . t . r̃ . e . i . ⁖Ɔ . de . v . car̃ tr̃e . m̃ teñ eṗs
W . ſep̄ . xvi . uitt . 7 ſep̄ . xii . bord̃ . ſemp . iiii . ſeru̇ . Tc̄ . ii . car̃ in dñio . m̃
iii . tc̄ . x . car̃ ~~omniũ~~ hoiũ m̃ . v . 7 v . poſſent ibi reſtaurari xii . ac̄ ṗti
tc̄ . ſilu̇ . ɔc . por̃ m̃ . cc . i . mot . i . æcctia . xii . ac̄ . 7 . iiii . eɋ . ɋñ . rec̄ . & m̃
ſemp . vi . añ . S̄ep xxvi . porc̃ . cc . oūs . Tc̄ uat cū ſoc̄ . xii . tib̃ . m̃ . xvi .
reddid̃ Sup ſerting de almehã tit W . eṗs . ſocã 7 ſacã p̄t hões Stigan
di eṗi . 7 B . Abb̃ . p teſtimoniũ hundreti . Habuit breuē de . e . r̃ . ɋd
ipſe habere debuit ſoc̄ 7 ſacã ſup tr̃ã ſc̃i edmundi . & ſui hõcs.

⌐ In barſhã . xvi . ac̄ . & . ii . bord̃ . & dim̃ . car̃ . & uat . ii . ſot.

379 b

⌐HERTESMARA . H̄ . In Iacheſlea . 7 in thrandeſtuna teñ Almarus
EṖC . t . r̃ . e . i . car̃ tr̃æ . p mañ . S̄ep . v . bord̃ . & . i . car̃ . ii . ac̄ ṗti . 7 uat xx

.XVIIII.

⌐FEVDV̇ EṖI
DE TEDFORT;

ſot . & ptiñ ad æcctiã de hoxna.

⌐ In Seilanda . i . tib̃ hõ . Stigandi . ii . car̃ terræ . & xii . bord̃ . & . ii . car̃ in dñio
Tc̄ . iiii . car̃ . hoium . m̃ . ii . & . v . ac̄ ṗti . ſilua . de . lx . porc̃ . & . i . mot .

ſēp uat . lx . ſot.

⌐ tĩ teñ Ailmar . Erfaſtus.

WANGFORD Hundred
4 Bishop Aelmer held HOMERSFIELD before 1066; 1 manor at 5
   carucates of land. Now Bishop William holds (it).
      Always 16 villagers; always 12 smallholders; always 4 slaves.
      Then 2 ploughs in lordship, now 3; then 10 men's ploughs, now 5,
         and 5 could be restored there.
      Meadow, 12 acres; woodland, then 600 pigs, now 200; 1 mill.
      1 church, 12 acres.
      3 horses when he acquired (it) and now. Always 6 cattle. Always
         26 pigs; 200 sheep.
   Value then, with the jurisdiction, £12; now it pays [£] 16.
   Bishop William has full jurisdiction over the Ferthing of (South)
   Elmham, except over Bishop Stigand's men; and Abbot B(aldwin),
   according to the testimony of the Hundred, had a writ from King
   Edward (stating) that he himself ought to have full jurisdiction over
   St. Edmund's land and his men.

5 In BARSHAM 16 acres.
      2 smallholders.
      ½ plough.
   Value 2s.

HARTISMERE Hundred   379 b
6 In YAXLEY and in THRANDESTON Bishop Aelmer held 1 carucate of
   land as a manor before 1066.
      Always 5 smallholders;
      1 plough. Meadow, 2 acres.
   Value 20s.
      It belongs to the church of Hoxne.

19   THE BISHOP OF THETFORD'S HOLDING

[BISHOP'S Hundred]
1 In SYLEHAM 1 free man of Stigand's; 2 carucates of land.
      12 smallholders.
      2 ploughs in lordship; then 4 men's ploughs, now 2.
      Meadow, 5 acres; woodland at 60 pigs; 1 mill.
   Value always 60s.
      Aelmer held this, (and) Erfast.

Menneham . teñ Vlfus teinn̄ . tēpore . reg̃ . e . I . car̄

tr̄æ . p̃ Ailmar & Erfaſtus . ſemp . I . uiłł . & . x . borđ . & . I . car̄ in dñio . Tc

III . car̄ . m̄ . I . & dim̄ . 7 . vi . ac̄ p̃ti . ſilua de . Lx . porc̄ . 7 . I . moliñ . & . II . liƀ ho

xi . ac̄ cōmđ & dim̄ . car̄ . Octaua pars ecctiæ . de xL ac̄ . 7 dim̄ car̄ . Plus

tr̄æ ptīn ſed in breuiata in norfolc . Tc uał . xxx . ſoł . m̄ Lx .

In denham . v . liƀi hoes . Almari cm̄da . Lx . ac̄ . & . I . car̄ . 7 uał . x . ſoł .

In horan . vii . liƀi hoes . comđ xLii . ac̄ . 7 ſēp . I . car̄ 7 dim̄ . Silua de xvi . porc̄ .

In Wilebi . I . liƀ hō . x . ac̄ In Ciccheliga . I . liƀ hō . xvi . ac̄ . 7 . II . borđ . ſemp

dimiđ . car̄ . Ecctia . de viii . ac̄ . Toł uał . xx . ſoł .

In horan . II . liƀi hoes cōmđ 7 ſoca . xix . ac̄ & dim̄ . car̄ . 7 uał . III . ſoł 7 . x . đ .

In Wilebey . I . liƀ hō . xL . ac̄ comđ . 7 ſoc̄ . ſemp . I . borđ . Tc . I . car̄ . & . II . ac̄ p̃ti

ſilua xx . porc̄ . Tc uał . x . ſoł . m̄ . viii .

In Wighefelda . I . liƀ hō c̄om 7 ſoca . x . ac̄ . 7 uał . xx . đ .

In Cicheling . I . liƀ hō c̄omđ . xx . viii . ac̄ . 7 . III . borđ . ſemp dim̄ . car̄ 7

2 Ulf, a thane, held MENDHAM before 1066; 1 carucate of land. Later
Aelmer and Erfast [held it].
　Always 1 villager; 10 smallholders;
　1 plough in lordship. Then 3 [men's] ploughs, now 1½.
　Meadow, 6 acres; woodland at 60 pigs; 1 mill.
　2 free men under patronage; 11 acres. ½ plough.
　The eighth part of a church with 40 acres. ½ plough.
　More land belongs, but (it is) listed in Norfolk.
Value then 30s; now 60[s].

3 In DENHAM 5 free men; Aelmer (had) the patronage; 60 acres. 1 plough.
Value 10s.

4 In HORHAM 7 free men under patronage; 42 acres. Always 1½ ploughs.
　Woodland at 16 pigs.

5 In WILBY 1 free man; 10 acres.
In CHICKERING 1 free man; 16 acres.
　2 smallholders.
　Always ½ plough.
　A church with 8 acres.
Value of the whole 20s.

6 In HORHAM 2 free men under patronage and jurisdiction; 19 acres.
½ plough.
Value 3s 10d.

7 In WILBY 1 free man under patronage and jurisdiction; 40 acres.
　Always 1 smallholder.
　Then 1 plough.
　Meadow, 2 acres; woodland, 20 pigs.
Value then 10s; now 8[s].

8 In WINGFIELD 1 free man under patronage and jurisdiction; 10 acres.
Value 20d.

9 In CHICKERING 1 free man under patronage; 28 acres.
　3 smallholders.
　Always ½ plough.

ual . v . fol . In ead lib hō xl . aċ . 7 dim car . filua de xii ; porċ . dim aċ
p̄ti . 7 ual . vi . fol . 7 . viii . d . In ead . i . liba femina . viii . aċ . ante ē Rodꝉ.
malet cindation . t . r . e . 7 ual xvi . d . Almarus foċ 7 faċ.

> In badingelelda . ii . libi hoēs . xxx . aċ comd . 7 . i . car . Tē ual . vi . fol.
> m̄ . x .

380 a

> H̄ . DELOSA . In Framalingaham . i . liꝉ hō . c̄omd . Almari ep̄i . xx . aċ
> trǣ . & dim car . & ual . iiii . fol .

> HERTESMARA . H̄ . In acle . i . liꝉ hō . Algarus comd . fco Edmundo . t . r .
> e . xiiii . aċ . & dim car . & dim aċ p̄ti . & ual . ii . fol . Drogo teñ de ep̄o

> WANEFORDA . H̄ . Humbresfelda . teñ . i . liꝉ hō comd Ælmari . xl
> aċ ꝑ mañ . Semp . ii . bord . Tē . ii . car . modo . i . ii . aċ p̄ti . i . æcclia . de xxx .
> aċ . Tē ual . vi . fol . 7 viii . d . m̄ . ix . 7 . iiii . d . Adhuc in ead uilla . xxiii .
> libi hoēs . lxxx . aċ . Tē . vi . car . m̄ . v . Tē ual . xl fol . Ꝏ xxx . & ħt in
> longo . i . lḡ . 7 dim in lat . 7 de gelt xx . d .

Value 5s.

In the same (Chickering) a free man; 40 acres. ½ plough.
Woodland at 12 pigs; meadow, ½ acre.

Value 6s 8d.

In the same (Chickering) 1 free woman; 8 acres. Robert Malet's predecessor (had) the patronage before 1066.

Value 16d.

Aelmer (had) full jurisdiction.

10 In BEDINGFIELD 2 free men under patronage; 30 acres. 1 plough.
Value then 6s; now 10[s].

Hundred of LOES

11 In FRAMLINGHAM 1 free man under the patronage of Bishop Aelmer; 20 acres of land. ½ plough.

Value 4s.

HARTISMERE Hundred

12 In OAKLEY 1 free man, Algar, under the patronage of St. Edmund's before 1066; 14 acres. ½ plough.
Meadow, ½ acre.

Value 2s.

Drogo holds (this) from the Bishop.

WANGFORD Hundred

13 1 free man under the patronage of Aelmer held HOMERSFIELD; 40 acres as a manor.
Always 2 smallholders.
Then 2 ploughs, now 1. Meadow, 2 acres.
1 church with 30 acres.

Value then 6s 8d; now 9[s] 4d.

Also in the same village, 23 free men; 80 acres. Then 6 ploughs, now 5.

Value then 40s; now 30[s].

It has 1 league in length and ½ in width; 20d in tax.

In halmeha . 1 . lib hō comd . 7 foc Ælmari epi . ꝑ man . xl . ac . 7 . 1111 .
bord . Sep . 1 . car . & . 11 . ac ꝓti . filua ad v111 . porc . 1 . æcclia . v1 . ac . 7 fub
eo . 111 . libi comd eide . v1 . ac & dim . car . Tc ual . x . fol . m̄ reddid x11 .
In ead uilla . 1 . lib hō . Aluuin . cmd 7 foc . Almari xl . ac . ꝑ man . & . 11 . bord .
Tc . 1 . car . m̄ dim . 11 . ac ꝓti . Tc ual . v1 . fol . m̄ . x . 7 . v111 . d . Adhuc in ead
x . libi hoes cmd & foc eide lx . ac . Sep . 1 . car . 11 . ac ꝓti . Tc ual . x . fol . m̄
reddid . x1111 . fol . In ead . x . libi hoes comd | eide . xxx . 1111 . ac . Tc . 111 . car
m̄ . 11 . Tc ual . x . fol . m̄ reddid . xx . 7 ħt in longo . 1 . lg 7 dim . in lato . &
de gelt . xx . d . Alii ibi tenent .

In fiixtuna . 1 . lib hō . Ofketellus cōmd & foca . Stigandi epi . ꝑ man
xxx . ac . & . 1 . bord . Sep . 1 . car . 11 . ac ꝓti . q̄nta pars uni mol . Tc ual . v111 . fol .
m̄ . x . reddd . 7 . v111 . d . In ead . v111 . libi hoes cmd 7 foca 7 faca Almari
epi . c . 7 . v11 . ac . Tc . 11 . car . m̄ . 1 . 7 dim . dim æcclia x11 . ac . Tc ual . x .
fol . m̄ reddidit . xxx1 . & . 1111 . d .

Almea teñ Willm de epo . Qd tenuit Aluuin . t . r . e . lib hō . cmd

380 b

In Wari tcin . 11 . car tr̄æ . 7 . xx . ac . Tc uill . m̄ . 1111 . Tc . x1 . bord . m̄ xx . Tc . 1111 .
feru . Tc in dñio . 111 . car . m̄ dim . 1 . runc . 7 v11 . an . 7 xxx . porc . 7 x111 . ous .
7 xxx . cap̄ . Tc houm . v1 . car . m̄ . 111 . 7 dim . 7 x1 . ac ꝓti . filua ad xxx . porc .

14 In (South) ELMHAM 1 free man under the patronage and jurisdiction
of Bishop Aelmer; 40 acres as a manor.
> 4 smallholders.
> Always 1 plough.
> Meadow, 2 acres; woodland at 8 pigs.
> 1 church, 6 acres.
> Under him, 3 free [men] under the patronage of the same man;
6 acres. ½ plough.
Value then 10s; now it pays 12[s].
In the same (South Elmham) 1 free man, Alwin, under the patronage
and jurisdiction of Aelmer; 40 acres as a manor.
> 2 smallholders.
> Then 1 plough, now ½. Meadow, 2 acres.
Value then 6s; now 10[s] 8d.
Also in the same (South Elmham) 10 free men under the patronage
and jurisdiction of the same man; 66 acres. Always 1 plough.
> Meadow, 2 acres.
Value then 10s; now it pays 14s.
In the same (South Elmham) 10 free men under the patronage and
jurisdiction of the same man; 34 acres. Then 3 ploughs, now 2.
Value then 10s; now it pays 20[s].
> It has 1 league in length and ½ in width; 20d in tax. Others hold
there.

15 In FLIXTON 1 free man, Askell, under the patronage and jurisdiction
of Bishop Stigand; 30 acres as a manor.
> 1 smallholder.
> Always 1 plough.
> Meadow, 2 acres; the fifth part of one mill.
Value then 8s; now it pays 10[s] 8d.
In the same (Flixton) 8 free men under the patronage and full
jurisdiction of Bishop Aelmer; 107 acres. Then 2 ploughs, now 1½.
> ½ church, 12 acres.
Value then 10s; now it pays 31[s] 4d.

16 William holds from the Bishop (South) ELMHAM. Alwin, a free man
under the patronage of Ingvar, a thane, held it before 1066; 2   380 b
carucates of land and 20 acres.
> Then 10 villagers, now 4; then 11 smallholders, now 20; then
>   4 slaves.
> Then 3 ploughs in lordship, now ½ plough.
> 1 cob, 7 cattle, 30 pigs, 13 sheep, 30 goats.
> Then 6 men's ploughs, now 3½.
> Meadow, 11 acres; woodland at 30 pigs.

. I . æcclia . XL . ac libæ t̄ræ . 7 dim̄ . car̄ . Tc uat . fot . m̄ . IIII . lib . In ead . I . lib homo
Bondus com̄d Ailmari eṗi . LX . ac ꝑ man̄ . 7 . II . uitti 7 . II . bord̄ . 7 . I . car̄ in dn̄io.
Tc hoūm . I . car̄ . m̄ dim̄ . II . ac ṗti . 7 ſub ſe . II . libi hoes . VII . ac . Tc . I . car̄ . m̄
dim̄ . Tc uat . x . fot . m̄ . XIII . Adhuc in ead . I . lib hō com̄d 7 ſoc 7 ſacā . Sti —
gandi . XXX . ac . ꝑ man̄ . Sep̄ . II . uitt . 7 . I . car̄ . & hoūm . I . car̄ . II . ac ṗti . Silua
ad VIII . porc̄ . Tc uat . VIII . fot . m̄ . x . & . VIII . d̄ . In ead . I . lib hō . Aluuı . com̄d . Edri
de laxefella . t . r . e . XXX . ac ꝑ man̄ . Tc . II . bord̄ . m̄ . III . Semper dimid car̄
. I . ac ṗti . Silua ad VIII . porc̄ . 7 ſub eo . II . libi hoes . IIII . ac 7 d̄ . car̄ . Tc uat . x . fot .
modo ſimilit̄ . Witt malet . erat ſaiſitus die qua obiit . In ead . XX . v .
lib hoes . com̄d Almaro eṗo . I . car̄ terræ 7 dimid . Tc . VIII . car̄ . m̄ . VI . 7 VI .
ac ṗti . filua ad XVI . porc̄ . Tc uat . XXX . fot . m̄ XL . fot . III . æcliæ . XXX . ac .
7 uat . v . fot .
Fnflixtuna . I . lib hō Briht nothus . com̄datus Almaro . XXX . ac . ꝑ man̄ . 7 . IIII .
bord̄ . Sep̄ . I . car̄ . 7 hoū dim̄ . II . ac ṗti . filua ad IIII . porc̄ . Tc uat . v . fot .
7 . IIII . d̄ . m̄ . XX . fot . Adhuc . III . libi hoes . cm 7 ſoc 7 ſac . Almaro . XXXVIII . ac .
Sep̄ . I . car̄ . 7 dim̄ . filua ad . IIII . porc̄ . III . ac ṗti . Tc uat . VI . fot . m̄ . XI . 7 VIII . d̄ .

1 church, 40 acres of free land. ½ plough.
Value then ... ; now £4.
In the same (South Elmham) 1 free man, Bondi, under the patronage
of Bishop Aelmer; 60 acres as a manor.
2 villagers; 2 smallholders.
1 plough in lordship; then 1 man's plough, now ½. Meadow,
   2 acres.
Under him, 2 free men; 7 acres. Then 1 plough, now ½.
Value then 10s; now 13[s].
Also in the same (South Elmham) 1 free man under the patronage
and full jurisdiction of Stigand; 30 acres as a manor.
Always 2 villagers;
1 plough; 1 men's plough.
Meadow, 2 acres; woodland at 8 pigs.
Value then 8s; now 10[s] 8d.
In the same (South Elmham) 1 free man, Alwy, under the patronage
of Edric of Laxfield before 1066; 30 acres as a manor.
Then 2 smallholders, now 3.
Always ½ plough.
Meadow, 1 acre; woodland at 8 pigs.
Under him, 2 free men; 4 acres. ½ plough.
Value then 10s; now the same.
William Malet was in possession on the day he died.
In the same (South Elmham) 25 free men under the patronage of
Bishop Aelmer; 1½ carucates of land. Then 8 ploughs, now 6.
Meadow, 6 acres; woodland at 16 pigs.
Value then 30s; now 40s.
3 churches, 30 acres; value 5s.

17 In FLIXTON 1 free man, Brictnoth, under the patronage of Aelmer;
30 acres as a manor.
4 smallholders.
Always 1 plough; ½ [men's] plough.
Meadow, 2 acres; woodland at 4 pigs.
Value then 5s 4d; now 20s.
Also 3 free men under the patronage and full jurisdiction of Aelmer;
38 acres. Always 1½ ploughs.
Woodland at 4 pigs; meadow, 3 acres.
Value then 6s; now 11[s] 8d.

ħ totū teñ Wﬂmus de noers . de epo . Adhuc in ead uiﬂt . I . liƀ hō comd
7 ſoc Stigandi xxx . ac ꝑ mañ . Tc . II . borđ . m̃ . VIII . Tc . I . cař . m̃ . II . II . ac p̃ti.
ſiluæ ad . IIII . porc . 7 ſub eo . I . liƀ hō xvi . ac . 7 dim̃ . cař . tc꞉ modo . II . bou.
Tc uaﬂt . x . ſoﬂt . 7 m̃ ſimiﬂt . ide W.

Ⅴ In barſſſſ . x . liƀi hōes . ex eis habuit Aluric . 7 Guert coind . de . VIII . 7 dim̃.

381 a

& ex aliis . Almari ep̃i . LX . ac . Tc . II . cař . modo . I . & dim̃ . II . ac p̃ti . tc uaﬂt . VIII.
ſoﬂt . modo . x . Ⅴ HERTESMARA . H̃ . In Jacheſlea 7 in Thrandeſtuna
XL . liƀi hōes . I . cař . terræ . 7 . xIx . ac . Tc . III . cař . m̃ . III . 7 dim̃ . II . ac p̃ti.
Sēp uaﬂt . XL ſoﬂt . Ep̃s ſoc 7 ſacā . hoc teñ . Othem de epo.

Ⅴ In brō . I . liƀ hō . comdatus . cuidā comd . Almari ep̃i . vi . ac꞉ 7 uaﬂt . xII . đ.

Ⅴ DIM̃ . H̃ . In ſlixtuna . tenuit ſēs michahel in elemoſinā . t . r . e . I . cař
terræ . Tc . xIII . borđ . m̃ . VIII . Sēp . I . dñio . I . cař . Tc hōiū . IIII . cař . m̃ . I.
Silua . ad VIII . porc . IIII . ac p̃ti . dim̃ moliñ . Sēp uaﬂt . xx . ſoﬂt . Soca . Stigndo.

★ Ⅴ TERRE EP̃I ROVENSIS . LACFORDA . Hundret.   . Xx
Frakenaham teñ Orthi teinus heroldi . t . r . e . 7 pea derotionatus ē . Lan -
francus iuﬀu regis . i ep̃atū rouenſem . ꝑ mañ . x . cař træ . Semp xvi . uiﬂt.
& VIII . borđ . 7 . vi . ſeru . 7 ſemp . v . cař . in dñio . 7 . vi . cař hoiu . ſed . VIII . poſs

William of Noyers holds the whole of this from the Bishop.
Also in the same village 1 free man under the patronage and
jurisdiction of Stigand; 30 acres as a manor.
 Then 2 smallholders, now 8.
 Then 1 plough, now 2.
 Meadow, 2 acres; woodland at 4 pigs.
 Under him, 1 free man; 16 acres. Then ½ plough, now the same.
Value then 10s; now the same.
 William also holds (this).

18 In BARSHAM 10 free men; of these, Aelfric and Gyrth had patronage
 over 8 and a half, and Bishop Aelmer (had it) over the others; 60   381 a
 acres. Then 2 ploughs, now 1½.
  Meadow, 2 acres.
 Value then 8s; now 10[s].

HARTISMERE Hundred
19 In YAXLEY and in THRANDESTON 40 free men; 1 carucate of land and
 19 acres. Then 3 ploughs, now 3½.
  Meadow, 2 acres.
 Value always 40s.
 The Bishop (had) full jurisdiction.
 Otheri holds this from the Bishop.

20 In BROME 1 free man under the patronage of someone under the
 patronage of Bishop Aelmer; 6 acres.
 Value 12d.

Half-Hundred [of LOTHINGLAND]
21 In FLIXTON St. Michael's held in alms 1 carucate of land before 1066.
  Then 13 smallholders, now 8.
  Always 1 plough in lordship. Then 4 men's ploughs, now 1.
  Woodland at 8 pigs; meadow, 4 acres; ½ mill.
 Value always 20s.
 The jurisdiction belonged to Stigand.

LANDS OF THE BISHOP OF ROCHESTER
20

LACKFORD Hundred
1 Orthi, a thane of Harold's, held FRECKENHAM before 1066; later on
 Lanfranc by the King's command adjudged (it to be) in the Bishopric
 of Rochester; 10 carucates of land as a manor.
  Always 16 villagers; 8 smallholders; 6 slaves.
  Always 5 ploughs in lordship; 6 men's ploughs, but 8 could be

reſtaurari.7.xx.ac̄ p̄ti.7.i.mot.7.ii.piſcaꝛ.Eccłia.xx.ac̄.7.iii.cq̄.7
an̄.&.xl.porc̄.&.cc.xxx.ous.7.vi.uaſa apū.Tc̄ uał xii.lib.m̄.xiiii.h̄
1 leug in lōg.7 dimid̄ in lato.& de gelto.xx.d̄.Huic man̄ addidit
com̄s Rad̄.iiii.libos hoēs q̄s inuaſit de.viii.ac̄ tr̄æ.Sēp dim̄ car̄.7 uał&
viii.d̄.Soc̄ hui man̄ habeb̄ id eꝑs.7 de libis hōibꝫ h̄t Sc̄s Edmundus.

.XXI. SVTHFVLC TR̄Æ SC̄E ALDREDE; TheWARDESTREV.

HVNDRET.Rateſdane ten̄ ſc̄a Aldreda.t.r.e.ꝑ.vi.car̄ terræ Semp xviiͬ.
uiłł.Tc̄ xx.bord̄.Ⓜ.xx.vii.Tc̄.vi.ſerui.m̄.iiii.Sēp.iii.car̄ in dn̄i.
Tc̄.xii.car̄ hōiū.m̄.iii.Silua.xx.iiii.porc̄.7 xvi.ac̄ p̄ti.Sēp.v.run-.
Tc̄ m̄ xii.an̄.7 lxxx.7.x.ous.xl.porc̄.m̄.xi.cap̄.Semp uał.x.lib.
.i.æcclia.xxiiii ac̄.7.xv.ac̄.ten̄ hunfridus hō.W.de.Wār.& goſce-
linus homo comitis.de moritonio.ii.h̄t.xvi.q̄r in longo.7 x.in lato.
7 de gelto uiginti denarios.Soca ſc̄e.ealdrede.

Ⅴ In eadem.i.liber homo ſc̄æ aldrede cōm̄d 7 ſoca.t.r.e.iii.ac̄.&
uał.vi.d̄.Ⅴ In Rateſdana.i.liber homo ſc̄e aldrede ſoca & ſaca
viii.ac̄ tr̄æ.7 uał.ii.ſoł.falco homo ſc̄i edmundi habuit has.viii.
ac̄.dū abbatia ſc̄e aldrede.ēet in manu regis & uſqꝫ huc tenuit.
f̣ negat ſe detinuiſſe ſeruitiū.

Ⅴ Drinceſtona ten̄ ſc̄a.A.t.r.e.ii.car̄ terræ.7.i.æcclia.xii.ac̄
Tc̄.xv.bord̄.m̄.vii.Tc̄.vi.ſeru.m̄.iiii.femp.ii.car̄ in dominio.Tc̄
iii.car̄ hominū.m̄.i.Silu de.c.porc̄.7 vi.ac̄ p̄ti.Sēp.ii.æqui.in halla.
.x.an̄.xxx.ii.porc̄.xxx.ous.viii.cap̄.Tc̄ uał xl.ſoł.m̄ lx.f̣ fuit
ad firmā.c.ſoł.& n̄ potuit reddere.h̄t.viii.q̄r in longo.& vii.i lato.
Et de gelto.xi.d̄.

restored.

Meadow, 20 acres; 1 mill; 2 fisheries.

A church, 20 acres.

3 horses, 13 cattle, 40 pigs, 230 sheep, 6 beehives.

Value then £12; now [£] 14.

It has 1 league in length and ½ in width; 20d in tax.

To this manor Earl Ralph added 4 free men with 8 acres of land, whom he annexed. Always ½ plough.

Value 8d.

The Bishop also has the jurisdiction of this manor; St. Edmund's has (jurisdiction) over the free men.

21   SUFFOLK LANDS OF ST. ETHELDREDA'S   381 b

THEDWESTRY Hundred

1 St. Etheldreda's held RATTLESDEN before 1066 for 6 carucates of land.

Always 18 villagers. Then 20 smallholders, now 27; then 6 slaves, now 4.

Always 3 ploughs in lordship. Then 12 men's ploughs, now 3.

Woodland, 24 pigs; meadow, 16 acres. Always 5 cobs. Then [and] now 12 cattle; 80 and 10 sheep; 40 pigs. Now 11 goats.

Value always £10.

1 church, 24 acres.

Humphrey, W(illiam) of Warenne's man, holds 15 acres; Jocelyn, the Count of Mortain's man, (holds) 2 (acres).

It has 16 furlongs in length and 10 in width; 20d in tax. The jurisdiction (is) St. Etheldreda's.

In the same (Rattlesden) 1 free man of St. Etheldreda's, under patronage and jurisdiction before 1066; 3 acres.

Value 6d.

2 In RATTLESDEN 1 free man of St. Etheldreda's, under full jurisdiction; 8 acres of land.

Value 2s.

Falc, a man of St. Edmund's, had these 8 acres while the Abbey of St. Etheldreda's was in the King's hand, and he has held (them) until now; but he denies that he has withheld the service.

3 St. Etheldreda's held DRINKSTONE before 1066; 2 carucates of land.

1 church, 12 acres.

Then 15 smallholders, now 7; then 6 slaves, now 4.

Always 2 ploughs in lordship. Then 3 men's ploughs, now 1.

Woodland at 100 pigs; meadow, 6 acres. Always 2 horses at the hall, 10 cattle, 32 pigs, 30 sheep, 8 goats.

Value then 40s; now 60[s]; but it was at a revenue for 100s and could not pay.

It has 8 furlongs in length and 7 in width; 11d in tax.

⌐ *THINGOHOV*. H̃. In reda . xx . ac̃ in dñio . & . IIII . borđ . II . ac̃ p̃ti.
& dim̃ . car̃ foca & faca sc̃e aldrede . & . ual . IIII . fol.

⌐ *LACFORDE* . H̃ . Brandona . ten̄ sc̃a . Aldrede . t . r . e . 7 m̃ .p . mañ.
v . car̃ terræ . Semp . VIII . uill̃ . & . IIII . borđ . VII . ferui . femp . III.
★ car̃r in dñio . Tc̃ . IIII . car̃ . hou̇m . m̃ . III . ac̃ p̃ti . 7 . I . pifcar̃.

382 a

&. II . afini . & . xi . añ . 7 . cc . ous̄ . 7 xx . por̃c . Ecclia . xxx . ac̃ . Tc̃ ual . vi . lib̃.
m̃ . VIII . h̃t . I . l̃g in lōgo . 7 dimiđ lati . 7 de gelto . xx . đ.

⌐ Laringahetha . ten̄ sc̃a aldređ . t . r . e . .p mañ . III . car̃r træ . Sep̃
vi . uill̃ . & . v . borđ . & . IIII . feru̇ . Tc̃ . III . car̃r in dominio . m̃ . II.
Semper . II . car̃r hou̇ . 7 . v . ac̃ p̃ti . 7 dim̃ molin̄ . 7 . II . pifcar̃.
7 . II . æqui in halla . & . v . añ . c . ous̄ . 7 XVII . por̃c . Ecclia . LX . ac̃.
Tc̃ ual . IIII . lib̃ . modo . vi . h̃t . I . l̃g in longo . 7 dim̃ in lato . Et de gelto
xx . den̄ . ⌐ Lundale . I . car̃r terre . ten̄ sc̃a alđ . 7 . III . borđ . 7 IIII.
feru̇ . Semp . II . car̃r in dñio . 7 XIII . ac̃ p̃ti . & . II . pifcar̃ . & . I . æq̇ . & . xx.
IIII . añ . 7 . LX . II . ous̄ . Semp ual . xx . fol . Ecclia fine tr̃a . h̃t . II . qr̃ in lōgo
& . II . iu lato . Gel̃t in Laringeheta.

⌐ In du̇hā dim̃ lib̃ hõ sc̃e aldređ cu̇ foca dim̃ car̃r tr̃æ . 7 . III . borđ . 7 . I . ac̃
p̃ti . Sẽp dim̃ car̃ . 7 ual . v . fol.

THINGOE Hundred

4 In REDE 20 acres in lordship.
    4 smallholders.
    Meadow, 2 acres.
    ½ plough.
    The full jurisdiction (is) St. Etheldreda's.
  Value 4s.

LACKFORD Hundred

5 St. Etheldreda's held BRANDON before 1066, and now, as a manor;
  5 carucates of land.
    Always 8 villagers; 4 smallholders; 7 slaves.
    Always 3 ploughs in lordship. Then 4 men's ploughs, now 3.
    Meadow, [3] acres; 1 fishery. 2 asses, 11 cattle, 200 sheep,   382 a
      20 pigs.
    A church, 30 acres.
  Value then £6; now [£] 8.
    It has 1 league in length and ½ in width; 20d in tax.

6 St. Etheldreda's held LAKENHEATH before 1066 as a manor; 3
  carucates of land.
    Always 6 villagers; 5 smallholders; 4 slaves.
    Then 3 ploughs in lordship, now 2; always 2 men's ploughs.
    Meadow, 5 acres; ½ mill; 2 fisheries. 2 horses at the hall, 5
      cattle, 100 sheep, 17 pigs.
    A church, 60 acres.
  Value then £4; now [£] 6.
    It has 1 league in length and ½ in width; 20d in tax.

7 St. Etheldreda's held UNDLEY; 1 carucate of land.
    3 smallholders; 4 slaves.
    Always 2 ploughs in lordship.
    Meadow, 13 acres; 2 fisheries. 1 horse, 24 cattle, 62 sheep.
  Value always 20s.
    A church without land.
    It has 2 furlongs in length and 2 in width. Tax in Lakenheath.

8 In (Santon) DOWNHAM a half free man of St. Etheldreda's, with the
  jurisdiction; ½ carucate of land.
    3 smallholders.
    Meadow, 1 acre.
    Always ½ plough.
  Value 5s.

⊢In Liuermera . III . libi hões sce . Aldrede commd . tnt . t . r . e . in soca sci . e.
XXIX . ac træ . Sep dim car . 7 ual . v . sol

⊢Babga duo h . Clamesford ten sca ald . t . r . e . & . m p manerio
VIII . car tre . Sep . XVI . uilt . 7 XVIII . bord . & . v . seru . semp . III . car
in dnio . 7 VII . car hoiu . 7 XII . ac pti . Silua . v . porc . & . I . molin .
semp . III . eq . in halla . & . VIII . an . & . m . cc . ous . 7 . XXX . II . porc . Eclia
de . xxx ac libe træ . 7 . I . soc . de . VIII . ac . Tc ual . x . lib . m . XVI . ht . I . lg
in longo . 7 . VIII . qr . in lato . & de gelto xv . d.

⊢Herteft ten sca Aldrede . t . r . e . p man . v . semp XII . uilt . & . XIIII .
bord . 7 IIII . seru . temp . II . car in dnio . Tc . v car hoium . m . VI . 7 . x,
ac pti . Silua de . VI . porc . Sep . IIII . equi . in halla . 7 XX . animalia.

382 b

7 XX . v . porc . 7 LX . ous . Eclia de LXXX . ac libe terre . Tc ual . VI . lib . m . XI .
lib . ht . I . lg in longo 7 dim in lato . & de gelto . x . d.
In ead . IIII . soc . de XXX . ac træ . 7 dim . car . 7 ual . v . sol . Adhuc c . I . soca de . I
car træ . semp . I . car . 7 ual XX . sol . hc ten bner baliftari de sca Aldred.

⊢Stohu . H . In Ciltuna ten sca Aldreda . II . soc . de . XXX . VI . ac .
sed n pot uende . fine licnca abbis . 7 . I . bord . Tc . I . car . m . nulla . 7 dim
ac pti . 7 ual . v . sol.

⊢In bukeffalla . I . soc . de . x . ac . forefacte tre . 7 . I . bord . de . v . ac 7 ual
. x . d . In finebga ten Roger de oburuilla de sca aldreda . III . soc
de . xxx . IIII . ac træ . 7 ual . IIII . sol . In ead uilla VII . ac de dnio . in
bkinges . saca 7 foca sce aldre.

9 In (Great) LIVERMERE 3 free men of St. Etheldreda's, under patronage
only before 1066, in the jurisdiction of St. Edmund's; 29 acres of
land. Always ½ plough.
Value 5s.

BABERGH Two Hundreds
10 St. Etheldreda's held GLEMSFORD before 1066, and now, as a manor;
8 carucates of land.
Always 16 villagers; 18 smallholders; 5 slaves.
Always 3 ploughs in lordship; 7 men's ploughs.
Meadow, 12 acres; woodland, 5 pigs; 1 mill. Always 3 horses at
the hall, 8 cattle. Now 200 sheep, 32 pigs.
A church with 30 acres of free land.
1 Freeman with 8 acres.
Value then £10; now [£] 16.
It has 1 league in length and 8 furlongs in width; 15d in tax.

11 St. Etheldreda's held HARTEST before 1066 as a manor; 5 carucates
of land.
Always 12 villagers; 14 smallholders; 4 slaves.
Always 2 ploughs in lordship. Then 5 men's ploughs, now 6.
Meadow, 10 acres; woodland at 6 pigs. Always 4 horses at the
hall, 20 cattle, 25 pigs, 60 sheep.
A church with 80 acres of free land.
Value then £6; now £11.
It has 1 league in length and ½ in width; 10d in tax.
In the same (Hartest) 4 Freemen with 30 acres of land. ½ plough.
Value 5s.
Also there is 1 [Freeman] with 1 carucate of land. Always 1 plough;
Value 20s.
Berner the crossbowman holds this from St. Etheldreda's.

382 b

STOW Hundred
12 In CHILTON St. Etheldreda's held 2 Freemen with 36 acres; but they
could not sell without the Abbot's permission.
1 smallholder.
Then 1 plough, now none. Meadow, ½ acre.
Value 5s.

13 In BUXHALL 1 Freeman with 10 acres of forfeited land.
1 smallholder with 5 acres.
Value 10d.

14 In FINBOROUGH Roger of Auberville holds from St. Etheldreda's 3
Freemen with 34 acres of land.
Value 4s.
In the same village 7 acres of the lordship of Barking.
The full jurisdiction (is) St. Etheldreda's.

$\mathcal{F}$ *DIM.* $\bar{H}$. De gepeſwiz . Stoches tenuit . S . A . III . car̄ trǣ . ꝓ man̄.
t . r . e . femp . IX . uilt . 7 tē . v . bord . modo . xv . Tē . I . ſerū . femp . II . car̄ in
dn̄io . 7 VI . car̄ hoiūm . & . I . æccłia . de . XL . ac̄ libe trǣ . 7 . I . molin̄.
7 xx . ac̄ p̄ti . 7 XII . an̄ . 7 xx . porc̄ . 7 xx . IIII . oūs . & . XIIII . cap̄ . & adhuc
ht̄ ſc̄a . Al . medietat̄ ſoche quǣ ē ułt pontē . Tē uał . IIII . lib̄ . m̄ . c . ſoł.
ht̄ . VI . qr̄ in lonḡ . 7 VI . in lat̄ . 7 . IIII . đ . in gelto . de xx ſoł

$\mathcal{F}$ Boſemera . $\bar{H}$. Berchingas ten̄ . Sc̄a . A . c̄ ſoca 7 ſaca . t . r . e . ꝓ man̄.
VII . car̄ trǣ . Tē xxVII . uiłti . m̄ . xxv . Tē . xx . IIII . bord . m̄ . xxx . Tē
. v . ſerū . m̄ . IIII . ſēp . III . car̄ in dn̄io . Tē xx . IIII . car̄ hominū . m̄ . xv.
Eccłia LXXX . III . ac̄ libǣ trǣ 7 . II . car̄ . 7 . L . II . ac̄ p̄ti . Silua . de . L . porc̄,
ſemp . I . moł . 7 unā excluſā Alti molini . 7 in excluſa alti moł.
ht̄ Rob̄ . malet parte . 7 . II . arpen . . . . uinee . In dn̄io . XI . runc̄.
7 xx . III . an̄ . 7 xxx . porc̄ . 7 . c . oūs . 7 XLVIII . cap̄ . 7 IIII . lib̄i.

383 a

Hoies . de . VI . ac̄ . 7 ħnt . I . car̄ . Iſti additi ſt̄ huic manerio . t . r . e . Will.
& uał . II . ſoł . Rex & com̄s ſoca . Vnum 7 dim̄ . ex his ꞏ habuit harduin̄
q̄do forisfecit . m̄ ten̄ abbas . Tē uał mān̄riū . xvi . lib̄ . & abbas dedit
ad firmā ꝓ . xx . lib̄ . ħt . I . łḡ . & . IIII . qr̄ in longo 7 . VIII . qr̄ . in lat̄ . 7
xx . đ . de gt̄.

$\mathcal{F}$ In dermodeſduna . tenuer̄ . xxv . lib̄ lib̄i hoes . I . car̄ trǣ . ex quibₔ
habuit ſc̄a . Al . com̄ 7 ſoca . t . r . e . Tē . VI . car̄ . modo . II . & . III . ac̄ p̄ti
7 uał . xx . ſoł . Roger bigot tenet de abbate quia abbas eam derationauit ſuꝑ eū . cora epo de ſc̄o Laudo ſ̧ ꝑ tam̄ tenebat de rege

$\mathcal{F}$ In b̄chingas tenet . Roḡ . c . xvIII . ac̄ . de abb̄e de ſuo dn̄io . 7 . I . æccłiā
de . VI . ac̄ . & uał . x . ſoł.

Half-Hundred of IPSWICH

15 St. Etheldreda's held STOKE; 3 carucates of land as a manor before 1066.

Always 9 villagers. Then 5 smallholders, now 15; then 1 slave.
Always 2 ploughs in lordship; 6 men's ploughs.
A church with 40 acres of free land.
1 mill; meadow, 20 acres. 12 cattle, 20 pigs, 24 sheep, 14 goats.
Also St. Etheldreda's has the half of the jurisdiction which is beyond the bridge.
Value then £4; now 100s.
It has 6 furlongs in length and 6 in width; 4d in a tax of 20s.

BOSMERE Hundred

16 St. Etheldreda's held BARKING with full jurisdiction before 1066 as a manor; 7 carucates of land.

Then 27 villagers, now 25; then 24 smallholders, now 30; then 5 slaves, now 4.
Always 3 ploughs in lordship. Then 24 men's ploughs, now 15.
A church, 83 acres of free land. 2 ploughs.
Meadow, 52 acres; woodland at 50 pigs; always 1 mill, and a dam of another mill, and in the dam of the other mill Robert Malet has a share; 2 *arpents* of vines. In lordship 11 cobs, 23 cattle, 30 pigs, 100 sheep, 48 goats.
4 free men with 6 acres. They have 1 plough. These (free men)   383 a
were added to this manor after 1066.
Value 2s.
The King and the Earl (have) the jurisdiction.
Of these (free men), Hardwin had one and a half when he forfeited; now the Abbot (holds them).
Value of the manor then £16; the Abbot granted it at a revenue for £20.
It has 1 league and 4 furlongs in length, and 8 furlongs in width; 20d in tax.

17 In DARMSDEN 25 free men held 1 carucate of land; over whom St. Etheldreda's had patronage and jurisdiction before 1066. Then 6 ploughs, now 2.

Meadow, 3 acres.
Value 20s.
Roger Bigot holds (this) from the Abbot, because the Abbot established his claim to it against him before the Bishop of St. Lô; but later, however, he held (it) from the King.

18 In BARKING Roger holds 118 acres from the Abbot in his lordship.

1 church with 6 acres.
Value 10s.

⟩ In horſwalda . ı . lib hō . com̃ 7 ſoca . t . r . e . de . xx . ıı . aē 7 dim̃ . 7 dim̃
car . & dimid . 7 ual . ııı . ſot . hē tenuit . Roḡ de otburuilla
de rē . 7 abbas derationauit ſup eū m̃ ten̄ de abb̄e .

⟩ In badeleıā tenuit . ſc̄a . A . xxx . aē ın dn̄io . t . r . e . hōē ın p̄tio de ꝏ
chingis

⟩ In hamingeſtuna . ı . ſoē ſc̄e . A . de . xıı . aē . Wiꞁꞁ de ſcoies . ten̄ de
abb̄e . & c̄ in p̄tio de blachā .

⟩ In hamingeſtuna . ı . lib̄ hō . Iricus . c̄omdatus abb̄i 7 in ſoca eı
xv . aē . 7 . ıı . bord . 7 ual . ıı . ſot . 7 vı . d .

⟩ In Vledana . ı . lib̄ hō . Aluricus . c̄om̃ tn̄t . ı . aē . 7 d . 7 ual . ııı . d . rex
7 . c . ſoē . hoc eſt in dominio .

⟩ In Codenhā . xvı . aē . dn̄ice trǣ . & fuit in p̄tio de ꝏcham .

⟩ In haſſa . ı . lib̄a femina . Liſteua . comendata abb̄i . ı . aē . 7

383 b

ual & . ıı . den̄ . R . 7 . c . ſoē .

⟩ In ead . ı . lib̄ hō com̃dation̄ tn̄t dim̃ . aē . 7 ual . ı . d . R . 7 . c . ſoē .

⟩ *CLAINDVNE . H̄ .* Bercham tenuit ſc̄a . A . t . r . e . ıııı . car t̄re
p man̄ . ſemp xxıııı . uiꞁꞁ . m̃ . ıx . bord . Tē . vı . ſeru . modo . ıı . Tē . ııı .
car in dn̄io . modo . ı . Tē . vııı . car hoıū . m̃ . vı . Ecclia . de xvı . aē .
ſemp . ı . moliñ . & . xıı . aē p̄ti . Tē ſilua . c . porē . m̃ . xvı . m̃ . ıx . porē .
7 xvıı . ouſ . 7 . ı . ſoē . xxx . aē . ſēp ı . carr . Tē ual . xıı . lib . modo . c . ſoꞁ .
ht̄ . ı . lḡ in longo 7 vıı . qr̄ 7 dim̄ in lat̄ . 7 . xx . d de gꞁ .

19 In HORSWOLD 1 free man under patronage and jurisdiction before 1066, with 22½ acres. ½ plough.
Meadow, ½ acre.
Value 3s.
Roger of Auberville held this from the King. The Abbot established his claim against him. Now he holds (it) from the Abbot.

20 In BADLEY St. Etheldreda's held 30 acres in lordship before 1066. This is in the assessment of Barking.

21 In HEMINGSTONE 1 Freeman of St. Etheldreda's, with 12 acres. William of Écouis holds (this) from the Abbot.
It is in the assessment of Blakenham.

22 In HEMINGSTONE 1 free man, Eric, under the patronage of the Abbot and in his jurisdiction; 15 acres.
2 smallholders.
Value 2s 6d.

23 In 'OLDEN' 1 free man, Aelfric, under patronage only; 1½ acres.
Value 3d.
The King and the Earl (have) the jurisdiction.
This is in lordship.

24 In CODDENHAM 16 acres of lordship land.
It was in the assessment of Barham.

25 In ASH(BOCKING) 1 free woman, Licteva, under the patronage of the Abbot; 1 acre.
Value 2d.
The King and the Earl (have) the jurisdiction.
In the same (Ashbocking) 1 free man under patronage only; ½ acre.
Value 1d.
The King and the Earl (have) the jurisdiction.

383 b

CLAYDON Hundred
26 St. Etheldreda's held BARHAM before 1066; 4 carucates of land as a manor.
Always 24 villagers. Now 9 smallholders. Then 6 slaves, now 2.
Then 3 ploughs in lordship, now 1; then 8 men's ploughs, now 6.
A church with 16 acres.
Always 1 mill. Meadow, 12 acres; woodland, then 100 pigs, now 16. Now 9 pigs, 17 sheep.
1 Freeman, 30 acres. Always 1 plough.
Value then £12; now 100s.
It has 1 league in length and 7½ furlongs in width; 20d in tax.

ꝑ In ead . ı . lib̄ hō . xxx . v . ac̄ . in ſoca & cōm̄datione abb̄is . Tc̄ . ı . carr̄ .
modo dim̄ . Tc̄ . ı . bord̄ . m̄ . ıı . 7 . ııı . ac̄ p̄ti . 7 . ı . moliñ . Tc̄ uat̄ . x . ſot.
m̄ . xx . Roḡ de otburuilla tenebat de rege m̄ de abb̄e.

★ ꝑ In Eſcarletuna . ııı . libi . hōes in ſoca 7 cōm̄d abb̄is . vııı . ac̄ . 7 . ıı . bou.̄
Tc̄ uat̄ . xx . d̄ m̄ . ıı . ſot . hoc tenuit . W . de ſcoies de rege . m̄ de abb̄e.

ꝑ Wineſtunā tenuit ſc̄a . A . t . r . e . ı . car̄ trǣ in dn̄io . 7 xL . ac̄ ꝑ mañ .
ſēp . vı . uitt . 7 . ııı . bord̄ . Tc̄ . ıı . car̄ . m̄ . ı . ſēp . ııı . car̄ houm̄ . vı . ac̄
p̄ti . Tc̄ ſilua . c . porc̄ ; m̄ . Lx . Ecct̄ia . vııı . ac̄ . ıı . runc̄ . 7 . ıııı . an̄ .
& xx . porc̄ . & . L . ou̅s . Tc̄ . uat̄ . ıııı . lib̄ . m̄ . ıııı . 7 x . ſot . Et . ı . lib̄
homo additus Alsi . huic manerio xxx . ac̄ . ꝑ mañ . in ſoca &
cōm̄dtione abb̄is . femp . ıı . bord̄ . 7 . ı . car̄ . 7 uat̄ . x . ſot . ht̄ . ı .
lḡ in longo . 7 . ııı . qr̄ in lat̄ . 7 xııı . d̄ . & obot̄ de gt̄.

ꝑ In Weſtrefelda tenuit Aſeret . ı . ſoc̄ abb̄is . xx . v . ac̄ . ſēp . ı . car̄
& . ı . ac̄ p̄ti . 7 uat̄ . v . ſot . Herueus teñ de abbate iuſſu regis.

In ead̄ . Turchillus lib̄ hō cōm̄ . vııı . ac̄ . 7 uat̄ . xvı . d̄ .
hc̄ tenuit herueus de rege . & m̄ de abb̄e iuſſu reḡ ſic ipſe dicit

384 a
Soca reḡ

In the same (Barham) 1 free man in the jurisdiction and patronage of the Abbot; 35 acres. Then 1 plough, now ½.
Then 1 smallholder, now 2.
Meadow, 3 acres; 1 mill.
Value then 10s; now 20[s].
Roger of Auberville held (this) from the King; now [he holds it] from the Abbot.

27 In SHARPSTONE 3 free men in the jurisdiction and patronage of the Abbot; 8 acres. 2 oxen.
Value then 20d; now 2s.
W(illiam) of Écouis held this from the King; now [he holds it] from the Abbot.

28 St. Etheldreda's held WINSTON before 1066; 1 carucate of land in lordship and 40 acres as a manor.
Always 6 villagers; 4 smallholders.
Then 2 ploughs in lordship, now 1; always 3 men's ploughs.
Meadow, 6 acres; woodland, then 100 pigs, now 60.
A church, 8 acres.
2 cobs, 4 cattle, 20 pigs, 50 sheep.
Value then £4; now [£] 4 10s.
1 free man, Alsi, in the jurisdiction and patronage of the Abbot, was added to this manor; 30 acres as a manor.
Always 2 smallholders;
1 plough.
Value 10s.
It has 1 league in length and 3 furlongs in width; 13½d in tax.

29 In WESTERFIELD Aseret, 1 Freeman of the Abbot's, held 25 acres.
Always 1 plough.
Meadow, 1 acre.
Value 5s.
Hervey holds (this) from the Abbot by order of the King.
In the same (Westerfield) Thorkell, a free man under patronage; 8 acres.
Value 16d.
Hervey held this from the King; now [he holds it] from the Abbot by order of the King, as he says.
The jurisdiction (is) the King's.

384 a

In Petehaga Idē turchillus . dim̄ cōm Abƀi . t . r . e . & dim̄.
Guert . xx . aē . & . 1 . aē p̄ti . & . 1 . uiłł . & dim̄ . caʀ . & uał . v . foł . hē &iā
tenuit herueus de rege . & m̄ de abƀe iuſſu regis ſiē ipſe dicit
Dim̄ foca abƀis . & ante ceſſoris hugonis.

/ In depłohā dim̄ lib hō foca & cōmdatioē . 1111 . aē . & . uał . viii . đ.
hē tēnuit . Roƀte . malet . de rege . m̄ de abƀe.

/ In Aſſefelda . 1 . lib hō fóc & commendatione . iii . aē . & uał
viii . dēn.

/ In Henlea . 1 . lib . hō comđ . & foé . dimiđ . aē . & . uał . 1 . đ.

/ In torp . Alſi lib hō . foca & commendé . x . aē . 7 uał . xx . đ.

/ In Scaruetuna . 1 . lib homo foca & commendation . 11 . aē
& . uał . 1111 . đ . Gałt tēn.

/ Perehā̃ . dim̄ . H̃ . In Blacheſſala . v . liƀi hóes
in foca & comendation Abƀis . xx . vi . aē . femper dimidia caʀ
7 ualet . 1111 . foł.

/ In Wanteſdena . xii . aē de dñio de Sutburne 7 uał . xx
1111 dēn . In eadē tēn . Moruuinus lib homo . 11 . aē . & uał
1111 . dēn . Idē moruuinus tēn de abƀe.

30 In PETTAUGH the same Thorkell, half under the patronage of the
Abbot and half (under that) of Gyrth before 1066; 20 acres.
  Meadow, 1 acre.
  1 villager.
  ½ plough.
Value 5s.
  Hervey also held this from the King and now [holds it] from the
Abbot by the King's order, as he says.
  The jurisdiction (was) half the Abbot's and (half that) of Hugh's
predecessor.

31 In DEBENHAM a half free man under jurisdiction and patronage;
4 acres.
Value 8d.
  Robert Malet held this from the King; now [he holds it] from
the Abbot.

32 In ASHFIELD 1 free man under jurisdiction and patronage; 3 acres.
Value 8d.

33 In HENLEY 1 free man under patronage and jurisdiction; ½ acre.
Value 1d.

34 In THORPE (Hall) Alsi, a free man under jurisdiction and patronage;
10 acres.
Value 20d.

35 In SHARPSTONE 1 free man under jurisdiction and patronage; 2 acres.
Value 4d.
  Walter holds (this).

PARHAM Half-Hundred
36 In BLAXHALL 5 free men in the jurisdiction and patronage of the
Abbot; 26 acres. Always ½ plough.
Value 4s.

37 In WANTISDEN 12 acres of the lordship of Sudbourne.
Value 24d.
In the same (Wantisden) Morewin, a free man, held 2 acres.
Value 4d.
  Morwin also holds (this) from the Abbot.

⟨V⟩ *PLVMESGATᾱ. H̃.* Sudburnhā teñ S̃ca. A . t . r . e.

ꝓ mañ . vi . caꞧ t̃re . femp . xiiii . uitł . T̃c xv . borđ . modo xxi.

T̃c . ii . feru̇ . T̃c . iii . caꞧ in dñio . m̃ . i . T̃c . xii . caꞧ . houm . modo.

vi . & . vi . poffent reftauꞧ . iiii . a͡c p̃ti . Silua . de xii . porc̃.

⟨: m̃. ii.⟩
T̃c . i . ruñ : femp . vii . añ . 7 xvii . porc̃ . & . c . xx . ou̅s . 7 se̅p

⟨Eccłia . viii . a͡c.⟩
uał . vii . liƀ . h̃t . i . l̅g in lōngo . & dimiđ in lato . 7 xx . đ
|de gelto.

384 b

⟨V⟩ *HERTESMARA. H̃.* Weringhefetᾱ . teñ . S̃ca . A . t . r . e . iiii . caꞧ.

terre ꝓ mañ . m̃ teñ& . Rađ de fauigni q̃rtᾱ ; de . R . peurel . femp

x . uitł . & . ix . borđ . T̃c . iiii . feru̇ . modo . se̅p . ii . caꞧ in dñio . & . iii . caꞧ

houm . & . iiii . a͡c p̃ti . T̃c filua . ꝺ . porc̃ . m̃ . cccc . Ecclia . xvi . a͡c . &

dim̃ . caꞧ . & . ii . runc̃ . & . viii . añ . 7 xxx . porc̃ . & . c . vii . ou̅s . 7 . xviii . cap̃.

T̃c uał . x . liƀ . 7 m̃ fimilit̃ . In ead̃ . iiii . liƀi hoes c͡om . Gotwinus

Brictmar . Ofulfus . DeRolfus . xl . a͡c . femp . ii . caꞧ . 7 uał . x . foł . S̃ca.

Ałd . focᾱ . h̃t . i . l̅g 7 dim̃ in longo 7 . i . l̅g in lat̃ . 7 . ix . deñ de gelto.

Alii ibi tenent.

⟨V⟩ *RISEBRVGE . H̃.* Cedeberia . ii . caꞧ terre . ꝓ . ii . b̦ maneriis

. ii . liƀi hoes . t . r . e . T̃c . ii . borđ . m̃ . v . femp . iiii . feru̇ . T̃c . ii . caꞧ in dñio.

modo . iiii . 7 dim̃ caꞧ hoium . viii . a͡c p̃ti . filua . de xii . porc̃ . hoc

teñ frodo de abƀe . Quando recepit . iiii . runc̃ . modo nullus.

T̃c viii . añ . m̃ . xiiii . T̃c xx . ou̅s . Tota hec t̃ra iacebat in dñio abba-

tiæ . tpr regis eduardi c̅ o̅i confuet̃ . p̅t fex forisfactas s̃ci . e . T̃c uał

xl . foł . m̃ . lx . & h̃t dim̃ l̅g in longo . 7 . iii . q̃r in lato . 7 . i . deñ . 7 . i.

ferdig . de g̅ . Alii ibi teñ.

⟨V⟩ In Copletuna . iii . liƀi hoes . xx . a͡c . S̃ca . A . foc̃ 7 facᾱ 7 c͡om 7 uał . ii.

foł . S̃cs . e . vi . forisfaĉturas.

PLOMESGATE Hundred

38 St. Etheldreda's held SUDBOURNE before 1066 as a manor; 6 carucates of land.
  Always 14 villagers. Then 15 smallholders, now 21; then 2 slaves.
  Then 3 ploughs in lordship, now 1; then 12 men's ploughs, now 6, and 6 could be restored.
  Meadow, 4 acres; woodland at 12 pigs. Then 1 cob, now 2.
    Always 7 cattle, 17 pigs, 120 sheep
Value always £7.
  A church, 8 acres.
  It has 1 league in length and ½ in width; 20d in tax.

HARTISMERE Hundred   384 b
39 St. Etheldreda's held WETHERINGSETT before 1066; 4 carucates of land as a manor. Now Ralph of Savenay holds a fourth (part) from R(anulf) Peverel.
  Always 10 villagers; 9 smallholders. Then 4 slaves, now 2.
  Always 2 ploughs in lordship; 3 men's ploughs.
  Meadow, 4 acres; woodland, then 500 pigs, now 400.
  A church, 16 acres. ½ plough.
  2 cobs, 8 cattle, 30 pigs, 107 sheep, 18 goats.
Value then £10; now the same.
In the same (Wetheringsett) 4 free men under patronage, Godwin, Brictmer, Oswulf, Derwulf; 40 acres. Always 2 ploughs;
Value 10s.
  St. Etheldreda's (has) the jurisdiction. It has 1½ leagues in length and 1 league in width; 9d in tax. Others hold there.

RISBRIDGE Hundred

40 2 free men held CHEDBURGH before 1066; 2 carucates of land as 2 manors.
  Then 2 smallholders, now 5; always 4 slaves.
  Then 2 ploughs in lordship, now 4; ½ men's plough.
  Meadow, 8 acres; woodland at 12 pigs.
Frodo holds this from the Abbot.
  When he acquired it, 4 cobs, now none; then 8 cattle, now 14; then 20 sheep.
The whole of this land lay in the Abbey's lordship before 1066, with every customary due, except for the 6 forfeitures of St. Edmund's.
Value then 40s; now 60[s].
  It has ½ league in length and 3 furlongs in width; 1¼d in tax. Others hold there.

41 In CLOPTON 3 free men; 20 acres.
  St. Etheldreda's has full jurisdiction and patronage.
Value 2s.
  St. Edmund's (has) the 6 forfeitures.

⌐ *DĪM. H̄*.de Cosforda Hecham.teñ.Sc̄a.A.t.r.e.xī.car̓

træ.Tc̄ xxx.uiłł.modo.xxx.vi.Tc̄ xviii.borđ.m̄.xx.vi.

femp.viii.feru̓.Tc̄.iiii.car̓ in dñio.modo.iii.Tc̄ xx.

car̓ hoium.modo xvi. 7 xvi.ac̄ p̓ti.filua.de xx.porc̄.

femp.xi.runc̄.&.xxx.añ,7.clxxv.ou̅s. 7 lx.porc̄. 7 xl.ii.cap̄.

385 a   ~Æcłia.ii.ac̄.

&.ii.uafa apu̅.Tc̄ uał.xx.lib.modo xl.h̄t.i.lg̅. 7.iiii.qr̓ in long̓. 7

.i.lg̅ in lat̓. 7 xv.deñ.de gelt.Alii ibi tenent.

⌐Niedingā teñ.S.A.t.r.e.iii.car̓ træ.Tc̄.viii.uiłł.m̄.vi.Tc̄.vi.borđ.

m̄.ix.Tc̄.iii.ferui.m̄.i.femp.iii.car̓ in dñio.Tc̄.ii.car̓ hoium.m̄

.i.viii.ac̄ p̓ti.Silua vi.porc̄. 7.i.moł. 7.ii.runc̄. 7 xiiii.animał.

.c.ou̅s.& xx.porc̄. 7 æcc̄lia.vii.ac̄. 7.ii.foc̄.de.xiiii.ac̄.Tc̄.i.car̓.

modo.ii.bou̅.Tc̄ uał.iiii.lib.m̄.viii.h̄t.i.lg̅ in longo. 7.iii.qr̓ in lat̓.

7.ii.deñ.& oboł de gł.

⌐In hecham.v.foc̄.lx.ac̄.Tc̄.ii.car̓.&.dim̄.m̄.i. 7.iii.ac̄ p̓ti. 7 uał

x.foł.Rog̅ bigot tenet. ⌐In eađ...cxx ac̄ de dñio. 7.iii.borđ.

7.i.carr̓. 7.i.ac̄ & dim̄.p̓ti. 7 uał.x.foł.In eađ.i.foc̄.xl.ac̄. 7 uał

.v.foł.hoc tenet.Ricard̓ filǐ.G.comitis.

⌐Biffcopes.*H̄*.Wineḃgā teñ.lib̓ hõ de q̃.fc̄a.A.c̄omenđ.t.r.e.

ii.carr̓ træ. 7.vii.borđ.Tc̄.ii.car̓ in dominio.m̄.i.fēp.ii.car̓ houm.

xi.ac̄ p̓ti.filua.c.xl.porc̄.Tc̄.ii.runc̄.m̄.i. 7.i.añ.Tc̄.lx.porc̄.

m̄.xx. 7 xx.ou̅s. 7.ii.rufc̄.Ecc̄lia xx.iiii.ac̄. 7 uał.iiii.foł.

Half-Hundred of COSFORD

42 St. Etheldreda's held HITCHAM before 1066; 11 carucates of land.
Then 30 villagers, now 36; then 18 smallholders, now 26; always
8 slaves.
Then 4 ploughs in lordship; now 3; then 20 men's ploughs, now 16.
Meadow, 16 acres; woodland at 20 pigs. Always 11 cobs, 30 cattle,
175 sheep, 60 pigs, 42 goats, 2 beehives.
A church, 2 acres.
Value then £20; now [£] 40.
It has 1 league and 4 furlongs in length and 1 league in width;
15d in tax. Others hold there.

43 St. Etheldreda's held NEDGING before 1066; 3 carucates of land.
Then 8 villagers, now 6; then 6 smallholders, now 9; then 3 slaves,
now 1.
Always 3 ploughs in lordship. Then 2 men's ploughs, now 1.
Meadow, 8 acres; woodland, 6 pigs; 1 mill. 2 cobs, 14 cattle,
100 sheep, 20 pigs.
A church, 7 acres.
2 Freemen with 14 acres. Then 1 plough, now 2 oxen.
Value then £4; now [£] 8.
It has 1 league in length and 3 furlongs in width; 2½d in tax.

44 In HITCHAM 5 Freemen; 60 acres. Then 2½ ploughs, now 1.
Meadow, 3 acres.
Value 10s.
Roger Bigot holds (this).
In the same (Hitcham) 123 acres of [land in] lordship.
3 smallholders.
1 plough. Meadow, 1½ acres.
Value 10s.
In the same (Hitcham) 1 Freeman; 40 acres.
Value 5s.
Richard son of Count Gilbert holds this.

BISHOP'S Hundred

45 A free man, over whom St. Etheldreda's had patronage before 1066,
held WINGFIELD; 2 carucates of land.
7 smallholders.
Then 2 ploughs in lordship, now 1; always 2 men's ploughs.
Meadow, 11 acres; woodland, 140 pigs. Then 2 cobs, now 1;
1 cattle; then 60 pigs, now 20; 20 sheep; 2 [bee] hives.
A church, 24 acres; value 4s.

& xiii . libi hoes . lxxx . ac . ex uno habuit antec . Rob . male& cõ
m̃ . Tc . iiii . car . m̃ . iii . Tc ual& . iiii . lib . 7 xiii . fol . 7 . iiii . d . m̃
iiii . lib . H̃ reclamat Ro . bigot . de dono regis . fed abbas de eli de
rationauit fup eũ . m̃ ten . Rog̃ p refpectũ . foca in hoxa.
In Lon . i . Leug 7 . ii . qr . & . in lat . iiii . qr . & . xi . d . & obol . de gt
Alii ibi tenent.

⫫In Sahā . i . lib hõ cõmdation . i . car . trǣ . & . ii . uilt . 7 . iii . bord.
femp . ii . car . & . v . ac . p̃ti . filua . x . porc . Tc ual xx . fol . m̃ . xxv.

385 b

foca In oxa . hoc tenuit Robt mal& . de rege ; Abbas derationaũ
& eā Rob de eo teñ.

⫫In blidinga . H̃ . teñ sca adeldrida Alnetne . p man̄ . t . r . e . ii . car
trǣ . Tc . ix . uilt . modo . vii . femp . xiii . bord . femp . i . fer . femper
ii . car in dominio . 7 . iii . car hoium . 7 dim̄ . Æcclia . de . ii . ac.
filua ad vi . porc . ii . ac p̃ti . 7 . i . runc . & . viii . añ . 7 xxviii . ous.
& viii . porc . 7 xvi . cap̄ . Huic manerio ptinet lxxx . burgenfes.
★ in dunewic . 7 manent . iii . xiiii . ac . sẽp ual . c . fol.
In eat . iii . libi hoes ptinent manentes in befemera de xiiii . ac.
& . i . car . & ual . iii . fol . S . A . focā . 7 facā.

⫫H̃ . DECOLENESSE . In moreftuna . i . lib hõ . Vluiet
de . v . ac . cõmd . Æ . sca . t . r . e . 7 ual xvi . d . h̃ ten& de sca . R . mat.
⫫In trelega . i . lib hõ . Leuuricus . de xl . ac . p man̄ . cõmd abbis.
t . r . e . hunc ten& Rog̃ bigot de rege . Abbas derationauit & eam
. R . de eo ten& . 7 . i . car . 7 . iii . bord . i . ac p̃ti . 7 . i . lib hõ fub fe.
de . iiii . ac . 7 ual xx . fol.

13 free men; 80 acres. Robert Malet's predecessor had patronage over one of them. Then 4 ploughs, now 3.

Value then £4 13s 4d; now £4.

Roger Bigot claims this by the King's gift, but the Abbot of Ely established his claim against him. Now Roger holds (it) through a postponement.

The jurisdiction (is) in Hoxne. It has 1 league and 2 furlongs in length, and 4 furlongs in width; 11½d in tax. Others hold there.

46 In (Monk) SOHAM 1 free man under patronage; 1 carucate of land.
2 villagers; 3 smallholders.
Always 2 ploughs.
Meadow, 5 acres; woodland, 10 pigs.
Value then 20s; now 25[s].
The jurisdiction (is) in Hoxne.

385 b

Robert Malet held this from the King. The Abbot established his claim to it. Robert holds (it) from him.

In BLYTHING Hundred
47 St. Etheldreda's held *ALNETERNE* as a manor before 1066; 2 carucates of land.
Then 9 villagers, now 7; always 13 smallholders; always 1 slave.
Always 2 ploughs in lordship; 3 men's ploughs.
½ church with 2 acres.
Woodland for 6 pigs; meadow, 2 acres. 1 cob, 8 cattle, 28 sheep, 8 pigs, 16 goats.
To this manor belong 80 burgesses living in Dunwich; they dwell [on] 14 acres.
Value always 100s.
In the same (*Alneterne*) belong 3 free men who dwell in Bosmere, with 14 acres. 1 plough.
Value 3s.
St. Etheldreda's (has) full jurisdiction.

Hundred of COLNEIS
48 In MORSTON 1 free man, Wulfgeat, under the patronage of St. Etheldreda's before 1066, with 5 acres.
Value 16d.
R(obert) Malet holds this from St. (Etheldreda's).

49 In TRIMLEY 1 free man, Leofric, under the patronage of the Abbot before 1066, with 40 acres as a manor. Roger Bigot holds this (free man) from the King. The Abbot established his claim and Roger holds it from him. 1 plough.
3 smallholders.
Meadow, 1 acre.
1 free man under him, with 4 acres.
Value 20s.

In Waletuna . I . liƀa femina . Alueua . XVI . aᴄ . ᴄomᵭ . abƀis . & . II .
borᵭ . 7 diṁ . caᵲ . & uaɫ . III . foɫ . h . berruari̓ ten& de abbate
& tenuit de rege . fed abbas derationauit . 7 In plūgeard . I . liƀ
hō . Æ . Edwin . de . II . aᴄ . 7 uaɫ . IIII . ᵭ . 7 ṁ ten& iᵭ . H . de abƀe .

In Kenebroc . I . liƀ hō . Edeldridæ . Godricus . VII . aᴄ . 7 II boū
7 uaɫ . XX . ᵭ . hᴄ tenuit . Roᵹ . bgot de rege . fed abbas derationauit . & eū . Roᵹ . bigot . de eo ten . fᴄa Edeldridā . focā
ex . V . hunᵭ . 7 diṁ . 7 reddet illi XI . liƀ ;

. H̃ . DE CARLEFORDA . Kẏngeſtunā . teñ fᴄa . E̓ . t . r . e .
II . caᵲ terre . ℈ mã . Tᴄ . VIII . uiɫɫ . ṁ . v . ṁ . VIII . borᵭ . Tᴄ . II . feᵲu .
ṁ . I . Sep in dominio . II . carᵲ . 7 . III . carᵲ hoṁ . & . VIII . aᴄ
& diṁ p̓ti . filua ad . v . porᴄ . Semp . I . runᴄ . 7 . IIII . aniaɫ
& XXX oūs . 7 XII . porᴄ . femper ualet XL . foɫ . & ɧt in longo .
IIII . qᵲ . 7 . III . in laᵲ . 7 . III . ᵭ in gelᵲ . Alii ibi tenent .

Brihtewella teñ . Sᴄa . t . r . e . ℈ maɦ . II . caᵲ . terre .
Tᴄ . VI . uiɫɫ . ṁ . v . Semp . III . borᵭ . Tᴄ . v . feᵲu . ṁ . II . Semp in
dɦio . II . caᵲ . Tᴄ hoṁ . IIII . caᵲ . ṁ . III . 7 . I . æcᴄlia . fine tᵲa .
& VI . aᴄ p̓ti . 7 . II . moliɦ . Semp . I . runᴄ . 7 . XL . oūs . 7 VIII . porᴄ
& . I . foᴄ . de XII . aᴄ . ~~& manet~~ & manet in neubrumna . 7 femp
uaɫ . XL . foɫ . & ɧt in longo . X . qᵲ . 7 VI . in lato . & de gelᵲ . IIII . deɦ .
& . I . ferding . Alii ibi teɦeᵲ .

In grundeſburc . teñ Algaᵲ liƀ hō . S . e̓ . t . r . e . I . caᵲ terræ . ℈ ṁ .
& . XXX . aᴄ . femp . II . uiɫɫ . & . v . borᵭ ꞉ femp in dɦiꝋ . II . caᵲ . 7 houm .
. I . caᵲ . IIII . aᴄ p̓ti . Sep . III . runᴄ . 7 . V̓I . aɦ . 7 XVI . porᴄ . 7 LXX oūs .

50 In WALTON 1 free woman, Aelfeva, under the patronage of the Abbot; 16 acres.
    2 smallholders.
    ½ plough.
Value 3s.
    H(ervey) of Berry holds this from the Abbot. He held (it) from the King but the Abbot established his claim.

51 In 'PLUMGEARD' 1 free man of (St.) Etheldreda's, Edwin, with 2 acres.
Value 4d.
    Now H(ervey) also holds (this) from the Abbot.

52 In KEMBROKE 1 free man of (St.) Etheldreda's, Godric; 7 acres. 2 oxen.
Value 20d.
    Roger Bigot held this from the King, but the Abbot established his claim and Roger Bigot holds him from him.
    St. Etheldreda's (has) the jurisdiction of the 5½ Hundreds; it is worth £11 to it.

Hundred of COSFORD   386 a

53 St. Etheldreda's held KINGSTON before 1066; 2 carucates of land as a manor.
    Then 8 villagers, now 5; now 8 smallholders; then 2 slaves, now 1.
    Always 2 ploughs in lordship; 3 men's ploughs.
    Meadow, 8½ acres; woodland for 5 pigs. Always 1 cob, 4 cattle, 30 sheep, 12 pigs.
Value always 40s.
    It has 4 furlongs in length and 3 in width; 3d in tax. Others hold there.

54 St. (Etheldreda's) held BRIGHTWELL before 1066 as a manor; 2 carucates of land.
    Then 6 villagers, now 5; always 3 smallholders. Then 5 slaves, now 2.
    Always 2 ploughs in lordship. Then 4 men's ploughs, now 3.
    1 church, without land.
    Meadow, 6 acres; 2 mills. Always 1 cob, 40 sheep, 8 pigs.
    1 Freeman with 12 acres; he dwells in Newbourn.
Value always 40s.
    It has 10 furlongs in length and 6 in width; 4¼d in tax. Others hold there.

55 In GRUNDISBURGH Algar, a free man of St. Etheldreda's, held before 1066; 1 carucate of land as a manor and 30 acres.
    Always 2 villagers; 5 smallholders.
    Always 2 ploughs in lordship; 1 men's plough.
    Meadow, 4 acres. Always 3 cobs, 6 cattle, 16 pigs, 70 sheep,

&.iii.uaſa apū.Tc ual& xx.ſot.m̄.xL.ſot.h̄ ten& her-

★ ueus.deberuari⁹ ~~deberuari~~.dè.Sc̄a.ẽ.7 h̄t.x.qr̄ in lōngum

&.vi.in latū.& de gelt xv.d.

⌠In Grundeſburgh.iii.dimidii.h̄oes.cōm.Algari.t.r.e.

vii.ac̄.7 ual xii.deñ.

⌠In haſcetuna.xx.ii.ac̄.&.ual.iiii.ſot.

⌠In Thiſteldena.teñ.ı.lib̄ hō.Vlmarus.cōm.ſc̄e.ẽ.Lx.ac̄.

p̱.mañ.7.v.lib̄i hōes ſub ſe.Ex his fuer̄.ıı.cōm̄d ante.c.G.de magna uitt.

386 b

Tc̄.i.car &.dim̄.m̄.ı.&.iii.ac̄ p̄ti.Tc̄ ual.x.ſot.modo xii.Qn̄do

recep̄.ı.runc.7 m̄.Tc̄.v.añ.7 m̄;xv.porc̄.7 L.ōus.7 xii.cap̄.

7.v.uaſa apum.

⌠In parua belinges.ıı.lib̄i hōes.dè xx.ac̄.cōm̄ d̄at.Sc̄e.E.7 dimid̄.

car.& ual.iii.ſolidoS.

⌠In foxehola.xv.ac̄.7 ual.ıı.ſot.Iñ bucleſh̄a.v.ac̄.7 ual viii.dener̄.

⌠In Riſhemara.teñ Turchillus lib̄ hō.t.r.e.cōm̄d dim̄ ſc̄e.Æ.&

dim̄.Guerti Lxxx.ac̄ tr̄æ.p̱ mañ.Tc̄.ı.car.m̄ dim̄.v.ac̄ p̄ti.

Tc̄ ual.xx.ſot.modo x.⌠In eadc̄.ı.lib̄ hō.Edric cōm̄d.

ſic ali de.xx.ac̄.Tc̄.ı.carr.modo.dim̄.7 dimidia ac̄.p̄ti.

Tc̄ ual.x.ſot.modo.vi.Ad hūc in ead.v.lib̄i.hōes com̄.Turchillus

xv.ac̄.Tc̄.dim̄.car.m̄.nulla.Tc̄ ual.xxx.d.m̄.iii.ſot.

⌠In Todenh̄a.ı.lib̄.hō.Aluric⁹.iiii.ac̄.cōm̄d.cuiuſd̄a cōm̄d.ſc̄e.Æ.

7 ual.viii.d.hoc totum tenet heruéu deberruariū.de.ſc̄a Æ.

3 beehives.
Value then 20s; now 40s.
Hervey of Berry holds this from St. Etheldreda's.
It has 10 furlongs in length and 6 in width; 15d in tax.

56 In GRUNDISBURGH 3 half [free] men under the patronage of Algar
before 1066; 7 acres.
Value 12d.

57 In HASKETON 22 acres.
Value 4s.

58 In THISTLETON 1 free man, Wulfmer, under the patronage of St.
Etheldreda's, held 60 acres as a manor.
5 free men under him; of these, 2 were under the patronage of
Geoffrey de Mandeville's predecessor. Then 1½ ploughs, now 1.   386 b
Meadow, 3 acres.
Value then 10s; now 12[s].
When he acquired it and now, 1 cob; then and now 5 cattle.
15 pigs, 50 sheep, 12 goats, 5 beehives.

59 In LITTLE BEALINGS 2 free men under the patronage of St.
Etheldreda's, with 20 acres. ½ plough.
Value 3s.

60 In FOXHALL 15 acres.
Value 2s.

61 In BUCKLESHAM 5 acres.
Value 8d.

62 In RUSHMERE (St. Andrew) Thorkell, a free man half under the
patronage of St. Etheldreda's and half (under that) of Gyrth, held
before 1066; 80 acres as a manor. Then 1 plough, now ½.
Meadow, 5 acres.
Value then 20s; now 10[s].
In the same (Rushmere St. Andrew) 1 free man, Edric, under the
same patronage as the other, with 20 acres. Then 1 plough, now ½.
Meadow, ½ acre.
Value then 10s; now 6[s].
Also in the same (Rushmere St. Andrew) 5 free men under the
patronage of Thorkell; 15 acres. Then ½ plough, now none.
Value then 30d; now 3s.

63 In TUDDENHAM 1 free man, Aelfric, under the patronage of someone
under the patronage of St. Etheldreda's; 4 acres.
Value 8d.
Hervey of Berry holds the whole of this from St. Etheldreda's.

⟍In Kalletuna teñ iſaac . VIII . libo hoes cõmdat . Sce . Æ . I . car terre
& . II bord . Tc . III . car . m̄ . I . IIII . ac p̃ti . 7 ual . XVI . ſol . 7 hab& in
long . VI . q̃r . & . II . in lat . & de gelt . II . deñ . & obolū . ~~homo teñ&~~ Iſaac
de abbe.

⟍In ingolueſtuna . I . lib homo . de . XVI . ac . 7 dim̄ . ac p̃ti . 7 dim̄ . car .
7 ual . III . ſol . hoc tenet . R . malet . de abb.

⟍In isLeueſtuna . I . liba femina . cõmd . Sce . E . XXX . ac . Tc . I . car . m̄
dim̄ . II . bord . IIII . ac p̃ti . 7 . I . lib ~~homo . de~~ . X . ac . 7 ual . IIII . ſol.

⟍In burh . VI . ac . 7 ual XII . deñ . ⟍In biſchelea . IIII . ac . 7 ual . VIII .
d . ⟍In riſemara . I . lib homo . Leuric Cõmd . S . Æ . XL . ac . 7 VII . bord.

& . I . car . 7 dim̄ . I . ac p̃ti . 7 ual . X . ſol.

★ ⟍In fineſford . I . liba femina keueua . cõmdat . Sce . Æ . XL . ac . 7 . I . car .
7 IIII . bord . 7 ual . VI . ſol.

⟍*H . DE WILEFORDA* . In Suttuna . Ro . mal& . teñ . dim̄.
lib hõ . Goduuinus . cõmd . S . e . de . XII . ac . p man̄ . 7 dim̄ bord . Tc
dim̄ car . 7 modo . I . ac p̃ti . Tc ual . II . ſol . modo . V . In ead . IX . lib
hõ ſub eo . 7 . I . lib hõ cõmd Sce . Æ . XL . ac . Tc . I . car . m̄ . ſimil . dim̄ .
ac p̃ti . Tc ual . IIII . ſol . modo . VII.

64 In *KALLETUNA* Isaac held 8 free men under the patronage of St. Etheldreda's; 1 carucate of land.
    2 smallholders.
    Then 3 ploughs, now 1. Meadow, 4 acres.
  Value 16s.
    It has 6 furlongs in length and 2 in width; 2½d in tax.
    Isaac [holds this] from the Abbot.

65 In *INGOLUESTUNA* 1 free man with 16 acres.
    Meadow, ½ acre.
    ½ plough.
  Value 3s.
    R(obert) Malet holds this from the Abbot.

66 In ISLETON 1 free woman under the patronage of St. Etheldreda's; 30 acres. Then 1 plough, now ½.
    2 smallholders.
    Meadow, 4 acres.
    1 free man with 10 acres.
  Value 4s.

67 In BURGH 6 acres.
  Value 12d.

68 In BIXLEY 4 acres.
  Value 8d.

69 In RUSHMERE (St. Andrew) 1 free man, Leofric, under the patronage of St. Etheldreda's; 40 acres.
    7 smallholders.
    1½ ploughs. Meadow, 1 acre. 387 a
  Value 10s.

70 In 'FINESFORD' 1 free woman, Leofeva, under the patronage of St. Etheldreda's; 40 acres. 1 plough.
    4 smallholders.
  Value 6s.

Hundred of WILFORD
71 In SUTTON Ro(bert) Malet holds a half free man, Godwin, under the patronage of St. Etheldreda's, with 12 acres as a manor.
    A half smallholder.
    Then and now ½ plough. Meadow, 1 acre.
  Value then 2s; now 5[s].
In the same (Sutton) 9 free men under him and 1 free man under the patronage of St. Etheldreda's; 40 acres. Then 1 plough, now the same.
    Meadow, ½ acre.
  Value then 4s; now 7[s].

⨍ In Capeles . iii . libi . hões 7 dim̃ cõmd̃ . Scæ . e . xv . ac̃ . tr̃e . Tc̃ . i . car̃.
m̃ dim̃ . Tc̃ . ual& . ii . ſot . modo . iiii . 7 In Scoteſhā . i . liɓ hõ 7 dimiɗ
cõmd̃ eiɗe . vii . ac̃ . 7 ual . xii . ɗ.

⨍ In bramesſwella . i . liɓ hõ 7 dim̃ . cõmend̃ . S . æ . viii . ac̃ . dim̃ . carr̃.
7 ual . xvi . den̄ . ħ ten& . R . mal& . de sc̃a Æ.

⨍ In bredefelda . iii . liɓos hões . integros . 7 . iii . dim̃ 7 quarta parte . i . liɓi
xx . iiii . ac̃ . Tc̃ . ii . car̃ . m̃ dim̃ . 7 ual . vi . ſot . 7 ii . den̄ . Roɓ . malet . de sc̃a æ.
7 . i . liɓ hõ . farmann . xii . ac̃ . in ſoc̃ . 7 cõmdatione aɓɓis . 7 ual . ii . ſot.

⨍ In baldeſeia . ii . liɓi cõmd̃ . S̃ . e . vii . ac̃ . 7 ual . xii . ɗ . ⨍ In alretuna
xii . ac̃ . 7 ual& . ii . ſot . ⨍ In carsfelda . ii . liɓi hões cõmdat̃ . S̃ . e . xxx.
iii . ac̃ . 7 . i . car̃ . i . ac̃ p̃ti . 7 ual . v . ſot . ⨍ In Capeles . i . liɓ hõ 7 in bradefelda alt̄ . xxx . ii . ac̃ tr̃æ . 7 abbas de heli cõmd̃ . Tc̃ . i . car̃ . m̃ dimiɗ car̃.
ſemper ual& . v . ſot . hoc ten& Ro . malet de abbate de heli.

72 In CAPEL (St. Andrew) 3 free men and a half [free man] under the patronage of St. Etheldreda's; 15 acres of land. Then 1 plough, now ½.
Value then 2s; now 4[s].

73 In SHOTTISHAM 1 free man and a half [free man] under the same patronage; 7 acres.
Value 12d.

74 In BROMESWELL 1 free man and a half [free man] under the patronage of St. Etheldreda's; 8 acres. ½ plough.
Value 16d.
    R(obert) Malet holds this from St. Etheldreda's.

75 In BREDFIELD 3 whole free men and 3 half [free men] and the fourth part of 1 free man; 24 acres. Then 2 ploughs, now ½.
Value 6s 2d.
    Robert Malet [holds this] from St. Etheldreda's.
1 free man, Farman, in the jurisdiction and patronage of the Abbot; 12 acres.
Value 2s.

76 In BAWDSEY 2 free men under the patronage of St. Etheldreda's; 7 acres.
Value 12d.

77 In ALDERTON 12 acres.
Value 2s.

78 In CHARSFIELD 2 free men under the patronage of St. Etheldreda's; 33 acres. 1 plough.
    Meadow, 1 acre.
Value 5s.

79 In CAPEL (St. Andrew) 1 free man and in BREDFIELD another; 32 acres of land. The Abbot of Ely (has) the patronage. Then 1 plough, now ½ plough.
Value always 5s.
    Ro(bert) Malet holds this from the Abbot of Ely.

Meltuna habbis de heli . II . car̄ tr̄æ . ꝓ mañ . Tc̄ . xvIII . uiℓℓ . m̄ . Ix.
Tc̄ . vI . borđ . modo . xIII . Tc̄ . II . feru̇ . m̄ . nuℓℓ . femper . II . car̄ in dn̄io.
Tc̄ . v . car̄r̄ hoi̇um . m̄ . III . 7 dim̄ . xvII . ac̄ p̄ti . I . runc̄ . 7 . I . moliñ.

xI . porc̄ . xxx . vII . ou̇s ; & huic manerio p̄tinet Balderefeia . bereuuita.
& enumerata . & . IIII . fochemanos ; de xxx . II . ac̄ terræ . terr̄a dare non
potuer̄ nec uende . Tc̄ . II . car̄ . m̄ . I . & dim̄ . II . ac̄ p̄ti ι Sep xL . foℓ . uaℓ.
7 ℓit . I . lḡ . I . lḡ in longo . 7 . Ix . q̄r de dim̄ de laℓ . 7 xxvII . den̄ . de gelℓ.
In eađ balderefeia . v . libi hȯes xIx . ac̄ tr̄æ abbas de eli cōmđ femp uaℓ
In hoi̇ . I . lib hō de xIx ac̄ tr̄æ femp dim̄ car̄ . I . ac̄ p̄ti . sēp̱ uaℓ . v̇ ⌐ foℓ. xL . den̄.
In hundeftuf . I . lib homo de . vI . ac̄ terre . Abbas de eli cōmđ . xII . den̄ uaℓ.
In brumefuelle . II . libi hȯes de . x . vI . ac̄ tr̄e . 7 abb̄ de eli cōmđ . xII . đ uaℓ.
In eađ uilla . I . æccℓia de . xvI . ac̄ terræ & uaℓ . II . foℓ . Ehoc eft
dominiu̇ abbatis . Et in eađ uilla ten̄ herueu . Lxx . lib̄ȯ hȯes.

tunde abb̄s habuit foc̄a & faca 7 om̄s confuetudines Ex his habuit
antec̄ . R . bigot̄ . cōmđ . de . I . cu̇ . vI . ac̄ . 7 ṁodo xL . v . II . car̄
terræ . 7 xvI . ac̄ . Tc̄ . xII . car̄ . modo . vI . 7 . III . ac̄ p̄ti . Tc̄ uaℓ . xL . foℓ.
7 modo Lx . In eadem . IIII . libi . homines c̄ōmđ abb̄i . Lx . & xvI.
ac̄ tr̄æ . Tc̄ . IIII . car̄ . modo . III . 7 . IIII . ac̄ p̄ti . 7 . II . runc̄ . vI . porc̄.
L . vII . ou̇s . Tc̄ uaℓ . xx . foℓ . 7 modo fimiℓ.
In berdesfella . III . libi . hȯes . cōmđ abb̄ . Lxx . vI . ac̄ tr̄æ ι Tc̄ . III.
car̄ . modo . II . 7 fub eis . III . libi homines de . v . ac̄ . dim̄ ac̄ prati̇.
Tc̄ uaℓ . xv . foℓ . modo . xx.

80 The Abbot of Ely's MELTON; 2 carucates of land as a manor.
Then 18 villagers, now 9; then 6 smallholders, now 13; then
   2 slaves, now none.
Always 2 ploughs in lordship. Then 5 men's ploughs, now 3½.
Meadow, 17 acres. 1 cob. 1 mill. 11 pigs, 37 sheep.
To this manor belongs an outlier, BAWDSEY, and [it has] been
counted.
4 Freemen with 32 acres of land. They could not grant or sell the
land. Then 2 ploughs, now 1½.
Meadow, 2 acres.
Value always 40s.
It has 1 league in length and 9[½] furlongs in width; 27d in tax.
In the same BAWDSEY 5 free men; 19 acres of land. The Abbot of Ely
(has) the patronage.
Value always 40d.

81 In HOO 1 free man with 19 acres of land. Always ½ plough.
Meadow, 1 acre.
Value always 5s.

82 In 'HUNDESTUF' 1 free man with 6 acres of land. The Abbot of Ely
(has) the patronage.
Value 12d.

83 In BROMESWELL 2 free men with 10 acres of land. The Abbot of Ely
(has) the patronage.
Value 12d.
In the same village, 1 church with 16 acres of land; value 2s.
This is (part of) the Abbot's lordship.
In the same village Hervey holds 70 free men over whom the Abbot
had patronage, full jurisdiction and all customary dues. Of these
(free men), R(oger) Bigot's predecessor had patronage over 1 with 6
acres. Now 45 [with] 2 carucates of land and 16 acres. Then 12
ploughs, now 6.
Meadow, 3 acres.
Value then 40s; now 60[s].
In the same (Bromeswell) 4 free men under the patronage of the
Abbot; 60 and 16 acres of land. Then 4 ploughs, now 3.
Meadow, 4 acres. 2 cobs, 6 pigs, 57 sheep.
Value then 20s; now the same.

84 In BREDFIELD 3 free men under the patronage of the Abbot; 76 acres
of land. Then 3 ploughs, now 2.
Under them, 3 free men with 5 acres.
Meadow, ½ acre.
Value then 15s; now 20[s].

In berdefelda . vi . ac qte ante . Ro . mal& . modo ten&.

Herueu de berruarius de abb . hoc totum ten& herueus de abb.

Adhuc in ead . i . æcclia xxx . i . ac . libe terræ . & . ii . ac pti . & ual

In bromefwella herueus . ii . libi hoes . comd . Sce . e . ⌐ . v . fol.

xxii . ac . Tc . ii . car . modo dim . i . ac dim ac pti . Tc ual . iiii . fol.

⌐ m . v.

388 a

In bradefelda . herueus . ii . libi . comd . S . e . iiii . ac . & ual . xii d.

In brumefwella . R . malet ten& . iii . libo . hoes . comend . S . e .

iiii . ac . & ual . ii . fol . In Scotefha . i . ac . & ual . ii . den.

In usforda ten p man . Almar lib ho . t . r . e . comd . Edrici

dim . 7 dim sce . e . lx . ac . Tc . iiii . bord . modo . ii . Tc . i . car .

& dim . m dim . iiii . ac . pti . & . i . molin . Seper ual . x . fol.

In ead . ix . libi hoes . comd eid . pt . ii . Ipfi fuer comd . S . e .

xxv . ac . & . ii . ac pti . Sep . i . car . Semp ual . iiii . fol.

In Ludha . dim lib homo . Morewinus . comd sce . e . xx . ac 7

dim bord . & dim . car . 7 . vii . libi hoes . fub eo . de xx . ac . ii . ac . & dim

pti . Tc . i . car . modo dim . Semp ual . x . fol.

In hora pola . dim . ii . libi hoes . de xiii . ac & dim . & ual xx . den.

85 In BREDFIELD 6 acres which Ro(bert) Malet's predecessor held. Now
Hervey of Berry holds (it) from the Abbot.
    Hervey holds the whole of this from the Abbot.
Also in the same (Bredfield) 1 church, 31 acres of free land.
    Meadow, 2 acres.
Value 5s.

86 In BROMESWELL Hervey [holds]; 2 free men under the patronage of
St. Etheldreda's; 22 acres. Then 2 ploughs, now ½.
    Meadow, 1½ acres.
Value then 4s; now 5[s].

87 In BREDFIELD Hervey holds; 2 free men under the patronage of St.   388 a
Etheldreda's; 4 acres.
Value 12d.

88 In BROMESWELL R(obert) Malet holds 3 free men under the patronage
of St. Etheldreda's; 4 acres.
Value 2s.

89 In SHOTTISHAM 1 acre.
Value 2d.

90 In UFFORD Aelmer, a free man half under the patronage of Edric and
half under (that of) St. Etheldreda's, held 60 acres as a manor
before 1066.
    Then 4 smallholders, now 2.
    Then 1½ ploughs, now ½.
    Meadow, 4 acres; 1 mill.
Value always 10s.
In the same (Ufford) 9 free men under the patronage of the same
man, except for 2 who were under the patronage of St. Etheldreda's;
25 acres.
    Meadow, 2 acres.
    Always 1 plough.
Value always 4s.

91 In LOUDHAM a half free man, Morewin, under the patronage of St.
Etheldreda's; 20 acres.
    A half smallholder.
    ½ plough.
7 free men under him, with 20 acres.
    Meadow, 2½ acres.
    Then 1 plough, now ½.
Value always 10s.

92 In HARPOLE half 2 free men, with 13½ acres.
Value 20d.

ꟼIn meltuna . ı . liƀ hő . S . e . ıı . aꝶ . 7 ual . ıııı . deñ.

ꟼIn horepolo . dım̃ . liƀ homo . S̷ . e . xv . aꝶ . 7 tꝶ . dimidia caꝛr . modo
nulla . 7 ualet . ııı . fol.

Γ . H̃ . DELOSA . HOV . tenuit sꝶa . e . t . r . e . ꝓ mañ . ııı .
caꝛ terræ . Tꝶ xvııı . uıll . modo . x . Tꝶ . ı . borꝺ . modo . xvı . Tꝶ . vı . feru̷ .
modo . ıı . Tꝶ . in dñio . ııı . caꝛ . modo . ıı . Tꝶ . vı . caꝛ hominũ . m̃ . v . Silua
ad . xx . porꝶ . vıı . aꝶ ꝓti . ı . molĩ . & vıı . añ . xxıııı . porꝶ . & xxx . oũs . 7 xL .
capre . Tꝶ ual . c . fol . m̃ . ıııı . liƀ . 7 . ı . ex his caꝛr . cep̄ . W . debu uilla .
. ı . ꝓq derationata ē p ꝓceptũ regis . 7 faifita æcclıæ . fed dominiũ fuum
G . de magna uilla reuocat ad tutoꝛe̷ . 7 dedit inde uadē . modo
eſt t̃ra in manu regis . Huic manerio iacent . ıııı . liƀi hões . comdat
S̷ . Æ . vı . aꝶ t̃re . & ual . xıı . ꝺ . ı . æcclıa . vııı . aꝶ 7 dimiꝺ . & ual xvı . deñ.

7 l̃t in longo . vııı . q̃r . 7 in lato . ıııı . 7 de gelt . ııı . deñ & oboł.

ꟼIn brandeſtuna . ı . liƀ hő . teñ herueus de bituricenfis . S̷ . Æ . vııı . aꝶ . 7 ual
. ıııı . fol . ꟼIn Letheringaham . ııı . aꝶ & dim̃ . de dñio & ual . vı . deñ.

ꟼIn gretingahã . ı . uilla xvı . aꝶ 7 dim̃ . caꝛ . 7 ual . ııı . fol . ꟼIn dalingehou
ıııı . liƀi hões . comꝺ . S̷ æ . dim̃ . caꝛ terræ . Tꝶ . ıı . caꝛ . modo . ı . aꝶ ꝓti . Tꝶ
ual . vııı . fol . modo fimilit̃.

ꟼIn vdebriga . vıı . liƀi hões . t . r . e . modo . ıı . commend . S̷ . Æ . xL . aꝶ .
Tꝶ . ı . caꝛ . Tꝶ ual . vı . fol . modo . v . In ead uilla . Ro mal & . ı . liƀ hő
xvı . aꝶ . 7 dim̃ . 7 dim̃ caꝛ . 7 ual . v . fol.

ꟼIn dalingahou . dim̃ liƀ hő . xvı . aꝶ . 7 ual . ıı . fol . 7 . vııı . ꝺ .

93 In MELTON 1 free man of St. Etheldreda's; 2 acres.
Value 4d.

94 In HARPOLE a half free man of St. Etheldreda's; 15 acres. Then ½
plough, now none.
Value 3s.

Hundred of LOES
95 St. Etheldreda's held HOO before 1066 as a manor; 3 carucates of
land.
 Then 18 villagers, now 10; then 1 smallholder, now 16; then
  6 slaves, now 2.
 Then 3 ploughs in lordship, now 2; then 6 men's ploughs, now 5.
 Woodland for 20 pigs; meadow, 7 acres; 1 mill. 7 cattle, 24 pigs,
  30 sheep, 40 goats.
Value then 100s; now £4.
 W(illiam) of Bouville took 1 of these carucates. It was afterwards
adjudged by the King's command and put in the possession of the
Church; but he recalls his lord, G(eoffrey) de Mandeville, as guarantor
and he gave a pledge for it. Now the land is in the King's hand.
To this manor belong 4 free men under the patronage of St.
Etheldreda's; 6 acres of land.
Value 12d.
 1 church, 8½ acres; value 16d.
 It has 8 furlongs in length and 4 in width; 3½d in tax.   388 b

96 In BRANDESTON Hervey of Bourges holds; 1 free man belonging to
St. Etheldreda's; 8 acres.
Value 4s.

97 In LETHERINGHAM 3½ acres of lordship (land).
Value 6d.

98 In CRETINGHAM 1 villager; 16 acres. ½ plough.
Value 3s.

99 In DALLINGHOO 4 free men under the patronage of St. Etheldreda's;
½ carucate of land. Then 2 ploughs, now 1.
 Meadow, [1] acre.
Value then 8s; now the same.

100 In WOODBRIDGE 7 free men before 1066, now 2, under the patronage
of St. Etheldreda's; 40 acres. Then 1 plough.
Value then 5s; now 5[s].
In the same village, Ro(bert) Malet [holds]; 1 free man; 16½ acres.
½ plough.
Value 5s.

101 In DALLINGHOO a half free man; 16 acres.
Value 2s 8d.

Ⱶ In reslesħa

diħ liƀ ħō . vi . ac̄ . 7 ual . xii . đ . Ⱶ In vdebrige . ii . bord . x . ac̄ . & ual . ii . sol.

Ⱶ In mungedena . i . liƀ ħō . 7 in ceres felda . alt . xviii . ac̄ . 7 ual . iii . sol.

Ⱶ PLVCATA . H̄ . In aldeburc . v . ac̄ . 7 est in dn̄io . 7 ual . x . đ . Normann.

.XXII . Ⱶ TR̄A . Gisleƀti ep̄i . ebroicensis . Wilefort Hund . Vdeħa

tenuit Turmod p̄ uno man . de . ii . car̄ . tr̄æ . Tc̄ . ii . uill . m̄ . vii . Sep̄

. ii . car̄ . in dn̄io . 7 . i . car̄ . hom . 7 . x . ac̄ . p̄ti . i . mol . i . runc̄ . vii . an.

lvi . porc̄ . Tc̄ ual . xl . sol . m̄ . xii . liƀ.

Ⱶ Capescia tenuit brictmar . i . soc̄ . sc̄e Adelđ . l . ac̄ . p . c̄ɔ̄ . 7 n̄ potuit

uend t dare t̄ra . sua . sep̄ . i . uill . 7 . iii . bor . tc̄ . i . car̄ . ii . ac̄ . p̄ti . Tc̄ . i . mol.

7 . reddit . xxxv . sol . in supiori p̄tio . In Ludham xxx liƀi ħōes

cōm̄d Turmodo . ex ħ fuere . xv . cm̄dati Edrici . 7 un̄ fuit cm̄d . Sc̄æ

. A . c̄ . xx . ac̄ . it totu . ħnt . i . car̄ tr̄e . 7 . đ . tc̄ . vi . car̄ . m̄ . iii . vi . ac̄ . p̄ti . Val.

viii . liƀ . 7 . i . eccla . lx . ac̄ . 7 . ual . v . sol . plures ibi parciunt.

389 a

⋆ Ⱶ TR̄A ABB̄IS DE BERNAI ; STOV . H̄ . In cratinga . i . liƀ ħō . de xx . ac̄ . XX.

dim ecclia . x . ac̄ . 7 . i . uill . 7 . ii . bord . Semp . i . car̄ . int oēs . & . ii . ac̄ p̄ti.

102 In RENDLESHAM a half free man; 6 acres.
Value 12d.

103 In WOODBRIDGE 2 smallholders; 10 acres.
Value 2s.

104 In MONEWDEN 1 free man and in CHARSFIELD another; 18 acres.
Value 3s.

PLOMESGATE Hundred
105 In ALDEBURGH 5 acres. It is in lordship.
Value 10d.
Norman [holds this].

22   LAND OF GILBERT, BISHOP OF EVREUX

WILFORD Hundred
1 Thormod held 'UDEHAM' as one manor at 2 carucates of land.
Then 2 villagers, now 7.
Always 2 ploughs in lordship; 1 men's plough.
Meadow, 10 acres; 1 mill. 1 cob, 7 cattle, 56 pigs.
Value then 40s; now £12.

2 Brictmer, 1 Freeman of St. Etheldreda's, held CAMPSEY (Ash); 50
acres as a manor. He could not sell or grant his land.
Always 1 villager; 3 smallholders.
Then 1 plough.
Meadow, 2 acres; then 1 mill.
It pays 35s in the above assessment.

3 In LOUDHAM 34 free men under the patronage of Thormod. Of
these, 15 were under the patronage of Edric and 1 was under the
patronage of St. Etheldreda's with 20 acres. Between them all they
have 1½ carucates of land. Then 6 ploughs, now 3.
Meadow, 6 acres.
Value £8.
1 church, 60 acres; value 5s.
Several have a share there.

23   LAND OF THE ABBOT OF BERNAY   389 a

STOW Hundred
1 In CREETING (St. Peter) 1 free man with 20 acres.
½ church, 10 acres.
1 villager, 2 smallholders.
Always 1 plough between them all. Meadow, 2 acres.

App̃tiata eſt in cratinga in alio. h̃. In ead̃. I. lib̃ hõ. de. v. ac̃. ap̃tiata c̃
Rex dedit. de feudo harduini.

⁋ BOSEALARA. H. Cratingas teñ Aluricus lib̃ homo. I. carr̃ terræ
& dim̃. p man̄. femp. IIII. uilli. 7 XII. bord. &. II. ferũ. Tc̃. II. carr̃ in dñio.
m̃. I. Tc̃. II. car̃ hoũm. m̃. I. &. IIII. ac̃ p̃ti. 7 VI. an̄. 7 XV. porc̃. Tc̃. c. oũs.
m̃. XXX. VI. Tc̃ ual. c. fol. modo. VI. lib̃. Niwetuñã. teñ Aluuricus. I. car̃
træ. p man̄. t. r. e. femp. III. uill. 7 XII. bord. 7. I. ferũ. 7. I. car̃ in dominio.
Tc̃. II. car̃ hoiũm modo. I. v. ac̃ p̃ti. filua de. VI. porc̃. 7. II. mol̃. 7 ual. LX. fol.
⁋ In Cratingas. XX. IIII. lib̃i hões. I. carr̃ terræ. 7. I. uirg̃. Tc̃. III. car̃. modo
. I. & dimid. 7 ual XX. fol. Æcclia. de. XII. ac̃ Niuetuna ht̃. VI. qr̃ in lõgo
7. III. in lat. &. v. den̄ de gelt̃. Rex & comes de toto foc̃ã In Vledana Aluuĩ
. II. lib̃ hões. XI. ac̃. Tc̃ dim̃. car̃. m̃ nichil. in eod̃ p̃tio;

★ ⁋ T̃RE ABBATIÆ. DE CETE.. HT. DIMID. H. de cosfort.   ; XXIIII
Carefcia tenuit. Sc̃a maria t. r. e. III. car̃ træ. 7 dim̃. femp. VI.
uilti. 7 XVIII. bord. 7. I. ferũ. &. II. car̃ in dominio. 7. IIII. car̃ hoũm. &.
. IIII. ac̃ p̃ti. filua. LX. porc̃. 7. I. molin̄. 7. I. runc̃. &. X. an̄. &. XXX. VI.
porc̃. 7. c. XL. oũs. 7. III. uafa ap̃. Ecclia. III. ac̃. &. I. foc̃. II. ac̃. 7. I. lib̃ hõ
XX. ac̃. 7. I. ũcar̃. 7. I. ac̃ p̃ti. Tc̃ ual h̃ man̄. IIII. lib̃. modo. c. fol. 7
Lib̃ hõ. IIII. fol. IIII. d̃. min̄. ht̃. VIII. qr̃ in longo. 7. VI. in lato. 7 VII.
den̄ & obol de gelt̃;

RISBRIDGE Hundred

1 Aelfric held CLARE as a manor; 24 carucates of land before 1066.
   Then 40 villagers, later 35, now 30; then and later 10
      smallholders, now 30; always 20 slaves.
   Then 12 ploughs in lordship, later 6, now 7; then 36 men's
      ploughs, later 30, now 24.
   Meadow, 37 acres; woodland at 12 pigs; always 1 mill. now
      5 *arpents* of vines. Always 6 cobs. Then 10 cattle, now 14;
      then 12 pigs, now 60; then 60 sheep, now 480; 12 beehives.
   Always 1 market; now 43 burgesses.
   Aelfric son of Withgar gave this manor to St. John's before 1066
with the assent of his son and placed therein a certain Ledmer the
priest and others with him. When a charter had been made, he
committed the Church and the whole place to the custody of Abbot
Leofstan and into the protection of his son Withgar. The clerics
could not grant this land or alienate it from St. John's. But after
King William came, he took possession of it into his own hand.
To this manor have always belonged 5 Freemen with every
customary due; 1½ carucates of land. Always 1½ ploughs.
   Meadow, 6 acres.
Value then £40; now the same. It has 2 leagues in length and 1 in
width; 15d in tax.

2 HUNDON; Withgar [held it] before 1066 as a manor; 25 carucates of
land and 20 acres.
   Then and later 54 villagers, now 41. Always 30 smallholders;
      14 slaves.
   Then 9 ploughs in lordship, later 4, now 7; then 31 men's ploughs,
      later and now 23.
   Meadow, 45 acres; woodland at 160 pigs; always 1 mill.
   A church, ½ carucate of free land. Another church, 4½ acres.
Always 1 plough.
   Meadow, 3 acres. Then 2 cobs, now 6; then 14 cattle, now 31;
      then 130 pigs, now 160; then 80 sheep, now 480; now 17
      beehives.
Value then £30; later and now [£] 40 4s.
   It has 2 leagues and 2 furlongs in length, and 1 league in width;　　390 a
15d in tax. Others hold there.

Defelingā tenuit . Wifcar . p man̄ . t . r . e . xx . car̄ terræ . femp

xxviii . uilt . 7 lxxx . xi . bord̄ . 7 xx . ferū . & . x . car̄ in dn̄io . 7 xxx.

ii car̄ . hominū . & xv . ac̄ p̄ti . Silua lxxx . porc̄ . Tc̄ . v . molin̄ . m̄.

iiii . Duæ æcclïæ . i . car̄ terræ 7 dimid . 7 . i . car̄ & dim̄ . Tc̄ . viii . runc̄.

m̄ . v . Tc̄ . xviii . an̄ . m̄ . xl . tc̄ . c . porc̄ . modo lxxx . Tc̄ ɒccc . xl . ous . m̄ . ɒccc

& . ix . uafa apū . Tc̄ ual . xxx . lib̄ . P̊ 7 modo . xl . Sed tn̄ dedit cuidā

p̄pofito ad firmā ꝓ lx . v . lib̄ . fed maneriū non potuit pati . Et h̄t

. ii . lḡ 7 dim̄ in longo . 7 . i . lḡ in lat̄ . 7 xxx . vii . den̄ de gelto . in duob₃ h̄.

h̄ · ten̄ . Rob̄. In danerdeftuna . i . foc̄ . ii . car̄ terræ . 7 . x . ac̄ . p man̄ . 7 . iii . bord̄.

7 . ii . ferū . Tc̄ . iii . car̄ . modo . ii . & . ii . ac̄ p̄ti . filua . de . x . porc̄ . modo

ii . runc̄ . 7 xiii . an̄ . 7 xx . viii . porc̄ . 7 xxx . ii . ous . 7 . iiii . cap̊ . Tc̄ 7 p̊

ual xl . fot . modo . l.

In Cleptuna . ii . foc̄ . i . car̄ terre . 7 lxxx . 7 . i . ac̄ . & dimid . &

. ix . bord̄ . & . ii . ferū . Tc̄ . ii . car̄ in dn̄io . m̄ . iii . & dimidia . car̄ hoūm.

& . iii . ac̄ p̄ti . filua de . iiii . porc̄ . femp . ii . runc̄ . Tc̄ . vi . an̄ . m̄ . xii . m̄

xxx . porc̄ . Tc̄ xl . ous . modo . lxxx . & . iii . uafa apū . Tc̄ ual xx . fot.

m̊ . xl . Danardeftuna h̄t . i . lḡ in lonḡ . & . iii . qr̄ . in lat̄ . 7 . ii . &

obot . de gelt̄ . Et Cloptuna h̄t . i . lḡ in longo . & . iii . qr̄ . in lat̄.

& . vi . d̄ . & obot de gelt̄.

In dalham . i . foc̄ . ii . car̄ terre . & . i . uilt . & . v . bord̄ . & . ii . ferū . & . ii.

car̄ in dn̄io . Tc̄ . ii . car̄ hominū . modo . i . & dimidia . & . ii . ac̄ p̄ti.

filua lx . porc̄ . femp . ii . runc̄ . & . x . an̄ . modo . xvi . Tc̄ xxiiii . porc̄.

m̄ . xxx . Tc̄ . c . ous . modo . cl . 7 . l . cap̊ . Tc̄ ual xl . fot . m̄ . lx . i . æcclia

xl . ac̄ libæ tr̄æ & dimidia car̄ . 7 ual . v . fot . H̄ ten̄ Wilłmus peccatū.

In denhā . ii . foc̄ . iii . car̄ terre . femp . v . uilt . & . xiii . bord̄ . & . i . ferū . Tc̄.

iiii . car̄ in dominio . modo . iii . femp . iiii . car̄ hom̄ . vi . ac̄ p̄ti . filua xx.

porc̄ . Ecclia abfq₃ tr̄a . h̄ ten & . W . hurant . Tc̄ . i . eq̄ . m̄ . ii . m̄ . iiii.

an̄ . Tc̄ xv . porc̄ . modo . xxx . iii . 7 lxxii . ous . 7 xxx . viii . cap̊ . Tc̄ ual

iii . lib̄ . modo . iiii . 7 x . fot.

3 Withgar held DESNING as a manor before 1066; 20 carucates of land.
    Always 28 villagers; 91 smallholders; 20 slaves;
    10 ploughs in lordship; 32 men's ploughs.
    Meadow, 15 acres; woodland, 80 pigs; then 5 mills, now 4.
    2 churches, 1½ carucates of land. 1½ ploughs.
    Then 8 cobs, now 5; then 18 cattle, now 40; then 100 pigs,
        now 80; then 840 sheep, now 960; 9 beehives.
Value then £30; later and now [£] 40; nevertheless he gave it to a
reeve at a revenue for £65, but the manor could not bear it.
    It has 2½ leagues in length and 1 league in width; 37d in tax in
two Hundreds.
    Robert holds this.

4 In DENSTON 1 Freeman; 2 carucates of land and 10 acres as a manor.
    3 smallholders, 2 slaves.
    Then 3 ploughs, now 2. Meadow, 2 acres; woodland at 10 pigs.
        Now 2 cobs, 13 cattle, 28 pigs, 32 sheep, 4 goats.
Value then and later 40s; now 50[s].

5 In CLOPTON 2 Freemen; 1 carucate of land and 81½ acres.
    9 smallholders, 2 slaves.
    Then 2 ploughs in lordship, now 3; ½ men's plough.
    Meadow, 3 acres; woodland at 4 pigs. Always 2 cobs. Then 6
        cattle, now 12; now 30 pigs; then 40 sheep, now 80; 3 beehives.
Value then 20s; now 40[s].

5a   Denston has 1 league in length and 3 furlongs in width; 2½d in tax.
    Clopton has 1 league in length and 3 furlongs in width; 6½d in tax.

6 In DALHAM 1 Freeman; 2 carucates of land.
    1 villager; 5 smallholders, 2 slaves.
    2 ploughs in lordship; then 2 men's ploughs, now 1½.
    Meadow, 2 acres; woodland, 60 pigs. Always 2 cobs. [Then] 10
        cattle, now 16; then 24 pigs, now 30; then 100 sheep, now
        150; 50 goats.
Value then 40s; now 60[s].
    1 church, 40 acres of free land. ½ plough. Value 5s.   390 b
    William Peche holds this.

7 In DENHAM 2 Freemen; 3 carucates of land.
    Always 5 villagers; 13 smallholders; 1 slave.
    Then 4 ploughs in lordship, now 3; always 4 men's ploughs.
    Meadow, 6 acres; woodland, 20 pigs.
    A church, without land.
William Hurant holds this.
    Then 1 horse, now 2; now 4 cattle; then 15 pigs, now 33; 72
        sheep, 38 goats.
Value then £3; now [£] 4 10s.

In auo Keduna.ɪ.foc͂.ɪ.car̄ terræ.femp.&.ɪɪ.uiłł.7.ɪ.feru̅.&.ɪ.car̄.
in dn̄io.7 dim̅ car̄ hou̅m.7 uał.xx.foł.hoc ten̄ Gifłeƀ.

In auo Keduna.ɪ.foc͂.ɪ.car̄ terræ.&.modo.ɪɪɪ.borđ.&.ɪ.feru̅.femp
.ɪ.car̄ in dn̄io.&.ɪɪɪɪ.ac͂ p̄ti.femp uał.xx.foł.Hoc ten& fulkeredus.

In Wratinga.ɪ.foc͂.ɪ.car̄ terræ.femp.ɪ.uiłł.&.ɪɪɪ.borđ &.ɪ.car̄
in dominio.Tc͂ dim̅.car̄ hom̅.modo.ɪɪ.bou̅.7.ɪɪɪɪ.ac͂ p̄ti.Ecłia
xxx.ɪɪ.ac͂.liƀæ t̄ræ.femp.uał.xx.foł.Vlmarus femp tenet.

In ftanesfelda.ɪ.foc͂.ɪ.carr̄ t̄ræ.7.ɪɪ.borđ.7 femp.ɪ.car̄.7.ɪɪɪ.ac͂.
prati.Roḡ ten̄.Quando recepit.ɪɪɪ.run͂c.7 modo fimiłiſ.
Tc͂.ɪɪɪɪ.an̅.modo. vɪ.Tc͂.vɪɪ.porc͂.modo.xxx.Tc͂ xʟ.ou̅s.m̊.ʟxxx.
Tc͂ uał.xx.foł.modo.xxx.

In hvnedana.ɪ.foc͂.ɪ.car̄ terræ.femp.ɪɪ.borđ.&.ɪ.car̄ Hamo ten̄
Tc͂ xxx.ou̅s.modo.ʟ.7 uał& xx.folidos.In eade͂.x.foc͂.ɪ.car̄
terræ.femp.ɪ.car̄.&.ɪɪ.ac͂ p̄ti.7 uał.xx.foł. In farleia.ɪ.foc͂
vɪɪ.ac͂.& uał xɪɪɪɪ.đ.In brochola.ɪ.foc͂.dim̅.car̄ terræ.femp.ɪ.car̄
&.ɪɪ.ac͂ p̄ti.Tc͂ uał.vɪɪɪ.foł.m̊.xvɪ.

In Kidituna.ɪ.foc͂.xxx.ac͂.& đ.car̄.7 uał v.foł.

8 In HAWKEDON 1 Freeman; 1 carucate of land.
　　Always 2 villagers; 1 slave;
　　1 plough in lordship; ½ men's plough.
　Value 20s.
　　Gilbert holds this.

9 In HAWKEDON 1 Freeman; 1 carucate of land.
　　Now 3 smallholders; 1 slave.
　　Always 1 plough in lordship. Meadow, 3 acres.
　Value always 20s.
　　Fulcred holds this.

10 In WRATTING 1 Freeman; 1 carucate of land.
　　Always 1 villager; 3 smallholders; 1 slave;
　　1 plough in lordship. Then ½ men's plough, now 2 oxen.
　　　Meadow, 4 acres.
　　A church, 32 acres of free land.
　Value always 20s.
　　Wulfmer has always held it.

11 In STANSFIELD 1 Freeman; 1 carucate of land.
　　2 smallholders.
　　Always 1 plough. Meadow, 3 acres.
　Roger holds (this).
　　When acquired, 3 cobs, now the same; then 4 cattle, now 6; then
　　　7 pigs, now 30; then 40 sheep, now 80.
　Value then 20s; now 30[s].

12 In HUNDON 1 Freeman; 1 carucate of land.
　　Always 2 smallholders.
　　1 plough.
　Hamo holds (this).
　　Then 30 sheep, now 50.
　Value 20s.
　In the same (Hundon) 10 Freemen; 1 carucate of land. Always 1
　plough.
　　Meadow, 2 acres.
　Value 20s.

13 In FARLEY 1 Freeman; 7 acres.
　Value 14d.

14 In BROCKLEY 1 Freeman; ½ carucate of land. Always 1 plough.
　　Meadow, 2 acres.
　Value then 8s; now 16[s].

15 In KEDINGTON 1 Freeman; 30 acres. ½ plough.
　Value 5s.

ac̄ . & . ɪɪɪ . borđ . sēp . ɪ . car̄ . & . ɪɪ . ac̄ p̄ti . 7 ual̄ . x . fol . ⟨In Stoches . ɪ . foc̄.

391 a

xxx . vɪɪ . ac̄ . Tc̄ dimiđ . car̄ . modo . ɪɪ . bou̇ . 7 . ɪɪɪ . ac̄ p̄ti . 7 ual̄ . vɪ . fol.
& . ɪɪ . đ . Hos fochemanos tenuit Wifgar . t . r . e . cū ōi c̄fuetuđne.
p̄t . vɪ . forisfacturas sc̄i eadmundi.

⟨RISEBRVGE . H̃ . In Wimundeftuna . ɪɪɪ . foc̄ . ᴌxv . ac̄ . & dim̄.

car̄ . 7 ual̄ . x . fol . Ex his hab̄ . fuus ante c̄ omēm . c̄fuet̄ . ⟨DIM . H̃.
De cosfort . In Wecefhā ten̄ Vluricus lib̄ hō . t . r . e . ᴌxxx . ac̄.
hoc eft de feudo phinci . femp . ɪɪɪ . bor . & . ɪ . feru̇ . & . ɪ . car̄ in dn̄io . & . ɪ . ac̄
& dim̄ p̄ti . Tc̄ . ɪɪɪ . runc̄ . m̄ . v . Tc̄ . vɪɪɪ . an̄ . m̄ . xɪ . Tc̄ . ɪɪɪ . porc̄ . modo
xx . v . c̃) ᴌxxx . ou̇s . 7 ual̄ . xx . v . fol . Sc̄s . e . focȧ . In ead̄ . ɪ . lib̄ homo . xv.
ac̄ . & ual̄ . ɪɪ . fol . 7 vɪ . đ . Wifgarus focȧ . Sc̄s . e . vɪ . forisfacturas ;
⟨In hetchā . ɪɪ . lib̄i hōes . ɪ . car̄ terræ . ɪɪɪɪ . borđ . & . ɪɪ . ferui . Tc̄ . ɪɪ . car̄
m̄ . ɪ . & . ɪɪɪɪ . ac̄ p̄ti . 7 ual̄ . xx . fol . hoc tenet Ailuardus filius belli.

⟨BLAKE . brune . H̃ . In b̄deuuella . ɪ . lib̄ hō c̄omđ . xxx . ac̄ . & . ɪ . borđ.
Tc̄ dim̄ . & ual̄ . v . fol . ⟨In Stou . ɪ . foc̄ . xxvɪɪɪ . ac̄ . tc̄ . dim̄ car̄ & ual̄
ɪɪɪ . fol . Ḣ ten& Rob̄ . blunđ . sc̄s . edmunđ foc̄ . ⟨

16 In BOYTON 1 Freeman; 60 acres.
   3 smallholders.
   Always 1 plough. Meadow, 2 acres.
   Value 10s.

17 In STOKE (by Clare) 1 Freeman; 37 acres. Then ½ plough, now 2 oxen.   391 a
   Meadow, 3 acres.
   Value 6s 2d.
   Withgar held these Freemen before 1066 with every customary
   due, except for the 6 forfeitures of St. Edmund's.

RISBRIDGE Hundred
18 In *WIMUNDESTUNA* 3 Freemen; 65 acres. ½ plough.
   Value 10s.
   His predecessor had every customary due from these (Freemen).

Half-Hundred of COSFORD
19 In WATTISHAM Wulfric, a free man, held 80 acres before 1066. This
   is part of Finn's Holding.
   Always 3 smallholders; 1 slave.
   1 plough in lordship.
   Meadow, 1½ acres. Then 3 cobs, now 5; then 8 cattle, now 11;
      then 3 pigs, now 25; now 80 sheep.
   Value 25s.
   St. Edmund's (has) the jurisdiction.
   In the same (Wattisham) 1 free man; 15 acres.
   Value 2s 6d.
   Withgar (had) the jurisdiction. St. Edmund's (has) the 6
   forfeitures.

20 In HITCHAM 2 free men; 1 carucate of land.
   3 smallholders; 2 slaves.
   Then 2 ploughs, now 1. Meadow, 4 acres.
   Value 20s.
   Aethelward son of Bell holds this.

BLACKBOURN Hundred
21 In BARDWELL 1 free man under patronage; 30 acres.
   1 smallholder.
   Then ½ plough.
   Value 5s.

22 In STOW (LANGTOFT) 1 Freeman; 28 acres. Then ½ plough.
   Value 3s.
   Robert Blunt holds this.
   St. Edmund's (has) the jurisdiction.

⟨ *WILEFORD*. *H̃*. In Bredefella . xii . ac̃ trǣ . 7 . i . uiłł . & uał
. ii . soł . h̃ ten̄ . Normannus . de . R.

⟨ *HER*tesmera . h̃ . In cotetuna . ten̄ . sader . vii . ac̃ . 7 uał . xiiii . d̃.
Galł diaconus ten&.

⟨ *THEWARDESTRE* . *H̃*. In timeworda . i . lib̃ hõ . Withgari . t.
r . e . antecessoris Ricardi com̃dation̄ tantũ . lx . ac̃ . Tc̃ . i . car̃ . 7 uał
. x . soł . Soc̃ sc̃i Edmundi . In rastedena . ii . soc̃ . vii . ac̃ 7 uał xii . den̄.

⟨ *THINGEHOV*. *H̃*. In Westlea . iii . libi hões . Withgari . com̃d . lxxx.
ac̃ cũ soca pt̃ . vi . foresfac̃turas . sc̃i edmundi . 7 . i . bord̃ . Semp . ii . car̃.

391 b

& . ii . ac̃ pt̃i . Ecclia viii . ac̃ . Silua de ix . porc̃ . 7 due partes . i . moł.
& uał . x . soł . In eađ uilla . i . lib̃ hõ . sc̃i . e . com̃d . cũ soca dim̃ car̃ terrǣ.
. iii . ac̃ pt̃i . Sep̃ . i . car̃ . Semp uał . x . soł . ⟨ In Saxham . i . soc̃ . Wisgari.
de xv . ac̃ . Semp̃ dim̃ car̃ . & uał . iii . soł . ⟨ In horningeserda . i . soc̃ . ei
dẽ de . xx . ac̃ . 7 . ii . bord̃ . femp . i . car̃ . & uał . iiii . soł . ⟨ In hersteda . ii.
libi hões . Wisgari cũ saca sed poterant uende fine licencia . xv ac̃.
Semp dim̃ car̃ . & uał . iii . soł.

WILFORD Hundred

23 In BREDFIELD 12 acres of land.
   1 villager.
   Value 2s.
      Norman holds this from Richard.

HARTISMERE Hundred

24 In COTTON Fathir held 7 acres.
   Value 14d.
      Walter the deacon holds [this].

THEDWESTRY Hundred

25 In TIMWORTH 1 free man, under only the patronage of Withgar,
   Richard's predecessor, before 1066; 60 acres. Then 1 plough.
   Value 10s.
      The jurisdiction (is) St. Edmund's.

26 In RATTLESDEN 2 Freemen; 7 acres.
   Value 12d.

THINGOE Hundred

27 In WESTLEY 3 free men under the patronage of Withgar; 80 acres,
   with the jurisdiction except for the 6 forfeitures of St. Edmund's.
      1 smallholder.
      Always 2 ploughs. Meadow, 2 acres.   391 b
      A church, 8 acres.
      Woodland at 9 pigs; two parts of 1 mill.
   Value 10s.
   In the same village 1 free man of St. Edmund's, under patronage
   with the jurisdiction; ½ carucate of land.
      Meadow, 3 acres.
      Always 1 plough.
   Value always 10s.

28 In SAXHAM 1 Freeman of Withgar's, with 15 acres. Always ½ plough;
   Value 3s.

29 In HORRINGER 1 Freeman of the same man's, with 20 acres.
      2 smallholders.
      Always 1 plough.
   Value 4s.

30 In HAWSTEAD 2 free men of Withgar's, with the jurisdiction but they
   could sell without permission; 15 acres. Always ½ plough.
   Value 3s.

In maneſtuna . ɪ . liƀ hõ dim̄ car terræ
ſub Witgaro . cũ ſoca . t . r . e . Tc̄ . ɪɪɪ . borđ . modo . ɪ . Tc̄ & p̄ . ɪ . car . m̄ dim̄.
& . ɪɪ . ac̄ p̄ti . 7 ſemp ual . x . ſol . In Redũ . vɪɪ . liƀi hões . Wiſg . cũ
ſoca & ſaca ſed po�remt uenđe . ɪ . car . terræ . & . vɪ . borđ . Tc̄ & poſt . ɪɪɪ,
car . modo . ɪ . & dim̄ . & . ɪɪɪɪ . ac̄ p̄ti . Silua . ɪɪɪ . porc̄ . Tc̄ & p̄ ual xxx
ſol . modo . xL . Eccłia xɪɪ . ac̄ t̄rræ libere.

LAC . FORDA . H̄ In ƀtona teñ . godeua . ɪ . liƀa femina
Wiſgari com̄ tantũ in ſoca ſc̄i . edm̄ . t . r . e . Lx . ac̄ t̄ræ & . ɪɪɪɪ . borđ.
& . ɪ . ſerũ . ſemp dim̄ . car in dñio . 7 . ɪ . ac̄ p̄ti . 7 ual . v . ſol . In eađ
. ɪ . ſoc̄ Witḡ . Lx ac̄ . & . ɪɪɪɪ . borđ . Sēp dim̄ . car . & . ɪ . ac̄ p̄ti . & ual
. v . ſol . Witḡ . ſoc̄ . Haluedona teñ Leuiet . liƀ hõ ſub Wit -
garo . t . r . e . co:nđ . tantũ in ſoca ſc̄i . e . ꝓ mañ . ɪɪ . car terræ
Tc̄ . ɪɪɪɪ . uitt . m̄ . ɪɪ . & ſemp . ɪɪɪ . borđ . 7 . ɪ . ſerũ . Tc̄ . ɪɪ . car in dñio.
p̄ 7 m̄ . ɪ . 7 dimiđ . car hom̄ . & q̄rta pars piſcr . ſemp . ɪ . æq . &
xɪɪ . porc̄ . 7 . c . L . ous̄ . Tc̄ ual . ſol . xxx . & p̄ 7 modo ſimilit̄ . Æc
cłia . xv . ac̄ liƀe t̄ræ ; Canauathã teñ Wi:gar ante
ceſſor . Ricardi ƀwitã in deſelinga . ꝓ . v . car . terræ . cũ ſoca . ſēp
xx . v . uitt . 7 . v . car . Æcclia . Lx . ac̄ liƀ terræ . & . tc̄ . v . mot . m̄ . ɪɪɪɪ.

392 a

& . ɪɪɪ . ac̄ p̄ti . tit . ɪ . leuͨg in longo . & . ɪɪɪɪ . q̄r in lato . & de gelto . xx . đ ;

31 In MANSTON 1 free man under Withgar, with the jurisdiction before
1066; ½ carucate of land.
   Then 3 smallholders, now 1.
   Then and later 1 plough, now ½. Meadow, 2 acres.
Value always 10s.

32 In REDE 7 free men of Withgar's, with full jurisdiction but they
could sell; 1 carucate of land.
   6 smallholders.
   Then and later 3 ploughs, now 1½.
   Meadow, 4 acres; woodland, 3 pigs.
Value then and later 30s; now 40[s].
   A church, 12 acres of free land.

   LACKFORD Hundred
33 In BARTON (Mills) Godiva, 1 free woman under only the patronage
of Withgar [but] in the jurisdiction of St. Edmund's before 1066,
held 60 acres of land.
   4 smallholders, 1 slave.
   Always ½ plough in lordship. Meadow, 1 acre.
Value 5s.
In the same (Barton Mills) 1 Freeman of Withgar's; 60 acres.
   4 smallholders.
   Always ½ plough. Meadow, 1 acre.
Value 5s.
   Withgar (had) the jurisdiction.

34 Leofgeat, a free man only under the patronage of Withgar before
1066 [but] in the jurisdiction of St. Edmund's, held ELVEDEN as a
manor; 2 carucates of land.
   Then 4 villagers, now 2. Always 3 smallholders; 1 slave.
   Then 2 ploughs in lordship, later and now 1; ½ men's plough.
   The fourth part of a fishery. Always 1 horse; 12 pigs; 150 sheep.
Value then 30s; later and now the same.
   A church, 15 acres of free land.

35 Withgar, Richard's predecessor, held CAVENHAM as an outlier in (the
lands of) Desning for 5 carucates of land, with the jurisdiction.
   Always 25 villagers;
   5 ploughs.
   A church, 60 acres of free land.
   Then 5 mills, now 4; meadow, 3 acres.
   It has 1 league in length and 4 furlongs in width; 20d in tax.

392 a

⌐In Lakingahethe . 1 . cař terræ . & . viii . uiłł . Tč . 1 . cař in dñio.
modo . 1 . & dim̃ . & . iiii . pifcař . in eli . 7 . 1 . nauis ad pifcandum . &
. 1 . ač p̃ti . hæ . ii . terre sũ in p̃tio de defilinges . ⌐Totenhã teñ id anteč.
~~comiñe~~ Ricardi . 1 . cař terræ 7 dim̃ . 7 . ix . uiłłi . Sẽp . ii . cař . 7 . ač
& dim̃ p̃ti . & Reddit . l . foł . ⌐In ƀtona xxx . ač tře in dñio . Wit
gari . & . ii . boů . & uał . iii . foł . ⌐In mudenehalla . ii . foč de . lx . ač.
7 . 1 . borð . & femp . ii . cař . & uał . v . foł . & ptiñ in defelinga . & non
poť uend . ⌐In hernigawella . iii . foč . Wit . de lx . ač Semp dim̃
cař . apptiata ẽ . in defelinga . In eað . 1 . foč . Wisg̃ cũ medietať
tře . foca . tefte . hund . 7 medietať sći . edm̃ . cũ foca . & h̃t . 1 . cař tře
& . v . borð . Semp . 1 . cař . inť oẽs . 7 uał . xv . foł.
⌐In Wamforda . iiii . foč eidẽ cũ foca de . 1 . cař tře . & . 1 . borð . Sẽp
. ii . cař . inť oñs . & . iii . ač p̃ti . 7 uał . x . foł . & iacẽt in defilinges.

36 In LAKENHEATH 1 carucate of land.
    8 villagers.
    Then 1 plough in lordship, now 1½.
    4 fisheries in Ely; 1 fishing-boat; meadow, 1 acre.
These 2 lands are in the assessment of Desning.

37 Richard's same predecessor held TUDDENHAM; 1½ carucates of land.
    9 villagers.
    Always 2 ploughs. Meadow, 1½ acres.
It pays 50s.

38 In BARTON (Mills) 30 acres of land in Withgar's lordship. 2 oxen.
Value 3s.

39 In MILDENHALL 2 Freemen with 60 acres.
    1 smallholder.
    Always 2 ploughs.
Value 5s.
    It belongs in (the lands of) Desning. They could not sell.

40 In HERRINGSWELL 3 Freemen of Withgar's, with 60 acres. Always ½
plough.
It has been assessed in Desning.
    In the same (Herringswell) 1 Freeman of Withgar's with a half of
the land and the jurisdiction, as the Hundred testifies; and a half of
the land (is) St. Edmund's with the jurisdiction. He has 1 carucate
of land.
    5 smallholders.
    Always 1 plough between them all.
Value 15s.

41 In WANGFORD 4 Freemen of the same man, with the jurisdiction,
with 1 carucate of land.
    1 smallholder.
    Always 2 ploughs between them all. Meadow, 3 acres.
Value 10s.
    It lies in (the lands of) Desning.

BABERGA.DVO. $\bar{H}$. In bure ten& Witḡ.T.R.E.xvɪɪɪ.libi hŏes.

de cōmd 7 foca 7 faca 7 poterant uend trā.T.R.E. fine licencia

ei &.ɪɪɪɪ.foc̄ qui non poterant uende.& xvɪɪɪ.h̄nt.ɪ.car̄ trǣ

7 dim̄.&.ɪɪɪ.foc̄.ɪ.car̄.& dim̄ trē.7 hi tres h̄nt fubfe ɪ uilt.7.vɪɪ.

bord.7 ɪɪɪ.carr̄.7.ɪɪɪɪ.ac̄ p̄ti.7 ual.xxx.fot.7 hi xvɪɪɪ libi

h̄nt.fub fe.x.bord.Semp.ɪɪ.car̄.7.ɪɪɪɪ.ac̄ p̄ti.Silua.vɪ.porc̄.

7 ɪ.molin̄ 7 ual.xxx.fot.Bura h̄t.ɪ.lḡ in longo 7 dimid

in lato.7 de gelto xxɪɪɪɪ.đ.S7 alii ten̄ ibi.Eccłia de.xvɪɪɪ.

ac̄ libe trǣ. *In cormerda.vɪɪ.libi hŏes Wifgari cōmd*

& focā & faca.t.r.e.ɪɪ.car̄ trǣ.7.ɪ.bord.Tc̄.ɪɪɪ.car̄ p̄ƴ & m̄ƭ.ɪɪ.

392 b

7.v.ac̄ prati.7 ual& xxvɪ.fot.7.vɪɪɪ.den̄. *In Coresfella.vɪɪ.libi*

cōmd 7 fac̄ 7 foc̄ eidd.ɪɪɪ.car̄.7 dim̄ terrǣ.xxv.ac̄.7 x.bord.Semp

ɪɪɪ.car̄.inter om̄s.& xɪɪɪ.ac̄ p̄ti.& ual.ɪɪɪ.lib̄. *In ilelega.vɪɪ.libi*

hŏes cōmd 7 fac̄ 7 foc̄ eid lx.ac̄ trǣ.Semper.ɪ.car̄ inter omnes.&

.ɪ.mot.7 ual.x.fot. *In Waldinga fella.ɪɪɪ.libi hŏes cōmd 7 focā*

7 facā eid.ɪ.car̄ terrǣ.7 xlv.ac̄.7 ɪx.bord.Tc̄.ɪɪɪ.car̄.p.ɪɪ.m̄.ɪ.

7.ɪɪɪ.ac̄ p̄ti.7.ɪ.runc̄.7.ɪɪ.an̄.7 lxxx.xɪɪɪ.ous̄.Silu de.ɪɪɪ.porc̄.

7 ual.l.fot. Ꝋ ten̄ elinant.ƭcia pars.ǣcctie.x.ac̄ libǣ trǣ.

BABERGH Two Hundreds

42 In BURES Withgar [held] 18 free men before 1066, with the patronage and full jurisdiction; they could sell the land before 1066 without his permission. Also 4 Freemen who could not sell. The 18 (free men) have 1½ carucates of land. 3 Freemen (have) 1½ carucates of land.
The 3 (Freemen) have under them
    1 villager, 7 smallholders.
    3 ploughs. Meadow, 4 acres.
Value 30s.
The 18 free men have under them
    10 smallholders.
    Always 2 ploughs.
    Meadow, 4 acres; woodland, 6 pigs; 1 mill.
Value 30s.
    Bures has 1 league in length and ½ in width; 24d in tax. But others hold there.
    A church with 18 acres of free land.

43 In CORNARD 7 free men under the patronage and full jurisdiction of Withgar before 1066; 2 carucates of land.
    1 smallholder.
    Then 3 ploughs, later and now 2. Meadow, 5 acres.
Value 26s 8d.

392 b

44 In *CORESFELLA* 7 free men under the patronage and full jurisdiction of the same man; 3½ carucates of land [and] 25 acres.
    10 smallholders.
    Always 3 ploughs between them all. Meadow, 13 acres.
Value £3.

45 In ELEIGH 7 free men under the patronage and full jurisdiction of the same man; 60 acres of land.
    Always 1 plough between them all. 1 mill.
Value 10s.

46 In WALDINGFIELD 3 free men under the patronage and full jurisdiction of the same man; 1 carucate of land and 45 acres.
    9 smallholders.
    Then 3 ploughs, later 2, now 1.
    Meadow, 3 acres. 1 cob, 2 cattle, 93 sheep. Woodland at 3 pigs.
Value 50s.
    Now Elinant holds (this).
    The third part of a church, 10 acres of free land.

⁊In Ranauadiſc . ix . liƀi . hōes cōm̄d . ⁊ ſoca ⁊ ſaca eidē . iii . caᵣr tᵣæ
& . v . borđ . ⁊ . i . ſeru . ⁊ . iii . caᵣ . ⁊ xiiii . ac̄ p̄ti . ⁊ . iiii . an̄ . ⁊ . i . æquus
m̄ . xv . porc̄ . ⁊ xl . vi . ōus . ⁊ ual̄ . iii . liƀ . Roᵍ de ſc̄o germ̄ . ten̄.

⁊In herterſt . ii . liƀi hōes . com̄ & ſocā ⁊ ſacā eidē de . ii . caᵣ terræ
⁊ . iii . borđ . Semp . ii . caᵣ . & . viii . ac̄ p̄ti . ⁊ ual̄ . ii . liƀ.

⁊In Walingaſella . ii . liƀi hōes & . un̄ fuit rotƀti . filii Witmar -
ce . com̄d . āƀo Wiſgari ⁊ ſoca ⁊ ſacā & . ħnt . ii . caᵣ . terræ . & . ix
ac̄ p̄ti . ⁊ . ii . caᵣ . m̄ . ix . an̄ . ⁊ xxxvii . porc̄ . ⁊ lxix . ōus . & . xi . cap̄.
⁊ ual̄ . l . ſol̄ . ħ⁊ . iiii . qᵣ . in longo . & . iiii . in lato . & de gelto . vi . đ.
qui cūq̛ ibi tēnent . ⁊In grotena . i . liƀ hō . cōm̄d ⁊ ſacā . & ſocā
⁊ ħ⁊ . x . ac̄ tᵣæ . ⁊ ual̄ . xx . đ.   ⁊*STOHV . HVNÐ.*

In Sellanda ten̄ find .. antec̄ Ri . xx . iii . ac̄ . ⁊ . iiii . borđ . ſemp
dimidia caᵣ . & . ii . boū . ⁊ ual̄ . v . ſol̄ . ⁊*DIMIDIVM . H̄.*

·Degepeſwiz . In burgo de gepeſwiz tenuit Wiſgarus . i . æcc⁊ā
ſc̄i petri . t . r . e . cui pertinebant . Tc̄ ⁊ m̄ . vi . caᵣ tᵣæ ⸌p man̄.

47 In CAVENDISH 9 free men under the patronage and full jurisdiction of the same man; 3 carucates of land.
>5 smallholders, 1 slave.
>3 ploughs.
>Meadow, 14 acres. 4 cattle, 1 horse; now 15 pigs; 46 sheep.
>Value £3.
>Roger of St. Germain holds (this).

48 In HARTEST 2 free men under the patronage and full jurisdiction of the same man, with 2 carucates of land.
>3 smallholders.
>Always 2 ploughs. Meadow, 8 acres.
>Value £2.

49 In WALDINGFIELD 2 free men; one was under the patronage of Robert son of Wymarc, both (were) under the full jurisdiction of Withgar. They have 2 carucates of land.
>Meadow, 9 acres.
>2 ploughs.
>Now 9 cattle, 37 pigs, 69 sheep, 11 goats.
>Value 50s.
>It has 4 furlongs in length and 4 in width; 6d in tax, whoever holds there.

50 In GROTON 1 free man under patronage and full jurisdiction. He has 10 acres of land.
>Value 20d.

STOW Hundred
51 In SHELLAND Finn, Richard's predecessor, held 23 acres.
>4 smallholders.
>Always ½ plough and 2 oxen.
>Value 5s.

Half-Hundred of IPSWICH
52 In the Borough of IPSWICH Withgar held 1 church, St. Peter's, before 1066 to which belonged, then and now, 6 carucates of land as a manor.

ii . car̄ in dominio . Tc . iii . car̄ . modo . iiii . Tc ſilu̅ . viii . porc̄ . m̄
iiii . ſemper . i . molin̄ . 7 . iii . ac̄ . p̄ti . m̄ . i . run̄ . & . i . an̄ . 7 . ix . porc
7 lxxx . ou̅s p̱tinent adhuc huic æccliæ . v . burgenſes . 7 . in burgo .
xv . ac̄ libe t̄ræ . 7 vi . manſure uacue . Ex ſup̄dictis . vi . car̄ t̄c . ca -
lu̅pniat̄ . Roger uicecomes . c . ac̄ . 7 . v . uill . & . i . mol . ad maneriu̅
regis de branfort . & . v . uill . de eodẽ manerio teſtantur ei . & . offert
legẽ qualẽ quis iudicauerit . ſed dimidiu̅ hundret de gepeſwiz te -
ſtantur qđ hoc iacebat ad ecclia̅ . t̄ . e . & Wiſgar tenebat . & offert
derationari . Tc ual . c . ſol . modo . xv . lib . cu̅ aliis terris que iacent
huic æccliæ . In eođ burgo h̄t Ricardus . xiii . burgenſes . quos tenuit
Phin . t . r . e . ſuper . iiii . ex his habebat ſoca̅ & ſaca̅ . 7 co̅mđ . un̅ eoꝛ
ē ſeruus . 7 ſup xii . comđ tn̅t ſed manebant in̅ ſua ꝓpa t̄ra . & red -
debāt in burgo totā conſuetudinẽ . 7 Hoc eſt de honore ſint .

V̄ BOSEMARA . H̄ . Badeleia̅ ten̄ Aſchil . t . r . e . modo . R . in dn̄io
ꝓ ii . carr̄ terræ . 7 xx . ac̄ . ꝓ man̄ . ſemp . iiii . uill . 7 . iiii . borđ . 7 . v . ſeru̅ .
7 . ii . car̄ in dominio 7 . ii . carr̄ hominu̅ . viii . ac̄ p̄ti . 7 dim̄ molin̄ . 7 .
ii . runc̄ . & xx . vi . anial . 7 xxx . ii . porc̄ . Tc . lx . ou̅s . modo . c . Ecclia . xiiii .
ac̄ . Tc ual lx . ſol . modo . iiii . lib . Ex hac t̄ra calu̅pniat̄ Ab̄b̄ dim̄ . car̄ .
teſte . h̄ . Rex & comes ſoca̅ . Huic manerio additi ſ̄ . t . r . . . xx . vi . uiłłi
lib̄i hoẽs . i . car̄ terræ 7 xl . v . ac̄ . hos om̄s ten̄ Ricar̄ . ad hoc maneriu̅
quod tenuit ſint . 7 ipſe phin tenebat eos p acommodatione̅ . | Tc 7 p̄ꝰ
v . car̄ . modo . ii . Tc ual xl . ſol . modo . xl . vii . Rex 7 comes ſoca̅ & ſaca̅ .
h̄t . x . qr̄ in longo . & . v . in lato . 7 . x . den̄ de gelto .

V̄ In ſtanham . v . ac̄ terræ . 7 ſilua . iiii . porc̄ . in p̄cio . de . xv . lib . eſt .

Then and later 6 villagers, now 8; then and later 5 smallholders, now 15; then 4 slaves.

Always 2 ploughs in lordship. Then 3 [men's] ploughs, now 4.

Woodland, then 8 pigs, now 4; always 1 mill. Meadow, 3 acres. Now 1 cob, 1 cattle, 9 pigs, 80 sheep.

Also to this manor belong 5 burgesses, 15 acres of free land in the Borough and 6 empty dwellings.

Of the above-mentioned 6 carucates of land, Roger the Sheriff claims 100 acres, 5 villagers and 1 mill for the King's manor of Bramford, and 5 villagers of the same manor testify for him and they offer (to prove it by) any law, whoever should give judgment. But the Half-Hundred of Ipswich testify that this belonged to the church before 1066 and Withgar held it, and they offer (to let it) be proven.

Value then 100s; now £15, with other lands which belong to this church.

In the same Borough, Richard has 13 burgesses whom Finn held before 1066. Over 4 of these, (Finn) had full jurisdiction and patronage. One of them is a slave. Over 12 (he had) only the patronage, but they dwelt on their own land and they paid the whole of the customary due in the Borough. This is (part) of Finn's Honour.

BOSMERE Hundred

53 Askell held BADLEY before 1066, now Richard [holds it] in lordship, for 2 carucates of land and 20 acres as a manor.

Always 4 villagers; 4 smallholders; 5 slaves.

2 ploughs in lordship; 2 men's ploughs.

Meadow, 8 acres; ½ mill. 2 cobs, 26 cattle, 32 pigs; then 60 sheep, now 100.

A church, 14 acres.

Value then 60s; now £4.

Of this land, the Abbot claims ½ carucate as the Hundred testifies. The King and the Earl (have) the jurisdiction.

To this manor 26 free men were added after 1066; 1 carucate of land and 45 acres. Richard holds all these men for this manor which Finn held. Finn himself held them on lease from the Sheriff, as the Sheriff himself says. Then and later 5 ploughs, now 2.

Value then 40s; now 47[s].

The King and the Earl (have) full jurisdiction. It has 10 furlongs in length and 5 in width; 10d in tax.

54 In STONHAM 5 acres of land.

Woodland, 4 pigs.

It is in the assessment of £15.

Flochetunā tenuit Godmanus.t.r.e.Wiſgarus habuit cōm̄d
7 rex & comes ſocā.hoc ten& Germundus.de.R.p̄ man̄.&.ii.car
terræ.ſemp.iiii.bord.&.i.ſeru.&.ii.carr in dominio.7.ix.ac̄ p̄ti.
Tc̄.i.runc.Tc̄.iiii.an̄.m̄.viii.Tc̄.iiii.porc̄.Tc̄.xv.ou̅s.modo lx.
Tc̄ ual̄.iiii.lib.modo.lx.ſol.l̄t dim̄ l̄g in longo.7.iiii.qr̄ in lato.
&.ii.den̄ de gelto.Huic manerio addidit Germundus.xv.ac̄.t.r.
Wil̄li.q̄s lib̄e tenebat quidā p̄br.t.r.e.in ſoca regis 7 comit.& ual̄
ii.ſol.&.vi.den̄. Brieſetā ten̄.Bondo lib̄ hō.t.r.e.7 regina
edeua habuit cōm̄d tant.ſed.R.clamat ad feudū Wiſgari 7 Rex
& com̄s ſocā.modo.Roḡ.p̄.i.car trǣ.7 p̄ man̄.ſemp.i.uill̄.&.i.bord.
&.i.car in dominio.&.tc̄.i.car hou̅m.Tc̄ ual̄.xx.ſol.modo xxx.
Hanc terrā reclamat.Roḡ deramis de donσ regis & inde ſaiſitus
fuit. In ead̄e id̄e ten̄.Roḡ de orhec.ii.liberos.hōes.de xv.ac̄.& ual̄
xxx.d̄.hoc etiā calūpniatur Rḡ de ramis.ſc̄ ſuperius.ſ7 Ric̄ Reclamat ad feudū Wiſgari.In ead̄ ten&.Ran̄ piperellus.iiii.ac̄.quæ
iacebant ſup̄dic̄to manerio.t.r.e.Hoc reclamat ad feudū phin.
In Rigneſeta tenuit Hardechinus lib̄ hō.c.ac̄.p̄ m̄.t.r.e.modo
ten& Goisfridus.ſemp.ii.uill̄.&.iiii.bord.&.i.car in dominio
Tc̄ dimidia car hominū.vii.ac̄ p̄ti.Silua.tc̄ xxx.porc̄.modo xvi.
Et ual̄.tc̄.xx.ſol.modo xxx.v.In ead̄ tenet Godricus lib̄ hō.t.r.e.
lx.ac̄.p̄ man̄.ſemp.i.car.Tc̄ ual̄.x.ſol.modo.xx.In ead̄ Codui
lib̄ hō tenuit lx.ac̄.p̄ man̄.Tc̄.i.car.Tc̄ ual̄.x.ſol.modo.xv.

55 Godman held FLOWTON before 1066, Withgar had the patronage and
the King and the Earl (had) the jurisdiction. Germund holds this
from Richard as a manor and 2 carucates of land.
> Always 4 smallholders; 1 slave;
> 2 ploughs in lordship.
> Meadow, 9 acres. Then 1 cob; then 4 cattle, now 8; then 4 pigs,
>   then 15 sheep, now 60.

Value then £4; now 60s.
> It has ½ league in length and 4 furlongs in width; 2d in tax.

To this manor after 1066, Germund added 15 acres which a priest
held freely before 1066 in the jurisdiction of the King and the Earl.
Value 2s 6d.

56 Bondi, a free man, held BRICETT before 1066; Queen Edith had only
the patronage; but Richard claims (it) for Withgar's Holding. The
King and the Earl (have) the jurisdiction. Now Roger [holds this]
for 1 carucate of land, as a manor.
> Always 1 villager; 1 smallholder;
> 1 plough in lordship. Then 1 men's plough.

Value then 20s; now 30[s].
> Roger of Rames claims back this land by the King's gift and he

was in possession of it.
In the same (Bricett) Roger of Orbec also holds 2 free men, with
15 acres.
Value 30d.
> Roger of Rames claims this too, as above, but Richard claims

(it) back for Withgar's Holding.
In the same (Bricett) Ranulf Peverel holds 4 acres which belonged
to the above-mentioned manor before 1066. This he claims back
for Finn's Holding.

57 In *RIGNESETA* Hardekin, a free man, held 100 acres as a manor
before 1066. Now Geoffrey holds (it).
> Always 2 villagers; 4 smallholders;
> 1 plough in lordship. Then ½ men's plough.
> Meadow, 7 acres; woodland, then 30 pigs, now 16.

Value then 20s; now 35[s].
In the same (*Rigneseta*) Godric, a free man, [held] 60 acres before
1066 as a manor. Always 1 plough.
Value then 10s; now 20[s].
In the same (*Rigneseta*) Godwy, a free man, held 60 acres as a manor.
Then 1 plough.
Value then 10s; now 15[s].

Totū ten& Goisfridus 7 dedit ad firmā ꝑ LXX.ſol.ſed ñ poꝱ habe
niſi LX.ſol.Huic manerio addidit phin.t.r.Wiꝉꝉ.III.liꝭos.

hões de XX.aē.Tē.I.car.hoc ē in eod ꝓtio.ħt.VIII.qᷓ in longo.&.III.
in laꝫ.&.V.deñ de gelto.Rex & comes ſocā. ⸜ In facheduna.I.liꝭ
hō Comitis Algari.ten& XXX.aē.t.r.e.in̅ Vl̅maꝛ de Ricardo.ſemꝑ
.I.caꝛ & uaꝉ.V.ſoꝉ.rex & comes ſocā. ⸜ Aſſiam tenuit Vluricus
liꝭ hō.LX.aē ꝑ man̅ ſemp.II.uiꝉꝉ 7.II.ſoē.de.VII.aē.&.II.borꝺ.
&.I.caꝛ in dominio.& dimidia car hoūm.&.II.aē ꝑti.Tē uaꝉ
XX.ſoꝉ.modo XXX.7 Rex & comes ſocā.In ead ten Iric liꝭ homo
LX.aē ꝑ man̅.&.II.borꝺ.& ſemp.I.caꝛ.&.I.aē ꝑti.7 uaꝉ.XXX.
ſoꝉ.R.7.c.ſocā In ead ten& Edricus.liꝭ hō.t.r.e.XL aē ꝑ man̅.
Tē.I.caꝛ.&.I.aē ꝑti.Rex 7 comes ħt ſocā.7 uaꝉ XX.ſoꝉ.huic manerio addidit phin.t.r.Wiꝉꝉi.VIII.liꝭos hões.de XXX.V.aē.& ſoē.
de.XII.aē.qui ñ potuiꝼ recedere de ſcā aeldreda.7 inꝼ eos
habebant.Tē.III.caꝛ.modo.II.Tē uaꝉ.XV.ſoꝉ.modo.XX.Totū
ten Oſbnus de wanceio.& Ricardus reclamat ad feudū phin.
Rex & com̅s ſocā.Duos ex his liꝭis hōibꝫ calūpniatur Roḡ
de ramis ad ſuū feudū.& inde ſaiſitus fuit.Toꝫ ħꝼ.VI.qᷓ in longo
7.II.in lato.7 VI.deñ.de gelꝫ.Ex hoc toto nichil habuit
Phin.tᷓe.regis.e.

Geoffrey holds the whole of this and gave it at a revenue for 70s; but he could only have 60s.

To this manor after 1066, Finn added 3 free men with 20 acres. Then 1 plough.

This is in the same assessment.

It has 8 furlongs in length and 3 in width; 5d in tax. The King and the Earl (have) the jurisdiction.

58 In *FACHEDUNA* 1 free man of Earl Algar's [held] 30 acres before 1066. Now Wulfmer [holds it] from Richard. Always 1 plough. Value 5s.

The King and the Earl (have) the jurisdiction.

59 Wulfric, a free man, held ASH(BOCKING); 60 acres as a manor.

Always 2 villagers; 2 Freemen with 7 acres; 2 smallholders; 1 plough in lordship; ½ men's plough. Meadow, 2 acres.

Value then 20s; now 30[s].

The King and the Earl (have) the jurisdiction.

In the same (Ashbocking) Yric, a free man, held 60 acres as a manor.

2 smallholders.

Always 1 plough. Meadow, 1 acre.

Value 30s.

The King and the Earl (have) the jurisdiction.

In the same (Ashbocking) Edric, a free man, [held] 40 acres as a manor before 1066. Then 1 plough.

Meadow, 1 acre.

The King and the Earl have the jurisdiction.

Value 20s.

To this manor after 1066, Finn added 8 free men with 35 acres, and a Freeman with 12 acres who could not withdraw from St. Etheldreda's. Between them they had then 3 ploughs, now 2.

Value then 15s; now 20[s].

Osbern of Wanchy holds the whole of this and Richard claims it back for Finn's Holding.

The King and the Earl (have) the jurisdiction.

Roger of Rames claims two of these free men for his own Holding and was in possession of them.

The whole has 6 furlongs in length and 2 in width; 6d in tax.

Finn had nothing of the whole of this before 1066.

CLAINDINE. *H̃*. In Toroluestuna. in dñio xvIII. liɓi hões. Ex
his fuer̃. xII. 7 dim̃ cõmdati Alurico p̃ro cõmdato Wisgari
int̃ tot̃ hñt. lxIIII. ac̃. Et ex aliis scil̃. v. & dim̃. ñ haɓ ante
cessor Ricardi. commd̃. de alurico. Walduino. Haroldo. Go-
duino. Vlmaro. Alurico. Isti habebant. xxIIII. ac̃. t̃. r̃. e. hos
hões ideo tenet Ricardus quia eos tenebat Arfast̃us ep̃c.

394 b

q̃do Ricardus derationauit æcclĩa sc̃i petri de gipeswiz sup eũ.
sed modo nesciebat eos ñ ptinere ad suũ feudũ. Int̃ totũ hñt. semp. III.
car̃. & . I. ac̃ p̃ti. Supiores. xII. ual&. Tc̃ vI. sol̃. & . vIII. denarios. & Alii.
IIII. sol̃. & . I. den̄. Rex 7. cõms h̃t socã de toto.

In helminghẽa de tr̃a sin tenuit Turi⁹ teinn⁹. reg̃. E. I. car̃ tr̃æ
p̃ mañ. semp. I. car̃. & . II. car̃ houm. 7. III. uitt. & v. borđ. & . III. ac̃ p̃ti.
Tc̃ silua. de. xx. porc̃. m̃. x. & . II. runc̃. & . IIII. añ. & . xx. IIII. porc̃. 7 xL
oũs. 7. II. uasa apũ. Tc̃ ual xvI. sol̃. m̃ xx. h̃t. I. lg̃ in longo. & . vII.ᵃ˒⁴ᵗ in-
lato. 7 xx. den̄ de gelt. Alii ibi ten̄. Rex. 7 cõms h̃t socã. Galf̃ de cadomo.

IN TVROL uestuna. lxxxxI ac̃. ptinentes æccliæ sc̃i petri de
Gipewiz. 7 ual. xv. sol̃. 7 h̃ ẽ in p̃tio de sup̃dictis. xv. liɓ. h̃t. x. qr̃ in
longo. & . vI. in lato. 7 xx. den̄. de gel. alii jbi tenet.

SANFORT. *H̃*. 7 dim̃. Alwartunã ten̄ de tr̃a phin Turi⁹
teinnus reg̃. p̃ mañ. I. car̃ tr̃æ. 7 dim̃. Tc̃. vIII. uitti. m̃. III. Tc̃. IIII. borđ.
modo. vII. semp. I. car̃. 7 dim̃ in dñio. Tc̃. IIII. car̃ in dñio. modo. I.
& . III. ac̃ p̃ti. t̃cia pars piscinæ. Tc̃. I. runc̃. m̃. II. Tc̃.ᵛ·ᴵ· añ. modo
vIII. Tc̃. xx. porc̃. modo. xxvI. semp. lxxx. oũs. modo. IIII.
cap̃. Tc̃ ual. xL. sol̃. modo. xxx. Rog̃ ten&. de Ricardo. Idẽ Tu
Ri⁹ socã.

CLAYDON Hundred

60 In THURLESTON 18 free men in lordship. Of these, 12 and a half were under the patronage of Aelfric father of Withgar; in total, they have 64 acres. Of the others, that is 5 and a half, Richard's predecessor did not have patronage over Aelfric, Waldwin, Harold, Godwin, Wulfmer (and) Aelfric; these had 24 acres before 1066. Richard holds these men because Bishop Erfast held them when Richard established his claim to the church of St. Peter's, Ipswich, against him, but now (he says that) he did not know that they did not belong to his Holding. In total, they have always had 3 ploughs.

394 b

Meadow, 1 acre.

Value of the above 12 (free men) then 6s 8d; (value of) the others 4s 1d.

The King and the Earl (have) jurisdiction over the whole.

61 Of Finn's land, Thuri, a thane of King Edward's, held 1 carucate of land in HELMINGHAM as a manor.

Always 1 plough; 2 men's ploughs;
3 villagers; 5 smallholders.
Meadow, 3 acres; woodland, then at 20 pigs, now 10. 2 cobs,
   4 cattle, 24 pigs, 40 sheep, 2 beehives.
Value then 16s; now 20[s].
It has 1 league in length and 7 furlongs in width; 20d in tax.
Others hold there. The King and the Earl (have) the jurisdiction.
Walter of Caen [holds this].

62 In THURLESTON 91 acres which belong to the church of St. Peter's, Ipswich.
Value 15s. This is in the assessment of the above-mentioned £15.
It has 10 furlongs in length and 6 in width; 20d in tax. Others hold there.

SAMFORD Hundred and a Half

63 Of Finn's land, Thuri, a thane of the King's, held ERWARTON as a manor; 1½ carucates of land.
Then 8 villagers, now 3; then 4 smallholders, now 7.
Always 1½ ploughs in lordship. Then 4 ploughs in lordship,
   now 1.
Meadow, 3 acres; the third part of a fish-pond. Then 1 cob,
   now 2; then 6 cattle, now 8; then 20 pigs, now 26; always
   80 sheep. Now 4 goats.
Value then 40s; now 30[s].
Roger holds (this) from Richard.
Thuri also (had) the jurisdiction.

⌐In Scoteleia tenuit Celeolt . t . r . e . comdat Alurico
LX . ac̄ p̄ man̄ . ſemp . 1 . uiłł . & . 1 . borđ . & dim̄ . car̄ . & uał . x . ſoł . Idē
Roḡ; Soca in bercolt . In torp . tenuit Osḃnus liḃ hō Alurici . c . ac̄ . p̄ man̄
t . r . e . ſemp . 111 . borđ . & . 1 . car̄ . 7 . 111 . ac̄ p̄ti . 7 uał . xx . ſoł . Soca in ḃcolt .
Idē Osḃnus de ricardo . Purte p̄ẏt ten jđ Osḃnus . t . r . e . LX . ac̄
p̄ man̄ . ſemper . 111 . uiłł . & . 11 . borđ . & . 11 . ſerū . & dim̄ car̄ in dn̄io .

395 a

& . 11 . car̄ hom̄ . 7 uał . x . ſoł . Idē Osḃnus Soca in bercolt ⁊
⌐In Cherchetuna tenuit . Edmundus liḃ hō LX . ac̄ . p̄ man̄ . t . r . e .
ſemp dimiđ . car̄ . & . 1 . ac̄ p̄ti . 7 tē uał xx . ſoł . modo xx . 111 . ſoł . &
11 . den̄ . In eađ Strangulfus liḃ hō . tenuit . LX . ac̄ p̄ man̄ . t . r . e .
ſemp dimidia . car̄ . & uał . 1111 . ſoł . In Eađē Turi liḃ hō . Guert
LX . ac̄ . p̄ man̄ . t . r . e . ſemp . 1111 . borđ . & dimidia . carr̄ . Tē
uał . x . ſoł . modo . xı . ſoł . 7 . v . den̄ . In eađ . 11 . liḃi . hōes . Hun̄ .
7 Godric̄ . xv . ac̄ . t . r . e . 7 . 11 . boū . Tē . uał . v . ſoł . modo . v111 .
Soca in ḃcolt . ħt . v1 . q̄r̄ in longo . 7 . v . in lato . 7 . 1111 . đ . de gelto .
⌐In Eure Wardeſtuna tenuit Ailḃnus liḃ hō . LX . ac̄ . p̄ maner̄ .
ſemp dim̄ . car̄ . 7 uał . v111 . ſoł . In eduineſtuna . tenuit Godric̄
liḃ homo . xxx . ac̄ . p̄ m̄ . ſemp dimidia . car̄ . Tē uał . v . ſoł . modo
111 . Soca in ḃcolt .

70 Also in the Hundred, Richard has 3 free men, Godric, Edwin, Leofric; 33 acres. Always ½ plough.
Value then 5s; now 6s 6d.
   The jurisdiction (is) in (East) Bergholt.

71 In BURSTALL Aelfric Starling, under the patronage of Gyrth, held 40 acres as a manor before 1066.
   Always 2 smallholders.
   Then 1 plough, now ½. Meadow, 2 acres.
Value 8s.

72 In BOYNTON Leofstan, a free man under the patronage of Finn, held 50 acres before 1066.
   Always 3 smallholders.
   Then 1 plough, now ½. Meadow, 3 acres.
Value then 10s; now 11s 5d.
   The jurisdiction (is) in (East) Bergholt.

73 In TOFT Alwin, a free man under the patronage of Asgar the Constable; 20 acres.
   In the same (*Toft*) Alfgeat, a free man; 8 acres. Always ½ plough.
Value then 5s; now 20[s] 4d.
   The jurisdiction (is) in (East) Bergholt.

74 In RAYDON Leofric, a free man, held 30 acres as a manor. Always ½ plough.
   Meadow, 2 acres.
Value then 5s; now 11s 5d.
   Richard holds the whole of this in lordship.   395 b

75 In HIGHAM Godric, a free man, held 1 carucate of land as a manor before 1066.
   Always 1 villager; 2 smallholders;
   1 plough in lordship. Meadow, 6 acres.
   A church, 4 acres.
Value then 20s; now 25[s].
   Osbern holds (this).

From all these free men, Finn, Richard's predecessor, had nothing before 1066 except for patronage only over one alone. The jurisdiction of the whole (is) in (East) Bergholt. Richard holds them as of Finn's Honour.

76 Robert son of Wymarc held FRESTON before 1066. Roger of Abenon holds 6 carucates of land as manor.
   Always 24 villagers; 4 smallholders;

& . ii . car in dominio . Tc . viii . car hom . modo . vi . viii . ac . pti . & .

. i . mol . Quedā æcclia . Tc . xi . añ . m̂ . iii . Tc . xl . porc . modo . iii .

Tc . c . xl . ous . m̂ . ci . Tc ual viii . lib . modo . xi . & . x . fol . ħt . i . lḡ

in long . 7 dim̄ in lato . & . x . deñ . de gelto . Idē Rob . focā .

⌐In Burgheftala . Leuricus . commendatus Algaro Comiti . t . r .

e . xvii . ac . 7 ual . iii . fol . ħ Reuocat Ricardus ad irā fin . Vlmar

teñ de ricardo . foca in bcolt .

⌐RISEBRVGE . H̄ . Ifti s̄ libi hoēs qui . t . r . e . poterant terras fuas

ucndere & donare . Wifgar ante ceffor Ricardi habuit commd

& focā & facā p̄t vi . foris facturas . sci eadmundi . ⌐In Stanesfelda

teñ Edric fpuda . i . lib ho . ii . car . terræ . & . ii . bord . 7 . iii . ferui .

femp . ii . car . & . ii . ac pti . m̂ . xiiii . añ . Tc . iiii . ous . modo . lxxx .

& xxv . porc . Tc ual . xl . fol . modo . lx . ħ tenet Giflebertus .

⌐In ead . teñ Vlflet . i . lib ho . i . car terræ . femp . i . car . & . iiii . ac

pti . Tc ual . xx . fol . modo . xxx . Rob . ten & . In ead Crawa

. i . lib ho . lx . ac træ . & . i . feru . femp . i . car . & . iiii . ac . & dim̄ p̄ti .

396 a

femper . i . moliñ . & tc ual . x . fol . modo . xv . ħ tenet . Roḡ .

Ecclia de xv . ac libæ træ . Tota ftenesfelda . ħt xii . q̄r in longo . & . vi .

in lato . & xiii . d̄ & obolū de gl .

2 ploughs in lordship. Then 8 men's ploughs, now 6.
Meadow, 8 acres; 1 mill.
A church.
Then 11 cattle, now 3; then 40 pigs, now 3; then 140 sheep, now 101.
Value then £8; now [£] 11 10s.
It has 1 league in length and ½ in width; 10d in tax.
Robert also (had) the jurisdiction.

77 In BURSTALL Leofric, under the patronage of Earl Algar before 1066; 17 acres.
Value 3s.
Richard avouches this as Finn's land. Wulfmer holds (it) from Richard.
The jurisdiction (is) in (East) Bergholt.

RISBRIDGE Hundred
THESE ARE THE FREE MEN WHO COULD SELL AND GRANT THEIR LANDS BEFORE 1066; WITHGAR, RICHARD'S PREDECESSOR, HAD PATRONAGE AND FULL JURISDICTION (OVER THEM), EXCEPT FOR THE 6 FORFEITURES OF ST. EDMUND'S.

78 In STANSFIELD Edric Spud, 1 free man, held 2 carucates of land.
2 smallholders, 3 slaves.
Always 2 ploughs.
Meadow, 2 acres. Now 14 cattle; then 4 sheep, now 80; 25 pigs.
Value then 40s; now 50[s].
Gilbert holds this.
In the same (Stansfield) Wulfled, 1 free man, held 1 carucate of land. Always 1 plough.
Meadow, 4 acres.
Value then 20s; now 30[s].
Robert holds (this).
In the same (Stansfield) Crawa, 1 free man; 60 acres of land.
1 slave.
Always 1 plough.
Meadow, 4½ acres; always 1 mill.
Value then 10s; now 15[s].
Roger holds this.
A church with 15 acres of free land.
The whole of Stansfield has 12 furlongs in length and 6 in width; 13½d in tax.

396 a

$\digamma$ In depdana ten& . Briċtriċ

blacus . I . liƀ hō . II . ca̷ terræ . ſemp . VII . bord . & . I . ſeruus . & . II . ca̷ in dn̄io.
Tc̄ dimidia ca̷ hominū . 7 . III . ac̄ p̄ti . modo . I . runc̄ . Tc̄ . VII .
an̄ . modo XIIII . Tc̄ . XV . por̄c . modo XXX . tc̄ XXX . VII . ōus . modo
LXXX . modo . X . cap̄ . & . III . uaſa apū . Semp . ual . LX . ſol . Frodo
fr̄ Abƀis ten& . $\digamma$ In eadē . II . liƀi hoēs . Blacuinus 7 Godwinus
II . liƀi hoēs . II . ca̷ terræ . & . III . bord . Tc̄ . I . caȓ . & . dim̄ . modo . II .
& . III . ac̄ p̄ti . Tc̄ . I . runc̄ . Semp . VI . an̄ . Tc̄ XVI . porc̄ . m̄ . XX . VI . tc̄
XL . ōus . Tc̄ ual XXX . ſol . modo . L . Osƀnus ten̄ .

$\digamma$ In Cloptuna ten̄ Leuiet . I . liƀ hō . I . caȓ & dim̄ træ . & . I . uiłł . & .
. I . bord . 7 . III . feru̷ . Tc̄ . I . caȓ . modo . II . 7 . IIII . ac̄ p̄ti . ſemper . I . runc̄ .
7 . X . an̄ . m̄ . XXX . IIII . porc̄ . 7 LXXX . III . ōus . Tc̄ ual . XX . ſol . modo
XXX . Roḡ ten& . $\digamma$ In Vratinga . Goda . I . liƀa femina . II . caȓ
træ . 7 XXX . ac̄ . ſemp . IX . bord . 7 . II . caȓ in dominio . & dimidia caȓ.
hoın . VII . ac̄ p̄ti . 7 . I . moliñ . Tc̄ . I . runc̄ . modo . II . Tc̄ . IIII . an̄ . m̄
X . Tc̄ . I . porc̄ . m̄ . L . II . Tc̄ LXXX . ōus . m̄ . C . Tc̄ . IIII . cap̄ . modo . XL .
Tc̄ ual . XXX . ſol . m̄ . XL . Paganus ten& . Tota ħt . I . łḡ in longo
& dim̄ in lato . & . XII . den̄ de gelto . $\digamma$ In hauer hella ten& frede -
ƀnus . I . liƀ hō . V . bord . & ħnt LXXX . ac̄ . 7 . I . caȓ in dn̄io . 7 . II . boū
hoıum . 7 . II . ac̄ p̄ti . Tc̄ ual . XIII . ſol . & . IIII . d . modo . XV . ſol . Idē
paganus ten& . $\digamma$ In haningehæc . ten̄ Alvvinus . I . liƀ hō . C . ac̄ .
& . I . bord . & . I . caȓ . & . II . ac̄ p̄ti . Tc̄ ual . X . ſol . modo . XV ;

79 In DEPDEN Brictric Black, 1 free man, [held] 2 carucates of land.
Always 7 smallholders; 1 slave;
2 ploughs in lordship. Then ½ men's plough.
Meadow, 3 acres. Now 1 cob; then 7 cattle, now 14; then 15 pigs,
now 30; then 37 sheep, now 80; now 10 goats; 3 beehives.
Value always 60s.
Frodo, the Abbot's brother, holds (this).
In the same (Depden) 2 free men, Blackwin and Godwin; 2 carucates
of land.
3 smallholders.
Then 1½ ploughs, now 2.
Meadow, 3 acres. Then 1 cob; always 6 cattle. Then 16 pigs,
now 26; then 40 sheep.
Value then 30s; now 50[s].
Osbern holds (this).

80 In CLOPTON Leofgeat, 1 free man, held 1½ carucates of land.
1 villager; 1 smallholder; 3 slaves.
Then 1 plough, now 2.
Meadow, 4 acres. Always 1 cob; 10 cattle. Now 34 pigs; 83 sheep.
Value then 20s; now 30[s].
Roger holds (this).

81 In WRATTING Goda, 1 free woman; 2 carucates of land and 30 acres.
Always 9 smallholders.
2 ploughs in lordship; ½ men's plough.
Meadow, 7 acres; 1 mill. Then 1 cob, now 2; then 4 cattle, now
10; then 1 pig, now 52; then 80 sheep, now 100; then 4 goats,
now 40.
Value then 30s; now 40[s].
Payne holds (this).
The whole has 1 league in length and ½ in width; 12d in tax.

82 In HAVERHILL Fridebern, 1 free man, [held] 5 smallholders; they
have 80 acres.
1 plough in lordship; 2 men's oxen. Meadow, 2 acres.
Value then 13s 4d; now 15s.
Payne also holds (this).

83 In HANCHET Alwin, 1 free man, held 100 acres.
1 smallholder.
1 plough. Meadow, 2 acres.
Value then 10s; now 15[s].

⟨ In Vrdresfelda. Vlmarus teñ . ı . liƀ hõ . L . ı . aꞓ . & . ı . borꝺ . & dim̃
car̄ . & . ı . aꞓ prati . ꝺ uat . vııı . fot . Idẽ Paganus ten& . In eaꝺ . ı . liƀ
hõ Leuiara . c . aꞓ . ꝺ . ı . borꝺ . ꝺ . ı . car̄ . ꝺ uat . xx . fot . Godart tenet.

In eaꝺ . ı . liƀ hõ Aluuinus . ııı . car̄ trǽ . & . ıı . uitt . & . xı . borꝺ . & . ııı . feru̅ .
& . ııı . car̄ in dñio . Tꞓ . ı . car̄ hom̃ . m̊ . dim̃ . & . ıı . aꞓ . p̃ti . filua . xx . porꞓ.
Tꞓ . ıı . runꞓ . modo . ııı . Tꞓ xx . ıı . añ . m̊ . xx . Tꞓ Lx . porꞓ . modo xL . v .
Tꞓ Lx . ou̅s . modo . cxxııı . Tꞓ . Lx . cap̃ . m̊ . Lvıı . Sẽp uat . Lx . fot . Wilard
ten& . Tota h̅t . ı . lg̅ in longo ꝺ dim̃ in lato . ꝺ vı . ꝺ . de gelto.

⟨ In Wratinga . ı . liƀ hõ alƀnus . ııı . car̄ trǽ . & . v . uitti . & . x . borꝺ . Tꞓ
ııı . car̄ in dñio . modo . ıı . femper . ı . car̄ hom̃ . & . xıı . aꞓ p̃ti . Silua
vııı . porꞓ . ꝺ . ı . molm̅ . Tꞓ . ıı . runꞓ . modo . ııı . Tꞓ . ıx . añ . m̊ . xııı .
Tꞓ xx . ıııı . porꞓ . modo . xL . vııı . Tꞓ . Lx . ou̅s . m̊ . vıı . c . ꝺ . vı . uafa apu̅ .
ꝺ fub eo . ıx liƀi hoẽs dim̃ car̄ trǽ . Tꞓ dim̃ . car̄ . & . ı . aꞓ p̃ti . Æcctia . xııı .
aꞓ . Tꞓ uat . L . fot . m̊ . Lx . ⟨ In cileburna . teñ . Godwiñ . ı . liƀ hõ
ıı . car̄ terrae . ı . uitt . & . ıııı . borꝺ . Tꞓ . ıı . car̄ . m̊ . ı . ꝺ . vı . aꞓ . p̃ti . & . ı . mot .
femp . ı . runꞓ . Tꞓ uat . xL fot . modo . L . Goisfridus fili hamonis ten& .

⟨ In Poflingeorda . ı . liƀ hõ . edricus . xxx . v . aꞓ . & dim̃ car̄ . & . ıı . aꞓ
p̃ti . & uat vııı . fot Loher ten& . In boituna . ı . liƀ hõ Vlgar . vııı .
aꞓ . ꝺ uat xvı . ꝺ . Radulfus ten& .

84 In WITHERSFIELD Wulfmer, 1 free man, held 51 acres.
    1 smallholder.
    ½ plough. Meadow, 1 acre.
    Value 8s.
    Payne also holds (this).
In the same (Withersfield) 1 free man, Leofwaru; 100 acres.
    1 smallholder.
    1 plough.
    Value 20s.
    Godard holds (this).
In the same (Withersfield) 1 free man, Alwin; 3 carucates of land.
    2 villagers, 11 smallholders, 3 slaves.
    3 ploughs in lordship; then 1 men's plough, now ½.
    Meadow, 2 acres; woodland, 20 pigs. Then 2 cobs, now 3; then
        22 cattle, now 20; then 60 pigs, now 45; then 60 sheep, now
        123; then 60 goats, now 57.
    Value always 60s.
    Wilard holds (this).
    The whole has 1 league in length and ½ in width; 6d in tax.

85 In WRATTING 1 free man, Ailbern, 3 carucates of land.
    5 villagers, 10 smallholders.
    Then 3 ploughs in lordship, now 2; always 1 men's plough.
    Meadow, 12 acres; woodland, 8 pigs; 1 mill. Then 2 cobs, now 3;
        then 9 cattle, now 13; then 24 pigs, now 48; then 60 sheep,
        now 700; 6 beehives.
Under him, 9 free men; ½ carucate of land. Then ½ plough.
    Meadow, 1 acre.
    A church, 13 acres.
    Value then 50s; now 60[s].

86 In CHILBOURNE Godwin, 1 free man, held 2 carucates of land.
    1 villager, 4 smallholders.
    Then 2 ploughs, now 1.
    Meadow, 6 acres; 1 mill. Always 1 cob.
    Value then 40s; now 50[s].
    Geoffrey son of Hamo holds (this).

87 In POSLINGFORD 1 free man, Edric; 35 acres. ½ plough.
    Meadow, 2 acres.
    Value 8s.
    Lother holds (this).

88 In BOYTON 1 free man, Wulfgar; 8 acres.
    Value 16d.
    Ralph holds (this).

⁊ In alia boituna ten̄ Ajuuar̄ . I . lib̄

Hō . xxIIII . ac̄ . ⁊ ual . IIII . fol . W . peret . ten̄ . ⁊ In hauo keduna . Ten̄

Aluuin̄ . I . lib̄ hō . xL . ac̄ . ⁊ dim̄ . car̄ . ⁊ . II . ac̄ . p̄ti . & . ual . vI . fol . & . vIII . d̄.

Folkered ten̄ . ⁊ In CloPtuna . I . lib̄ . hō . Roc . de . xIII . ac̄ . & ual .

II . fol . Wiłłm peccatū ten̄ . ⁊ In Bradeleia . femp . II . lib̄i hōes . Lx .

vIIII . ac̄ . ⁊ . I . ac̄ . p̄ti . Semp . I . car̄ . & ual . xvII . fol . & . vI' . d̄.

⁊ In Tridiauua femp . x . lib̄i hōes . I . car̄ tr̄æ . & . I . car̄ . ⁊ . I . ac̄ p̄ti . Æc

cłia xxvIIII . ac̄ . ⁊ ual . x . fol . Tota ħt . I . łg in longo . & . I . qr̄ in lato . &

xII . d̄ de gelto . ⁊ In Kidituna . femp . x . lib̄i . hōes . I . car̄ terræ . & . II .

car̄ . & . ual . xx . fol . ⁊ In hauerhella . femp . xIII . lib̄i hōes . I . car̄ terræ

⁊ Lx . ac̄ . ⁊ . I . car̄ ⁊ dim̄ filua . vII . porc̄ . ⁊ ual & . xxx . fol .

⁊ In Wedresfelda . Ix . lib̄i hōes . I . car̄ terræ . ⁊ dim̄ . femp . II . car̄

& dim̄ . Tc̄ ual xx . fol . modo . xxx . ⁊ In ftoches femp . xx . I . lib̄i hōes

. I . car̄ terræ . Lx . vIII . ac̄ . Tc̄ . I . car̄ . & . dim̄ . modo . II . & . x . ac̄ . p̄ti .

Tc̄ ual . xx . fol . modo . xxx . I . ⁊ . IIII . den̄ . Ecclia Lx . ac̄ . & . ual . x .

fol . ⁊ In poflingewrda femp . vI . lib̄i hōes . Lxxx . v . ac̄ . & . III . bord .

& . I . carr̄ . & ual & . xIIII . fol . & . II . d̄ .

89 In the other BOYTON Ainuar, 1 free man; 24 acres.
Value 4s.
    William Peret holds (this).

90 In HAWKEDON Alwin, 1 free man, held 40 acres. ½ plough.
    Meadow, 2 acres.
Value 6s 8d.
    Fulcred holds (this).

91 In CLOPTON 1 free man, Roc, with 13 acres.
Value 2s.
    William Peche holds (this).

92 In BRADLEY always 2 free men; 69 acres.
    Meadow, 1 acre.
    Always 1 plough.
Value 17s 6d.

93 In THURLOW always 10 free men; 1 carucate of land. 1 plough.   397 a
    Meadow, 1 acre.
    A church, 29 acres.
Value 10s.
    The whole has 1 league in length and 1 furlong in width; 12d
in tax.

94 In KEDINGTON always 10 free men; 1 carucate of land. 2 ploughs.
Value 20s.

95 In HAVERHILL always 13 free men; 1 carucate of land and 60 acres.
1½ ploughs.
    Woodland, 7 pigs.
Value 30s.

96 In WITHERSFIELD 9 free men; 1½ carucates of land. Always 2½
ploughs.
Value then 20s; now 30[s].

97 In STOKE (by Clare) always 21 free men; 1 carucate of land [and]
68 acres. Then 1½ ploughs, now 2.
    Meadow, 10 acres.
Value then 20s; now 31[s] 4d.
    A church, 60 acres; value 10s.

98 In POSLINGFORD always 6 free men; 85 acres.
    3 smallholders.
    1 plough.
Value 14s 2d.

| In Wichā . femp . I . liƀ homo
LX . aē . 7 . II . borđ . 7 . I . car̄ . 7 . IIII . aē p̄ti . 7 ual& . x . fol . *|* In Stra
tefella femp . xvI . liƀi . hōes . I . car̄ terræ . femp . III . car̄ . & . II . aē p̄ti,
& ual& . xx . fol . Æcclia . xxx . aē . & ual . v . fol . *|* In hauokeduna
femp . vIII . liƀi hōes xxx . aē . & . II . borđ . 7 . I . car̄ . 7 ual . xIII . fol . 7 . IIII đ.
| In hauerha . II . liƀi hōes xxvI . aē . 7 ual . IIII . fol . & dim̄ . Ifti
om̄s pot̄ uenđe 7 dare tr̄as fuas . fed Wifgarus ħt . t̄ . r̄ . e̅ . 7 focā 7
facā p̄t̄ . vI . forisfaɕuras sc̄i eadmundi . ut fupius diximus.
| In bradeleia . IIII . liƀi . hōes . Vluuinus . Leuricus . 7 Leuuinus . & ħnt
xv . aē . Quartus bundo . & . ħt . I . car̄ . terræ . femp . II . car̄r . 7 . II . aē
prati . 7 ual . xx . II . fol . 7 vI . deñ . Ex his n̄ habuit ante c̄ Ricardi.
c̄om̄đ . t . r . e . Sc̄s . edm̄ . totā focā . *|* In Tridlauua . II . foē . edeuæ
cū om̄i c̄fuetudine . q̄s tenebat . Rađ q̄do forisfecit . & ħnt xxv.
aē . & femp dim̄ car̄ . & . ual IIII . fol . & . IIII . deñ . ħ teñ Widardus.

| In Wimundeftuna . vI . liƀi hōes . de fexto qui uocatur briɕtricus.
nefcit hunđ fi potuit tr̄a fuā uenđe ł . non . t . r . e . fed teftatur
qđ uiđer̄ eū iurare qđ non poterant dare uenđe tr̄a fuā ab ante
ceffore Ricardi . & ħnt . II . car̄ . terræ . 7 xI . aē . femp . II . car̄ . vII . aē
p̄ti . m̄ . II . runc̄ . Tc̄ . II . uaē . modo . III . Tc̄ . vI . porc̄ . modo xxx . Tc̄.
xvI . oūs . modo . LxII . Tot̄ ual xL . fol . hoc teñ . Giroldus.

| DIMIDI . H̄ . DE COSFORT . In hechā . xIIII . liƀi hōes . Lx . aē
Tc̄ . II . car̄ . modo . I . & . II . aē p̄ti . 7 ual . x . fol.

99 In WICKHAM(BROOK) always 1 free man; 60 acres.
    2 smallholders.
    1 plough. Meadow, 4 acres.
    Value 10s.

100 In STRADISHALL always 16 free men; 1 carucate of land. Always 3
ploughs.
    Meadow, 2 acres.
    Value 20s.
    A church, 30 acres; value 5s.

101 In HAWKEDON always 8 free men; 30 acres.
    2 smallholders.
    1 plough.
    Value 13s 4d.

102 In HAVERHILL 2 free men; 26 acres.
    Value 4½s.

All these (free men) could sell and grant their lands but Withgar had
full jurisdiction before 1066, except for the 6 forfeitures of St.
Edmund's, as we said above.

103 In BRADLEY 4 free men. Wulfwin, Leofric and Leofwin; they have
15 acres. The fourth, Bondi, has 1 carucate of land. Always 2
ploughs.
    Meadow, 2 acres.
    Value 22s 6d.
    Over these (free men), Richard's predecessor did not have
patronage before 1066; St. Edmund's (had) full jurisdiction.

104 In THURLOW 2 Freemen of Edeva's with every customary due. (Earl)
Ralph held them when he forfeited. They have 25 acres. Always
½ plough.
    Value 4s 4d.
    Widard holds this.

105 In *WIMUNDESTUNA* 6 free men. Concerning the sixth, called Brictric,   397 b
the Hundred does not know if he could sell his land or not before
1066 but it testifies that they saw him swear that he could not
grant or sell his land away from Richard's predecessor. They have
2 carucates of land and 11 acres. Always 2 ploughs.
    Meadow, 7 acres. Now 2 cobs; then 2 cows, now 3; then 6 pigs,
        now 30; then 16 sheep, now 62.
    Value of the whole 40s.
    Gerald holds this.

    Half-Hundred of COSFORD
106 In HITCHAM 14 free men; 60 acres. Then 2 ploughs, now 1.
    Meadow, 2 acres.
    Value 10s.

★ ⟨In halefheia . vɪ . libi hǒes . ɪ . car ́ terræ . & . vɪ . borđ . & . ɪɪ . car ́ . & . ɪɪ . ac̄
prati . & . ual . xx . fot . ⟨In carefeia . ɪ . lib . v . ac̄ . 7 ual . x . đ . fuus antēc
foca & cōm ́ . ⟨In brettham . vɪɪɪ . libi hǒes . xxx . ac̄ . & . ɪ . car ́ . & ual
v . fot . ⟨In Rifebroc . ɪɪ . libi hǒes . x . ac̄ . & . ual . xx . đ.

⟨In Watefelda . ɪɪɪ . libi hǒes ʟx . ac̄ . & . ɪɪɪ . borđ . Tc̄ . ɪ . car ́ . & dim ́ . moɗo
. ɪɪ . 7 ual . x . fot . Ex ħ . hab̄ fuus ante c̄ c̄mđ . t . r . e . 7 foca & faca . S̄ . e.
vɪ . foris facturas . ⟨In Staneftrada . ɪ . lib̄ homo . xxɪɪɪɪ . ac̄ . & ual
ɪɪɪɪ . fot . Ante c̄ . dimiđ . c̄omđ . & Abb̄ . de eli aliā . Dim ́ hanc
terrā calūpniat ́ . R . peurel 7 fuit ei lib̄ata in Lofa . S̄ . E . focā ;

398 a

398 a

⟨TERRE WILLMI DE WARENA :~ Thewardeftreu . H̃ . .XXVI.

In ratefdana tenuer ́ . ɪɪ . libi hǒes . fce aldrēde ; c̄ foca 7 faca.
un eoʒ poteraṇt uendere ˛ terrā . 7 alt n̄ poterat . Qui po
terat uende . habebat . xʟ . ac̄ . 7 . v . borđ . & alt qui non poterat
ʟx . Semper . ɪɪ . borđ . Semp int eos . ɪɪ . carr ́ . & . ɪɪ . ac̄ p̄ti . 7 ual . xx.
fot . & ē de efcangio Lewes . Hoc ⟨ In gedinga . ɪɪ . libi hoes fci . e . c̄om ́
       ten& humfrid' fit' Roderici.
7 foca ʟx . ac̄ . træ . & . ɪɪɪ . borđ . Tc̄ . ɪ . car ́ . moɗo nulla . & . v . ac̄ p̄ti.
& ual . v . fot . DE efcangio Lewes.

107 In LINDSEY 6 free men; 1 carucate of land.
6 smallholders.
2 ploughs. Meadow, 2 acres.
Value 20s.

108 In KERSEY 1 free man; 5 acres.
Value 10d.
His predecessor (had) the jurisdiction and patronage.

109 In BRETTENHAM 8 free men; 30 acres. 1 plough.
Value 5s.

110 In RUSHBROOKE 2 free men; 10 acres.
Value 20d.

111 In WHATFIELD 3 free men; 60 acres.
3 smallholders.
Then 1½ ploughs, now 2.
Value 10s.
Over these (free men) his predecessor had patronage before 1066,
and full jurisdiction. St. Edmund's (had) the 6 forfeitures.

112 In STONE STREET 1 free man; 24 acres.
Value 4s.
His predecessor (had) half the patronage and the Abbot of Ely
(had) the other half.
R(anulf) Peverel claims half this land and it was delivered to him
in Loose.
St. Edmund's (has) the jurisdiction.

26   LANDS OF WILLIAM OF WARENNE

398 a

THEDWESTRY Hundred

1 In RATTLESDEN 2 free men of St. Etheldreda's held with full
jurisdiction. One of them could sell the land, the other could not.
The one who could sell had 40 acres; 5 smallholders. The other who
could not (sell had) 60 (acres); always 2 smallholders. Always 2
ploughs between them.
Meadow, 2 acres.
Value 20s.
It is in exchange (for) Lewes.
Humphrey son of Rodric holds this.

2 In GEDDING 2 free men of St. Edmund's under patronage and
jurisdiction; 60 acres of land.
3 smallholders.
Then 1 plough, now none. Meadow, 5 acres.
Value 5s.
(It is) in exchange (for) Lewes.

⍌*LACFORDA*. H̃. ⍌In heluedana teñ.ı.lib homo s̃ce Aldrede
com̃d tantũ.in foca s̃ci.e.ıı.car̃ terræ ⍵ efcangio de Lewes.qd teñ
Nicolaus.de.W.T̃c & p̃.ıııı.uiłł.modo.ııı.Semp.ıı.bord.&.ı.feru.
T̃c & p̃.ıı.car̃ in dominio.modo.ı.Semp.ı.car̃ hom̃.& quarta
pars pifcariæ.&.ı.æccłiæ.xv.ac̃.terræ.T̃c.ıııı.porc.modo.ıı.T̃c
cc.oũs.modo.ccc.T̃c.l.cap̃.m̃.c.vı.minus.t̃c & p̃ uał.xxx.fol.
modo.l.fol. ⍌In herninga Roḡrus teñ&. wella teñ& ⍵pofitus 7 fuit tohe
lib ħo f7 non poterat.uend.ı.car̃ terræ.&.ıı.bord.Semp.ı.carr
& lx.oũs.& uał xvı.fol.De feudo frederici in foca s̃ci.ed.
In ead teñ lib homo antc frederici in foca s̃ci.e.xl.ac̃.qd teñ&
nicolaus de.W.T̃c dim̃ car̃.modo nulla.& uał.xl.deñ.

⍌*STOV*. H̃. In bureffalla hunfrid' teñ& monulfus p̃fbit h̃o s̃ce aldrede com̃ -
d in foca regis dimidia car̃ terræ.& xx.ac̃.m̃ teñ Wiłłmus
⍵ efcangio Lewes.t̃c & p̃.ıı.bord.modo.vıı.T̃c 7 femp.ı.car̃ in do -
minio.Semp.ıı.boŭ houm̃.&.ıı.ac̃ p̃ti In ead.ıııı.libi h̃oes eid
monulfi com̃d.ıı.ac̃.&.uał.xıı.fol.

398 b
⍌*BOSEMARA*. H̃.Toneftala nicolau' teñ tenuit.Lefwinus lib homo.ı.car̃
terræ.7 xx.ac̃ ⍵ mañ.t.r.e.femp.ı.uiłł.T̃c.ıı.car̃ in dominio.P̃ 7 modo
.ı.&.ıı.ac̃ p̃ti.modo.ı.runc̃.7.ı.uac̃.T̃c.xxx.oũs.modo.lx.T̃c uał
xxıııı.fol.modo.xxv.Rex & comes focã

LACKFORD Hundred

3 1 free man of St. Etheldreda's, under patronage only (but) in
jurisdiction of St. Edmund's, held in ELVEDEN; 2 carucates of land
in exchange for Lewes. Nicholas holds (it) from William.
>Then and later 4 villagers, now 3. Always 2 smallholders; 1 slave.
>Then and later 2 ploughs in lordship, now 1; always 1 men's
>plough.
>The fourth part of a fishery.
>1 church, 15 acres of land.
>Then 4 pigs, now 2; then 200 sheep, now 300; then 50 goats,
>now 100 less 6.
Value then and later 30s; now 50s.

4 Roger holds in HERRINGSWELL; a reeve [held], he was a free man of
Toki's but could not sell; 1 carucate of land.
>2 smallholders.
>Always 1 plough; 60 sheep.
Value 16s.
It is (part) of Frederick's Holding, in the jurisdiction of St.
Edmund's.
In the same (Herringswell) a free man of Frederick's predecessor,
in the jurisdiction of St. Edmund's, held 40 acres. Nicholas holds
it from William. Then ½ plough, now none.
Value 40d.

STOW Hundred

5 Humphrey holds in BUXHALL; Munulf the priest, a man of St.
Etheldreda's under patronage (but) in the jurisdiction of the King,
[held] ½ carucate of land and 20 acres. Now William holds (it) in
exchange (for) Lewes.
>Then and later 2 smallholders, now 7.
>Then and always 1 plough in lordship; always 2 men's oxen.
>Meadow, 2 acres.
In the same (Buxhall) 4 free men of the same Munulf's under
patronage; 2 acres.
Value 12s.

BOSMERE Hundred
6 Nicholas holds in TUNSTALL; Leofwin, a free man, held (it); 1
carucate of land and 20 acres as a manor before 1066.
>Always 1 villager.
>Then 2 ploughs in lordship, later and now 1. Meadow, 2 acres.
>Now 1 cob; 1 cow. Then 30 sheep, now 60.
Value then 24s; now 25[s].
The King and the Earl (have) the jurisdiction.

teñ de Wiłłmo . ı . lib h̃m . xxxvııı . ac̃ . ſemp . ı . car̃ . Tc̃ ual . vııı . ſoł . modo . x.

⅂ *BRADEMARA* . *H̃* . BERHAM . teñ Hugo fiłi goldæ quod tenuit
Boſteinn . t . r . e . Dım̃ car̃ . træ . ᵽ mañ . ſemp . ııı . borđ . & . ıı . ſerui.
& . ı . car̃ in dño . Tc̃ dım̃ . car̃ hom . modo . ıı . boũs . Tc̃ . ıı . runc̃.
modo . ı . Tc̃ . xııı . porc̃ . Tc̃ ʟxxx . v . oũs . Modo . x . c . ⁊ ııı . libi h̃oes.
ıııı . ac̃ . & . dım̃ . car̃ . ex his habuit ſuus ante ceſſor c̃om̃d . Tc̃ ual
xvı . ſoł . Modo . xx.

⅂ *RISEBRVGE* . *H̃* . ᴅᴇ FEVDO FEDRICI . --
Depdanã teñ hugo de Wanceio qđ tenuit Toka teinnus . t . r . e . ᵽ m̃.
ııı car̃r terræ . ſemp xvı . uiłł . ⁊ vıı . borđ . Tc̃ . ıııı . ſerù . Tc̃ & ᵽ
ıı . car̃r in dominio . modo . ıııı . ſemper . ıııı . car̃ hom . xıı . ac̃ p̃ti.
Silù . de . c . porc̃ . ſemper . ıı . runc̃ . Tc̃ xx . ıı . añ . modo . xvıı.
Tc̃ . xʟ porc̃ . ꝏ . ʟxx . ıı . Tc̃ . xxıııı . oũs . modo . c . xıı . modo
xııı . uaſa apũ . Ecclia . xx . ıııı . ac̃ . libæ træ . Tc̃ ual . ıııı . lib.
Modo . vı . h̃t . ı . lēg . in longo . & . vııı . q̃r . in lat̃ . ⁊ . v . đ . ⁊ ob̃lũ de gelto.
⅂ Wedresfeldã . teñ . Wimer quã tenuit idē . t . r . e . ᵽ manerio
ıı . car̃ ᴛᴇʀræ . ſemp . v . uiłł . & . v . borđ . Tc̃ . ııı . ſerù . Tc̃ . ıı . car̃
in dominio . modo . ııı . ſemper . ı . car̃ . hominũ . ıı . ac̃ prati.
Silua . xx . porc̃ . Tc̃ . ıı . runc̃ . modo . ııı . Tc̃ . ıııı . añ . modo.
xıı . Tc̃ xx . porc̃ . modo . xxx . Tc̃ ʟxxx . oũs . ꝏodo . c . ſemᵽ

399 a

xvı , cap̃ . ⁊ vı . uaſa apũ . Tc̃ ual ʟxx . ſoł . modo . ıııı . lib . In eadē
. ı . lib h̃o . xx . ıııı . ac̃ . ſemp dım̃ car̃ . ⁊ ual . ıııı . ſoł.
⅂ In Cloptuna teñ . hugo . quam tenuit idē tocha . ı . car̃r . træ
ſemper . ı . car̃r . & . ıı . ac̃ . prati . Semper ual & . xx . ſoł.

7 In CREETING Humphrey holds from William 1 free man; 38 acres. Always 1 plough.
Value 8s; now 10[s].

BRADMERE Hundred

8 Hugh son of Gold holds BARNHAM; Bosten held it before 1066; ½ carucate of land as a manor.
    Always 3 smallholders; 2 slaves;
    1 plough in lordship. Then ½ men's plough, now 2 oxen.
    Then 2 cobs, now 1; then 13 pigs; then 85 sheep, now 90.
3 free men, 4 acres. ½ plough. Over these (free men) his predecessor had patronage.
Value then 16s; now 20[s].

RISBRIDGE Hundred
(PART) OF FREDERICK'S HOLDING

9 Hugh of Wanchy holds DEPDEN; Toki, a thane, held it before 1066; 3 carucates of land as a manor.
    Always 16 villagers; 7 smallholders. Then 4 slaves.
    Then and later 2 ploughs in lordship, now 4; always 4 men's ploughs.
    Meadow, 12 acres; woodland at 100 pigs. Always 2 cobs. Then 22 cattle, now 17; then 40 pigs, now 72; then 24 sheep, now 112; now 13 beehives.
    A church, 24 acres of free land.
Value then £4; now [£] 6.
It has 1 league in length and 8 furlongs in width; 5½d in tax.

10 Wigmer holds WITHERSFIELD; he also held it before 1066; 2 carucates of land as a manor.
    Always 5 villagers; 5 smallholders. Then 3 slaves.
    Then 2 ploughs in lordship, now 3; always 1 men's plough.
    Meadow, 2 acres; woodland, 20 pigs. Then 2 cobs, now 3; then 4 cattle, now 12; then 20 pigs, now 30; then 80 sheep, now 100.
    Always 16 beehives.
Value 70s; now £4.
In the same (Withersfield) 1 free man; 24 acres. Always ½ plough.
Value 4s.

399 a

11 Hugh holds in CLOPTON; Toki also held it; 1 carucate of land. Always 1 plough.
    Meadow, 2 acres.
Value always 20s.

⌐ *HVND DE BLEDINGA*. Wretham tenuit. Edricus

lib̄ hō . t . r . e . ii . carr̄ . terræ . p̄ mañ . femp . v . uitt . femp xi . bord̄.

Tc̄ . vi . ferui . modo . iii . Tc̄ car̄ & dim̄ in dn̄io . modo . ii . Tc̄ . iii.

car̄ hoūm . modo . ii . femp̄ filua ad xx . porc̄ . femper . ii . ac̄ prati.

mo . ii . runc̄ . modo xiii . añ . modo . xii . porc̄ . modo ⁚ c . xiii . oūs.

modo xx . cap̄ . 7 v . uafa apū . 7 . i . æcctia . de . xl . ac̄ . femp uat . xl . fot⁚

7 iftū mneriū teñ Rodb̄tus de petro ponte de eo . In eadē uilla

tenuit Turchillus . lib̄ hō . t . r . e . femper . ii . carr̄ . terræ . p̄ . i . ma

nerio 7 femper . v . uitt . 7 femp̄ xi . bord̄ . ii car̄ . poffunt fieri in

dominio . 7 . i . quando recepit . ii . ac̄ . p̄ti . filua ad xx . porc̄.

femp uat . xl . fot . Et hanc terrā ipfe met . R . ten&.

⌐ In ead̄ villa . teñ Wluric̄ lib̄ homo . ii . car̄ terræ p̄ manerio.

femp . v . uitt . 7 xi . bord̄ . i . car̄ in dominio . & altera poteft fieri.

& . ii . carr̄ . hominū . ii . ac̄ prati . filua ad xx . porc̄ . femp uat . xl.

fot . 7 . i . æcctia . de . viii . ac̄ . 7 hoc teñ id̄e . R.

In ead̄ Villa . xx . libi homiñ manfer̄ . de . ccc . lx . ac̄ . & . ii . bord̄.

7 femp . vi . car̄ in dominio . femp uat . lx . fot . In . i . de iftis hominib᷄

hī Cōms Alanus dim̄ ēmendationē . 7 dim̄ trā 7 focā & facā.

7 totū h̄ h̄t Rodb̄tus de Wittmo . de Warena . de tota hac trā iac̄

foca & faca in blideburg . H̃.

399 b

⌐ Adhuc h̄t Wittm⁹ in ead̄e uilla . i . maneriū ⸱ ᴵᴵᴵ ᶜᵃⁱ ᵗⁱᵃᵉ quod tenuit halden⁹

. i . lib̄ homo . Tc̄ . vi . uitt . 7 mo . iiii . Tc̄ xi . bord̄ . modo . xiii . Tc̄ . iii . feru.

modo . i . femp . iii . car̄ in dominio . Tc̄ & modo . ii . car̄ hoūm . ii.

ac̄ p̄ti . filua ad xl . porc̄ . modo . vii . añ . modo . xxiiii . porc̄.

quat xxti . oūs . modo . xxx . cap̄ . T . R . E . uat . iiii . lib̄ . & modo

iii . 7 hoc teñ Wittmus fili⁹ Rainaldi . de . W . de Warene.

Hundred of BLYTHING

12a Edric, a free man, held WRENTHAM before 1066; 2 carucates of land as a manor.

Always 5 villagers; always 11 smallholders. Then 6 slaves, now 3. Then 1½ ploughs in lordship, now 2; then 3 men's ploughs, now 2. Woodland, always for 20 pigs; meadow, always 2 acres. Now 2 cobs, now 13 cattle, now 12 pigs, now 113 sheep; now 20 goats, 5 beehives. 1 church with 40 acres.

Value always 40s.

Robert of Pierrepont holds this manor from him.

In the same village Thorkell, a free man, held before 1066; always 2 carucates of land as 1 manor.

Always 5 villagers; always 11 smallholders. 2 ploughs possible in lordship; when acquired, 1. Meadow, 2 acres; woodland for 20 pigs.

Value always 40s.

The same Robert holds this land.

In the same village Wulfric, a free man; 2 carucates of land as a manor.

Always 5 villagers; 11 smallholders; 1 plough in lordship, another possible; 2 men's ploughs. Meadow, 2 acres; woodland for 20 pigs.

Value always 40s.

1 church with 8 acres.

Robert also holds this.

In the same village dwell 20 free men, with 300 acres. 2 smallholders. Always 6 ploughs in lordship.

Value always 60s.

Over 1 of these men, Count Alan has half the patronage, half the land and full jurisdiction.

Robert has the whole of this from William of Warenne.

The full jurisdiction over the whole of this land lies in Blythburgh.

12b Also in the same village William has 1 manor; 3 carucates of land.   399 b
Haldane, 1 free man, held it.

Then 6 villagers, now 4; then 11 smallholders, now 13; then 3 slaves, now 1. Always 3 ploughs in lordship. Then and now 2 men's ploughs. Meadow, 2 acres; woodland for 40 pigs. Now 7 cattle; now 24 pigs; fourscore sheep; now 30 goats.

Value before 1066 £4; now [£] 3.

William son of Reginald holds this from William of Warenne.

In eadē villa manſit . I . liƀ hō . 7 dimidia . car̔ terre teñ ꝓ ma-
nerio. ᵠᵈ ᵗᵉⁿ& ⁱᵈᵉ· 7 ſubſe habuit . II . liƀo homines . de . x . ac̄ . & . I . bord̄ . ſemp . I . ca͘r̔
in dominio . 7 dimid̄ car̄ hoūm . ſilua . ad . IIII . porc̄ . 7 dim̄ ac̄
prati . II . runc̄ . VI . añ . x . porc̄ . xxx . oūs . xx . cap̄ . Tc̄ ual . x . ſoł .
7 modo ſimiłr̄ . ⫽ In eadē uilla teñ Aluricus de ſanford
. L . ac̄ ꝓ manerio . ſemp . II . bordarii . ſemp . I . car̔ . in dominio
. I . ac̄ prati . 7 . I . runc̄ . IIII . añ . VIII . porc̄ . LX . oūs . VII . cap̔ .
ſemp ualuit . x . ſoł . ⫽ In eadē uilla manent . VIII . liƀi hŏes
7 tenēt . car̔ 7 dim̄ . 7 x . ac̄ terræ . 7 . tenē . I . bord̄ . ſemp . II .
car̔ in dominio . ſemper ual̔ . xII . ſoł . 7 hoc totū ten&
uuiłłmus fili⁹ rainaldi . ſub . W . de uuarena.
⫽Heneſtede . I . bereuuite de uueretehā . I . car̔ terræ . ſemp .
IIII . uiłłi . 7 ſemper . IX . bord̄ . 7 ſemp . I . car̔ in dominio . 7 ſemp
II . car̔ hominū . 7 . VI . añ . 7 xL . oūs . XII . porc̄ . xx . cap̄ . ſemp
ual̔ . xx . ſoł . 7 modo ſunt additi . II . liƀi . hŏes . de . xxx . ac̄ tr̄æ .
7 h̄nt . I . car̔ . in dominio . 7 ual̔ . III . ſoł . 7 has . II . terras ten&
Godefridus de ⌈ᵖᵉᵗʳᵒ ponte . ſub . Wiłłmo de Warenna . Et om̄s hæ
terræ . h̄nt . III . łḡ in longo . & . II . de lato . 7 reddit . II . ſoł . de geldo

400 a

regis ꝑ ꝉotā hanc terrā h̄t Rex ſocā 7 ſacā p̄t dōminium
Aldani . ꝛ de terra hac s̄t ablate . VI . ac̄ . terræ . comiti . Alano
q̂s homines Wiłłmi ſibi abſtuleꝛ teſte hundreto . 7 Turkil de uue-
reteham fuit hō edrici ante ceſoris Rodb̄ti malet.

In the same village 1 free man dwelt and held ½ carucate of land as a manor. He also holds it.

Under him he had 2 free men, with 10 acres. 1 smallholder.

Always 1 plough in lordship; ½ men's plough.

Woodland for 4 pigs; meadow, ½ acre. 2 cobs, 6 cattle, 10 pigs, 30 sheep, 20 goats.

Value then 10s; now the same.

In the same village Aelfric of *Sanford* held 50 acres as a manor.

Always 2 smallholders.

Always 1 plough in lordship.

Meadow, 1 acre. 1 cob, 4 cattle, 8 pigs, 60 sheep, 7 goats.

Value always 10s.

In the same village 8 free men dwell and hold [1]½ carucates and 10 acres of land. They hold

1 smallholder.

Always 2 ploughs in lordship.

Value always 12s.

William son of Reginald holds the whole of this under William of Warenne.

12c HENSTEAD, 1 outlier of Wrentham; 1 carucate of land.

Always 4 villagers; always 9 smallholders.

Always 1 plough in lordship; always 2 men's ploughs.

6 cattle, 40 sheep, 12 pigs, 20 goats.

Value always 20s.

Now 2 free men have been added, with 30 acres of land. They have 1 plough in lordship.

Value 3s.

Godfrey of Pierrepont holds these two lands under William of Warenne.

12d All these lands have 3 leagues in length and 2 in width; 2s in the King's tax.

Through the whole of this land the King has full jurisdiction, 400 a except (in) Haldane's lordship.

From this land 6 acres of land were taken away from Count Alan which William's men took away for themselves, as the Hundred testifies.

Thorkell of Wrentham was a man belonging to Edric, the predecessor of Robert Malet.

MIdeltuna . teñ Rannulfus nepos ᵠᵈ ᵗᵉⁿᵘⁱᵗ· | Aluricus . I . liƀ homo .p . I.

manerio . modo W . de Warena . ~~in dñio~~ teñ . II . caŕ terræ . fem -

per . II . uilli . femp . VIII . borđ . Tc̄ . IIII . ferui . 7 . modo . I . Tc̄ . II . caŕ

in dñio . 7 m̄ dim̄ . caŕ hom̄ . VI . ac̄ p̃ti . Tc̄ . I . runc̄ . 7 modo . II . 7

modo . II . uaccas . 7 XX . porc̄ . 7 L . ou̅s . 7 tc̄ ual . XL . fol . 7 modo . &.

. I . æcclia de XV . ac̄ . 7 ual . II . fol . 7 huic manerio s̄t additi . V . liƀi hoĕs

7 dim̄ pƀr . 7 teñ . L . V . ac̄ . 7 dim̄ . & . I . caŕ 7 dimid in dñio . 7 . II . ac̄

p̃ti . 7 . X . fol ual . 7 ħt . VIII . q̄r in longū 7 . VII . in lat̄ quicūq̄ ibi

terrā hab& . 7 Reddit . VII . đ . & obolū . 7 fup hos . VI . hoĕs hab& Rex

& Comes focā 7 facā . 7 Aluricus qui hunc maneriū teñ

fuit homo Edrici ante cefforis Rodƀti . & Will mal& . 7 Rodƀti . 7

fuerunt faifiti . de tr̄a hac.

Torintuna . teñ Aluricus liƀ h̄omo . p̄ mañ . t . r . e . m̄

ten& Godefridus de petroponte de Will . deuarena femper

II . caŕ terræ . femp . V . uill . XI borđ . Tc̄ III . feru̅ . modo . II . Tc̄ . II . caŕ &

modo III . in dominio . & femper . IIII . caŕ hom̄ . filua ad VI . porc̄ . II.

ac̄ prati: 7 VI . añ . otiofa . 7 XL . porc̄ . 7 . c . 7 XX . ou̅s . & . IIII . uafa apum.

7 ual LX . fol . Et hanc terrā reclamat Rodƀtus malet ficut

alterā . hoc teftatur hun~~d~~ret . 7 Rex 7 Comes focā 7 facā

Norhals teñ . t . r . e . Edricus liƀ h̄o .p . I . manerio . II . caŕ tr̄æ.

400 b

Tc̄ . V . borđ . modo . VI . Tc̄ . I . feru̅ . Tc̄ . II . caŕ in dominio . modo caŕ & dim̄

7 dimid caŕ hom̄ . I . ac̄ p̃ti . Tc̄ . I . runc̄ . 7 modo . I . 7 VIII . poŕc.

7 . c . V . ou̅s . 7 tc̄ ual XL . fol . & . modo . XX . huic manerio funt ad

dite . c . ac̄ terræ q̄s tenuer̄ XIIII . liƀ omines . Tc̄ . II . caŕ . ~~modo~~ . modo

. I . 7 . I . ac̄ p̃ti . 7 ual . X . folidos . Et totā hanc terrā teñ Willmus fili⁹

Rainaldi . de . W . de Warena . 7 II . dimidios de iftis . XIIII . hominib₇

h̄nt fafitos h̄oĕs Willelmi fup comite Alanū.

400 a, b

13 Ranulf, his nephew, held MIDDLETON. Aelfric, 1 free man, held it as 1 manor. Now William of Warenne holds (it); 2 carucates of land.

Always 2 villagers; always 8 smallholders. Then 4 slaves, now 1. Then 2 ploughs in lordship; now ½ men's plough.
Meadow, 6 acres. Then 1 cob, now 2; now 2 cows, 20 pigs, 50 sheep.
Value then and now 40s.
1 church with 15 acres.
Value 2s.
To this manor were added 5 free men and half a priest. They held 55½ acres. 1½ ploughs in lordship.
Meadow, 2 acres.
Value 10s.
It has 8 furlongs in length and 7 in width, whoever has land there; it pays 7½d. The King and the Earl (have) full jurisdiction over these 6 men.
Aelfric who held this manor was a man belonging to Edric, the predecessor of Robert and of William Malet, and of Robert; they were in possession of this land.

14 Aelfric, a free man, held THORINGTON as a manor before 1066. Now Godfrey of Pierrepont holds (it) from William of Warenne. Always 2 carucates of land.

Always 5 villagers; 11 smallholders. Then 3 slaves, now 2. Then 2 ploughs in lordship, now 3; always 4 men's ploughs.
Woodland for 6 pigs; meadow, 2 acres. 6 idle cattle, 40 pigs, 120 sheep, 4 beehives.
Value 60s.
Robert Malet claims this land back like the other; the Hundred bears witness to this.
The King and the Earl (have) full jurisdiction.

15 Edric, a free man, held COVEHITHE before 1066 as 1 manor; 2 carucates of land.

Then 5 smallholders, now 6; then 1 slave.   400 b
Then 2 ploughs in lordship, now [1]½ ploughs; ½ men's plough.
Meadow, 1 acre. Then 1 cob, now 1; 8 pigs, 105 sheep.
Value then 40s; now 20[s].
To this manor were added 100 acres of land which 14 free men held.
Then 2 ploughs, now 1.
Meadow, 1 acre.
Value 10s.
William son of Reginald holds the whole of this land from William of Warenne. Of the 14 free men, William's men have 2 half (free men of whom) they have taken possession from Count Alan.

⨍ H̄. DE EARLAFORDA. In burhe.tenuit Alricus lib̃ homo
t.r.e.i.car̃.terræ.⁊ xx.ac̃.p̃ man̄.Tc̃.ii.bord̃.modo.vii.Tc̃
.i.car̃.modo.ii.Tc̃.hom̃ dim̃.car̃.modo.i.iiii.ac̃ prati.⁊.i.runc.
&.vii.aniat.Tc̃.xvi.porc̃.modo.xii.⁊ xvii.ous̃.Tc̃ uat.xx.ſot
modo.xxx.In eadē.xi.libi hoẽs.integros.&.iii.dim̃.Cōm̃d eid̃
Alrici.de.l.ac̃.⁊.ii.bord.Tc̃.ii.car̃.modo.i.dimid.ac̃.p̃ti.
Tc̃ uat.x.ſot.modo.viii.ſot.h̃ totū recep̃.W.p̃.i.car̃.terræ
&.R.de glā uitt de eo.⁊.i.æcctia.de.viii.ac̃.⁊ plures h̃nt
⨍ H̄.DE WILEFORDA.   ⨍partem.
              Rob̃ ten&
In bulges.i.lib̃ homo.cōm̃d.Ailrici.t.r.e.⁊.xiii.ac̃.⁊ dim̃
car̃.⁊ uat.ii.ſot. ⨍In depebecs.i.lib̃ hõ.cōm̃ eidē.iiii.ac̃.
⁊ uat.viii.d̃. ⨍In torſtaneſtuna.vi.ac̃.⁊ uat xii.deñ.hoc
ten&.R.de glam uilla.de.W.de uarena
    ⨍In b̃defelda teñ Ailric̃ lib̃ hõ.iii.ac̃.&.uat.vi.d̃.Idē Rob̃.

401 a
⨍TR̃A SVANI DESCESSE JN SVDFVLCH.   .XXVII.

TINGOOV.H̄.In Riete.i.ſoc̃.de xx.ac̃.&.i.bord.&.dim̃.car̃.
&.i.ac̃ p̃ti.& uat.v.ſot.Soca s̃cs.e.
⨍In maneſtuna.i.ſoc̃.de.xx.ac̃.&.i.bord.&.dimid.car̃.&.i.ac̃
prati.⁊.uat.v.ſot.

Hundred of CARLFORD

16 Aethelric, a free man, held in BURGH before 1066; 1 carucate of land and 20 acres as a manor.
> Then 2 smallholders, now 7.
> Then 1 plough, now 2; then ½ men's plough, now 1.
> Meadow, 4 acres. 1 cob; 7 cattle; then 16 pigs, now 12; 17 sheep.
> Value then 20s; now 30[s].
> In the same (Burgh) 11 whole free men and 3 half (free men) under the patronage of the same Aethelric, with 50 acres.
> 2 smallholders.
> Then 2 ploughs, now 1. Meadow, ½ acre.
> Value then 10s; now 8s.
> William acquired the whole of this as 1 carucate of land, and R(obert) of Glanville [holds it] from him.
> 1 church with 8 acres. Several have a share.

Hundred of WILFORD

17 Robert holds in BOULGE; 1 free man under the patronage of Aethelric before 1066; 13 acres. ½ plough.
> Value 2s.

18 In DEBACH 1 free man under the patronage of the same man; 4 acres.
> Value 8d.

19 In 'TORSTANESTUNA' 6 acres.
> Value 12d.
> R(obert) of Glanville holds this from William of Warenne.

20 In BREDFIELD Aethelric, a free man, held 3 acres.
> Value 6d.
> Robert also [holds this].

27   SWEIN OF ESSEX'S LANDS   401 a

THINGOE Hundred

1 In REDE 1 Freeman, with 20 acres.
> 1 smallholder.
> ½ plough. Meadow, 1 acre.
> Value 5s.
> St. Edmund's (has) the jurisdiction.

2 In MANSTON 1 Freeman, with 20 acres.
> 1 smallholder.
> ½ plough. Meadow, 1 acre.
> Value 5s.

/ B̶A̶b̶e̶g̶a̶ : D̶I̶O̶ . H̄ . Stokes tenet Rotb̄t . t . r . e . ꝑ mañ
iiii . car̄ tr̄æ cū ſoca . Tc̄ . xx . v . uiłł . modo . xv . Tc̄ . xxx . ii . borᵭ .
modo xxiii . Tc̄ . viii ; ſeru̇ . modo . vi . Tc̄ . ii . carr in dn̄io . modo . iiii;
Tc̄ . xii . car̄ hominū . modo . vii . modo . ii . molin̄ . 7 . xx . v . ac̄ . p̄ti .
Silua . lx . por̄c . modo . iii . equi . modo . viii . an̄ . modo xx . por̄c . modo
lxx . ous̄ . modo . iiii . cap̄ . Tc̄ uał . x . lib̄ . modo . xii ; Eccłia de . lx . ac̄
libere , terræ . In cad uilla . xi libi ; homines Rotb̄ti comᵭ . 7
ſoca jnt̄ oēs . i . car̄ . terræ . ſed pot uenᵭe ; 7 . i . lib̄ . homo . de . xii .
ac̄ comenᵭ . Rot . ſ7 ſaca 7 ſoca . sc̄i . e . jnt̄ oēs . i . car̄ . 7 dim̄ tc̄ .
modo . i . 7 uał& . xxx . ſoł . ht̄ . viii . qr̄ ; in longo . 7 . iiii . in lato .
& . de gelto . xx . den̄ .
/ Withermers ten̄ Rotb̄ par̄ ſueni . t . r . e . ꝑ ; mañ . iiii . car̄
terræ . cū ſoca . Tc̄ . xx . vii . uiłł . modo . xx . iiii . Tc̄ . xxx . ii .
borᵭ . modo . xxvii . Tc̄ . ii . ſeru̇ . modo . i . Tc̄ ; iii . car̄ in dominio .
modo . ii . Tc̄ , xiii . car̄ . hominū . modo . viii . Semꝑ . i . molin̄ . 7
xxx . ac̄ . p̄ti . m̄ . ii . equi . 7 xx . an̄ . modo . xx . iiii . por̄c . 7 xv ; æq̄
ſiluatice . modo . lxxx . ous̄ . Tc̄ uał . x . lib̄ . modo ; xii . ht̄ viii . qr̄ in
longo . 7 iiii . in lato . 7 de gelto xx . ᵭ .
/ Poleſteda ten̄ iᵭ Rotb̄tus par̄ ſueni . t . r . e . ꝑ mañ . iiii . car̄

401 b

car̄ terræ cū ſoca . Tc̄ . xx . vi . uiłł . modo . xx . i ; Tc̄ . xxx . vi . borᵭ .
modo xxx . ſemp . i . ſeru̇ Tc̄ . 7 ſemp . ii . car̄ in dn̄io . Tc̄ . xv . carr
hominū . modo . ix . Semper . i . moł . Silua . lxxx . por̄c .
. xxx
7 . i . ac̄ prati . modo . viii . equi . in halla . modo xxviii ; an̄ ; modo
xl . por̄c . modo c . l . ous̄ . Tc̄ uał . x . lib̄ . modo . xii . lib . ht̄ viii .
qr̄ in longo . 7 iiii . jn lato ; 7 de gelto . xx . ᵭ . quicūq̄ ibi ten̄ .

BABERGH Two Hundreds

3 In STOKE (by Nayland) Robert [held] before 1066; 4 carucates of land as a manor, with the jurisdiction.

Then 25 villagers, now 15; then 32 smallholders, now 23; then 8 slaves, now 6.

Then 2 ploughs in lordship, now 3; then 12 men's plough, now 7.

Now 2 mills; meadow, 25 acres; woodland, 60 pigs. Now 3 horses; now 8 cattle; now 20 pigs; now 70 sheep, now 4 goats.

Value then £10; now [£] 12.

A church with 60 acres of free land.

In the same village 11 free men under the patronage and jurisdiction of Robert; 1 carucate of land between them all, but they could sell. 1 free man with 12 acres, under the patronage of Robert but the full jurisdiction (was) St. Edmund's.

Between them all, then 1½ ploughs, now 1.

Value 30s.

It has 8 furlongs in length and 4 in width; 20d in tax.

4 Robert, Swein's father, held WITHERMARSH before 1066 as a manor; 4 carucates of land, with the jurisdiction.

Then 27 villagers, now 24; then 32 smallholders, now 27; then 2 slaves, now 1.

Then 3 ploughs in lordship, now 2; then 13 men's ploughs, now 8.

Always 1 mill. Meadow, 30 acres. Now 2 horses; 20 cattle; now 24 pigs; 15 wild mares; now 80 sheep.

Value then £10; now [£] 12.

It has 8 furlongs in length and 4 in width; 20d in tax.

5 Robert, Swein's father, also held POLSTEAD before 1066 as a manor;   401 b
4 carucates of land, with the jurisdiction.

·Then 26 villagers, now 21; then 36 smallholders, now 30; always 1 slave.

Then and always 2 ploughs in lordship; then 15 men's ploughs, now 9.

Always 1 mill. Woodland, 80 pigs; meadow, 31 acres. Now 8 horses at the hall; now 28 cattle; now 40 pigs; now 150 sheep.

Value then £10, now £12.

It has 8 furlongs in length and 4 in width; 20d in tax, whoever holds there.

Ƿ Eilanda teñ idē Rodbť pat̄.fueñ,t.r.e.p̄.mañ.ıı.car̄ terræ

cum foca.Semp.vı.uiłł.Tc̄.xx.bord̄.modo,xvıı,Tc̄.vı.feru̅.

modo.ıı.Semp.ı.car̄ in dominio.Tc̄.ıııı.car̄ hominū.m̄.

ııı.Semp.ı.moliñ.7.x.ac̄ prati.modo.ııı.equi in halla.

modo.xxx.ı.animał.modo.xL.v.porc̄.modo.Lxxx.ous̄.modo

xxxv.cap̄.Tc̄ uał.vı.liƀ.modo.vııı.liƀ.h̄t dim̄ łḡ in lango.

7.ıı.q̄r̄.in lato.7 de gelto.xıı.deñ.

Ƿ Aluenelega teñ brungar liƀ h̄o Rotƀti com̄d tantum.

t.r.e.p̄ mañ.ı.car̄ tr̄æ.cū foca Semp.ı.uiłł.7.x.bord̄.

femp.ıı.car̄ in dñio.7 dim̄ car̄ hominum.Silua.vı.porc̄.

7 ıııı.ac̄ prati.7.ı.moliñ.7.ı.æquus in halla.7 modo.xıııı.

amał.modo xL.ıx.porc̄.7 Lxxx.vıı.ous̄.Tc̄.uał.xx

foł.p̄ 7 modo.xxx.foł.h̄t.vı.q̄r̄ in longo.7 ııı.in lato

7 de gelto.ııı.deñ.Sup̄ hanc habuit.ses̄.e.foc̄ & fac̄a.t.r.e.

7 Rodƀtus filı̄ Wimarce 7 pat̄ fueni.com̄d tantū.Eodē

t̄p̄r fuer̄ furati equi inuenti.in domo ıftı̄ brungarı.ita

qd̄ abbas cuius fuit foca 7 faca & Rodbť qui habuit com̄

datione fup̄ ıftū.uener̄ de hoc furto ad placitū 7 fīc H̄.teftat̄.

Difceffer̄ amicabiliť fine iuditio qd̄ uidiffed hundr̄t.

Ƿ Dımı̄ᵭ.H̄.DEGEPES Wız.In burgo habuit.Roƀ.

t.r.e.xLı.burgenfes cū foca 7 faca.7 com̄d.7 rex habebat

alias confuetudines.Ex ıłł mortui funt.xv,amifit commen-

datione fed foc̄a 7 fac̄a hab&.& de aliis fimiliť.& rex alias con

fuetudines.haƀ.

Ƿ SANFORT.H̄.Stratfort tenuit Roƀ.t.r.e.p̄ mañ

ııı.car̄ terræ.femp xx.uiłł.Tc̄.vııı,bord̄.modo.x.Tc̄.ıııı.feru̅.

Tc̄.ıı car̄ in dominio.modo.ı.Tc̄.x.car̄.hominū.modo.v.7.v.poffent

reftaurari.7.xvı.ac̄ p̄ti.filua xvı.porc̄.femp.ı.moliñ.Eccłia.xx

ac̄.liƀæ terræ.7 dim̄.car̄.&.ı.runc̄.&.vı.aniał.7 xxx.vı.porc̄.7

L.ous̄.femp uał.vı.liƀ.Roƀ de eo.Sueñ.foc̄a.h̄t vıı.q̄r̄ in longo

&.v.in lato.7.ıx.deñ de gelto.

6 Robert, Swein's father, also held NAYLAND before 1066 as a manor; 2 carucates of land, with the jurisdiction.

    Always 6 villagers. Then 20 smallholders, now 17; then 6 slaves, now 2.

    Always 1 plough in lordship. Then 4 men's ploughs, now 3.

    Always 1 mill. Meadow, 10 acres. Now 3 horses at the hall; now 31 cattle; now 45 pigs; now 80 sheep; now 35 goats.

Value then £6; now £8.

    It has ½ league in length and 2 furlongs in width; 12d in tax.

7 Brungar, a free man under the patronage only of Robert, held AVELEY before 1066 as a manor; 1 carucate of land, with the jurisdiction.

    Always 1 villager, 10 smallholders.

    Always 2 ploughs in lordship; ½ men's plough.

    Woodland, 6 pigs; meadow, 4 acres; 1 mill. 1 horse at the hall; now 14 cattle; now 49 pigs; 87 sheep.

Value then 20s; later and now 30s. It has 6 furlongs in length and 3 in width; 3d in tax.

    Over this (land), St. Edmund's had full jurisdiction before 1066 and Robert son of Wymarc, Swein's father, (had) patronage only. At that time stolen horses were found in the home of Brungar, and so the Abbot, who had full jurisdiction, and Robert, who had patronage over him, came about this theft to the assembly, as the Hundred testifies. They left in a friendly manner without a trial that the Hundred had seen.

402 a

Half-Hundred of IPSWICH

8 In the Borough (of IPSWICH) Robert had 41 burgesses before 1066 with the full jurisdiction and the patronage, and the King had the other customary dues.

    Of these (burgesses), he has lost the patronage over 15 (who) are dead but he has full jurisdiction, and the same with the others; the King has the other customary dues.

SAMFORD Hundred

9 Robert held STRATFORD (St. Mary) before 1066 as a manor; 3 carucates of land.

    Always 20 villagers. Then 8 smallholders, now 10; then 4 slaves.

    Then 2 ploughs in lordship, now 1; then 10 men's ploughs, now 5, and 5 could be restored.

    Meadow, 16 acres; woodland, 16 pigs; always 1 mill.

    A church, 20 acres of free land. ½ plough.

    1 cob, 6 cattle, 36 pigs, 50 sheep.

Value always £6.

    Robert holds [this] from him.

Swein (has) the jurisdiction. It has 7 furlongs in length and 5 in width; 9d in tax.

ꟼ Painetunā ten&. Roƀ. T.R.E.

ɪɪ.caꝛ̃ terræ. ꝑ mañ. Tc̃.ɪɪɪ.uiłł.femp.ɪɪɪ.borđ.Tc̃.ɪɪ.caꝛ̃ in dominio.
modo.ɪ.Tc̃.ɪɪɪ.caꝛ̃.hominū.&.x.ac̃ p̃ti.Ecclie.ɪɪɪ.ac̃.liƀe.tꝛ̃e.
modo.ɪ.falina.&.vɪɪɪ.aniał.&.xx.porc̃.7 ʟxxx oũs.7 xx.vɪɪɪ.
cap̃.Tc̃ uał.xʟ.fol.modo.xxx.Hꞇ.v.qꞃ̃ in long.&.ɪɪɪɪ.in lat̃.
&.ɪɪɪɪ.đ.&.ɪ.ferding de gł.Roƀꞇ foc̃ Algarus de fueno.

ꟼ Weruefta tenuit Toli liƀ hō.commendatus.Roƀto.ɪ.caꝛ̃ terræ
&.ɪ.borđ.&.ɪ.caꝛ̃.&.ɪɪɪ.ac̃ p̃ti.&.v.porc̃.7 xxx.oũs.&.xɪɪɪɪ.
cap̃.Tc̃ uał.x.fol.7 modo fimilit̃.Suen in dn̄io.

ꟼ In frifetuna.ten̄.Roƀ.t.r.e.xxx.ac̃.de dn̄io.femp.ɪ.caꝛ̃.&.ɪ.
ac̃ p̃ti.7 uał.x.fol.Ernulfus de fueno.Idē Roƀ foc̃ā;

402 b

ꟼ H̄.ᴅᴇ *WILEFORDA* Peituna tenuit Godricus
comđ heroldi.t.r.e.ꝑ mañ.ɪɪɪ.caꝛ̃.terræ.Tc̃.x.uiłł.modo vɪɪɪ.
Tc̃.ɪɪɪɪ.borđ.7 modo; Tc̃.ɪ.feru.Semp in dn̄io.ɪɪ.caꝛ̃.& hom̄.
.ɪɪɪ.caꝛ̃.ɪɪɪ.ac̃ prati.7.ɪ.molin̄.Tc̃.ɪɪ.runc̃.Tc̃.ɪɪɪɪ.an̄.modo.ɪɪ.
Tc̃.ɪ.porc̃.modo.vɪ.7 xxvɪɪ.oũs.Tc̃ uał.ʟx.fol.modo xʟ.7 hꞇ
★ in longo.ɪ.leugā.7.in lat̃.ɪɪɪɪ.qꞃ̃.7 de gelto.xɪɪɪ.den̄.7 oƀlū.
In eadē ptinent.xx.liƀi.hoes.comđ eidē.ʟxxx.ac̃.tꞃ̃æ.7
ɪɪ.ac̃ p̃ti.Semp.ɪɪ.caꝛ̃.Tc̃ uał xɪɪɪ.fol.modo.xv.

10 Robert [held] PANNINGTON before 1066; 2 carucates of land as a manor.

Then 3 villagers; always 3 smallholders.
Then 2 ploughs in lordship, now 1; then 3 men's ploughs.
Meadow, 10 acres.
A church, 3 acres of free land.
Now 1 salt-house; 8 cattle, 20 pigs, 80 sheep, 28 goats.
Value then 40s; now 30[s].
It has 5 furlongs in length and 4 in width; 4¼d in tax.
Robert (had) the jurisdiction.
Algar [holds this] from Swein.

11 Toli, a free man under the patronage of Robert, held WHERSTEAD; 1 carucate of land.

1 smallholder.
1 plough.
Meadow, 3 acres. 5 pigs, 30 sheep, 14 goats.
Value then 10s; now the same.
Swein [holds this] in lordship.

12 In FRESTON Robert held before 1066; 30 acres in lordship. Always 1 plough.

Meadow, 1 acre.
Value 10s.
Arnulf [holds this] from Swein.
Robert also (had) the jurisdiction.

Hundred of WILFORD

13 Godric, under the patronage of Harold, held PEYTON before 1066 as a manor; 3 carucates of land.

Then 10 villagers, now 8; then and now 4 smallholders; then 1 slave.
Always 2 ploughs in lordship; 3 men's ploughs.
Meadow, 3 acres; 1 mill. Then 2 cobs; then 4 cattle, now 2; then 1 pig, now 6; 27 sheep.
Value then 60s; now 40[s].
It has 1 league in length and 4 furlongs in width; 13½d in tax.
In the same (Peyton) 20 free men, under the patronage of the same man; 80 acres of land.
Meadow, 2 acres.
Always 2 ploughs.
Value then 13s; now 15[s].

⫟**T**ERRÆ EEVDONIS DAPIFERI IN SVTFVLC⫶

Lacforda . h̄ . Herefwella teñ godwinus teinus . reḡ . E . p̄⁻
mañ . vi . car̄ trǣ . Tc̄ xi . uiłłi . p̄ . x . modo . xi . 7 femp . iiii . borđ .
Semp . xi . feru . Tc̄ 7 p̄ . v . car in dn̄io . modo . iii . Semp . v . hom .
7 xiiii . ac̄ p̄ti . & . ii . moł . 7 dim . Eccłia . lx . ac̄ trǣ . ii . pifcar .
Semp . ii , equi in halla . Tc̄ . xx . añ . modo . xiii . Tc̄ xl . porc̄ . m̄ . xx .
Tc̄ . ꝺ . cccc . oū . m̄ . ꝺ . ccc . Tc̄ & p̄ uał . x . liƀ . m̄ . xvi . hꝉ . i . lḡ in loḡg .
7 . vi . qr̄ in lato . 7 de gelto . x . đ . ⫟ Huic iac& . i . ƀeuita cocles -
worda . viii . car̄ . terre . Eccłia lx . ac̄ . Tc̄ 7 poſt . xv . uiłł . modo
xi . uiłł . Semp . iiii . borđ . Tc̄ 7 p̄ , xi . feru . modo . viii . 7 xx . ii .

403 a

ac̄ prati . Tc̄ 7 p̄ v . eaꝛ . Tc̄ & p̄ . v . car . in dominio . modo . iiii .
Tc̄ 7 poſt . vi . car̄ . homin̄ . modo . v . 7 . ii . equi . in halla . Tc̄ . cc . oūs .
modo . ꝺ . cccc . xx . minus . Tc̄ & p̄ uał xii . liƀ . modo . xxiiii .
hꝉ . i . lḡ in longo . 7 . viii . qr̄ in lato . 7 de gelto . vii . đ .
Socā & facā . ſcs edm̄ .

⫟In Lakingaheda 7 in brantona . vi . foc̄ . Aldrede cū foca qd n̄
pot̄ uende . Libati fueꝛ lifie ante ceſſori eudonis . p̄ . ii . car̄ terræ
ſed tam̄ poſtea recognoū de ſc̄a aldreda 7 Eudo tenuit eos cū
foca & faca . 7 . iiii . borđ . femp . iii . car̄ . 7 . iii . ac̄ . p̄ti . 7 . ii . pifcr̄ .
Tc̄ 7 poſt uał . xxx . folidos modo reddit lxx . foł .

⫟**T**odenhā teñ Canut liƀ h̄o comit̄ algari p̄ mañ . iii . car̄ t̄ræ
Tc̄ . vi . uiłł . p̄ iiii . m̄ . vi . 7 Tc̄ . iiii . feru . modo . i . Tc̄ . iii . car in do -
minio . p̄ dim . modo . ii . 7 . i . car̄ . 7 dim hominū . 7 . iii . ac̄ . p̄ti .
7 . i . molin̄ . i . pifcina fuit f7 modo n̄ c̄ . Eccłia . xxx . ac̄ . modo . x .
equi . in halla . 7 modo . xl . porc̄ . 7 . xi . añ . Tc̄ . cc . oūs . modo . lx .

Value then and later £4; now 100s.
It has 1 league in length and 6 furlongs in width; 20d in tax.

4 In CAVENHAM 1 free man under the patronage only of Canute (and) in the jurisdiction of St. Edmund's; 60 acres.
    1 smallholder.
    Always 1 plough.
Value always 5s.

SAMFORD Hundred and a Half
5 In RAYDON Swarting, a free man, held 17 acres.
    Value 3s.
        Osbern holds [this] from Eudo.
        The jurisdiction (is) in (East) Bergholt.

PLOMESGATE Hundred
6 Wulfric, half under the patronage of the Abbot of Ely and half (under that) of Malet's predecessor, held (Great) GLEMHAM; 2 carucates of land as a manor before 1066. William Malet was in possession of it.
    Always 7 smallholders;
    2 ploughs in lordship; ½ men's plough.
    Meadow, 8 acres; 1 mill.
    ½ church, 10 acres.
    Then 9 pigs, now 16; then 5 sheep, now 40.
Value then 40s; now 50[s].
In the same (Great Glemham) were added 10 free men under the patronage of Wulfric; 53 acres. 1 plough.
Value 10s 10d.
        Pirot holds [this] from Eudo.
        The jurisdiction (is) the Abbot of Ely's.
        William Malet was in possession of the whole of it.
        It has 12 furlongs in length and 6½ in width; it pays 20d in tax.

403 b

Half-Hundred of COSFORD
7 Aelfric Kemp held LAYHAM before 1066; 4 carucates of land as a manor.
    Always 15 villagers; 3 smallholders; 1 slave.
    Always 2 ploughs in lordship. Then 6 men's ploughs, later and now 3.
    Meadow, 12 acres; woodland, 10 pigs; 1 mill.
    A church, 40 acres. Meadow, 1 acre. 1 plough.
    Always 1 cob, 20 cattle, 36 pigs, 180 sheep, 23 goats.
Value always £6.
    (It has) 8 furlongs in length and 6 in width; 7½d in tax.

In fineɓga teñ Leuefuna liɓ hō gut mundi ante c̄ hugoñ
de monte forti commd tant . ɪɪ . car̄ tr̄e . 7 Tc̄ . ɪɪɪɪ . borđ . p̄ 7 m̄
ɪɪɪ . Semp . ɪɪ . car̄ in dn̄io . Silŭ de . xɪɪ . porc̄ . 7 xvɪ . ac̄ p̄ti.
7 . ɪ . moliñ . Ecclia de . xxx . ac̄ liɓe . terræ . 7 . ɪ . ac̄ p̄ti . Tc̄ . ɪ . runc̄ ;

404 a

M nuil . Semp vɪɪɪ . añ . Tc̄ . xx . porc̄ . modo . vɪ . Tc̄ xxx . ōūs . mc̄do.
. c . Tc̄ ual . ɪɪɪɪ . liɓ . p̄ . ɪɪ . m̄ . ʟx . fol . h̄t . ɪ . lḡ in longo . & vɪɪɪ ; qr̄
in lato . 7 de gelto xx . ɪɪ . deñ . & obolŭ . In eod̄ manerio . xvɪɪɪ . liɓi
homines eid̄e Leuefune commendant̄ . tant̄ . ɪ . car̄ terræ . ɪ̄ . foc̄ . reḡ
7 comī . Tc̄ 7 p̄ . ɪɪɪ . car̄ . modo . ɪ . 7 . ɪɪɪ . ac̄ p̄ti . 7 dim̄ . Hos ten& Roḡ
.p efcangio . In eađ . vɪ . foc̄ ptinentes in tornei manerio regis . Ed.
cū comd 7 faca 7 foca 7 ſūmagio . 7 ñt ʟx . v . ac̄ 7 dim̄ . terræ . &
. ɪ . borđ . Tc̄ & p̄ . ɪɪɪ . car̄ . int̄ ōes modo . ɪ . 7 . ɪɪɪ . ac̄ p̄ti . & hos ten& .p
efcangio . In eađ . ɪɪ . liɓi h̄oes gut mundi ante hugonis comdat
tant̄ ʟxxx . ac̄ in foca reḡ 7 comit̄ . Tc̄ . ɪ . car̄ & dim̄ . p̄ 7 modo . nuil.
& hos ten& fimiliī . Adhuc in eađ . ɪ . liɓ hō comd ante c̄ euſtachii
ɪɪɪɪ . ac̄ . In eađ . ɪ . liɓ homo Leuſtani de lofa comd . ɪɪɪɪ . ac̄ . In eađ
. ɪ . liɓ hō Adhuc reḡ comd 7 foca 7 faca in hunđ . xx . ac̄ . Tc̄ dim̄ car̄ .
7 . ɪ . ac̄ p̄ti . In eađ . ɪ . liɓ homo Wiſgari Ante Ricardi comd . fed in
hunđ . xxx . ac̄ . 7 . ɪ . uiil Tc̄ . ɪ . car̄ . p̄ 7 modo nichil . & . ɪɪ . ac̄ p̄ti.
In eađ . ɪɪɪɪ . liɓi h̄oes . foca in hunđ xvɪ . ac̄ . Tc̄ . ɪ . car̄ . 7 dim̄ . p̄ 7
modo . nichil . hos ten& .p efcangio . Tc̄ 7 p̄ ual ōms iſti liɓi . ɪɪɪɪ.
liɓ . modo . xʟ . fol.

BOSMERE Hundred

2 Leofcild held SOMERSHAM in lordship; 1 carucate of land as a manor before 1066. Always 1 plough.
> Meadow, 1 acre.

Value 30s.

3 Dot, a free man, [held] *PILEBERGA*; 60 acres as a manor before 1066. Now Roger [holds it] in lordship.
> 1 smallholder.
> Always 1 plough. Meadow, 1 acre.

Value 20s.
> The King and the Earl (have) the jurisdiction.

In the same (*Pileberga*) 5 free men; 30 acres.

(It is) in the same assessment.
> The King and the Earl (have) the jurisdiction.

4 In FLOWTON Godman, 1 free man, held 20 acres in lordship before 1066 and still holds (them) from Roger.   404 b

Value 40d.

In the same (Flowton) 2 free men, Wilgrip and Edric, one (with) 40 acres, the other with 10 acres. Always 1 plough.
> Meadow, 1 acre.

Value 16s.
> The King and the Earl (have) the jurisdiction.

5 In BLAKENHAM Wulfward, 1 free man, held 30 acres in lordship. Always ½ plough.
> Meadow, 1 acre.

Value 14s.

6 In *ELLA* 1 free man, Alfgeat; 12 acres in lordship. 2 oxen.

Value 7s.

In the same (*Ella*) 1 free man; 3 acres.

It is in the assessment of Somersham.

7 In OFFTON Waldwin, 1 free man, under the patronage of Leofric Hobbeson. He [had] 20 acres.
> 1 smallholder.
> Then ½ plough.

Value then 40d; now 4s.
> William holds (this) from Roger.

8 In BRICETT Leofric, 1 free man, under the patronage of Godric of Ringshall, William of Auberville's predecessor. He [had] 10 acres. Then 2 oxen.

Value 20d.
> Gilbert holds (this) from Roger.
> The King and the Earl (have) the jurisdiction.

$\digamma$ In horſwalda . ii . libi hōes

hardinc͛ . 7 toui͆ com͆dati regis . ten̄ . xx . ii . ac̄ . 7 dim̄ . modo Witt . ten̄

de Rog͠o . ſemp dim̄ car͛ . & dim̄ . ac̄ ꝓti . 7 uaͭ . v . ſoͭ . 7 . x . den̄ . Rex &

Coms̄ . ſoca͞ . hanc tra͞ ten̄ Roger͆ de abͫe de eli ꝓcepto epi de

sco Laudo . ut ipſe Rog͡ dicit. $\digamma$ In Langhedana . i . lib homo

Wlbolt xxiiii . ac̄ . ꝓ man̄ . & . i . ac̄ & . dim̄ ꝓti . 7 in tcio anno q̄rta

pars mot . 7 uaͭ . 7 ualuit . v . ſoͭ . 7 . viii . den̄.

$\digamma$ CLAINDVNE . H͠ . Henleia͞ tenuit Tepechinus lib homo

t . r . e . com͆d heroldo . ii . car͛ terræ . ꝓ man̄ . 7 xvi . bord . Tc̄ . iiii . ſerui .

Tc̄ . iiii . car͛ in dominio . modo . ii . Tc̄ . iiii . car͛ hom̄ . modo . iii . viii .

ac̄ . ꝓti . ſilua . vi . porc̄ . 7 . vii . an̄ . 7 . xiiii . porc̄ . 7 xxx . ous̄ . Eccliæ

. ii . ac̄ . Tc̄ . uaͭ . iiii . lib . modo . iii . Eudo dapifer ten& in ſuo dn̄io.

In ead . iiii . libi homines additi . viii . ac̄ . & . ii . bou͞ . 7 uaͭ . ii . ſoͭ . Rex 7 coms̄

$\digamma$ ſocam ;

405 a

$\digamma$ DIMID͞ . H͞ . DE COSFORT . Elmeſ͛ta͞ ten̄ Thou͛.

teinnus ꝓ man̄ . t . r . e . vi . car͛ . tra͞æ . 7 xl . ac̄ . Tc̄ & ꝓ .͛ xi . uitt . m̄

. ii . ſemp . xii . bord . Tc̄ . iiii . ſeru͞ . ſemp . ii . car͛ . in dn̄io . Tc̄ & ꝓ.

xii . car͛ hominu͞ . modo . iiii . Ecctia . de . xv . ac̄ . 7 dim̄ . car͛ . Tc̄ . ii . run̄.

Tc̄ . xvi . an̄ . m̄ . iiii . Tc̄ . xxx . porc̄ . modo . xx . Tc̄ . cc . xl . ous̄ . modo.

. cc . Tc̄ uaͭ . x . lib . m̄ . vii . ht͞ . x . q̄r in longo . 7 vii . in lat͞ . 7 . xv . den̄

den̄ de gelto . Scs͞ . e . dim̄ ſocam.

$\digamma$ In Wateſelda . i . lib hō . lx . ac̄ . 7 . ii . bord . Tc̄ 7 poſt . i . car͛ . modo

dim̄ . 7 . i . ac̄ . ꝓti . 7 uaͭ . x . ſoͭ . scs͞ . e . com͆d 7 ſoca͞.

404 b, 405 a

9 In HORSWOLD 2 free men, Harding and Tovi, under the patronage of
the King, held 22½ acres. Now William holds (it) from Roger.
Always ½ plough.
    Meadow, ½ acre.
Value 5s 10d.
    The King and the Earl (have) the jurisdiction.
Roger holds this land from the Abbot of Ely by command of the
Bishop of St. Lô, as Roger himself says.

10 In *LANGHEDANA* Wulfbold, a free man; 24 acres as a manor.
    Meadow, 1½ acres; in (every) third year, the fourth part of a mill.
The value is and was 5s 8d.

CLAYDON Hundred
11 Tepekin, a free man, under the patronage of Harold, held HENLEY
before 1066; 2 carucates of land as a manor.
    16 smallholders; then 4 slaves.
    Then 3 ploughs in lordship, now 2; then 4 men's ploughs, now 3.
    Meadow, 8 acres; woodland, 6 pigs. 7 cattle, 14 pigs, 30 sheep.
    A church, 2 acres.
Value then £4; now [£] 3.
    Eudo the Steward holds (this) in his lordship.
In the same (Henley) 4 free men (were) added; 8 acres. 2 oxen.
Value 2s.
    The King and the Earl (have) the jurisdiction.

Half-Hundred of COSFORD   405 a
12 Tovi, a thane, held ELMSETT as a manor before 1066; 6 carucates of
land and 40 acres.
    Then and later 11 villagers, now 2; always 12 smallholders. Then
        4 slaves.
    Always 2 ploughs in lordship. Then and later 12 men's ploughs,
        now 4.
    A church with 15 acres. ½ plough.
    Then 2 cobs; then 16 cattle, now 4; then 30 pigs, now 20; then
        240 sheep, now 200.
Value then £10; now [£] 8.
    It has 10 furlongs in length and 7 in width; 15d in tax.
    St. Edmund's (has) half the jurisdiction.

13 In WHATFIELD a free man; 60 acres.
    2 smallholders.
    Then and later 1 plough, now ½. Meadow, 1 acre.
Value 10s.
    St. Edmund's (has) the patronage and the jurisdiction.

$\mathcal{f}\bar{H}$. *DE CARLEFORD.* In Finesford . teñ . Tepekin . xxiiii . ac̄.
& . i . ac̄ prati . Tc̄ dim̃ . car̄ . 7 . i . liba femina de dim̃ . ac̄ . Semp ual . iiii . ſol.

★ $\mathcal{f}$TRA WILLI FR̃IS . ROGERI DE OTBURVILLA.　　　　.XXX.

Boſemara . $\bar{H}$. Ringeſhalam tenuit Godui lib homo . i . car̄ terræ
7 xl . ac̄ . ꝑ mañ . Tc̄ . i . uill . Tc̄ . ii . car̄ modo dim̃ . & iiii . borđ . 7 . vi.
ac̄ prati . ſilua . viii . porc̄ . dim̃ Ecclia . xii . ac̄ . Tc̄ . iiii . runc̄ . modo.
. i . 7 xiii . porc̄ . & lx . oũs . 7 xxxii . capr̄ . 7 ual xl . vii . ſol . Ex hac terra teñ quidã com̃dtus abbatis sc̄i . eadm̃ . xi . ac̄ . t . r . e ; De hoc
manerio teñ hugo . xl . ac̄ . 7 in eod ꝓtio ual . v . ſol . In ead . i . lib homo
Vluricus teñ . lxxx . ac̄ . ꝑ mañ . Tc̄ . i . car̄ . 7 . iiii . ac̄ prati . Tc̄ ual&
. xx . ſol . modo . viii . Fulcho ten& de Willmo . Rex 7 Com̃s ſoc̃.

405 b

In eađ Trumuinus lib hõ regis . tenuit xviii . ac̄ . t . r . e . modo
Witt . in dñio . Tc̄ dim̃ car̄ . & ual . iii . ſol . $\mathcal{f}$ In Ringhes hala . Edric̃
lib homo . com̃đ ante ceſſori . Willi . ten& . v . ac̄ . m̃ Witt . in dominio
7 ual& xii . deñ ; $\mathcal{f}$ In Brieſeta Fulcho tenet de Witto . Anſchillius
lib homo com̃đ Leurico obbeſune ten& lx ac̄ . t . r . e . ꝑ mañ . Ex his
ħt Wittmus xl . ac̄ ſed totũ ſimul ſibi libatũ fuit in hac terra . eſt.
. i . borđ . & ſemp . i . car̄ . 7 ual . x . ſol . Rex & com̃s ſoc̃ . Ex ſupiorib;
lx . ac̄ . tulit hugo de hoſdenc xx . ac̄ ut Wittmus dicit . 7 hunđ
ſed ipſe hugo ē in captione regis & idõ non potuit dare reſpoñſũ.

Hundred of CARLFORD
14 In FINESFORD' Tepekin held 24 acres.
    Meadow, 1 acre.
    Then ½ plough.
    1 free woman with ½ acre.
  Value always 4s.

30   LAND OF WILLIAM BROTHER OF ROGER OF AUBERVILLE

BOSMERE Hundred
1 Godwy, a free man, held RINGSHALL; 1 carucate of land and 40 acres
as a manor.
    Then 1 villager. Then 2 ploughs, now ½. 4 smallholders.
    Meadow, 6 acres; woodland, 8 pigs.
    ½ church, 12 acres.
    Then 4 cobs, now 1; 13 pigs, 60 sheep, 32 goats.
  Value 47s.
Of this land, a man under the patronage of the Abbot of St.
Edmund's held 11 acres before 1066.
Of this manor, Hugh held 40 acres.
(It is) in the same assessment; value 5s.
In the same (Ringshall) Wulfric, 1 free man, held 80 acres as a
manor. Then 1 plough.
    Meadow, 4 acres.
Value then 20s; now 8[s].
    Fulk holds (this) from William.
    The King and the Earl (have) the jurisdiction.
In the same (Ringshall) Trumwin, a free man of the King's, held 18   405 b
acres before 1066. Now William [holds it] in lordship. Then ½
plough.
Value 3s.

2 In RINGSHALL Edric, a free man under the patronage of William's
predecessor, [held] 5 acres. Now William [holds it] in lordship.
Value 12d.

3 In BRICETT Fulk holds from William. Askell, a free man under the
patronage of Leofric Hobbeson, [held] 60 acres before 1066 as a
manor. Of these, William has 40 acres, but the whole (of it) was
delivered to him altogether. On this land is
    1 smallholder.
    Always 1 plough.
Value 10s.
    The King and the Earl (have) the jurisdiction.
Of the above 60 acres, Hugh of Houdain took 20 acres so William
and the Hundred say; but Hugh himself is under the King's arrest
and has therefore not been able to give a reply.

.XXXI. ⌐TERRÆ.HVGONIS DE MONTE FORTI. ⌐BRADEmara . H̃.

In berham in dominio . ix . liɓi homines . xvi . ac̃ . & dim̃ . car̃.

⌐In Watefelda in dñio . ix . liɓi homines . xvi . ac̃ . & dim̃ car̃ . & ualēt

xv . ſot . Sc̃s eadmundus ſoc̃ . Duo ex his fuer̃ ſc̃i eadm̃ . ad com̃d . t . r . e.

& . vii . ante ceſſoris hugonis comitis.

⌐BISSCOPES . H̃ . SAHAM . tẽ . Oſlac teinnus . t . r . e . p̃ man̄

. i . car̃ terre Rog̃ dē Candos tẽ . ſemp . i . uiłt . & . iii . borð . & . i . ſeru̅.

& . i . car̃ in dominio . & dim̃ . car̃ hom̃ . & . iiii . ac̃ p̃ti . ſilua x . porc̃.

406 a

Tc̃ . x . porc̃ . modo . xii . 7 . v . añ . Tc̃ . iiii . ou̅s . modo . xii . ſemp ual̅ xx . ſoł.

★ Soca ep̃i . ⌐In borant . idẽ tẽ . i . liɓ homo com̃d . xiiii . ac̃ & dim̃

car̃ . & ual̅ . iii . ſoł . ⌐In badinga felda . v . liɓi homines . cõm̃d

lx . ac̃ . 7 . ii . borð . & . i . car̃ . 7 dim̃ . 7 . ii . ac̃ p̃ti . 7 ual̅ . x . ſoł . Ep̃s ſoc̃a.

⌐In Badingafelda . id̅ . vii . uiłt . lx . ac̃ . & . i . car̃ 7 dim̃ . ſilua . xl . porc̃.

h̃ iac̃& inacolt . 7 in p̃tio ſoca ep̃i.

⌐In Blidinga . H̃ . In Stouone tẽ& Hugo de montfort in dñio . l.

ac̃ . tr̃æ . q̃s tenuc̃r̃ . iiii . liɓi hões . t . r . e . 7 modo . iii . dim̃ . ac̃ p̃ti.

& . i . car̃ in dñio . 7 vii . ſoł . & dim̃ . ual̅ . ſemp . 7 . c . allec̃tia . 7 rex

7 comes habuer̃ ſoc̃a 7 ſac̃a ſup hos . iiii . hões.

405 b, 406 a

Hundred of COLNEIS

8 In NACTON Guthmund held in lordship before 1066; 2 carucates of
land as a manor.
　　Always 6 villagers.
　　Always 2 ploughs in lordship. Then 3 men's ploughs, now 2.
　　Woodland for 8 pigs; meadow, 2 acres; then 1 mill, now none.
　　　　Then 4 cobs, now 1; 1 cattle; then 8 pigs, now none; then 23
　　　　sheep, now 123; then 30 goats, now none.
Value always is and was 70s. It has 1½ leagues in length and 1 in
width; 2d in tax.

9 In [*BRIHTOLUESTUNA*] 18 free men under the patronage of Guthmund,
with 1 carucate of land and 20 acres.
　　4 smallholders.
　　Then 10 ploughs, now 5.
　　Meadow, 2 acres; woodland at 2 pigs.
　　A church with 6 acres.
　　It has ½ league in length and 2 furlongs in width; 10d in tax.

10 In LEVINGTON 3 free men under the patronage of the same man;
20 acres. Then 2 ploughs, now 1.

11 In *CULUERDESTUNA* 5 free men under the patronage of the same man;
21½ acres. Then 2 ploughs, now 1.
　　It has 3 furlongs in length and 2 in width; 2d in tax.

12 In *ISTEUERTONA* 4 free men under the patronage of the same man;
18 acres. Then 2 ploughs, now 1.
　　Meadow, 1 acre.
Value £4 10s.
　　St. Etheldreda's (has) jurisdiction over the whole of this land.

13 In WALTON 1 free man, Lurk by name, under the patronage of N.;　　406 b
24 acres.
Value 3s.
　　Norman holds (this) from Hugh.
　　St. Etheldreda's (has) the jurisdiction.

13a Guthmund held the above-mentioned manor of NACTON from St.
Etheldreda's in 1066 in such a way that he could not sell or grant
it away from the Church, (and) on the agreement that after his
death it ought to return to the Church in lordship; the Hundred
testifies to this.

Hundred of CARLFORD

14 In BIXLEY in lordship; 3 free men under the patronage of Guthmund
before 1066; 29 acres. 1 plough.
　　Meadow, 1 acre.
They are in the assessment of *Brithtoluestuna*.

In burg.ɪ.liƀ hō.cōmđ dim.sc̄e.e.t.r.e.

7 dim̄ ante cefforis.Roƀ.malet.modo.ɪɪɪ.hōes.xx ac̄.terræ.Tc̄.ɪ.car̄.

modo.dim̄.ɪɪ.ac̄ p̄ti.Tc̄ ual.x.fol.modo.v.In eadē.ɪ.liƀ homo

cōmđ.dimiđ.sc̄e.æ.7 dim̄.Edrici grimma de.x.ɪx.ac̄ terræ.7.ɪ.

borđ.Tc̄.ɪ.car̄.modo dim̄.ɪ.ac̄ p̄ti.7 ual.ɪɪɪɪ.fol.7.ɪx.den̄.

In Parua belinges.ɪ.liƀ hō.cōmdat dim̄.Sc̄e.æ.7 dim̄.Edrici.ɪɪɪɪ.

ac̄.7 dim̄.7 ual.vɪɪɪ.den̄. In clopetuna.ɪɪ.liƀ hō.7 dim̄ cōmđ

Sicuti alii ut.fup̄.xɪɪɪɪ.ac̄.Tc̄ dim̄.car̄.m̄.nult.& ual.ɪɪ.fol.7 vɪɪ.đ.

.H.de Wileford.In Keresfelda in dn̄io.x.liƀi homines cōmđ Edrici.

& dim̄.Sc̄e.Æ.ʟx.ac̄.&.ɪ.ac̄ p̄ti.Tc̄.ɪɪ.car̄.modo.ɪ.Tc̄ ual xxɪɪɪɪ.fol.

modo xx.ɪɪ.fol.& vɪɪɪ.den̄.

.H.DE LOSA.In ceres felda.ɪɪ.liƀi hōes.com.S.e 7 de.ɪ.cōmđ

habuit dim̄ ante c̄.hugonis de monte forti.vɪɪ.ac̄.7 ual xvɪ.đ.

In gretingahā tenuit Aluric liƀ hō heroldi.t.r.e.ɪɪ.car̄ terræ 7 dim̄.

7 xv.ac̄.Semp.vɪ.uilt.7 xxɪ.borđ.Tc̄.ɪɪ.fer.7.in dn̄io.ɪɪ.car̄.7.vɪ.

car̄ hom̄.7 vɪɪɪ.ac̄ p̄ti.Silua ad vɪɪɪ.porc̄.ɪ.molin̄.Tc̄.ɪ.runc̄.7.ɪɪ.an̄.

7 xx.ōus.7 xx.porc̄.Tc̄ ual.c.fol.modo.vɪɪɪ.liƀ.7.ɪ.uncea auri.&

ħt in longo.ɪ.lḡ.7.ɪɪɪ.qr̄ in lato.&.de gelto.xɪ.đ.Alii ibi tenent.

In eađ.x.liƀi homines.cōmđ eiđ xʟvɪ.ac̄.ɪx.ac̄ & dim̄.calūpniatur.

Wiłłmus de arcis.&.ɪɪ.dim̄ hōes.Semp.ɪ.car̄.& ual.xx.fol.ɪ.ex iſtis.fuit

cōmđ.Edrici de laxa fella.7 Wiłł.malet inde fuit faiat die qua

obiit.ħ ten&.R.de hugone.

15 In BURGH 1 free man before 1066, half under the patronage of St. Etheldreda's and half (under that) of Robert Malet's predecessor's; now 3 men; 20 acres of land. Then 1 plough, now ½.
Meadow, 2 acres.
Value then 10s; now 5[s].
In the same (Burgh) 1 free man, half under the patronage of St. Etheldreda's and half (under that) of Edric Grim, with 19 acres of land.
1 smallholder.
Then 1 plough, now ½. Meadow, 1 acre.
Value 4s 9d.

16 In LITTLE BEALINGS 1 free man, half under the patronage of St. Etheldreda's and half (under that) of Edric; 4½ acres.
Value 8d.

17 In CLOPTON 2 free men, half under patronage like the others above; 14 acres. Then ½ plough, now none.
Value 2s 7d.

Hundred of WILFORD
18 In CHARSFIELD in lordship; 10 free men, half under the patronage of Edric and half (under that) of St. Etheldreda's; 60 acres.
Meadow, 1 acre.
Then 2 ploughs, now 1.
Value then 24s; now 22s 8d.

Hundred of LOES
19 In CHARSFIELD 2 free men under the patronage of St. Etheldreda's and Hugh de Montfort's predecessor had half the patronage over 1; 7 acres.
Value 16d.

20 Roger of Candos holds in CRETINGHAM; Aelfric, a free man of Harold's, held (it) before 1066; 2½ carucates of land and 15 acres.
Always 6 villagers; 21 smallholders. Then 2 slaves.
2 ploughs in lordship; 6 men's ploughs.
Meadow, 8 acres; woodland for 8 pigs; 1 mill. Then 1 cob, 2 cattle, 20 sheep, 20 pigs.
Value then 100s; now £8 and 1 ounce of gold.   407 a
It has 1 league in length and 3 furlongs in width; 11d in tax.
Others hold there.
In the same (Cretingham) 10 free men under the patronage of the same man; 46 acres. William of Arques claims 9½ acres and 2 half (free) men. Always 1 plough.
Value 20s.
One of these (free men) was under the patronage of Edric of Laxfield; William Malet was in possession on the day he died.
Roger holds this from Hugh.

$\int$ *WANNEFORDA*. $\tilde{H}$. In Willinga hā ~~teñ~~ in dñiū . xv . libi hões

coñ Burcardi . t . r . e . 1 . caꝛ terræ 7 diñ . 7 xviii . aē . Semp . 11 . uiłł.

Tē . vii . caꝛ . modo . vi . filua ad x . porc . 1 . aē . p̃ti . 1 . æcclia . xl . aē . 7 uał . vꝛꝛ.

foł . plures ibi participantur . Tē uał . lx . foł . modo xxx . foł . 7 xxx . đ.

7 . iii . miłł alleđiū . Rex 7 Coñs foca.

$\int$ In Weftuna . 1 . lib hō . xvi . aē . coñd eiđ . & diñ caꝛ . 7 uał . v . foł.

& . cccc . alleđium . $\int$ In Wellingaham . 1 . lib hō coñd . Burckardi

7 non potuit uendere terrā nec dare . iii . aē libe terræ . 7 . uał xviii.

đ . 7 . c . alleđi . In ^{h}atheburgfelda . vi . libi hões . commđti Burcardo

lx . aē . Tē . 11 . caꝛ . modo . 1 . & diñ . Tē uał . x . foł . modo . xi . 7 viii . deñ.

7 . ꝺ . cccc . alleđi . $\int$ In Warlingahā . v . libi hões . 7 diñ . coñđ.

Guerti . lx . aē . Semp . 11 . caꝛ . & . 1 . borđ . 11 . aē prati . Semp uał . x . foł.

7 . vi . đ . 7 . 1 . miłł . alleđi

$\int$ *LVDINGA*. $\tilde{H}$. In beketuna in dñio . vi . libi hões . coñđ . Burchardi.

. l . aē tꝛe . Tē . 1 . caꝛ . modo diñ . Tē uał . iiii . foł . modo xxi . 7 iiii . đ . 7 i.

miłł 7 diñ . alleđi.

$\int$ In Keffingelanda . 1 . lib hō . coñd . Edrici de Laxefella . xxx . aē . ꝓ m̃.

Semp . 1 . caꝛ . & . 1 . aē p̃ti . Tē uał . v . foł . modo . viii . foł . In eađ . iiii . libi hões

407 b

. 1 . coñdatus Edrici . & . iii . coñdati . Burckardi . t . r . e . lxxx . 7 x.

aē . & . 11 . borđ . Semp . 11 . caꝛ . 7 . 1 . aē p̃ti . Tē uał . x . foł . modo . xxii.

miłł alleđi .

WANGFORD Hundred

21 In WILLINGHAM in lordship; 15 free men under the patronage of
Burghard before 1066; 1½ carucates of land and 18 acres.
  Always 2 villagers.
  Then 7 ploughs, now 6.
  Woodland for 10 pigs; meadow, 1 acre.
  1 church, 40 acres; value 7s. Several have a share there.
Value then 60s; now 30s 30d and 3000 herrings.
The King and the Earl (have) the jurisdiction.

22 In WESTON 1 free man under the patronage of the same man; 16
acres. ½ plough.
Value 5s and 400 herrings.

23 In WILLINGHAM 1 free man under the patronage of Burghard; he
could not sell the land nor grant; 3 acres of free land.
Value 18d and 100 herrings.

24 In *HATHEBURGFELDA* 6 free men under the patronage of Burghard;
60 acres. Then 2 ploughs, now 1½.
Value then 10s; now 11[s] 8d and 900 herrings.

25 In WORLINGHAM 5 free men and a half under the patronage of Gyrth;
60 acres. Always 2 ploughs;
  1 smallholder.
  Meadow, 2 acres.
Value always 10s 6d and 1000 herrings.

LOTHING Hundred

26 In *BEKETUNA* in lordship; 6 free men under the patronage of Burghard;
60 acres of land. Then 1 plough, now ½.
Value then 4s; now 21[s] 4d and 1500 herrings.

27 In KESSINGLAND 1 free man under the patronage of Edric of Laxfield;
30 acres as a manor. Always 1 plough.
  Meadow, 1 acre.
Value then 5s; now 8d.
In the same (Kessingland) 4 free men, 1 under the patronage of   407 b
Edric and 3 under the patronage of Burghard before 1066; 80 and
10 acres.
  2 smallholders.
  Always 2 ploughs. Meadow, 1 acre.
Value then 10s; now 22[s and] 1000 herrings.

⌐In Rodenhala . I . lib hō Aſlacus . comd̄ Burcardi
XL . ac̄ . ꝑ man̄ . Semp . IIII . bord . Semp in dominio . I . car̄ . 7 hōu dim̄
car̄ . ſilua ad . III . porc̄ . I . ac̄ & dim̄ p̄ti . Tc̄ ual . v . ſol . modo . IX . 7 VI . ccntos
allecti . Totum in dn̄io.

⌐In Wimundahala . II . libi hōes comd̄ Burckardi . XII . ac̄ . Semp dim̄
car̄ . Tc̄ ual . II . ſol . modo . III . 7 dim̄ mitt allecti.

In Giſleha̅ . II . lib hō comd̄ eid̄ . I . ac̄ . 7 dim̄ . 7 ual . II . ſol . 7 VI . den̄.
7 . cc alleci . In ead . I . lib hō comd̄ eid̄ . VI . ac̄ . 7 dim̄ car̄ . 7 ual . v . ſol.
7 ccc . allecii . ⌐In hornes . I . lib hō . comendatiō . Guerti . t . r.
. v . ac̄ . 7 ual . III . ſol . 7 . c . 7 LX . allecii.

⌐In carletuna . II . libi hōes comd̄ . Burchardi . XXX . ac̄ . Semp . I . carr̄.
& ual . III . ſol . cccc . allec̄ . In ead . I . lib hō comd̄ . eid̄ . XXX . ac̄ . Tc̄
. I . car̄ . modo nut . dimid̄ ac̄ p̄ti . Tc̄ ual & modo . v . ſol . 7 . ccc . allecti

⌐In kirkelea . I . lib homo comd̄ . dim̄ . Burchardi 7 dimid̄ . Vlſi . XII.
ac̄ . Tc̄ dim̄ car̄ . modo nutt . Tc̄ ual . II . ſol . modo . III . 7 . cc . allecti.

⌐In riſcemara . I . lib homo . com̄ . Guerti . XVI . ac̄ . Tc̄ . I . car̄ . modo dim̄.
& ual . v . ſol . 7 . ccc . allecti . Ḣ totū ten̄ . H in ſuo dominio . 7 q̄rta
pars . I . æccliæ . VIII . ac̄ . 7 ual . XVI . d . Rex 7 Comes ſoca . quattuor ex his
ſupradictis hōibƷ teſtatur hund qd̄ Walter de doai . fuit ſaiatus
die qua ſe forisfecit . 7 p̄t hug Coms . modo ten̄ hugo de monte
forti . ſed n̄ ten& p libationē teſte hund . 7 hōes hug de mut.
dicunt qd̄ ipſe . W . tenuit de eo.

28 In *RODENHALA* 1 free man, Aslac, under the patronage of Burghard;
40 acres as a manor.
    Always 4 smallholders.
    Always 1 plough in lordship; ½ men's plough.
    Woodland for 3 pigs; meadow, 1½ acres.
Value then 5s; now 9[s] and 600 herrings.
    The whole (is) in lordship.

29 In *WIMUNDAHALA* 2 free men under the patronage of Burghard;
12 acres. Always ½ plough.
Value then 2s; now 3[s] and 500 herrings.

30 In GISLEHAM 2 free men under the patronage of the same man;
1½ acres.
Value 2s 6d and 200 herrings.
In the same (Gisleham) 1 free man under the patronage of the same
man; 16 acres. ½ plough.
Value 5s and 300 herrings.

31 In *HORNES* 1 free man under the patronage of Gyrth [before 1066];
5 acres.
Value 3s and 160 herrings.

32 In CARLTON (Colville) 2 free men under the patronage of Burghard;
30 acres. Always 1 plough.
Value 3s [and] 400 herrings.
In the same (Carlton Colville) 1 free man under the patronage of
the same man; 30 acres. Then 1 plough, now none.
    Meadow, ½ acre.
Value then and now 5s and 300 herrings.

33 In KIRKLEY 1 free man half under the patronage of Burghard and
half (under that) of Wulfsi; 12 acres. Then ½ plough, now none.
Value then 2s; now 3[s] and 200 herrings.

34 In RUSHMERE 1 free man under the patronage of Gyrth; 16 acres.
Then 1 plough, now ½.
Value 5s and 300 herrings.
    Hugh holds the whole of this in his lordship.
    The fourth part of 1 church, 8 acres; value 16d.
    The King and the Earl (have) the jurisdiction.
The Hundred testifies that Walter of [Dol] was in possession of
four of the above-mentioned men on the day he forfeited; later Earl
Hugh (was in possession); now Hugh de Montfort holds [them].
But he does not hold them through a delivery, as the Hundred
testifies; and Hugh de Montfort's men say that William himself held
(them) from him.

HERTESMARA. H̄. In cotintuna . I . lib̄ hō Saxwinus
com̄d . Buchardi . xx ac̄ . t . r . e . Tc̄ . I . car̄ . modo dimid . dim
ac̄ prati . filua ad II . porc̄ . 7 ē in p̄tio in dn̄io de neutūn .

⫟ In Wluertheftuna . ten̄ herueus . II . libo hōes com̄d Burchardi
xviii . ac̄ . filua ad . II . porc̄ . 7 uat̄ . iiii . fot̄ .

⫟ In caldecoten ten̄ . in dn̄io . I . lib̄ hō . II . ac̄ & dim̄ . 7 uat̄ . vi . den̄ .

⫟ In Giffingahā . ten̄ Giffeb̄ . I . libā feminā c̄m . Gutmundi . xv .
ac̄ . 7 . I . ac̄ p̄ti . 7 uat̄ . II . fot̄ . In caldecotan . in dn̄io . III . ac̄ 7 dim̄
7 uat̄ . vi . d̄ .

⫟ *LACFORDA* . H̄ . Lluermera ten& hugo de beuerda ~~ten&~~ de
hugone quā tenuit Gutmundus . t . r . e . fub s̄cā aldreda qd̄ non
poter̄ uende ‚p manerio . II . car̄ terræ . Semp̄ iiii . uitti . & . III . bord̄ .
Tc̄ . III . ferui . modo . I . Semp̄ II . car̄ in dn̄io . Tc̄ & p : II . car̄ . hom .
modo . I . 7 iiii . ac̄ p̄ti . 7 . I . pifcar̄ . Semp̄ . I . eq̄ . 7 . III . an̄ . Tc̄ . x . porc̄ .
modo . III . clx . ou̅s . modo . c . Soc̄ 7 fac̄ s̄cā aldred̄ . & . III . libi hōes
gutmundi comd̄ 7 foc̄ 7 fac̄ s̄ci edm̄ . lxxx . ac̄ terræ 7 medietate
comd̄t uni cū tr̄a habuit s̄cs . e . t . r . e . Int oēs femp̄ . II . car̄ & . I . ac̄
p̄ti . Man̄ uat̄ . xl . fot̄ . 7 libi homines xiii . fot̄ . h̄t vi . qr̄ in longo
& . iiii . in lato . & de gelto . iiii . d̄ .

HARTISMERE Hundred

35 In COTTON 1 free man, Saxwin, under the patronage of Burghard; 20 acres before 1066. Then 1 plough, now ½.
Meadow, ½ acre; woodland for 2 pigs.
It is in the assessment of the lordship of (Old) Newton.

36 In WYVERSTONE Hervey holds 2 free men [who were] under the patronage of Burghard; 18 acres.
Woodland for 2 pigs.
Value 4s.

37 In CALDECOTEN he holds in lordship; 1 free man; 2½ acres.
Value 6d.

38 In GISLINGHAM Gilbert holds 1 free woman [who was] under the patronage of Guthmund; 15 acres.
Meadow, 1 acre.
Value 2s.

39 In CALDECOTAN 3½ acres in lordship.
Value 6d.

LACKFORD Hundred

40 Hugh de *Beuerda* holds (Great) LIVERMERE from Hugh; Guthmund held (it) before 1066 under St. Etheldreda's, so that he could not sell; 2 carucates of land as a manor.
Always 4 villagers; 3 smallholders. Then 3 slaves, now 1.
Always 2 ploughs in lordship. Then and later 2 men's ploughs, now 1.
Meadow, 4 acres; 1 fishery. Always 1 horse; 3 cattle. Then 10 pigs, now 3; [then] 160 sheep, now 100.
The full jurisdiction (is) St. Etheldreda's.
He also holds 3 free men of Guthmund's under the patronage and full jurisdiction of St. Edmund's; 80 acres of land. Before 1066 St. Edmund's had the half of the patronage of one (free man) with the land. Always 2 ploughs between them all.
Meadow, 1 acre.
Value of the manor 40s; (value of) the free men 13s.
It has 6 furlongs in length and 4 in width; 4d in tax.

/ *BABERGA DVO*. H̃. Staneſteda tᶜñ ĩ dñio gutmund⁹
teinñ.t.r.e.ꝑ mañ.v.caȓ terræ cũ ſoca.Tc̃.iiii.uiȟ.ꝑ⁹7 m̃
.iii.7.x.borḋ.Tc̃ 7 ꝑ⁹ꞈ x.ſerú.modo.vi.Tc̃.iiii.caȓ in dñio.
ꝑ⁹7 modo.iii.Semp.ii.caȓ hominũ.&.xvi.ac̃ p̃ti.&.i.moliñ.
Silua de.xx.poȓc̃.Tc̃.iii.equi.modo.iiii.Semp xvi.añ.

&.lx.porc̃.7.c.oũs Tc̃ ual & ꝑ⁹.vi.liȟ.m̃ reddit.xii.liȟ.hȓ.i.lg̃ in
longo.7 iiii.qȓ in lato.7 de gelto.vii đ & obolũ.quicuq̃, ibi ten&.
Eccłia de xx.v.ac̃ liȟæ terre.

/ *STOV*. H̃.Hagala teñ Gut mundus.ſub.R.E.ꝑ manerio.viii.
caȓ terræ cũ ſoca & ſaca ſuꝑ dñium hallæ tñtũ.Tc̃ xxx.ii.uiȟ.
ꝑ⁹7 modo xxx.7.viii.borḋ.7 tc̃.x.ſerú.ꝑ⁹vi.m̃.iii.Semp.iiii.caȓꞈ.
in dñio.Tc̃ 7 poſt xxiiii.caȓ hoiũ.modo.viii.Silua.cc.porc̃.7
xlii.ac̃ prati.Eccłia de.xxxi.ac̃ liȟe terræ.7 dim̃ ac̃ prati.
Semp.vi.equi in halla.7 xviii.añ.7 lxxx.porc̃.~~lxxxxvi~~·ᶜˣˡᵛⁱ·.oũs.
7 lxxx.caꝑ.7 in dño.vi.ſoc̃.eidē Gut mundi de quibȝ ſoca eſt.in
hunḋ 7 ñ poꞇ uenḋe trã.Tc̃ dim̃ caȓ terræ.7 xx.ac̃.7 ſemper.Tc̃ 7
ꝑ⁹.ii.caȓ.modo nulla.Tc̃ totũ ual.xvi.liȟ.ꝑ⁹xii.modo xx.liȟ.
De h̃ mañ.teñ herueus.i.caȓ.&.xxx.ac̃.7 ual.lxiii.ſoł.7 Radul-
fus.i.caȓ.de.xx.ſoł.Turoldus.i.caȓ.de xxx.ſoł.Peſſerera.dim̃.caȓ
de.x.ſoł.Rotbȓ.xx.ac̃.de.v.ſoł.Ricarḋ.xxx.ac̃.de.v.ſoł.Totũ ē
in p̃tio manerii.ȟt.i.lg̃ in longo 7 dim̃ in lato.& de gelto xvii.đ.
/ In daga worda teñ hugo in dñio.vii.liȟos homines quã teñuiꞇ
Gutmundus Ante cũ hugoñ com̃ḋ tantũ.ii.caȓ terræ in ſoca reg̃
& comit 7 ſub eis xvii.borḋ.Tc̃.7 ꝑ⁹.v.caȓ.inꞇ oēs.modo.iiii.Silua
xii.porc̃.&.viii.ac̃ p̃ti.Tc̃ & ꝑ⁹ual.xl.v.ſoł.7 modo xl.v.

BABERGH Two Hundreds

41 Hugh holds STANSTEAD in lordship; Guthmund, a thane, [held it] before 1066 as a manor; 5 carucates of land, with the jurisdiction.

Then 4 villagers, later and now 3; 10 smallholders; then and later 10 slaves, now 6.

Then 4 ploughs in lordship, later and now 3. Always 2 men's ploughs.

Meadow, 16 acres; 1 mill; woodland at 20 pigs. Then 3 horses, now 4; always 16 cattle, 60 pigs, 100 sheep.

Value then and later £6; now it pays £12.

It has 1 league in length and 4 furlongs in width; 7½d in tax, whoever holds there.

A church with 25 acres of free land.

STOW Hundred

42 Guthmund held HAUGHLEY under King Edward as a manor; 8 carucates of land, with full jurisdiction only over the lordship of the hall.

Then 32 villagers, later and now 30; 8 smallholders; then 10 slaves, later 6, now 3.

Always 4 ploughs in lordship. Then and later 24 men's ploughs, now 8.

Woodland, 200 pigs; meadow, 42 acres.

A church with 31 acres of free land. Meadow, ½ acre.

Always 6 horses at the hall; 18 cattle, 80 pigs, 146 sheep, 80 goats. Also in lordship, 6 Freemen of the same Guthmund's, jurisdiction over whom is in the Hundred; they could not sell the land. Then and always ½ carucate of land and 20 acres. Then and later 2 ploughs, now none.

Value then of the whole, £16; later [£] 12; now £20.

Of this manor, Hervey holds 1 carucate and 30 acres; value 63s. Ralph (holds) 1 carucate of land at 20s. Thorold (holds) 1 carucate [of land] at 30s. Pesserera (holds) ½ carucate [of land] at 10s. Robert (holds) 20 acres at 5s. Richard (holds) 30 acres at 5s. The whole is in the assessment of the manor.

It has 1 league in length and ½ in width; 17d in tax.

43 In DAGWORTH Hugh holds in lordship 7 free men; Guthmund, Hugh's predecessor, held it with only the patronage, in the jurisdiction of the King and Earl; 2 carucates of land.

Under them, 17 smallholders.

Then and later 5 ploughs between them all, now 4.

Woodland, 12 pigs; meadow, 8 acres.

Value then and later 45s; now 45[s].

In daga warda eadē teñ in dñio . vi . foc ptinentes in tornei . mañ reg.
de regiōe cū omi confuetudine . & hñt inf oms . i . car terræ . & . iiii . bord.
Tc 7 poft . iii . car . modo . ii . 7 . v . ac pti . Tc & p ual . xxx . fol . modo xx.
dim' æcclia . de xxv . ac libæ terræ
7 hos . vi . foc reclamat hugo ex libatione ; Daga worda ht . i . lg 7 dim

in lato . & de gelto xxx . d . Quicūq ibi teneat.
i dñio
In Watdena xvii . libi hoes gut mundi antc hugonis comd tñi.
& hñt . ii . car terræ in foca regis 7 comit . Tc . x . bord . 7 femp . Tc . v.
Dim' æcclia de . xv . ac libe træ . de . i . ac pti
car . poft . iiii . modo . v . inf oms . Silua . iiii . porc . 7 . vi . ac pti . Tc & p
ual . l . fol . modo xl . ht . i . leug . in longo 7 dim in lato & de gelto xxx .
deñ . quicūq ibi teñ.
In erueftuna . x . libi homines gut mundi antec . . . . hugoñ . cō
mendat tñtū dim car terræ in foca reg 7 comit . 7 ii bord.
Tc & p . iii . car inf oms . modo uix hñt . i . car . 7 iiii . ac pti . Tc
& p ual . xx . fol . modo . x . Ecclia . x . ac . libæ terræ . ht . x . qr in
longo . & . vi . in lato . 7 de gelto . x . deñ . qcūq ibi teñ.
In torpe . xvi libi hoes ante c comd tñtū . i . car træ in fac reg 7 comit.
7 . ii . bord . fub eis . Tc 7 p . iii . car . inf oms . modo . i . 7 . iii . ac . prati.
Tc 7 p ual . xxx . fol . modo . uix ual . x . fol . ht . v . qr . in longo . 7
. iii . in lato . & de gelto . viii . d . quicūq ibi teñ.
i dñio
In Vltuna . iii . libi hoes eid gudmund comm tñtū . dim car terræ
in foca reg 7 coms . 7 xiii . ac . Tc 7 p . iii . bord . modo . i . Semp . i . car.

44 In the same DAGWORTH he holds in lordship 6 Freemen who belong
to the King's manor of Thorney, belonging to the Realm, with every
customary due. They have between them all 1 carucate of land.
4 smallholders.
Then and later 3 ploughs, now 2. Meadow, 5 acres.
Value then and later 30s; now 20[s].
½ church with 25 acres of free land.
Hugh claims [to hold] these 6 Freemen by a delivery.
Dagworth has 1 league [in length] and ½ in width; 30d in tax,
whoever holds there.

409 a

45 In WETHERDEN in lordship; 17 free men belonging to Guthmund,
Hugh's predecessor, under patronage only, in the jurisdiction of the
King and the Earl. They have 2 carucates of land.
Then and always 10 smallholders.
Then 5 ploughs, later 4, now 5 between them all.
Woodland, 4 pigs; meadow, 6 acres.
½ church with 15 acres of free land. Meadow, 1 acre.
Value then and later 50s; now 40[s].
It has 1 league in length and ½ in width; 25d in tax, whoever
holds there.

46 In *ERUESTUNA* 10 free men belonging to Guthmund, Hugh's
predecessor, under patronage only, in the jurisdiction of the King
and the Earl; ½ carucate of land.
2 smallholders.
Then and later 3 ploughs between them all, now they have
scarcely 1 plough. Meadow, 4 acres.
Value then and later 20s; now 10[s].
A church, 10 acres of free land.
It has 10 furlongs in length and 6 in width; 10d in tax, whoever
holds there.

47 In *TORPE* 16 free men [of Hugh's] predecessor, under patronage
only, in the jurisdiction of the King and the Earl; 1 carucate of land.
Under them, 2 smallholders.
Then and later 3 ploughs between them all, now 1. Meadow,
3 acres.
Value then and later 30s; value now scarcely 10s.
It has 5 furlongs in length and 3 in width; 8d in tax, whoever
holds there.

48 In *VLTUNA* in lordship; 3 free men of the same Guthmund's, under
patronage only, in the jurisdiction of the King and the Earl; ½
carucate of land and 13 acres.
Then and later 3 smallholders, now 1.
Always 1 plough.

7 . IIII . ac p̄ti . 7 . I . moliñ . ſed medietatē calūpniatur. Cōm̄s de mo

retoñ . 7 . H̄ . teſtatur. Tc̄ & p̄ ual̄ XII . ſol̄ . & modo ſimilit̄.

⊦ In Ciltuna 7 in torſtuna ten& hugo iñ dñio . ex libatione ut dic̄.

XVI . ſoc qui p̄tinebant in tornei maner̄ regis . e . cū ōi conſuetudiñ

teſte hund̄ . & h̄nt . I . car̄ terræ 7 . VII . bord̄. Tc̄ 7 p̄ . IIII . car̄ . int̄ ōm̄s.

modo . III . 7 . VI . ac p̄ti . Tc̄ 7 p̄ ual̄ . L . ſol̄ . modo XXX . Tot̄ h̄t . IIII.

q̄r in longo . & . III . in lato . & de gelto . VIII . d̄ . Et ōes iſti . libi hoc̄s ē

409 b

7 ſoca fuer̄ libati ſic̄ ōm̄s hugonis dicunt ‚p . II . mañ . V . car̄t tr̄æ.

⊦ In dagaworda teñ breme lib̄ h̄o . Reg . e . qui fuit occiſ in bello ha -

ſtingenſi & h̄t . I . car̄ terræ 7 dim̄ ſed libata fuit hugoñ ‚p dimid car̄

de eſcangio . 7 ſoca reg . 7 cōm̄s . Semp . XI . bord̄ . 7 III . ſeru . Tc̄ 7 ſemp

II . car̄ . in dñio . Tc̄ & p̄ . II . car̄ hominū . modo . I . Silua LX . porc̄ . 7 IX.

ac prati . & . I . moliñ . I . Eccl̄ia ſine terra 7 dim̄ eccl̄ia . XXX . ac terræ.

★ Tc̄ . I . ac & dim̄ prati . Tc̄ XIII . añ . modo . X . 7 XII . porc̄ . 7 XVI . ōus.

7 XL . cap̄ . Semp ual̄ . LX . ſol̄ . In eod̄ manerio . I . lib̄ h̄o bremere

cōm̄d tantū . 7 h̄t . XI . ac & dim̄ . & . I . bord̄ . Tc̄ & p̄ dim̄ . car̄ . modo

nulla . 7 ual̄ . III . ſol̄ . hoc mañ ten& . Wil̄l fil̄i groſſe de hugone

de monte forti.

               in dñio

⊦ In newetuna . ten& Alwinus de melleſſam . I . lib̄u hoe dim̄

car̄ terræ modo ten& hugo ‚p eſcangio . ſub eo . II . bord̄ . Semp

. I . car̄ . 7 . I . ac 7 dimid p̄ti . & modo . XL . ōus . & . III . porc̄ . Semp

ual̄ . XL . ſol̄ . In ead̄ teñ hugo in dñio . ex libat̄ ‚p eſcangio . II.

libos hoes de quib; ſoc erat in hundret & h̄nt XXVII . ac . Semp

dim̄ car̄ . & ual̄ . V . ſol̄ . ⊦ In dago Worda teñ hugo . dim̄ lib̄u homi -

nē . XX . ac . & ual̄ . III . ſol̄.

                                     409 a, b

Meadow, 4 acres; 1 mill, but the Count of Mortain claims a half
and the Hundred testifies [to this].
Value then and later 12s; now the same.

49 In CHILTON and in *TORSTUNA* Hugh holds in lordship, by a delivery so
he says, 16 Freemen who belonged to King Edward's manor of
Thorney with every customary due, as the Hundred testifies. They
have 1 carucate of land.
  7 smallholders.
  Then and later 4 ploughs between them all, now 3. Meadow,
    6 acres.
Value then and later 50s; now 30[s].
  The whole has 4 furlongs in length and 3 in width; 8d in tax.
  All these free men, ... and the jurisdiction were delivered, as all
of Hugh's (men) say, for 2 manors, 5 carucates of land.

409 b

50 In DAGWORTH Breme, a free man of King Edward's, held, who was
killed in the Battle of Hastings; he had 1½ carucates of land but it
was delivered to Hugh for ½ carucate by an exchange. The
jurisdiction (is) the King's and the Earl's.
  Always 11 smallholders; 3 slaves.
  Then and always 2 ploughs in lordship; then and later 2 men's
    ploughs, now 1.
  Woodland, 60 pigs; meadow, 9 acres; 1 mill.
  1 church without land. ½ church, 30 acres of land. Meadow,
    1½ acres.
  Then 13 cattle, now 10; 12 pigs, 16 sheep, 40 goats.
Value always 60s.
In the same manor 1 free man; Breme had only the patronage. He
has 11½ acres.
  1 smallholder.
  Then and later ½ plough, now none.
Value 3s.
  William son of Gross holds this manor from Hugh de Montfort.

51 In (Old) NEWTON in lordship; Alwin of Mendlesham [held] 1 free
man; ½ carucate of land. Hugh now holds (it) by exchange.
  Under him, 2 smallholders.
  Always 1 plough.
  Meadow, 1½ acres. Now 40 sheep, 3 pigs.
Value always 40s.
In the same (Old Newton) Hugh holds in lordship by delivery 2 free
men by exchange, jurisdiction over whom was in the Hundred. They
have 27 acres. Always ½ plough.
Value 5s.

52 In DAGWORTH Hugh holds a half free man; 20 acres.
Value 3s.

¶ In torneia teñ Rog̃ . de candos . i.

car̃ terræ de hugone . que fuit de dñio manerio foca regis . tē : pore
. r . e . fed fuit libata . ꝑ . i . car̃ terræ . hanc habuit . Rad ſtalra in ua
dimonio de uice comite . Toli . ut hundreto audiū dr̃e f7 non uidit
breues neq̄ libatorē . & tenebat die qua rex . e . fuit mortuus . & p̃
Radulfus filius ei . & ħt . iiii . uiłł . 7 . iii . bord̃ . & . ii . ſer̃ . Tc̃ . ii . car̃
in dominio . m̃ . i . ſemp . ii . car̃ hoim̃ . & . iiii . ac̃ prati . & . i . moliñ

410 a
Silua . iiii . porc̃ . modo . x . porc̃ . & xxx . ous̃ . Semp uał lx ſoł.
Et in ead id̃ . teñ . ii . libi hŏes . xx . ac̃ . Tc̃ & poſt . i . car̃ . modo dim̃.
& uał . xl . deñ . Hæc eſt de eſcangio.

¶ THEWARDESTEV . H̃ . In begatona . teñ . i . lib hŏ Ediue
diuitis . xl . ac̃ tr̃æ . t . r . e . modo teñ hugo de monte forti ꝑ eſcang̃.
Semp dim̃ . car̃ . 7 uał . v . ſoł.

¶ DIMID̃ . H̃ . DEGERES WIZ . In burgo ħt . Hugo in dñio
. i . manſurā 7 iacet in nechetuna . Rex ħt totā conſuetudinē.

¶ BOSEMARA . H̃ BETESFORT . ten& Rog̃ de candos de . hug̃.
quā tenuit Aluricus lib hŏ . t . r . e . ꝑ mañ . i . car̃ . terræ . ſemp . viii.
bord̃ . Tc̃ . ii . car̃ in dominio . modo . i . & dim̃ . car̃ . hom̃ . vi . ac̃ p̃ti.
filua de xx . porc̃ . Dim ecclia . xx . ac̃ . modo . i . runc̃ . 7 iiii . animał.
& xii . porc̃ . & . xxi . ous̃ . & . iiii . cap̃ . 7 uał . xxx . ſoł . Huic mañ.
addidit hugo . v . libos hŏes . i . car̃ terræ . & . x . ac̃ . iii . bord̃.
Tc̃ . iii . car̃ . modo . i . car̃ & dim̃ . vi . ac̃ p̃ti . filua.
v . porc̃ . 7 uał . xx . ſoł . ħ ē ꝑ eſcangio de tr̃a ſci au-
guſtini . Rog̃ de candos teñ . Rex . 7 Coms̃ ſocā.
ħt . x . qr̃ iu longo . & . v . in lato . Alii ibi tenent.
7 . x . deñ . de gł.

53 In THORNEY Roger of Candos holds 1 carucate of land from Hugh which was in the lordship of the manor in the jurisdiction of the King before 1066, but it was delivered for 1 carucate of land. Ralph the Constable had this in pledge from the Sheriff, Toli, as the Hundred has heard say, but it did not see the writs nor a deliverer; he held (it) in 1066. Later Ralph, his son [held it]. It has
    4 villagers, 3 smallholders, 2 slaves.
    Then 2 ploughs in lordship; now 1; always 2 men's ploughs.
    Meadow, 4 acres; 1 mill; woodland, 4 pigs. Now 10 pigs, 30 sheep.   410 a
Value always 60s.
In the same (Thorney) he also holds; 2 free men; 20 acres. Then and later 1 plough, now ½.
Value 40d.
    This is by exchange.

THEDWESTRY Hundred
54 In BEYTON 1 free man of Edeva the Rich's held 40 acres of land before 1066. Now Hugh de Montfort holds (it) by exchange. Always ½ plough.
Value 5s.

Half-Hundred of IPSWICH
55 In the Borough (of IPSWICH) Hugh has 1 dwelling in lordship and it belongs to Nacton.
    The King has the whole of the customary due.

BOSMERE Hundred
56 Roger of Candos holds BATTISFORD from Hugh; Aelfric, a free man, held it before 1066 as a manor; 1 carucate of land.
    Always 8 smallholders.
    Then 2 ploughs in lordship, now 1; ½ men's plough.
    Meadow, 6 acres; woodland at 20 pigs.
    ½ church, 20 acres.
    Now 1 cob, 4 cattle, 12 pigs, 21 sheep, 4 goats.
Value 30s.
To this manor Hugh added 5 free men; 1 carucate of land and 10 acres.
    3 smallholders.
    Then 3 ploughs, now 1½ ploughs.
    Meadow, 6 acres; woodland, 5 pigs.
Value 20s.
    This is by exchange for land of St. Augustine's.
    Roger of Candos holds (this).
    The King and the Earl (have) the jurisdiction.
    It has 10 furlongs in length and 5 in width. Others hold here; 10d in tax.

Ⅴ In dermo—desduna. Vluricus . ɪ . liƀ
homo . comd . t . r . e . xvɪɪɪ . aͨ . & dim car . & . ual . ɪɪ . sol.
7 . vɪɪ . d̄.

Ⅴ CLAINDVNE . H̃ . In Westrefelda . ten̄ hugo . in dn̄io.
quem tenuit Ordricus liƀ hō . vɪɪɪ . aͨ . & ual xvɪ . den̄ . In Saham
ɪɪ . aͨ tr̄æ de dn̄io . 7 ual ɪɪɪɪ . den̄.

Ⅴ HERTESMere H̃ . Acolt.tenuit Gutmundus de ulurico fr̄e suo
abƀe de eli . ɪ . car terræ 7 xʟ . aͨ . pro man̄ m̄ ten& Roḡ de candos
de hugone . semp . v . uill . 7 vɪɪɪ . bord . Tͨ . ɪɪ . serui . Tͨ 7 p̄ . ɪɪ . carr
in dominio . m̄ . ɪ . Tͨ . ɪɪ . car hom . P̄ 7 modo . ɪ . 7 dim . & . ɪɪɪ . aͨ p̄ti.
silua . xʟ porͨ . Ecclia de . vɪɪɪ . aͨ . 7 dim car . semp . ɪ . runͨ . Tͨ . vɪɪɪ.
an̄ . Tͨ . ʟx . porͨ . modo . xɪɪɪ . Tͨ . xʟ . ous . modo . xxvɪɪɪ . & xxɪ.
cap̄ . Tͨ ual . ʟx . sol . Post . ɪɪɪɪ . liƀ . modo . c . sol . Et huic manerio
additi sunt . vɪɪɪ . liƀi hões xʟ . aͨ . Tͨ & post . ɪɪ . car modo . ɪ . & dim.
Ecclia xɪɪ . aͨ . 7 ual . x . sol . Gud mundus de toto socā . ħt x . qr̄.
in longo . & . vɪɪɪ . in lato 7 . ɪx . den̄ de gelto ;

Ⅴ TRA GOSFRIDI DE MAGNA VILLA . ᷊ ᷊
Stohu . H̃ . In cratinga ten̄ Witgarus liƀ homo abƀis de eli com̄
d tn̄tū . t . r . e . ɪɪ . car terræ . in soca regis 7 comit . Gosfridus ħt
p man̄ . ex dono reg . & sub eo Willmus de boe uilla sed non per-
tenuit ad feudū ansgari ante c̄ gosfridi . Semp . vɪ . bord . Semp
ɪɪ . car in dn̄io . Tͨ 7 p̄ dim car hominū . m̄ nichil . 7 v . aͨ p̄ti.
7 q̄rta pars . ɪ . mol . 7 medietas altr̄ mol . semp . ɪɪ . equi . in halla
7 v . an̄ . & . vɪɪɪ . por . Tͨ xx . ous . modo xxx . Semp ual xxx . v̄ . xl. sol.

57 In DARMSDEN Wulfric, 1 free man under patronage before 1066; 18 acres. ½ plough.
Value 2s 7d.

CLAYDON Hundred
58 In WESTERFIELD Hugh holds in lordship what Ordric, a free man, held; 8 acres.
Value 16d.

59 In (Earl) SOHAM 2 acres of land in lordship.
Value 4d.

HARTISMERE Hundred   410 b
60 Guthmund held OCCOLD from his brother Wulfric, the Abbot of Ely; 1 carucate of land and 40 acres as a manor. Now Roger of Candos holds (it) from Hugh.
　　Always 5 villagers; 8 smallholders. Then 2 slaves.
　　Then and later 2 ploughs in lordship, now 1; then 2 men's ploughs, later and now 1½.
　　Meadow, 3 acres; woodland, 40 pigs.
　　A church with 8 acres. ½ plough.
　　Always 1 cob. Then 8 cattle; then 60 pigs, now 13; then 40 sheep, now 28; 21 goats.
Value then 60s; later £4; now 100s.
To this manor were added 8 free men; 40 acres. Then and later 2 ploughs, now 1½.
　　A church, 12 acres.
Value 10s.
　　Guthmund (had) jurisdiction over the whole. It has 10 furlongs in length and 8 in width; 9d in tax.

32　　　　　　LAND OF GEOFFREY DE MANDEVILLE   410 a
STOW Hundred
1 In CREETING (St. Peter) Withgar, a free man of the Abbot of Ely's under patronage only, in the jurisdiction of the King and the Earl, held before 1066; 2 carucates of land. Geoffrey has it as a manor by the King's gift, and William of Bouville under him; but it did not belong to the Holding of Asgar, Geoffrey's predecessor.
　　Always 6 smallholders.
　　Always 2 ploughs in lordship. Then and later ½ men's plough, now nothing.
　　Meadow, 5 acres; the fourth part of one mill, and a half of another mill. Always 2 horses at the hall; 5 cattle, 8 pigs. Then 20 sheep, now 30.
Value always 40s.

7 in ead . v . libi homines eidē Witg cōmd tñtū . ix . aē terræ in foca
regis 7 comit . & dim car . & ual& . ii . fol . In eod mañ . i . lib hō
edrici . anteē . Rotbti mal& cōmd tant . modo teñ Willm de
boe uilla fub gosfrido . 7 ht . xvi . aē . & . i . bord . & dim car . & . i . aē
pti . 7 ual& . xxx . vi . den .

V CLAINDVNE . H̃ . In Weftrefelda tenuit Langfere
lib hō cōmd haldein xiiii . aē . & ual . ii . fol . Id Witt . Rex 7 cōms
focā . *V* SANFORT . H̃ . 7 dim . Holetunā teñ Aufgar .
t . r . e . ii . car terræ . p mañ . femp . xiii . uitt . & . ii . bord . Tē . iiii . feru
modo . iii . femp . ii . car in dominio . Tē . v . car hom . modo . iii . &
xxiiii . aē prati . Ectia . Tē . ii . runc . modo . i . & . ii . an . Tē xii .
porc . modo . vi . Tē lx . oūs . m̃ lxxiiii . Tē ual . lx . fol . m̃ . xl .
ht . vi . qr in longo . & . iiii . in lato . 7 . vii . den de gelto . Id Aufgar focā .
V Reindunā ten& . Angar . ii . car terræ . p mañ . t . r . e . femp
viii . uitti . & . iii . bord . & . iii . feru . & . ii . car in dominio . Tē . vii .
car hom . modo . iiii . vi . aē pti . filu . xvi . porc . Tē . ii . runc .

411 b
modo . i . Semp . v . añ . & . xii . porc . Tē . xxx . oūs . modo . l . Semp ual
viii . lib . In dñio . *V* De eadē terra ten& Aluredus . i . uitt . de
xxx . aē . 7 ual& . v . fol . Angarus focā . Dead terra ten& Giflebt
pbr . i . uitt . de . xxx . aē . 7 dimid car . & ual . v . fol .

In the same (Creeting St. Peter) 5 free men of the same Withgar's under patronage only, in the jurisdiction of the King and the Earl; 9 acres of land. ½ plough.
Value 2s.
In the same manor 1 free man belonging to Edric, Robert Malet's predecessor, under patronage only. Now William of Bouville holds (him) under Geoffrey. He has 16 acres.
1 smallholder.
½ plough. Meadow, 1 acre.
Value 26d.

CLAYDON Hundred

2 In WESTERFIELD Langfer, a free man under the patronage of Haldane, held 14 acres.
Value 2s.
William also [holds this].
The King and the Earl (have) the jurisdiction.

SAMFORD Hundred and a Half

3 Asgar held HOLTON (St. Mary) before 1066; 2 carucates of land as a manor.
Always 13 villagers; 2 smallholders. Then 4 slaves, now 3.
Always 2 ploughs in lordship. Then 5 men's ploughs, now 3.
Meadow, 24 acres.
A church. Then 2 cobs, now 1; 2 cattle; then 12 pigs, now 6; then 60 sheep, now 74.
Value then 60s; now 40[s].
It has 6 furlongs in length and 4 in width; 7d in tax. Asgar also (had) the jurisdiction.

4 Asgar [held] RAYDON; 2 carucates of land as a manor before 1066.
Always 8 villagers; 3 smallholders; 3 slaves;
2 ploughs in lordship. Then 7 men's ploughs, now 4.
Meadow, 6 acres; woodland, 16 pigs. Then 2 cobs, now 1. Always   411 b
5 cattle; 12 pigs. Then 30 sheep, now 50.
Value always £8.
(It is) in lordship.
Of the same land, Alfred holds 1 villager with 30 acres.
Value 5s.
Asgar (had) the jurisdiction.
Of the same land, Gilbert the priest holds 1 villager with 30 acres.
½ plough.
Value 5s.

ꝼIn belefteda tenuit Olf.& adhuc ten& lib hō.t.r.e.cōm
dt̃⁹ Anſgaro.Lxxx,ac̄.femp.i.uilł.&.ii.borđ.Tc̄.i.car̄.modo
dim̃.& ii.ac̄ p̃ti.Tc̄.i.moliñ.Quarta pars æcclɨæ.Tc uał.x.fol
modo.vii.Soca in bcolt.
ꝼScottunā ten Rainelmus ten& de Gosfr̄.quā tenuit frieber-
nus teinnus reḡ.t̃.r̃.e.ii.terræ.p̃ mañ.femper.ii.uiłł.&.x.
borđ.Tc̄.ii.feru̅.modo.femp.i.car̄ in dominio.&.i.car̄ hom̄.
&.iiii.ac̄ p̃ti.Tercia paʀs ecclɨæ.de xv.ac̄.m̄.vii.añ.Tc̄.ii.por̄.
modo.xiii.7 Lx.ou̅s.7.i.fał.7.ii.uafa apu̅.& uał.foł.ɦt.vi.
qr̄ in longo.& iiii.qr̄ in lato.&.iiii.deñ.de głId Frieb.focā
ꝼIn Gipe Wiz.i.manfurā.& p̃tin& in mofa.
ꝼIn rienduna.Eduinus.7 Brictmarus libi homines cōmđti
Anſgaro.t.r.e.&.dim̃.car.7 uał.v.fol.Soca in bcolt.
ꝼH̃.DE WILEFORD.In cerefelda.i.liba femina.Le
ueua cōmdatus.Haldeini.t.r.e.xxx.ac̄.7 ii.borđ.Semp
.i.car̄.ii.ac̄ p̃ti.Tc̄ & femp uał.x.fol.In eađ.i.lib homo
cōmdatus eiđe.xi.ac̄.& uał.ii.fol.
ꝼIn depeBek.i.lib hō.cōmd.cuiufdā cōm.R.ftalra.vi.ac̄.
& uał.xii.deñ.ꝼIn bulges.i.lib hō.cōm.haldeini xvi.ac̄.
Tc̄.i.car̄.modo.ii.bou̅.7 uał,ii.fol.In eađ.i.lib homo cōmđ.

412 a
Haldeini.7 Vlurici.vi.ac̄.& uał.xii.deñ.

5 In BELSTEAD Vlf, a free man under the patronage of Asgar before 1066, held and still holds 80 acres.
 Always 1 villager; 2 smallholders.
 Then 1 plough, now ½.
 Meadow, 2 acres. Then 1 mill.
 The fourth part of a church.
Value then 10s; now 7[s].
 The jurisdiction (is) in (East) Bergholt.

6 Rainalm holds STUTTON; he holds (it) from Geoffrey. Fridebern, a thane of the King's, held it before 1066; 2 [carucates] of land as a manor.
 Always 2 villagers; 10 smallholders. Then 2 slaves, now ... .
 Always 1 plough in lordship; 1 men's plough. Meadow, 4 acres.
 The third part of a church with 15 acres.
 Now 7 cattle; then 2 pigs, now 13; 60 sheep; 1 salt-house;
  2 beehives.
Value 40s.
 It has 6 furlongs in length and 4 furlongs in width; 4d in tax.
Fridebern also (had) the jurisdiction.

7 In IPSWICH 1 dwelling; it belongs to Moze.

8 In RAYDON Edwin and Brictmer, free men under the patronage of Asgar before 1066; 15 acres. ½ plough.
Value 5s.
 The jurisdiction (is) in (East) Bergholt.

Hundred of WILFORD
9 In CHARSFIELD 1 free woman, Leofeva, under the patronage of Haldane before 1066; 30 acres.
 2 smallholders.
 Always 1 plough. Meadow, 2 acres.
Value then and always 10s.
In the same (Charsfield) 1 free man under the patronage of the same man; 11 acres.
Value 2s.

10 In DEBACH 1 free man under the patronage of someone under the patronage of R(alph) the Constable; 6 acres.
Value 12d.

11 In BOULGE 1 free man under the patronage of Haldane; 16 acres.
 Then 1 plough, now 2 oxen.
Value 2s.
In the same (Boulge) 1 free man under the patronage of Haldane and of Wulfric; 6 acres.
Value 12d.

412 a

ℱ In Wikam . ɪ . lib homo commend heldeini . ɪɪɪ . ac . & ual& . vɪ . den ;

ℱ In meltuna . ɪɪ . libi hocs . comd . heldeini . ɪɪɪɪ . ac . & ual& . vɪɪɪ . den.
h̄ ten& . W . fili fahuala . de . G . de magna uilla.

ℱ . H̃ . DE LOSA . Ledringaham tenuit . haldeinus . t . r . e . emd heroldi.
ʟxxx . ac p̧ man̄ . Tc . v . bord . modo . x . Tc . ɪ . feru . modo . ɪɪ . Semp
in dominio . ɪɪ . car . 7 hou . ɪɪ . car . Silua ad . ɪɪɪɪ . porc . vɪ . ac p̃ti . ɪ . mol.
Semp . ɪɪ . run̄ . 7 . vɪ . an̄ . 7 xxx . porc . 7 ʟxxx . cap̄ . 7 . v . uafa apū . ɪ.
æcclia . de xx . ac . 7 ual . xʟ . d . Tc ual& . xx . fol . modo fimil.
In ead . xɪɪɪ . libi hoes 7 . ɪɪ . dim . comd eid . p̃t . vɪ . fuer comd . S . æ -
deldryde . ʟx . ac . Semp . ɪɪɪɪ . car . ɪɪ . ac p̃ti . Tc ual xvɪɪ . fol . m̄ fimil.
Adhuc in ead . ɪ . lib ho . com dim S æ . 7 dim haldeini . ʟx . ac . p̧ man̄
7 ɪɪ . bord . 7 . ɪ . car . ɪɪɪɪ . ac p̃ti . Semp ual . xx . fol.

ℱ In udebrige . ɪɪ . libi hoes comd eide haldeini . xxxɪɪɪ . ac . & dim
car . & . ɪ . bord . & ual . ɪɪɪ . fol . h̄ ten& ide . Willmus . de . G . de magna uill.

ℱ WAINEFORDA . H̃ . Scadena fella . ten& haldein . lib homo . co
md heroldi . ɪ . car terræ p̧ man̄ . Semp . ɪ . uill . 7 x . bord . Tc in dn̄io . ɪɪ.
car . modo . ɪɪ . Semp hou . ɪ . car . ɪɪɪɪ . ac p̃ti . filua ad . xx . porc . & . ɪ . ru.
& . xɪ . porc . 7 ʟxxx . ous . 7 . ɪɪ . uafa apū . Tc ual& . x . fol . modo . xx.

12 In WICKHAM (Market) 1 free man under the patronage of Haldane; 3 acres.
Value 6d.

13 In MELTON 2 free men under the patronage of Haldane; 4 acres.
Value 8d.
    W(illiam) son of Saxwalo holds this from Geoffrey de Mandeville.

Hundred of LOES
14 Haldane held LETHERINGHAM before 1066 under the patronage of Harold; 80 acres as a manor.
    Then 5 smallholders, now 10. Then 1 slave, now 2.
    Always 2 ploughs in lordship; 2 men's ploughs.
    Woodland for 4 pigs; meadow, 6 acres. 1 mill. Always 2 cobs,
      6 cattle, 30 pigs, 80 goats, 5 beehives.
    1 church with 20 acres; value 40d.
Value then 20s; now the same.
In the same (Letheringham) 13 free men and two half (free men) under the patronage of the same man, except for 6 who were under the patronage of St. Etheldreda's; 60 acres. Always 4 ploughs.
    Meadow, 2 acres.
Value then 17s; now the same.
Also in the same (Letheringham) 1 free man half under the patronage of St. Etheldreda's and half (under that) of Haldane; 60 acres as a manor.
    2 smallholders;
    1 plough. Meadow, 4 acres.
Value always 20s.

15 In WOODBRIDGE 2 free men under the patronage of the same Haldane; 33 acres. ½ plough.
    1 smallholder.
Value 3s.
    William also holds this from Geoffrey de Mandeville.

WANGFORD Hundred
16 Haldane, a free man under the patronage of Harold, [held]
SHADINGFIELD; 1 carucate of land as a manor.
    Always 1 villager; 10 smallholders.
    Then 2 ploughs in lordship, now 2; always 1 men's plough.
    Meadow, 4 acres; woodland for 20 pigs. 1 cob, 11 pigs, 80 sheep,
      2 beehives.
Value then 10s; now 20[s].

In ead . I . lib hō comd . Stigandi epī . I . car . terræ . ꝑ man . Tc . I . uill
modo similit . Tc . v . bord . modo . IIII . Tc in dominio . I . car . Tc hoū . II .
car . modo . I . Tc ual& xx . fot . m̄ similit . Hic hō fuit derationatus
7 faiatus ad opus regis . 7 poſtea faiſiuit . eū Waleram . 7 inde dedit uadc .
Adhuc in ead . II . libi hōes cm̄d haldeini . xxxII . ac 7 dim̄ ꝑ man . Semp

dim̄ car . & ual . v . fot . 7 . vIII . d .

⌐ In Weſtuna . I . lib hō . v . ac . 7 ual& xvI . d . ⌐ In Wichedis . I . lib hō . I . ac . &
ual& . IIII . d . ⌐ . H̄ . DE BLIDIGGA . Turintuna ten& aldenus
t . r . e . III . car terræ ꝑ man . Tc vIII . bord . modo . xIII . femp . II . ferū .
Tc . II . car in dnio . modo . IIII . femp . III . car hcū . filua ad xx . porc .
vII . ac p̄ti . Tc . I . runc . modo . II . 7 modo . xIIII . porc . Tc Lx 7 xII . oūs .
modo . q̄t xx 7 xII . 7 modo . IIII . uafa apū . 7 xv . cap̄ . 7 . I . molin̄ . 7
. I . æcclia de . vIII . ac . Tc ual xL . fot . modo Lx . Wiłłmus de boe uilla
ten& de . G . de magna uilla . 7 non ē de honore Anfgari .
⌐ Huic manerio iac& . II . libi hōes . de . c . ac . 7 xx . terræ . II . bordarii
IIII . ac p̄ti . Tc . II . car in dnio . m̄ nułł . Tc ual . I . marcā . m̄ . vIII . fot .
Ił terra h̄t . I . lḡ . & dim̄ in long . 7 in latū leugā & dim̄ . 7 vII . d
& obolū reddit de geldo .
⌐ In norhals . xx . ac terræ . q̄s ten̄ . I . lib homo . t . r . e . de ſtigando .
modo ten̄ . W . de boe uilla . de . G . de magna uilla . femp dim̄ . car .
7 ual . IIII . fot .

⌐ . H̄ . DE CARLEFORDA . In torp tenet halden lib hō . t . r . e .
. III . car terræ . ꝑ man . Semp . IIII . uiłł . 7 xI . bord . Tc II . ferū . modo .
. I . Semp in dnio II . car . Tc hoū . II . car . modo . I . vII . ac p̄ti . & . II .
runc . 7 vII . an . 7 xII . porc . 7 . c . oūs . Tc ual xx . fot . modo . xL . &

In the same (Shadingfield) 1 free man under the patronage of
Bishop Stigand; 1 carucate of land as a manor.
Then 1 villager, now the same; then 5 smallholders, now 4.
Then 1 plough in lordship; then 2 men's ploughs, now 1.
Value then 20s; now the same.
This (free) man was adjudged and taken for the King's use; later
on Waleran was in possession of him and gave a pledge for him.
Also in the same (Shadingfield) 2 free men under the patronage of
Haldane; 32½ acres as a manor. **Always ½ plough.**   412 b
Value 5s 8d.

17 In WESTON 1 free man; 5 acres.
Value 16d.

18 In *WICHEDIS* 1 free man; 1 acre.
Value 4d.

Hundred of BLYTHING
19 Haldane [held] THORINGTON before 1066; 3 carucates of land as a
manor.
Then 8 smallholders, now 13; always 2 slaves.
Then 2 ploughs in lordship, now 3; always 3 men's ploughs.
Woodland for 20 pigs; meadow, 7 acres. Then 1 cob, now 2; now
14 pigs; then 60 and 12 sheep, now fourscore and 12; now 4
beehives; 15 goats. 1 mill.
1 church with 8 acres.
Value then 40s; now 60[s].
William of Bouville holds (this) from Geoffrey de Mandeville.
It is not (part) of Asgar's Honour.
To this manor belong 2 free men, with 120 acres and 20 of land.
2 smallholders.
Meadow, 4 acres.
Then 2 ploughs in lordship, now none.
Value then 1 mark of silver; now 8s.
This land has 1½ leagues in length and 1½ leagues in width; it
pays 7½d in tax.

20 In COVEHITHE 20 acres of land which 1 free man held from Stigand
before 1066. Now W(illiam) of Bouville holds (it) from Geoffrey de
Mandeville. Always ½ plough.
Value 4s.

Hundred of CARLFORD
21 In THORPE Haldane, a free man, [held] before 1066; 3 carucates of
land.
Always 4 villagers; 11 smallholders. Then 2 slaves, now 1.
Always 2 ploughs in lordship. Then 2 men's ploughs, now 1.
Meadow, 7 acres. 2 cobs, 7 cattle, 12 pigs, 100 sheep.
Value then 20s; now 40[s].

hł in longo.VIII.qr̃.7 VI.in lat̃.&.xv.đ.de gelt̃.Alii ibi tenent.

╔ In burcg.VIII.libi hoes.comđ eid.halden.LIIII.ac̄.Semper
II.cař.II.ac̄ prati.7 uał.x.fol.

╔ In grundesburg.IIII.libi hoes comđ.halden.T.r.e.de xxvi.ac̄

ťræ.7.I.cař.dim̃ ac̄ p̃ti.7 uał.IIII.fol.In ead.I.lib hõ.Almarus
comđ Eilrici de burg.de.VIII.ac̄.dim̃ ac̄ prati.7 uał xvi.đ.

╔ In hafhetuna.III.dim̃ hoes.7.I.integru.̄com halden.t.r.e.de xxII
ac̄.terræ.&.I.cař.& dim̃ ac̄ p̃ti.& uał.III.fol.

★ ╔ In netkemara.II.libi hoes comđ.Alden.de xx.ac̄.7 dim̃ cař.dim̃ ac̄
p̃ti.& uał.II.fol. ╔ In ingoluestuna.I.lib homo.Godric̃ com dimiđ
halden.7 dim̃.Sc̄a.Æ.xx.ac̄ terræ.II.ac̄ p̃ti.& uał.II.fol.

╔ In Ifleuestuna.I.fochemañ.halden.xv.ac̄.&.I.borđ.Tc̄.I.cař.modo
.I.bou.I.ac̄ p̃ti.7 uał.II.fol. In burg.III.libi hoes.t.r.e.̄comđ hal
den.L.ac̄ terre.Tc̄.II.cař.m̃.I.I.ac̄ 7 dim̃ p̃ti.7 uał.x.fol.In ead
.I.lib hõ.Brichtricus.comđ Alric deburch.x.ac̄.7 uał.xx.đ.Adhuc
in eadc̄.I.lib hõ.Brihtuoldus mufla.comđ dim̃.ante c̄.herueu
deberu.7 dim̃ ante c̄.R.mal&.xxIIII.ac̄.Tc̄.I.cař.modo ñ.I.ac̄ p̃ti.

It has 8 furlongs in length and 6 in width; 15d in tax. Others hold there.

22 In BURGH 8 free men under the patronage of the same Haldane; 54 acres. Always 2 ploughs.
Meadow, 2 acres.
Value 10s.

23 In GRUNDISBURGH 4 free men under the patronage of Haldane before 1066, with 26 acres of land. 1 plough.
Meadow, ½ acre.
Value 4s.

In the same (Grundisburgh) 1 free man, Aelmer, under the patronage of Aethelric of Burgh, with 8 acres.
Meadow, ½ acre.
Value 16d.

24 In HASKETON 3 half (free) men and 1 whole (free man) under the patronage of Haldane before 1066, with 22 acres of land. 1 plough.
Meadow, ½ acre.
Value 3s.

25 In [NECKEMARA] 2 free men under the patronage of Haldane, with 20 acres. ½ plough.
Meadow, ½ acre.
Value 2s.

26 In INGOLUESTUNA 1 free man, Godric, half under the patronage of Haldane and half (under that) of St. Etheldreda's; 20 acres of land.
Meadow, 2 acres.
Value 2s.

27 In ISLETON 1 Freeman of Haldane's; 15 acres.
1 smallholder.
Then 1 plough, now 1 ox. Meadow, 1 acre.
Value 2s.

28 In BURGH 3 free men before 1066 under the patronage of Haldane; 50 acres of land. Then 2 ploughs, now 1.
Meadow, 1½ acres.
Value 10s.
In the same (Burgh) 1 free man, Brictric, under the patronage of Aethelric of Burgh; 10 acres.
Value 20d.
Also in the same (Burgh) 1 free man, Brictwold Muffle, half under the patronage of Hervey of Berry's predecessor and half (under that of) R(obert) Malet's predecessor; 24 acres. Then 1 plough, now none.
Meadow, 1 acre.

7 ual. v. fol. & lit in longo. ix qr. & vii. in lato. 7 xv. d̄ de gelt. Alii

ibi tenent. ⫽In culfola. iii. libi hōes. ii. com̄ halden. & 7 icius com̄.

Scæ Edeld. xxx. ac̄ tr̄æ &. i. bord. Tc̄. ii. car. modo nulla. ii. ac̄ p̄ti.

& ual. v. fol.

⫽In hobbeſtuna. i. lib hō com̄d. e. 7 uxor ei. com̄d. halden. t. r. e. xxx.

ac̄. Tc̄. i. car. modo. n̄. i. ac̄ p̄ti. Semp ual. v. fol. In ead. i. foc. Topi. com̄

S. æ. xv. 7 ual. iii. fol.

⫽In finlesforda. ii. ac̄. halden. t. r. e. 7 ual. iiii. d̄. li totū ten&. Willm̄

fili ſahala debou uilla. de. G. de magna uilla. sc̄a. Æ. p totā fochā

huius hundreti;

413 b

.XXXIII. ⫽TR̄Æ RADVLFI. BAIGNARDI. RISEBRVGE. Ĩ.

Kiditunam tenuit Ailad. t. r. e. p man. v. car. terræ. Tc̄ & p̄ xiii.

uill. modo. xi. Tc̄ & p̄. i. bord. modo. ii. Tc̄ & p̄. ix. ſer. modo nullus.

Tc̄ & p̄. iii. car in dominio. modo. ii. Tc̄ & p̄. viii. car hominum.

modo. ii. & dim. xx. ac̄. p̄ti. Tc̄. i. molin. Tc̄. iiii. runc. modo. iii.

Tc̄. xv. an̄. modo. iiii. Tc̄ xxvii. porc. modo. xviii. Tc̄. lii. ous.

modo. c. l. modo. vi. uaſa apū. Tc̄ ual. vi. lib. modo vii. &. v. fol.

Value 5s.

It has 9 furlongs in length and 7 in width; 15d in tax. Others hold there.

29 In CULPHO 3 free men, 2 under the patronage of Haldane and the third under the patronage of St. Etheldreda's; 30 acres of land.
1 smallholder.
Then 2 ploughs, now none. Meadow, 2 acres.
Value 5s.

30 In *HOBBESTUNA* 1 free man under the patronage of (St.) E(theldreda's) and his wife under the patronage of Haldane before 1066; 30 acres.
Then 1 plough, now none.
Meadow, 1 acre.
Value always 5s.
In the same (*Hobbestuna*) 1 Freeman, Topi, under the patronage of St. Etheldreda's; 15 acres.
Value 3s.

31 In 'FINLESFORDA' 2 acres; Haldane [held it] before 1066.
Value 4d.
William son of Saxwalo of Bouville holds the whole of this from Geoffrey de Mandeville.
St. Etheldreda's (has) the whole of the jurisdiction of this Hundred.

33 THE LANDS OF RALPH BAYNARD

RISBRIDGE Hundred

1 Aethelgyth held KEDINGTON before 1066 as a manor; 5 carucates of land.
Then and later 13 villagers, now 11; then and later 1 smallholder, now 2; then and later 9 slaves, now none.
Then and later 3 ploughs in lordship, now 2; then and later 8 men's ploughs, now 2½.
Meadow, 20 acres; then 1 mill. Then 4 cobs, now 3; then 15 cattle, now 4; then 27 pigs, now 18; then 52 sheep, now 150; now 6 beehives.
Value then £6; now [£] 7 5s.

In Ead̄ xxv.libi hōes.ii.car̄ terræ.&.v.bord̄.&.ii.feru.femp
xi.car̄.7 vi.ac̄ p̄ti.& ual xl fol.fuus ante c̄ com̄d 7 foca &
facā.p̄t vi.forisfacturas fc̄i eadmundi.& de uno habuit ante
c̄.Ricardi filii giflebti.comitis com̄d.S7 baign̄ totū reclamat
‿p efcangio.Ecclia de.xl ac̄ libæ tr̄æ.7.i.ac̄ & dim̄ p̄ti.7 ual.vi.
fol.h̄t in longo xii.q̄r.7 vi.in lato.7 xii.den̄.de gelto.Alii ibi tenēt.
In Poflingewrda.iii.libi.hōes.de iftis duob;̄ habuit fuus antec̄
com̄.t.r.e.7 focā & facā.p̄t vi.forisfact̄.fc̄i.e.7 idē.fc̄s eadmund̄
com̄ de tc̄io.t.r.e.& rex conceffit ei.t̄rā.ex h̄ uidimus breuē
& h̄nt.i.car̄ terræ.&.xx.ac̄.&.vii.bord̄.&.i.car̄ & dim̄.filua de
.v.porc̄.femp ual xxx.i.fol. In eadē.i.lib.hō.i.car̄ terræ & di-
mid̄.femp.vi.bord̄.7.i.car̄ in dn̄io.h̄ tēn Noriolt.Tc̄.ii.run̄.
7 modo fimilit̄.7 vi.an̄.7 xvi.porc̄.&.xx.ous̄.Tc̄ ual xx.fol.
modo xxv. In ead̄.i.lib hō.i.car̄ terre & dim̄.&.iii.bord̄.
7.i.car̄ & dim̄.&.iiii.ac̄ p̄ti.modo.ii.runc̄.7.iiii.an̄.7 xx.
porc̄.7 xxviiii.ous̄ h̄ tēn.Walt̄.7 ual.xxx.fol.In ead.ii.
libi hōes.c.lx.ac̄.7 viii.bord̄ 7.i.car̄.7 ual xxvi.fol.&.viii.d̄.

414 a
H̄ ten& Ricer̄.Ecclia.xl.ac̄ libæ terr̄æ & ual.vi.fol.Sc̄s.e.vi.
forisfacturas.baign̄.focā.h̄t xiii.q̄r in longo.7 xii.in lato.
& xv.d̄.de gelto.Alii.ibi tenent.h̄ eft ‿p efcangio.

In the same (Kedington) 25 free men; 2 carucates of land.
5 smallholders; 2 slaves.
Always 11 ploughs. Meadow, 6 acres.
Value 40s.

His predecessor (had) the patronage and the full jurisdiction,
except for the 6 forfeitures of St. Edmund's; and of one, the
predecessor of Richard son of Count Gilbert had the patronage.
But Baynard claims the whole by exchange.

A church with 40 acres of free land. Meadow, 1½ acres. Value 6s.

It has 12 furlongs in length and 6 in width; 12d in tax. Others
hold there.

2 In POSLINGFORD 3 free men. Of these, his predecessor had the
patronage over two before 1066 and the full jurisdiction, except
for the 6 forfeitures of St. Edmund's; St. Edmund's also had
patronage over the third before 1066. The King granted the land
to him; and we have seen the writ for this. They have 1 carucate
of land and 20 acres.
7 smallholders.
1½ ploughs. Woodland at 5 pigs.
Value always 31s.
In the same (Poslingford) 1 free man; 1½ carucates of land.
Always 6 smallholders;
1 plough in lordship.
Norigold holds this.
Then 2 cobs, now the same; 6 cattle, 16 pigs, 20 sheep.
Value then 20s; now 25[s].
In the same (Poslingford) 1 free man; 1½ carucates of land.
3 smallholders.
1½ ploughs.
Meadow, 4 acres. Now 2 cobs, 4 cattle, 20 pigs, 29 sheep.
Walter holds this.
Value 30s.
In the same (Poslingford) 2 free men; 160 acres of land.
8 smallholders.
1 plough.
Value 26s 8d.
Richere holds this.

A church, 40 acres of free land; value 6s.

414 a

St. Edmund's (has) the 6 forfeitures; Baynard (has) the
jurisdiction. It has 13 furlongs in length and 12 in width; 15d in tax.
Others hold there.
This is by exchange.

Wltefkeou ten&. Godwinus. tein nus . t . r . e . ꝓ man . iii . car terre.
& xv . ac . femp . vi . uilt. Tc . iiii . bord . modo . v . Tc . vi . feru . modo,
. iiii . Tc 7 p̃ iii . car in dominio. modo . ii . femp . ii . car . & dim
hom . filua . x . porc . xii . ac p̃ti . femp . i . molin . Tc . ii . runc.
Tc . xxiiii . an . modo xii . Tc xl porc . modo . xii . Tc lx . ous . modo
xl . & . v . uafa apu . Eclia . v . ac . & . ii . libi hoes xxv . ac . i . car.
& . i . ac p̃ti . Suus ant comd . 7 foc . S . e . vi . forisfacturas . Tc & p̃
ual lxxx . iii . fol . & modo fimilit . ht dim lg in longo . & . iii.
q̃r & dim in lato . 7 iii . den . de gelto . Alii ibi tenent.

BIDINGA . H̃ . Rienduna ten& Toret . v . car terræ . tc 7 p̃
xiiii . uilt. modo . v . Tc & p̃ xvi . bord . modo . xx . Tc . ii . ferui,
modo . i . Tc 7 p̃ iii . car in dnio . modo . ii . Tc & p̃ . xi . car hom . in
vii . filua de . lx . porc . Tc . ii . runc . modo . i . Tc . xii . an . modo . v.
Tc xl . porc . modo . xxx . fep . c . x . ous . modo . xv . cap . Tc ual . c . fol
modo . vii . lib . 7 x . fol . In ead . xxx . libi hoes . ii . car terre . & . v . ac.
& . ii . bord . Tc 7 p̃ . viii . car . modo . vi . 7 ual . xii . lib . 7 x . fol . ex . h
fuus ante c comd & foc & faca . t . r . e . In ead . ii . libi hoes comd
xvi . ac . & dim car . & ual . x . fol . Rex & coms foca . hoc eft ꝓ efcangio
ht . i . leug . 7 . iii . q̃r in longo . 7 . i . lg in lato . 7 . iii . pcas . 7 . vi . d
& obolu de gelto . ii . ecclie . i . car . tre . ual . x . fol.

3 Godwin, a thane, [held] WIXOE before 1066 as a manor; 3 carucates of land and 15 acres.

> Always 6 villagers. Then 4 smallholders, now 5; then 6 slaves, now 4.
>
> Then and later 3 ploughs in lordship, now 2; always 2½ men's ploughs.
>
> Woodland, 10 pigs; meadow, 12 acres; always 1 mill. Then 2 cobs; then 24 cattle, now 12; then 40 pigs, now 12; then 60 sheep, now 40; 5 beehives.
>
> A church, 5 acres.

Also 2 free men; 25 acres. 1 plough.

> Meadow, 1 acre.

His predecessor (had) the patronage and jurisdiction; St. Edmund's (had) the 6 forfeitures.

Value then and later 83s; now the same.

It has ½ league in length and 3½ furlongs in width; 3d in tax. Others hold there.

BLYTHING Hundred

4 Thored [held] REYDON; 5 carucates of land.

> Then and later 14 villagers, now 5; then and later 16 smallholders, now 20; then 2 slaves, now 1.
>
> Then and later 3 ploughs in lordship, now 2; then and later 11 men's ploughs, now 7.
>
> Woodland at 60 pigs. Then [3] cobs, now 1; then 12 cattle, now 5; then 40 pigs, now 30; always 110 sheep; now 15 goats.

Value then 100s; now £7 10s.

In the same (Reydon) 30 free men; 2 carucates of land.

> 2 smallholders.
>
> Then and later 8 ploughs, now 6.

Value £12 10s.

Over these (free men) his predecessor had patronage and full jurisdiction before 1066.

In the same (Reydon) 2 free men under patronage; 16 acres. ½ plough. Value 10s.

The King and the Earl (have) the jurisdiction.

This is by exchange.

It has 1 league and 3 furlongs in length and 1 league and 3 perches in width; 6½d in tax.

2 churches, 1 carucate of land; value 10s.

In brantuna . xi . libi h̃oes c̃omd . t . r . e . m̃ . x . ii . car̄ tr̃x.

& lx ac̄ . Tc̄ ii . uitt . modo . i . Tc̄ viii . bord̄ . modo xvii . Tc̄ . ix . car̄ . m̃
vii . filua xx . porc̄ . & ii . ac̄ p̃ti . Tc̄ uat xxx . fot . modo xl . Rex &
cõns foc̄ . p̃ efcangio . In ead̄ . i . foc̄ . ii . car̄ terre . & ii . uitt . & . viii .
bord̄ . & . iii . car̄ . filua . iii . porc̄ . & . ii . ac̄ p̃ti . & ual & xxx . fot . Ecctia
xvi . ac̄ . 7 uat . xvi . d̄ . Rex & cõns foc̄.

Froxedena ten̄ & toret . p̃ man̄ . iii . car̄ terræ . t . r . e . femp x . uitti .
Tc̄ xiiii . bord̄ . modo . xx . Tc̄ . ii . feru̅ . femp . ii . car̄ in dominio . femp
. i . port maris . Tc̄ & p̃ ix . car̄ hom̃ . modo . vii . filu̅ xl porc̄ . Tc̄ . i . nulla.
& . iii . ac̄ p̃ti . Tc̄ . ii . runc̄ . modo . i . Tc̄ . x . an̄ . modo . vi . Tc̄ lx . porc̄ . m̃
xiii . 7 lx . ou̅s . 7 xx . iiii . cap̃ . 7 . ii . uafa apu̅ . femp uat . iiii . lib̄ . Rex
7 Cõns foc̄a vi . forisfac̄turas . In ead̄ . viii . libi h̃oes . t . r . e . modo . iii .
c . xiii . ac̄ . Tc̄ . iii . car̄ . modo . i . & dim̃ ac̄ p̃ti . Tc̄ uat . x . fot . m̃ . xiiii .
p̃ efcagio . Rex & Cõns foc̄a . In longo . i . lg̃ . 7 xx . iiii . pcas . 7 in lat . x . qr̃
& . vii . pcas . 7 . iiii . d̄ de gelto . Ran̄ ten̄ . ii . ecctiæ . xxviii . ac̄ . vat . iii . fot

Wankeford̄a ten̄ . Toret . p̃ man̄ . t . r . e . ii . car̄ terræ femp . viii .
uitt . Tc̄ & poft . xiii . bord̄ . modo . xxi . Tc̄ . ii . feru̅ . femp ii . car̄ in dn̄io .
Tc̄ . viii . car̄ hom̃ . m̃ . vii . filua lx . porc̄ . & . ii . ac̄ prati . femp . i . mot .
Tc̄ . i . falina . Tc̄ . ii . runc̄ . Tc̄ xxiiii . an̄ . m̃ . xvii . Tc̄ . xxx . v . porc̄.

5 In BRAMPTON 11 free men under patronage before 1066, now 10; 2
carucates of land and 60 acres.
   Then 2 villagers, now 1; then 8 smallholders, now 17.
   Then 9 ploughs, now 7.
   Woodland, 20 pigs; meadow, 2 acres.
   Value then 30s; now 40[s].
   The King and the Earl (have) the jurisdiction.
   (This is) by exchange.
In the same (Brampton) 1 Freeman; 2 carucates of land.
   2 villagers; 8 smallholders.
   3 ploughs.
   Woodland, 3 pigs; meadow, 2 acres.
   Value 30s.
   A church, 16 acres; value 16d.
   The King and the Earl (have) the jurisdiction.

6 Thored [held] FROSTENDEN as a manor; 3 carucates of land before
1066.
   Always 10 villagers. Then 14 smallholders, now 20; then 2 slaves.
   Always 2 ploughs in lordship. Always 1 seaport. Then and later
      9 men's ploughs, now 7.
   Woodland, 40 pigs; then 1 salt-house, now none; meadow, 3
      acres. Then 2 cobs, now 1; then 10 cattle, now 6; then 60 pigs,
      now 13; 60 sheep, 24 goats, 2 beehives.
   Value always £4.
   The King and the Earl (have) the 6 forfeitures.
In the same (Frostenden) 8 free men before 1066, now 3; 113 acres.
Then 3 ploughs, now 1.
   Meadow, ½ acre.
   Value then 10s; now 14[s].
   (This is) by exchange.
   The King and the Earl (have) the jurisdiction. It has 1 league and
24 perches in length, and 10 furlongs and 7 perches in width; 4d
in tax.
   Ranulf holds (this).
   2 churches, 28 acres. 1 plough. Value 3s.

7 Thored held WANGFORD as a manor before 1066; 2 carucates of land.
   Always 8 villagers. Then and later 13 smallholders, now 21; then
      2 slaves.
   Always 2 ploughs in lordship. Then 8 men's ploughs, now 7.
   Woodland, 60 pigs; meadow, 2 acres; always 1 mill. Then 1
      salt-house. Then 2 cobs; then 24 cattle, now 17; then 35 pigs,

modo . xvii . Tc . c . ous . m̃ lxxx . 7 viii . cap̃ . & . v . uaſa apũ . abold⁹

ten& . ſemper ual . iiii . lib . jn log . i . lg . 7 . i . qr . in lat . ix . qr . 7 . vii.

d . de gelto . alii ibi tenent . Rex 7 Coms . vi . foriſfacturas.

In henhã . i . lib . homo Aluin⁹ cmd . i . car træ ꝓ man . ſemp . iiii.

uiłł . Tc . xi . bord . modo . xiiii . Tc . ii . car in dñio . p⁹ . i . m̃ . ii . Tc 7

poſt . v . car hominũ . modo . iii . ſilu . xl . porc & dim̃ ac prati.

ſemp . i . molin̄ . modo . i . runc . 7 . viii . an . Tc . iiii . porc . m̃ . xiiii.

Tc xx . ous . modo . xl . ſemp . xvi . cap̃ . modo . iiii . uaſa apũ . ſemp

ual . xl . ſoł . Rex 7 coms ſoca . h̃ ten . Rob de blideburc . h̃ e ꝓ eſcago.

BLIDINGA . H̃ . Vpbeſtunã . ten . toret . t . r . e . ꝓ man . iii . car.

: te . iiii . bor . Poſt . v . m̃ . xx . te . ii . ſer' . m̃ . i . te 7 p' . ii . car' in dñio . m̃ . iii.

træ . Tc xv . uiłł . p⁹ vii . modo . iii . Tc 7 p̃ ix . car hom . m̃ . x . ſilua

de . clx . porc . 7 vii . ac p̃ti . Tc . i . runc . modo . ii . Tc xvi . an . modo

xviiii . ſemp xxx . porc . Tc . xii . ous . m̃ . lxxxxii . ſemp ual . c . ſoł.

In huic man̄ iacent . iii . libi hoes de . xlii . ac . 7 . i . bord . 7 . i . car 7 ſilu

ad xvi . porc . & . i . ac . p̃ti . Tepore . r . e . ual . vi . ſoł . 7 viii . d . modo.

viii . ſoł 7 . i . æcclia . de . iii . ac . 7 ual . iii . d . 7 tota hæc terra hab&

vii . qr in longo . & iiii . in lato . & reddit de geldo regis . iii . den̄.

now 17; then 100 sheep, now 80; 8 goats; 3 beehives.
Anbold holds (this).
Value always £4.
(It has) 1 league and 1 furlong in length, and 9 furlongs in width;
7d in tax. Others hold there. The King and the Earl (have) the 6
forfeitures.

8 In HENHAM 1 free man; Alwin, under patronage; 1 carucate of land
as a manor.
Always 4 villagers. Then 11 smallholders, now 14.
Then 2 ploughs in lordship, later 1, now 2; then and later 5 men's
ploughs, now 3.
Woodland, 40 pigs; meadow, ½ acre; always 1 mill. Now 1 cob, 415 a
8 cattle; then 4 pigs, now 14; then 20 sheep, now 40; always
16 goats. Now 4 beehives.
Value always 40s.
The King and the Earl (have) the jurisdiction.
Robert of Blythburgh holds this. This is by exchange.

BLYTHING Hundred
9 Thored held UBBESTON before 1066 as a manor; 3 carucates of land.
Then 15 villagers, later 7, now 3; then 4 smallholders, later 5,
now 20; then 2 slaves, now 1.
Then and later 2 ploughs in lordship, now 3; then and later 9
men's ploughs, now 10.
Woodland at 160 pigs; meadow, 7 acres. Then 1 cob, now 2;
then 16 cattle, now 19; always 30 pigs. Then 12 sheep, now 92.
Value always 100s.
In this manor belong 3 free men, with 42 acres.
1 smallholder.
1 plough.
Woodland for 16 pigs; meadow, 1 acre.
Value before 1066, 6s 8d; now 8s.
1 church with 3 acres; value 3d.
The whole of this land has 7 furlongs in length and 4 in width;
it pays 3d in the King's tax.

In Cratafelda tenuit tored ꞏ T . ɼ ꞏe ꞏ iii ꞏ car' & dim̃ ꞏ terræ ꞏ ꝓ mañ.
femp . v . uilt . Tc & p̃ ꞏ ix ꞏ bord̃ . 7 m̃o . xxxi . fenp . i . fer' . ſep . in dñio
. ii . car' . Tc hom̃ . vii . car' . modo . x . filua ad . cc . & dim̃ porc̃ . iii . ac̃ &
dim̃ p̃ti . Tc 7 modo . i . runc̃ . Tc . viii . añ . modo . xiiri . Tc xl . porc̃.
modo xlvii . Tc xx . vi . cap̃ . modo . xxxii . 7 . i . æcclia . de . vi . ac̃.
7 ual . vi . d . femp . iiii . lib̃ . 7 huic manerio iacent . v . franci . hões . de
xxvi . ac̃ . 7 femp . ii . car' . & filua ad vi . porc̃ . 7 ual . vi . fot . 7 viii . deñ.
Et ifti redd̃ foca huic mañ p̃terea . ii . hões . de . xl . ac̃ . 7 . i . car' . 7 ual
v . fot . 7 foca de iftis duob₇ in bledeburc . Et has . ii . manfiones ten&
uuilielmus bainardus de radulfo auunculo ei . In ead̃ uilla ten&
quidã francus . i . Mañ . de . xl . ac̃ . 7 . iii . bord̃ . femp . i . car' . filua ad vi . porc̃.
. i . ac̃ & dim̃ p̃ti . T . R . e . ual . x . fot . modo . xx . Et iftud mañ eft in dñiũ
radulfi . Et tota h̃ terra ħt . viii . qr̃ in longo . 7 . v . in lato . 7 reddit

de gelto regis . iii . deñ . 7 obolum.

Ⅴ . H̃ . de Wanneford . Infcadenafella . i . lib̃ homo . Toredi . xx . ac̃ ɼ̃ræ
Tc . i . car' . modo . nulla . & ual& . iii . fot.

Ⅴ THEWARDESTREⅤ . H̃ . In ftanfella teñ elflet . i . lib̃a femiñ.
fub fc̃o . e . t . r . e . i . car' terræ . M̃ ten& bainardus . ꝓ efcangio . Tc
. i . bord̃ . modo . iii . Tc . ii . ferũ . modo . i . tc̃ . ii . car' in dominio . p̃
dim̃ . modo . i . 7 . v . ac̃ p̃ti . modo . i . moliñ . Tc ual xxx . fot . modo . xl.
In ead̃ . iii . libi hões . eid̃e efflet c̃omd̃ . xxx . ac̃ . ɼ̃ræ in foca fc̃i . E.
femp . i . car' . & . i . ac̃ p̃ti . femp ual& . v . fot.

10 In CRATFIELD Thored held before 1066; 3½ carucates of land as a manor.
> Always 5 villagers. Then and later 9 smallholders, now 31.
>> Always 1 slave.
>
> Always 2 ploughs in lordship. Then 7 men's ploughs, now 10.
> Woodland for 250 pigs; meadow, 3½ acres. Then and now 1 cob;
>> then 8 cattle, now 14; then 40 pigs, now 47; then 26 goats, now 32.
>
> 1 church with 6 acres; value 6d.

[Value] always £4.
To this manor belong 5 free men with 26 acres. Always 2 ploughs.
> Woodland for 6 pigs.

Value 6s 8d.
> And the (freemen) pay suit to this manor.

In addition, 2 men with 40 acres. 1 plough.
Value 5s.
> Over these two (men), the jurisdiction (is) in Blythburgh.
> William Baynard holds these two manors from Ralph, his uncle.

In the same village a free(man) [held] 1 manor, with 40 acres.
3 smallholders.
> Always 1 plough.
> Woodland for 6 pigs; meadow, 1½ acres.

Value before 1066, 10s; now 20[s].
> That manor is in Ralph's lordship.
> The whole of this land has 8 furlongs in length and 5 in width;

it pays 3½d in the King's tax.

415 b

Hundred of WANGFORD
11 In SHADINGFIELD 1 free man of Thored's; 20 acres of land. Then 1 plough, now none.
Value 3s.

THEDWESTRY Hundred
12 In STANNINGFIELD Aelfled, a free woman, held under St. Edmund's before 1066; 1 carucate of land. Now Baynard holds (it) by exchange.
> Then 1 smallholder, now 3; then 2 slaves, now 1.
> Then 2 ploughs in lordship, later ½, now 1.
> Meadow, 5 acres; now 1 mill.

Value then 30s; now 40[s].
In the same (Stanningfield) 3 free men under the patronage of the same Aelfled, in the jurisdiction of St. Edmund's; 30 acres of land.
Always 1 plough.
> Meadow, 1 acre.

Value always 5s.

Γ*BABENBERGA*.duo hund.Simplinga teñ ailith liƀa
femina fub glofo.R.e.p mañ.vi.car terræ.7 dim.Tc ix.uilt
modo.xii.Tc xii.bord.modo xvi.Tc.iii.ferui.modo.null Tc
& p.iiii.car in dominio.modo.iii.Tc.vii.car hom.modo.vi.
Silua.c.porc.7 xvii.ac pti.Tc.iiii.eq.modo.v.Tc.vii.añ.
modo.v.Tc lx.porc.m xxx.iii.Tc lxxx.oũs.modo.c.Tc xvi.
cap.modo xxiiii.Ecclia de.lx.ac libæ tre.&.i.bord.&.
.i.car.7 dim ac pti.Tc ual.x.liƀ.p 7 modo.xii.ħt.i.lg in lõg.
7 dim in lato.& de gelto.xv.d.In ead uilla.i.liƀ hõ Alith
comd in foca sci.e.xxx.ac.&.i.bord.femp.i.car 7.i.ac 7 dim
prati.Semper ual x.fol.7 hc bainardus p efcangio;

Γ*TERRE RANVLFI PEVRELLI LACFORDA.H̃.* ₒXXXIIII.

In etclingaham teñ Sewardus de melduna fub rege.e.fed foca
& faca.sci.e.p mañ.iii.car terræ Semp.vi.uilt.Tc.ii.bord.modo.
.i.Tc & poft.iiii.ferui.m.iii.Semp.iii.car in dominio.7.ii.car hom.
&.i.molin.Tc.i.æqus.modo nullus.7 tc.iii.añ.modo.ii.Tc xxx.
porc.modo.xxi.tc.cc.l.oũs.modo.ccc.l.Tc & p ual.iiii.liƀ.
modo.c.fol.Socā scs.e.

BABERGH Hundred[s]

2 Siward of Maldon, a thane, held ACTON before 1066 as a manor; 12 carucates of land, with full jurisdiction.

> Always 23 villagers; always 38 smallholders; always 17 slaves.
> Then 8 ploughs in lordship, later and now 6; then 20 men's ploughs, later and now 14.
> Meadow, 50 acres; woodland, 40 pigs; then and later 2 mills, now 1. Then 8 horses at the hall, now 11; then 34 cattle, now 31; then 200 pigs, now 160; then 300 sheep, now 423 sheep; then 9 beehives, now 7.

A church to which are attached 30 acres of free land.

Value then and later £20; now [£] 30.

In ACTON 4 free men whom Ranulf acquired for land; 50 acres. In WALDINGFIELD 5 free men; 72 acres. In the other WALDINGFIELD 3 (free men), with 50 acres. In HONILEGA 1 (free man), with 50 acres. In MANTON 1 free man, with 50 acres.

> Between them all they have 7 smallholders.
> Then and later 5 ploughs, now 4.

Value of the free men then and later £4; now 60s.

Of all these (free) men, 11 could sell their lands and 4 could not; but Ranulf's predecessor had patronage over them all, and jurisdiction, except for one who is in the jurisdiction of St. Edmund's.

Ranulf acquired them all for land.

Acton has 1 league in length and 1 in width; 13d in tax.

3 Siward, Ranulf's predecessor, also held ASSINGTON as a manor; 8 carucates of land with full jurisdiction before 1066.   416 b

> Then and later 14 villagers, now 5; then and later 21 smallholders, now 55; then and later 14 slaves, now 12.
> Then and later 7 ploughs in lordship, now 6; then and later 13 men's ploughs, now 12.
> Woodland, 30 pigs; meadow, 15 acres; 1 mill. Then 6 horses at the hall, now 5; then 24 cattle, now 23; then 100 pigs, now 60; then 210 sheep, now 90; then 14 beehives, now 6; now 12 goats.

A church with 30 acres of free land.

In the same (Assington) 5 free men under the same Siward's patronage and jurisdiction, but they could not sell their land while still remaining in the jurisdiction. Between them all they have 30 acres of land.

> Meadow, 1 acre.

Semp . ɪ . caʳ . Adhuc in eadē . ɪ . lib̄ hō libatus ⸝ꝑ terra ſed ñ ꝑtin&

mañ de q̄ antec̄ Rañ habuit com̄d cū ſoca . & h̄t . xxx . ac̄ . ſemꝑ

. ɪ . caʳ . Tc̄ ual x . lib̄ . 7 ꝑ xɪɪ . modo xx . ſed ñ pot̄ redde . de . c . ſoł .

De iſtis xx . lib̄ . ſt̄ xx . ſoł . ſuꝑ iſtos libos hōes . h̄t . ɪ . lḡ in longo . vɪɪɪ . q̄r

in lato . & de gelto . vɪɪ . đ.

Ƒ In Clamesforda . teñ blacuiñ . c̄om̄datus . Siwardo . xxx . ac̄ . ⸝ꝑ m̄

t . r . e . & ual& . vɪ . ſoł . Garinus tenet . Sc̄a . A . ſoc̄a .

Ƒ LOSAM ten& Leuſtañ teñ ſub rege glorioſo . e . ⸝ꝑ mañ . ɪ . caʳ . & dim̄

terræ dei caʳ fuit ſoca ʲ trinitatis in cantuariā . Semp . vɪ . bord̄ . Tc̄ . ɪɪ .

feru . Semp ɪɪ . caʳ in dominio . & nulla hoū . 7 vɪ . ac̄ p̄ti . Tc̄ . ɪɪ . equi .

modo nullus . Tc̄ . x . añ . m̄ nulł Tc̄ . xxx . porc̄ . m̄ . nulł . Tc̄ ʟx . ɪɪɪɪ . oūs

modo nullus . Tc̄ & poſt ual xʟ . ſoł . 7 modo . h̄t dim̄ lḡ in longo & . ɪɪɪɪ .

q̄r in lato . & de gelto . ɪ . đ.

Ƒ Stohu . h̄ . Anuhus teñ ketel tegñ . Reḡ . e . ⸝ꝑ . ɪ . caʳ & dim̄ . & xx . ac̄ .

cū ſoca . Semp . vɪɪɪ . bord̄ . & . ɪɪɪɪ . feru . Tc̄ & ꝑ ⸌ ɪɪɪ . caʳ in dñio . modo . ɪɪ .

& ſemp . ɪ . caʳ hom̄ . & . xɪɪ . ac̄ p̄ti . Silua de . vɪ . porc̄ . & . ɪ . runc̄ . &

vɪ . añ . Tc̄ xvɪ . porc̄ . modo . xxx . Tc̄ xʟ . oūs . m̄ . ʟxxx . vɪɪ . 7 xxɪɪ . cap̄ .

Eccła de . ɪɪɪ . ac̄ libæ terre . Tc̄ & ꝑ ual xʟ ſoł . modo . ʟ . h̄t . v . q̄r in

longo . & . ɪɪɪ . in lato . & de geldo . vɪ . đ & obolū .

Ƒ In Aneus ꝑtinuer . t . r . e . xxvɪ . ac̄ . & modo ten& osb̄tus maſculus

in æccłia ſtou . & tenuit anteq̄ Ranulfus habuiſſ& mañ anulus .

★ Ƒ BOSEMARA . H̄ . Burgheſtalā . teñ Rad de ſauigneio . de . Radulfo .

quā tenuit Turchillus teinnus . t . r . e . ⸝ꝑ mañ . xxvɪɪɪ . ac̄ . modo . ɪɪ . bord̄ .

ſemp . ɪ . caʳ in dominio . & . ɪɪ . ac̄ p̄ti . ſemp . ɪ . runc̄ . & . ɪ . añ . modo . ɪx .

porc̄ . Tc̄ . xɪɪɪɪ . oūs . modo . xxx . Tc̄ ual . v . ſoł . & . ɪɪɪɪ . đ . m̄ . vɪɪɪ . ſoł .

8 In BRICETT Ralph son of Brian holds what Leofstan held before
1066; 2 carucates of land and 4 acres as a manor.
>Always 1 villager; 10 smallholders; 2 slaves;
>3 ploughs in lordship.
>Meadow, 6 acres; woodland, 10 pigs.
>Then 2 men's ploughs, now 1.

Of this land, 54 acres belonged to a church. Ralph son of Brian now
holds them in his lordship.
>Then 2 cobs, now 5; then 10 cattle, now 15; then 30 pigs, now
>50; then 80 sheep, now 140.

In the same (Bricett) 4 Freemen, with 41 acres. Then 1½ ploughs,
now 2 oxen.
>The King and the Earl (have) the jurisdiction.
>Value then 60s; now 100[s].

9 Humphrey son of Aubrey holds CODDENHAM; he holds (it) from
Ranulf. Leofric, a free man, held it before 1066; 60 acres as a manor.
>Always 3 smallholders;
>2 ploughs.
>Meadow, 4 acres; woodland at 60 pigs.
>A part of 3 churches.
>1 cob; then 8 cattle, now 6; 14 pigs, 12 sheep.

Value then 20s; now 40[s].
>A church, 3 acres; value 6d.

10 In MICKFIELD Ralph of Savenay holds 12 acres.
>3 smallholders.
>½ church, 2½ acres.

They are in the assessment of Ulverston.
>The King and the Earl (have) jurisdiction over the whole.

11 In STONHAM the fourth part of a church, 7½ acres; value 15d.

CLAYDON Hundred

12 Saxi held DEBENHAM; 1 carucate of land as a manor, and 22 acres.
Of these 22 acres, Robert Malet's predecessor had 8 acres before
1066 in the jurisdiction and under the patronage of the Abbot.
>Then 4 villagers, now 2; always 19 smallholders. Then 1 slave.
>Always 2 ploughs in lordship.
>The third part of St. Mary's Church, with 10 acres.
>Always 2 ploughs in lordship. Then and later 3 men's ploughs,
>now 2.
>Meadow, 4 acres; woodland then at 100 pigs, now 40. Then 1
>cob, 4 cattle. [Then] 40 pigs, now 28; 27 goats; then 40
>sheep, now 30.

30 acres in lordship in Loes Hundred.
Value then 60s; now 50[s].
>Ralph of Savenay holds (this).

Vlueſtune tenuit Idē Saxo . 7 eođ modo ꝑ mañ.

. I . caŕ terræ . t . r . e . Tc̄ . & p̄ . III . uiłł . modo . I . Tc̄ & p̄ ꞓ IX borđ . modo

XIIII . Tc̄ & p̄ . II . caŕ in dn̄io . modo . I . Tc̄ & p̄ . III . caŕ hom . modo

II . Tc̄ . I . runc̄ . Tc̄ XIIII . añ . Tc̄ LX . porc̄ . modo XXII . Tc̄ XXII . oūs .

modo . XXX . Tc̄ & p̄ ual . XL . ſoł . modo XXX . Huic mañ ꝑtinebant

VIII . ac̄ . de dominio . t . r . e . q̄s modo ten& mat̄ Rob̄ti malet .

łt . I . łḡ in longo . & . VII . q̄r in lato . & XXVI . đ & ob̄ . de geldo Alii ibi teꝧ.

Dim̄ . ħ . DE COSFORT ꞉In Watefelda . XX . ac̄ . tenuit . Leſtanus &

ual XX . đ . sc̄s . e . ſoc̄a

H̄ . DE CARLEFORD . In Clopetuna . teñ . Edric̄ grim . t . r . e .

. I . caŕ terræ . 7 XLII . ac̄꞉comd dim̄ . S̄ æ . 7 dim̄ ante c̄ . R . malet .

Semp . II . uiłł . & XIII . borđ . Tc̄ in dn̄io . III . caŕ . modo . II . ſed poteſt fieri ,

Tc̄ hom̄ . II . caŕ . m̄ . I . v . ac̄ p̄ti . ſilua ad . x . porc̄ . & . I . runc̄ . Tc̄ . VIII .

añ . modo . III . modo . XXX . porc̄ . Tꝭ LXXX . oūs . modo XX . Tc̄ ual

LX . ſoł . modo . L . hoc teñ . Toroldus . de . R . I . æccłia . XV . ac̄ . de quat

tuor dominationib꜓ & ual . II . ſoł .

H̄ . DE WILEFORDA . In depebꝰs . XV . ac̄ . & ꝑtinent ad clopetuna

418 a
& ual . III . ſoł .

HERTESMARA . H̄ . In Tuſemera . I . caŕ terræ . de dn̄io abb̄is de eli .

qd tenuit ſaxo . t . r . e . ꝑ ſuis ſolidatis . Tc̄ & p̄ . I . caŕ . modo nichil .

& te ual XX . ſoł . modo . x . Rađ de ſauigni teñ .

In Aſpella XVI . ac̄ . de dn̄io . Vlueſtune . 7 IIII . borđ . & dim̄ caŕ .

In ead tc̄ia pars æcctiæ . & t̄cia pars feriæ .

13 Saxi also held ULVERSTON in the same way as a manor; 1 carucate of land before 1066.

> Then and later 3 villagers, now 1; then and later 9 smallholders, now 14.
>
> Then and later 2 ploughs in lordship, now 1; then and later 3 men's ploughs, now 2.
>
> Then 1 cob; then 14 cattle; then 60 pigs, now 22; then 22 sheep, now 30.

Value then and later 40s; now 30[s].

To this manor before 1066 belonged 8 acres in lordship. Now Robert Malet's mother holds them.

> It has 1 league in length and 7 furlongs in width; 26½d in tax. Others hold there.

Half-Hundred of COSFORD

14 In WHATFIELD Leofstan held 20 acres.

Value 20d.

> St. Edmund's (had) the jurisdiction.

Hundred of CARLFORD

15 In CLOPTON before 1066 Edric Grim, half under the patronage of St. Etheldreda's and half (under that) of R(obert) Malet's predecessor, held 1 carucate of land and 42 acres.

> Always 2 villagers; 13 smallholders.
>
> Then 3 ploughs in lordship, now 2, but [another] possible; then 2 men's ploughs, now 1.
>
> Meadow, 5 acres; woodland for 10 pigs. 1 cob; then 8 cattle, now 3; now 30 pigs; then 80 sheep, now 20.

Value then 60s; now 50[s].

> Thorold holds this from Ranulf.
>
> 1 church, 15 acres from four lordships; value 2s.

Hundred of WILFORD

16 In DEBACH 15 acres; they belong to Clopton.

Value 3s.

418 a

HARTISMERE Hundred

17 In *TUSEMERA* 1 carucate of land of the Abbot of Ely's lordship. Saxi held it before 1066 as his wages. Then and later 1 plough, now nothing.

Value then 20s; now 10[s].

> Ralph of Savenay holds (this).

18 In ASPALL 16 acres of the lordship of Ulverston, and in the assessment.

> 4 smallholders.
>
> ½ plough.

In the same (Aspall) the third part of a church. And the third part of a fair.

Lauenham teñ Vlwinus teinn . reg̃ . e . ꝓ mañ . vi . car̓ . terræ .

cū ſaca & ſoca . Tc̄ & p̊ xi . uiłł . modo vii . Tc̄ & p̊ xxiiii . borđ . modo

xxx . viii . Semꝓ . vi . feru̓ . Semꝓ . iiii . car̓ in dominio . Tc̄ & poſt

ix . car̓ hoɱ . modo vii . &. x . ac̄ p̃ti . Silu̓ . de . c . porc̃ . Tc̄ . v . eꝗ . in halla

modo . i . Tc̄ xxiiii . añ . modo xxv . Tc̄ c . lx . porc̃ . modo lx . v . Tc̄ &

ſemper . cc . ou̅s . Tc̄ lx . cap̅ . modo . lxxx . Tc̄ . v . uaſa apū . modo . vi .

i . arpentū uineæ . & . i . ſoc̄ ꝗ non pot̓ dare nec uende . de . i . car̓ i̅ræ

& . v . borđ . Semꝓ . ii . car̓ . modo . i . moł . & . iii . ac̄ p̃ti . Tc̄ 7 p̊ totū

uał x . lib . m̅ . xv . ħt . i . leg̅ in longo . & di̅ɱ in lato . & de gelto . vii . đ & oboł .

V Walingafella teñ ide̅ ulwinus antec̓ albrici . ſub rege . e . ꝓ mañ .

ii . car̓ terræ cū ſoca & ſaca . Semꝓ . iiii . uiłł . & . x . borđ . & . iiii . feru̓ ſemꝓ

. ii . car̓ in dñio . & . ii . car̓ hoɱ . & iiii . ac̄ p̃ti . Silua de . iiii . porc̃ . Semꝓ

. i . eꝗ in halla . 7 iii . añ . 7 xvi . porc̃ . Semꝓ . c . ou̅s . Semꝓ uał . v . lib . ħt

xii . qr̓ in longo . & . iii . in lato . & de gelto . vi . đ .

V *SANFORT* . *H̃.* Belſteđa̅ tenuit Tocha lib̅ ho̅ coɱđ . tantū .

lxxx . ac̄ ꝓ mañ . Tc̄ . ii . uiłłi . modo . ii . borđ . ſemꝓ . i . car̓ . & . ii . ac̄ p̃ti .

Tc̄ . i . molin . Tc̄ uał xvi . ſoł . p̊ 7 m̅ xv . fermeus ten& . Soca in ꞗcolt .

In eade̅ teñ Turgiſus lib̅ homo . coɱđ tantū . lxxx . ac̄ . ꝓ mañ . ſe̅p

. ii . uiłłi . & . i . borđ . Tc̄ & p̊ . i . car̓ . m̅ . nichil . & . ii . ac̄ p̃ti . Tc̄ uał . xvi .

ſoł . P̊ & modo xv . Soca in ꞗcolt . ħt . v . qr̓ in longo . & . iii . in lato . & vi . đ

& oboł de gelto . hæc duo mañ derationata ſunt . Rađ taillebofc .

7 Phin in manu reg̓ . & poſt accepit ea . Albicus ſine liꞗatione . ſic

ꝑpoſit . & hunđ . di̅c̄ .

BABERGH Two Hundreds
1 Wulfwin, a thane of King Edward's, held LAVENHAM as a manor;
6 carucates of land, with full jurisdiction.
> Then and later 11 villagers, now 7; then and later 24 smallholders,
> now 38; always 6 slaves.
> Always 4 ploughs in lordship. Then and later 9 men's ploughs,
> now 7.
> Meadow, 10 acres; woodland at 100 pigs. Then 5 horses at the
> hall, now 1; then 24 cattle, now 25; then 160 pigs, now 65;
> then and always 200 sheep; then 60 goats, now 80; then 5
> beehives, now 6. 1 *arpent* of vines.
> 1 Freeman who could not grant or sell, with 1 carucate of land.
> 5 smallholders.
> Always 2 ploughs.
> Now 1 mill. Meadow, 3 acres.
Value of the whole then and later £10; now [£] 15.
It has 1 league in length and a ½ in width; 7½d in tax.

2 Wulfwin, Aubrey's predecessor, also held WALDINGFIELD under King   418 b
Edward as a manor; 2 carucates of land, with full jurisdiction.
> Always 4 villagers; 10 smallholders; 4 slaves.
> Always 2 ploughs in lordship; 2 men's ploughs.
> Meadow, 4 acres; woodland at 4 pigs. Always 1 horse at the hall;
> 3 cattle; 16 pigs; always 100 sheep.
Value always £5.
It has 12 furlongs in length and 3 in width; 6d in tax.

SAMFORD Hundred
3 Toki, a free man under patronage only, held BELSTEAD; 80 acres as
a manor.
> Then 2 villagers; now 2 smallholders.
> Always 1 plough.
> Meadow, 2 acres; then 1 mill.
Value then 16s; later and now 15[s].
> Fermeus holds (this).
The jurisdiction (is) in (East) Bergholt.
In the same (Belstead), Thorgils, a free man under patronage only,
held 80 acres as a manor.
> Always 2 villagers; 1 smallholder.
> Then and later 1 plough, now nothing. Meadow, 2 acres.
Value then 16s; later and now 15[s].
> The jurisdiction (is) in (East) Bergholt.
> It has 5 furlongs in length and 3 in width; 6½d in tax.
These 2 manors were adjudged from Ralph Tallboys and Finn
into the King's hand; later Aubrey received them without a
deliverer, so the reeve and the Hundred say.

¶In Canepetuna ten̄ Brunnuin̓ focheman̓ de b̄colt manerio regis.
.iiii.ac̄.& ual xii.d̄.

¶HERTESMERA. H̄.Burgatā tenuit Vluuinus lib̄ hō.t.r.e.
p man̄.v.car̓ terre & femp xxii.uiłł.7 xxxiii.bord̄.Tc̄.iiii.feru̓.
femp.iii.car̓ in dominio.Tc̄ 7 p̓ xv.car̓.modo.x.7 iii.ac̄ & dimid̄.
p̓ti.Tc̄ filua.c.porc̓.modo xl.Æccliæ.de.xxix.ac̄.& dim̓ car̓.
Tc̄ vii.an̄.modo.xii.Tc̄ xxiii.porc̓.modo lxxx.Tc̄ lxiii.oūs.
m̊ clxxvi.Tc̄ xl.cap̄.m̊.lvii.&.ix.foc̄.cxlii.ac̄.&.iiii.bord̄.
femp.v.car̓.&.iii.ac̄ & dim̓ p̓ti.filua de.vi.porc̓.Q̇rta pars
æccliæ.i.ac̄.Tc̄ ual totū.xvi.lib̄.modo xix.7 iiii.fol.ħt.i.łg in lōgo

419 a

7 vii.q̇r̓ in lato.7.v.den̄.de gelto.Vluuin̓ habuit foca̓.Totū ten̄&
Adelolm̓ de alb̄ico.

¶DIM̀.H̄.de cosfort.Ialelham ten̄.Vluuinus.t.r.e.p man̄.
v.car̓ terræ & dim̓.Tc̄ vii.uiłł.modo.iiii.Tc̄ vi.feru̓.modo.ii.Tc̄.
iiii.car̓ in dn̄io.modo.iii.Tc̄ vi.car̓ hom̓.modo.iiii.vii.ac̄ p̓ti.
Silua viii.porc̓.femp.ii.molin̄.& iii.runc̓.Tc̄.x.an̄.modo.xviii.
Tc̄ lxxx.porc̓.modo lx.Tc̄.c.xl.oūs.M lx.Ecclia.de.vii.ac̄.Tc̄ ual
.viii.lib̄.modo xv.In cadē.i.lib̄ hō.v.ac̄.com̓ tantū.s̄es ead foca̓
7 ual.x.den̄.ħt viii.q̇r̓ in łongo.& vii.in lato; & v.den̄ de gelto;

4 In *CANEPETUNA* Brunwin, a Freeman from the King's manor of
(East) Bergholt, held 4 acres.
Value 12d.

HARTISMERE Hundred
5 Wulfwin, a free man, held BURGATE before 1066 as a manor; 5
carucates of land.
    Always 22 villagers; 33 smallholders. Then 4 slaves.
    Always 3 ploughs in lordship. Then and later 15 [men's] ploughs,
       now 10.
    Meadow, 3½ acres; woodland, then 100 pigs, now 40.
    ... churches with 29 acres. ½ plough.
    Then 7 cattle, now 12; then 23 pigs, now 80; then 63 sheep,
       now 176; then 40 goats, now 57.
  9 Freemen; 142 acres.
    4 smallholders.
    Always 5 ploughs.
    Meadow, 3½ acres; woodland at 6 pigs.
    The fourth part of a church, 1 acre.
Value of the whole then £16; now [£] 19 4s.
    It has 1 league in length and 7 furlongs in width; 5d in tax.   419 a
    Wulfwin had the jurisdiction.
    Adelelm holds the whole (of this) from Aubrey.

Half-Hundred of COSFORD
6 In ALDHAM Wulfwin held as a manor before 1066; 5½ carucates of
land.
    Then 7 villagers, now 4; then 6 slaves, now 2.
    Then 4 ploughs in lordship, now 3; then 6 men's ploughs, now 4.
    Meadow, 7 acres; woodland, 8 pigs; always 2 mills. 3 cobs; then
       10 cattle, now 18; then 80 pigs, now 60; then 140 sheep,
       now 60.
    A church with 7 acres.
Value then £8; now [£] 15.
In the same (Aldham) 1 free man, under patronage only, St.
Edmund's (had) the jurisdiction; 5 acres.
Value 10d.
    It has 8 furlongs in length and 7 in width; 5d in tax.

/ $\tilde{H}$ERTESMERA. $\tilde{H}$. In burgata liƀa femina . milda 7 Iin

wordam . ix . liƀi h̅o̅es Beſo . Aluuiñ . Godwinus Vluiet Botius.

Ordricus . Stanart . Godric . / In Strandeſtuna . ii . liƀi h̅o̅es

Fulcardus . Aluiñ . / In metles . iiii . liƀi homines . & dim̅ . Leuric.

Godric . Vluara . Leuũiñ . benne. Furcardus dim̅ . / In torham

. i . liƀ h̅o̅ . Vlmar̅ . In Richinge hala . i . liƀ h̅o̅ . Briƈtmar̅ . In gis

lingehā liƀ h̅o̅ Edricus . / In Wordhā . i . liƀ h̅o̅ . Colemanus . In metles

. i . liƀa femina Menleua . & habebat . xiiii . ac̅ . liƀæ terræ . 7 . t . r . e.

concefferat. illā terrā sc̅o eadmundo . In̅t totu̅ h̅nt alii lxxxx . ac̅

femp . vi . car̅ . & dim̅ . &̅ . i . ac̅ p̊ti . Semp ual lx . fol̅ . Totu̅ ten&

Adelalmus de alƀico. ex his liƀis hominibȝ habuit ante c̅ Alƀici

foca̅ . & comd . t . r . e . / In Giſlinghehā . iii . liƀi h̅o̅es . Vlmar̅ . Leſta r̅,

Lefquena xxiii . ac̅ . &̅ . i . car̅ . 7 ual iiii . fol̅ . 7 viii . den̅ . Ide̅ Adelaln̅

ten& de aƀico.

419 b

.XXXVI . / TERRA ROBERTI GRENONIS . S⸱nfort . h̅ . & dim̅.

Cercesfort tenuit Scapi teinnus Haroldi . ⱷ man̅ . i . car̅ terræ.

t . r . e . modo ten& Wittm de alno . de Roƀto . Tc̅ vi . uitt . modo

iiii . Tc̅ . iiii . borđ . modo . iii . Tc̅ . ii . feru̅ . m̊ . i . Tc̅ . ii . car̅ in dn̅ioȷ

modo . i . Tc̅ . i . car̅ & dim̅ hom̅ . modo . i . vii . ac̅ p̊ti . modo . i . mol̅.

Tc̅ . ii . runc̅ . & vi . an̅ . & c . xl . oūs . modo nichil . Tc̅ & p̊ ual lx.

fol̅ . modo . xl . h̅t . vi . qr̅ in longo . & . ii . in lato . & . iiii . den̅.

de gelto . Scapi habuit foca̅ fub haroldo.

/ Stotunā tenuit Ide̅ Scalpi t . r . e . ii . car̅ terræ . ⱷ man̅.

Tc̅ . viii . uitt . modo . v . Tc̅ . iiii . borđ . modo . v . Tc̅ . vi . feru̅ . modo . iii.

HARTISMERE Hundred

7 In BURGATE a free woman, Mild; and in WORTHAM 9 free men, Besi, Alwin, Godwin, Wulfgeat, Boti, Ordric, Stanhard, Godric. In THRANDESTON 2 free men, Fulcard, Alwin. In MELLIS 4 free men and a half (free man); Leofric, Godric, Wulfwaru, Leofwin Benne, and Fulcard the half (free man). In THORNHAM (Magna) 1 free man, Wulfmer. In RICKINGHALL (Superior) 1 free man, Brictmer. In GISLINGHAM a free man, Edric. In WORTHAM 1 free man, Coleman. In MELLIS 1 free woman, Menleva; she had 14 acres of free land, and before 1066 she had given that land to St. Edmund's. Between them all the others have 90 acres. Always 6½ ploughs.
   Meadow, 1 acre.
Value always 60s.
   Adelelm holds the whole (of this) from Aubrey.
   Over these free men Aubrey's predecessor had jurisdiction and patronage before 1066.

8 In GISLINGHAM 3 free men, Wulfmer, Leofstan, Leofcwen; 23 acres. 1 plough.
Value 4s 8d.
   Adelelm also holds (this) from Aubrey.

LAND OF ROBERT GERNON

SAMFORD Hundred and a Half

1 Scalpi, a thane of Harold's, held CHURCHFORD as a manor; 1 carucate of land before 1066. Now William *de Alno* holds (it) from Robert.
   Then 6 villagers, now 4; then 4 smallholders, now 3; then 2 slaves, now 1.
   Then 2 ploughs in lordship, now 1; then 1½ men's ploughs, now 1.
   Meadow, 7 acres; now 1 mill. Then 2 cobs, 6 cattle, 140 sheep; now nothing.
Value then and later 60s; now 40[s].
   It has 6 furlongs in length and 2 in width; 4d in tax. Scalpi had the jurisdiction under Harold.

2 Scalpi also held STUTTON before 1066; 2 carucates of land as a manor.
   Then 8 villagers, now 5; then 4 smallholders, now 5; then 6 slaves, now 3.

Tc & p̄.ii.car̄ in dn̄io.modo.i.ſemp.ii.car̄ hom̄.v.ac̄ p̄ti.ſilua
xvi.porc̄.ſemp.i.mol.&.ii.ſalinæ.dim̄ ecclia xv.ac̄.Tc̄.ii.
runc̄.Tc̄ xvi.an̄.modo.ii.Tc̄ xl.porc̄.modo.xiiii.Tc̄.clxxxx,
ōus.modo xxxv.Tc̄ & p̄ ual vi.lib.modo.lx.ᵸſol.ᷗt vi.q̄r
in longo.& iiii.in lato.&.iiii.d̄ de gelto.Id̄ē Wiᵵᵵm̄.Soca eod̄ m̄.

⌐In branthā.i.lib̄ ᷉h̄ Mauua com̄d tantū.v.ac̄ & dim̄.7 ual
   xii.d̄.Id̄ē Wiᵵᵵ haʀoldu̇s ſocā.

⌐Manesfort tenuit Sc̄s benedic̄tus de ɾameſeia ᴉn dn̄io.t̄.r̄.c̄,
   modo id̄ē.W.p̄ man̄.i.car̄ terræ.7 dim̄ ſemper.ii.uiᵵt.Tc̄.iiii.
   bord̄.modo.v.Tc̄ & p̄ ii.car̄ in dn̄io.modo.i.Semp.i.car̄ hom̄,
   iii.ac̄ p̄ti.&.i.mol.Tc̄.ii.runc̄.Tc̄.v.an̄.modo.iii.Tc̄ xv.
   porc̄.modo.v.ſemp.xxx.ōus.Tc̄ & p̄ ual xl.ſol.modo.xx.
   ᷗt vi.q̄r in longo.& iii.ᴉn lato.7 iii.den̄ &.i.ferding de gelto,
   Sc̄s.benedic̄tus.ſocam.

420 a
⌐ In alfildeſtuna.tenuit.Aluuiᵰ liḃ᷉ com̄datus Alurico ante ceſſori
   Roḃti.xxx.ac̄ terræ ꝑ man̄.t.r.e.ſemp dim̄ car̄.& ual&.iiii.ſol.
   Haroldus ſocā.Id̄ē W.

⌐TVRchetleſtunā ten̄ Grimmus liḃ᷉ h̄ com̄datus Guert.i.car̄
   terræ ꝑ man̄.t̄.r̄.c̄.ſemp.ii.uiᵵt.&.ii.bord̄.Tc̄ & poſt.i.car̄.modo
   nichil.7.ii.parꞇ piſcariæ.ſemp.i.car̄ hom̄.Tc̄ ual xl.ſol.modo
   xxx.viii.Id̄ē W.hoc Reuocaꞇ Roḃ ꝓ eſcaᵑg.de terra hugoniſ
   de monte forti.haroldus ſocā.

Then and later 2 ploughs in lordship, now 1; always 2 men's ploughs.

Meadow, 5 acres; woodland, 16 pigs. Always 1 mill; 2 salt-houses. ½ church, 15 acres.

Then 2 cobs; then 16 cattle, now 2; then 40 pigs, now 14; then 190 sheep, now 35.

Value then and later £6; now 60s.

It has 6 furlongs in length and 4 in width; 4d in tax.

William also [holds this].

The jurisdiction [was held] in the same way.

3 In BRANTHAM 1 free man, Mawa, under patronage only; 5½ acres.

Value 12d.

William [holds this].

Harold (had) the jurisdiction.

4 St. Benedict's of Ramsey held MANESFORT in lordship before 1066.

Now William also [holds it] as a manor; 1½ carucates of land.

Always 2 villagers. Then 4 smallholders, now 5.

Then and later 2 ploughs in lordship, now 1; always 1 men's plough.

Meadow, 3 acres; 1 mill. Then 2 cobs; then 5 cattle, now 3; then 15 pigs, now 5; always 30 sheep.

Value then and later 40s; now 20[s].

It has 6 furlongs in length and 3 in width; 3¼d in tax. St. Benedict's (had) the jurisdiction.

5 Alwin, a free man under the patronage of Aelfric, Robert's predecessor, held ALFILDESTUNA; 30 acres of land as a manor before 1066. Always ½ plough.   420 a

Value 4s.

Harold (had) the jurisdiction.

William also [holds this].

6 Grim, a free man under the patronage of Gyrth, held TURCHETLESTUNA; 1 carucate of land as a manor before 1066.

Always 2 villagers; 2 smallholders.

Then and later 1 plough, now nothing. 2 parts of a fishery. Always 1 men's plough.

Value then 40s; now 38[s].

William also [holds this]. Robert claims this by exchange with the land of Hugh de Montfort.

Harold (had) the jurisdiction.

⌐Brantham tenuit Idē Grimus.lx.aē.ꝓ mañ.t.r.e.ſemp

.ɪ.borđ.Tē & poſt đim car.modo.ɪɪ.boū.ɪ.aē p̄ti.Tē & p̄ ual.x.

ſot.& vɪɪɪ đ.m̄.v.ſot.Idē W.hoc &iā reuocat Roƀ eođ m̄.harol-

⌐In hulfereſtuna ten& Aluret cōmdatus Scalpio ⌐dus ſocam.

lxxx.aē.ꝓ mañ.t.r.e.m̄ Roƀ in dominio.ſemp ɪɪɪ.borđ.

Tē & poſt.ɪ.car.in dn̄o.modo đim̄.&.ɪ.aē p̄ti.Tē ual xvɪ.ſot.

modo.x.

⌐In tatiſtuna.Trumuiñ 7 ulſius liƀi hós comđ.c.xx.aē.ꝓ

.ɪɪ.mañ.t.r.e.ſemp.ɪ.borđ.Tē & p̄.ɪɪ.car.modo.ɪ.&.ɪɪ.aē p̄ti.

Tē ual.x.ſot.modo.vɪɪɪ.

⌐In Stuttuna teñ Ætnod liƀ hō cm̄đ.lx.aē.ꝓ mañ.t.r.e.Tē

& p̄.ɪ.car.m̄ đim̄.&.ɪ.aē p̄ti.Tē ual.x.ſot.m̄.vɪɪɪ.

⌐In branthā.tela.liƀa femina.cōmđ.xxx.aē ꝓ mañ.t.r.e.

ſemp.ɪ.borđ.& dim̄ car.&.ɪ.aē p̄ti.Tē & p̄ ual.v.ſot.m̄.ɪɪɪ.

7 vɪ.deñ.& .obot.⌐In tatiſtuna.ten Aluricus liƀ homo.

comđ.xxx.aē ꝓ mañ.7.ɪɪ.borđ.Tē & p̄ dim̄.car.modo.ɪɪ.boū.

420 b

&.ɪ.aē p̄ti.Tunc ual xl deñ.modo xl.ɪɪ.

⌐In hercheſteda.Aluric liƀ hō comđ.xxx.aē.pro mañ.t.r.e.

Tē & p̄ dim̄ car.modo.ɪɪ.boū.& dim̄ aē p̄ti.Tē ual.v.ſot.m̄ xlɪɪ.đ.

⌐In eduineſtuna Spieta liƀ hō comđ.xxx.aē.ꝓ mañ.t.r.e.Tē

dim̄ car.Tē ual.v.ſot.m̄ xl.ɪɪ.đ.In h̄ hundreto.h̄t.vɪɪ.liƀ hóes

comđ Roƀ in dn̄io.cxx.aē.ſemp.ɪɪɪ.car.Tē ual xx.ſot.m̄ xxv.

Haroldus ſocam.

7 Grim also held BRANTHAM; 60 acres as a manor before 1066.
Always 1 smallholder.
Then and later ½ plough, now 2 oxen. Meadow, 1 acre.
Value then and later 10s 8d; now 5s.
William also [holds this]. Robert claims this in the same way.
Harold (had) the jurisdiction.

8 In WOLVERSTONE Alfred, under the patronage of Scalpi, [held] 80
acres as a manor before 1066. Now Robert [holds it] in lordship.
Always 3 smallholders.
Then and later 1 plough in lordship, now ½. Meadow, 1 acre.
Value then 16s; now 10[s].

9 In TATTINGSTONE Trumwin and Wulfsi, free men under patronage;
120 acres as 2 manors before 1066.
Always 1 smallholder.
Then and later 2 ploughs, now 1. Meadow, 2 acres.
Value then 10s; now 8[s].

10 In STUTTON Ednoth, a free man under patronage, held 60 acres as a
manor before 1066. Then and later 1 plough, now ½.
Meadow, 1 acre.
Value then 10s; now 8[s].

11 In BRANTHAM Tela, a free woman under patronage; 30 acres as a
manor before 1066.
Always 1 smallholder;
½ plough. Meadow, 1 acre.
Value then and later 5s; now 3[s] 6½d.

12 In TATTINGSTONE Aelfric, a free man under patronage, held 30 acres
as a manor.
2 smallholders.
Then and later ½ plough, now 2 oxen. Meadow, 1 acre.   420 b
Value then 40d; now 42[d].

13 In HARKSTEAD Aelfric, a free man under patronage; 30 acres as a
manor before 1066. Then and later ½ plough, now 2 oxen.
Meadow, ½ acre.
Value then 5s; now 42d.

14 In EDUINESTUNA Spieta, a free man under patronage; 30 acres as a
manor before 1066. Then ½ plough.
Value then 5s; now 42d.

15 In this Hundred Robert has in lordship 7 free men under patronage;
120 acres. Always 3 ploughs.
Value then 20s; now 25[s].
Harold (had) the jurisdiction.

$\digamma$ *COSFORT* . $\tilde{H}$. In Latham xx . aͨ . de d͠nio de ciꞇesfort qᵭ
tenuit Scapi⁹ . & uaɫ . ɪɪɪ . foɫ . Wiɫɫ de alno ꞉ ten&c.

$\digamma$ In Colenes . hunᵭ . ɪ . liɓ hͦ . ɪɪ . aͨ . liɓæ terræ . & uaɫ . ɪɪɪɪ . ᵭ . Idͤ ten&c.

.XXXVII. $\digamma$ **T**RÆ PETRI DE VALONIS. *BRADEMERA*. $\tilde{H}$. ★

Fachenham tenuit Aleſtaͦ teinnus ᵱ ma͠n . v . car̓ terræ . femp
xɪɪɪɪ . uiɫɫ . & vɪɪ . borᵭ . 7 . x . fer̓ . 7 femp . v . car̓ in d͠no . 7 ɪɪɪɪ . car̓ hͦm.
xvɪ . aͨ p̓ti . ſilua de . vɪɪɪ . porͨ . femp . ɪ . moli͠n . Tͨ . ɪɪɪɪ . runͨ . m̓ . ɪɪɪ.
7 xvɪ . equæ ſiluatice . femp . xɪɪ . an̓ Tͨ xl . porͨ . m̓ . xx . ſep̓ . ccc . oͧs.
Duæ æcclie xl . aͨ . 7 . ɪ . car̓ . & dim̓ aͨ p̓ti . huic ma͠n iacent . vɪ . foͨ
7 dim̓ . xxx . aͨ . femp . ɪ . car̓ . femp xɪɪɪ . liɓ . ħt . ɪ . l͡g in longo . &c . vɪɪɪ.

421 a

qr̓ in lato . 7 . ɪɪ . foɫ de gelto . In eaᵭ . xx liɓi hͦes de qᵭbᷟ habuit Aleſtaͦ
comᵭ . lxxx . aͨ . femp . ɪɪ . car̓ . & . ɪɪɪ . aͨ prati . & uaɫ xx . foɫ . hoc reclamat de dono regis . $\digamma$ In torp . ɪ . liɓ hͦ . Spauoc . xxx aͨ . hic fuit hͦ
regine edit . & dedit eͧ . petro⁹ . ᵱ mortͤ ei⁹ conceſſit ei . rex . ut dicͭ fui hͦes.

$\digamma$ In Sapeſtuna . ɪɪɪ . liɓi hoͤs . xɪɪɪ . aͨ . 7 dim̓ terræ inͭ eos femp . ɪ . car̓.
7 . ɪ . aͨ p̓ti . hoc eſt de dono regis . & uaɫ . v . foɫ.

5 In WYKEN Alan held 1 carucate of land as a manor before 1066.
    Always 5 smallholders. Then 2 slaves, now 1.
    Then 1 plough in lordship, now 2. Meadow, 3 acres; woodland at
        8 pigs. 2 men's oxen.
    Now 1 cob; then 3 cattle, now 11; then 7 pigs, now 13; then 40
        sheep, now 100.
    2 Freemen; 10 acres. Always 2 oxen.
    Value then 20s; now 30[s].
    In the same (Wyken) 8 free men under patronage; 1 carucate of land.
    11 smallholders.
    Always 2 ploughs.
    Meadow, 3 acres; woodland, 2 pigs.
    Value then 10s; now 20[s].
    He has this by a delivery and for land.

6 Auti and Ketel, free men (and) thanes, held RUSHFORD before 1066;
    2 carucates of land. Then 2 ploughs in lordship; now (the same).
    Meadow, 4 acres. Now 1 cob; then 1 cattle, now 5; then 11 sheep,
        now 80; 4 beehives.
    Those men held this land before 1066 as two manors.
    Value always 30s.
    In the same (Rushford) 8 free men; 1 carucate of land and 9 acres.
    7 under patronage and subject to fold-rights, and 1 under patronage
    only. Then and later 2 ploughs, now 1.
    Meadow, 4 acres.
    Value 10s.
    It has 6 furlongs in length and 3 furlongs in width; 11¼d in tax.
    St. Edmund's has jurisdiction over the whole Hundred.

HARTISMERE Hundred   421 b
7 In WESTHORPE 1 free man under patronage, Auti: 9 acres.
    Woodland for 2 pigs.
    Value 18d.

38   LAND OF ROGER OF RAMES

BABERGH Two Hundreds
1 In BURES Earl Algar held 1 carucate of land. Now Roger [holds it].
    1 villager, 3 smallholders, 1 slave.
    1 plough in lordship; 1 men's plough.
    Meadow, 2 acres; then ½ mill, now none. Always 1 horse, 30 pigs,
        100 sheep.
    Value 20s.

⌐In linhou . ten& uluric⁹ . fub alurico cāpo . t . r . e . 7 poterant uen -
dere . xxx . ac̄ . & . ɪɪɪɪ . bord . & . ɪɪɪ . boū . & ual . xvɪɪɪ . fol . Socā
7 facā . sc̄s . e.

⌐*DIMID* . *H̄* . De gepefwiz . In uilla de gepefuiz h̄t . Roḡ
. ɪ . ecc̄liā sc̄i georgii . 7 . ɪɪɪɪ . burḡnfes . 7 . vɪ . uaftatas manfuras
una ex his derationata . fuit ad op⁹ abb̄is de eli . & . inde faifit⁹
fuit . tefte hund̄ . fed Roḡ dicit qd̄ ten& de rege . Sup̄ dicte ecc̄liæ
ptin& . ɪ . ac̄ . t̄re . Totā ual . x . fol . Rex h̄t confuetudinē.

⌐*BOSEMERA* . *H̄* . In Crofelda . ten̄ Edricus lib̄ h̄o . t . r . e .
xx . ac̄ . Tc̄ . ɪ . car̄ . 7 m̄; Tc̄ . ɪɪɪɪ . runc̄ . modo nullus . Tc̄ . ɪɪ . an̄.
Tc̄ xɪɪ . porc̄ . 7 . v . ous̄ . m̄ int totū nichil femp ual xL . den̄.
In ead̄ ten̄ Wicolfus . lib̄e . t . r . e . xxxv . ac̄ qs tenebat ille . Edric̄
cū fua terra qd̄o lib̄ata fuit Roḡo . femp ɪɪɪɪ . bord . filua . x.
porc̄ . & . ɪɪ . ac̄ p̄ti . & ual . vɪɪɪ . fol.

⌐In Codehā . ɪɪɪ . lib̄i . h̄oes . xxx . ac̄ . & . ɪ . bord . Tc̄ & p̄ . ɪ . car̄ . modo
dim̄ . & . ɪ . ac̄ & dim̄ p̄ti . Tc̄ ual . vɪ . fol . modo . v . & qrta pars æcc̄lie
& qrta pars ex hoc qd̄ ecc̄liæ ptin& . hanc t̄rā tenuit Warenger⁹
de Rogero fed ipfe defaifiuit . Rex & coñs focā de toto.

⌐Eftenā ten̄ . ɪ . lib̄ h̄o . Aīlmarus fub Edrico ante ceffore Rob̄ . mal&
com̄d t̄ntū . t . r . e . p̄ mañ . Lx . ac̄ . femp . ɪ . bord . Tc̄ & poft . ɪ . car̄.
modo nulla . & . ɪɪ . ac̄ p̄ti . filua . de xxx . porc̄ . Ecc̄lia . de xɪɪɪɪ.
ac̄ . Tc̄ ual . xx . fol . m̄ . xv.

2 In *LINHOU* Wulfric [held] under Aelfric Kemp before 1066; they could sell; 30 acres before 1066.

>4 smallholders.
>3 oxen.
>St. Edmund's (has) full jurisdiction.

Half-Hundred of IPSWICH

3 In the town of IPSWICH Roger has 1 church, St. George's; 4 burgesses; and 6 destroyed dwellings. One of these (dwellings) was adjudged to be for the use of the Abbot of Ely and he was put in possession of it, as the Hundred testifies, but Roger says that he holds (it) from the King. To the above-mentioned church belongs 1 acre of land.

>Value of the whole, 10s.
>The King has the customary due.

BOSMERE Hundred

4 In CROWFIELD Edric, a free man, held 20 acres before 1066. Then 1 plough; now (the same).

>Then 4 cobs, now none. Then 2 cattle; then 12 pigs, 5 sheep; now nothing at all.
>Value always 40d.

In the same (Crowfield) before 1066 Wigulf held freely 35 acres which the same Edric held with his land when it was delivered to Roger.

>Always 4 smallholders.
>Woodland, 10 pigs; meadow, 2 acres.
>Value 8s.

5 In CODDENHAM 3 free men; 30 acres.   422 a

>1 smallholder.
>Then and later 1 plough, now ½. Meadow, 1½ acres.
>Value then 6s; now 5[s].
>The fourth part of a church and the fourth part of what belongs to the church.
>Warengar held this land from Roger but he dispossessed (him).
>The King and the Earl (have) jurisdiction over the whole.

6 Aethelmer, 1 free man under patronage only held STONHAM (Aspal) before 1066 under Edric, Robert Malet's predecessor, as a manor, 60 acres.

>Always 1 smallholder.
>Then and later 1 plough, now none.
>Meadow, 2 acres; woodland at 30 pigs.
>A church with 14 acres.
>Value then 20s; now 15[s].

In ead . i . lib hō . Aluuin̄ in ſoca regis . LXXXX . ac̄ . ꝑ man̄ . ſemp . i.

uiłł & . i . borđ . 7 tc̄ . ii . car̄ . in dn̄io . modo . i . & . iiii . ac̄ p̄ti . ſilu

xx . porc̄ . Tc̄ uał xL . ſoł . modo . xxv . Rex & Coms̄ ſoca.

In ead . lib hō . de Lx . ac̄ . & . i . borđ . & . i . uiłł . Tc̄ . & p . i . car̄ . modo

dim̄ . Tc̄ . i . car̄ hom̄ . modo dim̄ . & . i . ac̄ p̄ti . ſilua . xx . porc̄ . Tc̄

uał xx . ſoł . m̄ . xv . Rex & coms̄ ſoca . In ead lib hō de xxx . ac̄

& . i . borđ . Tc̄ & . p . i . car̄ . modo dim̄ . Silua de . x . porc̄ . Tc̄ uał . x.

ſoł . modo . v . Rex & coms̄ ſoca . In ead . viii . libi hōes . xxx . ac̄.

duo ex his fuer̄ com̄dati cuidā hōi com̄dato ante ceſſori Roƀ.

mał & . & Wiłłm̄ pat̄ ſuus inde ſaiſitus fuit . Int̄ eos oms̄ hnt

. i . car̄ . & uał . v . ſoł . h totū ten milo de Roḡ . & recepit . iiii . eq̄s

m̄ . i . Tc̄ . iii . an̄ . m̄ . iii . Tc̄ . xiiii . porc̄ . modo . xxxvi . Tc̄ xxxvi.

ōus . m̄ nułł . ht̄ dim̄ łg in longo . & dim̄ in lato . & . vi . đ . de gelto.

Alii ibi tenent . Rex ǀ coms̄ . ſoca.

In ead . R . ht̄ in dn̄io Eſtuna . xii . libi hōes . de . xL . ac̄ . in ſoca

reḡ . & comitis . Tc̄ & p . ii . car̄ . m̄ . i . car̄ & dim̄ . & . i . ac̄ p̄ti.

422 b
& uał & xv . ſoł.

In brieſeta . ten & Anſchetillus de Rogō . i . car̄ terræ ꝑ man̄ in

ſoca regis & comitis q̄ tenuit Goduuin liƀ hō . t . r . e . Tc̄ . ii . borđ.

modo . v . Ecclia de xv . ac̄ . ſemp . i . car̄ . in dn̄io . modo . ii . boū . hom̄.

& . ii . ac̄ p̄ti . 7 xL . ii . ōus . 7 xv . porc̄ . Tc̄ uał . xx . ſoł . modo xxv . Tota

ht̄ . i . łg in longo . & dim̄ in lato . & vi . đ & obolū de gelto . alii ibi tenēt.

In the same (Stonham Aspal) 1 free man, Alwin, in the King's jurisdiction; 90 acres as a manor.
   Always 1 villager; 1 smallholder.
   Then 2 ploughs in lordship, now 1.
   Meadow, 4 acres; woodland, 20 pigs.
Value then 40s; now 25[s].
   The King and the Earl (have) the jurisdiction.
In the same (Stonham Aspal) a free man, with 60 acres.
   1 smallholder, 1 villager.
   Then and later 1 plough, now ½; then 1 men's plough, now ½.
   Meadow, 1 acre; woodland, 20 pigs.
Value then 20s; now 15[s].
   The King and the Earl (have) the jurisdiction.
In the same (Stonham Aspal) 1 free man, with 30 acres.
   1 smallholder.
   Then and later 1 plough, now ½. Woodland at 10 pigs.
Value then 10s; now 5[s].
   The King and the Earl (have) the jurisdiction.
In the same (Stonham Aspal) 8 free men; 30 acres. Two of these were under the patronage of a man (who was) under the patronage of Robert Malet's predecessor, and William (Malet), his father, was in possession of that (patronage). Between them all they have 1 plough.
Value 5s.
   Miles holds the whole of this from Roger.
   He acquired 4 horses, now 1; 3 cattle, now 3; then 14 pigs,
      now 36; then 36 sheep, now none.
   It has ½ league in length and ½ in width; 6d in tax. Others hold there. The King and the Earl (have) the jurisdiction.

7 In the same STONHAM (Aspal) Roger has in lordship; 12 free men, with 40 acres, in the jurisdiction of the King and the Earl. Then and later 2 ploughs, now 1½ ploughs.
   Meadow, 1 acre.
Value 15s.

422 b

8 In BRICETT Ansketel holds from Roger 1 carucate of land as a manor, in the jurisdiction of the King and the Earl. Godwin, a free man, held it before 1066.
   Then 2 smallholders, now 5.
   A church with 15 acres.
   Always 1 plough in lordship. Now 2 men's oxen.
   Meadow, 2 acres. 42 sheep, 15 pigs.
Value then 20s; now 25[s].
   The whole has 1 league in length and ½ in width; 6½d in tax.
Others hold there.

⌐In Langhedana teñ filia Roḡ . ı . lib hm̃ . ıx . ac̄ . & ual xvııı . đ.
⌐In Codenhā . ı . lib hō Aluuiñ . ı . ac̄ . & ual . ıı . đ . & in ead . ıııı . ac̄
de dñio &   app̄ciate funt.

⌐*CLAINDVNE . H̃* . Achrehā tenuit Goduinus pb̄r . lib hō
t . r . e . ı . car̃ tr̃æ . 7 xx . ac̄ ꝑ mañ . modo filia Roḡ . Tc̄ in dñio . ıı . car̄.
m̃ . ııı . & . ıııı . ac̄ p̃ti . & . ıı . runc̄ . & . vıı . añ . & vı . porc᷃ . Tc̄ ual . xx
ıııı . fol . & m̃ fimilit̄ . In ead . ı . lib hō . Gotwin . c . ac̄ . ꝑ mañ . Tc̄.
ııı . borđ . 7 modo . ı . Tc̄ . ı . car̄ . & modo . & . ıı . ac̄ & dim̃ p̃ti . Tc̄ ual xvı.
fol . modo . xıx . 7 ıııı . đ . In ead . ı . lib hō Aluricus . c̄omdatus faxo aute
ceffori piperel xl . ac̄ . femꝑ . ı . car̄ . & . ı . ac̄ p̃ti . Tc̄ ual . vı . fol . 7 vııı . đ.
modo . x . In ead Sunwiñ lib hō tenuit Guert . c̄omđ . xxx̃ . ac̄.
ꝑ mañ . t . r . e . Tc̄ . ı . car̄ . & . ı . ac̄ & dim̃ p̃ti . & ual . vı . fol.
In ead Turbnus pb̄r lib hō tenuit . xxx . ac̄ . ꝑ mañ . t . r . e . Tc̄ . ı . car̄.
Tc̄ . ı . borđ . Tc̄ ual . v . fol . m̃ . x . 7 . x . đ . Rex & com̄s foca . & c̄omđ.
In ead . xxxv . libi hōes . cc . & . ııı . ac̄ . & dim̃ . & . ıı . ac̄ p̃ti . Tc̄ . vıı . car̄
m̃ dim̃ Tc̄ ual xl . fol . modo . v . lib . & ıx . fol . Rex et C . focā . hf̄ . ı . lḡ
in longo . & . vıı . qr̄ in lato . 7 xx . đ de gelto.
⌐In Weftrefelda . ııı . libi hōes . xx . vııı . ac̄ . Tc̄ & p̃ . ı . car̄ . modo

423 a
nichil . & . ı . ac̄ p̃ti . & ual . x . fol . Rex & com̄s focā.
⌐In toddenham . xx . ac̄ in dñio de totdenhā . & c̄ in p̃tio.

9 In *LANGHEDANA* Roger's daughter holds 1 free man; 9 acres.
Value 18d.

10 In CODDENHAM 1 free man, Alwin; 1 acre.
Value 2d.
In the same (Coddenham) 4 acres in lordship.
They have been assessed.

CLAYDON Hundred

11 Godwin the priest, a free man, held AKENHAM before 1066; 1 carucate
of land and 20 acres as a manor. Now Roger's daughter holds (it).
Then 2 ploughs in lordship, now 3.
    Meadow, 4 acres. 2 cobs, 7 cattle, 6 pigs.
    Three parts of a church, 12 acres.
Value then 24s; now the same.
In the same (Akenham) Godwin, a free man [under the patronage
of] Gyrth; 100 acres as a manor.
    Then 3 smallholders, now 1.
    Then 1 plough, now (the same). Meadow, 2½ acres.
Value then 16s; now 19[s] 4d.
In the same (Akenham) 1 free man, Aelfric, under the patronage of
Saxi, (Ranulf) Peverel's predecessor; 40 acres. Always 1 plough.
    Meadow, 1 acre.
Value then 6s 8d; now 10[s].
In the same (Akenham) Sunwin, a free man under the patronage of
Gyrth, held 36 acres as a manor before 1066. Then 1 plough.
    Meadow, 1½ acres.
Value 6s.
In the same (Akenham) Thorbern the priest, a free man, held 30
acres as a manor before 1066. Then 1 plough.
    Then 1 smallholder.
Value then 5s; now 10[s] 10d.
    The King and the Earl (have) the jurisdiction and the patronage.
In the same (Akenham) 35 free men; 203½ acres.
    Meadow, 2 acres.
    Then 7 ploughs, now ½.
Value then 40s; now £5 9s.
    The King and the Earl (have) the jurisdiction. It has 1 league in
length and 7 furlongs in width; 20d in tax.

12 In WESTERFIELD 3 free men; 28 acres. Then and later 1 plough, now
nothing.
    Meadow, 1 acre.
Value 10s.
    The King and the Earl (have) the jurisdiction.

423 a

13 In TUDDENHAM 20 acres of the lordship of Tuddenham.
It is in the assessment.

In Weſtrefelda . v . libi hões . xx . iii . aē . & . i . uirga . Tē & p̃ . i . caŕ.
modo nuℓℓ . 7 uaℓ . iiii . foℓ . Giroldus ten& . In ead . i . lib hõ . xvi.
aē . Tē & p̃ dim̃ . caŕ . modo . nuℓ . & uaℓ . xxx . ii . d . Rex & cõs focā,
Ernaldus teñ de eo.

In li hund . xx . aē quē p̃tinent eccℓiæ de totdenham.

Niuuetunã teñ ernaldus de roḡ . quē teñ Brictmarus lib hõ
t . r . e . c . ii . aē . p̃ mañ . t . r . e . Tē & p̃ . ii . uiℓℓi . & . ii . bord . modo . iiii.
bord . femp . i . caŕ in dñio . Tē & p̃ . ii . caŕ hom̃ . m̃ nichil . & . ii . aē
p̃ti . & . i . ruñ . Tē xx . porc̃ . modo xvi . Tē xx . oũs . modo xii.
7 uaℓ . xx . foℓ . In ead teñ Leuefunus . lib hõ cõmd . Stigando . xl.
aē . p̃ mañ . t . r . e . Tē & p̃ . i . caŕ . m̃ . ii . bou . & . i . aē . p̃ti . Tē uaℓ . xx . foℓ,
modo . x . Rad de Roḡ Rex & cõs de toto focā.

In Codeham teñ . Roḡ in dñio . vi . libos hões . xxvi . aē . in foc reḡ
& comitis . Tē & p̃ . ii . caŕ . modo . i . & . i . aē . p̃ti . 7 uaℓ . xii . foℓ . ii . d . miñ,

In helminchã . i . lib hõ Leuredus . xx . aē . Tē & p̃ . i . caŕ . modo nichil.
7 uaℓ . iii . foℓ . 7 . i . d . Rex & cõs de toto focā.

In eſtuna . xv . aē dñicæ terræ . & . in p̃tio . milo ten& de roḡo.

In Codehã teñ Aluric̃ . 7 boti . libi hões . boti ix . aē . & dim̃ . Tē . dim̃
caŕ . m̃ . ii . bou . 7 uaℓ . iii . foℓ . Idē milo.

14 In WESTERFIELD 5 free men; 23 acres and 1 pole. Then and later 1 plough, now none.
Value 4s.
　Gerald holds (this).
In the same (Westerfield) 1 free man; 16 acres. Then and later ½ plough, now none.
Value 32d.
　The King and the Earl (have) the jurisdiction.
　Arnold holds (this) from him.

15 In this Hundred, 20 acres which belong to the church of Tuddenham.

16 Arnold holds NEWTON from Roger; Brictmer, a free man, held it before 1066; 102 acres as a manor before 1066.
　Then and later 2 villagers and 2 smallholders; now 4 smallholders.
　Always 1 plough in lordship. Then and later 2 men's ploughs, now nothing.
　Meadow, 2 acres. 1 cob; then 20 pigs, now 16; then 20 sheep, now 12.
Value 20s.
In the same (Newton) Leofson, a free man under the patronage of Stigand, held 40 acres as a manor before 1066. Then and later 1 plough, now 2 oxen.
　Meadow, 1 acre.
Value then 20s; now 10[s].
　Ralph [holds this] from Roger.
　The King and the Earl (have) jurisdiction over the whole.

17 In CODDENHAM Roger holds in lordship 6 free men, in the jurisdiction of the King and the Earl; 26 acres. Then and later 2 ploughs, now 1.
　Meadow, 1 acre.
Value 12s less 2d.

18 In HELMINGHAM 1 free man, Leofred; 20 acres. Then and later 1 plough, now nothing.
Value 3s 1d.
　The King and the Earl (have) jurisdiction over the whole.

19 In STONHAM (Aspal) 15 acres of lordship land.
　(It is) in the assessment.
　Miles holds (this) from Roger.

20 In CODDENHAM Aelfric and Boti, free men, held 9½ acres. Then ½ plough, now 2 oxen.
Value 3s.
　Miles also [holds this].

⌐ *SANFORT*. $\tilde{H}$. & dim̃ . In heihã . teñ . firic̉ lib̃ hõ . xxx . ac̃ . ꝑ mañ.
t . r . e . femp dim̃ car̉ . & tc̃ ual& . v . fol . modo . viii . Garengerus teñ,
haroldus foca in b̃colt.

★ ⌐ $\tilde{H}$. De *CARLEFORDA*. In tudenhã Geroldus . i . lib̃ h̃m̃ Aluric
diaconv̄ com̃d Saxæ . de ab̃b̃e . t r . e . xii . ac̃ . ꝑ mañ . iii . bord̃.
Semp . i . car̉ . ii . ac̃ p̃ti . Tc̃ . i . runc̉ . 7 femp . ii . añ . & . xi . porc̉ . & xl.
oūs . & ual . iii . fol . 7 jn ead̃ . ii . libi h̃oes . com̃d . i . fc̃e Æ . & alter
com̃d . heroldi . x . ac̃ . 7 dim̃ car̉ . & ual . ii . fol . h̃ ten& . Geroldus.
de . R.

⌐ In Grundefbur Raulfus . xx . ac̃ & ꝑtinent ad neutuna . & in
p̃tio jn finlesford . vi . ac̃ . i . ac̃ de p̃to & ꝑtinent ad neutuna in
aliã hund . hoc ten& Radulfus.

⌐ In oteleia . iiii . ac̃ . & ꝑtinent ad eftuna . & in p̃tio h̃ teñ Milo de ◦
belefol.

⌐ *COLENESSE* . $\tilde{H}$. In kirketuna . ii . ac̃ . & ual . iiii . đ.

⌐ *LOSA* . $\tilde{H}$. In udebrige . i . lib̃ hõ . com̃d Aluuini . xi . ac̃ . dim̃
ac̃ p̃ti . & ual xxvii . đ.

SAMFORD Hundred and a Half

21 In HIGHAM Siric, a free man, held 30 acres as a manor before 1066.
Always ½ plough.
Value then 5s; now 8[s].
Warengar holds (this).
Harold (had) the jurisdiction in (East) Bergholt.

Hundred of CARLFORD 423 b

22 In TUDDENHAM Gerald [holds] 1 free man, Aelfric the deacon, under
the patronage of Saxi from the Abbot (of Ely) before 1066; 12 acres
as a manor.
3 smallholders.
Always 1 plough.
Meadow, 2 acres. Then 1 cob. Always 2 cattle, 11 pigs, 40 sheep.
Value 3s.
In the same (Tuddenham) 2 free men, 1 under the patronage of St.
Etheldreda's, the other under the patronage of Harold; 10 acres. ½
plough.
Value 2s.
Gerald [holds this] from Roger.

23 In GRUNDISBURGH Ralph [holds] 20 acres. They belong to Newton.
(They are) in the assessment.

24 In 'FINLESFORD' 6 acres.
Meadow, 1 acre.
They belong to Newton in another Hundred.
Ralph holds this.

25 In OTLEY 4 acres. They belong to Stonham (Aspal).
(They are) in the assessment.
Miles *de Belefol* holds this.

COLNEIS Hundred

26 In KIRTON 2 acres.
Value 4d.

LOES Hundred

27 In WOODBRIDGE 1 free man under the patronage of Alwin; 11 acres.
Meadow, ½ acre.
Value 27d.

.XXXVIIII./ TERRE . R . FRIS ILgeri . Coleneffe . h . In burg . 1 . lib homo Godricus . com . cuida com . horoldi xvi ac terræ . 11 bord . dim . car.
dim ac pti . ual . 111 . fol . 7 in tremelaia . 11 . ac . 7 . 1111 . d . ual.

/ In moreftona . 1 . lib ho . comd Brifmer . 1111 . ac . xii . d . ual.

/ In faltenam . xxvi . ac . ten ide . Bri . t . r . e . p man . Tc . 1 . car . 7 . 1.
runc . & . 1111 . an . & . xl . ous . modo int totu nichil . Tc ual . x.
fol . modo . v . fol . hic Brictmarus habuit plures terras . & queda

424 a

pars fuit libata ex parte regis ingelrico . Et alie partes . Randulfo
fri ilgeri . & tertia pars Radulfo pinello . 7 in ifta tertia parte fuit
ifta fup dicta terra delibata Rad fic ipfe dicit & ide pib& h . tefti
moni . quod ipfe fuit faifitus inpmis . f7 utru ex parte regis nec n
fuiff& faifitus illud ignorant . & dicunt etia . quod ifta terra . R.
calupniau fup radulfu . & uice coms . Rog denominauit illis confti
tutu tp . m . ut ambo adfuiffent . Ranulfo ad ueniente : de fuit Radulfus . & idcirco diiudicauer hoes hundreti . Rannulfu ee . faifitum.
qui modo ten& . f& Rad pinel negat qd n fuit fummonit de eo
placito . / Immo teftuna . 1 . liba femina . Vlueua . comd . Bric . x . ac.
Tc dim car . modo . null . & ual . 11 . fol.

COLNEIS Hundred

1 In BURGH 1 free man, Godric, under the patronage of someone under the patronage of Harold; 16 acres of land.
   2 smallholders.
   ½ plough. Meadow, ½ acre.
   Value 3s.
   In TRIMLEY (St. Martin) 2 acres.
   Value 4d.

2 In MORSTON 1 free man under the patronage of Brictmer; 4 acres.
   Value 12d.

3 In FALKENHAM the same Brictmer held 26 acres before 1066 as a manor. Then 1 plough;
   1 cob, 4 cattle, 40 sheep; now nothing at all.
   Value then 10s; now 5s.

   This Brictmer had several lands, and a part was delivered on the   424 a
   King's behalf to Engelric; other parts (were delivered) to Ranulf the brother of Ilger; and a third part (was delivered) to Ralph Pinel. The above-mentioned land was delivered in that third part to Ralph, so he himself says, and he also produces the testimony of the Hundred that he was at first in possession of it; but whether he was put in possession on the King's behalf or not they do not know. They say also that Ranulf claimed that land against Ralph, and Roger the Sheriff specified to them a set time that they should both be present; (although) Ranulf came, Ralph was absent and therefore the men of the Hundred judged that Ranulf should be in possession. He now holds (it), but Ralph Pinel denies that he was summoned concerning that assembly.

4 In MORSTON 1 free woman, Wulfeva, under the patronage of Brictmer; 10 acres. Then ½ plough, now none.
   Value 2s.

In halmelega . ı . lıƀ hõ brıƈtmar . cõm̃d dım̃ . Briht . & alıã medıetat̃
Sẽa Edeldrede . t . r . e . modo ten& . R . de rege p̃ lıƀatıonẽ ad fuũ
Dominıũ . fed abbas dicit q̃d ıpfe deb& de eo tenere medietatẽ . xx . ıı .
ac : m̃ . nuł . 7 . ı . borđ . ı . aẽ p̃tı . 7 . ı . feru . 7 uał . ıııı . foł . In eađ . ı . lıƀ hõ
Vlwardus . cõm̃d . Godrici . t . r . e . xx . aẽ . terræ . & . ıı . borđ . & . ı . car̃
dım̃ aẽ p̃tı . & uał . ıııı . foł . Adhuc in eađ . ı . lıƀ hõ . harduuinus
cuıdã cõm̃d . N . 7 . đ . com̃ . Edrici . t . r . e . v . aẽ træ . & dım̃ car̃ .
dım̃ aẽ p̃tı . & uał . xıı . đ . In eađ . ı . lıƀ hõ Brihtric̃ . cõm̃d dım̃ . Brih
mar̃ 7 dım̃ . Stanmar . t . r . e . ıx . aẽ 7 dım̃ car̃ . dım̃ aẽ pratı . 7 uał . ııı . foł,
æcclıa . vııı . aẽ . & uał . ıı . foł .
lı totũ ten̄ . R . fr̃ ilgeri p̃ lıƀatıonẽ regis . 7 Wıłłmus denomore
de eo sẽa edeld . focã .

H̃ . DE CARLA forda . In merlefham tenet Ædwoldus . t . r . e .

424 b

. ıı . car̃ terræ . & dım̃ . p̃ man̄ . Semp̃ . x . uıłł . & x . borđ . Tẽ . ıı . feru . Semp̃
in dn̄ıo . ıı . car̃ . & houm̃ . Tẽ . v . car̃ . modo . ıııı . xıı . a p̃tı . modo . ı . moł .
fılua ad xvı . porc̃ . Tẽ . ııı . runc̃ . modo . v . Tẽ xx . ıııı . an̄ modo . xx . Tẽ
xl . porc̃ . modo xxvıı . Tẽ . ccc . oũs . modo . cc . xıı . Tẽ xvı . cap̄ . Tẽ . vı .
uafa apũ . modo . xıı . Tẽ uał . xl . foł . modo fimilıt̃ . & ħt . in longo . ı . łg̃
& v . qr̃ in lato . & de gelto . vı . đ . In eađ . ı . æcclıa . de xxx . vı . aẽ . & uał . ııı .
foł . & . ı . lıƀ hõ Godric̃ nom̃ xvı . aẽ . & . ı . borđ . & dım̃ car̃ . 7 . ı . aẽ p̃tı .
& uał& . ıı . foł .

424 a, b

5 In HEMLEY 1 free man, Brictmer, half under the patronage of Brict and the other half (under that) of St. Etheldreda's before 1066. Now Ranulf holds from the King by a delivery, for his lordship, but the Abbot (of Ely) says that he ought to hold a half from him; 22 acres. Then 1 plough, now none.
    1 smallholder.
    Meadow, 1 acre; 1 slave.
Value 4s.
In the same (Hemley) 1 free man, Wulfward, under the patronage of Godric before 1066; 20 acres of land.
    2 smallholders.
    1 plough. Meadow, ½ acre.
Value 4s.
Also in the same (Hemley) 1 free man Hardwin, [half] under the patronage of N. and half under the patronage of Edric before 1066; 5 acres of land. ½ plough.
    Meadow, ½ acre.
Value 12d.
In the same (Hemley) 1 free man, Brictric, half under the patronage of Brictmer and half (under that) of Stanmer before 1066; 9 acres. ½ plough.
    Meadow, ½ acre.
Value 3s.
    A church, 8 acres; value 2s.
    Ranulf brother of Ilger holds the whole of this through the King's delivery, and William of Bosc [holds it] from him.
    St. Etheldreda's (has) the jurisdiction.

Hundred of CARLFORD

6 In MARTLESHAM Edwold [held] before 1066; 2½ carucates of land as   424 b a manor.
    Always 10 villagers; 10 smallholders. Then 2 slaves.
    Always 2 ploughs in lordship. Then 5 men's ploughs, now 4.
    Meadow, 12 acres; now 1 mill; woodland for 16 pigs. Then 3
        cobs, now 5; then 24 cattle, now 20; then 40 pigs, now 27;
        then 300 sheep, now 212; then 16 goats; then 6 beehives,
        now 12.
Value then 40s; now the same.
    It has 1 league in length and 5 furlongs in width; 6d in tax.
In the same (Martlesham) 1 church with 36 acres; value 3s.
Also 1 free man, Godric by name; 16 acres.
    1 smallholder;
    ½ plough. Meadow, 1 acre.
Value 2s.

⌐In Waldinga felda teñ Brihtmař liƀ hõ . t̕ . e . ɪ . caȓ terræ ꝓ mañ.
7 . ɪ . borđ . Tc̄ . ɪɪ . caȓ . m̂ . ɪ . & . ɪ . mot̕ . Tc̄ . ɪ . runc̄ . Tc̄ . c . oūs . m̂ xxvɪɪ . Tc̄
xx . fot̕ . modo . x . 7 h̄t in longo . vɪ . qȓ . 7 in lat̕ . ɪɪɪ . 7 de gelto . v . deñ.
In eađ . v . liƀi hões comđati . Brihmari . dim̂ . 7 dim̂ . fuæ matri . xʟ . ac̄ . 7
. ɪ . caȓ . 7 uat̕ . ɪɪɪɪ . fot̕

★ ⌐In Preftetuna . x . liƀi hoc̕s . com̄dati . dim̂ Brihmari 7 dim̂ . Quengeu&
mat̕ ei . uñ ex his fuit com̄dat dim̂ . sc̄e . Æ . ɪ . caȓ træ . m̂ . ɪx . borđ . fuƀ
eis . Tc̄ . ɪɪɪɪ . caȓ . modo . ɪɪ . ɪ . ac̄ p̄ti . Tc̄ uat̕ xx . fot̕ . modo . x . 7 h̄t . vɪ . qȓ
in longo . 7 ɪɪɪ . in lato . 7 de gelto . vɪ . đ.

⌐In hafpelega . v . liƀi hoes comđati eidē . Brichmari . ficuti alii . ɪ . caȓ tr̄e
& . v . borđ . 7 ɪɪɪ . caȓ . ɪɪ . ac̄ p̄ti . Tc̄ uat̕ . xxx . fot̕ . modo . xx . ɪ . ex iftis fuit
★ dim̂ hõ . Edrici 7 dim̂ hõ Normanni . ɪɪ . ex his fueȓ comđati . Quengeu&
t . r . e . & h̄t in longo . vɪ . qȓ; in lato . ɪɪɪ . & . v . đ . in gelt̕.

★ ⌐nnebrunna . xvɪ . liƀi hoes . com̄ . Brictmari . & quengeu& . t . r . e.
7 . ɪɪ . dim̂ com̄d . sc̄æ . Æ . de . ɪ . caȓ terræ . 7 xʟ . ac̄ . 7 fub eis . xɪɪɪɪ . borđ.
Tc̄ . ɪɪɪɪ . caȓ . modo . ɪɪɪ . ɪ . ac̄ . & đ p̄ti . Tc̄ uat̕ xʟ . fot̕ . m̂ . xx . fot̕ . ~~& h̄~~

425 a
. ɪ . æcct̕ia . xɪɪ . ac̄ . & uat̕ x̂vɪ . đ . & fuit normanni tefte huɲđ . 7 h̄t in ⎯
longo . vɪ . qȓ . & . v . in lato . & de gelto vɪɪ . đ . & obot̕.

⌐In Kingeſſanda . ɪ . caȓ terræ guafta tȓa & uat̕ . ɪɪ . fot̕ . & h̄t in longo . ɪɪɪɪ.
qȓ . 7 . ɪɪɪ . in lat̕ . 7 de gelto . v . đ . hoc totū teñ . W . de nemore . de . R . fȓe
ilgeri.

7 In WALDRINGFIELD Brictmer, a free man, held before 1066; 1 carucate
of land as a manor.
1 smallholder.
Then 2 ploughs, now 1.
1 mill. Then 1 cob; then 100 sheep, now 27.
Value then 20s; now 10[s].
It has 6 furlongs in length and 3 in width; 5d in tax.
In the same (Waldringfield) 5 free men half under the patronage of
Brictmer and half under his mother's; 40 acres. 1 plough.
Value 4s.

8 In PRESTON 10 free men half under the patronage of Brictmer and
half (under that) of Queneva his mother, and one of these was half
under the patronage of St. Etheldreda's; 1 carucate of land.
Now 9 smallholders under them.
Then 4 ploughs, now 2. Meadow, 1 acre.
Value then 20s; now 10[s].
It has 6 furlongs in length and 3 in width; 6d in tax.

9 In HASPLEY 5 free men under the patronage of the same Brictmer, as
the others; 1 carucate of land.
5 smallholders.
3 ploughs. Meadow, 2 acres.
Value then 30s; now 20[s].
1 of the (free men) was half Edric's man and half Norman's man,
(and) 2 of them were under the patronage of Queneva before 1066.
It has 6 furlongs in length and 3 in width; 5d in tax.

10 In NEWBOURN 16 free men under the patronage of Brictmer and
Queneva before 1066, and 2 half (free men) under the patronage of
St. Etheldreda's, with 1 carucate of land and 40 acres.
Under them, 14 smallholders.
Then 4 ploughs, now 3. Meadow, 1½ acres.
Value then 40s; now 20[s].
1 church, 12 acres; value 16d. It was Norman's, as the Hundred   425 a
testifies.
It has 6 furlongs in length and 5 in width; 7½d in tax.

11 In KINGSLAND 1 carucate of land. The land (is) waste.
Value 2s.
It has 4 furlongs in length and 3 in width; 5d in tax.

W(illiam) of Bosc holds the whole of this from Ranulf brother of
Ilger.

In Aluredeſtuna.tenuṫ.Durand lib̄ hō.antec̄ Ro.mal&.t.r.e.
.ı.car̄ terræ.7 ʟxxx.ac̄.m̄ ten& ſuo.de.R.fr̄e Ilgeri p̔ man̄.Semp.vıı.
uiłł.7.ııı.bord.Tc̄ in dn̄io.ıı.car̄.m̄.ı.ſemp hom̄.ııı.car̄.ıııı.ac̄ p̄ti.
&.ı.molin̄.7 ııı·an̄.7 ʟ.oūs.ı.æcclia de xıı.ac̄.& uał.xıı.đ.Tc̄ uał.ıııı.
lib̄.modo ʟx.ſoł.7 ħt in longo.vı.qr̄.&.ıııı.in lato.&.x.đ de gelto.
& in Gepeſwiz.ı.manſura.uacua.7 altā hoſpitata.7 reddit.vııı.đ.
In haſpelega.vıı.ac̄.7 ſt in p̄tio de almelega.In eduluestuna.ıx.ac̄.& uał
ıı.ſoł.In bulges.ı.uiłł.Vluric.ıııı.ac̄.& uał.vııı đ.

BABENBERGA.DVO.H̄.In Walingafella ten& uluricus teinn̄
reḡ.e.ı.car̄.terræ.modo ten̄ Ran̄ p̔ man̄ ex dono reḡ.W.cū ſoca & ſaca
ſemp.ı.uiłł.7.ııı.bord.Tc̄ & p̔.ı.car̄.m̄.ıı.inṫ om̄s 7.ıııı.ac̄ p̄ti.Sēp
.ıı.an̄.Tc̄ xıı.porc̄.modo xvı.Tc̄ xx.oūs.modo.xxx.Tc̄ 7 p̔ uał.xxx.
ſoł.modo.xʟ.

SANFORT.H̄.Branham tenuit Aluric̄ de Wenhou.ıı.car̄ tr̄æ
Tc̄ 7 p̔.ıııı.uiłł.m̄.ıı.Tc̄.ı.bord.modo.vııı.Tc̄.ıı.ſerū.modo.ı.Tc̄
7 p̔.ıı.car̄ in dn̄io.m̄.ı.ſēp.ı.car̄ hom̄.ſilū.xıı.porc̄.v.ac̄ p̄ti.7.ı.
ſalina.7.ı.moł.Tc̄.ı.runc̄.ſemp.xıı.an̄.7 xxıııı.porc̄.7 ʟx.oūs.7 uał
xʟ.ſoł.Aluric̄ ſocā ſub aroldo.Roḡ.de Ranulf.

12 In *ALUREDESTUNA* Durand, a free man, Ro(bert) Malet's predecessor, held before 1066; 1 carucate of land and 80 acres. Now Ivo holds (it) from Ranulf brother of Ilger as a manor.
    Always 7 villagers; 3 smallholders.
    Then 2 ploughs in lordship, now 1; always 3 men's ploughs.
    Meadow, 4 acres; 1 mill. 3 cattle, 50 sheep.
    1 church with 12 acres; value 12d.
Value then £4; now 60s.
    It has 6 furlongs in length and 4 in width; 10d in tax.
Also in IPSWICH 1 empty dwelling and another inhabited.
It pays 8d.

13 In HASPLEY 7 acres.
They are in the assessment of Hemley.

14 In *EDULUESTUNA* 9 acres.
Value 2s.

15 In BOULGE 1 villager, Wulfric; 4 acres.
Value 8d.

BABERGH Two Hundreds
16 In WALDINGFIELD Wulfric, a thane of King Edward's, [held] 1 carucate of land. Now Ranulf holds (it) as a manor by King William's gift, with full jurisdiction.
    Always 1 villager; 3 smallholders.
    Then and later 1 plough between them all, now 2.
    Meadow, 4 acres. Always 2 cattle. Then 12 pigs, now 16; then 20 sheep, now 30.
Value then and later 30s; now 40[s].

SAMFORD Hundred
17 Aelfric of *Wenhou* held BRANTHAM; 2 carucates of land.
    Then and later 4 villagers, now 2; then 1 smallholder, now 8; then 2 slaves, now 1.
    Then and later 2 ploughs in lordship, now 1; always 1 men's plough.
    Woodland, 12 pigs; meadow, 5 acres; 1 salt-house; 1 mill. Then 1 cob. Always 12 cattle, 24 pigs, 60 sheep.
Value 40s.
    Aelfric (had) the jurisdiction under Harold.
    Roger [holds this] from Ranulf.

.XL. Γ T̃ERROTĒTI FILII CORBVTIONIS . *TINGOV* . H̃. ★

★ Brode teñ Ricardus quā tenuit Saiardus lib̃ hō. fub ſc̄o edmundo . t . r . e . in ſoca ſc̄i edmund ſed non poterat uendere dim̄ car̄ tr̄æ
& . I . car̄ . 7 . I . ac̄ 7 dim̄ p̃ti . Tc̄ ual̄ . x . ſol̄ . m̄ . xv.

Γ B̃Aᵇᵉⁿbga duo . H̃ . Somerledetuna teñ . Rog̃ . quā tenuit ſtar̃ker
ſub glofo rege . e . p̃ mañ . I . car̄ terræ in ſoca ſc̄i . edmund . Semp . II
bord̃ . Tc̄ . IIII . feru̇ . m̄ . I . Tc̄ & p̃ . II . car̄ in dn̄io . modo . I . 7 III . ac̄
7 dim̄ p̃ti . modo . x . añ . Tc̄ xv . porc̃ . modo . VIII . Tc̄ Lx . oûs . modo
. L . modo . v . cap̃ . Tc̄ & p̃ ual̄ . xxx . ſol̄ . modo xL.

Γ S̃ANFORT . H̃ . & dim̄ Wenham tenuit Auti tenñ . t . r . e.
p̃ mañ . III . car̄ terræ . Tc̄ IX . uilt̃ . P̃ 7 modo . VI . Tc̄ 7 p̃ . IIII . bord̃.
m̄ . XIIII . femp . I . feru̇ . Tc̄ 7 p̃ . II . car̄ in dn̄io . modo dim̄ . Tc̄
. v . car̄ hom̄ . P̃ . IIII . modo . III . xI . ac̄ p̃ti . Tc̄ filu̇ de . x . porc̃.
femp . I . moliñ . Ecclia . de . xx . ac̄ . lib̃æ tr̄æ . femp dim̄ car̄ . Tc̄ . II.
runc̃ . 7 IIII . añ . & . xx . porc̃ . modo nichil . p̃t xx . III . oûs . Tc̄
& p̃ ual̄ VI . lib̃ . m̄ . c . ſol̄ . Auti habuit focā ſup ſuū dominiū.
7 ſoca de Wilt̃is erat in b̃colt . Γ Girardus teñ de h̃ manerio.
xxx . ac̄ . & ual̄ . v . ſol̄ 7 ſt̃ in eod̃ p̃tio.

Γ In Wenham teñ Godviñ . lib̃ homo . x . ac̄ . & ē additus huic
manerio . & ual̄ . II . ſol̄ . Soca in b̃colt . h̃t xII . qr̄ in longo . 7 VI . in
lat̄ . & . II . ſol̄ de gelto.

Γ · H̃ . DE *CARLEFORD* . In barcheſtuna teñ Depekin . lib̃ hō . cō
m̄d heroldi . I . car̄ terræ p̃ mañ . Tc̄ . VI . bord̃ . m̄ . IIII . Tc̄ . in dn̄io
. I . car̄ . modo nulla . Tc̄ hom̄ . VII . car̄ . modo nulla . v . ac̄ p̃ti . 7 VI . oûs.

Tc̄ ual̄ . xx . ſol̄ . modo xII . 7 h̃t in longo . VI . qr̄ . 7 . IIII . in lato . 7 de-
gelto . III . d̃.

THINGOE Hundred

1 Richard holds BROCKLEY. Saegard, a free man, held it under St. Edmund's before 1066; in the jurisdiction of St. Edmund's, but he could not sell; ½ carucate of land. 1 plough.

Meadow, 1½ acres.

Value then 10s; now 15[s].

BABERGH Two Hundreds

2 Roger holds SOMERTON. Starker held it under the glorious King Edward as a manor; 1 carucate of land; in the jurisdiction of St. Edmund's.

Always 2 smallholders. Then 4 slaves, now 1.

Then and later 2 ploughs in lordship, now 1.

Meadow, 3½ acres. Now 10 cattle; then 15 pigs, now 8; then 60 sheep, now 50; now 5 goats.

Value then and later 30s; now 40[s].

SAMFORD Hundred and a Half

3 Auti, a thane, held WENHAM before 1066 as a manor; 3 carucates of land.

Then 9 villagers, later and now 6; then and later 4 smallholders, now 14; always 1 slave.

Then and later 2 ploughs in lordship, now ½; then 5 men's ploughs, later 4, now 3.

Meadow, 11 acres; woodland then at 10 pigs; always 1 mill.

A church with 20 acres of free land. Always ½ plough.

Then 2 cobs, 4 cattle, 20 pigs; now nothing except for 23 sheep.

Value then and later £6; now 100s.

Auti had jurisdiction over his lordship; jurisdiction over the villagers was in (East) Bergholt.

Gerard holds 30 acres of this manor.

Value 5s; they are in the same assessment.

In WENHAM Godwin, a free man, held 10 acres; it has been added to this manor.

Value 2s.

The jurisdiction is in (East) Bergholt.

It has 12 furlongs in length and 6 in width; 2s in tax.

Hundred of CARLFORD

4 In BARKESTONE Tepekin, a free man under the patronage of Harold, held 1 carucate of land as a manor.

Then 6 smallholders, now 4.

Then 1 plough in lordship, now none; then 7 men's ploughs, now none.

Meadow, 5 acres. 6 sheep.

Value then 20s; now 12[s].

It has 6 furlongs in length and 4 in width; 3d in tax.

ᚱ*DIM̃.H̃ DE COSFORT*.In Watefeldā . I . ſoc̄ . ſc̄i eadmuđ
. c . ac̄ . 7 Tc̄ . I . car̄ . p̄ dim̃ . modo . nulla 7 uat . x . ſot . berardus . hō
Abbis ten& de abb̄æ.

ᚱ*SANFORT . H̃*.Torintunā tenuit Aluin̄ lib̄ hō . Stigandi
. t . r . e . II . car̄ terræ . p̄ man̄ . Tc̄ & p̄ . vI . uitt . modo . IIII . Tc̄ & p̄ . II . borđ.
m̄ . v . Tc̄ . II . ſeru̇ . p̄ & m̄ . I . femp . II . car̄ in dn̄io . Tc̄ & p̄ . III . car̄ hom̄.
m̄ . II . xx . ac̄ . p̄ti . femp . I . molin̄ . Ecctia . L . ac̄ . libe t̃ræ . m̄ . I . runc̄.
7 . vI . an̄ . Tc̄ . IIII . porc̄ . modo . xxx . 7 xx . ous̄ . 7 xxx . cap̄ . ſēp uat
. L . ſot . Idē ſocā habuit ſub ſtigando . ht̄ . vI . qr̄ in longo . 7 IIII . in
lato . & . v . đ de gelto . Gifardus ten̄ de Robto.

★ ᚱ TRE Galteri diaconi . *DIM̃.H̃*. de cosfort . Bileſtunā in dn̄io   .XL
tenuit Edid . regina . t . r . e . p̄ man̄ . vI . car̄ t̃ræ . femp . xIIII . uitt.
7 . vI . borđ . 7 vIII . ſeru̇ . & . III . car̄ in dominio . 7 . III . car̄ hom̄ . xx . ac̄
p̄ti . Silua de . x . porc̄ . 7 . III . runc̄ . & . x . an̄ . 7 xL . porc̄ . 7 Lxxx . ous̄
Ecctia xL . ac̄ . 7 . I . car̄ . 7 . I . ac̄ p̄ti . Tc̄ uat . vIII . lib̄ . modo . x . ſed reddit
. xII . ht̄ . I . lḡ in longo . & dim̄ in lato . & . v . den̄ de gelto.
ᚱ Claindune . H̃ . Suinlandā tenuit Regina . Edid . t . r . e . II.
car̄ terræ . 7 xL ac̄ . p̄ man̄ . femp vI . uitti . & . vI . borđ . & . I . ſeru̇.
& . II . car̄ in dominio . & . III . car̄ hom̄ . IIII . ac̄ p̄ti . filua . vI . porc̄.
Ecctia . de . v . ac̄ . & . I . runc̄ . & . vIII . an̄ . 7 xvIIII . porc̄ Tc̄ Lx . ous̄.

modo . c . Tc̄ uat . L . ſot . modo . Lxx . ht̄ . vI . qr̄ in longo . & . IIII . in lat̄.
7 xx . đ . de gt . Galt̄ in dn̄io . Regina ſocā.

Half-Hundred of COSFORD

5 In WHATFIELD'1 Freeman of St. Edmund's; 100 acres. Then 1 plough, later ½, now none.
Value 10s.
Berard, a man of the Abbot's, holds (this) from the Abbot.

SAMFORD Hundred

6 Alwin, a free man of Stigand's, held THORINGTON before 1066; 2 carucates of land as a manor.
Then and later 6 villagers, now 4; then and later 2 smallholders, now 5; then 2 slaves, later and now 1.
Always 2 ploughs in lordship. Then and later 3 men's ploughs, now 2.
Meadow, 20 acres; always 1 mill.
A church, 50 acres of free land.
Now 1 cob, 6 cattle. Then 4 pigs, now 30; 20 sheep; 30 goats.
Value always 50s.
He also had the jurisdiction under Stigand. It has 6 furlongs in length and 4 in width; 5d in tax.
Gifard holds (this) from Robert.

41   LANDS OF WALTER THE DEACON

Half-Hundred of COSFORD

1 Queen Edith held BILDESTON in lordship before 1066 as a manor; 6 carucates of land.
Always 14 villagers; 6 smallholders; 8 slaves;
3 ploughs in lordship; 3 men's ploughs.
Meadow, 20 acres; woodland at 10 pigs. 3 cobs, 10 cattle, 40 pigs, 80 sheep.
A church, 40 acres. 1 plough. Meadow, 1 acre.
Value then £8; now [£] 10, but it pays [£] 12.
It has 1 league in length and ½ in width; 5d in tax.

CLAYDON Hundred

2 Queen Edith held SWILLAND before 1066; 2 carucates of land and 40 acres as a manor.
Always 6 villagers; 6 smallholders; 1 slave;
2 ploughs in lordship; 3 men's ploughs.
Meadow, 4 acres; woodland, 6 pigs.
A church with 5 acres.
1 cob, 8 cattle, 19 pigs; then 60 sheep, now 100.
Value then 50s; now 70[s].
It has 6 furlongs in length and 4 in width; 20d in tax.
Walter [holds this] in lordship.
The Queen (had) the jurisdiction.

426 b

⊢In Turolueſtuna . I . liɓ hō xvɪ . ac̄ 7 ɪɪɪɪ . borđ . ſemp dim̄ car̄ . & . ɪ.
ac̄ p̃ti . 7 ual . ɪɪ . ſot . 7 vɪɪɪ . đ . dim̄ æcclia . v . ac̄

⊢In Weſtrefelda tenuit Almar liɓ hō . xxx . ac̄ . 7 ɪɪɪɪ . borđ . ſemp
. ɪ . car̄ . & . ɪɪ . ac̄ p̃ti . & ual . vɪɪɪ . ſot . Turſtin de Galtero de feudo te
drici . rex 7 . c . ſocā

⊢In Acrehā . ɪɪ . liɓi hões . Suen & Leuinus . ʟ . ac̄ . 7 ual . v . ſot . Turſtin
de Galtero . 7 ƀnardus . de eođ feudo.

⊢In Weſtrefelda . ɪɪɪ . liɓi hões xxvɪɪɪ . ac̄ . 7 tc̄ . dim̄ car̄ . 7 ual
xxx . vɪ . đ Bernard . 7 almar . ten& . Rex 7 Com̄s ſocā . In eađ . liɓ
hō vɪ . ac̄ . 7 ual& xɪɪ . đ . de eodē feudo . Normannus ten& Soca
Reg 7 comitis . ⊢HERTESMARA . H̄ . Bachetunam̄ . Leuuin
liɓ hō . heroldi . t . r . e . ɪɪɪ . car̄ terræ . 7 xʟ ac̄ . Tc̄ xvɪɪ . uilli . modo . vɪɪɪ.
Tc̄ . ɪɪɪ . borđ . modo . xɪɪ . Tc̄ . ɪɪ . ſeru . modo . ɪ . Semp in dn̄io . ɪɪ . car̄.
Tc̄ hom̄ . ɪɪɪ . car̄ . modo . ɪɪ . vɪ . ac̄ p̃ti . ſilu ad . c . porc̄ . Tc̄ . ɪ . x . runc̄.
modo . vɪɪɪ . Semp . vɪɪɪ . an̄ . Tc̄ ʟx . porc̄ . modo . xʟ . Tc̄ xvɪ . ous̄ . modo.
. c . Tc̄ . xʟ . cap̃ . modo . xxxvɪ . Tc̄ ual . vɪɪɪ . liɓ . modo . ɪx . liɓ . 7 x . ſot.
7 . xʟ . liɓi hões com̄d . Leuuino . t . r . e . ʟxx . ac̄ terræ . 7 . ɪ . borđ . Tc̄
. ɪɪɪ . car̄ . modo . ɪɪ . ɪ . ac̄ p̃ti . Tc̄ ual . xx . ſot . modo . ɪɪɪɪ . liɓ . 7 . x . ſot.
Rex & com̄s ſocā . 7 ħt ī longo . ɪ . lḡ . 7 . in lato . ɪɪɪɪ . qr̄ . & de gelto . vɪ . đ.

3 In THURLESTON 1 free man; 16 acres.
4 smallholders.
Always ½ plough. Meadow, 1 acre.
Value 2s 8d.
½ church, 5 acres.

4 In WESTERFIELD Aelmer, a free man, held 30 acres.
4 smallholders.
Always 1 plough. Meadow, 2 acres.
Value 8s.
Thurstan [holds this] from Walter, from Theodoric's Holding.
The King and the Earl (have) the jurisdiction.

5 In AKENHAM 2 free men, Swein and Leofwin; 50 acres.
Value 5s.
Thurstan [holds this] from Walter; and Bernard; from the same Holding.

6 In WESTERFIELD 3 free men; 28 acres. Then ½ plough.
Value 36d.
Bernard and Aelmer hold (this).
The King and the Earl (have) the jurisdiction.
In the same (Westerfield) a free man; 6 acres.
Value 12d.
(It is part) of the same Holding. Norman holds (it).
The jurisdiction (is) the King's and the Earl's.

HARTISMERE Hundred
7 [Walter holds] BACTON in lordship; Leofwin, a free man of Harold's, before 1066; 3 carucates of land and 40 acres.
Then 17 villagers, now 8; then 3 smallholders, now 12; then 2 slaves, now 1.
Always 2 ploughs in lordship. Then 3 men's ploughs, now 2.
Meadow, 6 acres; woodland for 100 pigs. Then 9 cobs, now 8; always 8 cattle. Then 60 pigs, now 40; then 16 sheep, now 100; then 40 goats, now 36.
1 church, 24 acres; value 3s.
Value then £8; now £9 10s.
And 40 free men under the patronage of Leofwin before 1066; 80 acres of land.
1 smallholder.
Then 3 ploughs, now 2. Meadow, 1 acre.
Value then 20s; now £4 10s.
The King and the Earl (have) the jurisdiction. It has 1 league in length and 4 furlongs in width; 6d in tax.

⁊ In caldecota . xix . aͨ . de dn̄io de bachetuna . 7 ual . iii . ſol . 7 iii . đ . 7
ħt in longo . ix . qͬ . 7 in lato . ii . 7 . v . ꝑce . 7 de gelto . vi . đ.
⁊ In Weſtorp . bricͭricus liħ hō cōm . vi . aͨ . 7 ual . xii . đ.

⁊ *BABENBͤGA . DⱵO . Ⱨ̄* . Mellinga ten̄ Galterͥ in dominio
quā tenuit Leuuinͦ de bagatona ten̄ . regͤ . e . ꝑ man̄ . ii . caͬ terræ
m̄ ten̄ Galͭ . & eſt de feudo thederici fͬis ſui Semp . vi . uiħi . & . vi .
borđ . 7 . iiii . ſeru . Semp ii . caͬ in dn̄io . Tͨ & pͦ⟋ iii caͬ hom . m̄ . i.
7 vi . aͨ ꝑti . Siluͦ de ⁚ vi . porͨ . & . i . moͭ . Semp . ii . eđ⟋ 7 vi . an̄ . modo.
vii . 7 xxii . porͨ . Tͨ . xl . oūs . modo . l . Tͨ . xii . caꝑ . modo xvi . Tͨ
7 pͦ ual . iiii . liħ . modo . vi . liħ . ħt vi . qͬ in longo . 7 iiii . in lato . 7 de₋
gelto . vii . đ . Ecͨħa . de xv . aͨ liħe terræ . Sup x . aͨ q̄s ħt . i . liħ
hō qđ poͭat uenđe ħt ſc̄s . e . ſoͨ 7 ſacā 7 ual . ii . ſol.
⁊ Stov . Ⱨ̄ ⁚ In dagaworda Wiħm ten̄ . i . liħ' hō de q̄ terⁱ antec̄
de barthetona habuit dim̄ cōmđ tanͭ . & gut mundus antec̄
hugon̄ de monte forti altaͥ medietaͭ . & poͭ ſine lic̄ncia eoͬ⁊
uenđe . terrā ſuā . 7 ħt lx . aͨ . & . i . borđ ⁚ Tͨ & pͦ . i . caͬ . 7 dim̄ ⁚ m̄
ii . boū . Silua x . porͨ . & . iii . aͨ ꝑti.
⁊ In Weledana xv ⁚ aͨ . de tͬa eiđ liħ hōis . 7 ii ⁚ aͨ ꝑti . Tͨ 7 pͦ
toͭ ual xx ⁚ ſoͭ . modo . v . hanc tͬā teoderic Anͭc̄ Walti diaͨoni
ſine liħatore teſte ħ . Rex & cōms ſocā 7 ſacā.
⁊ In Watͬdena . i ⁚ liħ hō in ſoca ħ . v . aͨ . & . ual . xii . đ.
⁊ *DIM̄* . ħ . de gepeſwiz . In burgo ħt ⁚ Galͭ . v . domos . 7 iii.
manſuras uacuas q̄s ten̄ . Regina . t ⁚ r . e . 7 redđͭ c̄ſuetđn̄e
7 ual xx . đ.

8 In *CALDECOTA* 19 acres of the lordship of Bacton.
Value 3s 3d.
It has 9 furlongs in length and 2 (furlongs) and 5 perches in width; 6d in tax.

9 In WESTHORPE Brictric, a free man under patronage; 6 acres.
Value 12d.

BABERGH Two Hundreds 427 a

10 Walter holds MILDEN in lordship. Leofwin of Bacton, a thane of King Edward's, held it as a manor; 2 carucates of land. Now Walter holds (it) and it belongs to the Holding of his brother Theodoric.
Always 6 villagers; 6 smallholders; 4 slaves.
Always 2 ploughs in lordship. Then and later 3 men's ploughs, now 1.
Meadow, 6 acres; woodland at 6 pigs; 1 mill. Always 2 horses. Then 6 cattle, now 7; 22 pigs; then 40 sheep, now 50; then 12 goats, now 16.
Value then and later £4; now £6.
It has 6 furlongs in length and 4 in width; 7d in tax.
A church with 15 acres of free land.
Over 10 acres which 1 free man has (and) which he could sell, St. Edmund's has full jurisdiction; value 2s.

STOW Hundred

11 William holds in DAGWORTH; 1 free man over whom Teri the predecessor of .... of *Barthetona* had only half the patronage and Guthmund, Hugh de Montfort's predecessor, (had) the other half, and he could sell his land without their permission. He has 60 acres.
1 smallholder.
Then and later 1½ ploughs, now 2 oxen.
Woodland, 10 pigs; meadow, 3 acres.
In *WELEDANA* 15 acres of the land of the same free man.
Meadow, 2 acres.
Value of the whole, then and later 20s; now 5[s].
Theodoric, Walter the Deacon's predecessor, had this land without a deliverer, as the Hundred testifies.
The King and the Earl (have) full jurisdiction.

12 In WETHERDEN 1 free man in the jurisdiction of the Hundred; 5 acres.
Value 12d.

Half-Hundred of IPSWICH

13 In the Borough (of IPSWICH) Walter has 5 houses and 3 empty dwellings which the Queen held before 1066. They pay the customary due.
Value 20d.

Ⱶ CLAINDVNE. H̃. Henleie tenuit Vluric lib hõ
. I . car terre . 7 LXX . ac̃ . p mañ . t . r . e . Tc̃ . II . bord . modo . VI .
Tc̃ 7 p̃ . II . car in dominio ; modo ; modo . I . femp . I . car hom . IIII . ac̃ p̃ti .

Tc̃ . III . runc̃ . Tc̃ . II . añ . m̃ . III . Tc̃ x . porc̃ . modo . II . Tc̃ XL . oũs
modo XLIIII . Ecclia de VIII . ac̃ . Tc̃ ual . XL . fol . 7 m̃ . XLVIII . Rog̃ .
de Galtero . Rex & cõms focã . In ead c̃omd . VI . libi hoes . XXXVI .
ac̃ . Tc̃ & p̃ . I . car . & dim ; modo ; I . car . Tc̃ ual . VI . fol . 7 . VIII . d̃ . m̃
VII . fol . Id . Rog̃ . Rex & cõms focã . In ead . I . lib hõ nõe Suenus,
tenuit . XL . ac̃ . p mañ . t . r ; e . femp . I ; car . & . I . bord . Tc̃ ual .
x . fol m̃ XVIII . Galt teñ . in dñio h̃t . I . lg̃ in longo . & dim̃
in lato . 7 xx d̃ . de gelto . Rex & cõms focã .
Ⱶ In Bruntuna tenuit Leuuin teinn . t . r . e . I . car terræ
& XL . ac̃ . p mañ . femp . IX . bord ; 7 . II . feru . Tc̃ & . p̃ . II . car .
modo . I . Tc̃ & p̃ . II . car hom ; modo . I . v . ac̃ p̃ti . Tc̃ . I . runc̃ .
Tc̃ xx . porc̃ . modo . x ; Tc̃ xx oũs . modo XVI . Tc̃ ual . XL . fol .
modo . xxx ; Rob de Galtro . Rex & cõms focã,
Ⱶ In Achehã . IIII . libi hoes . de xxx . II . ac̃ terræ ; Tc̃ . I . car . 7 ual
. v . fol . Rog̃ de galtero ; Rex & cõms focã .

CLAYDON Hundred
14 Wulfric, a free man, held HENLEY; 1 carucate of land and 70 acres as
a manor before 1066.
Then 2 smallholders, now 6.
Then and later 2 ploughs in lordship, now 1; always 1 men's
plough.
Meadow, 4 acres. Then 3 cobs; then 2 cattle, now 3; then 10 pigs,   427 b
now 2; then 40 sheep, now 44.
A church with 8 acres.
Value then 40s; now 48[s].
Roger [holds this] from Walter.
The King and the Earl (have) the jurisdiction.
In the same (Henley) 6 free men under patronage; 36 acres. Then
and later 1½ ploughs, now 1 plough.
Value then 6s 8d; now 7s.
Roger also [holds this].
The King and the Earl (have) the jurisdiction.
In the same (Henley) 1 free man, Swein by name, held 40 acres as
a manor before 1066. Always 1 plough;
1 smallholder.
Value then 10s; now 18[s].
Walter holds (this) in lordship.
It has 1 league in length and ½ in width; 20d in tax. The King
and the Earl (have) the jurisdiction.

15 In BRUNTUNA Leofwin, a thane, held 1 carucate of land and 40 acres
before 1066 as a manor.
Always 9 smallholders; 2 slaves.
Then and later 2 ploughs, now 1; then and later 2 men's ploughs,
now 1.
Meadow, 5 acres. Then 1 cob; then 20 pigs, now 10; then 20
sheep, now 16.
Value then 40s; now 30[s].
Robert [holds this] from Walter.
The King and the Earl (have) the jurisdiction.

16 In AKENHAM 4 free men, with 32 acres of land. Then 1 plough.
Value 5s.
Roger [holds this] from Walter.
The King and the Earl (have) the jurisdiction.

In Witdefhā tẽ Leuuin liƀ hõ . t . r . e . iii . caŕ t̃re . Semp . x . uitt . & . iiii . bord . 7 vi
feru . m̃ . v . femp . iii . caŕ in dominio . & hom . iiii . caŕ . x . ač p̃ti . & . iii . runc . & viii . añ.
& lxviii . porc̃ . 7 c . lxxx . oũs . & xxx . cap̃ . 7 vii . uafa apū . Tẽ uat lx . fot . m̃ xii . liƀ . &
longo . viii . qŕ . & . iiii . i lat̃ . & v . ɗ in glẽ . ∫ In finesforda in dñio . xxvi . libi hões . i . caŕ
cõmdti antecettori . Walt̃ . sc̃a . Æ . foc̃a . Tẽ int̃ eos . iii . caŕ . m̃ . ii . iiii . ač p̃ti .
7 uat . xl . fot . 7 ħt i lõg . x . qŕ . 7 . iii . in lato . 7 . x . ɗ . de gĩto . ∫ In otelega i dñio . vi ač 7 uat xix

.XLII. ∫Tr̃æ TEHELLI DE HERION . *B̃ãɮENBERGA* . ii . H̃.

Ilelega tẽ ulwaRdus liƀ hõ fubftigando . t . r . e . p̃ mañ . iii . caŕ
t̃ræ . Sẽp . v . bord . 7 . ii . fer̃ . femp . ii . caŕ in dñio . 7 . iii . ač p̃ti . & . i . met .
& . ii . eɋ . in halla . & . vi . añ . 7 xx . porc̃ . & . c . oũs . Tẽ uat . xl . fot . p̃ 7 m̃ .
lxxx . fot . ħt dim̃ lĩg in longo . 7 iiii . qŕ in lato . 7 de gelto . iii . ɗ . 7 obol ;

428 a

∫ *RISEBRVGE* . H̃ . Hauerhellā . tenuit Clareboldus . t . r . e . p̃
mañ . ii . caŕ terræ & dim̃ . Tẽ & p̃ vi . uitt . modo . i . Tẽ . & p̃ . iiii . borɗ .
modo . x . femp . x . feru . Tẽ & p̃ 7 femp . ii . caŕ in dominio . Tẽ & p̃
. i . caŕ . hom̃ . modo dim̃ . Silua de xx . porc̃ . vi . ač p̃ti . Tẽia pars
mercati in eo ? x . bord . æcctie . v . ač . Mañ uat & xl . fot . 7 mercatũ
xiii . fot . 7 . iiii . ɗ . ħt . i . lĩg in longo . 7 dim̃ in lato . & . vi . ɗ . de gelto .
Alii ibi tenent ;

Hundred of CARLFORD

17 In WITNESHAM Leofwin, a free man, held before 1066; 3 carucates of land.
> Always 10 villagers; 4 smallholders. [Then] 6 slaves, now 5.
> Always 3 ploughs in lordship; 4 men's ploughs.
> Meadow, 10 acres. 3 cobs, 8 cattle, 68 pigs, 180 sheep, 30 goats, 7 beehives.
> Value then 60s; now £12.
> It has 8 furlongs in length and 4 in width; 5d in tax.

18 In 'FINESFORDA' in lordship; 26 free men under the patronage of Walter's predecessor; 1 carucate of land. St. Etheldreda's (has) the jurisdiction. Then between them 3 ploughs, now 2.
> Meadow, 4 acres.
> Value 40s.
> It has 10 furlongs in length and 3 in width; 10d in tax.

9 In OTLEY, in lordship, 6 acres.
> Value 12d.

2 LANDS OF TIHEL OF HELLÉAN

BABERGH Two Hundreds

1 Wulfward, a free man under Stigand, held ELEIGH before 1066 as a manor; 3 carucates of land.
> Always 5 smallholders; 2 slaves.
> Always 2 ploughs in lordship.
> Meadow, 3 acres; 1 mill. 2 horses at the hall, 6 cattle, 20 pigs, 100 sheep.
> Value then 40s; later and now 80s.
> It has ½ league in length and 4 furlongs in width; 3½d in tax.

RISBRIDGE Hundred   428 a

2 Clarenbold held HAVERHILL before 1066 as a manor; 2½ carucates of land.
> Then and later 6 villagers, now 1; then and later 4 smallholders, now 10; always 10 slaves.
> Then and later and always 2 ploughs in lordship; then and later 1 men's plough, now ½.
> Woodland at 20 pigs; meadow, 6 acres; the third part of a market, in it 10 smallholders.
> 5 acres, belonging to the church.
> Value of the manor 40s; (value) of the market 13s 4d.
> It has 1 league in length and ½ in width; 6d in tax. Others hold there.

Hoketona ten& huthtradus fub heroldo . t . r . e . ꝑ mañ . ıı . caꞃ
terræ cū foca . Semꝑ . ı . uiℓℓ . & . ıı . borđ . & . v . feru̅ . Tc̅ . ııı . caꞃ in
dominio p̊ 7 modo . ıııı . Semꝑ dim̅ caꞃ hom̅ . Silua . de . xx . porc̅ .
7 . x . ac̅ ꝓti . Semꝑ . ı . æqus in halla . Tc̅ . ııı . añ . modo . nuℓℓ .
⫫Fineſteda ten& iđ uthtret . t . r . e . ꝑ . ı . caꞃ terræ . modo ten&
Rađ ꝑ ƀwita in hoketona . ab etgaro antece ceſſore fuo . Sēp
. ı . caꞃ in dominio . Hoketona Tc̅ uaℓ . ıııı . liƀ . modo . c . foℓ . 7 fin**e**
ſteda tc̅ & p̊ uaℓ . xx . foℓ . modo . xxx . fed e̅ . de . c . folidis . Totū
h̅ɪ . vııı . qꞃ in longo . & . ıııı . in lato . & de gelto . ıııı . đ .
⫫Rana uadifc ten̅ Normannus cū foca 7 faca fub rege . e .
ꝑ mañ . ıı . caꞃ tr̅æ . Ecclia . de xxx . ac̅ liƀæ tr̅æ . Semꝑ . v . uiℓℓ .
7 . vııı . borđ . 7 vıı . feru̅ . Tc̅ . ıı . caꞃ in dñio . p̊ 7 m̅ . ıııı . Sēꝑ . ııı .

428 b

caꞃ hom̅ . & . ı . moliñ . & . x . ac̅ ꝓti . Tc̅ . ııı . añ . modo xxıııı . Tc̅
xL . ōus . modo . c . x . Tc̅ xxx . porc̅ . m̅ . L . Huic mañ ptin& . ı . ƀwita
Rodenhā de . ıı . caꞃ tr̅æ . Tc̅ . v . uiℓℓ . 7 p̊ 7 m̅ . ııı . Tc̅ . ıııı . borđ . p̊
7 m̅ . xııı . Tc̅ 7 p̊: ıı . feru̅ . modo . ı . Tc̅ . ıı . caꞃ in dominio . p̊ & modo .
. ı . 7 . ı . caꞃ 7 dim̅ . hom̅ . Tc̅ dim̅ moℓ . p̊ 7 m̅ nuℓℓ . Ecclia de xx . ac̅ .
liƀæ tr̅æ . Tc̅ 7 p̊ uaℓ totū . c . foℓ . modo . x . liƀ . Rana uadis . h̅t dim̅
lg̅ in lōngo . 7 . ıııı . qꞃ in lato & de gelto . x . đ . Kodehā h̅t

★   7 vı . qꞃ̊ . in loñ . 7 . ııı . in laſ . 7 . ıııı . đ . 7
       obol de . gelto.
⫫Neuuetona ten̅ iđ uthtret fub heroldo . cū foca & faca ꝑ mañ .
. ıı . caꞃ terræ . Semꝑ . ııı . uiℓℓ . Tc̅ vıı . borđ . p̊ 7 modo xx . Tc̅ . ıııı .
feru̅ . p̊ 7 modo . ı . Semꝑ . ıı . caꞃ in dominio . Tc̅ & p̊ . ıı . caꞃ . hom̅ .
modo . ıı . & dim̅ . Silua . de . vı . porc̅ . 7 . ıııı . ac̅ ꝓti . Æcclia de
xxx . ac̅ liƀe tr̅æ . Tc̅ . ı . eq̅ . m̅ nuℓℓ . Tc̅ . ııı . añ . modo . vııı . Tc̅ xvıı porc̅ .

LANDS OF RALPH OF LIMÉSY

BABERGH Two Hundreds

1 Uhtred [held] HOUGHTON under Harold before 1066 as a manor; 2 carucates of land, with the jurisdiction.

    Always 1 villager; 2 smallholders; 5 slaves.

    Then 3 ploughs in lordship, later and now 4; always ½ men's plough.

    Woodland at 20 pigs; meadow, 10 acres. Always 1 horse at the hall. Then 3 cattle, now none.

Uhtred also [held] FENSTEAD before 1066 for 1 carucate of land. Now Ralph holds (it) as an outlier in (the lands of) Houghton. [Uhtred held it] from Edgar, his predecessor. Always 1 plough in lordship. Value of Houghton then £4; now 100s. Value of Fenstead then and later 20s; now 30[s], but it is (part) of the 100s.

    The whole has 8 furlongs in length and 4 in width; 4d in tax.

2 Norman held CAVENDISH, with full jurisdiction, under King Edward; as a manor, 2 carucates of land.

    A church with 30 acres of free land.

    Always 5 villagers; 8 smallholders; 7 slaves.

    Then 2 ploughs in lordship, later and now 4; always 3 men's ploughs.

    1 mill; meadow, 10 acres. Then 3 cattle, now 24; then 40 sheep, now 110; then 30 pigs, now 50.

To this manor belongs 1 outlier, CODDENHAM, with 2 carucates of land.

    Then 5 villagers, later and now 3; then 4 smallholders, later and now 13; then and later 2 slaves, now 1.

    Then 2 ploughs in lordship, later and now 1; 1½ men's ploughs.

    Then ½ mill, later and now none.

    A church with 20 acres of free land.

Value of the whole then and later 100s; now £10.

    Cavendish has ½ league in length and 4 furlongs in width; 10d in tax. Coddenham has 6 furlongs in length and 3 in width; [3]½d in tax.

3 Uhtred also held NEWTON under Harold, with full jurisdiction; as a manor, 2 carucates of land.

    Always 3 villagers. Then 7 smallholders, later and now 20; then 4 slaves, later and now 1.

    Always 2 ploughs in lordship. Then and later 2 men's ploughs, now 2½.

    Woodland at 6 pigs; meadow, 4 acres.

    A church with 30 acres of free land.

    Then 1 horse, now none; then 3 cattle, now 8; then 17 pigs,

428 b

modo.xx.Tc̄ lx.oūs.m̊.c.iii.Tc̄.xvii.cap̊.modo.xxx.v.di᷄ᵐ.æcc̄ľia
de.viii.ac̄ libæ terræ.In ead.i.lib̄ hō.dim̊ uthtredi & dimidi̊ sc̄i
E.c̄omd̄ f7 tot⁹ in ſoca sc̄i.e.Et pořat uend̄e ſine licencia.& ħt
xx.ac̄.Totū tc̄ ual.xl.ſoł.p̊⁹ 7 modo lx.ħt dim̊ lḡ in longo.7
iiii.qř in lato.Et de gelto.vi.d̄.& oboł.

Γ In Cornierda.i.lib̄ hō.Wiſgari.c̄omdatiō tantū.& ſoca de.i.
caŕ terræ.Semp.v.bord.Sēp.i.caŕ in dn̄io.7 vi.ac̄ p̊ti.Silua.
de.iiii.porc̄.Semp.v.an̄.Tc̄.x.porc.modo xx.Tc̄.xxx.oūs.m̊
lx.Semp ual.xx.ſoł.ħt dim̊ lḡ in longo 7 dim̊ in lato.& de gelto
.iii.d̄ & obolū.

Γ BISCOPES H̃.Bedinga f̣lda ten̄ Aluric̊ lib̄ hō heroldi
p̄ man̄.t.r.e.lxxxx.ii.ac̄.Tc̄.ii.bord.modo.iiii.ſemp̣.i.caŕ in dm̄io.

7.i.caŕ houm.ſilua.de.x.porc̄.7.i.ac̄ p̊ti.ſemp.xii.porc̄.7
xx.oūs.Q̊rta pars ecc̄liæ.vi.ac̄.Tc̄ ual.xxx.ſoł.m̊.xvi.7.viii.d̄.
In ead.vi.lib̄i hōes ex oīb꙯ aluric̊ c̄md̄ p̄t de dimidio.q̊ fuit ſub ante
c̄ Rob̄ mal& c̄omd̄ tant̄.& ħnt.xxx.v.ac̄.&.i.ac̄.p̊ti.ſemp̣.i.caŕ.
& ual.xl.d̄.

Γ H̃.DE LOSA.Framelingaham̊ ten̄ Bric̊tmar⁹ lib̄ hō.heroldi
.t.r.e.l.ac̄.třæ.p̄ man̄.Sēp.iii.bord.7.i.ſeru̇.7 in dn̄io.i.caŕ.& hom̊
dim̊.caŕ.Tc̄ ual & ſemp.xv.ſoł.

Γ HERTESMERA.H̃.Cranlea.ten̄.Aluricus.lib̄ hō.c.ac̄.p̄
man̄.t.r.e.ſemp.x.bord.&.i.caŕ in dn̄io.7.i.caŕ hom̊,Silua
vi.porc̄.7 ual.xx.ſoł.Aluric̊ habuit dim̊ ſocā.7 rex alia᷄ medietat̄.

now 20; then 60 sheep, now 103; then 17 goats, now 35.
½ church with 8 acres of free land.
In the same (Newton) 1 free man, half under the patronage of
Uhtred and half (under that) of St. Edmund's but wholly in the
jurisdiction of St. Edmund's; he could sell without permission.
He has 20 acres.
Value of the whole then 40s; later and now 60[s].
It has ½ league in length and 4 furlongs in width; 6½d in tax.

4 In CORNARD 1 free man of Withgar's, under patronage only and
jurisdiction, with 1 carucate of land.
Always 5 smallholders.
Always 1 plough in lordship.
Meadow, 6 acres; woodland at 4 pigs. Always 5 cattle. Then 10
pigs, now 20; then 30 sheep, now 60.
Value always 20s.
It has ½ league in length and ½ in width; 3½d in tax.

BISHOP'S Hundred
5 Aelfric, a free man of Harold's, held BEDINGFIELD as a manor before
1066; 92 acres.
Then 2 smallholders, now 4.
Always 1 plough in lordship; 1 men's plough.
Woodland at 10 pigs; meadow, 1 acre. Always 12 pigs, 20 sheep.
The fourth part of a church, 6 acres.
Value then 30s; now 16[s] 8d.
In the same (Bedingfield) 6 free men; over all of them, Aelfric had
patronage, except over half of one who, for patronage only, was
under Robert Malet's predecessor. They have 35 acres.
Meadow, 1 acre.
Always 1 plough.
Value 40d.

429 a

Hundred of LOES
6 Brictmer, a free man of Harold's, held FRAMLINGHAM before 1066;
50 acres of land as a manor.
Always 3 smallholders; 1 slave;
1 plough in lordship; ½ men's plough.
Value then and always 15s.

HARTISMERE Hundred
7 Aelfric, a free man, held CRANLEY; 100 acres as a manor before 1066.
Always 10 smallholders;
1 plough in lordship; 1 men's plough. Woodland, 6 pigs.
Value 20s.
Aelfric had half the jurisdiction, the King (had) the other half.

꓉In haſtelea.ıı.lıƀ hões.cõmđ.x.ac̄.7 ual.xx.đ.

꓉In Acolt.ı.lıƀ hō.cõmđ.vıɪɪ.ac̄ 7 ual xvı.đ.Totũ tēn Rađ in dñio.
Rex & cõms focā.In eađ.ı.lıƀ hō cõm abƀi de s̄co edmundo.ıı.ac̄.
& ual.ııɪɪ.đ.Rex & cõms focam;

★ ꓉**TERRÆ ROBERTI DE TODENIO.** *RISEBRVGE.* $\tilde{H}$.　　　.XLII.

Bradeleia.tenuit Olfus teinnus ₚ mañ.t.r.e.m̃.Roḡ.in dñio
tēn.vɪɪ.car terræ.femₚ.xɪɪɪɪ.uıℓℓ.7 xıı.borđ.&.vı.feru.&.ııɪ.car
in dominio.7 vɪɪ.car hom.& xııɪ.ac̄ p̃ti.filua.porc.femₚ.ı.
runc.Tc̄ xıı.añ.M̊ xvıɪɪ.Tc̄ Lx.porc.modo.L.ııɪ.Tc̄.xx.oũs.

429 b

M Lxııɪ.7 vɪɪ.cap̃.&.ı.uafa apũ.Ecclia.de.xv.ac̄.lıƀæ t̃ræ.Tc̄ ual
.vı.lıƀ.modo.vɪɪɪ.ħt.ı.lḡ in longo.7 vɪɪ.q̃r in lat̃.7 vı.đ de gelto.

꓉*BISCOPES.* $\tilde{H}$.Seilam tenuit cũ foca Olfus.t.r.e.ₚ mañ.ıı.car.
& dim t̃ræ.Tc̄ vɪɪɪ.uıℓℓ.modo.ııɪ.Tc̄ xıı.borđ.modo.xɪɪɪ.modo
.ı.feru.femₚ.ııɪ.car in dominio.Tc̄ & p̃.xıı.car hom.m̃.ıɪɪɪ.Silũ
c.L.porc.vɪɪɪ.ac̄.p̃ti.femₚ.ı.moℓ.Tc̄.ıı.runc.modo.ı.Tc̄.vɪɪɪ.añ.
modo.ıı.Tc̄ Lxxx.porc.m̃.xL,ıɪɪɪ.m̃.vɪɪ.oũs.&.ııɪ.cap̃.&.ı.uas
apũ.Tc̄ ual.c.foℓ.7 modo fimiℓt̃.In eađ.v.lıƀi hões.ante c̄.cõm
xxx.ac̄.Tc̄.ı.car.modo.dim.&.ı.ac̄.p̃ti.&.ual.v.foℓ.Ecclia.de.
xvı.ac̄.& ual.ıı.foℓ.In longo.ı.lḡ.&.vɪɪɪ.q̃r in lat̃.&.vɪɪ.đ.&.oƀoℓ
de geldo.foca in hox mañ.ep̃i.

8 In HESTLEY 2 free men under patronage; 10 acres.
Value 20d.

9 In OCCOLD 1 free man under patronage; 8 acres.
Value 16d.
    Ralph holds the whole of this in lordship.
The King and the Earl (have) the jurisdiction.
In the same (Occold) 1 free man under the patronage of the Abbot
of St. Edmund's; 2 acres.
Value 4d.
    The King and the Earl (have) the jurisdiction.

LANDS OF ROBERT OF TOSNY

RISBRIDGE Hundred
1 Ulf, a thane, held BRADLEY as a manor before 1066; now [Robert]
holds (it) in lordship; 7 carucates of land.
    Always 14 villagers; 12 smallholders; 6 slaves;
    3 ploughs in lordship; 7 men's ploughs.
    Meadow, 13 acres; woodland, 500 pigs. Always 1 cob. Then 12
        cattle, now 18; then 60 pigs, now 53; then 20 sheep, now 63;
        7 goats; 1 beehive.
    A church with 15 acres of free land.
Value then £6; now [£] 8.
It has 1 league in length and 7 furlongs in width; 6d in tax.

429 b

BISHOP'S Hundred
2 Ulf held SYLEHAM, with the jurisdiction, before 1066; as a manor,
    2½ carucates of land.
    Then 8 villagers, now 3; then 12 smallholders, now 13; now 1
        slave.
    Always 3 ploughs in lordship. Then and later 12 men's ploughs,
        now 4.
    Woodland, 150 pigs; meadow, 8 acres; always 1 mill. Then 2 cobs,
        now 1; then 8 cattle, now 2; then 80 pigs, now 44. Now 7
        sheep, 3 goats, 1 beehive.
Value then 100s; now the same.
In the same (Syleham) 5 free men under the patronage of [his]
predecessor; 30 acres. Then 1 plough, now ½.
    Meadow, 1 acre.
Value 5s.
    A church with 16 acres; value 2s.
    (It has) 1 league in length and 8 furlongs in width; 7½d in tax.
The jurisdiction (is) in the Bishop's manor of Hoxne.

⊬ *BLIDIGGA*. H̃. Mealla teñ mannig lib̃ hō ꝑ mañ. 7 modo
ħt Rodbt̃⁹ in dñio. iii . cař třæ . femp viii . uiłł . femp . xii . borđ . femp
iii . ferú . femp . ii . cař in dñio . iii . cař hom̃ . filua . ad . c . porč . v . ac̃
p̃ti . tc̃ . i . moł . modo . nułł . femp . ii . runč . vii . añ . xxx . porč . xvi .
ous̃ . Tc̃ uał . ʟ . foł . modo . ʟx . 7 ħt . x . qř in longū . & . vii . in łař .
& reddit . ii . đ . de gełdᵒ.

⊬ Gokesford teñ mannig ꝑ mañ . m̃ teñ . R . iñ dñio . v . cař ˒errǽ
Tc̃ xii . uiłł . modo . ix . Tc̃ . ii . borđ . m̃ . nul . femp . i . ferú . femp
. ii . cař in dñio . 7 hom̃ . iii . Silú . ad . xxx . porč . xx . ac̃ p̃ti . femp̃
˒i . runč . vii . añ . xxx . porč . 7 tc̃ uał xl . foł . modo . ʟx . 7 ħt . x.
qř in longo ˒ 7 vii . in łař . iii . đ . de gełto ;

★ ⊬ TERRA WALTERI GIFART ; *PERREHAM*.   .XLV.

DĨM . H̃ . In blacheffala . i . lib̃ . Codricus . dimiđi⁹ fub ꞇomdaꞇ
ante ceffori mał& . & dim̃ ab̃bi . de eli . x . ac̃ . & uał . xx . đ . Rad
de Langhetot teñ . Soca ab̃bis.

⊬ *PLVMESGATA . H̃ .* Gliemham . teñ . Starlinc . cʟxxx .
ac̃ . ꝑ mañ . t . r . e . dimiđi⁹ ꞇomdat⁹ Ab̃bi de eli & dimiđi⁹ . Wiłłmo
mał& . & inde faifitus fuit femp xi . borđ . & . ii . cař . in dñio .
& . i . cař hom̃ . & . i . ac̃ p̃ti . femp . ii . runč . Tc̃ xvi . por . modo
xxvi . Tc̃ xxx . ous̃ . modo . ʟ . Tc̃ uał xl . foł M̊ . ʟx . 7 st̃ additi
★ xxiiii . lib̃i hões ꞇomd . c . ac̃ . femp . iii . cař & uał . xl . foł .
ħt . i . łg̃ . in longo & dim̃ in lato . & xx đ . de gelto .

⊬ In Straffort . teñ . iđe . i . cař terrǽ . ꝑ mañ . t . r . e . femp . v . borđ .

BLYTHING Hundred

3 Manni, a free man, held MELLS as a manor; now Robert has (it) in lordship; 3 carucates of land.

Always 8 villagers; always 12 smallholders; always 3 slaves.
Always 2 ploughs in lordship; 3 men's ploughs.
Woodland for 100 pigs; meadow, 5 acres; then 1 mill, now none.
Always 2 cobs, 7 cattle, 30 pigs, 16 sheep.
Value then 50s; now 60[s].
It has 10 furlongs in length and 7 in width; it pays 2d in tax.

4 Manni held YOXFORD as a manor; now Robert holds (it) in lordship; 5 carucates of land.

Then 12 villagers, now 9; then 2 smallholders, now none; always 1 slave.
Always 2 ploughs in lordship; 3 men's [ploughs].
Woodland for 30 pigs; meadow, 20 acres. Always 1 cob, 7 cattle, 30 pigs.
Value then 40s; now 60[s].
It has 10 furlongs in length and 7 in width; 3d in tax.

5   LAND OF WALTER GIFFARD

PARHAM Half-Hundred

1 In BLAXHALL 1 free [man], Godric, half under the sub-patronage of Malet's predecessor and half (under that) of the Abbot of Ely; 10 acres.
Value 20d.

Ralph of Lanquetot holds (this).
The jurisdiction (is) the Abbot's.

PLOMESGATE Hundred

2 Starling held (Great) GLEMHAM; 180 acres as a manor before 1066; (he was) half under the patronage of the Abbot of Ely and half (under that) of William Malet (who) was in possession of it.

Always 11 smallholders;
2 ploughs in lordship; 1 men's plough.
Meadow, 1 acre. Always 2 cobs. Then 16 pigs, now 26; then 30 sheep, now 50.
Value then 40s; now 60[s].
24 free men under patronage were added; 100 acres. Always 3 ploughs.
Value 40s.
It has 1 league in length and ½ in width; 20d in tax.

3 In STRATFORD (St. Andrew) the same man held 1 carucate of land as a manor before 1066.

Always 5 smallholders;

&.ɪ.car̆ in dñio. 7 dim̄ car̆ hom̄.&.ɪɪɪɪ.ac̄ p̃ti.&.ɪ.mol̄.7 ual
xʟ.fol̄.In ead xɪɪɪ.libi hões. 7 dim̄.c̄omd̄.femp.ʟx.ac̄.7.ɪɪɪɪ.
&.ɪ.car̆.& dim̄. 7 ual̄.vɪɪ.fol̄. Totū ten&.Rad̄.de Langhetot.
Soca abbis de eli.

.XLVI. ⟨TERRE COMITISSE.DE ALBAMARLA.BABENɞga ⭑
duo.H̄. In Simplinga teñ Vluric̆ tenñ.reğ.e.p̃ mañ.v.car̆.terræ.
M̊ teñ comitiffa.de albamarla.Tc̄.v.uilt.modo.ɪɪɪ.Tc̄ & p̊.ɪɪɪɪ.bod̆r.
modo.x.femp.vɪ.feru̇.Tc̄ &.p̊.ɪɪɪ.car̆.in dñio.modo.ɪɪ.Semp.ɪɪɪ.
car̆ hom̄.Silu̇ vɪɪɪ.porc̄.&.x.ac̄ p̃ti.Sep̄.ɪ.eq̊.Tc̄ xɪɪɪɪ.añ.
m̊.vɪ.Tc̄ xʟ.porc̄.modo.xxɪɪɪɪ.Tc̄.c.xx.ōus.modo.c.Ecclia.de
xxx.ac̄.In ead̄.v.libi hões uluric̆ c̄omd̄ 7 foc̄a 7 fac̄a.sc̄i.e.t.r.e.
modo h̆t c̄omitiffa.ɪ.car̆ terre.&.ɪ.bord̄.&.ɪ.feru̇.Sep̄.ɪɪ.car̆.
&.ɪɪ.ac̄ p̃ti.Tc̄ & femp ual̄.ɪx.lib̄.h̆t.ɪ.lḡ in longo. 7 dim̄ in lato.
& de gelto.v.d̄.

⟨Scerdatra teñ id̄.ulricus.t.r.e.p̃ mañ.ɪ.car̆ terræ.Semp.ɪ.uilt
⭑ &.ɪɪɪ.bord̄.&.ɪɪɪ.fer.Tc̄.ɪɪ.car̆.in dñio.modo.nult.Semp.ɪ.car̆ h̊ou̇m̄
7.ɪɪɪ.ac̄ p̃ti.Semp ual̄.ʟx.fol̄.h̆t.ɪɪɪɪ.qr̄ in longo. 7.ɪɪ.in lato.
& de gelto.ɪɪ.d̄.& obol̄.

⟨SANFORT.H̄.7 dim̄.Belefted̄a tenuit Aluric̆ de Wein-
hou.ɪɪɪ.car̆ terræ. 7 xʟ.ac̄.p̃ mañ.femp.xɪɪ.uilt. 7.ɪɪɪ.bord̄.Tc̄
.v.feru̇.m̊.ɪ.Tc̄.ɪɪ.car̆ in dominio.m̊.ɪ.Tc̄.vɪɪɪ.car̆.P̊ 7 m̊.v.7.vɪ.
ac̄ p̃ti.Tc̄ filua.de xxx.porc̆.m̊.xx.Ecclia.de xxx.ɪɪɪɪ.ac̄ libe
terræ.modo xxvɪɪ.porc̆. 7 xxx.v.ōus.Tc̄ ual̄ vɪɪɪ.lib̄.modo.vɪ.

430 b

1 plough in lordship; ½ men's plough.
Meadow, 4 acres; 1 mill.
Value 40s.
In the same (Stratford St. Andrew) 13 free men and a half, under
patronage; always 60 acres and 4; 1½ ploughs.
Value 7s.
Ralph of Lanquetot holds the whole.
The jurisdiction (is) the Abbot of Ely's.

LANDS OF THE COUNTESS OF AUMÂLE

430 b

BABERGH Two Hundreds
1 In SHIMPLING Wulfric, a thane of King Edward's, held 5 carucates of
land as a manor. Now the Countess of Aumâle holds (it).
>
> Then 5 villagers, now 3; then and later 4 smallholders, now 10;
> always 6 slaves.
>
> Then and later 3 ploughs in lordship, now 2; always 3 men's
> ploughs.
>
> Woodland, 8 pigs; meadow, 10 acres. Always 1 horse. Then 14
> cattle, now 6; then 40 pigs, now 24; then 120 sheep, now 100.
>
> A church with 30 acres.

In the same (Shimpling) 5 free men; Wulfric (had) the patronage
and St. Edmund's (had) full jurisdiction before 1066; now the
Countess has (them); 1 carucate of land.
>
> 1 smallholder; 1 slave.
>
> Always 2 ploughs. Meadow, 2 acres.

Value then and always £9.
>
> It has 1 league in length and ½ in width; 5d in tax.

2 Wulfric also held CHADACRE before 1066 as a manor; 1 carucate of
land.
>
> Always 1 villager; 3 smallholders; [2] slaves.
>
> Then 2 ploughs in lordship, now 1; always 1 men's plough.
> Meadow, 3 acres.

Value always 60s.
>
> It has 4 furlongs in length and 2 in width; 2½d in tax.

SAMFORD Hundred and a Half
3 Aelfric of *Weinhou* held BELSTEAD; 3 carucates of land and 40 acres
as a manor.
>
> Always 12 villagers; 3 smallholders. Then 5 slaves, now 1.
>
> Then 2 ploughs in lordship, now 1; then 8 [men's] ploughs,
> later and now 5.
>
> Meadow, 6 acres; woodland then at 30 pigs, now 20.
>
> A church with 34 acres of free land.
>
> Now 27 pigs, 35 sheep.

Value then £8; now [£] 6.

Idē Aluricus focā . ħt . I . lḡ in longo . & . III . qr̄ . in lato . 7 de gelto
.VII . đ . ⫽Hercheſtedā . teñ . Edeua . faira . VII . car̄ t̄ræ ꝓ mañ . t . r . e
ſemp . XVII . uiłł . 7 VIII . borđ . Tc̄ . I . ſeru̅ . Tc̄ . III . car̄ . in dominio . P̄ 7 m̄
.II.ſemper . V . car̄ hom̄ . VIII . ac̄ p̄ti . filua . XXX . porc̄ . 7 . I . mol . Ec
clia XXIIII . ac̄ . & . IIII . añ . 7 XXIIII . porc̄ . 7 XL . ou̅s . 7 XXVII . cap̄ .

Tc̄ uał . X . liƀ . modo XIIII . ħt . I . leḡ in longo . 7 dimiđ in lat̄ . 7
XIIII . đ . de gelto;
⫽Gutthulues forđā ten& . Edeua . t . r . e . II . car̄ terræ ꝓ mañ .
ſemꝑ . I . uiłł & . VI . borđ . Tc̄ . II . car̄ hominu̅ . m̄ . I . 7 . III . car̄ poſſent reſtaurari . VIII . ac̄ p̄ti . Tc̄ filua . XX . porc̄ . Tc̄ . I . moliñ . Tc̄ia
pars æcclīæ . VIII . ac̄ . & uał . III . liƀ . ħt . VIII . qr̄ in longo . 7 . III . in lato .
& . V . đ de gelto . Edeua focā .
HVnđ . De coleneſſe . In helmelea . I . uiłł . de . IX . ac̄ . & uał . XX . đ .
& ꝑtin& ad cloptuna .
HVnđ de carleforda . In clopetuna tenuit Burric̄ liƀ hō . Radulfi
ſtalra . t . r . e . I . car̄ terræ . & XX . ac̄ ꝓ mañ . Semꝑ . XI . borđ . 7
in dñio . II . car̄ . Tc̄ hom̄ . II . car̄ . modo . I . IIII . ac̄ p̄ti . 7 X . porc̄
7 XXX . V . ou̅s . Semꝑ uał . XL . ſoł . In eađ . VI . ac̄ . q̄s ſeruat & ten&
Vluin pƀr . & uał . XII . đ .
⫽In burg . II . liƀi homines . I . cōmdation̄ . S . e . 7 alii cōm . R . comiti
de XXXVI . ac̄ . 7 . II . borđ . Tc̄ . car̄ ꝰ modo dim̄ . II . ac̄ p̄ti . 7 uał . VI . ſoł .
⫽In cloptuna . XII . liƀi hoes 7 dim̄ cōmdati . Burrici . t . r . e . LXXXXII .
ac̄ . & . II . borđ . Tc̄ . III . car̄ . modo . II . I . ac̄ p̄ti . 7 uał . XVI . ſoł . 7 . IIII . đ .

Aelfric also (had) the jurisdiction. It has 1 league in length and 3 furlongs in width; 7d in tax.

4 Edeva the Fair held HARKSTEAD; 7 carucates of land as a manor before 1066.
Always 17 villagers; 8 smallholders. Then 1 slave.
Then 3 ploughs in lordship, later and now 2; always 5 men's ploughs.
Meadow, 8 acres; woodland, 30 pigs; 1 mill.
A church, 24 acres.
4 cattle, 24 pigs, 40 sheep, 27 goats.
Value then £10; now [£] 14.
It has 1 league in length and ½ in width; 14d in tax.

431 a

5 Edeva [held] GUSFORD before 1066; 2 carucates of land as a manor.
Always 1 villager; 6 smallholders.
Then 2 men's ploughs, now 1; 3 ploughs could be restored.
Meadow, 8 acres; woodland, then 20 pigs; then 1 mill.
The third part of a church, 8 acres.
Value £3.
It has 8 furlongs in length and 3 in width; 5d in tax. Edeva (had) the jurisdiction.

Hundred of COLNEIS

6 In HEMLEY 1 villager, with 9 acres.
Value 20d.
It belongs to Clopton.

Hundred of CARLFORD

7 In CLOPTON Burgric, a free man of Ralph the Constable's, held before 1066; 1 carucate of land and 20 acres as a manor.
Always 11 smallholders;
2 ploughs in lordship. Then 2 men's ploughs, now 1.
Meadow, 4 acres. 10 pigs, 35 sheep.
Value always 40s.
In the same (Clopton) 6 acres which Wulfwin the priest looks after and holds.
Value 12d.

8 In BURGH 2 free men; 1 under the patronage of St. Etheldreda's, the other under the patronage of Earl R(alph); with 36 acres.
2 smallholders.
Then 2 ploughs, now ½. Meadow, 2 acres.
Value 6s.

9 In CLOPTON 12 free men and a half under the patronage of Burgric before 1066; 92 acres.
2 smallholders.
Then 3 ploughs, now 2. Meadow, 1 acre.
Value 16s 4d.

HVnd. *DE WILEFORD*. In depebes. iii. libi hões. com̃. Edrici
grim xx. ac̃. i. ac̃ p̃ti. Tc̃. i. car̃. 7 ual. iii. fol. i. æcclia. viii. ac̃. 7
ual. xvi. deñ. ⌐In bulges. i. lib̃ hõ dim̃ ac̃. & ual. ii. d̃.
⌐HVnd. De Lofa. In mungadena. v. ac̃. 7 in caresfella. iii. ac̃.
& ual. xii. d̃.

.XLVII. *H̃. DE COLONESE*. T̃RÆ WIL̃L̃ de arcis. In helmele. i. bord̃. ★
.v. ac̃. 7 p̃tinent ad cloptuna. 7 in precio.

*H̃. DE CARLE*ford. In cloptuna. teñ Ædmund p̃br. lib̃ hõ. s̃. Æ.
.t. r. e. i. car̃ terræ. 7 xx. ii. ac̃. p mañ. &. i. uill. &. vii. bord̃. Tc̃ in dñio
iii. car̃. modo. i. Tc̃ hom̃. i. car̃. modo dim̃. iiii. ac̃ p̃ti. modo. i. runc̃.
Tc̃. iiii. añ. Tc̃ xl porc̃. Tc̃ xxx. ou̅s. modo int̃ totũ nichil. Tc̃ ual
xxx. fol. modo. x. h̃ ten& Bernard de s̃co Audoeno. de W.
HVnd. DE LOSA Branteftuna. tenuit Ædmundus p̃br
com̃d. s̃. Æ. t. r. e. 7 terrã q̃ cepit. cũ uxore ei. de branteftuna
& de cloptuna. mifit in ecclia concedente muliere. tali conuentione qd̃ non potuit uendere nec dare. de æcclia. lx. ac̃. terræ p mañ
&. v. bord̃. &. ii. feru̅. 7 in dñio. i. car̃. 7 houm̃. i. car̃. v. ac̃ p̃ti. filu̅
ad vi. porc̃. Addite st̃ huic manerio. lxxx. ac̃. terræ p mañ. t. r. e.
Tc̃. iiii. bord̃. m̊. xii. bord̃. modo int̃ eos. i. car̃. Silua ad viii. porc̃.
7. iiii. ac̃ p̃ti. 7. i. moliñ. modo. i. runc̃. 7 xx. porc̃. 7 xvi. ou̅s. 7 xxx.
cap̅. 7 iii. uafa apu̅. Tc̃ ual totũ fimul. c. fol. modo. lx. fol.
h̃ h̃t Willm̃. p. i. mañ. fed. t. r. e. erant duo. i. æcclia. xii. ac̃. 7 ual
. ii. fol. 7 h̃t in longo. i. leuga. & in lato. iii. q̃r. 7 de gelto. v. d̃. & obol̃.

Hundred of WILFORD

10 In DEBACH 3 free men under the patronage of Edric Grim; 20 acres.
Meadow, 1 acre.
Then 1 plough.
Value 3s.
1 church, 8 acres; value 16d.

11 In BOULGE 1 free man; ½ acre.
Value 2d.

Hundred of LOES

12 In MONEWDEN 5 acres and in CHARSFIELD 3 acres.
Value 12d.

7   LANDS OF WILLIAM OF ARQUES   431 b

Hundred of COLNEIS

1 In HEMLEY 1 smallholder; 5 acres. They belong to Clopton.
(It is) in the assessment.

Hundred of CARLFORD

2 In CLOPTON Edmund the priest, a free man of St. Etheldreda's, held
before 1066; 1 carucate of land and 22 acres as a manor.
1 villager; 7 smallholders.
Then 3 ploughs in lordship, now 1; then 1 men's plough, now ½.
Meadow, 4 acres. Now 1 cob. Then 4 cattle, then 40 pigs, then
30 sheep; now nothing at all.
Value then 30s; now 10[s].
Bernard of St. Ouen holds this from William.

Hundred of LOES

3 Edmund the priest, under the patronage of St. Etheldreda's, held
BRANDESTON before 1066; and the land which he received with his
wife, (parts) of Brandeston and Clopton, he gave up to the Church
with his wife's consent by such an agreement that he could not sell
or grant (it) away from the Church; 60 acres of land as a manor.
5 smallholders; 2 slaves.
1 plough in lordship; 1 men's plough.
Meadow, 5 acres; woodland for 6 pigs.
80 acres of land, (held) as a manor before 1066, were added to this
manor.
Then 4 smallholders, now 12 smallholders.
Now 1 plough between them.
Woodland for 8 pigs; meadow, 4 acres; 1 mill. Now 1 cob, 20
pigs, 16 sheep, 30 goats, 3 beehives.
Value of the whole together then 100s; now 60s.
William has this as 1 manor, but before 1066 there were two.
1 church, 12 acres; value 2s.
It has 1 league in length and 3 furlongs in width; 5½d in tax.

★ **T**ERRA **D**ROGONIS DE BEVRERIA. *H͞VND*. de blidinga. .XLVI

Sudretunā. tenuit. Rada lib h͞o de heroldo . ıı . car̛ terræ . ꝑ man͞
M ten& franc̛ de drogone . Tc̄ & p̛꞉ xvı . borđ . modo xıx | ſeru.
Tc̄ & p̛꞉ ı . car̛ in dn͞io . m̊ . ıı . femꝑ . ııı . car̛ hom̛ . 7 . ıı . ac̄ p̛ti . ſilua
de . c . porc̛ . Eccłia.de . v . ac̄ . & . ı . run̛ . & . modo . ı . an͞ . Tc̄ . xıı . porc̛.
modo xxıııı . 7 xxv . o͞us . femꝑ xl . ſoł . ħt . ı . lg͞ in longo . & dim͞ in -
lato . 7 . ı . đ . 7 . ııı . ferdig . de gelto . Rada ante ceſſor drogonis
habuit ſocā & facā . huic manerio addidit hainfridus de Ꞅco b̄tino
. ı . lib͞u de . xıı . ac̄ . de q̊ habuit ſuus anteceſſor c͞md . t . r . e . femꝑ
. ı . borđ . & dim͞ . car̛ . & uał . ıı . ſoł.

★ **T**ERRE hugonis de Grentemeſnil . Dim͞ . *H̃* . De crosfort. .XLVII

Leiham ten& Alfnod de heroldo . t . r . e . ꝑ man͞ . ııı . car̛ terræ
femp . ıııı . uiłł . & . vıı . borđ . Tc̄ . v . ſeru . modo . vı . femꝑ . ıı . car̛ in dn͞io.
& . ıı . car̛ hom̛ . 7 xı . ac̄ p̛ti . 7 . ı . runc̛ . & . xv . an͞ . 7 xv . porc̛ . & . c.
o͞us . 7 xıx . cap̄ . Tc̄ uał lxx . ſoł . modo . c . ħt dim͞ lg͞ in longo &
dim͞ in lat̛ . & . ıııı . đ de gelto . & oboł . S̛ . e . ſocā.

★ **T**ERRÆ . Rađ . de felgeris . Eſtuteſtuna . tenuit Vlſi lib h͞o
c͞omđ . Guerti . ıı . car̛ terræ ꝑ man͞ . t . r . e . Semꝑ . ıııı . uiłł . &

ıııı . borđ . Tc̄ in dn͞io . ıı . car̛ . M̊ . ı . Sēp hom̛ . ı . car̛ . vı . ac̄ p̛ti . Tc̄ . ıı . an̈.
M̊ . ı . Tc̄ . v . porc̛ . Tc̄ uał lx . ſoł . m̊ . xl . ſoł . & ııı . lib͞i hŏes com̛ . Vlſi
xıı . ac̄ . & uał . ıı . ſoł . Rex & com͞s ſoc̛.
_F_ In frondeſtuna . vı . ac̄ . & uał . xıı . đ.

LAND OF DROGO OF BEUVRIÈRE

Hundred of BLYTHING

1 Rada, a free man, held SOTHERTON from Harold; 2 carucates of land
  as a manor. Now Frank holds (it) from Drogo.
   Then and later 16 smallholders, now 19; always 2 slaves.
   Then and later 1 plough in lordship, now 2; always 3 men's
      ploughs.
   Meadow, 2 acres; woodland at 100 pigs.
   A church with 5 acres.
   1 cob; now 1 cattle; then 12 pigs, now 34; 25 sheep.
Value always 40s.
   It has 1 league in length and ½ in width; 1¾d in tax. Rada,
Drogo's predecessor, had full jurisdiction.
   To this manor Humphrey of St. Bertins added 1 free [man] with
12 acres, over whom his predecessor had patronage before 1066.
   Always 1 smallholder;
   ½ plough.
Value 2s.

LANDS OF HUGH OF GRANDMESNIL

Half-Hundred of COSFORD

Alfnoth [held] LAYHAM from Harold before 1066 as a manor;
3 carucates of land.
   Always 4 villagers; 7 smallholders. Then 5 slaves, now 6.
   Always 2 ploughs in lordship; 2 men's ploughs.
   Meadow, 11 acres. 1 cob, 15 cattle, 15 pigs, 100 sheep, 19 goats.
Value then 70s; now 100[s].
   It has ½ league in length and ½ in width; 4½d in tax. St.
E(dmund's has) the jurisdiction.

LANDS OF RALPH OF FOUGÈRES

[Hundred of HARTISMERE]

Wulfsi, a free man under the patronage of Gyrth, held STUSTON;
2 carucates of land as a manor before 1066.
   Always 4 villagers; 4 smallholders.

   Then 2 ploughs in lordship, now 1; always 1 men's plough.
   Meadow, 6 acres. Then 2 cattle, now 1; then 5 pigs.
Value then 60s; now 40s.
3 free men under the patronage of Wulfsi; 12 acres.
Value 2s.
   The King and the Earl (have) the jurisdiction.

In THRANDESTON 6 acres.
Value 12d.

TERRA GALTERI DE SCO WALERICO. *STOV.* *H̃.* ★

In Cratinga ten̄ Aluric̄ lib̄ hō t . r . e . edrici ant̄ Rotb̄ti . mal.

com̄d tant̄ Rotb̄t̄ tenuit f7 p̄ fuit̄ defaitus . i . car̄ . & dim̄ tr̄æ

& . ii . uilt . 7 ix . bord . Semp . ii . car̄ & dim̄ in dn̄io . Tc̄ . i . car̄ . hom̄.

p̄ & modo dim̄ . Tc̄ filua xl porc̄ . m̄ . nult . 7 . i . mol . 7 vi . ac̄ p̄ti.

& dim̄ æcclia . x . ac̄ libæ tr̄æ . 7 . v . an̄ . 7 ix . ous̄ . 7 . xii . porc̄ . 7 ual̄

. c . fol . In ead ten̄ Galt̄ . i . lib̄ hō . Tholi com̄d . x . ac̄ . 7 dim̄ . Tc̄ 7 p̄

7 m̄ dim̄ car̄ . 7 ual̄ . iii . fol.

BOSEMERA . *H̃* . In Cratinga .. i . lib̄ hō .. lx . ac̄ . t . r . e . com̄dat

ante ceffori Robti mal& & pat̄ ei inde faifitus fuit femp . iiii.

uilt . 7 dim̄ car̄ h̄ iac& in Cratingis in hund de Stou & in p̄tio.

In ead . iiii . libi h̄oes cm̄ . vii . ac̄ jn Vledana . i . lib̄ hō . com̄d . iiii . ac̄.

& ual̄ . ii . fol . Rex & com̄s foca.

Hundred of CARLFORD

1 In OTLEY Aelfled, a free woman under the patronage of E(dric),
   Robert Malet's predecessor; 1½ carucates of land.
   Always 3 villagers; 10 smallholders.
   Then 2 ploughs in lordship, now 1½; then 3 men's ploughs,
     now 2.
   Woodland for 20 pigs; meadow, 2 acres. Always 2 cobs. Then 5
     cattle; then 40 pigs, now the same; always 100 sheep, 25
     goats, 6 beehives.
   Value then 100s; now £6.
   William Malet was in possession on the day he died; later Robert
   (was in possession), as the Hundred testifies.
   In the same (Otley) Lustwin, under the patronage of E(dric) before
   1066, held ½ carucate of land as a manor.
   Always 1 villager; 4 smallholders.
   Then 1 plough in lordship, now 1½; always 1 men's plough.
   Meadow, 2 acres; woodland for 5 pigs.
   Value then 20s; now 30[s].
   In the same (Otley) 16 free men and a half under the patronage of
   Leofled; 69 acres. Then 3 ploughs, and now (the same).
   Value then 20s; now 30s.
   1 church with 20 acres; value 4s.
   William Malet was in possession of the whole of this on the day
   he died, and later Robert (was in possession).
   The King and the Earl (have) the jurisdiction.
   In the same (Otley) Amund holds; 1 free man, Brictwold, under the
   patronage of Queen Edith; 30 acres.
   1 villager; 4 smallholders.
   Then 1 plough, now 1½.
   Meadow, 1 acre; woodland for 10 pigs.
   Value then 8s; now 10[s].

2 In CLOPTON 20 acres.
   1 smallholder.
   Value 5s.
   Amund holds this from Humphrey.

3 In OTLEY 6 free men under the patronage of Brictwold; 27 acres of
   land. Then 2 ploughs, now 1.
   Value then 10s; now the same.

4 In BURGH 1 free man, half under the patronage of the same man and
   half (under that) of St. Etheldreda's; 24 acres. ½ plough.
   Meadow, ½ acre.
   Value 10s.

433 b

LXXX.III.ac.p̄ man̄.Tc & modo.I.uiłł.&.I.bord.&.I.feru.
& in dn̄io.I.car.& hom̄ d̄.car.IIII.ac p̄ti.I.æcclia.VIII.ac.
7 uał.XVI.den̄.Semp III.runc.&.III.an̄.7 XXIIII.porc.
& XL.ous̄.7 XX.V.cap̄.7.IIII.uafa apū.Tc uał.XX.fol.m̄.
XXX.In eadē.VIII.libi hōes integros.7.IIII.dim̄.comd.eid.
LXVI.ac træ.Tc.II.car.modo.I.7 dim̄.I.ac p̄ti.Tc uał.XX.fol.
Modo.XXXI.fol.

HVNDRET^de *BOSEMERA*.In affa tenuit Aluuinus
lib hō.IIII.ac.Tc uał XVI.d.modo.VIII.In oteleia hunfrid
ten& in dn̄io.I.lib hm̄.III.uirg.& uał.III.d.In ead.I.liba
femina.Lifteua.I.ac.& uał&.II.d̄.

In brictices haga eft filua q̊ poterant pafci XVI.porc
t.r.e.modo IIII.& Amundus ten& de hunfrido 7 iacet
in gratinge ham.

Claindune.*HVNdret*.Elminghehā tenuit Grimolf
lib homo comdat regine.c.XX.ac træ & iac& in dn̄io
de oteleia.femp.I.uiłł.&.V.bord.7.I.car hominū.III.
ac p̄ti.Silu.L.porc.& ē in p̄tio de oteleia In ead in dn̄io
XI.libi hōes comdati fub ante ceffore p̄t duo q̊ fuerant
comdati brictuoldo.t.r.e.LXVIII.ac.t.r.e.femper
II.car.7 uał.XX.fol.In ead ten̄ lib homo Brictu
oldus.XL.ac.t.r.e.femp.II.uiłłi.7.III.bord
femp.II.car.III.ac|7 uał.XX.fol.Amund
ten& de hunfrido.Rex 7 Coms̄ foci.

Hundred of LOES

5 Amund holds CRETINGHAM; Brictwold held (it) under the patronage
of the Queen; 83 acres as a manor.

Then and now 1 villager, 1 smallholder, 1 slave;
1 plough in lordship; ½ men's plough.
Meadow, 4 acres.
1 church, 8 acres; value 16d.
Always 3 cobs, 3 cattle, 24 pigs, 40 sheep, 25 goats, 4 beehives.
Value then 20s; now 30[s].
In the same (Cretingham) 8 whole and 4 half free men under the
patronage of the same man; 66 acres of land. Then 2 ploughs,
now 1½.
Meadow, 1 acre.
Value then 20s; now 31s.

Hundred of BOSMERE

6 In ASH(BOCKING) Alwin, a free man, held 4 acres.
Value then 16d; now 8[d].

7 In OTLEY Humphrey holds in lordship 1 free man; 3 poles (of land).
Value 3d.
In the same (Otley) 1 free woman, Licteva; 1 acre.
Value 2d.

8 In *BRICTICESHAGA* there is woodland in which 16 pigs could be
pastured before 1066, now 4. Amund holds (it) from Humphrey.
It belongs to Cretingham.

CLAYDON Hundred

9 Grimwulf, a free man under the patronage of the Queen, held
HELMINGHAM; 120 acres. It belongs to the lordship of Otley.
Always 1 villager; 5 smallholders;
1 men's plough.
Meadow, 3 acres; woodland, 50 pigs.
It is in the assessment of Otley.
In the same (Helmingham) in lordship 11 free men, under patronage
under (his) predecessor, except for two who were under the
patronage of Brictwold before 1066; 68 acres before 1066. Always
2 ploughs.
Value 20s.
In the same (Helmingham) a free man, Brictwold, held 40 acres
before 1066.
Always 2 villagers; 3 smallholders.
Always 2 ploughs. Meadow, 3 acres.
Value 20s.
Anund holds (this) from Humphrey.
The King and the Earl (have) the jurisdiction.

In Affefelda . ıı . liɓi homs . ıııı . ac̄ & uaɫ . vııı . d̄ . Soca aɓɓis.

★ In bermefdena . tenuit . ıı . liɓ hões Anant . ⁷ ĭ cuñ. ɫxx . ac̄ t̄ . r̄ . e.

femp . ı . borð . Tc̄ . ı . car . ıı . ac̄ p̃ti . Tc̄ uaɫ xx . foɫ . modo xxx.

Hunfrið in dn̄io Rex & Com̄s foca Et . ı . liɓ hō addit̄ . ıııı.

ac̄ . & uaɫ . ıı . foɫ.

★ Terræ eVdonis filii spirVic . *Lacforda* H̃. .ı.ııı.

In ecclingaham Moruant ten& de eudone quā tenuit

Anant liɓ hō fub sc̄a aldreda . t̄ . r̄ . e. .p̱ mañ . ıı . car terræ

fed n̄ poterat uende . m̄ ten& eudo filī fpiruic ab henfrido

ante ceffore fuo . f⁊ foca & faca . sc̄ı . e . Tc̄ ⁊ p̃ . vıı . uiɫɫ . m̄

vı . ⁊ . vı . borð . & . ı . feru . Semp . ıı . car in dn̄io . ⁊ . ı . car hom̄.

& . v . ac̄ p̃ti . ⁊ . ı . moliñ . modo . ɫxxx . ıııı . ous̄ . Tc̄ uaɫ ıııı.

liɓ . modo . ɫx . foɫ.

BoSemera . ħ . Wledanā ten Siric̄ liɓ hō . t̄ . r̄ . e. .p̱ mañ

modo Wiɫ . ɫxx . ac̄ . femp . ıı . borð . Tc̄ . ıı . car . modo . ı . ⁊ d̄ . &.

. ıı . ac̄ p̃ti . Tc̄ . ıı . runc . modo xvı . porc̄ . ⁊ xxvııı . ous̄ . ⁊ uaɫ

xx . foɫ . In ead̄ . xııı . liɓi hões de duob₂ habuit ante ceffor.

Rog̃ı . com̄ðtion xɫ . ac̄ . & . ı . car̄ . ⁊ uaɫ x . foɫ . Rex . & com̄s

focā . ħt . ı . lg̃ in longo . & . ııı . qr̄ in laɫ . & . x . d̄ . de gelto.

Alii ibi tenent ;

10 In ASHFIELD 2 free men; 4 acres.
Value 8d.
The jurisdiction (is) the Abbot's.

11 In *BERMESDENA* Anund held 2 free men in patronage; [60] acres
before 1066.
Always 1 smallholder.
Then 1 plough. Meadow, 2 acres.
Value then 20s; now 30[s].
Humphrey [holds this] in lordship.
The King and the Earl (have) the jurisdiction.
1 free man has been added; 4 acres.
Value 2s.

53 LANDS OF EUDO SON OF SPIRWIC

LACKFORD Hundred
1 In ICKLINGHAM Morvant holds from Eudo what Anund, a free man,
held under St. Etheldreda's before 1066 as a manor; 2 carucates of
land. But he could not sell. Now Eudo son of Spirwic holds (it);
from Heinfrid, his predecessor. But the full jurisdiction (is) St.
Edmund's.
Then and later 7 villagers, now 6; 6 smallholders; 1 slave.
Always 2 ploughs in lordship; 1 men's plough.
Meadow, 5 acres; 1 mill. Now 84 sheep.
Value then £4; now 60s.

BOSMERE Hundred
2 Siric, a free man, held 'OLDEN' before 1066 as a manor; now William
[holds it]; 70 acres.
Always 2 smallholders.
Then 2 ploughs, now 1½.
Meadow, 2 acres. Then 2 cobs; now 16 pigs, 28 sheep.
Value 20s.
In the same ('Olden') 13 free men; Roger's predecessor had patronage
over two of them; 40 acres. 1 plough.
Value 10s.
The King and the Earl (have) the jurisdiction. It has 1 league in
length and 3 furlongs in width; 10d in tax. Others hold there.

Betesfort teñ Iarnagot quā tenuit Kerinc lib hō. t. r. e.

.ı.car terræ . 7 xx . ac̄ .p mañ . modo Jarnagod . & femp . v . borđ.
& . ı . feru . Tc̄ . ıı . car in dn̄io . modo . ı ; & đ car hom̄ . vı . ac̄ p̃ti . tc̄
filu̇ lx . porc; modo . x . Tc̄ . ıı . runc . modo . xx . porc . 7 . xı . ous̄.
7 xıı . cap̃ . 7 uat xxv . fot . In eadē . ııı . libi hoes . xx . ac̄ . de duobus
habuit fuus ante c̄ comđ . femp dim̄ car . & uat . v . fot . Rex
& com̄s focā.

In Codenham . Siric lib hō . v . ac̄ . 7 uat . x . đ . Soca regis.

HVnd . de Wanne forda . Flixtuna teñ Gosfridu̇ quā
tenuit . Offa . lib hō . com̄ . Stigando . t . r . e . ıı . car terræ . p mañ.
Tc̄ xvı . uitt . modo . x . Tc̄ . xı . borđ . modo . xıııı . Semp . ıı . feru̇.
& in dm̄io . ıı . car . Tc̄ hom̄ . xııı . car 7 dim̄ . modo . ıx . 7 dim̄.
Semp . ı . runc . & . ıı . an̄ . 7 . vı . porc . 7 xxvı . ous̄ . xıı . ac̄ p̃ti.
filu̇ ad xx . porc . dim̄ mot . Tc̄ uat . xl . fot . modo lx . dim̄ ecctia
x . ac̄ . 7 uat xvı . đ . In eađ . ıı . libi hoes . comđ eiđ . xxx . ac̄ . Semp
. ııı . borđ . 7 dim̄ . 7 . ıı . car & dim̄ . filu̇ . ad . ıı . porc . ııı . ac̄ . 7 dim̄.
p̃ti . Tc̄ uat . vıı . fot . modo . x . 7 vııı . đ . 7 ħt in longo . ı . lḡ . 7 dim̄
in lato . 7 de gelto xx . đ.

HERTES MARA . H̃ . Weft torp tenuit Vlricus hagana
. ı . car terre . p mañ . t . r . e . Semp . ı . borđ . & . ı . feru̇ . 7 in dn̄io.
. ı . car 7 dim̄ filua ad xıı . porc . vı . ac̄ p̃ti . 7 . ııı . runc . 7 . ıı . an̄.

3 Iarnagot holds BATTISFORD; Cynric, a free man, held it before 1066;   434 b
    1 carucate of land and 20 acres as a manor. Now Iarnagot (holds it).
        Always 5 smallholders; 1 slave.
        Then 2 ploughs in lordship, now 1; ½ men's plough.
        Meadow, 6 acres; woodland, then 60 pigs, now 10. Then 2 cobs;
           now 20 pigs, 11 sheep, 12 goats.
        ½ church, 20 acres.
    Value 25s.
    In the same (Battisford) 3 free men; 20 acres. His predecessor had
    patronage over two (free men). Always ½ plough.
    Value 5s.
        The King and the Earl (have) the jurisdiction.

4 In CODDENHAM Siric, a free man; in lordship, 5 acres.
    Value 10d.
        The jurisdiction (is) the King's.

Hundred of WANGFORD
5 Geoffrey holds FLIXTON; Offa, a free man under the patronage of
    Stigand, held it before 1066; 2 carucates of land as a manor.
        Then 16 villagers, now 10; then 11 smallholders, now 14. Always
           2 slaves;
        2 ploughs in lordship. Then 13½ men's ploughs, now 9½.
        Always 1 cob, 2 cattle, 6 pigs, 26 sheep. Meadow, 12 acres;
           woodland for 20 pigs; ½ mill.
    Value then 40s; now 60[s].
        ½ church, 10 acres; value 16d.
    In the same (Flixton) 2 free men under the patronage of the same
    man; 30 acres.
        Always 3 smallholders and a half;
        2½ ploughs.
        Woodland for 2 pigs; meadow, 3½ acres.
    Value then 7s; now 10[s] 8d.
        It has 1 league in length and ½ in width; 20d in tax.

HARTISMERE Hundred
6 Geoffrey also holds WESTHORPE; Wulfric Hagni held (it); 1 carucate
    of land as a manor before 1066.
        Always 1 smallholder; 1 slave;
        1½ ploughs in lordship.
        Woodland for 12 pigs; meadow, 6 acres. 3 cobs, 2 cattle,

7 xxx . i . porc . 7 . L . oũs . 7 xv . cap̃ . 7 . y . uafa apũ . Tc̃ ual xx . fol .
modo xxx . 7 xv . libi hoẽs . cõm . Vlurici . xxx . iii . ac̃ . Semp . i .
car . filua ad . ii . porc . ii . ac̃ p̃ti . 7 ual . x . fol . Sup h manerium

habuit Sc̃s eadmundus . t . r . e . Soc̃ 7 Sacã comd̃ . 7 non potuit uende nec dare ab eccłia . 7 ex xv . libis hõibʒ 7 fup Vlnoht
habuit . cõm . Ante ceffor . R . mał . tefte hund̃ . 7 ñ potuit uende
nee dare de eo . terrã fuã;

Γ DIM̃ . H̃ . De cosfort . In Weces hã . i . lib hõ . de quo abbas de eli
habuit cõm 7 focã . t . r . e . i . car terræ . 7 . iii . bord̃ . & . i . car̃ . & . iii . ac̃ p̃ti .
7 ual xx . fol . Sc̃s . E . vi . forisfac̃turas Iarnacotus ten& .

★ TERRÆ WIŁŁI . DE WATE VILLA . RISEBRVGE . H̃ .
Ligatã teñ Stori . p mañ . t . r . e . iiii . car terræ . 7 lx . ac̃ . Semp
ix . uitł . 7 xii . bord̃ . 7 . i . ferũ . & . ii . car in dñio . Tc̃ . iii . car hom̃ . m̃ .
ii . x . ac̃ p̃ti . filua de . xv . porc . femp . i . runc̃ . m̃ . v . añ . 7 xxv . porc .
Tc̃ xxx . iii . oũs modo . c . xL . 7 xiii . cap̃ . Tc̃ ual . Lxxx . fol . 7 m̃ fimił .
ħt . i . leuga in longo . & . viii . qr̃ in lato . 7 xiii . d̃ . & obol . de gelto . Alii
ibi tenent;

TINGOho . H̃ . Haragraua teñ Aluiet . i . liba femina . t . r . e . fub
sc̃o edmundo & ñ poterat uende . iiii . car træ . Tc̃ & p . vi . uitłi .
modo . viii . Tc̃ 7 p . iiii . bord̃ . modo . vii . Tc̃ . iiii . ferũ . modo . ii . Sẽp
. ii . car in dñio . Tc̃ 7 p . iiii . car hom̃ . m̃ . iii . Tc̃ . i . eq̃ . m̃ . nułł .
Tc̃ . ii . añ . modo . viii . Tc̃ . v . porc̃ . modo . xL . m̃ . c . oũs . & . iiii . ac̃
p̃ti . Silũ de . xvi . porc . Ecclia . xii . ac̃ libæ træ . Tc̃ 7 femp ual . iiii . lib .

Ħt viii . qr̃ in longo . & . v . in lato . & de gelto . vii . d̃ .

31 pigs, 50 sheep, 15 goats, 5 beehives.
Value then 20s; now 30[s].
15 free men under the patronage of Wulfric; 33 acres. Always 1 plough.
Woodland for 2 pigs; meadow, 2 acres.
Value 10s.
Over this manor before 1066 St. Edmund's had full jurisdiction and patronage. He could not sell or grant (it) away from the Church. R(obert) Malet's predecessor had patronage over the 15 free men and over Wulfnoth, as the Hundred testifies; he could not sell or grant his land away from him. 435 a

Half-Hundred of COSFORD
In WATTISHAM 1 free man over whom the Abbot of Ely had patronage and jurisdiction before 1066; 1 carucate of land.
3 smallholders.
1 plough. Meadow, 3 acres.
Value 20s.
St. Edmund's (has) the 6 forfeitures.
Iarnagot holds (this).

LANDS OF WILLIAM OF VATTEVILLE

RISBRIDGE Hundred
Stori held LIDGATE as a manor before 1066; 4 carucates of land and 60 acres.
Always 9 villagers; 12 smallholders; 1 slave;
2 ploughs in lordship. Then 3 men's ploughs, now 2. Meadow, 10 acres; woodland at 15 pigs. Always 1 cob. Now 5 cattle, 25 pigs; then 33 sheep, now 140; 13 goats.
Value then 80s; now the same.
It has 1 league in length and 8 furlongs in width; 13½d in tax.
Others hold there.

THINGOE Hundred
Aelfgyth, 1 free woman, held HARGRAVE before 1066, under St. Edmund's; she could not sell; 4 carucates of land.
Then and later 6 villagers, now 8; then and later 4 smallholders, now 7; then 4 slaves, now 2.
Always 2 ploughs in lordship; then and later 4 men's ploughs, now 3.
Then 1 horse, now none; then 2 cattle, now 8; then 5 pigs, now 40; now 100 sheep. Meadow, 4 acres; woodland at 16 pigs.
A church, 12 acres of free land.
Value then and always £4.
It has 8 furlongs in length and 5 in width; 7d in tax. 435 b

Lacheforda . $\bar{H}$. Bertunna teñ Alued . 1 . liƀ hõ . v . car̄ terre . & hanc
terrā teñ . W . de regina . modo teñ alwewe de rege . Tc̄ . x . uiłł.
modo . vii . modo . v . borđ . Tc̄ . ix feru̇ . Tc̄ . iiii . car̄ . in dominio . m̃
. 1 . Semp . iii . car̄ hom̄ . ii . piſcar̄ . ii . ac̄ p̃ti . Tc̄ . 1 . runc̄ . & modo
ii . eꝗ . Tc̄ . x . añ . modo . v̇ . Tc̄ . cc . oũs . modo . iii . Tc̄ xl . porc̄ . modo
iii . Tc̄ ual viii . liƀ . & p̃ : vi . liƀ . modo . xxx . ſol . 7 h̃t . 1 . lg̃ . in long
7 dim̄ in lato . 7 de gełto xx . đ . Soca 7 ſaca . ſc̄s . edmunđ.

TERRA JOH̄IS FILII WALERAMI . BAbenƀga duo . $\bar{H}$ ★
In bura teñ Vluric̄ fili̇ briꝗrici . t . r . e . ii . car̄ tr̄æ ſub rege . e.
Tc̄ . vii . feru̇ . 7 . 1 . faƀ . modo . iiii . feru̇ . 7 modo . ii . borđ . Semp . ii . car̄
in dñio . Silua de xl porc̄ . 7 . iiii . ac̄ p̃ti . modo . 1 . mol̄ . m̃ . ii.
eꝗ . 7 . ii . añ . Tc̄ lx . oũs . m̃ . c . xl . Tc̄ xl . porc̄ . modo . xx . m̃ . xxxv.
cap̃ . Tc̄ ual . lx . ſol . modo . xl . In eadē teñ toſti̇ liƀ hõ ſub rege.
. e . 1 . car̄ terræ . Tc̄ . 1 . uiłł . modo nułł . 7 m̃ . ii . borđ . 7 . 1 . ſer̄ . Sēp
. 1 . car̄ . Silua de . x . porc̄ . & . ii . ac̄ p̃ti . Tc̄ xl . porc̄ . m̃ xx . 7 xx.
oũs . modo . xv . cap̃ . 7 ual . xx . ſol . In ead̄ . ii . liƀi hóes herołdi.
& poterant uende . & h̃nt ꝉx . ac̄ . & . 1 . car̄ . & ual . v . ſol . & fuer̄
liƀati ad p̃ficiendū mañ.

436 a

★ TERRA HVNFRIDI FILII ALBBICI . STOV . $\bar{H}$. de eſcan -
gio normannie . In anehus . x . liƀi hóes Ketelli . com̄đ tantū
lx ac̄ . tr̄æ . & . 1 . borđ . Tc̄ . ii . car̄ . p̃ & modo . 1 . & iii . ac̄ p̃ti . 7
ual x . ſol . Rex & coms̄ ſoc̄.

LACKFORD Hundred

3 Alfgeat, 1 free man, held BARTON (Mills); 5 carucates of land.
William held this land from the Queen; now Aelfeva holds (it) from
the King.

    Then 10 villagers, now 8; now 5 smallholders; then 9 slaves.

    Then 4 ploughs in lordship, now 1; always 3 men's ploughs.

    2 fisheries; meadow, 2 acres. Then 1 cob, now 2 horses; then
       10 cattle, now 5; then 200 sheep, now 3; then 40 pigs, now 3.

Value then £8; later £6; now 30s.

    It has 1 league in length and ½ in width; 20d in tax. The full
jurisdiction (is) St. Edmund's.

55   LAND OF JOHN SON OF WALERAN

BABERGH Two Hundreds

1 In BURES Wulfric son of Brictric held before 1066 under King
Edward; 2 carucates of land.

    Then 7 slaves and 1 smith, now 4 slaves; now 2 smallholders.

    Always 2 ploughs in lordship.

    Woodland at 40 pigs; meadow, 4 acres; now 1 mill. Now 2 horses,
      2 cattle. Then 60 sheep, now 140; then 40 pigs, now 20; now
      35 goats.

Value then 60s; now 40[s].

In the same (Bures) Tosti, a free man under King Edward, held 1
carucate of land.

    Then 1 villager, now none. Now 2 smallholders; 1 slave.

    Always 1 plough.

    Woodland at 10 pigs; meadow, 2 acres. Then 40 pigs, now 20;
      20 sheep; now 15 goats.

Value 20s.

In the same (Bures) 2 free men of Harold's; they could sell. They
have 60 acres. 1 plough.

Value 5s.

    They were delivered to make up the manor.

56   LAND OF HUMPHREY SON OF AUBREY   436 a

STOW Hundred

1 (Part) of an exchange in Normandy; in ONEHOUSE 10 free men under
the patronage only of Ketel; 60 acres of land.

    1 smallholder.

    Then 2 ploughs, later and now 1. Meadow, 3 acres.

Value 10s.

    The King and the Earl (have) the jurisdiction.

⋎ Bosemera. H̃. In Codenham xi . liƀi hões . lxxx . ac̃
. ii . miñ . Tc̃ . ii . car̃ . modo . i . 7 đ . & ii . ac̃ p̃ti.
⋎ In Vledana . v . liƀi hões de . xx . ac̃ . femp dim̃ car̃.
⋎ In hauungeftuna . iii . liƀi . hões . ix . ac̃ . 7 totũ ual& . xxx . fot.
Rex & coms̃ focã . In Cadenham . viii . ac̃ . Aluric̃ liƀ homo
t . r . e . in eodẽ p̃tio.
⋎ Claindune . H̃ . In codenhã . i . liƀ hõ . iiii . ac̃ . & ual . viii . đ.
foca regis . 7 . c . De molino de belingesfort vii . fot . & . iiii . deñ.
⋎ In Eusfort . h̃ . In nordfolc.

★ Terra Huƀti de monte canefio . Hertes mera . hund.   .LVII .
Wiuerteftunã teñ Leuuiñ calu . t . r . e . i . car̃ terræ ꝑ mañ.
Tc̃ . iiii . borđ . m̃ . iii . Tc̃ ii . car̃ in dñio . Poft . i . m̃ . i . 7 dimidia
7 dim̃ car̃ hom̃ . 7 . iii . ac̃ p̃ti . Tc̃ Silũ . xl . porc̃ . modo . xx.
Æccfia . xvi . ac̃ . 7 dim̃ . car̃ . femꝑ . i . runc̃ . 7 . iii . añ . 7 xii.
cap̃ . & . x . porc̃ . 7 femp ual . xxx . fot . In eađ . vi . liƀi hões
c̃om̃dati . Leuuino . xxxvii . ac̃ . femꝑ . i . car̃ . & ual& . x . fot.

436 b
Hoc ten& totũ Ricardus de huƀto . Rex & coms̃ focã . h̃t . i . lg̃
in longo . 7 iiii . qr̃ & dim̃ in lato . & . viii . đ . de gelto.

436 a, b

BOSMERE Hundred

2 In CODDENHAM 11 free men; 80 acres less 2. Then 2 ploughs, now 1½.
Meadow, 2 acres.

3 In 'OLDEN' 5 free men with 20 acres. Always ½ plough.

4 In HEMINGSTONE 3 free men; 9 acres.
Value of the whole 30s.
The King and the Earl (have) the jurisdiction.

5 In CODDENHAM 8 acres; Aelfric a free man before 1066.
(It is) in the same assessment.

CLAYDON Hundred

6 In CODDENHAM 1 free man; 4 acres.
Value 8d.
The jurisdiction (is) the King's and the Earl's.
From the mill of Billingford 7s 4d.
In EYNSFORD Hundred in Norfolk

7 LAND OF HUBERT OF MONT-CANISY

HARTISMERE Hundred

1 Leofwin the Bald held WYVERSTONE before 1066; 1 carucate of land
as a manor.
Then 4 smallholders, now 3.
Then 2 ploughs in lordship, later 1, now 1½; ½ men's plough.
Meadow, 3 acres; woodland, then 40 pigs, now 20.
A church, 16 acres. ½ plough.
Always 1 cob, 3 cattle, 12 goats, 10 pigs.
Value always 30s.
In the same (Wyverstone) 6 free men under the patronage of Leofwin;
37 acres. Always 1 plough.
Value 10s.
Richard holds the whole of this from Hubert.   436 b
The King and the Earl (have) the jurisdiction.
It has 1 league in length and 4½ furlongs in width; 8d in tax.

TERRA . GONDWINI Camerarii . Sanfort . H̃ . & dim̃. ★

Hecham . tenuit Affeman . lib̃ hõ . comdat Robto filio Wi -
marce . ꝑ man̄ . I . car̃ terræ . femp . I . uiłł . & Tc̄ . III . bord̃ . p̃ 7 m̃
. II . Tc̄ . II . car̃ in dn̄io . P̃ nichil . m̃ . I . car̃ . Tc̄ . I . car̃ hom̃ . P̃ 7 m̃
dim̃ . VII . ac̄ pti . filua . x . porc̃ . femp . I . molin̄ . Pars æcctiæ . de.
. II . ac̄ . m̃ . III . an̄ . 7 VIII . porc̃ . 7 . VI . ous̄ . 7 VIII . cap̄ . 7 tc̄ uał
xxx . foł . modo . xx . f7 fuit ad firmã ꝑ xxx . foł . ħt . VIII . qr̄
in longo . & . VI . in lat̄ . 7 XII . d̃ . de gelto . Alii ibi ten& . Soca in
b̃colt.

TERRE SAISSELINI . *BRADEMERA . HVN̄D.* ★

Torp ten& Acolfus . t . r . e . teinn̄ . ꝑ man̄ . I . car̃ . træ . femp . II.
bord̃ . Tc̄ 7 p̃ . II . car̃ in dn̄io . m̃ . I . 7 dim car̃ hom̃ . VI . ac̄ . pti . Semp.
. I . molin̄ . Semp . II . an̄ . Tc̄ . x . porc̃ . modo . XVI . femp . xxx . ous̄.
7 IIII . libi ħoes . de qbȝ habuit fuu͞ ante c̄ comd̃ . t . r . e . 7 ħnt . XIII.
ac̄ . 7 dim̃ . car̃ . 7 uał . xx . foł . Sapeftuna ten̄ . Godman . teinn̄

437 a

t̃ . r̃ . e . dim̃ . car̃ . træ . femp . II . bord̃ . 7 . I . car̃ in dn̄io . v . ac̄ pti.
femp . I . molin̄ . 7 . II . an̄ . Tc̄ . III . porc̃ . m̃ . v̇ . Tc̄ xx . ous̄ . modo
xxxIII . femp uał . xv . foł . In ead̃ . VIII . libi ħoes comd̃ . xx . IIII.
ac̄ . 7 uał . III . foł . Sc̄s eadmundus de ħ 7 de toto hund̃ foc̄ 7 facã ;

LAND OF GUNDWIN THE CHAMBERLAIN

SAMFORD Hundred and a Half

1 Aescman, a free man under the patronage of Robert son of Wymarc, held HIGHAM before 1066; 1 carucate of land as a manor.
  Always 1 villager. Then 3 smallholders, later and now 2.
  Then 2 ploughs in lordship, later nothing, now 1 plough; then 1 men's plough, later and now ½.
  Meadow, 7 acres; woodland, 10 pigs; always 1 mill.
  Part of a church, with 2 acres.
  Now 3 cattle, 8 pigs, 6 sheep, 8 goats.
  Value then 30s; now 20[s]; but it was at a revenue for 30s.
  It has 8 furlongs in length and 6 in width; 12d in tax. Others hold there.
  The jurisdiction (is) in (East) Bergholt.

LANDS OF SASSELIN

BRADMERE Hundred

1 Acwulf, a thane, [held] (Ixworth) THORPE before 1066; 1 carucate of land as a manor.
  Always 2 smallholders.
  Then and later 2 ploughs in lordship, now 1; ½ men's plough.
  Meadow, 6 acres; always 1 mill. Always 2 cattle. Then 10 pigs, now 16; always 30 sheep.
  4 free men over whom his predecessor had patronage before 1066. They have 13 acres. ½ plough.
  Value 20s.

2 Godman, a thane, held SAPISTONE before 1066; ½ carucate of land.   437 a
  Always 2 smallholders;
  1 plough in lordship.
  Meadow, 5 acres. Always 1 mill; 2 cattle. Then 3 pigs, now 5; then 20 sheep, now 33.
  Value always 15s.
  In the same (Sapistone) 8 free men under patronage; 24 acres.
  Value 3s.
  St. Edmund's (has) full jurisdiction over this and over the whole Hundred.

★ **T**ERRA ROBERTI DE VERLI. *BL*ackebrune. *H̃.*

I Weſtunā tenuit Alsi lib̃ hō . t . r . e . ꝑ mañ . i . car̄ terræ . 7 . i . bord̄
7 . ii . ſerū . Tc̃ . ii . car̄ in dominio . P nichil . modo . i . ſemp . dim̃
car̄ hom̃ . iii . ac̃ . p̃ti . ſemp . i . molin̄ . modo . i . runc̄ . 7 . ii . añ . 7 viii .
porc̄ . 7 . L . oũs . 7 . vi . lib̃i hōes cm̃d . c . iii . ac̃ . Tc̃ . ii . car̄ . m̃ . i .
7 . i . ac̃ . p̃ti . Eccłia . xii . ac̃ . 7 dim̃ . car̄ . H̃ mañ ual& ſemp
xxv . ſoł . 7 Lib̃i hōes . v . ſoł.

★ **T**ERRA . RADVLFI PINEL . In Reinduna ten&   .LXI
. ii . lib̃i . hōes . Erniet . 7 Aluort . xL . ac̃ . ſemp . dim̃ car̄ . & . i . bord̄ .
7 uał . x . ſoł hanc tr̃ā tenuit Rad̄ de dono regis ſed ex ea ſeruiū .
Gosfrid̄ de magna uilla . Soca in b̃colt.

ꟼ *DIMID̄ . H̃ . DE COSFORT* . Laſham . teñ brich̃marus
t . r . e . xL . ac̃ . ſemp . i . bord̄ . 7 . i . ſerū . 7 . i . car̄ . 7 uał . x . ſoł ; ſc̃s . ed . ſocā

437 b

.LXII . **T**ERRA ISAC̃ . *BOSEMERA . H̃* . Offetunā . teñ Siric̃   ★
lib̃ hō . t . r . e . c . ac̃ . ꝑ mañ . ſemp . ii . bord̄ . 7 tc̃ . i . car̄ . modo dim̃ .
Eccłia . vii . ac̃ . 7 dim̃ . Tc̃ uał . xx . ſoł . modo xxx . Rex & com̃s .
focam.

0   LAND OF ROBERT OF VERLY

BLACKBOURN Hundred
1 Alsi, a free man, held (Market) WESTON before 1066; as a manor,
  1 carucate of land.
    1 smallholder; 2 slaves.
    Then 2 ploughs in lordship, later nothing, now 1; always ½ men's
      plough.
    Meadow, 3 acres; always 1 mill. Now 1 cob, 2 cattle, 8 pigs,
      50 sheep.
  6 free men under patronage; 103 acres. Then 2 ploughs, now 1.
    Meadow, 1 acre.
  A church, 12 acres. ½ plough.
  Value of this manor always 25s; (value) of the free men 5s.

1   LAND OF RALPH PINEL

[SAMFORD Hundred and a Half]
1 In RAYDON Erngeat and Alward, 2 free men, [held] 40 acres.
    Always ½ plough;
    1 smallholder.
  Value 10s.
    Ralph held this land by the King's gift but from it he gave service
  to Geoffrey de Mandeville.
    The jurisdiction (is) in (East) Bergholt.

Half-Hundred of COSFORD
2 Brictmer held LAYHAM before 1066; 40 acres.
    Always 1 smallholder; 1 slave;
    1 plough.
  Value 10s.
    St. Edmund's (has) the jurisdiction.

2   LAND OF ISAAC   437 b

BOSMERE Hundred
1 Siric, a free man, held OFFTON before 1066; 100 acres as a manor.
    Always 2 smallholders.
    Then 1 plough, now ½.
    A church, 7½ acres.
  Value then 20s; now 30[s].
    The King and the Earl (have) the jurisdiction.

★ ★ ⫷In Sumerſham tẽn Vluuin⁹ libomo.LX.ac̄.tr̃æ.p̃ man̄..t.r.e.
Tc̄.I.car̓.Tc̄ ual̓ xx.ſol̓.modo.xx.Rex & com̄s ſocā.In ead̄.Cole-
man.lib̄ homo.v.ac̄.& ual.xx̃.d̄.Rex & com̄s ſocā.
⫷In hamingeſtuna.IIII.ac̄.de dño.& ual.VIII.d̄.In ead̄
.I.lib̄ hõ dim̄ ac̄.& ual.I.d̄.Rex.7 com̄s ſocā.
Claindune.H̃.Hamingeſtunā tenuit.Leuric⁹ lib̄ hõ.t̓.
r̓.e.I.car̓ træ.p̃ man̄.ſemp.II.bord̓.Tc̄.II.car̓.m̄.I.&.IIII.
ac̄.p̃ti.Silua.II.porc̓.ſemp.I.runc̓.Tc̄.II.an̄.m̄.I.Tc̄.XI.
oũs.modo.xx.Tc̄.XIII.porc̓.m̄.xx.Tc̄.VII.cap̃.Tc̄ ual.xx.
ſol.modo.xxv.VIII.d̄ min̓.In ead̄.III.lib̄i.hoẽs.xxIIII.ac̄.
Tc̄ 7 p̃⁹.I.car̓.m̄ dim̄.7 ual.v.ſol.Rex 7 Com̄s ſocā.

*HERTESMERA.H̃.*Thorham tenuit Leuricus
com̄dat briſtrico p̃poſito ſc̄o eadmundi.t.r.e.I.car̓ terræ
p̃ man̄.ſemp.II.bord̓.Tc̄.II.car̓.P̃⁹ dim̄.m̄.I.II.ac̄ p̃ti.
Tc̄ ſilua.de xxx.porc̓.m̄.xx.Semp.II.runc̓.7 quarta
pars æccliæ.III.ac̄.7 dim̄.Tc̄ ual.xxx.ſol.modo xx.De hac
tr̃a habuit Abbas.tres partes ſochæ.7 Rex quartā.In ead̄
.III.lib̄i hoẽs.IIII.ac̄.7 dim̄.&.ual.VIII.d̄.h̃t VIII.qr̄ in longo
7.VIII.in lato.7 VIII.d̄ & obolũ de gelto.
Hvnd̄.de *CLAINDVNE*.In henleie.XVI.ac̄.lib̄e r̃æ

438 a
p̃tinentes in hamingeſtuna.& in p̃tio.

2 In SOMERSHAM Wulfwin, a free man, held 60 acres of land as a manor before 1066. Then 1 plough.
Value then 20s; now 20[s].
The King and the Earl (have) the jurisdiction.
In the same (Somersham) Coleman, a free man; 5 acres.
Value 20d.
The King and the Earl (have) the jurisdiction.

3 In HEMINGSTONE 4 acres in lordship.
Value 8d.
In the same (Hemingstone) 1 free man; ½ acre.
Value 1d.
The King and the Earl (have) the jurisdiction.

CLAYDON Hundred
4 Leofric, a free man, held HEMINGSTONE before 1066; 1 carucate of land as a manor.
Always 2 smallholders.
Then 2 ploughs, now 1.
Meadow, 4 acres; woodland, 2 pigs. Always 1 cob. Then 2 cattle, now 1; then 11 sheep, now 20; then 13 pigs, now 20; then 7 goats.
Value then 20s; now 25[s] less 8d.
In the same (Hemingstone) 3 free men; 24 acres. Then and later 1 plough, now ½.
Value 5s.
The King and the Earl (have) the jurisdiction.

HARTISMERE Hundred
5 Leofric, under the patronage of Brictric the reeve of St. Edmund's, held THORNHAM (Magna) before 1066; 1 carucate of land as a manor.
Always 2 smallholders.
Then 2 ploughs, later ½, now 1.
Meadow, 2 acres; woodland then at 30 pigs, now 20. Always 2 cobs.
The fourth part of a church, 3½ acres.
Value then 30s; now 20[s].
Over this land, the Abbot had three parts of the jurisdiction, and the King (had) the fourth (part).
In the same (Thornham Magna) 3 free men; 4½ acres.
Value 8d.
It has 8 furlongs in length and 8 in width; 8½d in tax.

Hundred of CLAYDON
6 In HENLEY 16 acres of free land belonging to Hemingstone. (They are) in the assessment.

438 a

HVN DE COSFORT.In Redles.dim̃ car̃ terræ.ten&.ı.foc
ftigango.Tc̃ & p̃.ı.car̃.modo nuł.7.ı.ac̃ p̃ti.7 uał&.xvııı.foł.
In hac terra iacebant.xıııı.ac̃ ſiluæ q̃s.W.de burnoluilla.inde
abſtulit.& m̃.ten&.

TERRA NORMANNI VICECOMITIS.Dim̃.h̃.de gepefwiz.   .LXIII
In burgo h̃t normannus.ıı.burgenſes.unũ in uadimonio.contra
eundẽ.& alterũ ᵱ debito.ſed Rex h̃t ſuas conſuetudines.

★ TERRA Iuichel p̃ori.*BOSEMERA*.H̃.In ſtanhã ten&   .LXIID
Aluricus lib̃ h̃o Edrici ante ceſſoris Robti mal&.ʟxxxx.ac̃
ᵱ mañ.7 inde fuit ſaiſitus.Rob.ſemp.vı.bord.&.ı.ſeru.&.ı.car̃
& dim̃ in dominio.& dim̃ car̃ hom̃.7.ıı.ac̃ p̃ti.ſilua.x.porc̃.
&.vıı.añ.Tc̃.ı.porc̃.modo.v.Tc̃.vıııı.oũs.modo.xʟ.&.v.libi
h̃oes.xx.ıııı.ac̃.& dim̃ car̃.& tc̃ uał.xx.ſoł.m̃ xxxv.In ead
.ı.lib̃ h̃o.xxıııı.ac̃.Tc̃.ı.car̃.& uał.v.ſoł.Rex & Cõms ſoc̃.
h̃t.ı.leuga in longo.7.ııı.q̃t in lato.Alii.ibi tenent.&.vıı.d.&
obolũ de gelto.

ꝟIn Stanham.ı.æcclia.xx.ac̃.q̃s ibi deder̃.ıx libi h̃oes ᵱ animab; fuis.

BISOPES.H̃.In horan.ı.car̃.tr̃æ.teñ Algar̃.t.r.e.lib̃ h̃o
ftigandi.7.ıı.alii.un h̃o Almari ep̃i.7 ałi h̃o Edrici de laxafelda

Hundred of COSFORD

7 In *REDLES* ½ carucate of land; 1 Freeman, belonging to Stigand,
[held it]. Then and later 1 plough, now none.
    Meadow, 1 acre.
Value 18s.
To this land belonged 14 acres of woodland which W(illiam) of
Bourneville took away from there and now holds.

63   LAND OF NORMAN THE SHERIFF

Half-Hundred of IPSWICH

1 In the Borough (of IPSWICH) Norman has 2 burgesses, one in pledge
to him, the other for a debt; but the King has his customary dues.

64   LAND OF JUDICAEL THE PRIEST

BOSMERE Hundred

1 In STONHAM Aelfric, a free man of Edric, Robert Malet's predecessor,
[held] 90 acres as a manor. Robert was in possession of it.
    Always 6 smallholders; 1 slave;
    1½ ploughs in lordship; ½ men's plough.
    Meadow, 2 acres; woodland, 10 pigs. 7 cattle; then 1 pig, now 15;
        then 8 sheep, now 40.
5 free men; 24 acres; ½ plough.
A church, 16 acres. ½ plough.
Value then 20s; now 35[s].
In the same (Stonham) 1 free man; 24 acres. Then 1 plough.
Value 5s.
    The King and the Earl (have) the jurisdiction.
    It has 1 league in length and 3 furlongs in width. Others hold
there. 7½d in tax.

2 In STONHAM 1 church; 20 acres which 9 free men granted there for
their souls.

BISHOP'S Hundred

3 In HORHAM 1 carucate of land; Algar, a free man of Stigand's, and
2 others, one a man of Bishop Aelmer's and the other a man of
Edric of Laxfield's, held (it) before 1066.

Semp vii . borđ . 7 . i . ſerú . 7 . i . car̄ in dn̄io . Silua . xxiiii . porc̄ . & . u.
ac̄ p̄ti . & . i . car̄ hom̄ . Tc̄ . ii . runc̄ . Tc̄ . viii . an̄ . ſemp xxiiii . porc̄.
Tc̄ xxiiii . ou̅s . 7 . i . uas . apū . 7 iiii . lib̄i hoes . xx . iiii . ac̄ . q̄s reclamat.
delib̄atione . Tc̄ dim̄ car̄ . m̄ . ii . bou̅s . Ecc̄lia de . xx . ii . ac̄ & uat̄
xxii . đ . Semp uat̄ . xx ſot̄ . Soca in hoxa ep̄i.

. LXV . **T**ERRE GIRoldi mareſchalchi . RiSeb̄ruge . H̄ . Damar -
deſtuna . ten̄ Com̄s Algar p̄ bereuuita in bademundesfelda.
t . r . e . ii . car̄ terrǣ . ſemp . iiii . uitt̄ . & . i . borđ . 7 . iii . ſerú . 7 ii . car̄ in
dn̄io . Tc̄ uat̄ . lx . ſot̄ . modo . lxx . ſemp . i . runc̄ . Tc̄ . ii . an̄ . modo.
xv . 7 xxiiii . porc̄ . 7 . xl . iiii . ou̅s.

. LXVI . **T**ERRǼ Rob̄TI . BLVNDI . B̄rademere . Hvnđ . Giſwor -
tham . ten̄ Achi p̄ man̄ . t . r . e . iii . car̄ terrǣ . ſemp . ii . borđ . Tc̄
. v . ſerú . m̄ . ii . ſemp . iii . car̄ in dn̄io . & . i . mot̄ . 7 xx . ac̄ p̄ti . Tc̄ . ii.
runc̄ . modo . i . Sep̄ . v . an̄ . Tc̄ . xl . porc̄ . modo . xx . ii . Tc̄ . viii . ou̅s.
modo lxxxx . ii . 7 iii . arpenni uinǣ . & un̄ parc̄ . Tc̄ uat̄ . lxxx.
ſot̄ . modo . vi . lib̄ . In eadē . xxv . lib̄i hoes . com̄ . ii . car̄ . & dim̄ terrǣ.
Tc̄ . v . car̄ . modo . iiii . & dim̄ . & . iiii . ac̄ p̄ti . ſemp uat̄ . xx . ſot̄ De toto
. H̄ . ſc̄s eadm̄ . ſac̄ & ſoca . In eadē . v . lib̄i hoes . com̄ . i . car̄ terrǣ . 7 lxxx.
ac̄ . Tc̄ . v . car̄ . m̄ . ii . 7 . iii . ac̄ p̄ti . Tc̄ uat̄ . xxx . ſot̄ modo xx.
Ǽcc̄lia lxxx . ac̄ lib̄ǣ terre . 7 . i . car̄ . & . i . ac̄ p̄ti . 7 uat̄ . v . ſot̄ . Totū

ht̄ . ii . lḡ in longo . & . vi . qr̄ in lat̄ . 7 xxii . đ & . iii . ferding . de geldo.

Always 7 smallholders; 1 slave; 438 b
1 plough in lordship. Woodland, 24 pigs; meadow, 2 acres;
1 men's plough.
Then 2 cobs; then 8 cattle; always 24 pigs. Then 24 sheep.
1 beehive.
4 free men, 24 acres, whom he claims by a delivery. Then ½ plough;
now 2 oxen.
A church with 22 acres; value 22d.
Value always 22s.
The jurisdiction (is) in the Bishop's (manor of) Hoxne.

5   LANDS OF GERALD MARSHAL

RISBRIDGE Hundred
1 Earl Algar held DENSTON as an outlier in (the lands of) Badmondisfield
before 1066; 2 carucates of land.
Always 4 villagers; 1 smallholder; 3 slaves;
2 ploughs in lordship.
Value then 60s; now 70[s].
Always 1 cob. Then 2 cattle, now 15; 24 pigs; 44 sheep.

6   LANDS OF ROBERT BLUNT

BRADMERE Hundred
1 Aki held IXWORTH as a manor before 1066; 3 carucates of land.
Always 2 smallholders. Then 5 slaves, now 2.
Always 3 ploughs in lordship.
1 mill; meadow, 2 acres. Then 2 cobs, now 1; always 5 cattle.
Then 40 pigs, now 22; then 8 sheep, now 92. 3 *arpents* of
vines; 1 park.
Value then 80s; now £6.
In the same (Ixworth) 25 free men under patronage; 2½ carucates
of land. Then 5 ploughs, now 4½.
Meadow, 4 acres.
Value always 20s.
St. Edmund's (has) full jurisdiction over the whole Hundred.
In the same (Ixworth) 5 free men under patronage; 1 carucate of
land and 80 acres. Then 5 ploughs, now 2.
Meadow, 3 acres.
Value then 30s; now 20[s].
A church, 80 acres of free land. 1 plough. Meadow, 1 acre. Value 5s.
The whole has 2 leagues in length and 6 furlongs in width; 22¾d 439 a
in tax.

Walſam.t.r.e.teñ Achi.ꝓ mañ.ii.caŕ t̅r̅æ.ſemp.iiii.borđ.
T̅c̅.ii.caŕ in dñio.modo.iii.7 dim.caŕ hom̃.&.v.ac̅ p̃ti.ſilua.xx.
porc̃.ſ͞ep.i.runc̃.T̅c̅.iii.añ.m̃.i.T̅c̅.xl.porc̃.m̃.xx.ix.T̅c̅.v.ou̅s.
modo.xxx.T̅c̅ ua̅t.xl.ſo̅t.m̃.lx.In eade̅.xx.li̅bi ho̅es.com̃đ.i.caŕ t̅r̅æ
ſemp.ii.caŕ.&.ii.ac̅ p̃ti.ſilua.x.porc̃.T̅c̅ ua̅t.x.ſo̅t.modo xx.In ea̅đ
.iii.li̅bi ho̅es 7 dim.i.caŕ terræ.T̅c̅ 7 p̃.iii.caŕ.7 dim.modo.ii.7.ii.
ac̅ & dim p̃ti.Silua de.iiii.porc̃.ſemp ua̅t.xx.ſo̅t.Ecc̅lia dimidia.
x.ac̅.&.i.ac̅ p̃ti.& ua̅t viii.đ.ħt.ii.leug in longo.&.vi.q̅r̅ in lato.
& xvii.đ de gelto.Alii ibi teneñt.

Eascefeldā teñ Achi.ꝓ mañ.t.r.e.iii.caŕ.t̅r̅æ.ſemp.ix.borđ.
T̅c̅.iiii.caŕ in dominio.modo.iii.& xii.ac̅ p̃ti.ſilua.lx.porc̃.
ſemper.ii.runc̃.&.ii.añ.T̅c̅ lx.porc̃.m̃odo.xv.T̅c̅ xxv.ou̅s.
modo.x.7.x.uaſa apu̅.ſemp ua̅t.lx.ſo̅t.In eade̅.xiiii.li̅bi
ho̅es.com̃đ.lxxx.ac̅.ſemp.i.caŕ.&.iiii.ac̅.p̃ti.ſilua.iiii.porc̃.
7 ua̅t.viii.ſo̅t.In eade̅.i.li̅b.ho̅ Chetel.~~i.li̅b ho̅~~.i.caŕ terræ
ꝓ mañ.ſemp.ii.borđ.7.ii.ſeru.7.ii.caŕ in dñio.7.iiii.ac̅ p̃ti.
ſilua xx.porc̃.7.iii.li̅bi ho̅es.ſub eo xxii.ac̅.7 dim.caŕ.ſemp.
ii.runc̃.T̅c̅.iiii.añ.T̅c̅.xxiiii.porc̃.m̃odo.xxiii.T̅c̅.xxii.ou̅s.
M̅.c.T̅c̅ xl.cap̅.modo.xii.ſemp ua̅l&.xxx.ſo̅t.ex ħ habuit antec̅.
Ro̅bti.cm̃đ.Wi̅ttm ten& de Ro̅bto.In ea̅đ.iii.li̅b ho̅es.com̃đ.i.caŕ

2 Aki held WALSHAM (le Willows) before 1066; as a manor, 2 carucates of land.
   Always 4 smallholders.
   Then 2 ploughs in lordship, now 3; ½ men's plough.
   Meadow, 5 acres; woodland, 20 pigs. Always 1 cob. Then 3 cattle, now 1; then 40 pigs, now 29; then 5 sheep, now 30.
Value then 40s; now 60[s].
In the same (Walsham le Willows) 20 free men under patronage; 1 carucate of land. Always 2 ploughs.
   Meadow, 2 acres; woodland, 10 pigs.
Value then 10s; now 20[s].
In the same (Walsham le Willows) 3 free men and a half; 1 carucate of land. Then and later 3½ ploughs, now 2.
   Meadow, 2½ acres; woodland at 4 pigs.
Value always 20s.
½ church, 10 acres. Meadow, 1 acre. Value 8d.
It has 2 leagues in length and 6 furlongs in width; 17d in tax.
Others hold there.

3 Aki held (Great) ASHFIELD as a manor before 1066; 3 carucates of land.
   Always 9 smallholders.
   Then 4 ploughs in lordship, now 3.
   Meadow, 12 acres; woodland, 60 pigs. Always 2 cobs, 2 cattle.
      Then 60 pigs, now 15; then 25 sheep, now 10; 10 beehives.
Value always 60s.
In the same (Great Ashfield) 14 free men under patronage; 80 acres.
Always 1 plough.
   Meadow, 4 acres; woodland, 4 pigs.
Value 8s.
In the same (Great Ashfield) 1 free man, Ketel; 1 carucate of land as a manor.
   Always 2 smallholders; 2 slaves;
   2 ploughs in lordship.
   Meadow, 4 acres; woodland, 20 pigs.
3 free men under him; 22 acres. ½ plough.
   Always 2 cobs. Then 4 cattle; then 24 pigs, now 23; then 32 sheep, now 100; then 40 goats, now 12.
Value always 30s.
   Robert's predecessor had this under patronage, William holds (it) from Robert.
In the same (Great Ashfield) 3 free men under patronage; 1 carucate

terræ . 7 . LX . ac̄ . 7 . I . borđ . ſemp . III . car̄ . 7 . IIII . ac̄ p̃ti . ſilua de . IIII .
porc̓ . 7 ſemp ual& . xxx . ſoł . h̃ tenent . II . miłites . Æccłia . ix . ac̄;

439 b

H̃ł . xi . q̓r in longo . 7 . xi . in lato . & . v . den̄ . & obolū de gelto . Alii
Wicā ten& Aki̇ . t . r . e . p man̄ . I . car̄ terræ Tc̄ . III . borđ ibi tenēt .
Tc̄ III . ſeru̇ . modo . II . ſemp . II . car̄ in dn̄io . 7 . III . ac̄ p̃ti . ſilu̇
x . porc̓ . Tc̄ . I . runc̓ . modo . II . ſem̃p . I . an̄ . Tc̄ . xiI . porc̓ . m̃ xx .
III . Tc̄ . xx . v . ou̅s . modo . xxxviii . ſem̃p uał . xxx . ſoł . & . v
łiɓi hoes . & dim̃ . com̃đ . I . car̄ tr̃æ . ſem̃p . II . borđ . 7 ſub eı̃s . II . łiɓi
hoes . IIII . ac̄ . ſemp . II . car̄ . & . vi . ac̄ p̃ti . 7 q̃rta pars m̃ol . Tc̄ uał
xx . ſoł . modo . xiii .
In Sapeſtuna . II . łiɓi hoes regis . e . xviii . ac̄ . 7 uał . iii . ſoł .
Langham ten̄ haret liɓ ho̅ de q̃ s̃c̃s eadmund . habuit em̃ -
t . r . e . III . car̄ terræ . Tc̄ . I . uiłł . ſem̃p . III . borđ . 7 . iii . ſeru̇ .
Tc̄ 7 p̃ . III . car̄ in dn̄io . modo . II . Tc̄ dim̃ car̄ hom̃ . xii . ac̄
p̃ti . ſilua . vi . porc̓ . Tc̄ . vii . runc̓ . modo . I . Tc̄ . viii . an̄ . m̃ . ii .
Tc̄ xxx . porc̓ . modo . xvi . Tc̄ . c̄ . xL . ou̅s . m̃ . xii . Tc̄ uał . Lxxx .
ſoł . modo . Lx . In ead̄ . II . łiɓi hoes . com̃đ . xx . ac̄ . Tc̄ dim̃ . car̄ .
modo . II . bou̇ . 7 uał . III . ſoł . h̃t . vii . q̓r in longo . 7 vi . in lato .
& . x . đ in gelt̓ .
In hepworda . dim̃ liɓ homo . xL . ac̄ . 7 . I . borđ . 7 ſemp dim̃
car̄ & dim̃ ac̄ p̃ti . 7 uał x . ſoł .
In Wica . I . liɓ ho̅ com̃đ . Lx . ac̄ . & . I . borđ . ſemp . I . car̄ .
7 uał& . x . ſoł .

of land and 60 acres.
  1 smallholder.
  Always 3 ploughs.
  Meadow, 3 acres; woodland at 4 pigs.
Value always 30s.
  2 men-at-arms hold (this).
  A church, 9 acres.
  It has 11 furlongs in length and 11 in width; 5½d in tax. Others   439 b
hold there.

4 Aki [held] WYKEN before 1066; as a manor, 1 carucate of land.
    Then 3 smallholders; then 3 slaves, now 2.
    Always 2 ploughs in lordship.
    Meadow, 3 acres; woodland, 10 pigs. Then 1 cob, now 2; always
        1 cattle. Then 12 pigs, now 23; then 25 sheep, now 38.
  Value always 30s.
  5 free men and a half, under patronage; 1 carucate of land.
    Always 2 smallholders.
  Under them, 2 free men; 4 acres.
    Always 2 ploughs.
    Meadow, 6 acres; the fourth part of a mill.
  Value then 20s; now 13[s].

5 In SAPISTON 2 free men of King Edward's; 18 acres.
  Value 3s.

6 Haret, a free man over whom St. Edmund's had patronage before
  1066, held LANGHAM; 3 carucates of land.
    Then 1 villager. Always 3 smallholders; 3 slaves.
    Then and later 3 ploughs in lordship, now 2; then ½ men's plough.
    Meadow, 12 acres; woodland, 6 pigs. Then 7 cobs, now 1; then
        8 cattle, now 2; then 30 pigs, now 16; then 140 sheep, now 12.
  Value then 80s; now 60[s].
  In the same (Langham) 2 free men under patronage; 20 acres. Then
  ½ plough, now 2 oxen.
  Value 3s.
    It has 7 furlongs in length and 6 in width; 10d in tax.

7 In HEPWORTH a half free men; 40 acres.
    1 smallholder.
    Always ½ plough. Meadow, ½ acre.
  Value 10s.

8 In WYKEN 1 free man under patronage; 60 acres.
    1 smallholder.
    Always 1 plough.
  Value 10s.

In Icſeẃrda . I . liƀ h̅o xl . a̅c ſemp . I . ċar

7 ual& . v . ſot Ex his o̅iƀȝ liƀis h̅oiƀȝ |rege̅ ad Waraṅt S̅c̅a̅

reuocat above rege̅

eadmund . de toto ſoc̅a̅ 7 ſac̅a̅.

440 a

In Icſeẃrda . tenuit Ketel liƀ h̅o . cc . a̅c . ꝑ mañ . ſemꝑ

II . bord . & . II . ſerů . & . II . car̅ in dñio . 7 vi . a̅c ꝑti . & . I . mot.

& ſub eo . vi . liƀi h̅oes . xxix . a̅c . Tc̅ . II . car̅ . modo . I . ſemꝑ ual&

lx . ſot . Ex h̅ habuit Angar̅ . ſtalra com̅d . t . r . e . Rad . fr̅ Roƀ

erat ſaiſitus quando fuit mortuus 7 Roƀ . recꝑit de rege.

DIMID̅ . H̅ . de Cosfort . In Watefella . v . liƀi h̅oes de uno

habuit s̅c̅s . e . com̅d 7 de o̅iƀȝ ſoc̅a̅ . antec̅ Roƀti nec c̅m̅d . & h̅nt

lx . a̅c . Tc̅ . II . car̅ . modo . I . ſemꝑ uat . vi . ſot . modo xx . In ead̅

. IIII . liƀi h̅oes lxIII . a̅c . Tc̅ . II . car̅ modo . dim̅ . 7 uat . x . ſot . 7 . vIII . d̅.

Blidinga . h̅ In Weſtledeſtuna . xxvII . a̅c . 7 dim̅ / ꝑ eſcang̅.

ten& Brunar̅ pƀr . T̅ . R . E . ſemꝑ dim̅ car̅ . 7 uat . IIII . ſot.

Herteſmera . H̅ . In Giſilmcham . xxx . a̅c de dñio de Waleſam

qd̅ tenuit Achi . & . I . a̅c ꝑti . 7 uat . vi . ſot . 7 vIII . d̅ . In ead̅ . III . liƀi

h̅oes com̅d . Achio Alger̅ . Godric . Goduuin̅ . lIII . a̅c . & . I . liƀ h̅o

ſub eis . I . a̅c . Tc̅ & ꝑ . II . car̅ . modo . dim̅ . & . I . a̅c ꝑti . filů xxIIII.

por̅c . & uat xvi . ſot . Sup̅ II . feminas iſtoȝ hominů habuit

Abbas s̅c̅i edmund̅ . dim̅ com̅d . 7 dim̅ ſoc̅

Herteſmara . H̅ . In Weſttorp . IIII . liƀi h̅oes com̅ Achi . t.

t̅ . e . IIII . a̅c . 7 dim̅ 7 uat . xvi . d̅ . In finingah̅a̅ . II . a̅c . de dñio

de Walſa̅.

9 In IXWORTH 1 free man; 40 acres. Always 1 plough.
Value 5s.
   Concerning all these free men he calls the King as warrantor.
   St. Edmund's (has) full jurisdiction over the whole.

0 In IXWORTH Ketel, a free man, held 200 acres as a manor.   440 a
   Always 2 smallholders; 2 slaves;
   2 ploughs in lordship.
   Meadow, 6 acres; 1 mill.
Under him, 6 free men; 29 acres. Then 2 ploughs, now 1.
Value always 60s.
   Over this, Asgar the Constable had patronage before 1066. Ralph,
   Robert's brother, was in possession when he died. Robert acquired
   (it) from the King.

Half-Hundred of COSFORD
1 In WHATFIELD 5 free men; St. Edmund's had patronage over one,
   and jurisdiction over all; and Robert's predecessor (did) not (have)
   patronage. They have 60 acres. Then 2 ploughs, now 1.
   Value always 6s; now 20[s].
In the same (Whatfield) 4 free men; 63 acres. Then 2 ploughs, now ½.
Value 10s 8d.
   (It is) by exchange.

BLYTHING Hundred
2 In WESTLETON 27½ acres. Brunmer the priest [held it] before 1066.
   Always ½ plough.
   Value 4s.

HARTISMERE Hundred
3 In GISLINGHAM 30 acres of the lordship of Walsham (le Willows)
   which Aki held.
      Meadow, 1 acre.
   Value 6s 8d.
In the same (Gislingham) 3 free men under the patronage of Aki;
Algar, Godric, Godwin; 53 acres. 1 free man under them; 1 acre.
Then and later 2 ploughs, now ½.
   Meadow, 1 acre; woodland, 24 pigs.
Value 16s.
   Over 2 of the wives of these (free) men, the Abbot of St. Edmund's
   had half the patronage and half the jurisdiction.

HARTISMERE Hundred
4 In WESTHORPE 4 free men under the patronage of Aki before 1066;
   4½ acres.
   Value 16d.

5 In FINNINGHAM 2 acres of the lordship of Walsham (le Willows).

In Wiuertheſtuna . ii . libi hões . cõmd Achi . t . r . e . xxx . ac
Tc dim . car . ſilua ad ii . porc . dim ac p̃ti . 7 ual . v . ſol . hoc tē
. R . ouethel . de . R . blond; STOV . H̃ . In eſcefella . iac& . i . bord
de . iii . ac . 7 redd . xii . d.

. LXVII . TERRA HERVEJ BITVRICENS . STOV . H̃ . In Tornei ten&
Euen de erueo . i . car terræ . quã tenuit briċtric blac ſub witgaro
antec Ricardi de clara . & non poŧ uendere ſine licencia eius.
modo ten& herueus ex dono regis . Tc . vi . bord . p 7 modo . iii . Tc.
ii . car . p nuŧ . & modo . i . car . & . iiii . ac p̃ti . Tc . ii . car hom . p &
modo nulla . Tc ual xxx . ſol . modo xlvii . ſol . Rex & cõms ſocam.
Boſemera . H̃ . Hamingeſtunã tē Rainaldus de herueho . quã
tenuit . Vlmarus lib hõ cõmdatus tant . Edrico . t . r . e . anteceſſori
Robti mal& . c . ac træ ₚ mañ . ſemp . vi . bord . & . i . car in dominio.
Tc . i . car hom . modo dim & . ii . ac p̃ti . & . i . lib hõ . iiii . ac . Totũ ual
xx . ſol . Rex & cõms ſocã . Ex hac terra fuit ſaiſitus . Wiŧ . mal& ea die
qua fuit mortuus 7 p̃ea Rob mal& fili ei.

16 In WYVERSTONE 2 free men under the patronage of Aki before 1066;
30 acres. Then ½ plough.
Woodland for 2 pigs; meadow, ½ acre.
Value 5s.
R. Oudkell holds this from Robert Blunt.

STOW Hundred
17 In (Great) ASHFIELD belongs 1 smallholder, with 3 acres.
He pays 12d.

7   **LAND OF HERVEY OF BOURGES**   440 b

STOW Hundred
1 In THORNEY Euen holds from Hervey 1 carucate of land. Brictric
Black held it under Withgar, Richard of Clare's predecessor; he
could not sell without his permission. Now Hervey holds (it) by
the King's gift.
Then 6 smallholders, later and now 3.
Then 2 ploughs, later none, now 1 plough. Meadow, 4 acres.
Then 2 men's ploughs, later and now none.
Value then 30s; now 47s.
The King and the Earl (have) the jurisdiction.

BOSMERE Hundred
2 Reginald holds HEMINGSTONE from Hervey. Wulfmer, a free man
under the patronage before 1066 only of Edric, Robert Malet's
predecessor, held it; 100 acres as a manor.
Always 6 smallholders;
1 plough in lordship. Then 1 men's plough, now ½. Meadow,
2 acres.
1 free man; 4 acres.
Value of the whole 20s.
The King and the Earl (have) the jurisdiction.
William Malet was in possession of this land on the day he died;
later on Robert Malet, his son, (was in possession).

V CLAINDVNE . H̄ . Pettehaga tenuit briƈtuolt in d̄nio . 1 . car᷎
terræ & . xxx . ac̄ . ꝑ man̄ . t . r . e Antecessor . Roƀ mal& . c᷎o᷎mdatione᷎
habuit Sēp . v . borđ . Tc̄ . 11 . car᷎ in d̄nio . P᷎̄ & modo . 1 . 111 . ac̄ p̄ti . semp
. 1 . runc᷎ . Tc̄ . 111 . an̄ . modo . 1 . Tc̄ . x111i . porc᷎ . modo . viii . Tc̄ . xxx . 11 . ou̅s . m̄
xx . Tc̄ ual lx . sol . modo . xl . In eade᷎ . v . liƀi homines . c᷎o᷎mđ . xviii .
ac̄ . Tc̄ . 11 . car᷎ . modo . 1 . Ecclia . de . 11 . ac̄ . & dim᷎ . & ual . v . sol . hoc fuit
ad firmā . ꝑ . 111 . liƀ . & xv . sol . sed h᷎oes inde fuer̄ confusi . & modo apꝑ -

tiatu̅ e᷎ . xlv . sol . Hꝉ . 1 . lḡ in longo . & . 111 . q̇r in lato . ꝰ . x . đ . de gelto .
Abbas de eli dimidiā socā & antecessor comitis hugonis dimidiā .
V In Affefelda . Godman᷎ . liƀ hō c᷎o᷎mđtus t . r . e . Roƀti mal&
ꝑ man̄ . xxx . ac̄ . 7 . 1 . borđ . 7 . tc̄ . 1 . car᷎ P᷎̄ . nichil . modo dim᷎ car᷎ . Ecclia
. 1111 . ac̄ . 7 . ual . x . sol . Rannulfus ten̄ . Soca aƀƀis . & hante cessoris
hugonis . Ex his duoƀƣ maneriis fuit saisitus Wiꝉꝉm᷎ mal& die
sui obitus . In eađ . 1 . liƀ hō . 11 . ac̄ . & ual& . 1111 . đ . Soca aƀƀis .
V Perreham dim᷎ h̄ . Brutge ten& Edricus . c᷎o᷎mdatus Edrico
Ante cessori . R . mal& . c . xx . ac̄ ꝑ man̄ . Tc̄ . 11 . car᷎ . p᷎̄ . 1 . modo
dim᷎ . 7 1111 . ac̄ p̄ti . semp . 1 . molin̄ . & q᷎rta pars ecclie᷎ . de . vi . ac̄ .

CLAYDON Hundred

3 Brictwold held PETTAUGH in lordship; 1 carucate of land and 30 acres as a manor before 1066. Robert Malet's predecessor had the patronage.

    Always 5 smallholders.

    Then 2 ploughs in lordship; later and now 1.

    Meadow, 3 acres. Always 1 cob. Then 3 cattle, now 1; then 14 pigs, now 8; then 32 sheep, now 20.

Value then 60s; now 40[s].

In the same (Pettaugh) 5 free men under patronage; 18 acres. Then 2 ploughs, now 1.

    A church with 2½ acres; value 5s.

This was at a revenue for £3 15s, but the men were thereby ruined and now it is assessed at 45s.

    It has 1 league in length and 4 furlongs in width; 10d in tax. The Abbot of Ely (had) half the jurisdiction, and Earl Hugh's predecessor (had) half.

441 a

4 In ASHFIELD Godman, a free man under the patronage of Robert Malet before 1066; as a manor, 30 acres.

    1 smallholder.

    Then 1 plough, later nothing, now ½ plough.

    A church, 4 acres.

Value 10s.

    Ranulf holds (this).

    The jurisdiction (belonged to) the Abbot and to (Earl) Hugh's predecessor.

    William Malet was in possession of these two manors on the day of his death.

In the same (Ashfield) 1 free man; 2 acres.

Value 4d.

    The jurisdiction (is) the Abbot's.

PARHAM Half-Hundred

5 Edric, under the patronage of Edric, R(obert) Malet's predecessor [held] BRUTGE; 120 acres as a manor. Then 2 ploughs, later 1, now ½.

    Meadow, 4 acres; always 1 mill.

    The fourth part of a church with 6 acres.

viii . porc̃ . Tc̃ ual . xl . ſoł . modo . xx . Abbas de eli ſocã . 7 Garneᵒ
ten& de herueo . In ead . viii . libi hoẽs . additi . xx . ac̃ . Tc̃ . i . caꝛ
p̃ dim̃ . modo . nichil . 7 ual& xl . deñ . de dimidio huiᵒ ꞇꝛæ herueus
conciliatus abb̃i . & p̃ eã de rege tenuit . ħt . viii . qꝛ̃ in longo
7 vi in lato . & xl . đ . de gelto.

Ᵹ In beureſhã . teñ Aluric̃ lib̃ hõ in ſoca & com̃d abb̃is de eli
lx . ac̃ . ꝓ mañ . Tc̃ . i . caꝛ . iii . ac̃ p̃ti . Tc̃ ual . xx . ſoł . P̃ & modo . v.

Ᵹ In ead . ii . libi hões com̃dati ſuꝓdicꞇo . alurico . x . ac̃ . Tc̃ dim̃ . caꝛ
p̃ 7 m̃ nichil . & ual . ii . ſoł . Id Garneꝛ ten& de herueo . 7 jpſe ẽ
c̃ciliatus abb̃i ex hoc꞉ ſuꝓdicꞇo . m̃.

Bɪꜱᴄᴏᴘᴇꜱ . Hᴠɴᴅʀᴇᴛ . In Cipbenhala in dñio . i . lib̃
hõ heroldi . lx . ac̃ . t . r . e . 7 ſemp . ii . uiłł . 7 . ii . caꝛ . & . ii . ac̃ p̃ti . ſilua
xxx . porc̃ . Tc̃ ual . x . ſoł . modo . xx . ħ tenuit . W . filiᵒ gorham .

Ᵹ In Coleſtuna . i . lib̃ hõ . c̃om̃đ . Edrici . xxx . ac̃ . 7 . iii . borđ . & dim̃ . caꝛ.

441 b

Tc̃ ual& . x . ſoł . modo xx . & p̃tiń& ad cranesfordã . ħ ten& Warⁱ-
narị . de heꝛ

Hᴠɴᴅ̃ de coleneſſe . In Kelebroc teñ Kenoldus de herueu
. i . lib̃ ħm̃ Vluricũ . com̃đ . ſce Æ . xiiii . ac̃ . dim̃ caꝛ . dim̃ moł.
. i . ac̃ p̃ti . & . ii . borđ . Tc̃ ual . v . ſoł . modo . ix . ſoł.

8 pigs.

Value then 40s; now 20[s].

The Abbot of Ely (has) the jurisdiction.

Warner holds (this) from Hervey.

In the same (*Brutge*) 8 free men were added; 20 acres. Then 1 plough, later ½, now nothing.

Value 40d.

Concerning half of this land Hervey came to an agreement with the Abbot; later he held it from the King.

It has 8 furlongs in length and 6 in width; 40d in tax.

6 In BEVERSHAM Aelfric, a free man in the jurisdiction and under the patronage of the Abbot of Ely, held 60 acres as a manor. Then 1 plough.

Meadow, 3 acres.

Value then 20s; later and now 5[s].

In the same (Beversham) 2 free men under the patronage of the above-mentioned Aelfric; 10 acres. Then ½ plough, later and now nothing.

Value 2s.

Warner also holds (this) from Hervey, who came to an agreement with the Abbot over this above-mentioned manor.

BISHOP'S Hundred

7 In CHIPPENHALL in lordship; 1 free man of Harold's; 60 acres before 1066.

Always 2 villagers;

2 ploughs.

Meadow, 2 acres; woodland, 30 pigs.

Value then 10s; now 20[s].

W. son of Gorham held this.

8 In COLSTON 1 free man under the patronage of Edric; 30 acres.

3 smallholders.

½ plough.

Value then 10s; now 20[s].

It belongs to Cransford. Warner holds this from Hervey.

441 b

Hundred of COLNEIS

9 In KEMBROKE Cynwold holds from Hervey 1 free man, Wulfric, under the patronage of St. Etheldreda's; 14 acres. ½ plough.

½ mill; meadow, 1 acre.

2 smallholders.

Value then 5s; now 9s.

*H*VND̃. de Carleforda. In grundeſburg. tenuit Godricus
lib̄ hō. t. r. e. heroldi. ɪ. car̓ terræ. ͵p mañ. Semp. ɪ. uiłł. &.
ɪɪɪɪ. bord̓. Semp. ɪ. car̓ in dominio. & hom̄. ɪ. car̓. ɪɪɪ. ac̄
p̓ti. Tc̄ uał xvɪ. fol̓. modo ſimiliͫ. In eadē. ɪɪɪ. dimidii
lib̓i hōes. c̄om eid̓. Godwinus Wluinus Leuericus. vɪɪ. ac̄ tr̄æ.
Tc̄ dim̄ car̓. modo. nułł. Tc̄ uał. ɪɪ. fol̓. modo. xɪɪ. d̓. Adhuc
in eadē in dñio. ɪɪ. lib̓i homines Burric̄. & ailric̄. com̄d̓. Aſchilli
huſcarli. t. r. e. v. ac̄. Tc̄ dim̄. car̓. modo. nulla. & uał. x. d̓.
In eadē in dñio. ɪ. lib̄ hō Brunus. c̄om̄d̓. e. ante c̄. Rob̄. mal &. xx.
ac̄. 7 has xx. ac̄. tenebat de. edrico. Tc̄. ɪ. car̓ modo. dim̄. ɪɪ. ac̄ 7 di -
m̄ p̓ti. Tc̄ uał. v. fol̓. modo. ɪɪɪɪ. fol̓.
F In belinges in dñio. x. lib̓i hōes. Blakemanus. Aluinus. Stanardus
Ana. Vluric̄. Turb̄tus. Edric̄. Godwinus Aleſtanus. Anundus. p̄b̄r.
7 de hoc haldena c̄om̄d̓. & de aliis. sc̄a Æ. de lxxx. ac̄ &. ɪɪɪɪ. ac̄
terræ. Tc̄. ɪɪɪɪ. car̓. modo. ɪɪ. car̓. vɪɪɪ. ac̄ p̓ti. Tc̄ uał. xx. fol̓. m̄ ſimił.
In eadē. ɪ. lib̄ hō. Vlmarus fuit hō. haldeni ante ceſs. Gaosfridri
de magna uilla. de. c. ac̄ tr̄æ in dñio ͵p mañ. & ipſe Vlmarus.
ħt ſubſe. ɪɪɪ. uiłł. Tc̄ ī dñio. ɪɪ. car̓. modo. ɪ. 7 hom̄. ɪ. car̓. 7. ɪɪɪ. ac̄
p̓ti. Tc̄. ɪɪ. runc̄. modͦ. ɪɪɪɪ. Tc̄. ɪɪɪɪ. añ. modo. ɪɪɪ. Tc̄. xvɪ. porc̄.

modo. xɪɪ. Tc̄ lxxx. ous̄. modo. lx. Tc̄ uał. xx fol̓. modo. xl. fol̓.
. ɪ. Æcclia. xx. ac̄. 7 uał. xl. d̓. Soca s̄. æ.
F In parua belinges teñ Gosfridus. ɪɪ. fochemanni. Glademanus
Brihtricus. ſup hos habuit Godwinus ſoca 7 ſaca 7 conſuetudinem
7. ɪ. Leofsi͛ dequo Edric̄ habuit c̄om̄. illi. ɪɪ. foc̄ hab̄. xxvɪɪɪ. ac̄. Tc̄
ɪ. car̓. m̄. nulla. ɪ. ac̄. p̓ti. &. uał. ɪɪ. fol̓. 7 Leoffi. in dñio. xx. ac̄.

Hundred of CARLFORD

10 In GRUNDISBURGH Godric, a free man of Harold's, held before 1066; 1 carucate of land as a manor.
  Always 1 villager; 4 smallholders.
  Always 1 plough in lordship; 1 men's plough. Meadow, 3 acres.
Value then 16s; now the same.
In the same (Grundisburgh) 3 half free men under the patronage of the same man; Godwin, Wulfwin, Leofric; 7 acres of land. Then ½ plough, now none.
Value then 2s; now 12d.
Also in the same (Grundisburgh) in lordship; 2 free men, Burgric and Aethelric, under the patronage of Askell, a guard, before 1066; 5 acres. Then ½ plough, now none.
Value 10d.
In the same (Grundisburgh) in lordship; 1 free man, Brown, under the patronage of E(dric), Robert Malet's predecessor; 20 acres. He held these 20 acres from Edric. Then 1 plough, now ½.
  Meadow, 2½ acres.
Value then 5s; now 4s.

11 In (Great) BEALINGS in lordship; 10 free men, Blackman, Alwin, Stanhard, Ani, Wulfric, Thorbert, Edric, Godwin, Alstan, Anund the priest; over the latter, Haldane had patronage, and over the others St. Etheldreda's (had it); with 80 and 4 acres of land. Then 4 ploughs, now 2.
  Meadow, 8 acres.
Value then 20s; now the same.
In the same (Great Bealings) 1 free man, Wulfmer, he was a man belonging to Haldane, Geoffrey de Mandeville's predecessor, with 100 acres of land in lordship as a manor; and Wulfmer himself [had] under him 3 villagers. Then 2 ploughs in lordship, now 1; 1 men's plough.
  Meadow, 3 acres. Then 2 cobs, now 4; then 4 cattle, now 3; then   442 a
  16 pigs, now 12; then 80 sheep, now 60.
Value then 20s; now 40s.
  1 church, 20 acres; value 40d.
  St. Etheldreda's (has) the jurisdiction.

2 In LITTLE BEALINGS Geoffrey holds; 2 Freemen, Gladman (and) Brictric, over whom Godwin had full jurisdiction and the customary due, and 1 (Freeman) Leofsi, over whom Edric had patronage.
  The 2 Freemen had 28 acres.
  Then 1 plough, now none. Meadow, 1 acre.
Value 2s.
  Leofsi (had) 20 acres in lordship.

Tc̄.ɪ.car̓.modo.nulla.ɪɪɪ.ac̄ p̓ti.ɪ.moliñ.7 ual̊.ɪ·ɪɪ.ſol̊.In ead.
in dñio.ɪɪ.libi hoes com̓d.Sc̄a.Æ.t.r̓.e.Leuric̓ 7 Brihtric̓.x.
ac̄.Semp.dim̓ car̓.dim̓ ac̄.p̓ti.7 ual̊.ɪɪ.ſol̊.Adhuc in eadem
in dñio.ɪɪ.libi hoes.com̓.eid̓.Æ.t.r̓.e.Vlmar̓.& boɴdus.ɪɪɪɪ.ac̄

★ & ual& vɪɪɪ.d̓.7 in ead dñio.hardekin lib hō com̓d Durandi
hō Edrici dim̓ 7 dim̓ heroldi.ɪɪɪ.ac̄.&.ual.vɪ.d̓.7 h̄t·in longo.vɪ.
qr̄.&.v.in lato.7 de gelto.vɪɪ.den̓.& obolũ.

╟ In nechemara.in dñio.ɪ.lib hō.Vlfwiñ.com Ingulfi haſcarli.
ɪɪɪ.ac̄.&.ual.vɪ.den̄.

╟ In Riſcemara in dñio.ɪ.lib hō Brunnuin̓.com̓d.Guerti.xxx.ac̄
Semp.ɪ.car̓.ɪ.ac̄ p̓ti.7 ual̊.ſemp.x.ſol̊.7 h̄t vɪɪɪ.qr̓ in longo
&.vɪɪ.in lato.7.xvɪ.d̓ de gelto.

╟ In tudeham in dñio.ɪɪɪɪ.ac̄.7 s̄t in belinges.& ual.vɪɪɪ.d̓.In ead
.ɪ.liba femina Aldeda.com̓d.E.de laxefella.vɪ.ac̄.7 ual.xɪɪ.d̓.

                                442 a

Then 1 plough, now none. Meadow, 3 acres; 1 mill.
Value 3s.
In the same (Little Bealings) in lordship; 2 free men, Leofric and
Brictric, under the patronage of St. Etheldreda's before 1066; 10
acres. Always ½ plough.
Meadow, ½ acre.
Value 2s.
Also in the same (Little Bealings) 2 free men, Wulfmer and Bondi,
under the patronage of the same (St.) Etheldreda's before 1066;
4 acres.
Value 8d.
In the same (Little Bealings) [in] lordship; Hardekin, a free man,
half under the patronage of Durand, a man of Edric's, and half
(under that) of Harold; 3 acres.
Value 6d.
It has 6 furlongs in length and 5 in width; 7½d in tax.

13 In *NECHEMARA* in lordship; 1 free man, Wulfwin, under the patronage
of Ingulf, a guard; 3 acres.
Value 6d.

14 In RUSHMERE (St. Andrew) in lordship; 1 free man, Brunwin, under
the patronage of Gyrth; 30 acres. Always 1 plough.
Meadow, 1 acre.
Value always 10s.
It has 8 furlongs in length and 7 in width; 16d in tax.

15 In TUDDENHAM in lordship; 4 acres. They are in (the lands of)
Bealings.
Value 8d.
In the same (Tuddenham) 1 free woman, Aldgyth, under the
patronage of E(dric) of Laxfield; 6 acres.
Value 12d.

In ead̃ ten̄ Bernardus de alencun . Lxxx ac̃ . qua tenuit Briht -
marus lib̃ hõ . t̃ . r̃ . e . comdatus Edrici de laxefet p̃ man̄ . Sẽp.
vi . bord̃ . & . i . feru . 7 . ii . car̃ in dñio . 7 . iiii . ac̃ p̃ti . Tc̃ . ii . tunc.
modo nutt . Tc̃ . iii . porc̃ . modo . v . Tc̃ . xv . oũs . m̃ . x . Tc̃ . vi . cap̃.

modo . nutt . Tc̃ uat . xx . fot . m̃ fimilit . 7 De h̃ manerio fuit ante
ceffor . R . mal& . Edric̃ faifitus . t̃ . r̃ . e . 7 W . mal& q̃ndo fuit mortuus.
& ñ poterat tr̃a fua dare i uende . alicui . & . v . lib̃i hões com̄ eid̃ Brih -
tmari . xiiii . ac̃ . Tc̃ . dim̃ . car̃ . modo . nutt . Tc̃ uat . xiii . fot . modo . iii.
fot . In ead̃ . ii . lib̃i hões un̄ comd̃ ante c̃ . R . frs ilgeri . 7 ali comd̃ . cu -
iufd̃a comd̃ . S . E . vii . ac̃ . Tc̃ dim̃ car̃ . modo . nutt . 7 uat . xvi . d̃ . &
ht in longo . x . qr̃ . & . vi . in lato . 7 xv . d̃ . de getto . h̃ totũ ten& Ber -
★ nardus de belencun̄ de . hejuehu.
⌐Thifteldena . i . lib̃ hõ . frana . com̄dat̃ . Edrici . t̃ . r̃ . e . xxx . ac̃ . tr̃æ.
Sẽp . ii . bord̃ . 7 . i . car̃ . ii . ac̃ p̃ti . 7 uat . viii . fot . hoc ten̄ Renoldus.
de heruehu . fed W . mal& inde fuit faifitus die qua obiit.
⌐In derneford . xi . lib̃i hões com̄dati Durandi hõ dim̃ . E . t̃ . r̃ . e . 7 dim̃.
Heroldi . lxxx . ac̃ . & . iii . bord̃ . Tc̃ . iiii . car̃ . modo . iii . & . ii . ac̃ p̃ti.
Tc̃ uat xl . fot . modo . xv.
⌐In ingolueftuna . xiii . lib̃i hões . t̃ . r̃ . e . modo . vi . com̄dti eid̃ . Duran -
di . i . car̃ terræ . & . iiii . ac̃ . Tc̃ . v . car̃ . modo . i . v . ac̃ p̃ti . & uat . x . fot.
⌐In ead̃ . i . lib̃ hõ comd̃ . eid̃ . Durandi . xii . ac̃ . & dim̃ . car̃ . & uat . xl . d̃.
& ht . in longo . vi . qr̃ . & . v . in lato . & . vii . d̃ . 7 obolũ de getto . hoc ten&
petrus . de paludel . de herueu.

In the same (Tuddenham) Bernard of Alençon holds 80 acres.
Brictmer, a free man under the patronage of Edric of Laxfield, held
it before 1066 as a manor.
> Always 6 smallholders; 1 slave;
> 2 ploughs in lordship.
> Meadow, 4 acres. Then 2 cobs, now none; then 3 pigs, now 5;
>> then 15 sheep, now 10; then 6 goats, now none.

442 b

Value then 20s; now the same.
> Of this manor, R(obert) Malet's predecessor, Edric, was in
possession before 1066, and W(illiam) Malet (was in possession)
when he died, and he could not grant or sell his land to someone else.
5 free men under the patronage of the same Brictmer; 14 acres.
Then ½ plough, now none.
Value then 4s; now 3s.
In the same (Tuddenham) 2 free men, one under the patronage of
the predecessor of R(anulf) brother of Ilger, and the other under the
patronage of someone under the patronage of St. Etheldreda's; 7 acres.
Then ½ plough, now none.
Value 16d.
> It has 10 furlongs in length and 6 in width; 15d in tax.
> Bernard of Alençon holds the whole of this from Hervey.

16 THISTLETON; 1 free man, Frani, under the patronage of Edric before
1066; 30 acres of land.
> Always 2 smallholders;
> 1 plough. Meadow, 2 acres.
Value 8s.
> Reginald holds this from Hervey, but W(illiam) Malet was in
possession of it on the day he died.

17 In *DERNEFORD* 11 free men under the patronage of Durand (who
was) half E(dric)'s man before 1066 and half Harold's; 80 acres.
> 3 smallholders.
> Then 4 ploughs, now 3. Meadow, 2 acres.
Value then 40s; now 15[s].

18 In *INGOLUESTUNA* 13 free men before 1066, now 6, under the
patronage of the same Durand; 1 carucate of land and 4 acres. Then
5 ploughs, now 1.
> Meadow, 5 acres.
Value 10s.
In the same (*Ingoluestuna*) 1 free man of the same Durand's; 12
acres. ½ plough.
Value 40d.
> It has 6 furlongs in length and 5 in width; 7½d in tax.
> Peter of Palluel holds this from Hervey.

HVNDRET . DE WILEFORDA . Berdefelda tenuit Suarting.

com ante c̄ . Rob . mal& . t . r . e . LXXX . ac̄ . & . i . bord . Tc̄ . i . car & dim̄.
modo . i . Tc̄ . ii . runc̄ . m̄ . ii . & . i . an . 7 XXVII . ous . Tc̄ ual XX . fol.
modo . XXX . 7 ht in longo . i . lḡ . 7 dim qr 7 . VI . qr in lato . & de gelto
XIII . den̄ . & obolū . In ead XXI . lib hoes com̄d Suartingi . t . r . e . i . car

443 a

trae . 7 XXII . ac̄ . Tc̄ . IIII . car . modo . iii . dim ac̄ pti . Tc̄ ual . XXX . fol.
modo fimil . Adhuc in ead . i . lib hō . com̄d . cuida com̄d . ante . c̄ . Rob
mal& . XII . ac̄ . femp . dim ear . & ual . ii . fol . Ex hoc erat . Will mal&
faifit die qua obiit.

In Wikham . ten̄ . i . lib hō . com Edrici . t . r . e . XXX . irf . ac̄ . p man̄.
(Rnnulfus) (Atser)
& . i . bord . iii . ac̄ pti . Tc̄ . i . car . modo . null . & . ii . libi hoes . fub fe . VIII.
ac̄ . Tc̄ dim . car . Tc̄ ual . x . fol . modo . VI . 7 ex h fimilit̄.

In futtuna . ten& ide atfer . t . r . e . LX . ac̄ . p man̄ . Semp . ii . bord
(Arcenbaldus)
Tc̄ & p . i . car . m̄ . dim . dim . ac̄ pti . Tc̄ ual . x . fol . m̄ fimilit . In ead
ten ide Arcebaldus . i . lib hō . com̄d . Edrici . VI . ac̄ . Sep . ii . bou . 7
tc̄ ual . ii . fol . m̄ fimilit ex hoc totide . fimil.

In horapola . ten odo . i . lib hm commendation . S . ae . & dim . Edrici
XVI . ac̄ . & ual& . iii . fol.

Hundred of WILFORD

19 Swarting, under the patronage of Robert Malet's predecessor, held
BREDFIELD before 1066; 80 acres.
    1 smallholder.
    Then 1½ ploughs, now 1.
    Then 2 cobs, now 2; 1 cattle, 27 sheep.
Value then 20s; now 30[s].
    It has 1 league and ½ furlong in length, and 6 furlongs in width;
13½d in tax.
In the same (Bredfield) 21 free men under the patronage of Swarting
before 1066; 1 carucate of land and 22 acres. Then 4 ploughs, now 3.   443 a
    Meadow, ½ acre.
Value then 30s; now the same.
Also in the same (Bredfield) 1 free man under the patronage of
someone under the patronage of Robert Malet's predecessor; 12
acres. Always ½ plough.
Value 2s.
    William Malet was in possession of this on the day he died.

20 In WICKHAM (Market) Ranulf holds; Azor, 1 free man under the
patronage of Edric before 1066; 33 acres as a manor.
    1 smallholder.
    Meadow, 3 acres.
    Then 1 plough, now none.
2 free men under him; 8 acres. Then ½ plough.
Value then 10s; now 6[s].
    Of this, likewise (William Malet was in possession on the day he
died).

21 In SUTTON Erchenbald holds; Azor also [held it] before 1066; 60
acres as a manor.
    Always 2 smallholders.
    Then and later 1 plough, now ½. Meadow, ½ acre.
Value then 10s; now the same.
In the same (Sutton) Erchenbald also holds; 1 free man under the
patronage of Edric; 6 acres. Always 2 oxen.
Value 2s; now the same.
    Of this, likewise (William Malet was in possession on the day he
died).

22 In HARPOLE Odo holds 1 free man [half] under the patronage of St.
Etheldreda's and half (under that) of Edric; 16 acres.
Value 3s.

★ ⌐In bredefella teñ petrus . i . lib homo̧ . com̛datione Durandi . de -
offetuna . xii . aꝭ . iii . boū . 7 xxiii . oūs . & ual& . ii . ſol . In eaꝫ . i . lib
homo comdation̛ Ailrici deburc . iiii . aꝭ & ual . viii . d̗.

⌐In Ludeham dm̄ lib hō comd Suartingi̧ . t . r . e xv . aꝭ & ual ; ii . ſol.

⌐In bulges . i . lib hō . comd Edrici . grim̄ . de . v . pꞇis terræ . & ual& . iiii d̗

⌐In horepolo . i . lib hō . comdatioñ . Edrici . v̇ . aꝭ ; & dim̄ aꝭ pꞇi . & ual . xii . d̗.

HVND . DE LOSA . Martele tenuit . Brihtmarus ; comd̛
heroldi . t̛ . r̛ . e̛ . ꝑ m̄ Lxxx . aꝭ Semp̧ . v ; bord . & ; iñ dñio ; ii . car̛ . ix . aꝭ
pꞇi . 7 . i . runc̛ . 7 . i . an̄ . & . ix . porc̛ . 7 . xvii . ꝯūs . 7 xxx cap̄ . Tꞓ ual . xL̗
ſol . modo xxx . 7 . x . libi homines . 7 ii . dim̄ comd eidē . Lx . aꝭ.
Semp . ii . car̛ . i . aꝭ & dim̄ pꞇi . & ual ; x ; ſol ; i . ex his calūpniat̛

443 b

Rob mal& . & hab& ; in longo . i ; leuga . & dim̄ in lato . & de
gelto ; xi . deñ.

⌐Campeſeia tenuer̄ . ii . libi hóes Suartingus , 7 edricus cꝰ
md Edrici . de laxefella . Lx . aꝭ . træ ꝑ man̄ , Semp . iii . uiſt̗
Semp . ii . car̛ . & d̗ . car̛ hominū . viii . aꝭ pꞇi . i ; molin̄ . & , ii̗
runc ; & . viii . porc̛ . & xx . ꝯūs ; & . iii . ruſcas ap̄ . Tꞓ ual . xx ; ſol̗
modo . xxx . & . xii . libi homines . comd̛ ; eiꝫ . xxxviii aꝭ . træ
Tꞓ . ii . car̛ . modo . i . Tꞓ ual viii ; ſol , modo . x , & ħt in longo
vi . qr̄ . & ; in lato ; iiii . & de gelto . vii , d̗ . Wiłłm mal& fuit
ſaiatus die q̊ obiit.

443 a, b

23 In BREDFIELD Peter holds 1 free man, the patronage was Durand of Offton's; 12 acres. 3 oxen.
 23 sheep.
Value 3s.
In the same (Bredfield) 1 free man under the patronage of Aethelric of Burgh; 4 acres.
Value 8d.

24 In LOUDHAM a half free man under the patronage of Swarting before 1066; 15 acres.
Value 2s.

25 In BOULGE 1 free man under the patronage of Edric Grim, with 5 perches of land.
Value 4d.

26 In HARPOLE 1 free man under the patronage of Edric; 5 acres.
 Meadow, ½ acre.
Value 12d.

Hundred of LOES
27 Brictmer, under the patronage of Harold, held MARTLEY before 1066; as a manor, 80 acres.
 Always 5 smallholders;
 2 ploughs in lordship.
 Meadow, 9 acres. 1 cob, 1 cattle, 9 pigs, 17 sheep, 30 goats.
Value then 40s; now 30[s].
10 free men and 2 half (free men) under the patronage of the same man; 60 acres. Always 2 ploughs.
 Meadow, 1½ acres.
Value 10s.
 Robert Malet claims 1 of these (men).   443 b
 It has 1 league in length and ½ in width; 11d in tax.

28 2 free men, Swarting and Edric, under the patronage of Edric of Laxfield, held CAMPSEY (Ash); 60 acres of land as a manor.
 Always 3 villagers.
 Always 2 ploughs; ½ men's plough.
 Meadow, 8 acres; 1 mill. 2 cobs, 8 pigs, 20 sheep, 2 hives of bees.
Value then 20s; now 30[s].
12 free men under the patronage of the same man; 38 acres of land. Then 2 ploughs, now 1.
Value then 8s; now 10[s].
 It has 6 furlongs in length and 4 in width; 7d in tax.
 William Malet was in possession on the day he died.

Renlefhã teñ Godgeua liɓa femina . comd . dim . sca . æ
& dim . Edrici de laxefella , Lx . ac . p mañ . Tc . ii . car . modo . i.
. ii . ac pti . & . i . uiɫɫ . Semp uaɫ xx . foɫ . & . i . liɓ hõ . & dim . x . ac
comd eidē . & dim . car . in eod ptio . H teṇ& Bernardus . de
Alencun . de herueu . Wiɫɫm fuit faifitus . die qua obiit . &
hɫ in longo . i . lg . & in lato . dim & de gelto . xiiii d.
Potesforda teñ odonus p mañ . Lxxx . ac ꝑ mañ quā tenuit
Wenningus . commd . dim . s . Æ . & dim . Edrici . Semp
ii . uiɫɫ . & . ii . bord , & , vi . ac pti . Tc . ii . car . m . i . i . runc . &
iiii . añ . & x . cap . Semp uaɫ xx . foɫ . 7 jn eadē . viii . liɓi hoes
. iii . ex iftis foris fecer fuā terrā cont abb . ne poftea uidit.
hundret qd eā redimer& . & qrtus fuit hõ abb . & ceɫi quat -
tuor . fuer comd . Wenningi . xxx . ac . hi oms dim car
. i . ac . & dim pti . Semp uaɫ . x . foɫ . & hɫ in longo . i . leuga

444 a

& dim in lato . & de gelto . xi . d . Wiɫɫ fuit faiatus die qua obiit
Glereuinges teñ Brihtmarus . comd Edrico . t . r . e . p mañ
xL ac . & . i . bord . & . i . car . iii . ac pti . i . moliñ . & . xx . oũs . Tc uaɫ
viii . foɫ . modo . x . In eadē uilla . xvii . liɓi homs . & dim . comd
eid . Lx . ac . Tc . ii . car . modo . i . i . ac pti . Tc uaɫ . xvii . foɫ . modo . xv.
W . mal& fuɫt faiatus die qua obiit . & . hɫ in longo . i . lg . & in
lato . dim . & de gelto . xxii . d . h ten& . Odo . de herueu.

29 Godiva, a free woman, half under the patronage of St. Etheldreda's
and half (under that) of Edric of Laxfield, held RENDLESHAM; 60
acres as a manor. Then 2 ploughs, now 1.
   Meadow, 2 acres.
   1 villager.
Value always 20s.
1 free man and a half (free man) under the patronage of the same;
10 acres. ½ plough.
(It is) in the same assessment.
   Bernard of Alençon holds this from Hervey. William (Malet) was
in possession on the day he died.
   It has 1 league in length and ½ in width; 14d in tax.

30 Odo holds POTSFORD; as a manor, 80 acres. Wynning, half under the
patronage of St. Etheldreda's and half (under that) of Edric, held it.
   Always 2 villagers; 2 smallholders.
   Meadow, 6 acres.
   Then 2 ploughs, now 1.
   1 cob, 4 cattle, 10 goats.
Value always 20s.
In the same (Potsford) 8 free men; 3 of these forfeited their land to
the Abbot and later on the Hundred did not see that they should
redeem it, and a fourth was the Abbot's man, and the other four
were under the patronage of Wynning; 30 acres. All of these [had]
½ plough.
   Meadow, 1½ acres.
Value always 10s.
   It has 1 league in length and ½ in width; 11d in tax.   444 a
   William Malet was in possession on the day he died.

31 Brictmer, under the patronage of Edric, held GLEVERING before
1066; as a manor, 40 acres.
   1 smallholder.
   1 plough.
   Meadow, 3 acres; 1 mill. 20 sheep.
Value then 8s; now 10[s].
In the same village 17 free men and a half under the patronage of
the same man; 60 acres. Then 2 ploughs, now 1.
   Meadow, 1 acre.
Value then 17s; now 15[s].
   W(illiam) Malet was in possession on the day he died.
   It has 1 league in length and ½ in width; 22d in tax.
   Odo holds this from Hervey.

F In delingahou . XL . aꝅ . qu̇d tenueꝛ . III . liƀi hőes . & ual . VI . fot.

In ead . II liƀi hȯes con̉d dim̉ . Suartingi & dim̉ . Brumani.

XX . aꝅ . Tꝅ dim̉ . caꝛ . & ual . III . fot . & ħt in longo . I . lg̅ . & in lato

III . qꝛ . & de gelto . VII . d & obolũ ; In eadē . II . dim̉ hȯes . com̉ . Edriꝛi

v . aꝅ . & ual . XII . d̃.

PLVMESGATE . *H̃* . Cranesforda . ten& . Atfur ꞇ con̉d . Edrici

de laxefella . LXXX . aꝅ tꝛæ . ꝓ man̅ . Semp . I . borḋ . Tꝅ ꞇ II . caꝛ

modo . I . I . aꝅ p̃ti . Tꝅ . II . runꝅ . Tꝅ . XXIIII . porꝛ . m̉ . I . 7 XVI . oũsꞇ

Tꝅ XL cap̃ . Tꝅ ual . XX . fot . m̃ XIII . & . IIII . d̃.

★ ## *T*ERRE GISLEBERTI BALASTARII . *BIDINGA* . *H̃.*   .LXVIII

In eftuna ten̅ Elricus fiłꝉ . Wluiat heroldi comiti con̉d . t . r . e

Ṁ . G . ꝓ man̅ . de rege . II . caꝛ terræ . Tꝅ . v . uiłt . modo . III . Semp

. v . borḋ . & . I . ferui . Tꝅ . I . caꝛ & dim̉ in dominio . modo nichil.

Semp hom̉ . III . caꝛ . filua . ad VIII . porꝛ . III . aꝅ p̃ti . Tꝅ . I . falina

444 b

Ṁ . nulla . Tꝅ . I . runꝅ . & . III . an̉ . & . II . porꝛ . & LXXX . oũs . m̃ nichil.

Tꝅ ual . XL . fot . modo XX . fot . Rex & com̅s focā . Adhuc in ugge ‑

cehala . I . uiłt . Vluricus de XX . aꝅ . & dim̉ caꝛ . ~~Rex & com̅s focā~~.

7 In cedeftan . I . uiłt ofketellus de XX . aꝅ . & dim̉ caꝛ . & in eoḋ p̃tioꞏ

de eftuna . Idē Gifleƀtus . ten& in cedeftan . I . liƀ hȯ Godricus

con̉d eid̉ . de XX . aꝅ . & . II . borḋ . & dim̉ caꝛ . & dim̉ aꝅ p̃ti . filua

ad . VI . porꝛ . & ual . IIII . fot . Et in eftuna . II . liƀi homines Godric̉.

& Ofketel . con̉d eidē . de XX aꝅ . tꝛæ . femp . I . caꝛ . & ual . IIII . fot.

32 In DALLINGHOO 40 acres. 3 free men held it.
Value 6s.
In the same (Dallinghoo) 2 free men, half under the patronage of
Swarting and half (under that) of Brunman; 20 acres. Then ½ plough.
Value 3s.
It has 1 league in length and 3 furlongs in width; 7d in tax.
In the same (Dallinghoo) 2 half [free] men under the patronage of
Edric; 5 acres.
Value 12d.

PLOMESGATE Hundred
33 Azor, under the patronage of Edric of Laxfield, [held] CRANSFORD;
80 acres of land as a manor.
Always 1 smallholder.
Then 2 ploughs, now 1.
Meadow, 1 acre. Then 2 cobs; then 24 pigs, now 1; 16 sheep;
then 40 goats.
Value then 20s; now 13[s] 4d.

LANDS OF GILBERT THE CROSSBOWMAN

BLYTHING Hundred
1 In EASTON (Bavents) Aelfric son of Wulfgeat, under the patronage of
Earl Harold, held before 1066; now Gilbert [holds it] as a manor
from the King; 2 carucates of land.
Then 5 villagers, now 3. Always 5 smallholders; 1 slave.
Then 1½ ploughs in lordship, now nothing; always 3 men's
ploughs.
Woodland for 8 pigs; meadow, 3 acres; then 1 salt-house, now   444 b
none. Then 1 cob, 3 cattle, 2 pigs, 80 sheep, now nothing.
Value then 40s; now 20s.
The King and the Earl (have) the jurisdiction.

2 Also in UGGESHALL 1 villager, Wulfric, with 20 acres. ½ plough. And
in CHEDISTON 1 villager, Askell, with 20 acres. ½ plough.
(This is) in the same assessment of Easton (Bavents).

3 Gilbert also holds in CHEDISTON; 1 free man, Godric, under the
patronage of the same man, with 20 acres.
2 smallholders.
½ plough.
Meadow, ½ acre; woodland for 6 pigs.
Value 4s.

4 And in EASTON (Bavents) 2 free men, Godric and Askell, under the
patronage of the same man, with 20 acres of land. Always 1 plough.
Value 4s.

Rex & coms focā. Eftuna hab̃.ɪ.lg̃ in longo.& dim̃ in lato.& de-
gelto.vɪ.đ.Alii ibi tenent.

HERTESMARA. H̃.Giflincham ten̄ Alsi lib̃ hõ.ɪɪ.cař trǣ

ꝑ mañ.&.ɪɪ.borđ.Tc̃ & ꝑ.ɪɪ.cař.in dñio.modo.ɪ.&.ɪɪ.ac̃ p̃ti.
Silua.ɪɪɪɪ.porc̃.7 uaɫ.xʟ.foɫ.h̃ manerıū fuit uiuente rege.
edwardo de dñio abb̃is Lefftani de sc̃o edmundo.7 Lefftanus abbas
eū acc̃omodauit Alfio & uxori fuæ tali conuentione qđ poft obitū
eoꝛ rehaberet Abbas fuū manerıū.& unū aliū mañ Alfi nõe
Euftuna Rex & Com̃s focā.In eađ.vɪɪɪ.lib̃i hões com̃đ Alfio
xvɪ.ac̃.Tc̃.ɪ.cař.modo.dim̃.& st̃ in fupiori p̃tio.In eađe.ɪɪɪ.
lib̃i hões com̃đ ante ceffori Alb̃ici de uer.vɪ.ac̃.& uaɫ.xɪɪ.đ.Rex
& com̃s focā.h̃t.ɪ.lg̃ in longo.&.vɪɪ.qř in lato.& x.đ.de gelto;

445 a

★ # TERRÆ RADVLFI BALISTARII. DIMIDIAM. H̃.   .ʟxvɪɪɪ

DELVDINGA LAND.Burch tenuit.Stigandus ep̃s.cū foca

t.r.e.ɪɪɪɪ.cař terræ ꝑ mañ.Semp.x.uiɫɫ.&.v.borđ.Tc̃.ɪɪ.feru.
modo nulla.Tc̃ in dñıõ.ɪɪɪ.cař.modo.ɪɪ.Tc̃ hõm.ɪɪɪɪ.cař.modo
.ɪɪɪ.x.ac̃ p̃ti.ɪɪɪ.faline.Semp.ɪɪɪ.runc̃.&.vɪ.an.7 xvɪɪ.porc̃.
&.c.ʟx.oũs.ɪ.æcclia.x.ac̃.&.ɪ.ac̃ p̃ti.Tc̃ uaɫ.c.foɫ.modo.c.&.vɪ.foɫ.
Caldecotan tenuit Bundus com̃đ.Guerti.t.r.e.ɪ.cař.terre.
ꝑ mañ.Tc̃.ɪ.borđ.modo.ɪɪɪ.Tc̃.ɪ.cař.modo.dim̃.Tc̃ uaɫ.x.foɫ.
modo.vɪɪɪ.

The King and the Earl (have) the jurisdiction.
Easton (Bavents) has 1 league in length and ½ in width; 6d in tax.
Others hold there.

HARTISMERE Hundred

5 Alsi, a free man, held GISLINGHAM; 2 carucates of land as a manor.
2 smallholders.
Then and later 2 ploughs in lordship, now 1.
Meadow, 2 acres; woodland, 4 pigs.
Value 40s.
During the reign of King Edward this manor belonged to the
lordship of Abbot Leofstan of St. Edmund's. Abbot Leofstan leased
it to Alsi and his wife with the agreement that after their death the
Abbot should have his manor back and one other manor of Alsi's,
Euston by name.
The King and the Earl (have) the jurisdiction.
In the same (Gislingham) 8 free men under the patronage of Alsi;
16 acres. Then 1 plough, now ½.
They are in the above assessment.
In the same (Gislingham) 3 free men under the patronage of Aubrey
de Vere's predecessor; 6 acres.
Value 12d.
The King and the Earl (have) the jurisdiction.
It has 1 league in length and 7 furlongs in width; 10d in tax.

69   LANDS OF RALPH THE CROSSBOWMAN   445 a

Half-Hundred of LOTHINGLAND

1 Bishop Stigand held BURGH (Castle) with the jurisdiction before
1066; 4 carucates of land as a manor.
Always 10 villagers; 5 smallholders. Then 2 slaves, now none.
Then 3 ploughs in lordship, now 2; then 4 men's ploughs, now 3.
Meadow, 10 acres; 3 salt-houses. Always 3 cobs, 6 cattle, 17 pigs,
160 sheep.
1 church, 10 acres. Meadow, 1 acre.
Value then 100s; now 106s.

2 Bondi, under the patronage of Gyrth, held CALDECOTT before 1066;
1 carucate of land as a manor.
Then 1 smallholder, now 3.
Then 1 plough, now ½.
Value then 10s; now 8[s].

In earetunà . i . liƀ hõ ; Ketelus comd . Vlfus . t . r . e . xl .

ac . Tc . i . bord . modo . nuⅼⅼ . Semp dim car . Sep uaⅼ . iiii . foⅼ .

In fumeRledeftuna . i . liƀ hõ ; Aluoldus comd Guerti . xxx ; ac . Tc
dim car . modo . nuⅼⅼ . Silua ad . v . porc . & uaⅼ . ii . foⅼ .

★ **TERRA RAINALDI BRITONIS** q̇ reuocat in elemofinà ⠀⠀⠀ . LXX

regis . *RISEBRVGE* . *H̃* . Litgatã . tenuer̃ . iii ; liƀi homines
p̄ . iiii . car . terræ . Tc . ix . uiⅼⅼ . p̄ . vii . m̂ . iii . Tc . i . bord . p̄ ; iiii . m̂ . vi .
Tc . iii . feru . p̄ ; i . m̂ . nuⅼ . Tc & p̄ . iii . car . m̂ . i . Tc & p̄ . vii ; car . hom̂ .
modo . ii . filuà . de . x . porc . x . ac p̃ti . Tc . ii . porc . m̂ . xxx . femp . vii ;
ous . Tc uaⅼ . lxxx ; foⅼ ; m̂ lx ; hanc tr̃à caⅼupniatur hoes de Wate
uiⅼla ad fuũ feudũ ;

445 b

. LXXI. TERRA . ROBERTI DE STRATFORT . *SAnfort* . *H̃*

Boitunã teñ . Suenus Suart . t . r ; e . i ; car terre . pro maner̃ .
Tc . ii . bord . modo . vi . Tc . ii ; car in dominio . femp . i . car hom̂ .
v . ac p̃ti . Tc uaⅼ . xl . foⅼ . modo xxx . Soca in ƀcolt . In eadẽ
tenuit brixi liƀ hõ . i . car . terræ p̄ man . t . r . e . Tc . i . bord .
modo ; ii . femp . i . car in dñio . & modo . i . runc . & . vi . ous . &
uaⅼ & . xx . foⅼ ſit . vii . q̃r in longo ; & . vi . in lato . 7 xiiii . d de gelto ;
Alii ibi tenent foca in ƀcolt .

3 In CORTON 1 free man, Ketel, under the patronage of Ulf before
1066; 40 acres.
Then 1 smallholder, now none.
Always ½ plough.
Value always 4s.

4 In SOMERLEYTON 1 free man, Alwold, under the patronage of Gyrth;
30 acres. Then ½ plough, now none.
Woodland for 5 pigs.
Value 2s.

0 **LAND OF REGINALD THE BRETON** which he claims as the King's alms

RISBRIDGE Hundred
1 3 free men held LIDGATE as 4 carucates of land.
Then 9 villagers, later 7, now 3; then 1 smallholder, later 4, now 6;
then 3 slaves, later 1, now none.
Then and later 3 ploughs, now 1; then and later 7 men's ploughs,
now 2.
Woodland at 10 pigs; meadow, 10 acres. Then 2 pigs, now 30;
always 7 sheep.
Value then 80s; now 60[s].
The men of (William of) Vatteville claim this land for his Holding.

1 **LAND OF ROBERT OF STRATFORD** 445 b

SAMFORD Hundred
1 Swein Swart held BOYNTON before 1066; 1 carucate of land as a
manor.
Then 2 smallholders, now 6.
Then 2 ploughs in lordship; always 1 men's plough. Meadow,
5 acres.
Value then 40s; now 30[s].
The jurisdiction (is) in (East) Bergholt.
In the same (Boynton) Brictsi, a free man; 1 carucate of land as a
manor before 1066.
Then 1 smallholder, now 2.
Always 1 plough in lordship.
Now 1 cob, 6 sheep.
Value 20s.
It has 7 furlongs in length and 6 in width; 14d in tax. Others hold
there. The jurisdiction (is) in (East) Bergholt.

In belefteda tenuit . Turi̷ LXXX . ac̄ ͵p man̄ . femp . III . uill . &
II . bord̄ . Tc̄ . I . car̷ . in dn̄io . femp . I . car̷ hom̄ . & ; II . ac̄ p̊ti ; & q̊rta
pars ecctiæ . & ual . XXIII . fol . foca in b̄colt.

. LXXII . TERRA STANARDI . filii alwii . Rifebruge . ħ In Vuefdana
xxx . ac̄ ten̄ Wifgar . t . r . e . femp . I . bord̄ . 7 . I . car̷ . & . II . ac̄ p̊ti.
7 ual xx fol.

. LXXIII . TERRA Wlmari ; Risebruge . H̄ . In Lafham . xxIIII . ac̄
& dim̄ . car̷ . & ual . IIII . fol . s̄es . e . foca . In ead̄e . Ix ac̄ . ten̄ id̄e
Vlmarus q̊s inuadauit . t . r . Witti de ante ceffore . Rad̄ pinel
pro . xxI . fol & ual xII . d̄ . Vicecom̄s Rog̊ habuit de patre
fuo herret̷.

446 a

TERRA VAVASORVM . BOSEMERA . H̄.   . LXXI

In hamingeftuna . I . lib̄ ho̅ . de xx ac̄ . in foca regis . & . v . bord̷.
femp . I . car̷ . & ual . v . fol.
In facheduna . III . libi ho̊es in foca regis . xxx . ac̄ . femp . I . car̷ . &
val& . v . fol . In eod̄ . ħ . In Betesfort . ten̄ . I . lib̄ ho̅ durandus . xxx.
ac̄ . t . r . e . M̊ . fiuuardus in foca regis . Tc̄ dim̄ car̷ . modo . II . boů.
& . II . ac̄.

2 In BELSTEAD Thuri held 80 acres as a manor.
Always 3 villagers; 2 smallholders.
Then 1 plough in lordship; always 1 men's plough. Meadow,
2 acres.
The fourth part of a church.
Value 23s.
The jurisdiction (is) in (East) Bergholt.

2   LAND OF STANHARD SON OF AETHELWY

RISBRIDGE Hundred
1 In OUSDEN 30 acres; Withgar held (it) before 1066.
Always 1 smallholder;
1 plough. Meadow, 2 acres.
Value 20s.

3   LAND OF WULFMER

RISBRIDGE Hundred
1 In *LAFHAM* 24 acres. ½ plough.
Value 4s.
St. Edmund's (has) the jurisdiction.
In the same (*Lafham*) Wulfmer also holds 9 acres which he annexed
after 1066 from Ralph Pinel's predecessor for 21s.
Value 12d.
Roger the Sheriff had the heriot from his father.

4   LAND OF VAVASSORS   446 a

BOSMERE Hundred
1 In HEMINGSTONE 1 free man in the King's jurisdiction, with 20 acres.
5 smallholders.
Always 1 plough.
Value 5s.

2 In *FACHEDUNA* 3 free men in the King's jurisdiction; 30 acres. Always
1 plough.
Value 5s.

3 In the same Hundred in BATTISFORD 1 free man, Durand, held 30
acres before 1066. Now Siward [holds it], in the King's jurisdiction.
Then ½ plough, now 2 oxen.
2 acres.

In Vledana.IIII.libi hões Rabboda.Leuricus.Edric̄.Vluric̄
VIII.ac̄.7 ual.XVI.d.isti st̄ additi.ad firmā.t.r.Wilti.& roḡ
&.R.nesciebat qd̄ ēent additi.
ē warat inde Vlmaro p̄posito.qui eos addidit & n̄ p̄tinebāt
ad ullā firmā.In ead.I.lib̄ hō.Vlmar̄.q̄rtā parte.uñi acre
&.ual.II.d.hunc tenuit brictmar̄.bedel.& dedit uadē.
Vlmarus p̄positus fide iussor.In ead.I.lib̄ hō Lewinus.II.ac̄.&
dim̄.& ual.VIII.d.

In hamigeftuna.I.lib̄ hō brictuolt.IIII.ac̄.& ual.VIII.d.

In Cratingis.Liba femina Aldid dim̄.ac̄.& ual.I.d.

HVND̄.DE CLAINDVNE.In haminghelanda.I.lib̄-
hō Aluuin Comdatus Guert.XXX.ac̄.Tc̄ dim̄.car̄.& ual.V.fol.
Vlmar̄ p̄posit adiunxit hunc libum hominē ad firmā regis
de brū for.& roḡ uicecoms ē ei inde warant.& reddit uno q̄q̄ an.
no.V.fol.7 rex & coms focā.

In Turolweftuna tenuit Rolf.t.r.e.m̄.Aluric̄ fili ei burgenfis
de gipefwiz.XII.ac̄.& ual.II.fol.Rex & coms focā.7 ex hac
fuit faifitus.R.coms quando forisfecit.Ide Aluric̄ ten& æcctiā.

446 b
Sc̄i iuliani jn burgo de gipefwiz.XX.ac̄.terræ.& ual.XL d.7 ex hac
ecctia fuit faifitus.R.coms.

In Claindune.ten̄.Alric̄ lib̄ hō.VI.ac̄.& dim̄.t.r.e.modo Idem Al.
uricus.& ual.XIIII.d.Rex & coms dimidiā focā 7 sc̄a Adeldreda
aliā medietate.hanc terrā tenuit ille Aluric̄ in uadimonio.&
non fit inde warant.Isti s̄ in manu regis.

4 In 'OLDEN' 4 free men, Radbod, Leofric, Edric, Wulfric; 8 acres.
Value 16d.
　These (free men) were added to the revenue after 1066 and
concerning them Roger is guarantor for Wulfmer the reeve
who added them. Roger did not know that they had been added.
They did not belong to any revenue.
　In the same ('Olden') 1 free man, Wulfmer; the fourth part of 1 acre.
Value 2d.
　Brictmer the beadle held this and gave a pledge. Wulfmer the
reeve (is) the surety.
　In the same ('Olden') 1 free man, Leofwin; 2½ acres.
Value 8d.

5 In HEMINGSTONE 1 free man, Brictwold; 3 acres.
Value 8d.

6 In CREETING a free woman, Aldgyth; ½ acre.
Value 1d.

Hundred of CLAYDON
7 In HEMINGSTONE 1 free man, Alwin, under the patronage of Gyrth;
30 acres. Then ½ plough.
Value 5s.
　Wulfmer the reeve added this free man to the King's revenue of
Bramford. Roger the Sheriff is guarantor for him concerning it.
He pays 5s each year.
　The King and the Earl (have) the jurisdiction.

8 In THURLESTON Rolf held before 1066; now his son Aelfric, a burgess
of Ipswich [holds it]; 12 acres.
Value 2s.
　The King and the Earl (have) the jurisdiction.
　Earl R(alph) was in possession of this when he forfeited.

9 Aelfric also holds St. Julian's church in the Borough of IPSWICH;　　446 b
20 acres of land.
Value 40d.
　Earl R(alph) was in possession of this church.

10 In CLAYDON Alric, a free man, held 6½ acres before 1066. Now
Aelfric also [holds it].
Value 14d.
　The King and the Earl (have) half the jurisdiction and St.
Etheldreda's (has) the other half. Aelfric held this land in pledge
and he does not have a guarantor for it.
　These are in the King's hand.

In Weſtrefelda . vi . liƀi hões Aluuinus flint . Aluuinus . Edricus . Vl -
uʀicus . Aleſtan . int eos . xv . ac . & . i . car . 7 uał xxx . đ . Vn ex his nõe
flint dedit uađ ex ħ qđ dix qđ dabāt firmā in Gipeſwiz . & ui -
cecoms derationauit qđ mentitus erat . & iđ uice comes de
eo ē fide iuſſor . Rex 7 coms focā . ⎾ xx . đ.
⎾In Turolueſtuna . i . liƀ hõ Godwin comdatus Stigand . x . ac 7 uał
⎾ In hoc hund ħt Rex . xxx . liƀos hões . cxlvii . ac 7 dim . & unā
æcclia in Widituna . de . x . ac . femp . iii . car . & . i . ac pti . & ual&
xl . foł . & . iiii . đ . Ħ ſt eoꝗ nõa . Aiſtan . Godric Goduuin . Offa.
Riȼtan . Gadinc . Aluric . Eſtrat Aluric . Touilt . Leuuinus Al -
uric . Gunequata . Vluric . Tchetel . Godric . Edieđ . Dirſi.
Briȼtmer . Leueua . Aluric . Vluric . Normann . Leuuric.
Saxlef . Aluuin . Vluuin . Edric Sigar . hos ten& uice coms in
manu regis . Rex & coms focā.
⎾ In Weſtrefelda . ten& femp Aluric pƀr . xii . ac . & . ii . ac . pti.
& uał . iii . foł . Rex & coms focā.
⎾ In Turueſtuna . ii . liƀi hões . Vluric . 7 Ormar . vi . ac . & uał
xii . đ . Soca Regis . Vice coms feruat in manu regis.

447 a

⎾ In Codenham . i . pƀr frieƀ . dim ac in elemofina . & uał . i . đ.

⎾ Iſti funt liƀi homines de Sudfulc ꝗ remanent in manu   . LXXV .
regis . *BRADEMERA* . *HVND* . In torp . i . liƀ hõ
xxx . ac . t . r . e . Tc & p dim car . modo . ii boues . & uał . ii . foł.
& . vi . đ . hunc tenuit Roƀ blund putans ēe . de feudo aƀƀis
& iđe hõ confirmabat ſe Roƀto eſſe de feudo abƀis . ſ7 abbas ex ħ
non ē ſibi warant . modo tandē recognouit illū non ēe de feudo
Aƀƀis dimifit eū in manu regis . 7 ex ħ dedit uađe.

1 In WESTERFIELD 6 free men, Alwin, Flint, Alwin, Edric, Wulfric, Alstan; between them 15 acres. 1 plough.
Value 30d.
 One of them, Flint by name, gave a pledge for what he said that they gave (to) the revenue in Ipswich and the Sheriff proved that he had lied. The same Sheriff is surety concerning it.
 The King and the Earl (have) the jurisdiction.

2 In THURLESTON 1 free man, Godwin, under the patronage of Stigand; 10 acres.
Value 20d.

3 In this Hundred the King has 30 free men; 147½ acres. And a church in WHITTON with 10 acres. Always 3 ploughs.
 Meadow, 1 acre.
Value 40s 4d.
 These are their names: Aethelstan, Godric, Godwin, Offa, Rictan, Goding, Aelfric, Estred, Aelfric, Tovild, Leofwin, Aelfric, Gunvati, Wulfric, Thorkell, Godric, Edith, Dersi, Brictmer, Leofeva, Aelfric, Wulfric, Norman, Leofric, Saxlef, Alwin, Wulfwin, Edric, Sigar. The Sheriff holds these (men) in the King's hand.
 The King and the Earl (have) the jurisdiction.

4 In WESTERFIELD Aelfric the priest has always held 12 acres.
 Meadow, 2 acres.
Value 3s.
 The King and the Earl (have) the jurisdiction.

5 In THURLESTON 2 free men, Wulfric and Ordmer; 6 acres.
Value 12d.
 The jurisdiction (is) the King's.
 The Sheriff looks after (this) in the King's hand.

6 In CODDENHAM 1 priest, Frideb... ; ½ acre as alms.   447 a
Value 1d.

THESE ARE THE FREE MEN OF SUFFOLK
WHO REMAIN IN THE KING'S HAND

BRADMERE Hundred
1 In (Ixworth) THORPE 1 free man; 30 acres before 1066. Then and later ½ plough, now 2 oxen.
Value 2s 6d.
 Robert Blunt held this (man), thinking he was of the Abbot's Holding, and the man himself confirmed to Robert that he was of the Abbot's Holding. But the Abbot was not his guarantor. Now at last he has recognized that that man is not of the Abbot's Holding and has given him up into the King's hand. He gave a pledge concerning this.

$\mathcal{V}$In Icſewrda.I.liƀ hō.xii.aͨ.& ual.ii.ſol.Sͨs eadmundus
dim cͦmđ.t.r.e.7 ſoca & ſaca.& ante ͨ.Petri de ualoniis dimidiā cͦmđ.Hunc tenuit Ricarđ hō Roƀti blundi & dedit uadē
Roƀ non ei warant.

*HVNĐ.*D*E BISCOPES;* In horan.i.liƀ hō.vi.aͨ.& ual
xii.đ.hͨ tenuit herƀtus blacun in manu regis iuſſu herfaſti
epi ſ7 iuchel.pƀr reclamat de dono regis.&.inde ſaiſitus
fuit.& ſuus antecͫmđ.t.r.e.Soca in hoxa.

$\mathcal{V}$In Iſteda.i.liƀ hō ꞉de quo habuit Ailmarus eps.cmđ.de.x.
aͨ.7.dim.7 q̃rta pₐrs molini.&.i.borđ.&.tͨ dim car.&
modo.ii.boū.& ual.ii.ſol.hoc tenuit.Wiⱡⱡ.malet.p̉ ea
Roƀ fili̦ ei̦ ſuus putans ēe de feudo patris ſui.

447 b

$\mathcal{V}$In baᵈlingafelda.ii.liƀi hoͤes q̃ remanent in manu regis
p̄ reſpeꝗtū placiti.int epm baiocens.& matrē Roƀti malⱦ
unus fuit cͦmđ.Stigando.& alͭ dim.Leurico.anteceſſori
Roƀti.malⱦ.& alia medietas Saxo.& ħnt.xl.aͨ.&.iii.
borđ.ſemp.i.car.filua.xx.porc.& ual.x.ſol.ſoca in hoxa.

.LXXVI.INVASIONES SVPER REGEM.*RISE*
*BRVGE.*H̃.Ricardus fili̦ Giſleƀti comitis.
In bradeleia.iiii.liƀi hoͤes.Vluuinus.Leuricus.Vluuinus.& ħnt.
xv.aͨ꞉& q̊rtus bundo.& ħt.i.car terræ.ſemp.ii.car.&.v.aͨ p̃ti.
& ualⱦ xxii.ſol.&.vi.deñ.Ex his nꝗ habuit ſuus ante ceſſor
cͦmđ.Malus uicinus tenⱦ carrucatā.Sͨs.e.totā ſocā.

447 a, b

BABERGH Two Hundreds

2 In GROTON Richard son of (Count) Gilbert holds; 1 free man of Robert son of Wymarc, under patronage only; 60 acres of land.
Then 4 smallholders, now 1.
Then and later 1 plough, now none. Meadow, 1 acre.
Value then and later 10s; now 18s.
Roger of Orbec annexed this and holds (it) under Richard son of (Count) Gilbert. Richard's men claim it for the Holding of Withgar, his predecessor. But, as the Hundred testifies, it never belonged [to the Holding] nor (did) the patronage or the jurisdiction.

3 In CAVENDISH Aelfric brother of Edric, a man of the said Withgar's, annexed a half of his brother's land; 60 acres. Now Roger of St. Germain holds (it) in Richard's Holding, but it never belonged to the Holding, (nor did) the patronage or the jurisdiction. 448 a
There has always been 1 villager and 1 smallholder.
Meadow, 1 acre.

4 In CORNARD before 1066 Aelfric Kemp [held] 2 free men under patronage only, in the jurisdiction of St. Edmund's; but after King William came, Withgar (Richard's) predecessor annexed (them) with the agreement of Richard who now holds (them). They have 2 carucates of land and 40 acres.
Then and later 4 smallholders, now 11; then 5 slaves, now 4.
Then 23 ploughs in lordship; now 3 between himself and the men.
Woodland, 30 pigs; meadow, 8 acres. Then 3 horses; now 4 cattle; now 30 pigs; now 110 sheep.
A church with 15 acres of free land.
Value then and later 20s; now it pays £6.
It has 8 furlongs in length and 4 in width; 24d in tax, whoever holds there.

5 In *SAIBAMUS* Richard holds; 1 free man of Robert son of Wymarc's under patronage; the full jurisdiction (was) St. Edmund's. Withgar held (him) when he forfeited. Now Richard, his successor, holds (him). He has 1 carucate of land.
3 smallholders; 2 slaves.
Always 1 plough.
Meadow, 7 acres. Now 50 sheep, 7 pigs.
Value 20s.

6 In CAVENDISH Alwold, 1 free man under the patronage and full jurisdiction of Harold before 1066, and after King William came. Now Richard has annexed (him). He has 1 carucate of land. Always 1½ ploughs.
Meadow, 2 acres.
Value 20s.

In eað inuafit Ricardus de clara . libū hoḿ . reḡ . e . fed ante
ceffor fuus nichil oīno in eo habuit . & ħt . i . caŕ . terræ . Tc̄ . iiii.
uiłł . p̉ & modo . ii . & . vii . borð . & tc̄ & p̉ : ii . caŕ . modo . i . &
. i . caŕ hoḿ . & . iiii . ac̄ p̉ti . & . modo . i . moliñ . Silua . x . porc̄.
& uał . xx . foł.

448 b

HVNĎ . DE BLACBRVNA . In Scantuna . i . liƀa femina
coḿd . sc̄o . e . t . r . e . xxx . ac̄ . & uał . v . foł.

ꝂIn gnedaffala . xxx . ac̄ teñ . sc̄s . e . t . r . e . & diḿ ḿoł . & uał . v . foł
ꝂIn beordewella manfiones cuïdā liƀi hòis . sc̄i . e . In eað . diḿ liƀ hō
sc̄i . e . viii . ac̄ . & uał xvi . ð . In eað . x . ac̄ . cuïdā liƀe . S̉ . e . 7 uał xx
ð . hoc totū inuafit . W de partenai fup aƀƀem . & teñ cōḿd uni̯
liƀ hòis

Ꝃ*HVNĎ DE BOSEMERA .* In fumerfam . i . liƀ hō . Vluricus
nòe de xii . ac̄ . 7 uał . iiii . foł . De hoc fuit faifitus . R . coḿs qdo
forisfecit . & fuus antec̉ habuit in nedefteda coḿdatione̅ . huic in
uafit Vlḿar̉ p̄pofitus r̉egis & dedit uadē . Roḡ bigot . fide iuffor.
& e̅ in manu regis . Rex & coḿs foca̅.

ꝂIn briefeta . sꝷ . xx . ac̄ . que̯ iacent in ma̍nerio Wiłłi de othobur
uilla . quod tenuit . Anfchillus . t . r . e . modo teñ eas Botilt que –
dā femina . & reuocat hugone̅ de hofdenc a̍d wa̍ra̍nt . fed ipfe
e̅ in captione regis . & non p̉o̍te̍ſt re̍ſpo̍nde̍ . ḿodo sꝷ in ḿanu
Regis & Vlmarus p̄po̍ḧt̯ e̍as cu̍ſtodit . & u̍ał . v . foł.

7 In the same (Cavendish) Richard of Clare annexed a free man of King Edward's, but his predecessor had nothing at all in relation to him. He has 1 carucate of land.
   Then 4 villagers, later and now 2; 7 smallholders.
   Then and later 2 ploughs, now 1; 1 men's plough.
   Meadow, 4 acres; now 1 mill; woodland, 10 pigs.
   Value 20s.

[WILLIAM OF PARTHENAY'S ANNEXATIONS]

Hundred of BLACKBOURN   448 b

8 In STANTON 1 free woman under the patronage of St. Edmund's before 1066; 30 acres.
   Value 5s.

9 In KNETTISHALL 30 acres; St. Edmund's held (it) before 1066.
   ½ mill.
   Value 5s.

10 In BARDWELL the dwellings of a certain free man of St. Edmund's.

11 In the same (Bardwell) a half free man of St. Edmund's; 8 acres.
   Value 16d.

12 In the same (Bardwell) 10 acres of a certain free (woman) of St. Edmund's.
   Value 20d.
   William of Parthenay annexed the whole of this in the Abbot's despite and holds patronage over one free man.

[WULFMER THE REEVE'S ANNEXATIONS]

Hundred of BOSMERE

13 In SOMERSHAM 1 free man, Wulfric by name, with 12 acres.
   Value 4s.
   Earl R(alph) was in possession of this when he forfeited, and his predecessor had the patronage in Nettlestead. Wulfmer, the King's reeve, annexed this. He gave a pledge; Roger Bigot is surety. (This) is in the King's hand.
   The King and the Earl (have) the jurisdiction.

[HUGH OF HOUDAIN'S ANNEXATION]

14 In BRICETT are 20 acres which belong to the manor of William of Auberville. Askell held (them) before 1066. Now a woman, Botild, holds them and calls Hugh of Houdain as guarantor, but he is in the King's custody and cannot answer. They are now in the King's hand and Wulfmer the reeve has charge of them.
   Value 5s.

ʃ In Belham.dim̅ eccłia.xii.ac̅ tenuit Regina Edeua.t.r.e.
& q̇diu uixit.Poſtea tenuit Willm̅ de burnoluilla.M̅ e̅ in manu regis & uał.ii.ſoł.ex h̅ d̅edit ꝟade.Turſtin̅ fiłi Guidonis fi̅de
iuſſor;

Hᵛnd̅.ꟿov. In finebga.i.liḃ h̅o̅ de quo ante ceſſor Rog̅ me-
dietate̅ com̅d euſtac.alia̅ medietate̅ com̅ ꞌ& p̅ tenuit Comes
de mauritanio;ſed Rog̅.tenuit eu̅ q̅ndo relinḋd terra̅.7 Rodḃ arbał

449 a

ſub eo.modo ten̅&.R.bigot In manu regis.q̇ ad uſq̟ derationaꞇ
ſit.& h̅t.xv.ac̅ tr̅æ.Tc̅ dim̅ car̅.modo nichil & uał.iii.ſoł.

Hᵛnd̅. Blidinga In Wiſeta.manerio comitis Alani.ꝑtinebat
.i.liḃ h̅o̅.iiii.ac̅ quæ iacent innorthala.& uał.viii.den̅.
h̅ inuaſ̅ Roḃ de curtun.hunc ten̅.R.c.q̇do forisfecit.ex hoc dedit
ꝟade.In ead̅.i.liḃ h̅o̅.viii.ac̅.& uał.xvi.d.de quo habu̅it abuit
ꞏante Willmi de War̅ com̅d.t.r.e.& h̅t de ſua tr̅a ꝑ eſcag̅.
Iſtas etia̅ inuaſit Roḃ.cu̅.iiii.ac̅ ſuꝑdictis.

ʃ In Wggeſſala.ii.liḃi h̅oes.Normannus.7 Ketel de xviii.ac̅.&
dim̅ car̅.& uał.iii.ſoł.h̅ inuaſit bereng̅ h̅o̅ sc̅i.e.7 e̅ in midia
regis hic infirmus erat.non potuit uenire ad placitu̅.m̅do ſunt
in cuſtodia uice comiꞇ.

[WILLIAM OF BOURNEVILLE'S ANNEXATION]

15 In BAYLHAM ½ church, 12 acres. Queen Edith held (it) before 1066 and while she lived. Later on William of Bourneville held (it). Now it is in the King's hand.
Value 2s.
He gave a pledge concerning this; Thurstan son of Guy (is) surety.

[ROGER (OF AUBERVILLE)'S ANNEXATION]

Hundred of STOW
16 In FINBOROUGH 1 free man over whom Roger's predecessor had half the patronage and Eustace had the other half of the patronage. Later the Count of Mortain held (him); but Roger held him when he gave up the land, and Robert the crossbowman under him. Now Roger Bigot holds him in the King's hand until it is adjudged. He has 15 acres of land. Then ½ plough, now nothing.
Value 3s.

449 a

[ROBERT OF COURSON'S ANNEXATIONS]

Hundred (of) BLYTHING
7 In Count Alan's manor of WISSETT 1 free man belonged; 4 acres which belong to Covehithe.
Value 8d.
Robert of Courson annexed this. Earl R(alph) held this (free man) when he forfeited. He gave a pledge for this.

8 In the same (Wissett) 1 free man; 8 acres.
Value 16d.
William of Warenne's predecessor had patronage over him before 1066. He has (it as part) of his land by exchange. Robert also annexed these (8 acres) with the above-mentioned 4 acres.

[BERENGAR'S ANNEXATION]

9 In UGGESHALL 2 free men, Norman and Ketel, with 18 acres. ½ plough.
Value 3s.
Berengar, a man of St. Edmund's, annexed this and is in the King's mercy. He was ill and could not come to the assembly; they are in the Sheriff's charge.

⁊ In Kanauadiſc teñ Radułf de limeſi . i . liƀ hõ heroldi quã tenuit
edricus diaconus Qui fuit mortuus cum eo in bello . & fuit liƀa ⸫
ta bainardo ‚p terra . Etgar addidit in ranauadiſc ꝑquã
bainardus ꝑdidit . modo ten& Raď de limeſi in dñio halle.

⁊ In Lauen Alƀicus deuer teñ . iii . liƀos Vlwini . antec̄ Alƀici
de uer c̄omď tantũ in ſoca . sc̄i . e . 7 h̄nt . l . ac̄ . Tc̄ inť om̄s . ii . car
modo . i . Semp uał . vi . ſoł.

⁊ In Kodenhã teñ antec̄ Galteri de sc̄o Walerico c̄omďatione

449 b

tantũ . ii . liƀi hões . modo teñ Roḡ deramis . ſed hunď neſcit
q̄m . Nec fuit aliquis ex parte ſua q̇ dicer& q̇modo . & h̄nt
xx . ac̄ . tr̄æ . Tc̄ & ꝑ uał& . x . ſoł . modo nichil.

HERTESMERA . H̃ . In eiam ten& . Roƀ mał&
. i . liƀum homem nõe Suartric . c̄omď haroldo . & in ſoca
eius ꞓ c . & xx . ac̄ . ‚p mañ . Semp . iiii . borď . & . i . car in dñio.
& . iiii . ac̄ ꝑti . Silua de . xiii . porꞓ . & uał xx . ſoł.

450 a

DE calvpniis Inť eꝑm baiocenſe & matr̃e Roƀti mał&.

H̃erteſmera . H̃ . In acołt . xx . ac̄ . teñ briꝗere liƀ hõ Stigandi.
ſeꝑ . i . borď . 7 uał . xl . ď . Hanc tr̄a dedit Stiganď matri Roƀti mał&.
7 ipſa eã ꝑa teñ de regina . m̃ . e.

[RALPH OF LIMÉSY'S ANNEXATION]

[BABERGH Two Hundreds]

In CAVENDISH Ralph of Limésy holds; 1 free man of Harold's, Edric the deacon, who died with him in the battle, held it. It was delivered to Baynard as an estate. Edgar added (it) to Cavendish after Baynard lost (it). Ralph of Limésy now holds (it) in lordship.

[AUBREY DE VERE'S ANNEXATION]

In LAVENHAM Aubrey de Vere holds 3 free (men) belonging to Wulfwin, Aubrey de Vere's predecessor, under patronage only, in the jurisdiction of St. Edmund's. They have 50 acres. Then 2 ploughs between them all, now 1.
Value always 6s.

[ROGER OF RAMES'S ANNEXATION]

In CODDENHAM Walter of St.Valéry's predecessor held 2 free men under patronage only. Now Roger of Rames holds (them), but the Hundred does not know how; nor was there anyone on his behalf who could say how. They have 20 acres of land.
Value then and later 10s; now nothing.

449 b

[ROBERT MALET'S ANNEXATION]

HARTISMERE Hundred

In EYE Robert Malet holds 1 free man, Swartrik by name, under the patronage of Harold and in his jurisdiction; 120 acres as a manor.
Always 4 smallholders;
1 plough in lordship.
Meadow, 4 acres; woodland at 13 pigs.
Value 20s.

7] CONCERNING THE DISPUTES BETWEEN THE BISHOP OF BAYEUX AND ROBERT MALET'S MOTHER

450 a

HARTISMERE Hundred

In OCCOLD Brictere, a free man of Stigand's, held 20 acres.
Always 1 smallholder.
Value 40d.
Stigand gave this land to Robert Malet's mother. Later on she held it from the Queen. Now the Bishop [holds it].

In eade ten Cheric lib ho dim fub cmdat
anteᵈ RoꝾ malet . 7 dimid comdat Saxo antec . Ra . piperelli ꞉́ xx . ac . 7 . ii . bo
7 . i ..car . 7 ual . xl . d.

Bifcopes . *H.* In badingefelda ten . Briꝰtere . 7 Cheric fuꝒdiꝉti xl . acr.
fuꝒdiꝉto m̊ . Tnc . i . car . m̊ dim . Silua . xl . porc . 7 . i . liꝾ ho cmdatus
Briꝰtredo . v . ac . totu ual xi . fol . ∕ Hertefmara . H̃ . In afpala . iiii . liꝾi
hoes . De rulf cmd . abꝾi de eli . 7 Turftan cmd . Saxa . 7 Marculf
cmd edrici antec . R . malet .. 7 Grunulf fubcmd antec . R . malet . lxxxvi . ac.
7 vii . bord . Seꝑ . iii . car . ii . ac ꝓti . Seꝑ ual . xl . fol . Ex hac tra fuit Witꞇm
malet faifit . fic hund teftaꞇ anꞇ qua eꝓc baiocſis ; 7 ꝑea uenit huꝾt de portu.
& deracionau liꝾam tram 7 faifiuit eꝑm ex hac tra qᵬ liꝾi hoes ea teneꞇbant.
7 die q̊ Rad com forisfec . Mat RoꝾti inde faifita erat tefte hund . 7 ufq̍
ad placitu de hodiha . m̊ . e . in pace reg . fic rex ꝓceꝑ it eꝑm . 7 matre RoꝾti.

ANNO ꟽILLESIMO OCTOGESIMO SEXTO . AB
INCARNATIONE DÑI . VIGESIMO V̊ REGNI
WILꞀI FACTA EST ISTA DESCRIPTIO . NON
SOLVM Ꝑ HOS TRES COMITATVS . SED &IÃ
Ꝑ ALIOS

2 In the same (Occold) Cynric, a free man, held; (he was) half under the sub-patronage of Robert Malet's predecessor, and half under the patronage of Saxi, Ranulf Peverel's predecessor; 20 acres.
    2 smallholders.
    1 plough.
    Value 40d.

BISHOP'S Hundred
3 In BEDINGFIELD the above-mentioned Brictere and Cynric held 40 acres in the above-mentioned manner. Then 1 plough, now ½.
    Woodland, 40 pigs.
    1 free man under the patronage of Brictere; 5 acres.
    Value of the whole 11s.

HARTISMERE Hundred
4 In ASPALL 4 free men; Derwulf, under the patronage of the Abbot of Ely; Thurstan under the patronage of Saxi; Marculf under the patronage of Edric, R(obert) Malet's predecessor; and Gunnulf under the sub-patronage of R(obert) Malet's predecessor; 86 acres.
    7 smallholders.
    Always 3 ploughs. Meadow, 2 acres.
    Value always 40s.
    William Malet was in possession of this land before the Bishop of Bayeux, as the Hundred testifies. Later on, Hubert of Port came; he proved the land (to be) free and put the Bishop in possession of this land because free men held it. On the day that Earl Ralph forfeited, Robert Malet's mother was in possession of it, as the Hundred testifies, and until the lawsuit at Odiham. Now it is in the King's peace, as the King commanded, between the Bishop and Robert's mother.

THIS SURVEY WAS MADE IN THE ONE THOUSAND AND EIGHTY SIXTH YEAR SINCE THE INCARNATION OF THE LORD, AND IN THE TWENTIETH OF THE REIGN OF WILLIAM, NOT ONLY THROUGH THESE THREE COUNTIES BUT ALSO THROUGH THE OTHERS.

SUFFOLK HOLDINGS
ENTERED ELSEWHERE IN THE SURVEY
The Latin text of these entries is given in the county volumes concerned

In CAMBRIDGESHIRE

EC 1

[1]   **LAND OF THE KING**   DB

In STAPLOE Hundred

12   In EXNING King William has 13½ hides. Land for 34 ploughs.
In lordship 7 ploughs; a further 3 possible.
> 35 villagers and 34 smallholders with 24 ploughs.
> 7 slaves; 3 mills, 20s and 7,000 eels; meadow for 4
> ploughs.

Total value £53; when Godric acquired it £12; before
1066 £56.

Edeva the Fair held this manor, and in this manor were
7 Freemen, Edeva's men; they could withdraw without her
permission, but she had jurisdiction of them herself; each
of them found cartage in the King's service, or 8d or a
pledge.

EC 2

14   **LAND OF COUNT ALAN**   DB

(In STAPLOE Hundred)

68   In EXNING Wymarc holds 1½ hides from the Count. Land
for 3 ploughs. In lordship 2 ploughs;
> 4 villagers have 1 plough;
> 8 slaves; 1 mill, 5s 4d; a fishery, 1,200 eels; meadow for
> 2 ploughs; pasture for the village livestock.

The value is and was 50s; before 1066, 60s.

Alsi, Edeva's man, held this land; he could withdraw'
without her permission.

In ESSEX

EE 1

1   **LANDS OF THE KING**   LD

Hundred of TENDRING

26   Harold held BRIGHTLINGSEA as a manor, for 10 hides. Now
King William (holds it) ...
Then Brightlingsea and Harkstead between them paid 2
nights' provisions; when P(eter) acquired (them) £25;
now £22. However, the outlier lies in Suffolk ...

189 b, d, 193 d, 195 c, LDB 1 b, 6 a

LAND OF RICHARD SON OF COUNT GILBERT

(Hundred of HINCKFORD)

27 In SUDBURY 5 burgesses who hold 2 acres.
They with all the above pay £15 6s 6d. The whole is in
Richard's lordship.

LANDS OF ROBERT GERNON

(Hundred of TENDRING)

40 William holds ARDLEIGH from Robert, which Scalpi held as
a manor, for ½ hide and 30 acres. It lies (in the lands of) a
manor in Suffolk; but it belongs in this Hundred ...

LANDS OF RANULF PEVEREL

(Hundred of HINCKFORD)

21 Thorold holds (Great) HENNY from Ranulf which Wulfwin,
a free man, held before 1066 as a manor for 2½ hides and
45 acres ...
To this manor belongs 12d of the customary due from
Sudbury ...

LAND OF AUBREY DE VERE

Hundred of HINCKFORD

5 Aubrey holds (Castle) HEDINGHAM in lordship, which
Wulfwin held as a manor, for 2 hides ...
Value then £13; now [£] 20.
To this manor are attached 15 burgesses in Sudbury;
they are assessed in the £20 ...

LAND OF JOHN SON OF WALERAN

(Hundred of HINCKFORD)

4 Roger holds HENNY from John, which a free man held
before 1066 as a manor, for 2½ hides ...
To this manor belongs a customary due of 22½d which
is from Sudbury ...

ENf 1

1 [LAND OF THE KING] LDB

GUILTCROSS Hundred

76 In KNETTISHALL 1 free man, at 30 acres of land. It appertains in Kenninghall.
2 villagers.
Meadow, 1 acre. Always ½ mill; ½ plough; 24 acres of land.
The whole is in the valuation of Kenninghall.

ENf 2

4 LANDS OF COUNT ALAN LDB

The Half-Hundred of EARSHAM

48 In Alburgh 12 acres of land; meadow, ½ acre. It belongs in Rumburgh.

ENf 3

7 LANDS OF ROBERT MALET LDB

(DEPWADE Hundred)

21 In HARDWICK 1 villager, at 5 acres. It is in the valuation of Eye ...

ENf 4

9 LAND OF ROGER BIGOT LDB

LODDON Hundred

49 In MUNDHAM Aelfric, a free man under Stigand, held 30 acres of land before 1066 ...
Value always 5s.
This Aelfric was outlawed and Ulfketel, the King's reeve, had possession of the land in the King's hand; Roger Bigot asked for it from the King and he granted it to him. Count Alan claims this because Earl R(alph) held it as part of his manor of Rumburgh; the men of the Hundred heard Ulfketel acknowledge this on one occasion during the year before R(alph) forfeited and likewise on one occasion after he forfeited, that he, Ulfketel, was doing service in Rumburgh, and finally the Hundred heard this same man say that he was doing service to Roger Bigot. Count Alan's men had 10s from there each year except for the last 4 years and this they are willing to prove by any means. Ulfketel holds.

42   LANDS OF GILBERT SON OF RICHERE

The Hundred of CLACKCLOSE

1   Aethelgyth held MILDENHALL before 1066.
       Then 2 ploughs, now 1.
       Always 15 villagers; 5 smallholders. Then 4 slaves, now 2.
       Then 2 men's ploughs, now 1. Then 1 cob. Then 16 pigs,
          now 8. 2 head of cattle. Always 29 sheep; meadow,
          10 acres.
       Value then £5; now 4.

NOTES ON THE TEXT AND TRANSLATION

ABBREVIATIONS used in the Notes

AN ... Anglo-Norman.

arr ... *arrondissement.*

Battle 1980 ... Proceedings of the Battle Conference on Anglo-Norman Studies III, 1980, ed. R. Allen Brown (Boydell Press, Woodbridge, Suffolk, 1981).

Björkman ... E. Björkman, *Nordische Personennamen in England in Alt- und Frumittelenglischer Zeit* (Halle 1910).

BT ... J. Bosworth and T. N. Toller, *An Anglo-Saxon Dictionary* (Oxford 1882-1898).

DB ... Domesday Book.

DBE ... H. C. Darby, *Domesday England* (Cambridge 1977).

DBS ... P. H. Reaney, *A Dictionary of British Surnames* (2nd edn. by R. M. Wilson, London etc. 1977).

DEPN ... E. Ekwall, *The Concise Oxford Dictionary of English Place-Names* (4th edn., Oxford 1960).

DG ... H. C. Darby and G. R. Versey, *Domesday Gazetteer* (Cambridge 1975).

Ellis ... Sir H. Ellis, *A General Introduction to Domesday Book* (2 vols. 1833, reprinted 1971).

Exon ... Exon. Domesday Book.

Farrer ... W. Farrer, *Honors and Knights' Fees* (3 vols. London and Manchester 1923-1925).

FB ... *The Feudal Book of Abbot Baldwin,* see Appendix II; references are to pages in FD.

FD ... D. C. Douglas (ed.), *Feudal Documents from the Abbey of Bury St. Edmunds* (London 1932).

von Feilitzen 1939 ... O. von Feilitzen, 'Notes on Old English bynames', *Namn och Bygd* xxvii (1939), 116-130.

von Feilitzen 1945 ... idem, 'Some unrecorded Old and Middle English personal names', *Namn och Bygd* xxxiii (1945), 69-98.

von Feilitzen 1963 ... idem, 'Some Continental Germanic personal names in England', in *Early English and Norse Studies presented to Hugh Smith,* edd. A. Brown, P. Foote (London 1963), 46-61.

von Feilitzen 1976 ... idem, 'The personal names and bynames of the Winton Domesday', *Winchester in the Early Middle Ages,* ed. M. Biddle (*Winchester Studies* i, Oxford 1976), 143-229.

Fellows Jensen ... G. Fellows Jensen, *Scandinavian Personal Names in Lincolnshire and Yorkshire* (Copenhagen 1968).

Forssner ... T. Forssner, *Continental-Germanic Personal Names in England in Old and Middle English Times* (Uppsala 1916).

Förstemann ... E. Förstemann, *Altdeutsches Namenbuch,* Band 1, *Personennamen* (2nd edn., Bonn 1900).

GDB ... Great Domesday Book.

Harmer, *ASWrits* ... F. E. Harmer, *Anglo-Saxon Writs* (Manchester 1952).

Hart ECEE ... C. R. Hart, *The Early Charters of Eastern England* (Leicester 1966).

HRH ... D. Knowles, C. N. L. Brooke, V. C. M. London (eds.), *The Heads of Religious Houses: England and Wales 940-1216* (Cambridge 1972).

ICC ... The Cambridgeshire Inquiry, *Inquisitio Comitatus Cantabrigiensis,* quoted from the same edition as IE, below; in it see further, Cambridgeshire, Introduction.

IE, IEAL, IEBrev, IENV ... For these texts see Appendix I; references are to pages in N.E.S.A. Hamilton (ed.), *Inquisitio Comitatus Cantabrigiensis* (London 1876); in the notes below, page numbers are not repeated when they are the same as those in the first reference in a particular LDB section.

J.M.D. ... Professor John McN. Dodgson, *in litteris.*

Lat ... Latin.

Latham ... R. E. Latham (ed.), *Revised Medieval Latin Word-List from British and Irish Sources* (London, 1965).

LDB ... Little Domesday Book.

LibEl ... E. O. Blake (ed.), *Liber Eliensis* (*Camden Society,* 3rd series, xcii, 1962).

Loyd ... C. T. Clay and D. C. Douglas (eds.), *The Origins of Some Anglo-Norman Families, by the late Lewis C. Loyd* (*Harleian Society* ciii, Leeds 1951).

MDB ... V. H. Galbraith, *The Making of Domesday Book* (Oxford 1961).

ME ... Middle English.

MLat ... Medieval Latin.

ModE ... Modern English.

MRH ... D. Knowles and R. N. Hadcock, *Medieval Religious Houses: England and Wales* (Revised edn., London 1971).

MS ... Manuscript.

NFr ... Norman French.

OBret ... Old Breton.

ODan ... Old Danish.

OE ... Old English.
OEB ... G. Tengvik, *Old English Bynames* (*Nomina Germanica* iv, Uppsala 1938).
OFr ... Old French.
OG ... Old German.
OLG ... Old Low German.
ON ... Old Norse.
OS ... Old Saxon.
O.S. ... Ordnance Survey.
OScand ... Old Scandinavian.
OSw ... Old Swedish.
OWScand ... Old West Scandinavian.
PNDB ... O. von Feilitzen, *The Pre-Conquest Personal Names of Domesday Book* (*Nomina Germanica* iii, Uppsala 1937).
Regesta i ... H. W. C. Davis (ed.), *Regesta Regum Anglo-Normannorum 1066-1154*, i, *1066-1100* (Oxford 1913).
Robertson, *AS Charters* ... A. J. Robertson (ed.), *Anglo-Saxon Charters* (Cambridge 1939).
Rom ... Romance.
Round FE ... J. H. Round, *Feudal England* (London 1895).
Sawyer ... P. H. Sawyer, *Anglo-Saxon Charters: An Annotated List and Bibliography* (*Royal Historical Society*, 1968).
Scand ... Scandinavian.
VCH ... *The Victoria History of the County of Suffolk*, i, ed. W. Page (London 1911), with Domesday translation adapted from that by Lord J. Hervey (Bury St. Edmunds 1888-1891).
VCH Cambridgeshire i ... *The Victoria History of the County of Cambridgeshire and the Isle of Ely*, i, ed. L. F. Salzman (London 1938).
Whitelock, *AS Wills* ... D. Whitelock (ed.), *Anglo-Saxon Wills* (Cambridge 1930).

The Editor is grateful to Miss Philippa Brown for a preliminary collation of the Suffolk text to FB and IE; and to the Suffolk County Record Office, Ipswich, for the use of maps of administrative divisions.
The text of the Domesday Survey for Suffolk is contained in Little Domesday Book (now preserved, with the larger volume, at the Public Record Office, London). The manuscript was written, by more than one scribe, on either side of leaves, or folios, of parchment (sheep-skin) measuring about 11 by 8 inches (28 by 20 cms). On each side, or page, is a single column, making two to each folio. The folios were numbered in the 17th century, and the two columns of each are here lettered a, b. Red ink was used to distinguish some chapter headings and most Hundred headings. Deletion was marked by putting a line (in the ink of the text) through incorrect words. The running title on the recto of folios was usually an abbreviatd form of the name of the Landholder whom the chapter concerned; the running title on the verso was an abbreviation of the county name.

SUFFOLK. *SVDFULC, -FVLCH, SVT(H)FVLC.* Abbreviated in the running title as *SV̄DF, SVD̄F, SVDF̄*.

References to text in other DB counties are to the Chapter and Section of the editions in this series. The Anglo-Saxon letter 'a'sh' is rendered *AE, ae*; the letter 'eth' by *th*.

GENERAL NOTES

L   LANDHOLDERS. See also folios 292a and 372a for partial lists of landholders which were used by the copyists as a running guide to the order of chapters before the full Suffolk list was constructed. The partial list on folio 372a was subsequently deleted. Similar partial lists occur in the Essex section of LDB on folios 9a and 17a. The presence of these partial lists in the MS reflects the way in which the county returns were put together from booklets relating to each of the major landholders.

1,1-60   LAND ... BELONGING TO THE REALM. *Terra regis de regione*; a similar phrase is used in 31,44 (referring to the same royal manor of Thorney). Swaffham in Norfolk (4,1) is also said to have belonged *ad regionem*. Round FE 119 dismissed the use of *de regione* as a copying error for *(de) regno*, but this is unlikely with the Swaffham example. It is more likely that *regio* is used as an alternative word for *Regnum*, 'realm, kingdom', which occurs with apparently similar usage in the heading before 1,120-121 below and in Norfolk 1,71; *regnum* is also used in connection with the King's lordship land in Devon in a heading in Exon., folio 83a.

1,1   ROGER BIGOT. The Sheriff, see 7 and note.
THORNEY. In Stowmarket.
KING EDWARD. The Confessor, died 5 January 1066.
ALWAYS. *Se(m)p(er)*; before 1066 and still in 1086.
THEN. *T(u)nc*; before 1066.
LATER ON. *Postea*; sometime between 1066 and 1086.
NOW NONE, BUT BEFORE 1066. MS *Regis.eW.*; Farley adds the abbreviation mark.
LATER. *P(ost)*; sometime between 1066 and 1086.
NOW 19. In the MS there is an erasure between *x* and *ix*, perhaps of an ampersand.
HUGH DE MONTFORT ... CLAIMS. See 31,44.
23 ACRES. In the MS there is an erasure between *xx* and *.iii.* Cf. the 25 acres mentioned in 31,44.
£15. The records of the Domesday Survey used the English currency system which lasted for a thousand years until 1971. The pound contained 20 shillings, each of 12 pence, abbreviated respectively as L(ibrae), s(olidi), d(enarii). Note however that, in common with other medieval records, the Domesday manuscripts frequently have instances where quantities of pence have not been converted into shillings, and quantities of shillings have not been converted into pounds. Sometimes a number of pennies was expressed in *orae* rather than shillings, see 1,94 note.
[£] 40 BLANCHED. A sample of coin was melted as a test for the presence of alloy or baser metal. Money could also be said to be blanched when, without a test by fire, a standard deduction from the face value was made to allow for alloying or clipping.
LEAGUE. Generally reckoned as a mile and a half.
15D IN TAX. That is, a sum of 15d in tax when the Hundred in which the manor lay was liable for £1.
HUGH DE MONTFORT. Cf. 31,44;53.
COUNT ROBERT. Of Mortain, see 2 and note.
ROGER OF AUBERVILLE. Cf. 29,1 where 6 Freemen belonging to this manor are mentioned.
FRODO. Possibly the brother of Abbot Baldwin of St. Edmund's, see 12 and note.
ROGER OF POITOU. Cf. 8,51;54.

1,2   BRAMFORD. See also 1,7.
VALUE THEN £ ... In the MS there is an erasure before *lib*; and *ual* has been corrected from *ual&* by subpuncting, although this is not shown by Farley.
BY WEIGHT. *ad pensu(m)*; that is the coins were weighed (although apparently not assayed) rather than being accepted at face value. This was to counteract any payment in coins which had been clipped.

1,5   'OLDEN'. Lost in Coddenham, see VCH 419,n.2.
AND A HALF. Half-shares in the rights over free men *(liberi homines)* or Freemen *(sochemanni)* are frequently found in the Suffolk and Norfolk folios of LDB.

1,6   BISHOP OF BAYEUX. For his lands in Stonham, see 16,15;22.

1,7   THIS ENTRY. Repeated at 74,7 under the lands of vavassors.
HEMINGSTONE. Here and at 62,4;6 and 74,7 assigned to Claydon Hundred, but elsewhere in the neighbouring Hundred of Bosmere. Both here and at 74,7 the form *haminghelanda* is used instead of *hami(n)gestuna*, showing alternation of OE *land* and *tun*, both with the meaning of 'estate'.

THIS MANOR. In the MS *monarium* has been altered to *monerium*, in error for *manerium*. Farley shows the *e* as suprascript but in the MS the *a* is merely altered to *e* by the addition of an extra loop.

1,90 VILLAGERS. LDB *Witti* is in error for *uill(an)i*.
MEADOW, 3 ACRES. In the MS there is an erasure after *.iii.*
IT HAS 1 LEAGUE. LDB has an otiose letter *E* at the beginning of the line.

1,92 REDENHALL. In Norfolk.
JURISDICTION ... HOXNE. The Bishop of Thetford's manor (18,1). Bishop's Hundred was renamed after it by 1191.

1,93 THORMOD OF PARHAM. See 1,75.

1,94 ORA. Literally an ounce, in Scandinavia a monetary unit and coin still in use; in the Domesday records valued at 16 (assayed) or 20 (unassayed) pence, see S. Harvey. 'Royal revenue and Domesday terminology', *Economic History Review*, 2nd series, xx (1967), 221-228.

1,96 PETER OF VALOGNES. Sheriff of Essex and Hertfordshire in 1086, see *37* and note. Here acting as Sheriff of Essex.
HAROLD. Earl of Wessex (1053-), King 1066. For his landholding, see Ann Williams, 'Land and power in the eleventh-century: the estates of Harold Godwineson', *Battle 1980*, 171-187. He is rarely given the title *comes* in LDB and never that of *rex*. Most of the instances of the name Harold in Suffolk probably refer to him.
BRIGHTLINGSEA. See Essex 1,26.

1,97-99 EARL MORCAR'S MOTHER. Aelfeva, wife of Earl Algar (see 8,33 note). She is named in 16,10. Morcar became Earl of Northumbria in 1065. He survived the Conquest but joined revolts against King William and was imprisoned first in Normandy and later at Winchester. He was still alive in 1087, and was freed by King William on his deathbed only to be imprisoned again by King William Rufus.
WILLIAM THE CHAMBERLAIN. Perhaps the same as the tenant of Westminster Abbey in North Ockendon, Essex 6,10.
OTTO THE GOLDSMITH. He held Gestingthorpe in Essex (81,1) which had formerly been held by Earl Algar. He was also holding Shalford and Finchingfield in the same county (1,11-12) on behalf of the King, both of which had been held by Earl Algar. In Colchester (Essex B3j) he had 3 houses which Countess Aelfeva used to hold. Before 1066 he married Leofgifu the widow of a citizen of London. He was the tenant of St. Edmund's Abbey at Hawstead (14,13). On him, and his son Otto, see FD cxxxix-cxli.

1,97 SUDBURY. In 1086 a detached part of Thingoe Hundred. Later in Babergh Hundred.
BURGESSES ... AT THE HALL. LDB *in d(omi)nio* deleted before *halle*. 'At the hall' has the same meaning in LDB as 'in lordship'.
ST. GREGORY'S CHURCH. This was the recipient of a bequest of Waldingfield in 1000 x 1002; Whitelock, *ASWills* no. 15, Sawyer no. 1486, Hart ECEE no. 64.

1,99 VALUE ... WHOLE. Of 1,98-99.

1,100- AELFRIC WAND. The byname is from OE *wand*, 'mole', OEB 367. Not necessarily the
106 same man as at Essex 25,24;26.

1,100 HAROLD. As 1,96 note.

1,101 EARL RALPH THE CONSTABLE. Earl of East Anglia from before March 1068. Father of Earl Ralph Wader (see 1,61-95 note). Died 1069/70. LDB *stalra* is from OE *st(e)allere*, 'staller, King's marshal', sometimes represented by Latin *constabularius*; OEB 270-271.
AFTER 1066. In the MS *T(empore). R(egis). Will(el)mi)*. has been altered from *T(empore). R(egis). E(dwardi)*.
[PARK] LDB *porc(us)* is in error for *parc(us)*. Cf. DBE 201-203. See also 6,83 note.

1,102 TO THIS MANOR ... The remainder of this entry probably refers to East Bergholt rather than to Shotley.
MALET. This could refer to both or either of Robert Malet (*6*) and his father William Malet.
ROBERT SON OF WYMARC. Father of Swein of Essex, see *27* and note.

1,103 HUNDRED AND A HALF. Of Samford.
OF GYRTH'S. In the MS the letter before *uert*, presumably *G*, has been smudged; Farley prints *.uert*.
AS A PREMIUM. LDB has an abbreviation mark, presumably to read as *gersu(m)ma*.
AS MUCH [THENCE]. Farley *m̃* is in error for *in* of MS, for *in̄(de)*.
AELFRIC THE REEVE ... THIS AELFRIC. The latter is probably Aelfric Wand, but not necessarily the former.

1

	DOES NOT REMAIN ... WHAT MAKES THAT PROFIT. The second negative of the Latin text is not translated.
	TAX OF 8D. Farley shows by means of dots an erasure in the MS after *gelt*.
1,105	AUBREY DE VERE. See *35* and note.
	1 FREEMAN. At *Canepetuna*, see 35,4.
	ALDHAM. See 35,6.
1,106	*CANAPPETUNAM*. The same as *CANEPETUNA* at 35,4 and *CANAPETUNA* at 3,80. Unidentified, DG 393. Consistently assigned to Samford Hundred.
	CHATTISHAM. Not elsewhere mentioned in LDB. Some text may have been omitted here.
1,107-119	STIGAND. Consecrated Bishop of Winchester in 1047, he held that See with the Archbishopric of Canterbury from 1052 until he was deposed in 1070. Died 1072.
	WILLIAM OF NOYERS. Probably from Noyers (Calvados), rather than Noyers (Eure), OEB 103. He was a tenant of the Bishop of Thetford, see 19,17.
1,107	20 ACRES. In the MS there is an erasure (? of x) after *xx*.
	PLOUGH, NOW ½. In the MS there is an erasure after *dimiđ*.
	1 COB. *.i.r.* MS; Farley adds the abbreviation mark.
	UNDER HIM. LDB *sub se* is in error for *sub eo*, referring to Thurstan.
1,108	COVEHITHE. Formerly 'North Hales'.
	ALL THIS. Probably meaning 1,107-108.
1,110	... CARUCATE. LDB omits the numeral.
	6 VILLAGERS ... 15 PIGS. In the MS between lines 18 and 19 of folio 288a and in the right margin several words have been erased.
	2 BROTHERS. LDB *fr(atr)is* is in error for *fr(atr)es*; in the MS it has been altered from *fr(atr)i*.
	EARL H(UGH). See *4* and note.
	60 ACRES. See 4,25.
	10 ACRES. 1 PLOUGH IN LORDSHIP. In the MS an ampersand has been erased after *car(uca)*.
	1 MEN'S PLOUGH. LDB has an otiose numeral *.i.* after *ho(min)u(m)* and an extra point before it.
1,111	PAT. The same personal name occurs in Cheshire 27,2 but is of obscure origin; PNDB 343.
	ALFGER. LDB *Alfger(us)* may represent ON *Álfgeirr* rather than OE Aelfgar; PNDB 173.
1,112	SMALLHOLDERS' PLOUGH. LDB *bordarii* (genitive singular) is in error for *bordariorum* (genitive plural); it is a variant of the usual *hominum*.
1,115	KING EDWARD GAVE ... ST. EDMUND'S. Mildenhall was granted by Edward the Confessor to St. Edmund's in 1043 x 1044; Harmer, *ASWrits* no. 9, Sawyer no. 1069, Hart *ECEE* no. 106. It appears to have been leased to Archbishop Stigand and taken back into royal hands by King William.
	THEN ... 30 VILLAGERS. In the MS there is an erasure after *xxx*; probably of *p(ost)* which, with the tironian nota for *et* (7), was subsequently inserted before the numeral.
	FISHERIES. LDB *piscat* is for *piscat(iones)*, replacing the more usual *piscina* or *piscaria*. For various types of fisheries in 1086, see DBE 279-286.
	WILD MARES. LDB *eque siluatice*, literally 'woodland mares'.
	11¼D IN TAX. In the MS there is an erasure before *ferdingu(m)*.
	BRAMFORD. Elsewhere in Bosmere Hundred, but placed here in the Hundred of Samford, probably because of its association with East Bergholt (1,100).
	HAROLD. As 1,96 note.
	BISHOP ERFAST. See 19,1-2 note.
1,120-121	BELONGING ... REALM. See 1,1 note.
	PICOT. Probably the Sheriff of Cambridgeshire.
	TRIBUTE. Translating *censu(m)*.
1,121	ALGAR. Earl Algar, see 65,1.
1,122a-122g	ROGER BIGOT. See 1,1-60 note.
1,122a-122b	THE QUEEN. Edith, wife of Edward the Confessor and daughter of Earl Godwin of Wessex.
1,122a	THIRD PART. Cf. 3,55 and reference there to the 'third penny'.
1,122b	GRANGE. Earl Gyrth also held a grange in Ipswich before 1066, see 3,55.
1,122c	POOR BURGESSES. Cf. the 'poor men' in Dunwich (6,84).

APART FROM ... HEADS. A similar poll-tax was levied at Colchester. see Essex
B3b.d.m.

1,122d ALWULF. LDB *Alnulfus* is in error for *Aluulfus*. see Forssner 23. s.n. *Alnoldus*. The
corrected form would represent OE *Aelfwulf*.

CULLING. The name also occurs among the burgesses of Colchester. Essex B3a. It
probably represents either the OE pers. n. *Colling*. also found as a byname (OEB 141-142.
von Feilitzen 1976, 153) or ON *Kullungr*. PNDB 307.

TUMBI. Perhaps ODan *Tumbi*. a short form of *Thurmoth*. *Thurmund*. see PNDB 388.

1,122f FEAST OF ST. JOHN. Probably 24 June. the Nativity of St. John the Baptist. rather than
29 August the Decollation.

COUNT ALAN. See *3* and note.

EARL RALPH. See 1.61-95 note.

IVO TALLBOYS. The byname is from OFr *tailgebosc*. 'cut wood'. OEB 388. He was the
brother of Ralph Tallboys. Sheriff of Bedfordshire. He commanded the siege of Hereward
the Wake at Ely in 1069. He was later Steward to King William Rufus and died about
1115.

AS (ITS) DELIVERER. That is, to bear witness that he had delivered ownership. on the
King's behalf. to Count Alan.

AESCHERE ... GODRIC ... 1 ACRE. This text is interlined in the MS. as shown by
Farley. but appears to have been inserted a few lines too early.

AESCHERE. An OE pers. n. *AEschere*. see von Feilitzen 1945. 72 and 73 n.1.

1,122g SESTERS. Usually 4. but sometimes 5 to 6 gallons. see R.E. Zupko. *A Dictionary of English
weights and measures from Anglo-Saxon times to the nineteenth century* (Univ. of Wisconsin Press.
1968). 155.

TO THE PREBENDARIES. For their food. cf. Essex B 6 (Colchester).

NOW IT PAYS. LDB repeats *modo reddit* in error.

2 ROBERT COUNT OF MORTAIN. A half-brother of King William. and younger brother
of Odo. Bishop of Bayeux (*16*).

2,1 ST. ETHELDREDA'S. See *21*.

ALWAYS 1½ PLOUGHS. IE (142) adds 'in lordship'.

2,2 JURISDICTION. IE (142). 'full jurisdiction'.

2,3 1 OX. That is, one eighth of a ploughteam of 8 oxen.

2,5 ALL THIS. Perhaps referring to 2,1-5.

COUNT BRIAN. Brother of Count Alan of Brittany (*3*).

2,7 NIGEL [HELD]. Farley prints *ten..t* for what in the MS is probably intended to be *tenuit*.
although some erasure has taken place. If he is the same Nigel as in 2.8 the past tense
appears appropriate.

2,8 CHURCH OF STOW(MARKET). Also at 34.6.

TO THE MANOR. LDB *man(us)* is in error for *man(erio)*.

IN THE CHURCH OF COMBS. In the MS *ta(m)bas* is in error for *ca(m)bas*; Farley silently
corrects.

2,9-10 ST. MARY'S OF GRESTAIN. The Benedictine Abbey in Normandy founded by Count
Robert's father. Duke Robert I.

2,9 7 CATTLE. In the MS *vii* has been altered from *vi*.

2,10 HARDWIN, THE EARL'S BROTHER. The Earl referred to is probably Ralph (cf. 7.67)
the Constable.

2,11 COUNT ... IN LORDSHIP. The two dots in the MS before *in*. shown by Farley. are
probably an anticipation of those either side of the following numeral.

VALUE [10]D. Farley prints *cv.đ.* but in the MS the *c* is an erroneous anticipation of the
bowl of *d* that follows the numeral.

2,12 ANUND. Added above the line in LDB.

[HELD IT]. Cf. below.

BELONGING TO THE CHURCH. Translating *Eccl(esi)ae*.

2,14 HELD. LDB *tenenuit* is in error for *tenuit*.

2,15 WHATFIELD. MS *gaWatefelda*; Farley *goWatefelda* in error. The place-name form should
be taken as *Watefelda*, with the *ga-* of the MS being an unerased false start with Norman *g*
for *w*.

2,16 2 FREE MEN ... PATRONAGE (OF) ST. ETHELDREDA'S. IE (144) adds, 'in full
jurisdiction'.

18 ACRES. IE (144) and IEAL (189). '14'.

IN TAX. In the MS *degelt(o)* altered from *det-*.

2,18 THORPE. In Trimley, VCH 432, n.20a.

2,19 'ALSTON'. Lost in Trimley, VCH 432, n.21. Also at 7,96;101;113.
NORMAN. LDB *normandNi* is in error for *normanni*. From OE *northmann*, originally designating a Scandinavian, especially a Norwegian, but by 1066 functioning as a pers. PNDB 331-332.

2,20 EUDO. Son of Nigel, as 2,16.
ALL THIS. 2,17-20.

Folio 292a, foot. A partial list of landholders (*3-4*) occurs here. This was a running guide to the contents of the quire which begins with this leaf. It should have been deleted after use like the one folio 372a, below. See further, note to List of Landholders, above.

3 COUNT ALAN. Of Brittany. He was the son-in-law of King William. His name is OBre *Alan*.

3,1 MANNI SWART. LDB *Mannius Suart*, from ODan *Manni* (PNDB 324) and the OWScand byname *suartr*, *suarti*, 'black' (OEB 338). For his son Ulf, see 6,109 and note.
1 [PLOUGH] WITH THE VILLAGERS. The formula is that found in ICC and IE, see Cambridgeshire, Introduction.
WESTON (COLVILLE). See Cambridgeshire 14,80 and note; and ESf.

3,2 IN THE ASSESSMENT OF RUMBURGH. The main entry for Rumburgh was omitted from LDB however. Cf. 3,105 and ENf2;4.
STONE (STREET). LDB places this in Bradmere Hundred. Geographically it is in Blything Hundred (as was RUMBURGH) and has been so mapped.

3,3 MEN'S PLOUGHS. In the MS the first *c* of *car(uce)* has been altered from *a*.
PIGS. LDB *pors*.
THE KING ... JURISDICTION. Misplaced in LDB in the middle of, rather than after, t value. It may perhaps have been interlined in an exemplar MS.
3¾D IN TAX. LDB has *seŕ* in error for *fer(dingi)*, 'farthings'.

3,4 THIS ASSESSMENT. In the MS *Hoe* in error for *Hoc*; Farley corrects.

3,5 16 SMALLHOLDERS. LDB *vxvi*, with an erroneous anticipation of the *v*.

3,7 (IT IS) ... JURISDICTION. Referring to 3,5-7 and the assessment of Bramfield mentioned in 3,4.

3,8 THORPE. In Blything Hundred. Near Heveningham, VCH 432, n.23. DG 413 places it Aldingham (*recte* Aldringham), but that is in Bishop's Hundred. Cf. 7,16 note.
WAS DELIVERED [TO HIM]. That is, the Count was put in lawful possession of him and the land. Cf. Bedfordshire 56,2 *quae sibi lib(er)ata fuit*.

3,9 8 CATTLE. In the MS *viii* has been altered from *vii*.
MAYNARD. OG *Maganhard*, *Mainard*, Forssner 181.

3,10 R(ALPH) THE CONSTABLE. Earl Ralph. LDB *Stabra* is in error for *Stalra*. See 1,101 note.
60 PIGS. In the MS the *L* of the numeral is written over an erased *x*.

3,13 IT IS ALL ... MANOR. That is, the 14 free men in 3,10 and the items in 3,11-13 are included in the assessment of Wissett in 3,10.
THE COUNT ... LENGTH ... TAX. These details refer to the whole manor of Wissett.

3,14 IN THIS CHURCH ... 12 MONKS. The Priory of Rumburgh, founded by Bishop Aelme and Abbot Thurstan of St. Benedict of Holme, see MRH 74. See also 3,105.
£20. See 3,10.

3,15 *WRABETUNA*. In Blything Hundred (also at 6,91;99;108. 7,11;28). Unidentified, DG 417 but referred to *temp.* Henry II (VCH 433, n.24).
HAMO OF VALOGNES. Probably from Valognes (La Manche). The LDB form *deuellen* may be compared to *de walenus* in 14,78 as a spelling for Peter of Valognes; cf. OEB 117.

3,16 COVEHITHE. As 1,108 note.

3,17 BEFORE 1066; [20] ACRES. In the MS *xxx* has been altered to *xx* by erasure; Farley prints *xxx* in error.
VALUE ALWAYS 4S. In the MS there is an erasure after *udť.*

3,20 (EARL) SOHAM. Identified DG 397.

3,21 IN CAPEL (ST. ANDREW). IE (147) and IEAL (185). 'In CAMPSEY (Ash)'.
EDRIC GRIM. The byname is OE *grimm*, 'fierce, savage', OEB 346-347.

3,24-27 EDRIC. Grim (IE 147).

3,26 IEAL (185) adds, '3 free men, 15 acres'.

3,27 26 ACRES. IEAL (185), 16.

3,28 'LITTLE' CHARSFIELD. LDB *parua ceresfella*.

3,29 E(DRIC). Grim (IE 147).

3,31 AETHELWOLD THE PRIEST. IE (148) and IEAL (185), '1 free man'.
50 ACRES. IEAL (185, in error), 1.
THEN 1 PLOUGH. IE 'Then 2 ploughs in lordship'.
ALL THIS. 3,21-31.

3,32	1 FREE MAN. IE (147) adds, 'of St. Etheldreda's' but omits the mention of patronage.
3,33	IN BOULGE. IE (147) and IEAL (185), 'in (Little) BEALINGS'.
	2 FREE MEN. IE adds, 'of St. Etheldreda's' but omits the patronage.
	THEY ... ASSESSMENT. Referring to 3,32-33.
3,34	EDRIC GRIM. IE (146) adds, 'a free man'.
	VALUE OF THE HEAD OF THE MANOR. That is, of the core. The total value, with the outliers, is given at 3,44.
	6 FREEMEN. IE adds, 'under the patronage of Edric Grim'.
	36 ACRES. IEAL (185), 30.
	2 FREE MEN ... ST. ETHELDREDA'S. In the MS an ampersand has been erased before *Eldre*.
3,35	12 FREE MEN AND A HALF. IEAL (185), 12.
3,36	ST. ETHELDREDA'S. In the MS *El* is written over an erasure.
	THE THREE OTHERS. IE (153), referring to these only, '15 acres. Value 3s.'
	1 CARUCATE. IEAL (185), 3.
3,39	5 WHOLE ... FREE MEN. IE (147) and IEAL (185), 6.
	W(ILLIAM) MALET. In the MS there is an erasure after *W*.
	WHEN HE DIED. Probably 1069 x 1071.
	34 ACRES. IE, 20.
3,40	AND A HALF. IE (147) and IEAL (185) omits.
	34 ACRES. IE, 30; IEAL, 4.
	EARL R(ALPH). Wader. He forfeited in 1075, see 1,61-95 note.
3,41	*BRODERTUNA*. Also at 6,278. Unidentified DG 392. In Loes Hundred.
	7 FREE MEN. IEAL (185), 6.
	HALF UNDER THE PATRONAGE ... LAXFIELD. IE (147), 'under the patronage of Edric Grim'.
	FORFEITED. In the MS *fec(it)* has been altered to *forisfec(it)*. He forfeited in 1075, see 1,61-95 note.
3,42	4½ ACRES. IE (147) and IEAL (185), 3.
3,44	8 ACRES. IE (147) and IEAL (185), 7.
	VALUE ... MANOR NOW £23 11S. IE, 'Value of the whole, £18. A church with 29 acres' IEAL, '11 churches, 29 acres'. The manor referred to is that of Kettleburgh, including 3,34-45.
3,45	ASSESSMENT. See preceding note.
3,46	ST. EDMUND'S. In the MS *.É.* altered to *.É.tmundi*, with two otiose abbreviation marks. IE (148), 'St. Etheldreda's'. IE uses the present tense here (*tenet*).
	(EARL) SOHAM. As 3,20 note.
	VALUE ... NOW £18 13S 4D. IE, 'Value £18'.
3,47	24 ACRES. IEAL (185), 23.
3,48	A HALF FREE MAN. IE (148) and IEAL (185), '1 free man'.
	THEY ... ASSESSMENT. Referring to 3,47-48.
3,49	2 VILLAGERS ... 50 ACRES. IE (148) adds 'under the patronage of Edric Grim'.
	50 ACRES. IEAL (185, in error), 1.
3,50	2 FREE MEN. IE (148) and IEAL (185), 1.
3,52	5 FREE MEN. Farley *libi* is in error for *liƀi* of the MS.
	ALL THIS ... KETTLEBURGH. Referring to 3,51-52.
3,53	WULFRIC. In the MS *Vlurici* has been altered from *Vlul-*.
3,54	BLUNDESTON. The LDB form *dunstuna* is corrupt.
3,55	TOWN OF IPSWICH. LDB *Gespeswiz* is in error for *Gepeswiz*.
	GRANGE. For another grange here, see 1,122b.
	THIRD PENNY. A third share in the profits of jurisdiction, traditionally the perquisite of the local Earl. Cf. 1,122a;g.
3,56	GAUTI. LDB *Gouti*, from ON *Gauti*, ODan *Gøti*; see PNDB 258, n.4 where this holder of the name is tentatively identified as *Gouti* in Whitelock *ASWills* no. 31 (and p. 136), Sawyer no. 1531, of A.D. 1043 x 1045. That man was associated however with Norfolk rather than Suffolk.
	ERLAND. In the MS *halanalt* has been altered from *halant*. The same man occurs as *harlenat* in 3,62. Both forms seem ultimately to derive from OG *Erland*, Förstemann 773 (J.M.D). Cf. Forssner 142, s.n. *Halanant*.
	ONLY THE PATRONAGE. LDB repeats *tantu(m)* in error.
	£7 10S. LDB *libi* is in error for *liƀ*, anticipating the 'free men'.

3,57	NARDRED. Possibly an OG name, but perhaps *Nardred(us)* is in error for *Hardred(us)* from OE *Heardred*; Forssner 193. THE JURISDICTION. IE (143), 'full jurisdiction and patronage from him'. HE WAS IN POSSESSION. Probably referring to Count Alan. (EARL) R(ALPH). Wader. See 1,61-95 note.
3,59	ABOVE LAND ... HUMPHREY HOLDS ... FORFEITED. This appears to refer to part of Nettlestead in 3,56 and to be misplaced here. BETWEEN WOODLAND AND OPEN LAND. Translating *int(er) silua(m) & planu(m)* which, however, probably stands for the OE formula *on wudu and on feld*, that is, it includes both sorts of terrain. WARENGAR. OG *Weringer*, Forssner 246. The LDB form has NFr *G-* for *W-*. Warengar also held from Roger Bigot in Essex (43,1-2). HE HELD (IT) LIKEWISE. Perhaps the subject of this is Count Alan, as in 3,57. (EARL) RALPH. Wader. See 1,61-95 note.
3,61	BARN. An ON byname, 'child', PNDB 192; cf. OEB 237. RALPH THE CONSTABLE BEFORE 1066. LDB *Radulf(us)* is in error for *Radulfo*, due to misreading of final *-o* as the abbreviation mark for *-us*.
3,62	ERLAND. See 3,56 note. NETTLESTEAD. 3,56. THIS ENTRY. IEAL (185) adds '3 free men; 50 acres'.
3,63	BEFORE 1066. In the MS, the text from *t.r.e.* (line 7) to the foot of folio 295a is in a different colour of ink to the preceding text on the page. 20 ACRES. In the MS *xx* has been altered from *xxx* by erasure.
3,64	SAME (THURLESTON). Although Westerfield is the last place named, the reference is back to the name at the beginning of the entry.
3,65	27 ACRES. In the MS *xxvii* has been altered from *xxvi*.
3,67	ERMENGOT. LDB *Erñiot*. The name is probably OG *Ermingaud, Ermengaut*, see Forssner 81.
3,68-69	EDEVA. Probably 'the Fair', cf. 3,67.
3,69	*BERIA*. Unidentified, DG 390.
3,70-71	FULCRIC. LDB *Furic*, representing OG *Fulcric* (PNDB 256-257) with AN loss of *l*.
3,71-74	EDEVA. As 3,68-69 note.
3,71	FULCRIC ... COUNT. This statement is out of place after the jurisdiction and is preceded by a paragraph marker, but seems to refer to Bentley.
3,73	TWO [MANORS]. Those in 3,72-73.
3,74	THEN 5 COBS. Farley adds the abbreviation mark above *r(uncini)*, which is not in the MS. IN LENGTH ... IN WIDTH. LDB *in longe, in latitudo* are in error for *in longo, in latitudine*. IN TAX. In the MS *get*has been altered (? from *gersumma*).
3,75	BEFORE 1066. In the MS *euardi* has been altered from *euau-*. Farley prints as *euaRdi*.
3,76-77	EDEVA. As 3,68-69 note.
3,76	THURSTAN. In the MS a word (? *tainus*, 'thane') has been erased after the pers. n. LDB *Suuart*, probably in error for *Siuuart, Siuuard(us)* from OE *Sigeweard* or ODan *Sigwarth*. Cf. PNDB 378.
3,79-80	
3,80	*CANAPETUNA*. See 1,106 note. ABOVE ASSESSMENT. Of Hintlesham in 3,79.
3,81	EDEVA. As 3,68-69 note.
3,83	SAME ASSESSMENT. Of Brantham in 3,82.
3,84	EDEVA. As 3,68-69 note.
3,86	PARHAM HALF-HUNDRED. The abbreviated form in LDB stands for *P(ER)REHAM*, c 1,75 etc. MALET. As 1,102 note.
3,88-89	HAMO. Perhaps 'of Valognes'', cf. 3,87.
3,89	BROTHER. LDB *Brotho*, from ON *Bróthir*, ODan *Brothir*; PNDB 208.
3,91	[HELD]. LDB *ten&* is in error for *tenuit*. EDHILD. A FREE MAN. The name is OE *Ēadhild* (feminine), PNDB 232. The descriptic of her as *lib(er) h(om)o* is not unusual since this was a description of status, not of gender which could be applied to either male or female.
3,92	BLAXHALL. In the MS *ii* has been erased after this place-name. It was probably written in anticipation of *iiii* further along the line.
3,93	3 FREE MEN. IE (148) adds, 'under him'.
3,94	SHEEP, NOW 170. In the MS *clxx* has been altered from *clxxx* by erasure.

IN LORDSHIP, 8 FREE MEN ... ABBOT OF ELY. Cf. IE (149), 'In the same village 3 free men under the patronage of Edric Grim; 60 acres. And 6 other (free men) under the patronage of St. Etheldreda's'. Cf. also IEAL 186, which assigns 1 carucate of land to the 6 (free) men.

8 FREE MEN. In the MS *in d(omi)nio* has been erased after *.viii.*

3,95   ABOVE-MENTIONED EDRIC. Grim, see 3,95. IE (149) adds, '1 free man'.

HUNEPOT. According to PNDB 296, the pers. n. may be OG *Hunbod* but could also be OE *Huna*/ON *Húni* with an added byname *pot* (*bot?*). The byname may be either OE *Pott* with a meaning 'plump' or 'stupid' (OEB 329-330) or OE *But(t)* 'cut off, truncated, short' (OEB 295-296), if *Hunebot* at 8,16 is the same name.

[4 ACRES]. In the MS *.iiii.* is written above *x* which has been erased. Farley prints both numerals.

1 LEAGUE. There is an erasure in the MS before *i.*

3,96   (LITTLE) GLEMHAM. LDB *Thieue gliemha(m)*. The affix may be OE *thīfe*, 'stolen', cf. BT 1058, s.v. *þīfe-feoh*.

3,98   85 ACRES. In the MS all except *Lx* is written over an erasure and is followed by *xvi* erased. Cf. note on 91 ACRES, below.

LATER AND NOW 1; ALWAYS. In the MS *p(ost) 7 m(odo) .i. se(m)p(er)* is written over an erasure.

2 MEN'S PLOUGHS. In the MS there is an erasure after *ho(m inu)m.*

91 ACRES. In the MS all except *lx* is written over an erasure and is followed by an erased numeral. Cf. note on 85 ACRES, above.

VALUE ... 60S. In the MS there is an erasure before *lx.*

HIS FATHER. William Malet.

60 ACRES. IEAL (186), 10.

ALWAYS 7 SMALLHOLDERS. In the MS *vii* has been altered from *vi.*

3,99   OSTULA. A derivative of OG *Ost-*, Forssner 201, PNDB 340.

3,100   THIS ENTRY. Cf. IE (149), '2 free men under the patronage of St. Etheldreda's, with 20 acres. Count Alan holds this.' Also IEAL (186), '3 free men; 20 acres'.

3,101   TUTFLED. LDB *Tutflet*. The second element of this feminine pers. n. is OE *-flǣd* but the first is obscure; PNDB 389.

MAGNI. LDB *magna*, perhaps from ON, ODan *Magni* (PNDB 323), but possibly from ODan *Manni*, OSw *Manne* (PNDB 324).

HIS FATHER ... POSSESSION. William Malet. In the MS there is an erasure after *fuit*, probably the words *ant(e)c(essori) malet* which were subsequently interlined in a different place.

3,102   WACRA. Perhaps a byname meaning 'watchful, vigilant', either from OE *Wacra* or from ON *Vakri*; PNDB 407.

HAMO ... ALL THIS. 3,99-102.

3,105   CHURCH OF RUMBURGH. See 3,14 note.

4   EARL HUGH. Hugh of Avranches, created Earl of Chester in 1071.

4,2-3   MANUUIC. Also at 6,19 and 16,32 (*MANEWIC*); all in Claydon Hundred. Unidentified, DG 405.

4,3   WAILOLF. LDB *Wailolf(us)*, IE (146) *Waiolf(us)*, probably from OG *Wadalulf*, see PNDB 408.

UNDER ... PATRONAGE ... ABBOT OF ELY. IE (146) adds, 'in the jurisdiction'.

4,4   YRIC. LDB *Iric(us)* is explained by PNDB (299-300) as an OE form for ON *Eyríkr*.

4,6-7   THORPE (HALL). In Ashfield.

4,6   HUGH ... HOLDS ALL THIS. 4,1-6.

4,10   SKULI. LDB *Scula*; ON *Skúli*, ODan *Skuli*, OSw *Skule*, see PNDB 366. Note that in the Nottinghamshire volume (10,23;52. 30,28) the spelling *Escul* for this name was incorrectly interpreted as Aswulf.

4,11   ... CARUCATE. LDB omits the numeral.

4,13   ; ALWAYS ...; Farley prints a curled dash before *se(m)p(er)*, representing what in the MS is a cross-bar to a capital *T* which was never completed. This was probably an anticipation of *T* in *T(u)nc* on the line below. The word *se(m)p(er)* also seems to be otiose, probably anticipating its occurrence further along the line.

BIGOT OF LOGES. From Loges (Calvados), OEB 95. Note that the first reference given in OEB is not however to Bigot but to Gerwy of Loges, see Gloucestershire 76,1. For the byname Bigot, see 7 note, with reference to Roger Bigot. Bigot of Loges may be identical with Roger Bigot, or with a relative of his, since Roger's son held land at Loges in 1133, see Loyd 14-15.

7½D IN TAX. Farley *gelt(o)* is in error for *get* of MS.

THROUGH HIS (OWN) POSSESSION. Translating *p(er) sua(m) sesina(m)* and referri~~n~~ to a public ceremony in which lawful possession had been transferred to Count Alan.

4,14 R(OBERT) OF COURSON. Cf. 7,8. He came from Courson (Calvados), OEB 85.

4,15 MUNULF. The name is either OSw or OG, see PNDB 331.

FROM HIM. From Munulf.

BRUNWIN. MS *Brunwin(us)* altered from *Buin Win(us)*, Farley *BRunWin(us)*.

MUNULF'S. LDB *Munolf* is in error for *Munolfi*.

ASMOTH. LDB *Esmoda*. The name is ODan, see PNDB 168.

TOLI THE SHERIFF. Of Suffolk and Norfolk under Edward the Confessor, see Harm~~er~~ *ASWrits* nos. 20, 25, 61; Sawyer nos. 1080, 1085, 1109; Hart ECEE nos. 115, 119, 135. S~~ee~~ Norfolk 1,229 etc.

BRICTMER, R(OBERT) MALET'S REEVE. Perhaps the same as Brictmer the Beadl~~e~~ 74,4.

INGOLD. This represents an Anglo-Scandinavian form of ON *Ingialdr*, ODan *Ingeld*, O~~E~~ *Ing(i)aeld*; PNDB 297-298.

WALTER OF CAEN. From Caen (Calvados), OEB 79.

WALTER OF DOL. From Dol or Dol-de-Bretagne (Ille-et-Villaine), OEB 86. He was exiled in 1075.

4.17 BURGH. In the MS *burh* has been altered from *burc*.

COUNTESS EDEVA. Probably the same as Edeva the Rich or Fair. See 1,61 note.

4,18 [HALF]. LDB omits *dim̃*.

4,19 5 CARUCATES ... BEFORE 1066. In the MS *t.r.e.* has been erased but is still partially visible. Farley retains it.

ALWAYS 3 CATTLE. In the MS there is an erasure after *an(imalia)*, as shown by Farle~~y~~ gaps on this line and the next.

40 ACRES AS 1 MANOR. In the MS *m(anerio)* is interlined above a blotted attempt at alteration which precedes an erasure.

SUMMERLED. LDB *Sumerlet*, from ON *Sumarlithr*; PNDB 377-378.

FOURTH PART OF 1 MILL. In the MS there is an erasure after *mol(endini)*, probably ~~o~~f *T(u)nc*, anticipating the next line.

4,20 WARIN SON OF BURNIN. LDB *Warin(us) filius Burn̄*; below (4,29) *-burnnini*. The forename is OG *Warin*, Forssner 246-247; this perhaps makes less likely the suggestion (OE~~B~~ 176) that the patronym is OE *Byrnwine*. Cf. also Burnin in 4,32.

4,24 THERE COULD BE ... LDB omits the numeral.

4,25 MANOR WHICH THE KING HOLDS. That at 1,110.

... WHOLE OF THIS. For the name, see 4,20 note.

4,29 WARIN SON OF BURNIN ... WHOLE OF THIS. For the name, see 4,20 note. This sentence probably refers to 4,21-29.

4,30 MUNDRED ... HELD. In the MS *q(uod)* is squeezed between *mundret(us)* and *ten(uit)* as ~~an~~ insertion, probably made at the same time as the overline insertion of *ten&*.

MUNDRED. Apparently OE *Mundrǣd*, PNDB 331. He may also have held the City of Chester and other lands from Earl Hugh in Cheshire (C24. 1,22;34. 2,13. 26,3). Note th~~at~~ the translated form in the Cheshire volume should read Mundred not Mundret.

ALWAYS 1 COB. In the MS *ea* has been erased before *r(uncinus)*. Farley shows the eras~~ure~~ by the use of dots, but no text seems to be missing.

4,31 *CROSCROFT*. Unidentified, DG 396.

SOTTERLEY ... TAX. Misplaced ere in 4,31 rather than in 4,30.

4,32 W. THE CONSTABLE. Not found elsewhere in LDB.

EARL R(ALPH). Wader, see 1,61-95 note.

HELD IT. LDB *qua(m)* either stands as a pronoun for *terra* or is in error for *que(m)* referring
to the free man.

BURNIN. Apparently the same name as that which formed the patronym of Warin in 4,20;29. It might refer to Warin's father, but could also be a short form for Warin son of Burnin himself.

4,33 *HETHEBURGAFELLA*. The same as *HATHEBURGFELDA* in 31,24. In Wangford Hundr~~ed~~ Unidentified, DG 400.

4,36 *RODENHALA*. Also at 31,28. In Lothing Hundred. Unidentified, DG 409.

R(ALPH) BAYNARD. See *33* and note.

4,39 FREE [MEN]. LDB *lib(er)os* has been corrected from *lib(er)is*.

HUGH ... HOLDS THE WHOLE OF THIS. 4,36-39.

4,41	SAME MAN. Probably Gyrth of 4,40. [16] ACRES. MS *xvi*; Farley prints *xv* in error.
4,42	R(OGER) BIGOT. In the MS the name is added in the inner margin. UNDER ... AELMER AND. In the MS there is an erasure from 7 to the end of the line. 6 WHOLE FREE MEN. LDB *integros lib(er)os* is in error for *integri lib(er)i*. IN THE SAME ... 1 FREE MAN. The numeral has been inserted between *eade(m)* and *lib(er)*. 1 VILLAGER. LDB *uill(an)i* is in error for *uill(an)us*. *ETHEREG.* Unidentified, DG 397. [ST.] ETHELDREDA'S. LDB *soca* is in error for *sancta*.
5	COUNT EUSTACE. Of Boulogne, brother-in-law of King Edward.
5,2	JURISDICTION. IE (141), 'full jurisdiction'. 60 ACRES. IEAL (189), 40. ALDRED. LDB *heldret*, from OE *Ealdrǣd*; cf. PNDB 241-242. 7 ACRES. IEAL, 6.
5,3-5	ENGELRIC. The predecessor of Count Eustace in many of his lands, particularly in Essex (chapter 20). The founder of St. Martin le Grand in London. See also 14,101 note.
5,4	(LITTLE) FINBOROUGH. Identified, VCH 444, n.51.
5,5	BUXHALL. FD no. 9 is a writ 1066 x 1087 of King William which orders that the men of Frodo in Buxhall taken away by Count Eustace's men are to be returned to the Abbot of St. Edmund's.
5,6	WITH 4 ACRES; 24 ... In the MS *de iiii acr(is)*. *7 xxiiii* has been written over an erasure; *ac.* follows but has been erased. RALPH OF MARCY. From Marcy (La Manche), OEB 97.
5,7	*STANFELDA.* Unidentified, DG 410. HATO. OG *Hatho, Hatto* ; Förstemann 790 (J.M.D.).
5,8	SAME ASSESSMENT. That in 5,7.
6	ROBERT MALET. Sheriff of Suffolk at same time between 1066 and 1086. The son of William Malet and member of a family which came from Graville-Ste-Honorine (Seine-Inf.), see Loyd 56. His extensive Holding, mainly in Suffolk, was later known as the Honour of Eye (cf. 6,191). The byname is OFr *malet*, a diminutive of *mal* 'evil', OEB 350-351. The main predecessor of William and Robert was Edric of Laxfield (6,305 and note). For Robert's mother, see 6,76-77 note.
6,1	WINTER MILL. *Mol(endinum) hyemal(e)*, a mill on a winterbourne, where the flow of water in summer was insufficient to turn the wheel.
6,2	THE COUNT. Presumably an error for Robert Malet. The scribe was no doubt affected by the three preceding comital chapters. PLOUGHS ... AND BETWEEN THE MEN. The meaning is probably 'a further 2 ploughs between the men'. THE SAME 3 FREE MEN. Translating *.iii. ide(m) lib(er)i ho(min)es*, but this may be in error for *in eade(m) .iii. lib(er)i ho(min)es*.
6,3	ROBERT OF GLANVILLE. From Glanville (Calvados), OEB 89-90.
6,4	PREDECESSOR. Farley shows an erasure in the MS after *antec(essor)* by the use of four dots. CUSTOMARY DUES. In the MS *consuetudins* has been altered from *consuetudine(m)*.
6,5	DAM. *excluse* (genitive singular) from *exclusa*. Probably a fish-weir.
6,7	'OLDEN'. As 1,5 note.
6,10-11	WILLIAM GOULAFRE. LDB *gulaf(f)ra*; the byname is OFr *goulafre, gouliafre*, 'glutton', OEB 347.
6,11	ABBOT. Of Ely. Cf. 21,31. In the present chapter, all unspecified references to 'the Abbot' refer to Ely. 30 ACRES ... IN ANOTHER HUNDRED. The precise significance is not apparent. Debenham (in Claydon Hundred) bordered on Bosmere, Hartismere, and Loes Hundreds. IN THE SAME ... 11 FREE MEN ... In the MS thre is an erasure after *xi*. SAXI, RANULF PEVEREL'S PREDECESSOR. Cf. 34,12.
6,12	THORPE (HALL). In Ashfield.
6,18	CHURCH OF ST. MARY. For the rest of it, see 16,28 and 34,12. TO ANSWER FOR. Translating *ad defendu(m)* and preserving the ambiguity of the Latin. This may refer to a fiscal liability on the part of Robert, or to a duty to maintain this proportion of the church. The contemporary cross in the left-hand margin of the MS (not shown by Farley) may have been meant to draw attention to this ambiguity.

CHURCH OF ST. ANDREW. For the rest of it, see 16,28.

6,19 MANUUIC. As 4,2-3 note.

6,20 UNDER PATRONAGE. In the MS there is an erasure after *co(m)m(en)d(ati)*.

6,21-22 JURISDICTION ... SAME WAY. Divided between the Abbot and Earl Hugh, as in 6,2

6,21;23 THORPE (HALL). In Ashfield.

6,23 TIGIER. LDB *Tiger(us)*; OFr *Tigier* from OG *Thiodger*, Forssner 234. The source of the surname *Tigar*, according to DBS 349.

6,25 THORPE (HALL). In Ashfield.

6,27 HUBERT HOLDS (THIS). This probably includes 6,26 too.

6,28 BRUTGE. Also at 67,5. In Parham Hundred. Unidentified, DG 393.
WALTER *DE RISBOIL*. Below (6,284), *de Risbou*. His place of origin is unidentified.

6,30 121 ACRES. These no doubt represent the land held by the 22 free men but were misplaced in LDB.
GILBERT OF WISSANT. From Wissant (Pas-de-Calais), OEB 120-121.
WILLIAM OF ÉMALLEVILLE. LDB *de malauill'*, below (6,33) *desmala uill'*. From Émalleville (Eure), OEB 114-115, Loyd 40.

6,32 NIUETUNA. Unidentified, DG 407.
[PLOUGH]. LDB omits *car(uca)*.
[ACRES]. LDB omits *ac(re)*.

6,33-34 Cf. IE (151), 'a half free man under the patronage of St. Etheldreda's; 10 acres. ½ plough. Value 3s. Also 1 free man; 12 acres. Value 2s. Another (free man); 2 acres. Valu 4d.'

6,34 OF HIS PREDECESSOR. That is, of Robert Malet's predecessor.

6,41-42 CHELETUNA, CHILETUNA. The same as *KELETUNA* in 6,288. In Plomesgate Hundred Unidentified, DG 394. Cf. VCH 447, n. 55 for a possible later reference.

6,43 OF THIS MANOR. Referring to *Chiletuna* in 6,42.

6,44 90 ACRES. In the MS the numeral and the 'acres' are written on either side of a hole (n repaired) in the parchment of folio 308a. See also 6,46 note.

6,45 OF HIS PREDECESSOR. As 6,34 note.

6,46 ROBERT OF CLAVILLE. From Claville-en-Caux (Seine-Inf.), Loyd 29; cf. OEB 82.
VALUE THEN 10S. In the MS on folio 308b *ual(uit)*. and *x. sol(idos)* are written on eithe side of the same hole which affects 6,44 on the other side of the leaf.
ROBERT SON OF FULCRED. The patronym is more probably OG **Fulcrad* than OE *Folcrǣd*; cf. Forssner 98-99.
AETHELWY. LDB *Ailwi*; OE *Aethelwīg*, PNDB 189.
HARDWIN. LDB *haruin(us)*; OG *Hardwin*, PNDB 286-287, Forssner 143.

6,48 5 SMALLHOLDERS. Misplaced in LDB among the ploughs.
ALWIN. It is not certain whether this is the name of the free man, or of the half free ma

6,49 ROBERT ... LIKEWISE. 'Likewise' may refer to the jurisdiction, belonging to the Abb as in 6,48.
LEOFRIC. Perhaps the name of one of the free men. As *Leuric(us)* is in the nominative i cannot (unless there is an error here) be associated with *co(m)mend(ati)*.

6,51 ALWYNN. LDB *Aluuem* is in error for *Aluuen*, from late OE *Alwynn* (feminine), PNDB 16 161.
FREE MAN. See note to 3,91 *sub* EDHILD.

6,54 UNDER PATRONAGE; 1½ ACRES. In the MS there is an erasure after *c(om)m(en)d(atus)*, perhaps of *xx*.

6,55 BADINGHAM. LDB *hadincha(m)* is in error for *b-*, cf. 6,306.

6,57 FROM ROBERT. Malet.
ROBERT BLUNT. Cf. 66,16.

6,59 SAME ASSESSMENT. Of Westhorpe in 6,58.

6,61 PENNIES. Translating *nu(m)mos*.
VALUE OF THE WHOLE OF THIS, 21S. It is not clear to what this refers.

6,62 4 COBS, 6 CATTLE. In the MS 7 .*iiii. r(uncini). 7 vi. an(imalia)* is written over an erasure.
RICKINGHALL. LDB *kikingahala* is in error for *R-*.
ST. E(DMUND'S). Cf. 14,46.

6,63 WILLIAM SHIELD. LDB *scutet*. The byname is from OFr **Escuet*, equivalent to Lat. *scutatus*, 'equipped with a shield', OEB 372. A man of this name was one of King William cooks, see *Regesta* i, no. 270 and Wiltshire 2,4 etc.

6,66 [HELD]. LDB *ten&* is in error for *tenuit*.

6,67 WILLIAM OF CAEN. Perhaps in error for Walter of Caen, cf. 6,5 etc.

6,143	12 FREE MEN. As 6,138 note.
6,144	*BURGESGATA.* Unidentified, DG 393.
6,145	*BURCH.* Unidentified, DG 393.
6,146	*INGOLUESTUNA.* Unidentified, DG 403. In Plomesgate Hundred. Perhaps distinct from the place of the same name in Carlford Hundred (21,65 etc).
6,147	*PRESTETUNA.* Unidentified, DG 408.
	[ACRE]. LDB omits *acr(a)*.
6,148	FISHERY. LDB *piscaī* is for *piscat(io)*. See 1,115 note.
	7D IN TAX. *p(er) totu(m) hundret* deleted in LDB after *.vii. d(enarii).*; *p(er) totu(m) Hund(ret)* was subsequently added on the next line after *soca(m)*.
6,150	1 ACRE. In the MS there is an erasure after *acr(is)*.
6,151	'LANEBURH'. The same as 'LANEBURC' at 6,173-174. Lost in Sutton, DG 404.
6,153	'TURSTANESTUNA'. Also at 11,2 ('THUR-') and 26,19 ('TOR-'). Lost in Bromeswell, DG 414.
6,154	THEY ARE ALL ... HOLLESLEY. That is 6,150-154.
6,155	LEOFSTAN. His land formed part of the same Holding as that of Osferth in 6,106 note. Apparently identical with Leofstan in 16,26.
6,156	'CULESLEA' Lost in Alderton, DG 396.
6,160	R(OBERT) OF GLANVILLE ... WHOLE OF THIS. Referring to 6,158-160.
6,164	12 ACRES. IE (162), '12 acres of the lordship (of St. Etheldreda's)'.
6,165	GODWIN. The other half of his patronage belonged to St. Etheldreda's, IE (162). He is called Godwin 'of Sutton' in 6,169.
	9 FREE MEN ... 1 FREE MAN. IE, '10 free men in the jurisdiction and patronage of St. Etheldreda's'.
6,167	ACRES. In the MS *acr(e)* has been altered from *ar-*.
6,168	WALTER ... ROBERT MALET. This sentence was added later to this entry in the MS.
6,169	6S 2D. IE (162), 7s 2d.
	MAYNARD. LDB *Menard(us)*; from OG *Maganhard, Mainard,* Forssner 181.
	CLAIMS. LDB *calu(m)piat(ur)* is in error for *calu(m)pniat(ur)*. In the MS the *p* has been altered from *n*.
	EARL R(ALPH). Wader, see 1,61-95 note.
	GODWIN OF SUTTON. Named from Sutton (6,165).
6,171	FREEMAN. MS *soćmanῡ*, for *soc(he)manu(m)*. Farley prints the abbreviation for *-us* above the *c* in error.
	AEDI. The form may represent an otherwise unrecorded OE *Ēadig*, PNDB 171-172.
6,172	HUMPHREY SON OF R. Cf. Humphrey son of Rodric in 26,1.
	... POSSIBLE. LDB omits the numeral.
6,173-174	'LANEBURC'. See 6,151 note.
	VALUE [12]D. Farley *xx* is in error for *xii* of MS.
	WALTER ... (THIS). *in d(omi)nio* 'in lordship' deleted in LDB after *tenῶ*.
6,176	'HALGESTOU'. Lost in Shottisham, DG 400.
6,177	MALET. Robert Malet.
6,179-180	FREE MEN. As 6,138 note.
6,179	CHARSFIELD. Here and at 31,18 assigned to Wilford Hundred, but elsewhere in the neighbouring Hundred of Loes.
	TO THE CHURCH. LDB *Ecl(es)iae* is in error for *Eccl-*. In the MS a capital *I* has been erased beneath *E-*.
6,181	WULFWIN. Farley *Wlfuiṁ*, although in the MS the final letter seems to be intended as *n* (followed by a partially erased otiose stroke).
6,183	FREE MEN. As 6,138 note.
6,187	[OF LAND]. LDB omits *t(er)rae*.
	1 PLOUGH, NOW 2. *nulla* 'none' deleted in LDB, *.ii.* interlined.
6,189	MEADOW ... ½ PLOUGH. The items are out of their usual order in LDB.
6,190	FREE MEN. As 6,138 note.
6,191	ROBERT ... IN LORDSHIP. In the MS there is an erasure after *d(omi)nio*.
	FISHERY. LDB *piscatio*. See 1,115 note.
	WALTER THE CROSSBOWMAN. MS *arbaῑ* with a single vertical stroke above the *r*, as in Farley. Perhaps an attempt to change the word to *Albaῑ*, for AN *alblaster*, instead of Latin *arbalistarius*; cf. OEB 234-235.
	THAT IS, WHAT THE BISHOP ... HAD. Interlined in LDB as an explanatory gloss; *habeb(er)e* is in error for *habuisse*.

THEN 4½ PLOUGHS. In the MS *7* has been erased after *T(u)nc*.

DYNECHAIE. This form is corrupt. J.M.D. suggests that it may be a misreading of *Dyrechaie*, standing for ODan *Thyri* with the byname *kai* 'left-handed'.

SWARTRIK. LDB *suartric(us)*, from ON **Svartríkr*; PNDB 380.

6,193 SMERT. Of uncertain origin according to PNDB 367; but perhaps LDB *Smert* is for *Siu* from OE *Sigefrith* (cf. 7,77 and PNDB 360).

WYNSTAN. LDB *Pinstan*, with *P-* in error for the Anglo-Saxon letter wynn; PNDB 429.

6,194 STUBHARD. LDB *Stubart*. The second element is OE *-heard* or OG *-hard*; the first elem may be OE *stubb*, 'stub, stump' but is not certain, see PNDB 376-377.

[AND]. LDB omits *7*.

6,195 MELLIS. The abbreviation mark in LDB, on the first *l*, is otiose.

[MAN]. LDB omits *h(om)o*.

FULCARD. The name is OG, PNDB 256.

6,196 YAXLEY. *Lacheleia* in Farley is in error for *I-* in the MS. Cf. 6,229 note.

6,199 IN THORNHAM PARVA. LDB *In paruo thornha(m)*.

6,200 THORNHAM MAGNA. LDB *Marthorham, Martonham* (6,214); *Mar-* represents OE *mǣr* 'greater', DEPN 467.

6,201 [HOLDS THIS] LDB omits *ten&*.

6,202 ALWARD. LDB *AWart, Alwart*; late OE *Alweard*, PNDB 155-157.

6,203 [HOLDS THIS]. As 6,201 note.

6,205 3S. In LDB *.vi.d(enarios)* has been deleted and *.iii. sol(idos)* interlined, along with the firs line of 6,206 which had previously been omitted.

6,207 FRESSINGFIELD. Geographically this is in Bishop's Hundred, although the previous Hundred rubric is that of Hartismere. It has been mapped in Bishop's Hundred. Cf. following note.

6,208 KNETTISHALL. Elsewhere this is placed in Blackbourn Hundred. Here both the previous and the subsequent Hundred rubric relates to Hartismere Hundred, suggesti that some intervening rubrics have been omitted from LDB. Cf. preceding note.

6,212 CALDECOTA. Probably identical with *KALDECOTES* 14,136; *CALDECOTA* 14,149; *CALDECOTEN* 31,37; *CALDECOTAN* 31,39; and *CALDECOTA* 41,8. Although the name of a common type, all these entries are assigned to Hartismere Hundred. Unidentified DG 393.

WALTER OF DOL ... FORFEITED. He was exiled in 1075. For the byname, see 4,15 note.

6,213 WULFEVA HAS THE JURISDICTION. LDB *hab&* may be in error for *habuit*, 'had', b Wulfeva was alive in 1075 (see 6,212 and preceding note).

6,214 THORNHAM MAGNA. See 6,200 note.

6,215 BRUNGAR. LDB *brungart*; OE *Brūngār*, PNDB 209.

WALTER OF DOL ... FORFEITED. In LDB *fecit fecit* has been deleted and *.forisfecit*. interlined. See also 6,212 note.

16 SHEEP. In the MS *v* has been erased before *xvi*.

6,216 ALSI NEPHEW OF EARL R(ALPH). Cf. 8,50 for the full name-form. Reference is probably to Earl Ralph the Constable.

RINGWULF. LDB *Ringulf(us)*; OE *Hringwulf*, PNDB 293.

BESI. Possibly from ODan *Bósi*, OSw *Bóse*; PNDB 201.

AUBREY DE VERE. Cf. 35,7-8.

SORCBES. According to PNDB 368, a corrupt form of a name with Scand. *Svart-* as firs element. Perhaps an Anglo-Scandinavian formation **Svart-thiofr* (J.M.D.).

VALUE 12D. In the MS *ual* has been erased above *ual(&)*.

CHIPPING. LDB *Chipinc*; OE *Cypping*, PNDB 221-222.

6,217 TEIT. ON *Teitr*, ODan, OSw *Tet*; PNDB 382.

6,218 IN THORNHAM PARVA. LDB *In paruo thornham*.

14 ACRES. In the MS *xiiij* has been altered from *xiii*.

6,222 9D IN TAX. In the MS there is an erasure before *ix*.

6,223 3 MEN'S PLOUGHS. In the MS the first letter of *ho(minu)m* has been altered (? from *e*)

[THEN] 200 PIGS. LDB omits *t(u)nc*.

6,226 BRICTMER BUBBA. The byname is probably an original OE nickname *Bubba*, denoti someone of a thickset stature, see OEB 296.

6,229 YAXLEY. As 6,196 note.

HAGRIS. Possibly as Scand. byname, **Há-Gríss*, 'the tall *Gríss*'; PNDB 282.

ROBERT'S MOTHER ... FROM THE QUEEN'S HOLDING. Referring to 6,209-229.

6,232	BEDINGFIELD. Here assigned to Hartismere Hundred. but elsewhere in the neighbouring Bishop's Hundred.
6,234	BROMESWELL. In the MS *brumeswella* has been altered from *bui-*.
6,238	GODRIC OF PEYTON. See 27,13.
6,242	EDRIC. LDB *edic* is in error for *edric(i)*.
6,247	14 FREE MEN. These appear to have been divided equally between Morewin and St. Etheldreda's, see IE (163) 'Under him, 7 free men with 20 acres. Meadow, 5 acres. Then 1 plough, now ½. Value 10s.'
6,250	['HUNDESTHOFT']. LDB *hundesthost* in error. The same as *HUNDESTUF* 21,82. The second element is ON *topt*, ODan, late OE *toft*, 'a house-plot'. Lost in Sutton. DG 402. FREE MEN. As 6,138 note.
6,254	SUTTON. LDB *stituna* is in error for *suttuna*.
6,256	[2] ACRES. Farley *viii* in error. In the MS *viii* has been altered to *ii* by erasure. VALUE 4D. The vertical line in Farley after the value is in error for *I* in the MS, being a false start for *In* of the following line.
6,261	FREE MAN. In the MS the first letter of *lib(eru)m* has been altered from *h-*.
6,264	EDRIC OF LAXFIELD. LDB *Edrici* is in error for *Edric(us)*. AND 14. Presumably 14 acres not included in the outlier. [PLOUGH]. LDB omits *car(uca)*. ASSESSMENT OF THE (PLACE) ABOVE. That is, of Dennington. FREEWOMAN. Translating LDB *soc(he)femina*. IEVA. Standing for OE *Gi(e)fu*, *Geofu*; PNDB 260. THORKELL. His land formed part of the same Holding as that of Osferth in 6,106 note.
6,265 6,266- 267	WILLIAM ALSO HOLDS. Apparently in error for Walter (of Caen), cf. 6,264. IN LORDSHIP. LDB *in d(omi)niu(m)* is in error for *in d(omi)nio*. See also 6,267 note.
6,267	HACHESTON. LDB *h& cetuna*, that is *h(et)cetuna*, is in error for *heccetuna*, from OE *Haecci* and *tūn*, see DEPN 209. AND 28. That is, 28 acres in some way separate from the 60 there. HE HOLDS (THIS) IN LORDSHIP. In the MS the words *& ten(et) i(n) d(omi)niu(m)* were added slightly later. See also 6,266-267 note.
6,270	SAME ASSESSMENT. Of Dennington, as in 6,269.
6,271	ALWAYS 1 PLOUGH. VALUE ... HUNA. This is an addition in the right-hand margin, much closer in to the main text than is shown in Farley. VALUE 7 ... LDB omits the unit of currency, probably shillings. TIGIER HOLDS IT. In LDB *q(uo)d ten& tiger(us)* was interlined at the same time as the addition was made in the right-hand margin. WOODBROWN. LDB *Vdebrun*, OE *Wudu-Brūn*, possibly 'Brūn who lives in the wood'; PNDB 417. THIS ENTRY. Cf. IE (151). 'In KENTON 1 free man, Edric, under the patronage of St. E(theldreda's); 30 acres. Value 5s. R(obert) Malet holds him, and R(oger) Bigot.' Also IEAL (183), in the Holding of Hamo of Saint-Clair, 'but Robert Malet had a half of the man'. Hamo, from Saint-Clair-sur-Elle (Manche), Loyd 88, is not named in LDB or IE, but occurs in IEAL.
6,274	CLACHESTORP. Also at 6,284. In Loes Hundred. Unidentified, DG 394.
6,276	[VALUE]. LDB omits *valuit*.
6,277	POSSEFELDA. Unidentified, DG 408.
6,278	BRODERTUNA. See 3,41 note.
6,283	THEN AND NOW 1 PLOUGH. The last line of folio 326b is inset in the MS, as shown by Farley, because of an irregularly shaped leaf.
6,284	CLACHESTORP. See 6,274 note. WALTER DE RISBOU. See 6,28 note.
6,287	IN WIDTH. In the MS *in longo* has been corrected to *in lato*.
6,288	KELETUNA. The same as CHELETUNA, CHILETUNA, see 6,41-42 note.
6,291	AND 17. That is, 17 acres.
6,295	HUNDRED [OF]. LDB omits *de*. THICCHEBROM. Unidentified, DG 412. Cf. VCH 466, n.78 for a later reference.
6,297	ICHEBURNA. Unidentified, DG 402.
6,301	WALTER OF CAEN. In the MS *Galter(us)*, altered from *W-*. 3 SMALLHOLDERS. MEADOW, 4 ACRES. In the MS there is an erasure between *bor(darii)* and *.iiii.*.

6,303   DENNINGTON. LDB *Binneuetuna(m)* is in error for *Dinueue-*.
           [FURLONGS]. LDB omits *q(ua)r(entinas)*.

6,304   17 SMALLHOLDERS. In the MS *xvii* has been written over an erasure.

6,305-   EDRIC. Of Laxfield (cf. 6,305). Predecessor of Robert (and William) Malet in many

306   entries in Suffolk and Norfolk. He was also known as Edric *Cecus*, 'the blind' (=Edric
           Blind, Wiltshire 67,53), see FD xc-xcii and no. 168.

6,305   VILLAGERS, LATER 8, NOW 6. In the MS *m(odo)* has been repeated in error; Farley
           prints it only once. Also, *vi* has been altered from *iji*.
           THEN 4 PLOUGHS. *semp(er)*, 'always' deleted in LDB before *.iiii*.
           LOERNIC. The LDB form is corrupt. It may perhaps be for *Leouric* FROM OE *Lēofric*, or
           from OG *Wenric*, Förstemann 1616 (J.M.D.).

6,306   IN LENGTH. In the MS *in lo(n)g(o)* has been altered from *in la-*.
           [£]10. LDB *sol(idis)* is in error for *lib(ris)*, see above.
           EDRIC HAS FULL JURISDICTION. LDB *hab&* may be in error for *habuit*, 'had', but
           Edric does appear to have been alive in 1086, see 6,305-306 note.

6,308   WINGFIELD. Cf. 21,45. The spelling *Wineb(er)ga* appears to represent an alternative
           second element for the place called *Wighefelda* in 19,8.
           WALTER HOLDS. In the MS *ten&* has been altered from *tet-*.

6,309   4 SMALLHOLDERS. In LDB *.7.i.ser(uus)*, 'and 1 slave', has been deleted after *bor(darii)*.

6,310   IT HAS ... IN TAX. The measurements and tax probably refer to Horham (6,309) in
           whose assessment Wilby was counted.

6,311   10 PLOUGHS. LDB repeats *7* in error before *x*.

6,313   [MEN'S] PLOUGHS. LDB omits *ho(minu)m*.

6,314   VALUE 10S. This may be the value of the 1 free man held by Walter, but may also be
           otiose here.

6,318   (WALTER SON OF GRIP) ALSO (HOLDS). In LDB *ide(m)* is interlined.

6,319   1 FREE MAN. In the MS *lib(er)* has been altered to *lib(eru)m*.
           VALUE 22S 8D. In the MS there is an erasure of three or four words after this value. The
           first two words erased may be *Rainald(us) pr(esbiter)*.Cf. perhaps the priest mentioned in
           6,319 as being in sub-patronage.

7   ROGER BIGOT. The ancestor of the Bigots, Earls of Norfolk. He came from a family
           with only a small amount of land in Calvados, Loyd 14-15. He was Sheriff of Suffolk and
           Norfolk in 1086, see 1,1-60;122 etc. His byname was OFr and meant 'bigot', OEB 342. He
           may possibly be the same as Bigot of Loges, see 4,13 note.

7,1   STANHARD. See following note. Cf. Stanhard son of Aethelwy (*72*).
           AETHELWY OF THETFORD. LDB *Ailwius*, for OE *AEthelwīg*. He was the father of
           Stanhard, the 1086 undertenant, and may have been Sheriff of Norfolk before 1066, see
           PNDB 189-190 n. 11.
           WILD MARES. As 1,115 note.
           160 SHEEP. In the MS there is an erasure (probably of *p*) after *.c.lx.*

7,2   [HAD]. LDB *hab&* is in error for *habuit*.
           ... OF HOUDAIN. Probably Houdain (Pas-de-Calais), but cf. also Houdeng-au-Bosc
           (Seine-Inf.) and Houdain (Nord); OEB 92-93. Cf. Hugh of Houdain (7,60 etc.).

7,3   (VALUE OF) THE OTHER MANOR. That is, value now of the manor formerly held by
           Wulfeva.

7,4   AITARD. The Rom. form of OG *Eidhart*, see Forssner 17-18. Note that the name given as
           Aethelhard in Cheshire 9,17 should also read Aitard.
           AITARD ALSO HOLDS HIM. LDB *qua(m)* is in error for *que(m)*. In the MS *ten&* has been
           altered from *p(er)tin&*.
           AITARD ALSO HOLDS HIM. LDB *qua(m)* for *que(m)* as above.
           AFTER THE KING ARRIVED. After 1066. Aelmer was deposed in 1070.

7,6   ... PLOUGH AND A HALF. LDB omits the numeral.

7,7   PADDA. A byname from late OE *pad(d)e* or ON *padda*, 'toad, frog'; PNDB 343.

7,9   G(ODRIC) THE STEWARD. Cf. 13,3.

7,10   [MEN'S] PLOUGHS. LDB *boū* is in error for *hoū ho(min)u(m)*.

7,11   *WARABETUNA*. See 3,15 note *sub WRABETUNA*.
           ROGER BIGOT. In the MS *Rog(ero)* has been altered from *Rob(erto)*.
           [SLAVE]. LDB *acr̄* is in error for *ser*.

7,12   COVEHITHE. Formerly 'North Hales'.

7,15   WILLIAM MALET ... DIED. Probably 1069 x 1071.
           LEDMAN. Perhaps more likely OE *Lēodmann* than OG *Liudman*; PNDB 309.
           STANHARD. LDB *Stauhart* is in error for *Stanhart*.

80 ACRES AND 16. 16 acres.

1 FREE MAN, AELFRIC. In the MS *lib(er)u(m) h(omine)m* has been altered from *lib(er) h(om)o*.

OF THIS FREE (MAN). In the MS *lib(er)i* has been altered from *lib(er)*.

7,76   [BELONGS]. LDB omits a verb such as *pertinet*.

15 FREE MEN. In the MS *xv* is written over an erasure and is followed by *iii* erased.

7,77   FREE MEN. *lib(er)i ho(min)es* is written in the left-hand margin in LDB, perhaps not strictly contemporary with the text. Cf. 7,23;55;96;136 notes.

SHEARMAN. LDB *Sereman(us)*, a byname from OE **scēarmann*, 'one who shears woollen cloth'; PNDB 355-356.

SWEETMAN. LDB *Suetman(us)* from OE **Swētmann*; PNDB 381-382.

AELFRIC STICKSTAG. LDB *stikestac* is probably an imperative nickname 'stick/stab stag'; OEB 387-388.

SIFRITH. LDB *Siuert(us)* from OE *Sigefrith*; PNDB 360.

13 FREE MEN. 14 men are named as being 'Roger Bigot's free men', 13 were probably taken over from Norman but one of them, Aelfric Stickstag, is stated below to have been half Edric's.

7,78   PASTURE COMMON TO ... THE HUNDRED. At present unidentified.

7,79   'MAISTANA'. Lost in Trimley, DG 405.

ALWAYS 3 PLOUGHS. In the MS *acr̊* was written first in error for *car̊* and the *a-* was then erased to leave *cr̊*. Farley shows the erasure by means of a dot. Cf. 7,138 note.

MAN OF EDRIC. LDB *Edric(us)* is in error for *Edrici*.

7,80   LUNDEN. The origin of the name is obscure according to PNDB 322. Probably an OScand name, ON **Lundinn*, ODan *Lunden* (J.M.D.). Cf. Lundi, Essex B3a.

THEY BELONG TO WALTON. Either the smallholders or the free men.

7,82   MOREGRIM. Possibly an Anglo-Scandinavian byname *Mōr-Grímr*, 'Grímr on the moor'; PNDB 328-329.

7,83   'TURSTANESTUNA'. In Colneis Hundred. Lost in Trimley, DG 414.

7,84   OTTI. ODan *Otti*, OSw *Otte*; PNDB 342.

7,85   'PLUMGEARD'. LDB *p̄lu(m)geard*, with an otiose abbreviation mark over the *p*. The same place as at 21,51. Lost in Trimley, DG 408 (s.n. *Plugeard*). For a later reference, see VCH 477 n.94.

BEFORE 1066, 2 PLOUGHS. Unusually, LDB here uses *t.r.e.* instead of *T(u)nc*.

7,86   RALPH OF TOURLEVILLE'S. LDB *Radulfi(us)* is in error for *Radulfi*. For the byname, see 7,73 note.

7,88   'STRUUSTUNA'. See 6,110 note.

7,89   'GUTHESTUNA'. Lost in Kirton, DG 400.

7,92   SPRETMAN. LDB *Spretman(us)* from OE **Sprēotmann*; PNDB 370.

7,93   'LEOFSTANESTUNA'. Also at 7,106;111. Lost in Trimley, DG 404. Cf. Leofstan, one of the free men here, after whom the place might have been named. For a later reference, see VCH 478 n.96.

STANFLED. LDB *Stanfleda* from OE **Stānflǣd* (feminine); PNDB 371.

7,96   'ALSTON'. See 2,19 note.

ALL OF THESE ... FREE MEN OF ROGER BIGOT. Those in 7,77;79-96; cf. the heading before 7,77.

7,98   OF THIS SWETING. In the MS *sueting* has been corrected from *suetingu(m)*.

7,99   HERMAN. LDB *Heremann(us)* from OG *Her(e)man*; PNDB 290, Forssner 149-150.

7,101   'ALSTON'. See 2,19 note.

7,102   PATRONAGE OF ALNOTH. LDB *Alnot(us)* is in error for *Alnoti*.

7,103   'STRUESTUNA'. See 6,110 note.

THORILD. LDB *Durilda* from ON *Thórhildr*, ODan *Thorild*; PNDB 393.

7,104   KETEL UVA. LDB *Keteluua* from ON *Ketill*, ODan *Ketil*, OSw *Kaetil* with the addition of a byname, possibly ON *úfi*, 'ruffled, rough, hostile'; PNDB 304-305.

7,105   'STRUESTUNA'. See 6,110 note.

HUSTEMAN. LDB *Husteman(us)*, possibly a form for OE **Ūhtmann*; PNDB 297.

7,106   'LEOFSTANESTUNA'. See 7,93 note.

BURGRIC. The LDB form *Burric(us)* may have been due to misreading of the combination
of letters *-rgr-* in insular minuscule script as *-rr-*.

7,109   LANGFER. The same name as *Langfere* at 32,2 below and *Lancfer* Huntingdonshire 19,13, *Langfer* Northamptonshire 3,1. Probably a byname from OE *lang-fēre, lang-fǣre*, 'long-lasting, enduring, old' (J.M.D.).

SEGAR. LDB *Fegar(us)* with a misreading of insular minuscule *s* as *f* (>F); OE **Sǣgār*, PNDB 352-353.

7,110 'MYCELEGATA'. See 6,111 note.

REGIFER. LDB *Regifer(us)*, possibly OG *Ragifred* or *Re(g)infrid*; PNDB 348.

7,111 'LEOFSTANESTUNA'. See 7,93 note.

THEODORIC. LDB *Teoddrrc(us)* is corrupt. OG *Theodric*; PNDB 383-384, Forssner 231-233. Cf. 8,56 note.

7,112 HILDFERTH. LDB *Hildeuert* from OE *Hildefrith*; PNDB 291.

UNDER THE PATRONAGE OF NORMAN. Perhaps referring only to Goda and Hildferth, since Derstan is treated separately. However, Derstan may have been under the sub-patronage of Wulfmer.

7,113 'ALSTON'. See 2,19 note.

7,114 EDRIC. Of Laxfield, cf. 6,128.

7,115 WILLIAM OF BOSC. LDB *de silua* here but below *de Nemore* (7,134.39,11), *de Nomore* (39,5). For the vernacular form *de Bosc* see Essex 37,17 and OEB 73-74. The place is unidentified, being a common name in Normandy. Cf. William *de More* in 16,1 and note. 10 FREE MEN. Only 9 are named in LDB.

7,117 WHITE. LDB *Whita* from OE *Hwīta*; PNDB 297.

7,118 *KULUERTESTUNA*. See 6,110 note.

7,119 ALSO ... 1 FREE MAN. In the MS *i* has been altered from *ii*. WHOLE OF THIS. 7,118-119.

7,120 'OXELANDA'. Lost in Trimley, DG 407.

7,121 14 FREE MEN. 15 are named.
[73] ACRES. Farley prints *LXIII* in error for *LXXIII* of the MS. WHOLE OF THIS. 7,120-121.
THIS LAND ASSESSED. LDB *pretiata* is in error for *pretiata(m)*.

7,122 WHOLE OF THIS LAND. This probably refers to the land and men formerly held by Norman (7,77;79-122).
EXCEPT ... WALTON. 7,76.

7,123 THORVOLD. LDB *Turnold(us)* is a scribal misreading for *Turuold(us)* from ON *Thorvaldr*, PNDB 397.

7,125 THURSTAN SON OF GUY. The spelling of the fore-name, *Sturstan(us)*, is corrupt in LDB. In the MS there is an erasure of two letters in the patronym between *Wid* and *donis*.

7,133 BRICTMER. LDB *Brihtmar(us)* is in error for *Brictmaru(m)*.
30 ACRES. IEAL (188), 35.
5 FREE MEN ... 16 ACRES. IE (152) and IEAL (183), '5 free men under him; 16 acres'.
EARL R(ALPH) ... W(ILLIAM) MALET ... POSSESSION. In the MS the text is arranged around a hole in the parchment which also affects 7,139 on the other side of the leaf. Earl Ralph Wader is meant here.
THURSTAN HOLDS ... FROM ROGER BIGOT. IE (152), 'Roger Bigot holds these (free men) under the Bishop of Bayeux'. Cf. IEAL (183) in the Holding of Hamo of Saint Clair (see 6,271 note).

7,136 FREE MEN OF ROGER BIGOT. The words *lib(er)i ho(min)es* are repeated in the right-hand margin. They are perhaps not strictly contemporary with the main text, cf. 7,23 note.
2 (UNDER THAT OF) THE ABBOT OF ELY. IE (151) adds 'Value 5s.'

7,137 EDHILD. LDB *Edilt* from OE *Ēadhild* (feminine); PNDB 232.

7,138 1½ [PLOUGHS]. LDB *acṙ* is in error for *car̃*, cf. 7,79 note.

7,139 This section is affected by the hole in the parchment mentioned in 7,133 note.

7,143 UNDER ... PATRONAGE OF NORMAN. LDB *normann(us)* is in error for *normanno*.
LEOFRIC SNIPE. The byname is probably from the OE or ON antecedent of ME *snipe*, perhaps describing a thin man, see OEB 366.

7,144 MALET. Here Robert Malet is meant.

7,145 5½S. That is 5s 6d.

7,147 SWEFLING. LDB *suest lingua* is in error for *sueftlinga*.

7,148 3 WERE. LDB *suere* in error for *fuere*.
GODRIC. LDB *Gadric* is in error for *Godric*.

7,151. IN (GREAT) GLEMHAM ... JURISDICTION. In the MS there is an erasure of text between lines 4 and 5 of folio 345b.

Folio 345b, line 6. The Hundred-rubric shown by Farley after 7,151 also occurs thus in the MS. It is not part of Chapter 7 however, being a false start for the first Hundred-rubric in Chapter 8.

8	ROGER OF POITOU. A younger son of Roger of Montgomery, Earl of Shrewsbury. He appears to have forfeited his lands in Lancashire, Derbyshire, Nottinghamshire, Norfolk and Suffolk (see 8,46) by 1086, possibly for supporting King William's rebellious son Robert of Normandy.
8,1	BEFORE THIS ENTRY. IE (149) has an additional entry, 'In PRESTON Roger of Poitou holds a half free man, Leofsi, under the patronage of St. Etheldreda's; 12 acres'. Cf. also IEAL (187), '1 free man; 12 acres'.
	80 ACRES. IEAL, 70.
	THEN 2 PLOUGHS IN LORDSHIP, NOW 3. IE, 'always 2 ploughs in lordship'. Cf. also IEAL.
	THEN 2 MEN'S PLOUGHS, NOW 1. IEAL, '2 belonging to the men'.
	COBS, NOW 1. In the MS *i* has been altered from *ii*.
8,2	THEN 1 PLOUGH, NOW NONE. IE (149), '1 plough in lordship'. IEAL (187), '2 ploughs in lordship'.
8,4	LICTWIN. LDB *Lihtwin(us)* from OE *Lēohtwine; PNDB 319.
	68 ACRES. IE (149) and IEAL (187), 80.
	50 ACRES. IEAL (in error), 1.
	THEN 3 PLOUGHS, NOW 2. IEAL, '3 ploughs'.
8,5	5 FREE MEN. IE (149) and IEAL (187), 4.
	21 [ACRES]. LDB has *car* in error for *acr*, cf. 7,79;138 notes. IE (149) and IEAL (187), '21 acres'.
8,6	20 ACRES. IE (149) and IEAL (187), 30. IE adds, 'In the same village the men of Roger of Poitou annexed 8 acres of the lordship. These belong to Kingston.' Cf. also IEAL.
	1½ ACRES. Repeated in error in LDB at the turning of the page.
	AETHELRIC OF BURGH. Probably named from Burgh in Carlford Hundred, cf. 32,28.
	2 FREE MEN, 1 UNDER ... ST. ETHELDREDA'S. Cf. IE, '1 free man under the patronage of St. Ethedreda's; 30 acres. 3 smallholders. 1 plough. Meadow, 1 acre. Value 5s.' Cf. also IEAL.
	1 FREE MAN OF ST. ETHELDREDA'S. Named in IE as Brictnoth.
8,7	MEADOW, 4 ACRES. Misplaced in LDB amongst the ploughs.
	ROGER SON OF ARNOLD HOLDS (THIS). Added slightly later than the main text in LDB. Cf. Roger son of Arnulf in 8,8.
8,8	ALWIN, A FREE MAN. IE (150) calls him a 'Freeman'.
	[WITH] 16 ACRES. LDB *dxvi* is in error, probably for *de xvi*. IEAL (187), 18.
	1 [FREE MAN] ... BROWN. LDB omits *lib(er)*. IE, '1 free man, Brown, under the patronage of St. Etheldreda's; 6 acres. Value 12d.' Cf. also IEAL.
	1 FREE MAN GIVEN TO ST. ETHELDREDA'S. 'Given', *dat(us)* is an alternative expression for 'under the patronage of', *commendatus*. See IE, '1 free man, Grimbold, under the patronage of St. Etheldreda's'. Cf. also IEAL, '2 free men, one with 16 acres, the other 8'.
	9½ ACRES. IE, 9. In the MS of LDB 7 *di(midia)* is squeezed in between *.ix. ac(re).* and the *dim(idia)* belonging to 'Meadow, ½ acre', probably having at first been omitted.
	ROGER SON OF ARNULF. Cf. Roger son of Arnold in 8,7.
8,9	8S. IE (150) adds, 'and a half'. That is, 6d.
	1 FREE MAN AND A HALF. In the MS 7 has been squeezed in between *.i.* and *dim(idius)*.
	1 FREE MAN ... 50 ACRES. IE names him as Edwy.
	VALUE ... NOW 11[S]. IE, 'Value 10s'.
8,10	MEADOW, 1 ACRE. IEAL (187), 2.
	VALUE ... NOW 7 [S]. IE (150), '2s' or '3s' in the different MSS.
8,11	PLOUGHS ... POSSIBLE. LDB omits the numeral.
8,12	1 UNDER ... ST. ETHELDREDA'S. IE (150) names him as Aelfric and assigns him '8 acres. Value 8d'. Cf. also IEAL (187).
	1 AND A HALF ... GRIMWULF. Perhaps they were under his sub-patronage.
8,14	GRENEWIC. Unidentified, DG 399.
8,15	BURNT ALBERT HOLDS THIS. 8,14-15. LDB *Alb(er)t(us) cremat(us)*, the byname being from Latin *cremare* 'to burn'.
8,16	HUNEBOT. See 3,95 note.
8,17	ROGER SON OF ARNOLD. LDB *AErloldi* stands for *AErnoldi* but has been the subject of AN dissimilation of *l* and *n*.
	VALUE THEN 8S; NOW THE SAME. IE (151), 'Value 10s'.
	1 FREE MAN OF ST. ETHELDREDA'S. IE names him as Godric.
	26 ACRES. IEAL (187), 27.

8,19	FREE [MEN]. LDB omits *homines*.
8,20	1 CARUCATE OF LAND AND 40 ACRES. IEAL (187) omits the carucate.
8,21	MEN'S [PLOUGH]. LDB omits *car(uca)*.
	1 FREE WOMAN. IE (152) and IEAL (182) adds 'under him, under the patronage of St. Etheldreda's'.
8,22	IN MONDEWDEN. IE (152) and IEAL (188) suggests that this entry relates to Kettleburgh.
	BEFORE 1066 14 FREE MEN AND A HALF, NOW 10. IE and IEAL 'there are 14 free men'.
	THEN 4 PLOUGHS, NOW 2. IEAL, '4 ploughs'.
	HUMPHREY THE CHAMBERLAIN. The byname is Latin *ca(m)barari(us)*.
	ERTALD. From the Rom. form *Hertald* of OG *Hardolt*, Forssner 143-144.
8,23	1 FREE MAN. IE (152) names him as Brictwold and adds, 'Edric; 16 acres. Value 30d.' Edric is credited with 15 acres in MSS B, C of IE; and with 20 acres in IEAL (188). IE places both these free men under Kettleburgh.
8,25	32 ACRES. In IE (152) and IEAL (188) the 4 free men are credited with 8 acres.
8,29	*CATESFELLA*. Unidentified, DG 394.
8,30	THRANDESTON. Elsewhere in Hartismere Hundred. It is possible that the rubric before 8,31 has been placed one entry too late.
8,32	LATER ..., NOW. Either a numeral or *7* has been omitted from LDB.
8,33	EARL ALGAR. Of East Anglia 1051-52, 1053-57; of Mercia 1057-62. He was probably dead by 1066, see Harmer, *ASWrits* 546-547. For his wife Aelfeva, mother of Earl Morcar, see 1,97-99 note.
	2 PLOUGHS IN LORDSHIP. In the MS there is an erasure after *car(uce)*.
8,35	VALUE THEN £6; NOW [£]4. In the MS *h(om)o* has been erased after *lib̄*. The scribe at first misconstrued *lib̄* as *lib(er)* 'free' rather than *lib(ras)* 'pounds'.
	NORMAN SON OF TANCRED. LDB *tauredi* is in error for *tanredi*. The patronym is OG *Thancrad, Tancrad* in the Norman form *Tancred*; Forssner 227-228.
	RICHARD. Son of Count Gilbert, see 25.
	THE 6 FORFEITURES. Certain profits of justice which were usually reserved to the King, but which were sometimes granted as a special privilege.
8,37	SELL. LDB *uend(er)ae* is in error for *uend(er)e*.
8,40	THEN ½ PLOUGH. LDB *T(un)c 7 dim(idia) car(uca)*; either *7* is otiose, or *post*, 'later' has been omitted.
8,45	OF THESE. LDB *histis* is in error for *istis*.
8,46	WHEN R(OGER) LEFT (IT). When Roger of Poitou forfeited, see *8* note.
	NORMAN ... CAVENDISH. Cf. 43,2.
	JURISDICTION OF WITHGAR. *saca* here stands as an alternative to *soca*; cf. Norfolk, Technical Terms.
8,47	RICHARD. As 8,35 note.
8,49	LEOFWIN CROC. He was also one of Roger of Poitou's predecessors in Essex (46,2). The byname is probably ON *krókr*, 'hook'; OEB 308. See also DBS, s.n. *Crook*. LDB *Leswin(us)* is in error for *Lefwin(us)*, due to confusion between *s* and *f* in insular minuscule script.
8,50	ALSI NEPHEW OF EARL RALPH. Probably Earl Ralph the Constable (see 1,101 note).
8,51	A DELIVERER. Anyone who had royal authority to transfer possession.
	GERALD. Perhaps Raymond Gerald, cf. 8,55.
8,55	WILLIAM OF WARENNE ... TUNSTALL. See 26,6.
	CHURCH, WITH 5 ACRES. *iiii* deleted in LDB, *v* interlined.
8,56	THEODORIC. LDB *Tednc(us)* is in error for *Tedric(us)*. Cf. 7,111 note.
	GODMAN. Cf. IE (144), '1 free man of St. Etheldreda's, Godman, with full jurisdiction and patronage, with 6 acres'.
8,59	ONE OF THESE. IE (144) names him as Algar.
	HERVEY OF BOURGES. Cf. 67,2.
	FINN, RICHARD'S PREDECESSOR. Finn the Dane, predecessor of Richard son of Count Gilbert (25). His widow Wulfeva was a landholder in Essex (84).
8,62	*LANGHEDENA*. See 1,68 note.
8,63	C(OUNT) G(ILBERT). Farley prints *C...* with a suprascript *G*. There is no erasure in the MS, which reads *C.G.* with another *G* suprascript. The *G* on the line was altered from *a*, rather unclearly, and the suprascript *G* was added to clarify the reading.
8,64	*LANGEDANA*. See 1,68 note.
	GINNI. Farley *Ghim(us)* is in error for *Ghini(us)* of the MS. From ODan *Ginni*, PNDB 261.

8,66	60 ACRES. IEAL (187), 40.
	GOSBERT. From OG *Gausbert*, etc.; Forssner 124.
8,68	ABBOT. Of Ely, see IE (146).
8,77	CODDENHAM. See 1,74 note.
8,81	*NORDBERIA*. Unidentified, DG 407.
	IN THE SAME ... Cf. IE (148), '50 free men who belong to Sudbourne, with 290½ acres. From them, the Abbot had full jurisdiction and patronage before 1066. 2 of these, Aelfric and Edwin, could not sell or grant their land'. Cf. also IEAL (187), which associates the men with Barham.
	UNDER THE PATRONAGE. LDB repeats *& c(om)m(en)datione* in error.
9	WILLIAM OF ÉCOUIS. From Écouis (Eure), Loyd 39-40, OEB 114.
9,1	BRUNARD. The name is OG; Förstemann 340.
9,2	HUARD OF VERNON. From Vernon (Eure), Loyd 110, OEB 119. The fore-name is an OFr form of OG *Hugihard*, Forssner 154-155.
	(MARKET) WESTON. LDB omits the abbreviation mark from above the final letter of *Westuna*, which should be in the accusative case.
	10 FREEMEN. In the MS *soc* has been altered from *soci*.
9,3	ROBERT OF VAUX. Cf. 7,24.
9,4	5 ... 'acres' has perhaps been omitted from LDB here.
	THIS ENTRY appears to have been written on a different occasion to 9,1-3.
10	HERMER OF FERRERS. From Ferrières-St.-Hilaire (Eure), OEB 88. The fore-name is OG *Her(e)mar*, Forssner 151.
10,1	[MEN'S]. LDB omits *ho(minu)m*.
11	RALPH OF BEAUFOUR. From Beaufour (Calvados), OEB 71.
11,2	'THURSTANESTUNA'. See 6,153 note.
11,4	RICHARD OF SAINT-CLAIR. Perhaps from Saint-Clair (La Manche), but cf. also Saint-Clair-sur-l'Elle (La Manche), Saint-Clair-sur-les-Monts (Seine-Inf.) and Saint-Clair-D'Arcy (Eure); Saint-Clair (Seine-et-Oise) is less likely. See OEB 112-113.
	MODGEVA. LDB *Modgeua* from OE *Mōdgifu*; PNDB 328.
	[ACRES]. LDB omits *acr(e)*.
12	FRODO THE ABBOT'S BROTHER. Brother of Abbot Baldwin of St. Edmund's (14,26 note). He also held land in Essex (56) where, however, in the Index of Persons he is wrongly described as brother of the Abbot of Ely. His fore-name is OG, Forssner 96.
12,1	MEADOW, 4 ACRES. In the MS *iiij* has been altered from *iii*.
12,2	6 FREE MEN. IE (142), 7.
	PLOUGHS, NOW 1. IE suggests that there still 3.
12,3	VALUE. LDB omits *ual(uit)*.
12,5	SIWARD OF MALDON. The predecessor of Ranulf Peverel in Essex (34,9 etc.) and Suffolk (34,1-2 below, etc.). Named from his tenure of Maldon in Essex (34,12).
12,6	NOW FRODO HOLDS (IT). In the MS there is an erasure after *ten*.
	HORSES. LDB *eq(uus)* is in error for *equi*.
	1½D IN TAX. Expressed in LDB as 'three halfpennies', *.iii. ob(oli)*.
13	GODRIC THE STEWARD. He held lands in Suffolk (1,61-95) and at Great Sampford in Essex (1,30) on the King's behalf. In the heading to the present chapter, *GODRICI* has been altered in the MS from *GODRID*-.
13,2	EDWIN ... CHURCH, 12 ACRES. Edwin bequeathed 4 acres of land to the church at Blyford in the mid-11th century, see Whitelock, *ASWills* no. 33, Sawyer no. 1516, Hart ECEE no. 94.
13,3	OTHULF. LDB *Odulf(us)* from ON *Authúlfr*, ODan *Øthulf*, OSw *Ødhulf*; PNDB 170.
13,4	UUARLE. Unidentified, DG 414. For a later reference, see VCH 491 n. 122.
13,6	IN LORDSHIP. In the MS the words *i(n) d(omi)nio* are written in the margin and may not be strictly contemporary with the main text.

Folio 356b. Most of the remainder of the Suffolk LDB text was written by a different scribe from that in the preceding chapters. His form of both minuscule and capital *e* has a distinctive downward stroke to complete the middle bar/ tongue of the letter. His abbreviated form for *tunc* is *t(un)c* rather than *t(u)nc* as used by the preceding scribe.

14	ST. EDMUND'S. Literally, 'St. Edmund' (see 14,167 note). The Abbey of Bury St. Edmunds, Suffolk. For a list of the food rents due from the Abbey's estates in Suffolk before 1066, see Robertson, *ASCharters* no. 104, Hart ECEE no. 108.
14,1	ALL ... AT FOLD. That is, they are subject to fold-rights (see Technical Terms).
	1 FREE MAN WITH [½] CARUCATE. LDB *ded* stands for *de d(imidia)*, cf. FB i (3). FB ii (24), '60 acres'.

1 SLAVE. FB ii (24), 2.

HE COULD GRANT ... THE LAND. LDB *t(er)re* is in error for *t(er)ram*.

14,2 COULD NOT GRANT OR SELL. The insular abbreviation for *uel* 'or' is used here in LDB.

ANOTHER HOLDS THERE. But LDB may have *ali(us)* here in error for *alii*.

14,3 9 SLAVES. LDB *serr* is in error for *seru(i)*.

6 FREE MEN ... 4 SMALLHOLDERS. Cf. FB ii (24), 'at HAWSTEAD Ralph holds 1½ carucates; 2 smallholders'. For the 30 acres and 4 smallholders which Ralph does not hold, cf. the preceding paragraph in LDB. VALUE ALWAYS 60S. In the MS there is an erasure after *sol(idos)*.

14,5-6 CHEVINGTON and SAXHAM. FB i (4) adds that these were among the manors formerly held by Brictwulf son of Leofmer. After Brictwulf's death King William granted his manors to Abbot Baldwin of St. Edmund's (see 14,26 note) to be granted out in return for military service. Baldwin retained Chevington and Saxham however in the church's lordship, since they were closest to Bury.

14,7 1 LEAGUE IN LENGTH. In the MS there is an erasure after *long*.

14,9 COULD NOT GRANT OR SELL THE LAND. LDB *t(er)rae* is in error for *t(er)ram* or *t(er)ras*.

14,10 ICKWORTH. LDB *KKewortha(m)* is probably a misreading of *Icke-*.

14,11 ALBERT AND FULCHER ... 8 SMALLHOLDERS. FB ii (16) 'Albert holds from St. (Edmund's) 1 carucate; 1 villager, 3 smallholders'. FB ii (17) 'Fulcher holds from St. (Edmund's) 1½ carucates of land; 7 villagers, 5 smallholders'.

FULCHER. Of Mesnières (Seine-Inf.), cf. Loyd 63. On him, see FD lxxxiv and n.4.

GRANT AND SELL THE LAND. LDB *t(er)re* is in error for *t(er)ram* or *t(er)ras*. [PERMISSION]. LDB omits *lic(entia)*.

OTHERS HOLD THERE. In the MS *Alii* has been altered by erasure.

14,12 6 SMALLHOLDERS. FB ii (17), '2 smallholders and a half'.

BETWEEN THEM ALL. In the MS *o(mn)es* has been altered from *ho(min)es*.

14,13 HAWSTEAD. See also 14,3 note.

OTTO. LDB *Odo*. Otto the Goldsmith (senior), see FD cxxxix-cxl and above 1,97-99 not A gift by Otto and his wife of land at Hawstead to St. Edmund's Abbey was confirmed by King Henry I 1102 x 1105, see FD no. 20. This was probably the former land of Otto's which was granted by Abbots Baldwin and Robert for the rebuilding of the Abbey, see F nos. 104, 106.

CLERIC, ALBOLD. Probably the same as Albold the priest who witnessed FD no. 104, relating to Otto's former land. Perhaps identical with Ailbold the priest in 14,39.

AGENET. LDB *Agenetus*. Probably a derivative in *-et*, from either the Scand. pers. n. *Haghni, Hagne* etc.(PNDB 282) or OG *Hagan*. (J.M.D.).

14,14 BROCKLEY and THEOBALD ... Cf. FB ii (18), 'Theobald the cleric holds from St. (Edmund's) 1 carucate of land; 1 villager, 3 smallholders, 3 slaves'.

3 FREEMEN. In the MS *lib(er)os* has been altered from *lib(er)i*.

MEADOW, 5 ACRES. In the MS *v* hs been altered from *xv*.

STILL BELONGED TO. In the MS there is an erasure after *rem*.

14,15 WARIN HAS. In the MS *hAb&* has been altered from *Ab-* (? the beginning of *Abbas*).

SELL THE LAND. LDB *t(er)rae* is in error for *t(er)ram*.

14,16 HENRY HAS FROM THE ABBOT ... 4 SMALLHOLDERS. FB ii (19) 'at REDE and at *UUILMUNDESTUN* Henry holds from St. (Edmund's) ½ carucate of land; 1 smallholder'. Cf. *WIMUNDESTUNA* at 25,18;105.

SELL THE LAND. As 14,15 note.

BERARD HOLDS ... 50 ACRES. FB ii (20), 'at REDE Berard holds from St. (Edmund's carucate of land; 3 smallholders; 1 free (man) with 20 acres'. Berard is OG or OFr, see Forssner 282, addendum.

7 FREE MEN. In the MS *lib(er)os* has been altered from *lib(er)i*.

14,17 WESTLEY. See also 25,27 note.

PETERS HOLDS 1 ... ABBOT. 5 SMALLHOLDERS. FB ii (19), 'At HORRINGER and WESTLEY Peter brother of Burghard holds from St. (Edmund's) 1 carucate of land; 3 smallholders'.

SELL THE LAND. As 14,15 note.

14,18 THEY COULD GRANT. In LDB *pot*, for *pot(uerunt)*, has been altered from *potuit*.

SELL THE LAND. As 14,15 note.

14,19 WANGFORD and WULFWARD. Wulfward of Wangford became the man of King Hen I in 1100 x 1107, see FD no. 26. He appears to have died by November 1120, see FD no. 38.

14,20	ELVEDEN. FB ii (17) states that Wulfward (of Wangford) 'holds'. SELL THE LAND. As 14,15 note.
14,21	FRODO. The Abbot's brother, see *12*. This was one of the manors formerly held by Brictwulf son of Leofmer (see 14,5-6 note) which Abbot Baldwin granted to his brother, see FB i (4-5). 9 FREE MEN. FB ii (23), '9 free (men) and a half'.
14,22	FULCHER HOLDS. FB ii (21), 'At (Great) LIVERMERE and at (Great) SNAREHILL (Norfolk 14,10) Fulcher the Breton holds 1 carucate of land; 3 smallholders'. FREE MEN. In the MS *lib(er)os* has been altered from *lib(er)i*.
14,23	OF THIS LAND. In the MS *t(er)ra* has been altered from *t(er)re*. 37 VILLAGERS. FB ii (5), 17. SMALLHOLDERS, NOW 10. FB, 30. [BEE] HIVES. LDB omits *apium*.
14,24	WINTER MILL. See 6,1 note. 80 AND 18 SHEEP. That is, fourscore and 18. 4 MEN HOLD. Only 3 are named here, but cf. FB ii (21), 'At COCKFIELD Gamilo holds from St. (Edmund's) 9 acres'. BERARD (HOLDS) 3 CARUCATES. FB ii (20, '(Berard) holds 1 carucate of land. 6 smallholders; 12 free (men) with 90 acres; 4 smallholders'. JAMES. LDB *Iames*, a very early occurrence in England of the OFr form of Latin *Iacobus*. Cf. DBS, s.n. *James*. COLEMAN. LDB *Goleman(us)* from OG *Coloman, Colman*; Forssner 55-56. BELONGED TO ST. (EDMUND'S). LDB *ei* is in error for *er(ant)*, cf. 14,27 etc.
14,25	1½ CARUCATES. The symbol in Farley between *&* and *d(imidia)* does not represent anything in the MS and appears to be a typographical error. WINTER MILL. See 6,1 note. [BUT] ST. EDMUND'S. LDB *r̃* (=*r(egis)*, cf. 14,29) is in error for *s(ed)*.
14,26	ARNULF. The name is interlined in LDB but appears to be the Abbey's 1086 tenant, as in 14,27. 3 FREEMEN ... LAND. FB ii (20) adds, '8 free men with 60 acres'.
14,27	ARNULF. In FB ii (20) he 'holds 3 carucates of land; 1 free (man) with 15 acres'.
14,28	FRODO. As 14,21 note. OTHERS HOLD THERE. LDB *ten&* is in error for *tenent*.
14,29	VALUE BEFORE 1066. LDB repeats *reg(is)* in error after *.t.r.e.* 6 [*ORA*]. LDB has *bo͡r* in error for *o͡r*. For the ora, see 1,94 note. If it were here worth 16d, then the value given would equal 96d. Such a value for 50 acres would be roughly proportionate to the 16d for 8 acres in 14,30.
14,30	3 FREEMEN. FB i (5), 4. [BUT]. LDB *7* is in error for *s7* (=*s(ed)*).
14,32	ADELUND. LDB *Aelons*. See 14,36 note. ALWAYS 3 VILLAGERS ... SMALLHOLDERS, NOW 10. Misplaced in LDB, amongst the resources. VALUE ... NOW [£]2½. That is, £2 10s.
14,35	RALPH HOLDS ... SMALLHOLDERS. FB ii (18), Ralph the Fat (*Crassus*) holds ½ carucate of land and 40 acres; 5 smallholders'.
14,36	ADELUND ... 23 ACRES. FB ii (21), 'Adelo holds from St. (Edmund's) 1 carucate of land; 12 villagers, 2 slaves; 11 free (men)with 23 acres'. ADELUND. [LDB here *Aelons* (also in 14,32), but below at 14,58 *Adelelund*' and at 14,98 *Adelund*'] is from OG *Adalland*, Förstemann 174. The FB form is from OG *Adelo*, Förstemann 159, apparently used as an alternative name for the same man (J.M.D.).
14,37	1 FREE MAN ... SMALLHOLDERS. FB ii (18), Ralph the Fat (*Crassus*) 'holds 60 acres; 3 smallholders'. FULL JURISDICTION AND PATRONAGE OVER THEM ALL ... WRITS AND SEAL. These documents have not survived but were no doubt sealed writs of Edward the Confessor, cf. Hart ECEE no. 96. They related to the free men in 14,35-37.
14,38	60 ACRES ...; 60 ACRES ... FB ii (16), '1 carucate of land'. 2 VILLAGERS; 1 VILLAGER. FB, 2. 3 SMALLHOLDERS; 1 SMALLHOLDER. FB, 6.
14,39	AILBOLD THE PRIEST. Perhaps the same as Albold, a cleric, in 14,13. The name-forms, here *Ailboldus* and at 14,13 *Alboldus*, are probably both from OG *Ailbald, Aglebald*, Förstemann 29 (J.M.D.). King Henry I granted the land at Stonham formerly of Ailbold the priest, with service, to St. Edmund's 1100 x 1107, see FD no. 25.

ENGELRIC. Probably the same as Engelric ('the priest' in FB) mentioned in 14,101 as one of the King's barons to whom the Abbot was in pledge. See 14,101 note.

WHEN THE ENGLISH BOUGHT BACK THEIR LANDS. Some Englishmen who survived the Norman Conquest, and who could afford to, appear to have been allowed t buy back some of their lands. Cf. 14,101 and note.

14,42 10 VILLAGERS; 19 SMALLHOLDERS. FB i (9), '9 villagers, 15 smallholders'.

24 FREE MEN ... 80 ACRES. FB, '23 free (men) with 50 acres of land; 12 smallholders; Freeman with 30 acres of land'.

14,44 12 FREE MEN AND 1 FREEMAN ... 30 ACRES. FB i (9), '14 free (men) with ½ carucate of land'.

14,45 4 CARUCATES ... 11 VILLAGERS ... 17 SMALLHOLDERS. FB i (10), '6 carucates of land; 1 villager; 19 smallholders'.

6 PIGS. In the MS *vi* has been altered from *xvi*.

29 FREE MEN. FB, 'Freemen'.

2 CARUCATES OF LAND LESS 12 ACRES. FB, '2 carucates of land'.

14,46 RICKINGHALL (SUPERIOR). Farley prints *Rachingehala* in error for *Richingehala* of the MS. FB i (9) has *Uprichingehale*.

14 FREE MEN ... 80 ACRES. FB, '9 free (men) with 50 acres of land'.

14,47 ST. EDMUND'S. In the MS there is an erasure (of about 3 letters) after *s(an)c(tu)s*.

14,48 THEDWESTRY HUNDRED. In the MS there is an erasure of two-thirds of a line of writing (ending *de s(an)c(t)o eadm(undo)*) before the name of the Hundred.

5 SMALLHOLDERS. FB i (5), 2.

7O FREE MEN. FB, 'Freemen'.

5 CARUCATES. In the MS *ii* has been erased before *v*.

BELONG TO THE FOLD. See 14,1 note.

14,49 PAKENHAM. An estate here had been granted to St. Edmund's by King Edward 1044 x 1047 and had formerly belonged to one Osgot, see Harmer, *ASWrits* no. 14, Sawyer no. 1074, Hart *ECEE* no. 111. This Osgot may perhaps have been identical with the free ma who leased ½ carucate for life from the Abbot, mentioned in this entry in LDB and in F i (5-6).

31 FREE MEN. FB i (5), 'Freemen'.

14,50 10 FREE MEN. FB i (6), 'Freemen'.

14,51 90 FREE MEN. In the MS *LXXXX* has been altered from *LXXX*. FB i (6), 'Freemen'.

14,52 3 FREE MEN. FB i (6), 'Freemen'.

THIS ENTRY. FB ii (20), 'At BRADFIELD Arnulf holds from St. (Edmund's) 1 carucat of land; 6 smallholders; 2 free (men) with 15 acres'.

14,53 PETER. The Steward (*Dapifer*), FB ii (18); he is said to hold '60 acres; 6 smallholders'.

OF THESE CARUCATES. LDB *histis* is in error for *istis*.

2 VILLAGERS (AND) 2 SMALLHOLDERS. FB, '1 villager, 10 smallholders, 1 Freema and a half'. The number of smallholders in FB probably includes those whom Peter held at Culford, see 14,70 and note.

HALL ... IN ANOTHER HUNDRED. Probably at Culford (in Bradmere Hundred), see 14,70.

14,54 RICHARD HOLDS ... ABBOT. FB ii (24) 'Richard the Bald (*Caluus*) holds 1½ carucates 'of land from St. (Edmund's)'.

8 FREE MEN. LDB *lib(er)i* is in error for *lib(er)os*.

VALUE OF THE WHOLE SUB-HOLDING. Translating *medietaƚ om(n)e ual(et)*; *medietaƚ* would appear to stand for *medietat(um)* and to refer to Richard's mesne-tenure. Cf. 14,78 note.

A CHURCH. The church at Thurston was confirmed to one Osward by Abbot Baldwin 1065 x 1098 and had previously been given to Osward's father, Aelfric the priest, by Abbot Leofstan, see FD no. 103.

VALUE ... ALWAYS £1½. That is, £1 10s.

14,55-57 THESE ENTRIES. A large part of the text covered by these entries was added to LDB after the preceding and following entries, but by the same scribe. Part of 14,55 and all of 14,56 are squeezed untidily into the main text-block, while 14,57 is written in the left-hand margin with a transposition sign directing it to its proper place after 14,56.

14,55 HALL ... IN ANOTHER HUNDRED. Woolpit is near the boundary between Thedwestr and Blackbourn Hundreds.

17 VILLAGERS. FB i (6), 18.

... IN LORDSHIP. The number of lordship ploughs seems to have been omitted from LDB.

JURISDICTION. Hart ECEE no. 103 (1042 x 1065) is a lost charter of Edward the Confessor which referred to Woolpit as being *de socagio*.

IN WIDTH. LDB repeats *in* in error.

14,56 1 CARUCATE OF LAND. LDB *.i. car(ucata) in t(er)rae*; the word *in* is otiose and is probably a repetition of the last word of the previous line.

6 SMALLHOLDERS. FB i (6), 11.

14,57 ½ CARUCATE. FB ii (20), '60 acres'.

ON HIM. Translating *sup(er) eu(m)*; that is, 'charge imposed on him'. This seems to be the value of a mesne-tenure here, cf. 14,54;78. A similar sub-value is given in 14,59;62.

14,58 ADELUND ... LAND. FB ii (21), '2 carucates of land; 3 smallholders'.

ADELUND. See 14,36 note.

... STILL BELONGED. Some text is missing from LDB here, giving details of the rights reserved to St. Edmund's.

14,59 RORIC ... ABBOT. FB ii (18) adds, '8 villagers; 4 smallholders; 5 slaves'. Forssner 219 takes the name to be OG *(H)Rodric*; note that the FB form is *Rerius* however.

FALC ... ½ CARUCATE. FB ii (19-20), '60 acres of land; 4 smallholders; a half Freeman with 2 acres of land'. For the name, cf. Forssner 87 s.n. *Falco* and n.1.

[ON] THEM. LDB *sub* seems to be in error for *sup(er)*, cf. 14,57;62 and notes.

54S. VCH 499 is probably incorrect in taking *soĉ* to be an error for *soĉ* from *sochemanni*.

SELL THEIR LANDS. *t(er)ras suas* was added in the margin in LDB, with a line to indicate its correct position in the text.

14,61 IN RATTLESDEN. The *I* of *In* has been omitted from LDB.

[HE HAS]. LDB *h(abe)nt* is in error for *h(abe)t*.

THIS ENTRY. Cf. FB ii (18), 'At RATTLESDEN Peter the Steward (*Dapifer*) holds from St. (Edmund's) 60 acres; 6 smallholders'.

14,62 ON HIM. As 14,57 note.

20 ACRES. FB ii (24), 30.

[VALUE]. LDB omits *ualuit*.

14,63 6 FREE MEN. In the MS *lib(er)os* has been altered from *lib(er)i*.

THIS ENTRY. FB ii (21) adds, 'At AMPTON and TIMWORTH Saer holds from St. (Edmund's) 80 acres; 2 smallholders; 12 Freemen with 12 acres'.

14,64 1 PLOUGH; VALUE 20S. In the MS there is an erasure before *uat*, possibly of *xx*.

AS ALMS. LDB *elemosine* is in error for *elemosina*.

7D IN TAX. In the MS there is an erasure before *.vii.*.

THIS ENTRY. See 14,63 note.

14,65 BEFORE 1066. LDB *.T.r.* is in error for *T.r.e.*

FRODO. As 14,21 note.

14,66 WARIN. LDB *Gaurincus* is from the Rom. form (*Gaurin*) of OG *Warin*; Forssner 246-247.

HOLDS 80 ACRES. FB ii (19), 'holds 1 carucate of land; 2 smallholders'.

14,68 (GREAT) LIVERMERE. Elsewhere placed in Lackford Hundred. The present entry, including 5 carucates, is the largest one however and the place is therefore mapped below in Thedwestry Hundred.

10 FREE MEN WITH 1 CARUCATE; 12 FREE MEN WITH 2 CARUCATES; 1 FREE MAN ... WITH 2 CARUCATES. FB i (6), '23 free men with 3 carucates of land'.

12 FREE MAN. In the MS *lib(er)os* has been altered from *lib(er)i*.

IN THE SAME. LDB *Iead(em)* is in error for *In ead(em)*.

1 FREE MAN. In the MS *lib(er)u(m)* has been altered from *lib(er)*.

WERNO OF POIX. Probably from Poix (Somme), OEB 105. The fore-name (LDB *Guernoni*, dative) is from OG *Werino, Werno*; Forssner 251.

HE GAVE THE LAND BACK. Between 1066 and April 1070 King William I granted the service from Livermere, until then held by Werno, to St. Edmund's, see FD no. 2.

THIS ENTRY. FB ii (22) adds, 'At (Great) LIVERMERE Hubert the Breton holds from St. (Edmund's) 2 carucates of land; 2 villagers; 4 smallholders; 2 slaves. In the same place, Reginald his brother holds 1½ carucates; 3 smallholders; 23 free men with 1½ carucates of land'. Reginald may be identical with Reginald the Breton (*70*).

14,69 WULFWY. Farley prints *Wlfiuus* in error for *Wlfuius* of the MS.

14,70 PETER. The Steward (*Dapifer*), FB ii (18) where the number of smallholders at Culford is not given, although they are probably included in the total for Fornham (St. Genevieve), see 14,53 and note.

[IN LORDSHIP]. LDB omits *in dominio*.

14,71 17D IN TAX. In the MS *xvii* has been altered from *xiiii*.

THIS ENTRY. FB ii (19) adds that Odard 'holds 2 carucates of land; 8 smallholders; 14 free (men) with 60 acres of land'.

14,72	7 FREE MEN. LDB *lib(er)os* is in error for *lib(er)i*.
	THIS ENTRY. FB ii (19) adds that in Stanton Burcard holds '3 free (men) with 31½ acres' and in Bardwell '5 free (men) and a half with 60 acres'.
14,73	[HELD]. LDB *ten&* is in error for *tenuit*.
	ANOTHER HOLDS THERE. As 14,2 note.
14,75	THESE (FREEMEN) ... PATRONAGE AND JURISDICTION. LDB repeats 'patronage in error after 'jurisdiction'.
	WHICH BELONG. LDB *p(er)tin&* (sing.) is in error for *p(er)tinent* (plural).
	OTHERS HOLD. LDB *tenet* is in error for *tenent*.
14,76	CONEY WESTON. This was granted to St. Edmund's 1051 x 1057, see Harmer, *ASWrit* no. 20, Sawyer no. 1080, Hart ECEE no. 115.
	[OF LAND]. LDB omits *terrae*.
	VILLAGERS; NOW AND ALWAYS 3 SMALLHOLDERS. However the ampersand (& might perhaps be an error in LDB for the number of villagers 'now'.
14,77	14 FREE MEN. FB i (7), 'Freemen', *sochemannos* (accusative).
14,78	FULCHER ... ABBOT. FB ii (17), Fulcher holds '80 acres of land and 10; 4 free (men) with 36 acres of land'.
	AS A WHOLE SUB-HOLDING. Translating *de omñe medietaĭ*. Cf. 14,54 and note. The abbreviation-sign above *omne* appears to be otiose.
	PETER OF VALOGNES. See *37* and note.
	30 ACRES. FB ii (24), 'a half free (man) with 30 acres'.
14,79	OF THIS LAND, RORIC ... 1 CARUCATE. FB ii (19), 'At WATTISFIELD and at HEPWORTH he holds 1 carucate of land; 3 smallholders; 3 free (men) with 8 acres of land'.
	OTHERS HAVE [LAND] THERE. Translating *Alii ibi h(abe)nt*.
14,80	FULCHER ... ½ CARUCATE. FB ii (17), he 'holds 60 acres of land; 4 smallholders'.
	ANOTHER HOLDS THERE. As 14,2 note.
14,81-82	BURCARD. Because of the context, LDB *bucardus* is taken to be from OG *Burghard, Burca* (Forssner 53-54), rather than OE *Burgheard* (PNDB 211-212).
14,81	FREE MEN ... 3. FB ii (19), 'Freemen', *sochemannos* (accusative).
	PETER OF VALOGNES ... 3 CARUCATES. Cf. FB ii (23), 'he holds 1 carucate of land; 10 villagers; 4 smallholders'. In LDB *& dim(idia)* has been deleted after *car(ucatis)*.
14,82	BARDWELL. The hyphen in the name-form in Farley represents a horizontal line in the MS correcting *beordewella* from two words to one.
	PETER OF VALOGNES HOLDS 10. FB ii (24), '10 free (men) and a half'.
	34¼D IN TAX. In the MS there is an erasure before the numeral.
	THIS ENTRY. FB ii (18) adds that at Bardwell Fulcher 'holds 60 acres of land; 1 smallholder'. FB ii (19) adds that Burcard 'holds from St. (Edmund's) 3 carucates of land 3 smallholders; 2 slaves'. See also 14,72 note.
14,83	PETER OF VALOGNES ... 4 WITH 80 ACRES. FB ii (23), 'he holds 6 free (men) with 8 acres and 9 acres'.
14,85	FREE [LAND]. LDB omits *terrae*.
	PETER HOLDS 1 CARUCATE. FB ii (23), 'Peter of Valognes holds from St. (Edmund's 1 carucate of land; 2 villagers; 2 free (men) with 70 acres; 9 free (men) with 60 acres'.
14,86	24 FREE MEN. FB i (8), 14.
14,87	7 FREE MEN. FB i (8), 6.
	STILL BELONG. LDB *remanet* (sing.) is in error for *remanent* (plural).
	WALTER HOLDS ... LAND. FB ii (20), 'Walter nephew of Peter the cleric holds from St (Edmund's) 1½ carucates of land; 2 smallholders; 1 free (man) with 3 acres'.
	3 FREE MEN. LDB *lib(er)i* is in error for *lib(er)os*.
14,89	FULCHER HOLDS 80 ACRES. FB ii (17), '1 carucate of land'.
14,90	THIS ENTRY. Cf. FB ii (17), Fulcher 'holds 80 acres of land; 2 smallholders; 8 free (men with 40 acres'.
14,91	2 FREE MEN. LDB *lib(er)os* is in error for *lib(er)i*.
14,92	WITH 3 CARUCATES OF LAND. In the MS there is an erasure after *car(ucatis)*, possibl of *acr̃*.
	STILL BELONG. LDB *reman&* is in error for *remanent*.
	ROBERT BLUNT ... LAND. FB ii (22) 'he holds 1½ carucates of land; 2 smallholders; 10 free (men) with 80 acres; over another 10 (free men) 3 carrying-services; a church with 8 acres; also the jurisdiction of the aforesaid villages (of Walsham le Willows and Great Ashfield)'.

14,93 ODARD ... 17 FREE MEN ... ACRES. FB ii (19), 'Odard holds from St. (Edmund's) 1 carucate of land; 5 smallholders; 13 free (men) with ½ carucate of land'. The fore-name Odard (LDB *Odar(us)*) represents the Rom. form of OG *Authart, Othard*; Forssner 194. ANOTHER HOLDS THERE. As 14,2 note.

14,95 4 SMALLHOLDERS. FB i (8), 3.
[VALUE]. LDB omits *uat̂*.
BURCARD ... 6 FREE MEN ... LAND. FB ii (19), Burcard 'holds 1 carucate of land; 4 smallholders and a half; 4 free (men) with 80 acres of land'. For Burcard, see 14,81-82 note.
6 FREE MEN. LDB has *lib(er)is* in error for *lib(er)os*.

14,96 PETER ... SMALLHOLDERS. FB ii (23), Peter of Valognes 'holds 1 carucate of land; 2 half free (men) with 45 acres; 8 villagers; 3 smallholders'.
FREE MEN. LDB *lib(er)i* is in error for *lib(er)os*.

14,97 PETER. FB ii (24), of Valognes.
60 ACRES OF LAND. FB adds, '1 villager'.

14,98 ADELUND ... LAND. FB ii (21), 'he holds 1 carucate of land; 5 smallholders; 1 free (man) with 1 acre'. For Adelund, see 14,36 note.
FREE MEN. As 14,96 note.
[VALUE]. As 14,95 note.
ANOTHER HOLDS THERE. As 14,2 note.

14,99 FULCHER ... SMALLHOLDERS. FB ii (18), Fulcher 'holds 60 acres of land; 8 smallholders'.

14,100 ROBERT BLUNT. In the MS *RodbErt(us)* has been altered from *Rod bl-*.
5 MEN. FB ii (21), '5 free (men)'.

14,101 9 FREE MEN. In the MS *lib(er)os* has been altered from *lib(er)i*.
1 FREE MAN. LDB *lib(er) h(om)o* is in error for *lib(er)u(m) ho(min)em*.
PUT THIS LAND IN PLEDGE TO. FB i (8), 'bought this land back from'. Cf. 14,39 and note.
BISHOP W(ILLIAM). Of Thetford (*18*).
ENGELRIC. The priest, FB. Probably he of 14,39 and to be identified with the royal official in Essex (1,19;24;27), where he is shown to be identical with the predecessor of Count Eustace, see above 5,3-5 note.
THIS ENTRY. Cf. FB ii (22), Robert Blunt 'holds 1 carucate of land; 7 free (men) and 2 half (free men) with 60 acres; a church with 12 acres.

14,102 [IT HAS]. LDB omits *Habet*.
10D IN TAX. In the MS there is an erasure before the numeral.

14,105 CHIPPENHALL. Given to St. Edmund's by Ulf son of Manni Swart, see 6,109 note.

14,106 FRODO. FB ii (23) adds, 'the Abbot's brother'. See *12* and note.
MENDHAM. This manor was given to Frodo by Abbot Baldwin in exchange for one of the manors formerly held by Brictwulf son of Leofmer (see 14,5-6 note), FB i (4, 10).
ABBOT. Baldwin, FB i (10).
19 ACRES OF LAND. FB i (10), 30.
THIS ENTRY. FB ii (23) combines the details of population and land with those given in another entry for Mendham, in Norfolk (14,19), which was also held by Frodo from Abbot Baldwin.

4,107 [HOLDS]. LDB omits *ten̂*.

4,108 BEFORE 1066. In LDB *reg(is)* is otiose after *TR.e.*
13 SMALLHOLDERS. FB i (9), 14.

4,109 BEFORE 1066. LDB *.t.r.e.r.* with an otiose *r*.
THEN AND NOW, ALWAYS. *t(un)c 7 m(odo)* in LDB is probably intended to be replaced by *se(m)p(er)*, but was not erased.
IN TAX. See 14,110 first note.

4,110 MEADOW, 6 ACRES. The words *de.ĝ.* after *.vi.* belong to the last sentence of 14,109. They were added to the MS later than the writing of the first line of 14,110.
BERARD ... LAND. FB ii (21), 'he holds 1½ carucates of land'.

4,111-14 BEFORE 1066. As 14,109 note.

4,111 NOW 50[S]. In the MS there is an erasure after the numeral.
BERARD ... FREE MEN. FB ii (21), 'he holds 1 carucate of land and 12 acres; 3 smallholders'. The 12 acres may perhaps be included in 14,112 which also relates to Whatfield.

14

IN THE SAME ASSESSMENT. In the MS the words *i(n) eod(em) p(re)tio* were added in th margin.

OTHERS HOLD. LDB *ten&* is in error for *tenent*.

14,112　FERTHING OF ALDHAM. FB i (9), 'Aldham'. The Ferthing (OE *feorthing*, 'a fourth part') represented a sub-division of the Hundred in E. Anglia into quarters, see O. S. Anderson. *The English Hundred-Names*, Lund 1934, xviii and note 5.

THEY HAVE 1½ CARUCATES. In LDB *vi* has been deleted before *h(abe)nt*.

VALUE OF THEIR LAND. Farley prints *uale7* in error for *ual7* of the MS.

BERARD ... 40 ACRES. Cf. note to 14,111 (with regard to Whatfield).

14,113　IN LINDSEY. LDB *n* is in error for *In*.

WHOEVER HOLDS THERE. This phrase is probably misplaced in LDB and should come after the details of tax.

14,114　KETTLEBASTON. Farley prints *bitel-* in error. In the MS the first letter is a *k* altered from *l*. The place-name form is thus *kitelbeornastuna*.

GAMAS ... CARUCATE. FB ii (21), 'At MANTON he holds 1½ carucates of land; 3 villagers; 2 smallholders'. The fore-name is obscure but may represent a scribal error for *Gamar* < Rom. *Guaimar* < OG *Weimar*, cf. Forssner 100.

14,115　BEFORE 1066. *re* in LDB after *.t.r.e.* is otiose.

ARNULF ... 30 ACRES. FB ii (20), 'At BRETTENHAM he holds 20 acres; 3 villagers'.

14,116　... [HOLDS]. LDB omits details of the holder, presumably St. Edmund's.

14,117　IN WALDRINGFIELD QUENEVA HELD. FB i (11), 'At WALDRINGFIELD 1 free (man)'. The fore-name (LDB *Quengeua*) is from OE *Cwengifu*, PNDB 220. She was the mother of Brictmer in 39,7-10.

ABBOT. Baldwin, FB.

14,118　AND A HALF. *& dim* in LDB; this appears otiose, unless it refers to a half free man not under the patronage of St. Edmund's. It does not appear in FB i (11).

14,119　DURAND. The cleric, of St. Edmund's and of Abbot Baldwin's, FB i (11). Cf. also FB ii (24).

FREE MEN. LDB *lib(er)i* is in error for *lib(er)os*.

14,120　... MEN'S PLOUGHS. LDB omits both *car* and the numeral.

HERRINGS. As 1,12 note.

14,121　BISHOP W(ILLIAM). Of Thetford (*18*).

14,122　10 ACRES. FB i (10), 20.

14,123　19 ACRES. FB ii (22), 16.

THIS ENTRY. See 14,151 note.

14,126　14 FREE MEN. FB i (10), 10.

14,129　IN OAKLEY ... HARTISMERE HUNDRED. *In ACLE* appears to have been written in error in LDB before the Hundred rubric, anticipating the following line and necessitatin the use of the preposition *DE*.

1 FREE MAN ... 90 ACRES ... 10 FREE MEN; 30 ACRES. FB i (10), '11 free (men) with carucate of land'.

14,130　5 FREE MEN ... 44½ ACRES. FB i (10), '4 free (men) with 30 acres of land'.

14,131　11 FREE MEN ... 68 ACRES. FB i (10), '6 free (men) with ½ carucate of land'.

ST. EDMUND'S. LDB *s(an)c(tu)s* is in error for *s(an)c(t)i*.

14,132　8 FREE MEN ... 60 ACRES. FB i (10), '6 free (men) with ½ carucate of land'.

14,133　LIKEWISE. That is, in the jurisdiction and under the patronage of the Abbot, as in 14,132.

14,134　6 FREE MEN ... 75 ACRES. See 14,151 note.

14,135　1 VILLAGER. FB i (10), '1 free (man)'.

14,136　*KALDECOTES*. See 6,212 note.

THEY ALL ... DUES. Probably referring to the men in 14,129-136, all in Hartismere Hundred as was Rickinghall (Superior).

14,137-
138　THESE ENTRIES. Cf. FB i (10), 'At OAKLEY and at STUSTON 16 free (men) with 1 carucate of land and 50 acres; 12 smallholders. Jocelyn, a man of Frodo's, holds this from St. Edmund's and Abbot Baldwin'.

14,138　LEOFSIDU. LDB *Leuseda* from OE *Lēofsidu*; PNDB 315 note 3.

4 PIGS. In the MS *iiij* has been altered from *iii*.

14,139　ANSELM. A man of Frodo's, FB i (10). Radfrid, FB ii (17).

ABBOT. Baldwin. FB i (10).

6 SMALLHOLDERS. FB i (10), 5. FB ii (17), 7.

12 FREE MEN AND A HALF; 42 ACRES. FB i (10), '13 free (men) and a half with 41 acres of land'. FB ii (17), '14 Freemen and a half with 45 acres of land'.

19,15	BISHOP STIGAND. Bishop Aelmer's brother, see 18,1 note.
	NOW IT PAYS 10[S] 8D. LDB *reddit* is in error for *redd(it)*.
	NOW IT PAYS 31[S] 4D. LDB *reddidit* is in error for *reddit*.
19,16	(SOUTH) ELMHAM. LDB *Almea(m)* altered to *Almeha(m)*.
	INGVAR. LDB *In Wari* (genitive), where it was apparently mistaken for a place-name. From ODan, OSw *Ingvar*; PNDB 298-299.
	1 COB ... 30 GOATS. Misplaced in LDB, among the ploughs, rather than after the woodland.
	VALUE THEN ... S. LDB omits the numeral.
19,17	WILLIAM OF NOYERS. See 1,107-119 note.
19,18	HAD PATRONAGE. LDB *habuit* is in error for *habuerunt*.
19,19	OTHERI. LDB *Othem(us)* is in error for *Otheri(us)*. From OG *Otheri, Authari*, Förstemann 195 (J.M.D.).
19,21	[OF LOTHINGLAND]. LDB omits the name.
20	BISHOP OF ROCHESTER. Bishop Gundulf, 1077-1108. In the MS there is a letter *f* in the right margin next to the chapter number, not shown by Farley; see *17* note.
20,1	ORTHI. Possibly OSw, see PNDB 338.
	FRECKENHAM. Sawyer no. 349, Hart ECEE no. 48, is a spurious charter of King Alfred granting Freckenham to the Bishop of Rochester. It may have been forged to back up the Bishop's claim to the estate which was the subject of dispute after 1066.
	LANFRANC. Archbishop of Canterbury, see *15* note.
	EARL RALPH. Wader, see 1,61-95 note.
21	ST. ETHELDREDA'S. Ely Abbey. For a list of food rents from its Suffolk (and other) manors, see LibEl 152-153.
21,1	MEN'S PLOUGHS, NOW 3. IE (153), 6. IEBrev (171), 6 or 5 in the different MSS. IENV (175), 15.
	MEADOW, 16 ACRES. IE, adds '2 beehives'.
	THEN [AND] NOW. LDB omits 7.
	VALUE ALWAYS £10. IE, 'Value then £8; now [£]10'.
	HUMPHREY. Son of Rodric, see 26,1.
	16 FURLONGS. IE, '1 league and 4 furlongs'.
21,2	FALC. Probably he of 14,59.
	ABBEY ... IN THE KING'S HAND. Probably during the vacancy in the Abbey, 1075/6-1082, see HRH 45.
21,3	SMALLHOLDERS, NOW 7. IE (154) and IEBrev (172), 8.
	MEN'S PLOUGHS, NOW 1. IEBrev and IENV (175), 2.
	HORSES. IE, 'cobs'.
21,4	THE FULL JURISDICTION. IE (154) adds, 'and patronage'.
	VALUE 4S. IEAL (182), '5s'.
	THIS ENTRY. IEAL, stated to be held by Henry, the Abbot of St. Edmund's man.
21,5	4 SMALLHOLDERS. IE (154) adds, 'and 1 in WANGFORD'.
	MEADOW, [3] ACRES. Farley omits *7.iii.* which is present in the MS. IE, 4; it adds,'½ mill' and 'always 2 cobs'.
	2 ASSES. The only ones mentioned in Domesday Suffolk.
21,6	5 SMALLHOLDERS. IE (154), 4.
	FISHERIES. An annual gift to Ely of 4000 eels from Lakenheath was confirmed by King Cnut in 1021 x 1023, according to Sawyer no. 980, Hart ECEE no. 86.
	HORSES. IE 'cobs'.
	20D IN TAX. IE, '10d'.
21,7	UNDLEY. LDB *Lundale* is in error for *Und-*.
	3 SMALLHOLDERS. IE (154), 'Always 5 smallholders'.
	2 PLOUGHS. IE, 1.
	HORSE. IE, 'COB'.
	24 CATTLE. IE, 23.
	THIS ENTRY. IEAL (181), Norman is stated to hold this manor from the lordship.
21,8	JURISDICTION. IE (155), 'full jurisdiction'.
21,9	IN (GREAT) LIVERMERE. IE (154) adds, 'and in WANGFORD'.
	IN THE JURISDICTION OF ST. EDMUND'S. IE, 'now under the patronage and in the full jurisdiction of St. Edmund's'.
21,10	18 SMALLHOLDERS. IE (155) and IEBrev (172), 16.
	7 MEN'S PLOUGHS. IE and IEBrev, 8.

HORSES. IE, 'cobs'.
8 CATTLE. IE, 18.
1 FREEMAN ... 8 ACRES. IE adds, 'Value 12d.'.

21,11   HORSES. IE (155), 'cobs'.
VALUE 5S. IE, '3s'.
[FREEMAN]. LDB *soca* is in error for *soc*.

21,12   NOT SELL. IE (157) adds, 'or grant'.

21,13   10 ACRES OF FORFEITED LAND. IE (157) '10 acres of land. He could not sell his lan

21,14   ROGER OF AUBERVILLE. Cf. 29,1.
34 ACRES OF LAND. IE (157) adds, 'which they could not sell. ½ plough'.
VALUE 4S. IE, '5s'.

21,15   THEN 1 SLAVE. IE (158) adds, 'now none'.
4D IN A TAX OF 20S. Stoke paid 4d when a tax of 20s was levied on the Half-Hundred
Ipswich.

21,16   MEN'S PLOUGHS, NOW 15. IENV (175), 6.
A CHURCH ... 2 PLOUGHS. IE (157), '1 plough'.
ARPENTS. A French measure of uncertain and probably variable size, usually applied t
vineyards in the Domesday records, but sometimes to meadow and woodland. See
Wiltshire 12,4 note. In the MS there is an erasure after *arpen,* probably of 7*i.*
IN LORDSHIP, 11 COBS. IE, 'and 1 part of BOSMERE. Always 11 cobs'.
AFTER 1066. LDB *.t.r.e. Will(elm)i* is in error for *.t.r. Will(elm)i.*
THE ABBOT ... FOR £20. IE, '(Value) now £20'.
THIS ENTRY. Cf. IEAL (181) which states that Sictric holds 1 carucate of land in
Barking from the lordship.

21,17   FREE MEN. LDB *lib(eri) lib(er)i ho(min)es* with an erroneous repetition of 'free'.
1 CARUCATE. IEAL (178), 2.
JURISDICTION. IE, 'full jurisdiction'.
BISHOP OF ST. LÔ. Also at 29,9. IE, 'Bishop of Coutances'.

21,18   ROGER. IE (157), Roger Bigot.

21,19   JURISDICTION. As 21,17 note.
ROGER OF AUBERVILLE. Cf. 29,9.

21,21   1 FREEMAN ... 12 ACRES. IE (158) adds, 'Value 8s'.

21,22   JURISDICTION. IE (158), 'full jurisdiction'.
THIS ENTRY. IE adds 'This belongs to Barham'.

21,23   'OLDEN'. As 1,5 note.
KING AND EARL ... JURISDICTION. IE (159), 'in the jurisdiction of the King'.

21,25   LICTEVA. LDB *Listeua,* from OE **Lēohtgifu;* PNDB 319.

21,26   BARHAM. According to LibEl 166 (Hart ECEE no. 116), Earl Algar (see 8,33 note)
granted Barham to the Abbot of Ely 1051 x 1057.
AS A MANOR. IE (159) adds, 'in lordship'.
PLOUGHS IN LORDSHIP, NOW 1. IEBrev (172), 2.
16 ACRES. IE adds, 'of free land'.
17 SHEEP. In the MS *xvij* has been altered from *xvi.* IE, 27 or 28, in the different MSS.
ALWAYS 1 PLOUGH. IE adds, 'Meadow, 2 acres'.
THEN 1 PLOUGH, NOW ½. IE, 'Always 1 plough'.
THEN 1 SMALLHOLDER, NOW 2. IE, '3 smallholders'.

21,27   IN SHARPSTONE. Farley prints *Escarletuna* in error for *Escarlestuna* of the MS. IE (159) '
the same village (of Barham)'. IEAL (181), 'In Barham'.

21,28   PLOUGHS IN LORDSHIP, NOW 1. IEBrev (172), 2.

21,29   ASERET. Probably from ON *Asrøthr;* PNDB 169.
25 ACRES. IE (159-160) adds, 'He could not sell his land'.
UNDER PATRONAGE. IE (160) adds, 'only'.

21,30   THORKELL ... 20 ACRES. IEAL (179), '1 free man with 21 (acres)'.
OF HUGH'S PREDECESSOR. IE (160), 'of the Earl'.

21,31   A HALF FREE MAN. IEAL (178), '1 free man'.

21,32   VALUE 8D. IE (160), '10d' or '9d' in the different MSS.

21,35   WALTER. IE (161), 'Walter the Deacon'.

21,36   IN BLAXHALL. IE (165) adds, 'St. Etheldreda's holds in lordship'.
½ PLOUGH. IE, 1.
THIS ENTRY. Cf. perhaps also IEAL (180) where it is stated that Hervey of Bourges
holds in Blaxhall, '5 free men with 16 acres'.

76 ACRES. IE, 71.

WITH 5 ACRES. IE adds, '2 smallholders'.

21,85   WHICH ... HELD. LDB *qte* is in error for *q(ue) ten(uit)*.

WHOLE OF THIS. Probably referring to 21,84-85.

21,86-88 UNDER THE PATRONAGE. IE (162), as 21,84 note.

21,86   THEN 2 PLOUGHS, NOW ½. IE, 'Then 2 ploughs, and now'.

21,87   HERVEY. IE (162), Hervey Bedruel (*bebruel*); see 67 note.

21,88   FREE MEN. In the MS *lib(er)os* has been altered from *lib(er)i*.

4 ACRES. IE (162) and IEAL (179), 12.

21,89   1 ACRE. IE (162) and IEAL (178) adds, 'of lordship (land)'.

21,90   THEN 4 SMALLHOLDERS, NOW 2. IE (162), '4 smallholders'.

IN THE SAME ... ST. ETHELDREDA'S. IE (162-163), 'Also 11 free men. In the same village under the patronage of St. Etheldreda's.

21,91   UNDER THE PATRONAGE. IE (163), as 21,84 note.

20 ACRES ... 1 PLOUGH. IE, '60 acres. 1 smallholder. Always 1 plough' and adds, 'Value 10s'.

MEADOW, 2½ ACRES. IE, '5 acres'.

21,92   HALF 2 FREE MEN. IEAL (179), '1 free man'. IE (163) adds, 'under the patronage of St. Etheldreda's.

13½ ACRES. IE (163) and IEAL (179), 12.

VALUE 20D. IE, 'Value 2s' and adds, 'R(obert) Malet holds this' referring to 21,88-92.

21,93   1 FREE MAN. IE (164), 'St. Etheldreda's holds 1 free man in its lordship, under patronage'.

21,94   A HALF FREE MAN. IE (164), 'R(obert) Malet holds from the Abbot a half free man, Bondi, under the patronage of St. Etheldreda's' and adds, 'Meadow, 1 acre'. IEAL (179), '1 free man'.

VALUE 3S. IE, '5s'.

21,95   PLOUGHS IN LORDSHIP, NOW 2. IEBrev (172), 3.

WILLIAM OF BOUVILLE. LDB *debu uilla*. See 16,11 note.

IT ... ADJUDGED. LDB .*i.* is probably in error for 7.

HIS LORD. LDB *dominiu(m)* is in error for *dominu(m)*.

AS GUARANTOR. Translating *ad tutore(m)*. William names his lord, Geoffrey de Mandeville, as the person from whom he had received the carucate.

VALUE 16D. IE (164), '12d' and adds, 'The whole of this is in the lordship of St. Etheldreda's.

21,98   1 VILLAGER. In the MS *uilla(nus)* has been altered from *uilla*.

21,99   PLOUGHS, NOW 1. MEADOW, [1] ACRE. LDB *car(uce). modo .i. ac(ra) p(ra)ti*, omitting one instance of the numeral .*i.* Cf. IE (164).

21,100 7 FREE MEN BEFORE 1066, NOW 2. IE (165) and IEAL (180), '7 free men'.

THEN 1 PLOUGH. IE adds, 'now none'.

VALUE ... NOW 5[S]. IE adds, 'Hervey Bedruel holds this from the Abbot', referring to entries 21,96-100. For Hervey, see 67 note.

1 FREE MAN. IE, 'a half free man, Aelmer, under the patronage of St. Etheldreda's'. IEAL (179), 'a half free man'.

16½ ACRES. IE, and IEAL (179), 15.

21,101-102 A HALF FREE MAN. IE (165) adds, 'under the patronage of St, Etheldreda's'.

21,102 RENDLESHAM. LDB *reslesha(m)* altered to *renslesha(m)*.

21,103 2 SMALLHOLDERS. IE (165) adds, 'of St. Etheldreda's'.

21,104 1 FREE MAN ... ANOTHER. IE (165), '2 free men under the patronage of St. Etheldreda's'.

VALUE 3S. IE adds, 'St. Etheldreda's holds these in its lordship', referring to 21,101-104 and to 21,38.

22   BISHOP OF EVREUX. Evreux (Eure). In the left margin of the MS, not shown by Farley, is the letter *f*, next to the chapter number. See 17 note.

22,1   'UDEHAM'. Lost, in Sutton, DG 414.

22,2   50 ACRES. IE (146) and IEAL (189), 60; IEAL (188), 40.

THIS ENTRY. IE adds before this entry, 'In WICKHAM (Market) 1 free man, Thorkell, under the patronage of St. Etheldreda's, with 20 acres'. IEAL (189) adds that Roger Bigot holds Wickham (Market) and Campsey (Ash) from the Bishop. Cf. also IEAL (188) where these two entries are included amongst the lands which Roger Bigot annexed from St. Etheldreda's.

23	ABBOT OF BERNAY. The Benedictine Abbey of Bernay (Eure). In the right margin of the MS, not shown by Farley, is the letter *f*, next to the chapter number. See *17* note.
23,1	ASSESSED ... IN ANOTHER HUNDRED. Probably with 23,2 in Bosmere Hundred. HARDWIN. Cf. 2,10.
23,2	CREETING (ST. MARY). As VCH 526.
23,4	1 VIRGATE. A quarter of a carucate is probably meant here.
23,6	'OLDEN'. As 1,5 note.
24	ABBEY OF CHATTERIS. The Benedictine Abbey of the B.V.M. at Chatteris, Cambs. founded 1007 x 1016 by Ednoth, successively Abbot of Ramsey and Bishop of Dorchester see LibEl 141. See also Cambridgeshire (*11*) and Hertfordshire (*12*). In the right margin the MS, not shown by Farley, is the letter *f*, next to the chapter number. See *17* note. CHATTERIS. The two dots printed by Farley in the middle of the name-form represent black blot in the MS. In Cambridgeshire (*11*) and Hertfordshire (*12*) the name is spelt *Cetriz, Cietriz*; above, in the List of Landholders, *ceterith*. The form beneath the blot here may have been *CETERIHT*.
24,1	ST. MARY'S. Literally, 'St. Mary'. 1 PLOUGH. LDB *ācaŕ* is in error for *caŕ*.
25	RICHARD SON OF COUNT GILBERT. In Kent (11,1) he was called Richard of Tonbridge, while in Suffolk (67,1. 76,6) he occurs as Richard of Clare (cf. 25,1); the places named being his important residences in the two counties. He was the son of Count Gilbert of Brionne. For the origin and distribution of his Holding, see R. Mortimer, 'The Beginnings of the Honour of Clare', *Battle 1980*, 119-141.
25,1	AELFRIC. Son of Withgar. His own son was also called Withgar, see below. On Aelfric see Robertson, *ASCharters* 425. *ARPENTS*. See 21,16 note. ST. JOHN'S. The collegiate church at Clare, founded by Aelfric *c*.1045, MRH 423. LEDMER THE PRIEST. See also Essex (23,4). CHARTER. This has not survived, see Hart ECEE 110. ABBOT LEOFSTAN. Of St. Edmund's, 1044-1065. WITHGAR. Richard's predecessor in most of his East Anglian estates, see Mortimer, 'Honour of Clare', 128-129 (see *25* note).
25,3	SHEEP ... NOW 960. In the MS *m(od)o. dcccclx.* was added in the margin. TAX IN TWO HUNDREDS. That is, Risbridge Hundred and Lackford Hundred (cf. 25,35-36; 39-41). ROBERT HOLDS THIS. Interlined in LDB, and taken to refer to 25,3 rather than 25,4 (as in VCH 527), since statements of the 1086 tenant usually occur at the end rather than at the beginning of entries in Suffolk.
25,6	[THEN] 10 CATTLE. LDB has *&* is in error for *T(un)c*. WILLIAM PECHE. LDB *peccatu(m)*, equivalent to OFr *peche*, 'sin'; OEB 353. He also held from Richard in Essex (23,4).
25,7	WILLIAM HURANT HOLDS THIS. The statement is misplaced among the resources rather than after the value, cf. 25,11-12. the byname is OFr *Hurand*, *-ant*, 'hairy, shaggy-haired'; OEB 318.
25,8	ALWAYS 2 VILLAGERS. LDB has an otiose *&* after *semp(er)*.
25,11	ROGER HOLDS (THIS). The statement is misplaced in LDB, see 25,7 note.
25,12	HAMO HOLDS (THIS). As preceding note.
25,17	THESE FREEMEN. Those in 25,4-17. 6 FORFEITURES. See 8,35 note.
25,18	*WIMUNDESTUNA*. Also at 25,105. In Risbridge Hundred. Unidentified, DG 416. Cf. 14,16 first note. 65 ACRES. In the MS *LXV* has been altered from *LV*.
25,19	FINN. The Dane, see 8,59 note. 3 SMALLHOLDERS. In the MS *bor* has been altered from *boū*. THEN 3 COBS. In the MS there is an erasure before *rūnć*, which has an otiose abbreviation-mark above *u*. 6 FORFEITURES. See 8,35 note.
25,20	AETHELWARD SON OF BELL. LDB *filius belli*. The patronym may be OE **Bell*, see OEB 173.
25,22	ROBERT BLUNT. See *66* and note.
25,24	FATHIR. LDB *fader* from ODan *Fathir*, OSw *Fadhir*; PNDB 250. WALTER THE DEACON. See *41* and note.

25,27	WESTLEY 3 FREE MEN. Richard's son Gilbert granted 2 free men here to St. Edmund's 1090 x 1098, see FD no. 170.
	6 FORFEITURES. See 8,35 note.
25,30	JURISDICTION. LDB has *saca* for *soca*, cf. Norfolk, Technical Terms.
25,35-36;39-41	DESNING. See 25,3.
25,36	FISHERIES. See 21,6 note.
	THESE 2 LANDS. That is, 25,35-36.
25,37	RICHARD'S SAME PREDECESSOR. Withgar. The meaning of the deleted word *comine* is not apparent.
25,42	WITHGAR [HELD]. LDB *ten&* is in error for *tenuit*.
25,44	*CORESFELLA*. Unidentified, DG 395.
25,46	ELINANT. The name is OG, Forssner 66-67. He also held from Richard in Essex (23,5).
25,47	CAVENDISH. LDB *Ranauadisc* is in error for *Kauan-*. Cf. 28,4 note on CAVENHAM; also 43,2 and note.
	ROGER OF ST. GERMAIN. From St. Germain-la-Campagne (Eure), Loyd 94. Cf. OEB 113.
25,49	2 PLOUGHS. Misplaced in LDB, after instead of before the meadow.
25,51	FINN. In the MS there is an erasure after *find*. The Dane, see 8,59 note.
25,52	ST. PETER'S. See also 1,122f and 25,60;62. Cf. 25,54 note.
	[MEN'S] PLOUGHS. LDB omits *hominum*.
	ROGER THE SHERIFF. Roger Bigot (7), cf. 1,122.
	KING'S MANOR OF BRAMFORD. 1,2 in Roger Bigot's custody.
	13 BURGESSES ... OVER 4 ... OVER 12. The numbers do not add up.
	HONOUR. A number of estates administered together.
25,53	THE ABBOT CLAIMS ½ CARUCATE. Apparently the Abbot of Ely, cf. IE (143), 'In BADLEY (Richard son of Count Gilbert) holds 70 acres of the Abbey's lordship which belong in (the lands of) Barking'. Cf. also IEAL (187).
	26 FREE MEN ... AFTER 1066. In the MS *t.r. Will(el)mi .xx.vi. lib(er)i ho(min)es* altered from *t.r.e. xx.vi. uill(an)i*.
25,54	ASSESSMENT OF £15. Probably that of St. Peter's, Ipswich, in 25,52.
25,55	GERMUND. The name is either ON or OG, see Forssner 108. He also held from Richard in Essex (23,15. 90,53).
25,56	ROGER. Of Orbec, see below. From Orbec (Calvados), Loyd 75, OEB 104.
	ROGER OF RAMES. Cf. 38,8.
	RANULF PEVEREL. Cf. 34,8.
	HE CLAIMS BACK. That is, Richard claims back as Finn's successor.
25,57	*RIGNESETA*. Unidentified, DG 409. Ringsett, VCH 531.
	HARDEKIN. LDB *Hardechinus*, from OG **Hardekin*; PNDB 286.
	GODRIC ... [HELD] ... BEFORE 1066. LDB *tenet* is in error for *tenuit*.
25,58	*FACHEDUNA*. Also at 74,2. In Bosmere Hundred. Unidentified, DG 398.
	1 FREE MAN ... [HELD] ... BEFORE 1066. LDB *ten&* is in error for *tenuit*.
25,59	YRIC. As 4,4 note.
	EDRIC ... [HELD] ... BEFORE 1066. LDB *ten&* is in error for *tenuit*.
	A FREEMAN WITH 12 ACRES. IE (143) adds, 'with every customary due'.
	WHO COULD NOT WITHDRAW. In LDB *potuit* has been altered to *pot*. IE has *pot(er)at*.
	OSBERN OF WANCHY. Possibly from Wanchy-Capval (Seine-Inf.), OEB 119.
25,60	UNDER THE PATRONAGE OF AELFRIC FATHER OF WITHGAR. The word *c̄omdato* is otiose.
	WALDWIN. The name is OG, PNDB 408.
	BISHOP ERFAST. Of Thetford. See 19,1-2 note.
25,60;62	ST. PETER'S, IPSWICH. See 25,52.
25,62	ABOVE-MENTIONED £15. In 25,52.
25,63	OTHERS HOLD THERE. LDB *tenet* is in error for *tenent*.
	PLOUGHS IN LORDSHIP. The second instance is probably in error in LDB for 'men's ploughs'.
25,64	CEOLWOLD. LDB *Celeolt* from *C̄eolweald*; PNDB 214.
25,65	*TORP*. In Samford Hundred and a Half. Unidentified, DG 413.
25,66	*PURTEPYT*. Unidentified, DG 408.
25,67	HUN. The name may be OE *Hūn* rather than either OE *Hūna* or ON *Húni*, ODan *Huni*, OSw *Hune*; PNDB 295.
25,69	*EDUINESTUNA*. Also at 36,14. In Samford Hundred and a Half. Unidentified, DG 397.

25,70	3 FREE MEN. In the MS *lib(er)os* has been altered from *lib(er)i*.
25,71	AELFRIC STARLING. The byname is OWScand *stari*, 'starling'; OEB 366.
25,73	*TOFT*. See 16,47 note.
	ASGAR THE CONSTABLE. LDB *stalre*, the same description as was given to Earl Ralph (see 1,101 note). See also 32,1 note.
25,74	RICHARD HOLDS THE WHOLE OF THIS. Referring to 25,67-74.
25,75	HONOUR. See 25,52 note.
25,76	ROGER OF ABENON. From Abenon (Calvados), Loyd 1, OEB 66.
25,78-102	Cf. 25,102 where the end of this group of entries is specified.
Heading	6 FORFEITURES. See 8,35 note.
25,78	EDRIC SPUD. LDB *spuda* from OE **Spudda*, probably denoting 'a short, thick-set person' OEB 336.
25,79	BRICTRIC BLACK. LDB *blacus*, probably from OE *blaec*, 'black, dark', rather *blāc*, 'bright pale'; OEB 292-293.
	[HELD]. LDB *ten&* is in error for *tenuit*.
	FRODO, THE ABBOT'S BROTHER. See *12* note.
	2 FREE MEN. LDB repeats *ii. lib(er)i ho(min)es* in error.
25,82	FRIDEBERN. LDB *Fredeb(er)nus*, from OG *Fridebern*, *Frithu-*, *Frethubern*; PNDB 253-254.
	[HELD]. As 25,79 note.
25,83	HANCHET. LDB *haningehaec*. DG 400, *Haningehest* is in error.
25,84	FREE MAN, LEOFWARU. LDB *Leuiara*, from OE *Lēofwaru* (fem.); PNDB 316. Here, as often in LDB, *liber homo* is used as a technical term without reference to gender.
	GODARD. LDB *Godart(us)*, from OFr *Godard*, see Forssner 120 s.n. **Godehard*.
	WILARD. From OG *Willihard*, *Wilhart*; cf. Forssner 255.
25,87	LOTHER. LDB *Loher(us)*, from OG *Lother*, *Lothar* (*Hlodochar*), Förstemann 852-853 (J.M.D.).
25,89	AINUAR. Farley prints *Ajuuar* in error for *Alnuar* of the MS. PNDB 142 suggests that the LDB form is a misreading of *Aimar*, from OE *Aethelmǣr*. Another possibility is that it is a misreading of *Aluuar*, from OE *Aelfwaru*.
	WILLIAM PERET. The byname probably stands for OFr *Per(r)ot*, a diminutive of the forename *Perre*, 'Peter'; OEB 224.
25,91	ROC. Probably from OE **Hrōc*, but perhaps ON *Hrókr*; PNDB 294.
25,92	69 ACRES. In the MS *Lx.viiij* has been altered from *Lx.viii*.
25,93	29 ACRES. In the MS *xxviiij* has been altered from *xxviii*.
25,102	4½S. That is, 4s 6d.
	ALL THESE (FREE MEN) ... SAID ABOVE. See 25,78-102 HEADING.
25,104	EDEVA. Probably Edeva the Fair, but cf. also Edith 1,90.
	(EARL) RALPH. Wader, see 1,61-95 note.
	WIDARD. From OG *Withard*, *Witard*; Forssner 253.
25,105	*WIMUNDESTUNA*. See 25,18 note.
	THAT HE COULD NOT GRANT. LDB *poterat* altered from *poterant* by subpuncting.
25,107	LINDSEY. Farley prints *halesheia* in error for *balesheia* of the MS. Cf. 14,113 *blalsega*.
25,108	HIS PREDECESSOR. Richard's predecessor.
25,111	6 FORFEITURES. See 8,35 note.
25,112	RANULF PEVEREL ... LOOSE. Cf. 34,5.
26	WILLIAM OF WARENNE. From Varenne near Bellencombre (Seine-Inf.), Loyd 111-112. He was created Earl of Surrey shortly after 16 April 1088, and died 24 June 1088.
26,1-3	IN EXCHANGE (FOR) LEWES. William appears to have acquired lands in Suffolk, Norfolk and Essex to compensate for estates he had lost in Sussex from his Rape of Lewes. See L. F. Salzman, 'The Rapes of Sussex', *Sussex Archaeological Collections* lxxii (1931), 25-26 and J. F. A. Mason, 'The Rapes of Sussex and the Norman Conquest', ibid cii (1964), 80-87.
26,1	2 FREE MEN ... 40 ACRES ... 60 (ACRES). IEAL (184), '4 score acres of land'.
	ONE OF THEM. In the MS the words *un(us) eor(um)* have been written over an erasure.
	COULD SELL. LDB *poterat* altered from *poterant* by subpuncting.
	HUMPHREY SON OF RODRIC. The patronym is OG *Hrodric*; OEB 196. See also 21,1.
	AND JURISDICTION. In the MS *sa* has been erased before *7 soca*.
26,3-4	NICHOLAS. He held Kennett, Cambridgeshire (18,8) from William and was a juror in Staploe Hundred there (Appendix A). In Suffolk, he also held from William at Herringswell (26,4) and Tunstall (26,6). See Farrer iii. 342.

26,4-5 [HELD]. LDB *ten&* is in error for *tenuit*.
26,4 TOKI. William's predecessor in Cambridgeshire (18,1;3;5-8), a thane of King Edward's.
FREDERICK. Called William's brother in Cambridgeshire (18,7) but apparently his brother-in-law, see L. C. Loyd, 'The origin of the family of Warenne', *Yorkshire Archaeological Journal* xxxi (1934), 111-113. He was killed in 1070.
26,5 MUNULF. LDB *monulfus*, from either OSw or OG *Munulf*; PNDB 331.
AND 20 ACRES. In the MS *xx* has been altered from *xxx*.
IN EXCHANGE (FOR) LEWES. See 26,1-3 note.
26,6 NICHOLAS. See 26,3-4 note.
26,7 FREE MAN. In the MS *h(o)m(inem)* has been altered from *h(om)o*.
26,8 HUGH SON OF GOLD. LDB *goldae* may be from either OE *Golda* (masc.) or *Golde* (fem.); OEB 184-185.
BOSTEN. LDB *Bosteinn(us)*. The name is OSw; PNDB 207.
26,9
Heading FREDERICK. See 26,4 note.
26,9 HUGH OF WANCHY. From Wanchy (Seine-Inf.), Loyd 111. Cf. OEB 119.
TOKI. See 26,4 note.
3 CARUCATES. In the MS *iij* has been altered from *ii*.
26,11 HUGH. Probably Hugh of Wanchy, cf. 26,9.
TOKI. See 26,4 note.
26,12a- THESE ENTRIES describe a large but fragmented unit of land in 1066, held by William
12d and his subtenants in 1086. The unit's measurements and fiscal liability are given at the end of 26,12d.
26,12a ROBERT OF PIERREPONT. From Pierrepont (Seine-Inf.), Loyd 78. Cf. OEB 106.
THORKELL. Called 'of Wrentham' in 26,12d.
BLYTHBURGH. The *H* (for 'Hundred') after the place-name is otiose in LDB.
26,12b WILLIAM SON OF REGINALD. He also held at Covehithe (26,15). On him, see Farrer iii. 327.
IN THE SAME VILLAGE ... DWELT. In the MS there is an erasure after *villa*.
HE ALSO HOLDS IT. Probably referring to William son of Reginald, but perhaps to the free man.
UNDER HIM ... 2 FREE MEN. In the MS *lib(er)os* has been altered from *lib(er)i*.
AELFRIC OF *SANFORD*. LDB *de sanford* may be from Samford Hundred and a Half (Suffolk) or from one of the Sampfords in Essex or from a lost OE name **sandford*.
[1]½ CARUCATES. LDB omits the numeral.
26,12c GODFREY OF PIERREPONT. See 26,12a note on ROBERT OF PIERREPONT.
26,13 RANULF ... HELD. LDB *teñ*, here apparently for *ten(uit)*; cf. following note.
WILLIAM ... HOLDS. LDB *teñ*, here apparently for *ten(et)*. The following words *in d(omi)nio* are deleted in LDB.
HALF A PRIEST. That is, half of the rights over him.
OF ROBERT ... OF ROBERT. The second instance is probably an erroneous repetition in LDB.
26,14 IDLE CATTLE. LDB *an(imalia) otiosa*; that is, not used for ploughing.
ROBERT MALET CLAIMS LIKE THE OTHER. Presumably referring back to 26,13.
26,15 COVEHITHE. Formerly 'North Hales'.
[1]½ PLOUGHS. LDB omits the numeral.
PLOUGHS, NOW 1. *modo* was written twice in LDB, but then the first instance was deleted.
26,16 HUNDRED OF CARLFORD. LDB *EARLAFORDA* is in error for *CARLAFORDA*.
Heading AETHELRIC. LDB *Alricus*. Called Aethelric of Burgh (from the manor in this entry) in 8,6;9 etc.
26,17 ROBERT. Of Glanville (see 6,3 note); Farrer iii. 424.
26,19 'TORSTANESTUNA'. See 11,2 note.
27 SWEIN OF ESSEX. Sheriff of Essex until at least 1075, in succession to his father Robert son of Wymarc (*24* and note).
27,3 ROBERT. Son of Wymarc, see preceding note.
[HELD]. LDB *tenet* is in error for *tenuit*.
CHURCH. A religious community existed here in the 10th and early 11th centuries (MRH 483). It received bequests of lands from Ealdorman Aelfgar and his daughters in Whitelock, *AS Wills* nos. 2,14-15; Sawyer nos. 1483, 1494, 1486. These bequests included Withermarsh, Polstead, Stratford St. Mary and Freston; cf. 27,4-5;9;12.

27,5   4 CARUCATES. *car(ucate)* was repeated in error in LDB, then the first instance was deleted.

                MEADOW, 31 ACRES. In LDB *.xxx* has been interlined above *.i.*

27,6   IN LENGTH. LDB *lango* altered from *lato*; for *longo*.

27,7   HAD SEEN. LDB *uidissed* is in error for *uidisset*.

27,8   ROBERT. Son of Wymarc, see *27* note.

                HE HAS LOST ... HE HAS. The subject here is Swein. He still retained rights over the property of the dead burgesses.

27,9   ROBERT. There are two men of this name in this entry. The first is Swein's father; the second is the 1086 subtenant, who is called Robert of Stratford in his own chapter *(71)*.

27,10-12   ROBERT. Son of Wymarc, see *27* note.

27,10   [HELD] ... BEFORE 1066. LDB *ten&* is in error for *tenuit*.

27,13   GODRIC. Called 'of Peyton' (from the manor in the present entry) in 6,238.

                1 LEAGUE. Farley prints *leugā* in error for what in the MS is *leuga* altered from *legu*.

28   EUDO THE STEWARD. The youngest son of Hubert of Ryes (Calvados; Loyd 40). Steward to King William. In the chapter-heading in LDB *EEVDONIS* is in error for *EVDONIS*.

28,1b   CHAMBERLAIN'S HALL. LDB *coclesworda*; DG 394.

                THEN AND LATER 5 PLOUGHS. In LDB *T(un)c 7 p(ost) .v. car(uce)* was repeated in error, then the first instance deleted.

28,2   6 FREEMEN. IEAL (187), 7.

                [WHO] COULD NOT. LDB *q(uo)d* is in error for *q(ui)*.

                LISOIS. Of Moutiers. He probably took his name from Moutiers-Hubert (Calvados), cf OEB 102. See also Essex (25,5 and note).

                EUDO HELD ... WITH FULL JURISDICTION. IE (142), 'Eudo held them and holds with full jurisdiction'.

                4 SMALLHOLDERS. IE adds, 'under them'.

                FISHERIES. See 21,6 note.

28,4   CAVENHAM. LDB *Ranauaha(m)* is in error for *Kauana-*. DG 394 *Kanaua-* is in error. Cf. 25,47 note on CAVENDISH.

28,6   PIROT. The LDB form may be in error for *Picot*. See Essex (25,11 and note), Cambridgeshire (25,1-2 and note) which suggest that this is Picot the Sheriff of Cambridgeshire.

                THIS ENTRY. Cf. IE (153), 'In North Glemham 1 free man, Wulfric son of Hugh *(Hugo sune, hugesune)*, under the patronage of St. Etheldreda's; 1½ carucates of land. Eudo the Steward holds this'. Cf. also IEAL (187), '1 free man with 1 carucate (of land)'.

28,7   1 SLAVE. In the MS there is an erasure after *ser*.

29   ROGER OF AUBERVILLE. Perhaps from Auberville-la-Renaut (Seine-Inf.); OEB 104-105. For his brother William, see *30*.

29,1   CARRYING-SERVICE. *Summagium*, the service of carriage by pack-animals, often commuted to a money payment. Parallel to *avera* in Cambridgeshire, etc.

                GUTHMUND. Brother of Abbot Wulfric of Ely, see 31,8 note.

                RICHARD'S PREDECESSOR. That of Richard son of Count Gilbert *(25)*.

29,3   [HELD]. LDB *ten&* is in error for *tenuit*.

                PILEBERGA. Unidentified, DG 408.

29,4   WILGRIP. LDB *Wilgripus*, from ODan *Vilgrip*; PNDB 405.

29,6   *ELLA*. Unidentified, DG 397.

29,7   LEOFRIC HOBBESON. The patronym is OE **Hobba*, a nickname meaning a lumpish o a stupid person; OEB 157-158. See also 30,3.

29,8   GODRIC OF RINGSHALL, WILLIAM OF AUBERVILLE'S PREDECESSOR. William Roger's brother, held lands at Ringshall (30,2-3) but a Godric is not named there.

29,9   BISHOP OF ST. LÔ. Also at 21,17.

29,10   *LANGHEDANA*. See 1,68 note.

29,11   TEPEKIN. LDB here *Tepechinus*, below (29,14) *Tepekin* and (40,4) *Depekin*. An OLG diminutive in *-kin*, perhaps added to a hypocoristic form of OS *Thiadbald, -bern*, etc.; PND 383.

29,12   15D IN TAX. In LDB *den(arii)* was written twice in error and the first instance then deleted.

29,14   'FINESFORD'. See 21,70 note.

                TEPEKIN. See 29,11 note.

30   WILLIAM BROTHER OF ROGER OF AUBERVILLE. For his brother, and the bynam see *29* and note. In the right margin of the MS, not shown by Farley, is the letter *f*, next t the chapter number; see *17* note.

30,1	RINGSHALL. See also Godric of Ringshall in 29,8.
	THEN 2 PLOUGHS, NOW ½. Misplaced in LDB, among the population details.
30,2-3	[HELD]. LDB *ten&* is in error for *tenuit*.
	LEOFRIC HOBBESON. See 29,7 note.
	HUGH OF HOUDAIN. See 7,60 note.
31	HUGH DE MONTFORT. From Montfort-sur-Risle (Eure); OEB 101, Loyd 68.
31,1	THIS ENTRY. LDB does not give a value.
31,2	EARL HUGH. Cf. 4,11.
31,3	ROGER OF CANDOS. From Candos (Eure, arr. Pont-Audemer), Loyd 26-27. Cf. OEB 81.
31,4-6	HE ALSO HOLDS. Roger of Candos, as 31,3.
31,4	HORHAM. Farley prints *borant* in error for *horant* of the MS.
31,7	7½S. That is, 7s 6d.
31,8-14	GUTHMUND. The brother of Abbot Wulfric of Ely. For the lands leased to him by his brother 1045 x 1066 (including Nacton, Great Livermere, and Occold, Suffolk; here 31,8;13a;40;60), see LibEl 166-167, 424-425. See also Essex 27,14 note.
31,8	23 SHEEP. 12 or 22 in the different MSS of IE (143).
	VALUE ... 70S. IE, 'Value £4'.
31,9	[*BRIHTOLUESTUNA*]. Farley prints *brihtoluestana* in error for *-tuna* of the MS. The place is also mentioned in 31,14. Unidentified, DG 392.
	AND 20 ACRES. IEAL (186), 'Meadow, 20 acres'.
	4 SMALLHOLDERS. IE (143), 3.
	PLOUGHS, NOW 5. MEADOW, 2 ACRES. In the MS there is an erasure before *.ii.* and *.v.* is interlined.
	6 ACRES. IE adds, 'of free land'. IEAL, 'with 5 acres of meadow'.
31,11	*CULUERDESTUNA*. See 6,110 note on *KYLUERTESTUNA*.
	THEN 2 PLOUGHS, NOW 1. IEAL (186), '2 carucates of land'.
	IT HAS 3 FURLONGS ... IN TAX. IE (144) gives these details as part of the entry equivalent to 31,12.
31,12	*ISTEUERTONA*. Unidentified, DG 403.
	VALUE. IE (143) adds, 'of all these free men'.
	JURISDICTION. IE, 'full jurisidiction and patronage'.
	WHOLE OF THIS LAND. Referring to 31,8-12; cf. IE (143-144).
	THIS ENTRY. Cf. IEAL (186), '6 free men; 2 carucates (of land) and 28 acres. Meadow, 1 acre. Always 4 ploughs in lordship'.
31,13	LURK. LDB *Lurc*, from ON *Lurkr*; a byname from the word for a cudgel, PNDB 322.
	PATRONAGE OF N. Perhaps for 'Norman', cf. elsewhere in Suffolk. In LDB *ei(us)d(em)* has been deleted before *.N.*.
31,13a	NACTON. See 31,8.
	THE HUNDRED. IE (144) adds, 'and the Shire'.
31,15	1 FREE MAN. IE (150), Stanhard.
	HALF UNDER ... ST. ETHELDREDA'S AND HALF ... EDRIC GRIM. IE, 'under the patronage of St. Etheldreda's'.
	19 ACRES. IE, 16. IEAL (186), 6.
	VALUE 4S 9D. IE, '4s'.
31,16	1 FREE MAN. IEAL (186), '2 free men'.
	VALUE 8D. IE (150), '6d'.
31,17	THIS ENTRY. Cf. IE (150), '2 free men under the patronage of St Etheldreda's; 14 acres. Value 2½s.' Cf. also IEAL (186).
31,18-19	THESE ENTRIES. IEAL (186) adds, 'Also in CHARSFIELD 1 free man; 6 acres. In the same (Charsfield) 2 Freemen; 8 acres of land'.
31,18	CHARSFIELD. See 6,179 note.
	10 FREE MEN ... ST. ETHELDREDA'S. IE (151), '11 free men ... 1 wholly, the others half under the patronage of St. Etheldreda's'. IEAL (186), '9 free men'.
	VALUE ... NOW 22S 8D. IE, 'Value 20s.'
31,19	2 FREE MEN ... HUGH DE MONTFORT'S PREDECESSOR ... OVER 1. IE (151), '1 free man and a half under the patronage of St. Etheldreda's'. IEAL (186), '1 free man'.
31,21	IN LORDSHIP. In LDB *ten* is deleted before *in d(omi)niu(m)*.
	30S 30D. That is, 32s 6d.
31,24	*HATHEBURGFELDA*. Altered from *athe-* in LDB. See 4,33 note.
31,26	*BEKETUNA*. See 1,29 note.
	1500 HERRINGS. Expressed in LDB as '1 thousand and a half herrings'.
31,28	*RODENHALA*. See 4,36 note.

ASLAC. LDB *Aslacus*, from ON *Áslákr*, ODan, OSw *Aslak*; PNDB 168.
WHOLE ... IN LORDSHIP. Referring to 31,27-28.
31,29   *WIMUNDAHALA*. See 7,53 note.
500 HERRINGS. Expressed in LDB as 'half a thousand herrings'.
31,31   *HORNES*. Unidentified, DG 402.
[BEFORE 1066]. LDB *t(empore). r(egis)*, omitting the name of the King.
31,34   WHOLE ... IN LORDSHIP. Referring to 31,29-34.
WALTER OF [DOL]. LDB *de doai*, 'of Douai' is in error here, cf. 4,15 etc. Walter of Dou
was still holding in 1086, see Essex *(52)*, etc.
31,36   VALUE 4S. In the MS *7.v*. has been erased after *sol(idos)*.
31,37   *CALDECOTEN*. See 6,212 note.
31,38   GUTHMUND. See 31,8-14 note.
31,39   *CALDECOTAN*. See 6,212 note.
31,40-43   GUTHMUND. See 31,8-14 note.
31,40   HUGH OF *BEUERDA*. The place is unidentified.
HOLDS. In LDB *ten&* has been repeated in error, then the second instance deleted.
ALWAYS 4 VILLAGERS. IE (142), 'Always 3 villagers'.
HORSE. IE, 'cob'.
[THEN] 160 SHEEP. LDB omits *T(un)c*.
VALUE ... 40S. IE, 'Value always 40s'.
31,42   146 SHEEP. In LDB *.cxlvi*. is interlined above *Lxxxvi* which is deleted.
PESSERERA. Obscure, but possibly an erroneous form of the OFr byname **Paisforiere*,
'pasture meadow', OEB 386 (J.M.D.).
31,43   GUTHMUND, HUGH'S PREDECESSOR, HELD. In LDB *tenuit* has been altered
(needlessly) to *teñ*. Ante *c̄ū* is in error for *Antecessor*.
31,44   KING'S MANOR OF THORNEY. See 1,1.
BELONGING TO THE REALM. See 1-60 note.
BY A DELIVERY. Translating *ex lib(er)atione*; by a lawful transfer of possession.
[IN LENGTH]. LDB omits *in longo*.
31,45-46   GUTHMUND. See 31,8 note.
31,45   17 FREE MEN ... UNDER PATRONAGE ONLY. In the MS *xvii* has been altered from
xviii. The last letter of *com̃t* has been written over an erasure.
31,46   *ERUESTUNA*. Unidentified, DG 397.
HUGH'S PREDECESSOR. In the MS there is an erasure after *antec(essoris)*.
31,47   *TORPE*. In Stow Hundred. Unidentified, DG 414.
[OF HUGH'S] PREDECESSOR. LDB omits *hugonis*. Probably meaning Guthmund, as i
31,46 and 31,48.
JURISDICTION. LDB uses *sac(a)* here for *soc(a)*, cf. Norfolk, Technical Terms.
31,48   *VLTUNA*. Unidentified, DG 414.
GUTHMUND'S. See 31,8 note.
31,49   *TORSTUNA*. Unidentified, DG 414.
BY A DELIVERY. As 31,44 note.
KING'S MANOR OF THORNEY. See 1,1.
... AND THE JURISDICTION. the meaning of *c̄*, the final word of folio 409a is not
apparent, but it might be in error for *c̄*, standing for *c(onsuetudines)*, 'the customary dues'
31,50   BREME. In this entry LDB has both *breme* and *bremere* as spellings of OE **Brēme*, the
second instance having an inorganic AN *re*; PNDB 207.
IN THE BATTLE OF HASTINGS. LDB *in bello hastingensi*; one of the few references to t
battle in the Domesday records.
MEADOW, 1½ ACRES. Farley prints *T(un)c* in error for *7* of the MS.
WILLIAM SON OF GROSS. The patronym is a nickname from OFr *gross(e)*, 'big, stout
OEB 185-186.
31,51   ALWIN OF MENDLESHAM. Perhaps identical with Alwin in 1,77.
[HELD]. LDB *ten&* is in error for *tenuit*.
31,53   MANOR ... OF THE KING. See 1,1.
RALPH THE CONSTABLE. See 1,101 note.
RALPH, HIS SON. Earl Ralph Wader, see 1,61-95 note.
DELIVERER. Someone who had the power to deliver possession of the land.
TO THIS MANOR ... 10D IN TAX. In the MS this part of the entry is written on either
side of a large hole in the centre of the leaf.
ST. AUGUSTINE'S. Ipswich, mentioned in 1,122d, rather than Canterbury.

31,57 THIS ENTRY is also written in the MS on either side of the hole which affects 31,56. The only reflection of this arrangement given by Farley is the hyphen in the place-name, which also occurs in the MS.

31,60 GUTHMUND. See 31,8 note.

WULFRIC, THE ABBOT OF ELY. ?1044 x 1045 - ?1066, HRH 45.

THEN 2 SLAVES. IE (153) adds, 'now none'.

THEN AND LATER 2 PLOUGHS IN LORDSHIP, NOW 1. IEAL (186), '2 ploughs in lordship'.

THEN 2 MEN'S PLOUGHS, LATER AND NOW 1½. IEAL, '2 ploughs belonging to the men'.

JURISDICTION OVER THE WHOLE. IE adds, 'under the Abbot'.

32 GEOFFREY DE MANDEVILLE. From Manneville (Seine-Inf.), Loyd 57; cf. OEB 96.

32,1 ASGAR. The Constable (see 25,73 note). Geoffrey's predecessor in a number of counties. On him, see Harmer, *ASWrits* 560-561 (s.n. Esgar, the staller); Ellis ii. 43.

VALUE ... 40S. In LDB *xxx.v.* has been deleted and *.xl.* interlined.

32,2 LANGFER. See 7,109 note.

32,3-5 ASGAR. As 32,1 note.

32,4 [HELD]. LDB has *ten&* in error for *tenuit*.

32,6 RAINALM. LDB *Rainelmus*, from *Rainalm* the Rom. form of OG *Raginhelm*; Forssner 210.

STUTTON. LDB *Scottuna(m)*. DG (412), omits this form.

2 [CARUCATES]. LDB omits *car(ucate)*.

SLAVES, NOW ... LDB omits either *7* before *modo*, or a numeral after it.

32,8 ASGAR. As 32,1 note.

32,9 UNDER THE PATRONAGE. LDB *co(m)m(en)datus* is in error for *co(m)m(en)data*, since the subject is female.

32,13 W(ILLIAM) SON OF SAXWALO. The same as William of Bouville, cf. 32,31. For the OG patronym, see OEB 197.

32,14 1 FREE MAN. IE (151), named as Ceolric (*Gelric(us)*, see PNDB 214), and stated there to be one of the 6 free men of the previous sub-entry in LDB.

1 PLOUGH. IE and IEAL (186), 1½.

32,15 WILLIAM. Son of Saxwalo, as 32,13.

HOLDS THIS. Probably referring to 32,14-15.

32,16 [HELD]. LDB *ten&* is in error for *tenuit*.

32,18 *WICHEDIS*. Unidentified, DG 416.

32,19 [HELD]. As 32,16 note.

ASGAR'S. That of Asgar the Constable, see 32,1.

1 MARK OF SILVER. 13s 4d.

32,20 COVEHITHE. Formerly 'North Hales'.

32,21 THORPE. In Dallinghoo, DG 413.

[HELD]. As 32,16 note.

32,23 AETHELRIC OF BURGH. See 32,28 note.

32,25 [*NECKEMARA*]. Farley prints *net-* in error for *nec-* of the MS. See 6,113 note.

32,26 *INGOLUESTUNA*. See 21,65 note. Cf. perhaps IE (145), 'In *GULUESTEHAM*, a half free woman, Mawa (*Maua*), with 20 acres, in the jurisidiction and under the patronage of St. Etheldreda's'.

32,27 OF HALDANE'S. LDB *halden*, uninflected. Cf. 32,22-24;26;28-30 for the use of a similar uninflected form for the genitive case.

32,28 AETHELRIC OF BURGH. Here *Alric*, but above (32,23) *Eilrici* (genitive). See 8,6 note.

BRICTWOLD MUFFLE. The byname is from OFr *mo(u)fle*, 'a winter glove'; OEB 371.

THIS ENTRY. Cf. IE (145), 'In BURGH 1 free man, Brictwold, half under the patronage and in the jurisdiction of St. Etheldreda's, with 40 acres'. Cf. also IEAL (186).

32,29 THE THIRD ... ST. ETHELDREDA'S. Cf. IE (145), 'In CULPHO 1 free man, Brictnoth, in the jurisdiction and under the patronage of St. Etheldreda's; 16 acres' or, in another MS, 'with 6 acres'. Cf. also IEAL (186), '1 free man; 6 acres'.

32,30 *HOBBESTUNA*. IE (145), *Hopestuna*. See 6,117 note *sub HOPESTUNA*.

IN THE SAME ... 1 FREEMAN. IE adds, 'who could not sell his land'.

TOPI. The name is ODan; PNDB 386.

15 ACRES. IEAL (186), 16.

32,31 'FINLESFORDA'. See 21,70 note *sub* 'FINESFORD'.

WHOLE OF THIS. Probably 32,21-31.

WHOLE OF THE JURISDICTION. In LDB *p(er)* is otiose.

33	RALPH BAYNARD. Sheriff of Essex at a date between 1066 and 1086, see Essex *33*. Castle Baynard in London was named after him. The patronym is OG *Beinhard, Beinhart*; OEB 213, Forssner 40-41.
33,1-3	6 FORFEITURES. See 8,35 note.
33,1	AETHELGYTH. LDB *Ailad*; PNDB 183-184.
33,2	WE HAVE SEEN THE WRIT. A rare use of the first person (plural) in LDB, *uidimus breue(m)*. NORIGOLD. LDB *Noriolt*, from OG *Norigaud*; Forssner 193. RICHERE. LDB *Ricer(us)*, from OG *Richer(e)*, OFr *Rich(i)er*; Forssner 214-215.
33,3-4	[HELD]. LDB *ten&* is in error for *tenuit*.
33,4-8	BLYTHING HUNDRED. LDB *BIDINGA* is in error for *BLIDINGA*.
33,4	THEN [3] COBS. Farley prints *ii* in error for *iii* of the MS. 3 FURLONGS IN LENGTH. In the MS the first two minims of *iii* are joined and the second one is elongated, perhaps intended as an alteration to *vi*.
33,6	[HELD]. As 33,3-4 note. THE KING ... 6 FORFEITURES. In LDB *soca(m)* has been deleted after *Com(e)s*. For the 6 forfeitures, see 8,35 note.
33,7	ANBOLD. LDB *ābold(us)*. Probably from OG *Aganbold*; Förstemann 38 (J.M.D.). 6 FORFEITURES. See 8,35 note.
33,9-10	BLYTHING HUNDRED. The Hundred rubric is otiose here.
33,9	IN THIS MANOR. LDB *In huic* is in error for either *In hoc* or *Huic*.
33,10	WOODLAND FOR 250 PIGS. Expressed in LDB as 'woodland for two and a half hundred pigs'. [VALUE]. LDB omits *ual&* after *semp(er)*. FREEMEN. Translating *franci ho(min)es*. FREE(MAN). Translating *francus*. [HELD]. As 33,3-4 note.
33,13	BAYNARD. In the MS *hainardus* in error for *bainardus*. Farley silently corrects.
34	RANULF PEVEREL. The byname is from OFr *peurel*, Latin *piperellus* 'pepper'; OEB 326.
34,1-2	SIWARD OF MALDON. See 12,5 note.
32,2	ACTON. LDB *ARetona* is in error for *Aketona* and *Aratona* for *Acatona*. RANULF ACQUIRED FOR LAND. Probably 'in exchange for land'. *HONILEGA*. Unidentified, DG 402.
34,3-4	SIWARD. Of Maldon, cf. 34,1-2.
34,3	REMAINING IN THE JURISDICTION. LDB *remanentēs* with an otiose abbreviation mark, having been altered from *remanente(m)*.
34,4	WARIN. LDB *Garinus*, from the OFr form of OG *Warin*; Forssner 246-247.
34,5	OVER 1 CARUCATE. LDB *dei* is in error for *de.i*. HOLY TRINITY IN CANTERBURY. See 15,2-3 note.
34,6	KETEL. His estate at Onehouse is referred to in his will, 1052 x 1066 (Whitelock, *AS Wills* no. 34, Sawyer no. 1519, Hart ECEE no. 118). On him see Whitelock, *AS Wills* 201-202. See also Norfolk (32,2-5) and below 37,6 note. OSBERT MALE. Cf. Osbern Male 1,12 and note. CHURCH OF STOW(MARKET). Cf. 2,8.
34,7	FROM [RANULF]. Farley prints *Radulfo* in error for *Ranulfo* of the MS.
34,8	AND 4 ACRES. See 25,56. WHAT LEOFSTAN HELD. In LDB *.i. lib(er) h(om)o* has been deleted before *qu(o)d*. In the MS *qu(o)d* has been altered from *que(m)*. NOW 2 OXEN. In LDB *bou(es)* is interlined above *car(uce) hom(inum)* which has been deleted.
34,9	A PART. In LDB *Queda(m)* was written twice in error, then the first instance deleted.
34,12	SAXI ... PATRONAGE OF THE ABBOT. Cf. IE (145), 'In DEBENHAM 1 free man, Saxi, [held] before 1066; 1 carucate of land as a manor. In the jurisdiction and under the patronage of St. Etheldreda's'. Cf. also IEAL (189). 8 ACRES. See 6,11 where '6 acres' and '2 acres' are treated as separate units both previously held by Saxi and by the Malets' predecessor. ALWAYS 2 PLOUGHS IN LORDSHIP. Repeated in LDB. The first instance was probably misplaced and should have been deleted when the phrase was interlined above its correct place. [THEN] 40 PIGS. LDB omits *T(un)c*.
34,15	BUT [ANOTHER] POSSIBLE. LDB omits a word here, perhaps *alia*.

CHURCH, 15 ACRES FROM FOUR LORDSHIPS. LDB ... *de quattuor dominationib(us)*. Presumably meaning that the church had been founded to serve four estates and had been endowed with land from each.

THIS ENTRY. IE (150-151), 'In the same (Clopton) a half free man ... under the patronage of St. Etheldreda's; 1 carucate of land and 30 acres, and 12 acres in *CAISNEID* ... Value 25s'. Cf. also IEAL (189), 'In Clopton 1 carucate and 30 acres. In *CAISNED* 12 acres as a manor. 3 ploughs in lordship; 2 [ploughs] belonging to the men'. *Caisne(i)d* is probably lost in Clopton.

34,17   *TUSEMERA.* Unidentified, DG 414.

AS HIS WAGES. Translating *p(ro) suis solidatis.*

35   AUBREY DE VERE. From Ver (La Manche), Loyd 110; cf. OEB 118.

35,1   *ARPENT.* See 21,16 note.

35,3   FERMEUS. Obscure, unless it represents a scribal error for Latin *seruiens* (J.M.D.).

RALPH TALLBOYS AND FINN. Both appear to have been dead by 1086. Ralph's wife occurs in Cambridgeshire *(42)* and Bedfordshire *(55)*. Finn's wife occurs in Essex *(84)*.

DELIVERER. See 31,53 note.

REEVE. Probably the Hundred-reeve.

35,4   *CANEPETUNA.* See 1,106 note.

35,5   [MEN'S] PLOUGHS. LDB omits *hominum* in error.

... CHURCHES. LDB omits the numeral.

ADELELM. LDB *Adelalm(us)*, from OG *Adalhelm, Adel(h)elm*; cf. Forssner 8, PNDB 184.

35,6   IN ALDHAM. LDB *Ialelham* is in error for *I(n) aldham.*

35,7   MILD. LDB *Milda*, from OE **Milde*; PNDB 328.

9 FREE MEN. Only 8 are named in LDB.

BESI. LDB *Beso*; a Scand. name of uncertain etymology, see PNDB 201.

BOTI. LDB *Botius*, from ON *Bóti*, OSw *Bote*; PNDB 207.

LEOFWIN BENNE. The byname is probably a patronym from OE *Bynna*; OEB 289.

FULCARD THE HALF (FREE MAN). LDB *Furcardus* has AN *-r-* for *-l-*; PNDB 256.

MENLEVA. LDB *Menleua*, probably from OG *Meginliuba, Megenlioba*; PNDB 327.

35,8   LEOFCWEN. LDB *Lefquena*, from OE *Lēofcwēn*, PNDB 311.

AUBREY. In the MS there is an erasure after *alb(er)ico.*

36   ROBERT GERNON. The byname is from OFr *grenon*, 'moustache'; OEB 314-315.

36,1-2   SCALPI, A THANE. The name is ON *Skálpi*, PNDB 365. Probably here referring to the same man as the Guard *(huscarl)* of that name mentioned in Essex (30,16) as having died after 1066 in outlawry in Yorkshire. The present Scalpi is definitely the same as he in Essex 32,40 who held at Ardleigh before William *(de Alno)*, see below EE 3.

THESE ENTRIES. See EE 3 note.

36,1   OF HAROLD'S. Of Earl Harold's, cf. Essex 30,16.

CHURCHFORD. LDB here *Cercesfort*, and 36,16 *Ciresfort*. Unidentified in DG (394).

WILLIAM *DE ALNO*. The place from which he took his name is so far unidentified, see OEB 67-68; DBS 94, s.n. *Dando*. He also held from Robert in Essex (32,40).

36,2-7   WILLIAM. *De Alno*, as 36,1.

36,3   MAWA. LDB *Mauua*. Of obscure etymology, perhaps related to OE *māwian* 'to mow' or *māēw* 'sea-gull'; PNDB 325.

36,4   ST. BENEDICT'S OF RAMSEY. See *17* note.

MANESFORT. Unidentified, DG 405.

36,5   *ALFILDESTUNA.* See 16,45 note.

36,6   *TURCHETLESTUNA.* Unidentified, DG 414.

36,7   IN THE SAME WAY. As in 36,6.

36,8   [HELD]. LDB *ten&* is in error for *tenuit.*

36,10   EDNOTH. LDB *AEtnod*, from OE *Ēadnōth*; PNDB 233.

36,11   TELA. Obscure, see PNDB 382.

36,14   *EDUINESTUNA.* See 25,69 note.

SPIETA. Perhaps ON *Spióti*, OSw *Spiute*; PNDB 370.

36,16   CHURCHFORD. See 36,1 note.

36,17   HE ALSO HOLDS. That is, William *de Alno.*

37   PETER OF VALOGNES. From Valognes (La Manche), OEB 117. Sheriff of Essex and Hertfordshire in 1086. In the MS there is a letter *f* in the left margin next to the chapter number, not shown by Farley; see *17* note.

37,1   [VALUE]. LDB omits *ual&.*

37,5   2 MEN'S OXEN. Misplaced in LDB; it should have been placed before the meadow.

FOR LAND. Probably meaning 'in exchange for land'.

37,6	AUTI. LDB *Alti(us)*, from ODan *Auti*; PNDB 169.
	KETEL. He bequeathed his estate at Rushford to his priest Aelfric, 1052 x 1066, in his will mentioned in 34,6 note.
38	ROGER OF RAMES. From Rames (Seine-Inf.), Loyd 84. Note that some earlier volumes in the present series followed OEB 109 in stating that he came from Raismes (Nord); they should be corrected to follow Loyd.
38,2	*LINHOU*. Unidentified, DG 404.
	[HELD]. LDB *ten&* is in error for *tenuit*.
38,6	MILES. Probably *de Belefol*, cf. 38,25.
38,8	BRICETT. See also 25,56.
38,9	*LANGHEDANA*. See 1,68 note.
	MAN. In the MS *h(omine)m* has been altered from *h(om)o*.
	VALUE 18D. In the MS *xviii* has been altered from *xiii*.
38,10	THEY ... ASSESSED. In LDB *ual* has been deleted before *app(re)ciate*.
38,11	[UNDER ... PATRONAGE OF] GYRTH. The name *Guert* is interlined in LDB, having probably at first been omitted during copying. The word *commenda tus* has also been omitted and would probably have followed *Gotwin(us)*.
	SUNWIN. LDB *Sunwin(us)*, from either OE **Sun(n)wine* or OG **Sunwin*; PNDB 378.
38,13	TUDDENHAM. Here placed in Claydon Hundred, but elsewhere in the neighbouring Hundred of Carlford. Cf. 38,15.
38,14	1 POLE. Translating *uirga*.
38,15	WHICH BELONG. LDB *quē* has an otiose abbreviation mark.
	CHURCH OF TUDDENHAM. Cf. 38,13 note.
38,19-20	MILES. Probably *de Belefol*, cf. 38,25.
38,20	AELFRIC AND BOTI, FREE MEN. LDB repeats *boti* in error after *ho(min)es*.
38,21	HAROLD. Earl Harold, see 1,100.
38,22-23	[HOLDS]. LDB omits *ten&* in error.
38,22	FREE MAN, AELFRIC. In the MS *h(omine)m* has been altered from *h(om)o*; *Aluric(us)* should have been altered to *Aluricum* but was not. Farley prints *Aluric(us)* of the MS.
	UNDER ... PATRONAGE ... FROM THE ABBOT (OF ELY). IE (151), 'under the patronage of St. Etheldreda's'.
	MEADOW, 2 ACRES. IE (151), 1 or 3 in the different MSS. IEAL (189), 4.
	1 UNDER ... ST. ETHELDREDA'S. IE names him as Edric and assigns to him '8 acres. Value 20d'. Cf. also IEAL.
38,24	'FINLESFORD'. See 21,70 note.
38,25	STONHAM (ASPAL). LDB *estuna*. DG 397 identifies this as Easton Bavents, but cf. 38,6-7;19, with two of which Miles (*de Belefol*) appears to be associated.
	MILES *DE BELEFOL*. His place of origin is unidentified.
39	RANULF BROTHER OF ILGER. Ranulf appears consistently in GDB and LDB as 'brother of Ilger', although in IE (149) he is called 'son of Ilger'. The name Ilger is from OG *Hilger*, see OEB 187.
39,1	16 ACRES. In the MS *xvi* has been altered from *xv*.
	2 SMALLHOLDERS. In the MS *ii* has been altered from *i*.
39,3	ROGER THE SHERIFF. Roger Bigot (7.
	A SET TIME. LDB *constitutu(m) t(em)p.m*, in error for *-t(em)pus* (neuter accusative sing.). In
	the MS *u* has been erased between *p* and *m* of the second word.
39,5	BRICT. Perhaps from OE *Beorht*, but possibly an abbreviated form of Brictmer, cf. 39,4. See PNDB 193.
	THE ABBOT (OF ELY) ... OUGHT TO HOLD. The half free man claimed by the Abbot may be the one at an unnamed place in IE (144), 'Ranulf brother of Ilger holds a half free man with 11 acres in the full jurisdiction and under the patronage of St. Etheldreda's. Value 2s.' In another MS, '9 acres'.
	[HALF]. In the MS *d(imidius)* has been erased before *cui(us)da(m)*, but should have been retained in preference to the latter.
	N. Probably Norman as in 39,9.
	STANMER. In the MS there is an erasure after *Stanmar*.
	VALUE 3S. In the MS this extends into the margin and was perhaps omitted at first.
	WILLIAM OF BOSC. LDB *de Nomore*; see 7,115 note.
39,6	[HELD]. LDB *tenet* is in error for *tenuit*.
	36 ACRES. In the MS *xxx.vi* has been altered from *xxx.iii*.
39,8-10	QUENEVA. See 14,117 note. Farley prints *Quengeu&* in error, with *&* standing for the Anglo-Saxon letter 'ash' of the MS. PNDB 220 and n. 2 is thus incorrect.

39,10   2 HALF (FREE MEN). IE (149) names them as Thorkell and Goda. IEAL (189), '3 free
men'.
VALUE ... 20[S]. In LDB *& h(abe)t* is deleted after the value. It probably represents an
erroneous anticipation of the last sentence of this entry.
39,11   W(ILLIAM) OF BOSC. LDB *de Nemore*; see 7,115 note.
WHOLE OF THIS. Referring to 39,6-11.
39,12   *ALUREDESTUNA*. Unidentified, DG 389.
39,14   *EDULUESTUNA*. Unidentified, DG 397.
39,15   BOULGE. Here placed in Carlford Hundred, but elsewhere in the neighbouring Hundred
of Wilford.
39,16   [HELD]. LDB *ten&* is in error for *tenuit*.
39,17   AELFRIC OF *WENHOU*. Also below at 46,3 (of *Weinhou*). His place of origin is
unidentified.
40   ROBERT SON OF CORBUCION. Also a landholder in Essex (*40*) and Norfolk (*35*). His
patronym is perhaps OFr *Corbucion* from Vulgar Latin *Corbutio*, an extended form of
Latin *corvus*, 'raven'; OEB 178-179. In the MS there is a letter *f* in the left margin next to
the chapter number, not shown by Farley; see *17* note.
40,1   BROCKLEY. Farley prints *Brode* in error for *Brocle* of the MS.
SAEGARD. LDB *Saiardus*, from OE *Sǣgeard*; PNDB 353.
40,3   OVER THE VILLAGERS. LDB *de Wiłłis* is in error for *de uill(an)is*.
40,4   TEPEKIN. See 29,11 note.
40,5   FROM THE ABBOT. The LDB form is in error for *abb(at)e*.
40,6   GIFARD. He also held from Robert in Norfolk (35,3;16-17). The name is OG; Forssner
113-114.
41   WALTER THE DEACON. Also a landholder in Essex (*42*). In the MS there is a letter *n̄* in
the right margin next to the chapter number, not shown by Farley; see *17* note.
41,4   THEODORIC'S HOLDING. That of Theodoric the predecessor and brother of Walter.
Also in Essex (42,1).
41,5-6   SAME HOLDING. Theodoric's, as in 41,4.
41,6   BERNARD AND AELMER HOLD. However, the verb in LDB is singular. The meaning
is probably rather that Aelmer *held* (cf. 41,4) and Bernard *holds*.
41,7   LEOFWIN. Probably Leofwin of Bacton, see 41,10 note.
3 CARUCATES. In the MS the *c* of *car(ucate)* has been written over a minim; *iii* has thus
been altered from *iiii*.
41,8   *CALDECOTA*. See 6,212 note.
41,10   LEOFWIN OF BACTON. Here described as a thane, but probably the same man as the
Leofwin, free man, in 41,7 at Bacton. Probably also the same as Young Leofwin in Essex
42,4 (cf. also 42,2;6).
41,11   TERI. LDB *Teri(us)*, possibly from OFr *Tier(r)i*, *Terri* from OG *Theodric* or perhaps ODan
Thyri; PNDB 383.
... OF *BARTHETONA*. The place is unidentified, unless it is a corrupt form of *Bachetona*,
from Bacton; cf. Leofwin of Bacton in 41,10.
GUTHMUND. See 31,8-14 note.
WELEDANA. Unidentified, DG 415.
41,15   *BRUNTUNA*. Unidentified, DG 392.
41,17-19   THESE ENTRIES are additions to this chapter, written by the same scribe but in a
compressed manner. They were squeezed into the space which had been left between
chapters *41* and *42*. In order to keep to the same text in each line as the MS, Farley
increased his line-length here.
41,17   [THEN]. LDB omits *T(un)c*.
41,18   'FINESFORDA'. See 21,70 note.
42   TIHEL OF HELLÉAN. Also called Tihel the Breton. From Helléan (Morbihan); OEB 91.
His byname has been fossilized in Helions Bumpstead (Essex 38,4) which he held in
1086. In the MS there is a letter *f* in the left margin next to the chapter number, not shown
by Farley; see *17* note.
42,2   CLARENBOLD. LDB *Clareboldus*, from OG *Clare(n)bald*; Forssner 54-55.
43   RALPH OF LIMÉSY. From Limésy (Seine-Inf.), Loyd 54, OEB 95. In the right margin of
the MS are the letters *f* and *r* next to the chapter number, not shown by Farley; see *17*
note.
43,1   [HELD]. LDB *ten&* is in error for *tenuit*.
EDGAR, HIS PREDECESSOR. That is, Ralph's predecessor.

43,2   CAVENDISH. LDB *Rana uadisc, Rana uadis* are in error for *Kauanadisc, Kauanadis*. Cf. 25,47
         and note.
         10D IN TAX. CODDENHAM. In the MS *.x.d̄. Kode...* is written over an erasure.
         [3]½D IN TAX. Farley prints *iiii* in error for *iii* of the MS.

43,9   RALPH HOLDS THE WHOLE ... LORDSHIP. This sentence may be misplaced in LDB
         It was perhaps intended to stand at the end of this entry and to refer to 43,1-9.

44   ROBERT OF TOSNY. From Tosny (Eure), Loyd 99, OEB 116. In the MS there are the
         letters *f* and *r* in the right margin next to the chapter number, not shown by Farley; see *17*
         note.

44,1   [ROBERT]. LDB *Rog(erus)* is in error for *Rob(ertus)*.

44,2   BISHOP'S MANOR OF HOXNE. See 18,1.

44,4   MEN'S [PLOUGHS]. LDB omits *car(ucate)*.

45   WALTER GIFFARD. Walter's father was a cousin of King William. Walter succeeded
         him before 1085 and was later created Earl of Buckingham, probably after 1093. The
         byname is either a patronym from OG *Gifard* or is a hereditary nickname from OFr *giffard*
         'the chubby-cheeked one'; OEB 219-220. In the MS there is a letter *f* in the right margin
         next to the chapter number, not shown by Farley; see *17* note.

45,1   1 FREE [MAN]. LDB *lib(er)*. IEAL (186), '1 Freeman'.
         RALPH OF LANQUETOT. From Lanquetot (Seine-Inf.), Loyd 53, OEB 94.

45,2   180 ACRES. IE (153), '1½ carucates'.
         THIS ENTRY. In the MS (folio 430a, lines 10-11) there is a contemporary note in the
         right margin: *q(ua)t(er) xx ac(re) 7 Lxx*, 'fourscore acres and 70'. Farley omits.

45,3   RALPH ... HOLDS THE WHOLE. Probably referring to 45,2-3.

46   COUNTESS OF AUMÂLE. King William's sister. In the left margin of the MS are the
         letters *f* and *r* next to the chapter number, not shown by Farley; see *17* note.

46,1   4 SMALLHOLDERS. LDB *bodr* is in error for *bord̄*.

46,2   [2] SLAVES. Farley prints *iii* in error for *ii* of the MS.
         PLOUGHS IN LORDSHIP, NOW 1. The interlined numeral *.i.* in LDB is here taken to
         be a correction for *null(a)* which should have been deleted.

46,3   AELFRIC OF *WEINHOU*. See 39,17 note.
         [MEN'S] PLOUGHS. LDB omits *hominum*.

46,4   EDEVA THE FAIR. In the MS *faira* has been altered from *feira*.

46,5   EDEVA. Probably the Fair, as 46,4.
         [HELD]. LDB *ten&* is in error for *tenuit*.

46,8   1 UNDER ... ST. ETHELDREDA'S. IE (150), '1 free man under the patronage of St.
         Etheldreda's; 16 acres. 2 smallholders. Meadow, 1 acre. Value 32d.' Cf. IEAL (189).

46,10   UNDER ... EDRIC GRIM. IE (148), 'under the patronage of St. Etheldreda's'.
         THIS ENTRY. IE adds, 'The Countess of Aumâle has 1 of these (free men)'. Cf. IEAL
         (185), where the three free men are stated to be held by Count Alan, and (189) where the
         meadow is said to be held by the Countess of Aumâle.

47   WILLIAM OF ARQUES. Probably from Arques (Pas-de-Calais), OEB 68-69. In the MS
         there are the letters *f* and *r* in the left margin next to the chapter number, not shown by
         Farley; see *17* note.

47,2   AND 22 ACRES ... 1 VILLAGER. IE (150), 'and 10 acres. He could not sell or grant it. 1
         villager; 12 acres'.
         THEN 1 MEN'S PLOUGH, NOW ½. IE, 'Then 2 ploughs belonging to the men, now 1'.
         BERNARD OF ST. OUEN. From St.-Ouen-sous-Bailli (Seine-Inf.), Loyd 91, OEB 112.

47,3   GAVE UP TO THE CHURCH. IE (152), 'gave to St. Etheldreda's'.
         WOODLAND FOR 6 PIGS. After this, IE adds, 'Value 20s'.

48   DROGO OF BEUVRIÈRE. From La Beuvrière (Pas-de-Calais), OEB 73. In the MS there
         is a letter *f* in the right margin next to the chapter number, not shown by Farley; see *17*
         note.

48,1   RADA. Perhaps OE **Hrada* from *hraed*, 'quick, alert' or ON *Hrathi*, ODan *Rathi*; PNDB
         344.
         FRANK. LDB *franc(us)* could be translated as 'a Frenchman', but cf. Norfolk (8,137)
         where 'a certain man of Drogo of Beuvrière, Frank by name' occurs. The name is OG
         Franco; Forssner 92.

49   HUGH OF GRANDMESNIL. From Le Grand-Mesnil (Calvados), Loyd 47, OEB 90. In
         the MS there is a letter *f* in the right margin next to the chapter number, not shown by
         Farley; see *17* note.

49,1   [HELD]. LDB *ten&* is in error for *tenuit*.

50 RALPH OF FOUGÈRES. From Fougères (Ille-et-Villaine), OEB 88-89. In the MS there is a letter *f* in the right margin next to the chapter number, not shown by Farley; see *17* note.

50,1 [HUNDRED OF HARTISMERE]. The rubric is omitted in LDB.

51 WALTER OF ST. VALÉRY. From St. Valéry-sur-Somme (Somme), OEB 114. In the left margin of the MS next to the chapter number are the letters *f* and *r*, not shown by Farley; see *17* note.

51,2 HIS FATHER. William Malet, father of Robert.

   'OLDEN'. See 1,5 note.

   THIS ENTRY. In the MS this is followed by an erasure of two and a half lines of writing.

52 HUMPHREY THE CHAMBERLAIN. In the right margin of the MS next to the chapter number is a letter *n̄*, not shown by Farley; see *17* note.

52,1-2 AMUND. LDB *Amund(us)*, from OSw *Aghmund*, cf. PNDB 141.

52,1 IN POSSESSION ... DIED; LATER. In the MS *saisitus* has been altered from *saiatus*.

52,2 FROM HUMPHREY. LDB *Winfrido* is in error for *Vmfrido*.

Folio 433a, the bottom corner of this folio is irregular in shape and affects the line-length of the text in part of 52,5.

52,5 8 WHOLE ... FREE MEN. LDB *lib(er)i ho(min)es integros* is in error; all three words should be in the nominative case.

52,7 LICTEVA. LDB *Listeua*, from OE **Lēohtgifu*; PNDB 319.

Folio 433b, the last four lines of the text of 52,8 are affected by the same irregular ity in the shape of the folio that affected 52,5.

52,8 *BRICTICESHAGA*. Unidentified, DG 392.

52,11 *BERMESDENA*. Unidentified, DG 390. For a later reference to the place, see VCH 568, n. 351.

   IN PATRONAGE. This is probably the meaning of the interlineation *7 i(n) cuñ*.

   [60] ACRES. Farley prints *LXX* in error. In the MS the second *X* has been erased.

53 EUDO SON OF SPIRWIC. Also a landholder in Lincolnshire and Norfolk (*29*). The patronym was taken to be OG in OEB 198, but may be Breton, see von Feilitzen 1939, 126. In the right margin of the MS next to the chapter number are the letters *f* and *r*, not shown by Farley; see *17* note.

53,1 MORVANT. He also held from Eudo in Norfolk (29,7). The personal-name (here *Moruant*, in Norfolk *Moruā*) has as first element the OE theme *Mor-* discussed in PNDB 328-329, but the second element is obscure (J.M.D.).

   HEINFRID. Also Eudo's predecessor in Norfolk (29,8). The name is OG *Heim-*, *Heinfrid*; Forssner 144-145.

   1 SLAVE. IE (142), '5 slaves'.

   MEADOW, 5 ACRES. IE, 'Meadow, 3 acres'.

53,2 'OLDEN'. See 1,5 note.

   ROGER. Perhaps Roger of Poitou, cf. 8,61.

53,3 IARNAGOT. LDB *Iarnagot(us)*, *Iarnagod* and (53,7) *Iarnacotus*. An Anglo-Scand. personal-name **Iarnagot* (J.M.D.).

   CYNRIC. LDB *Kerinc* is in error for *Kenric*, from OE *Cyneric*; PNDB 220-221, Forssner 171.

53,6 WULFRIC HAGNI. The byname (LDB *hagana*) is a patronym from ODan *Hag(h)ni*; PNDB 282, Fellows Jensen 122. Cf. OEB 221,186.

   WULFNOTH. Probably in error in LDB for Wulfric.

53,7 VALUE 20S. IE (142), 'Value 15s'.

   6 FORFEITURES. See 8,35 note.

   IARNAGOT. See 53,3 note.

54 WILLIAM OF VATTEVILLE. Probably from Vatteville (Seine-Inf.) but perhaps from Vatteville (Eure); OEB 120. In the right margin of the MS next to the chapter number is a letter *f*, not shown by Farley; see *17* note.

54,1 LIDGATE. William's men also claimed another estate here, see 70,1.

54,2 AELFGYTH. LDB *Aluiet*, from OE *AElfgyth*; PNDB 174.

54,3 ALFGEAT. LDB *Alued(us)*, from OE *AElfgeat*; PNDB 173.

   AELFEVA. LDB *alwewe*, from OE *AElfgifu*; cf. PNDB 173-174.

   ST. EDMUND'S. LDB *s(an)c(tu)s* is in error for *s(an)c(t)i*.

55 JOHN SON OF WALERAN. Also a landholder in Essex (*40*) and Cambridgeshire (*35*). In the left margin of the MS next to the chapter number is a letter *f*, not shown by Farley; see *17* note.

55,1 2 CARUCATES. In the MS *ii* has been altered from *iii*.

   1 SMITH. The only one mentioned in Domesday Suffolk.

56	HUMPHREY SON OF AUBREY. Also a landholder in Norfolk (*39*). In the right margin of the MS next to the chapter number is a letter *f*, not shown by Farley; see *17* note.
56,3	'OLDEN'. See 1,5 note.
56,4	VALUE ... JURISDICTION. Referring to 56,2-4.
56,6	CODDENHAM. See 1,74 note.
	MILL OF BILLINGFORD ... NORFOLK. Humphrey held Billingford in Eynsford Hundred in Norfolk (39,2), where the mill is listed but this value is not given. Although the present entry suggests that the mill was counted as part of Coddenham, it may be that it has simply been misplaced in Suffolk rather than in Humphrey's Norfolk chapter. Cf. Norfolk (ESf 7).
57	HUBERT OF MONT-CANISY. From Mont-Canisy (Calvados), OEB 100. In the right margin of the MS next to the chapter number is a letter *f*, not shown by Farley; see *17* note.
58	GUNDWIN THE CHAMBERLAIN. Perhaps the same as Gundwin in Essex (*80*) and Gundwin the keeper of the granaries (Wiltshire 68,29). The name is OG *Gund(e)win*; Forssner 135. In the left margin of the MS next to the chapter number is a letter *f*, not shown by Farley; see *17* note.
58,1	AESCMAN. LDB *Asseman(us)*, from OE *AEscmann*, possibly here a byname meaning 'sailor'; PNDB 182.
	OTHERS HOLD. LDB *ten&* is in error for *tenent*.
59	SASSELIN. Also a landholder in Essex (*57*). The name is a diminutive of OG *Saxo*; Forssner 223. In the left margin of the MS next to the chapter number is a letter *f*, not shown by Farley; see *17* note.
59,1	[HELD]. LDB *ten&* is in error for *tenuit*.
60	ROBERT OF VERLY. From Verly (Aisne), OEB 118. Also a landholder in Norfolk (*38*). In Essex (32,14-15;37;45) he held under Robert Gernon and gave his name to Virley (LDB *Salcota(m)*; 32,15). In the right margin of the MS next to the chapter number is a letter *f*, not shown by Farley; see *17* note.
60,1	WESTON. Before the name in LDB there is an otiose letter *I*. The scribe probably began writing *In* but stopped when he realised that *Westuna(m)* was the direct object of *tenuit* and not governed by a preposition.
61	RALPH PINEL. Also a landholder in Essex (*77*). The byname is OFr *pinel*, a diminutive of *pin*, 'a pine tree'; OEB 369. In the right margin of the MS next to the chapter number is a letter *f*, not shown by Farley; see *17* note.
61,1	[SAMFORD HUNDRED AND A HALF]. LDB omits the Hundred-heading.
	[HELD]. LDB *ten&* is in error for *tenuerunt*.
	GEOFFREY DE MANDEVILLE. Cf. 32,4;8.
62	ISAAC. Also a landholder in Norfolk (*47*). In the left margin of the MS next to the chapter number is a letter *f*, not shown by Farley; see *17* note.
62,2	WULFWIN, A FREE MAN. Farley prints *libomo* in error for *lihomo* of the MS (standing for *li(ber) homo*).
	MANOR BEFORE 1066. Farley prints an extra point between *man(erio)* and *.t.r.e.*, not present in the MS.
62,4	HEMINGSTONE. See 1,7 note.
62,5	OF ST. EDMUND'S. LDB *s(an)c(t)o* is in error for *s(an)c(t)i*.
62,6	HEMINGSTONE. See 1,7 note.
62,7	*REDLES*. Unidentified, DG 408.
	[HELD IT]. LDB *ten&* is in error for *tenuit*.
63	NORMAN THE SHERIFF. He also occurs in entries associated with two other Sheriffs of Suffolk, Robert Malet and Roger Bigot (6,91;290 and 7,36) and probably held the office before them.
64	JUDICAEL THE PRIEST. Also a landholder in Norfolk (*44*). His forename is OBret; PNDB 301, DBS 195 s.n. *Jekyll*. In the right margin of the MS next to the chapter number is a letter *f*, not shown by Farley; see *17* note.
64,1	[HELD]. LDB *ten&* is in error for *tenuit*.
64,3	7 SMALLHOLDERS. In the MS *vii* has been altered from *iii*.
	BISHOP'S (MANOR OF) HOXNE. See 18,1.
65	GERALD MARSHAL. In the left margin of the MS next to the chapter number is a letter *f*, not shown by Farley; see *17* note.
65,1	BADMONDISFIELD. See 1,121.
66	ROBERT BLUNT. Sheriff of Norfolk in 1086. His byname here is from OFr *blund, blond*, 'blonde, fair'; OEB 294. In Wiltshire (*60*) he has the Latin byname *flavus*, 'yellow, blonde'.

(OEB 313); in Northamptonshire (*33*) the Latin byname *albus*, 'white' (OEB 293); and in Norfolk (1,231. 26,3) the OFr byname *blanchart*, 'whitish' (OEB 293).

,1   *ARPENTS*. See 21,16 note.

,3   1 FREE MAN, KETEL. In LDB *.i. lib(er) h(om)o* was repeated in error after *Chetel*, then deleted.

THEN 32 SHEEP. In the MS the interlined *x* touches the first *x* of *xxii* and is much easier to recognize as an emendation of the numeral than the way it appears in Farley.

THIS ENTRY. FB ii (22), 'At (Great) ASHFIELD (Robert Blunt) holds 3 carrying-services (*aueres*) from 9 men'.

,4   [HELD]. LDB *ten&* is in error for *tenuit*.

THIS ENTRY. FB ii (22), 'At WYKEN (Robert Blunt) holds full jurisdiction over those who dwell on the King's land'.

,6   HARET. The second element is OE *-rāed*, but the first is obscure; PNDB 287.

ST. EDMUND'S HAD. In the MS there is an erasure after *eadmund(us)*.

,9   ALL THESE FREE MEN. Probably those in 66,5-9.

,12   BRUNMER. LDB *Brunar(us)*, from OE **Brūnmāer*; PNDB 210.

[HELD IT]. LDB *ten&* is in error for *tenuit*.

,13   WALSHAM ... AKI. See 66,2.

,15   WALSHAM (LE WILLOWS). See 66,2.

,16   WYVERSTONE ... AKI. Cf. 6,57.

R. OUDKELL. LDB *Ouethel*. The byname is from the Anglo-Scand. masc. personal-name *Authketill*, *Authkell*, see Fellows Jensen 39 (J.M.D.).

,17   (GREAT) ASHFIELD. Here placed in Stow Hundred which borders Blackbourn and Bradmere Hundreds to which it is assigned in 14,93 and 66,3.

HERVEY OF BOURGES. His byname *bict-*, *bituricensis*, *bituriensis* probably refers to Bourges (Cher); he also occurs as Hervey of Berry (*berruarius*, equivalent to OFr *berruier*, *beruier*, *barruier*), the province in central France in which Bourges is situated; see OEB 132. He also occurs in IE (158, 162, 165 etc) as Hervey Bedruel (*bebruel*, *bedruel*, *beruel*, *bredruel*); this byname was taken by OEB (132 n.1) to be an obscure local byname but is rather to be explained as an AN version of OFr *berruier*, 'of Berry' as above.

,1   EUEN. The name-form may represent **Euen(d)* from the OScand. masc. personal-name *Eyvindr* (Björkman 36), but might also be the OE fem. personal-name *Eawynn* (von Feilitzen 1945, 79) (J.M.D.).

,1   RICHARD OF CLARE'S PREDECESSOR. That of Richard son of Count Gilbert, see *25* note.

',3   ROBERT MALET'S PREDECESSOR. Probably Edric, as 67,2.

',4   1 FREE MAN. IE (146) adds, 'in the jurisdiction and under the patronage of St. Etheldreda's'.

',5   [HELD]. LDB *ten&* is in error for *tenuit*.

BRUTGE. See 6,28 note.

WARNER. LDB *Garner(us)*, from the OFr form of OG *Warinhari*; Forssner 247-248.

THIS ENTRY. Cf. IE (165), 'In *BRUGGE* 1 free woman under the patronage of St. Etheldreda's, with 80 acres as a manor. Then 1 plough, now ½. Meadow, 2 acres; ½ mill. Value then 20s; now 10[s]'. Cf. also IEAL (180).

',6   THEN 1 PLOUGH. IE (165) adds, 'now not'.

UNDER ... AELFRIC. IE, 'under the patronage of St. Etheldreda's'.

WARNER ... ABBOT. IE, 'Hervey Bedruel holds this from the Abbot', referring to 67,6 and to the entry in 67,5 note.

',7   W. SON OF GORHAM. The patronym may be OBret **Goron*; OEB 185.

',9   UNDER ... ST. ETHELDREDA'S. IE (144) adds, 'in full jurisdiction'.

VALUE ... NOW 9S. IE, 'Value 10s'.

',10   4 SMALLHOLDERS. In the MS the first minim of *iiii* is written over an erasure.

A GUARD. LDB *huscarli* (genitive) is here used as a descriptive term, probably denoting a trained soldier. For *Huscarl* used as a name, see 16,8 note.

',11   10 FREE MEN ... (HAD IT). IE (144), '9 free men over whom St. Etheldreda's had full jurisdiction and patronage'; eight of the LDB names are then given, excluding Wulfric and Edric.

ANI. LDB *Ana*, from ODan *Ani*; PNDB 161.

80 AND 4 ACRES. In LDB *ac(ris)* has been deleted between *LXXX* and *&*. For the 4 acres, cf. 67,15 and note.

WULFMER ... [HAD]. LDB *h(abe)t* is in error for *habuit*.

67,12 LEOFRIC AND BRICTRIC; and WULFMER AND BONDI. IE (144) adds 'over these the Abbot has full jurisdiction and patronage'.
[IN] LORDSHIP. In the MS *in ead(em) in d(omi)nio*. Farley omits the second *in*.
HARDEKIN. See 25,57 note.

67,13 *NECHEMARA*. See 6,113 note.
A GUARD. As 67,10 note.

67,15 4 ACRES ... BEALINGS. Cf. the 4 acres in 67,11 (Great Bealings) which is kept separa from the 80 acres therein.
BERNARD OF ALENÇON. From Alençon (Orne); OEB 67. Cf. below.
HE COULD NOT GRANT ... SOMEONE ELSE. The subject here is Edric.
THE OTHER UNDER ... SOMEONE UNDER ... ST. ETHELDREDA'S. Cf. IE (145) free man over whom the Abbot has full jurisdiction and patronage.'
BERNARD OF ALENÇON. In the MS *de belencún*; Farley prints *de belencuñ*. The LDB fc is in error for *de alencun*, as above.

67,16 FRANI. LDB *frana*, from ON *Fráni*; PNDB 252.
REGINALD. LDB *Renoldus*, from Rainald the Rom. form of OG *Raginald*; Forssner 208.

67,17 *DERNEFORD*. Unidentified, DG 396.

67,18 *INGOLUESTUNA*. See 21,65 note.
PETER OF PALLUEL. LDB *de paludel*. From either Palluel (Pas-de-Calais) or Paluel (Seine-Inf.); OEB 105.

67,20-21 AZOR. LDB *Atser(us)*, from ODan, OSw *Azur*; PNDB 170-171.
(WILLIAM MALET ... DIED). As in 67,19.

67,21 ERCHENBALD. LDB *Arce(n)baldus*, from OG *Ercanbald*, Rom. *Archembald*; Forssner 76.
[HELD IT]. LDB *ten&* is in error for *tenuit*.
OF THIS, LIKEWISE. In LDB *totide(m)* has been deleted after *ex hoc*.

67,22 FREE MAN. In the MS *h(omine)m* has been corrected from *h(om)o*.
[HALF] UNDER THE PATRONAGE. LDB omits the first *dim(idium)*.
THIS ENTRY. Cf. IE (146), '1 free man, *Wenelin(c)g*, half under the patronage of the Abbot, with 8 acres'. The name *Wenelin(c)g* is probably a patronymic derived from OG *Wenilo*; PNDB 411.

67,23 1 FREE MAN. In the MS *hom(ine)m* has been altered from *homo*. Farley prints as *homô*.

67,25 PERCHES. In the MS *p(erti)cis* has been altered from *p(erti)cas*.

67,27 17 SHEEP. In the MS *xvii* has been altered from *xiiii*.

67,28 ALWAYS 2 PLOUGHS. Presumably in lordship.
HIVES. The MLat term *rusca* is used here instead of the more usual *vas*.

67,29 UNDER THE PATRONAGE OF THE SAME. Either of Godiva or of Edric of Laxfield
1 FREE MAN AND A HALF. IE (148), '2 free men'. Cf. also IEAL (180).

67,30 ODO. LDB here *Odonus*, below (67,31) *Odo*. From OG *Odo*; Forssner 198-199. The first form appears to have a diminutive ending (perhaps it stands for *Odoinus*, with a Rom. suffix *-in*, cf. OEB 192).
AS A MANOR. The scribe repeated *p(ro) man(erio)* in LDB then deleted the second instance.
WYNNING. LDB *Wenningus*, from OE *Wynning*; PNDB 428. IE (148) calls him '1 free man'.
8 FREE MEN. IE, '8 free men and a half'.
THEY SHOULD REDEEM. LDB *redimer&* is in error for *redimerent*. IE has the correct form.

67,31 ODO. See 67,30 note.

67,32 HELD IT. In the MS *qu(o)d* has been altered from *qui*.

67,33 [HELD]. LDB *ten&* is in error for *tenuit*.

68 GILBERT THE CROSSBOWMAN. He also held land in Norfolk (*52*). Note that MLat *balistarius* has usually been translated as 'Gunner' in the present series but 'crossbowma is more accurate and is preferred here. In the right margin of the MS next to the chapte number is a letter *f*, not shown by Farley; see *17* note.

68,1-4 BLYTHING HUNDRED. LDB *BIDINGA* is in error for *BLIDINGA*.

68,1 AELFRIC SON OF WULFGEAT. LDB has here *Elricus* but he appears to be the same a *Aluricus* at 16,2-3; see PNDB 180 and n.2.

68,2 WULFRIC ... ½ PLOUGH. In LDB the words *Rex & com(e)s soca(m)* have been deleted after *car(uca)*.

68,3-4 PATRONAGE OF THE SAME MAN. Earl Harold, as in 68,1.

68,5 DURING THE REIGN OF KING EDWARD. Translating *uiuente rege.edwardo*, an alternative to *t.r.e.*

EUSTON. Cf. 14,98.
AUBREY DE VERE'S PREDECESSOR. Probably Wulfwin, cf. 35,7-8 and 35,1-2;5-6.
RALPH THE CROSSBOWMAN. He also held land in Norfolk (*53*). For the byname see
68 note. In the right margin of the MS near the chapter number is a letter *R*, not shown by
Farley; see *17* note.
,1 BISHOP STIGAND. See 1,107-119 note.
,3 CORTON. LDB *earetuna*, in error for *caretuna*.
REGINALD THE BRETON. The byname is MLat *Brito*, 'Breton'; OEB 133. In the right
margin of the MS next to the chapter number is a letter *f*, not shown by Farley; see *17*
note.
,1 (WILLIAM OF) VATTEVILLE. Cf. 54,1.
CLAIM. LDB *calu(m)pniatur* (sing.) is in error for *calu(m)pniantur* (plural).
ROBERT OF STRATFORD. From Stratford St. Mary (in Samford Hundred), which he
held from Swein of Essex, see 27,9; cf. OEB 51.
,1 SWEIN SWART. The byname is OWScand *Suartr*, *Suarti*, 'black'; OEB 338.
STANHARD SON OF AETHELWY. Possibly the same as Stanhard in Essex (*87*). Cf.
also Stanhard son of Aethelwy of Thetford (7,1).
WULFMER. Probably the same as Wulfmer the (King's) reeve in 1,7 and 74,4;7 and
76,13-14.
,1 *LAFHAM*. Unidentified, DG 404.
HERIOT. A payment due at the time of death from a warrior to his lord, representing the
return of his military equipment.
HIS FATHER. Wulfmer's father.
VAVASSORS. Undertenants. The obsolete term is retained here because of its rarity in
the Domesday records. It has been observed only here, in Buckinghamshire (12,30) and
on the Isle of Wight (Hampshire IOW 7,15).
,2 *FACHEDUNA*. See 25,58 note.
,3 2 ACRES. Probably of meadow, if *prati* has been omitted.
,4 'OLDEN'. As 1,5 note.
RADBOD. LDB *Rabboda*, from OG *Radbodo*, *Rabbodo*; PNDB 344, Forssner 205.
ROGER. Bigot, the Sheriff, see *7* and note.
WULFMER THE REEVE. See *73* and note.
BRICTMER THE BEADLE. The byname *bedel* is from OE *bydel*, Lat. *bedellus*, 'beadle';
OEB 240. He may perhaps be the same as Brictmer, Robert Malet's reeve, who is
mentioned in 4,15, since Robert Malet was Sheriff at one point, see *6* note.
,7 THIS ENTRY. This duplicates 1,7 under the King's lands.
,8-9 EARL R(ALPH). Wader, see 1,61-95 note.
,10 THESE ... KING'S HAND. Referring to 74,8-10.
,11 FLINT. A byname from OE *flint*, 'flint, rock'; PNDB 251.
,13 30 FREE MEN ... NAMES. Only 29 are named.
RICTAN. Of obscure origin. Perhaps a misreading.
ESTRED. LDB *Estrat*, from OE *Ēastrǣd*; cf. PNDB 244.
TOVILD. LDB *Touilt*, from ON *Tófa-Hildr*, 'Hildr the daughter of Tófi'; cf. PNDB 384
and Essex 90,72.
GUNVATI. LDB *Gunequata*, from ON *Gunnhvati*, cf. PNDB 277.
DERSI. LDB *Dirsi*, from OE *Dēorsige*.
SAXLEF. From OG *Sahsleib*, see von Feilitzen 1963, 57; (J.M.D.).
,16 FRIDEB... LDB *Frieb'*. This abbreviated form could represent OG *Fridebern/Fridebert* or OE
Frithubeorht.
FREE MEN ... IN THE KING'S HAND. These free men and their lands seem to have
been the subject of disputes, some of them as yet unresolved.
,1 THE ABBOT. Of St. Edmund's, cf. 14,100.
,3 HERBERT BLACUN. The byname is a patronym from OE *blaechūn*; OEB 214.
BISHOP ERFAST. See 19,1-2 note.
JUDICAEL THE PRIEST. Cf. 64,3.
,4 BISHOP AELMER. See 18,1 note.
,5 2 FREE MEN ... ROBERT MALET'S MOTHER. Probably Brictere and Cynric of 77,3.
ANNEXATIONS. For similar chapters, see Essex *90* and Norfolk *66*. The entries
represent instances of the unlawful occupation of lands, brought to light by the
Domesday Survey. They are grouped according to the landholder responsible for the
annexation.
,1-7 RICHARD SON OF COUNT GILBERT. See *25* and note.

76,1	BRADLEY. Cf. 25,92.
	MALUS VICINUS. A Lat. byname meaning 'bad neighbour', equivalent to OFr *mauveysin* which is the base of the medieval surname *Malveysyn, Mauueysyn, Mauvesyn*, etc. which appears in the reigns of Henry III and Edward III in W. Rye, *A calendar of the Feet of Fines Suffolk* (Ipswich, 1900), 47, 71, 196, 223 (sometimes printed therein as -*nn*-).
76,2	GROTON. Cf. 25,50.
	ROBERT SON OF WYMARC. As 1,102 note.
	ROGER OF ORBEC. As 25,56 note.
76,3	CAVENDISH. Cf. 25,47.
	SAID WITHGAR. In LDB *p(re)dicti* is misplaced after *Edrici* rather than after *Witgari*.
	ROGER OF ST. GERMAIN. As 25,47 note.
76,4	CORNARD. CF. 25,43.
	AELFRIC KEMP. As 16,41 note.
	[HELD]. LDB *ten&* is in error for *tenuit*.
	(RICHARD'S) PREDECESSOR ... AGREEMENT OF RICHARD. LDB *ante c(on)uention(e)* .*Ricardi* stands for *ante(c essor) c(on)uention(e)* .*Ricardi*, with *Ricardi* written o once although being governed by both of the preceding words. Cf. *ante* for *ante(cessor)* in 76,18.
76,5	*SAIBAMUS*. Unidentified, DG 409.
76,6-7	CAVENDISH. Cf. 25,47.
76,8-12	WILLIAM OF PARTHENAY. From Parthenay (Deux-Sèvres) or possibly Parthenay-d Bretagne (Ille-et-Vilaine); OEB 105.
76,8	STANTON. Cf. 14,72.
76,9	KNETTISHALL. Cf. 14,99.
76,10-12	BARDWELL. Cf. 14,82.
76,12	WHOLE OF THIS ... ABBOT'S DESPITE. Referring to 76,8-12 all of which was taken away from St. Edmund's.
76,13	WULFMER, THE KING'S REEVE. See *73* and note.
76,14	BRICETT ... 20 ACRES. See also 30,3.
	BOTILD. From ON *Bóthildr*, ODan,OSw *Bothild*, cf. PNDB 207.
76,15	BAYLHAM ... WILLIAM OF BOURNEVILLE. Cf. 7,58 where '½ church, 12 acres' is entered.
76,16	ROGER (OF AUBERVILLE). Cf. 29,1.
	EUSTACE. Count Eustace, cf. 5,4.
	COUNT OF MORTAIN. Robert, see *2* and note.
	HE GAVE UP. LDB *relinq(ui)d* is in error for *relinq(ui)t*.
	ROBERT THE CROSSBOWMAN. LDB *arbal(istarius)*; OEB 234-235. He was a minor landholder in Norfolk (*54*).
76,17-18	ROBERT OF COURSON. See 7,6-7 note.
	COVEHITHE. As 1,108 note.
	COUNT ALAN ... WISSETT. Cf. 3,10.
	EARL R(ALPH). Wader, the son of (Earl) R(alph) the Constable in 3,10. See 1,61-95 note.
76,18	WILLIAM OF WARENNE. See *26* and note.
76,19	UGGESHALL ... BERENGAR. Cf. 14,164 note.
76,20	RALPH OF LIMÉSY. See *43* and note.
	[BABERGH TWO HUNDREDS]. Omitted here before Cavendish, Lavenham and Coddenham.
	CAVENDISH. Cf. 43,2.
	IN THE BATTLE. Of Hastings, 1066.
	BAYNARD. Perhaps Ralph Baynard (*33*), or his nephew William (33,10).
	EDGAR. Probably Ralph's predecessor in 43,1.
	IN LORDSHIP. Translating *in d(omi)nio halle*.
76,21	AUBREY DE VERE. See *35* and note.
	LAVENHAM ... WULFWIN. Cf. 35,1.
76,22	ROGER OF RAMES. See *38* and note.
	CODDENHAM. Cf. 38,5.
	WALTER OF ST. VALÉRY. See *51* and note.
	FREE MEN. LDB *lib(er)i* is in error for *lib(er)os*.
	ON HIS BEHALF. In the MS *sua* has been altered from *suę*.
76,23	ROBERT MALET. See *6* and note.
	THIS ENTRY. This largely duplicates the last part of 6;191.

7]   DISPUTES ... This chapter is not included in the List of Landholders in the MS, although it has been inserted there in the present edition, see folio 281a. It is written by one of the scribes of LDB and is contemporary with the rest of the Suffolk text. The dispute is also mentioned in 75,5.

        BISHOP OF BAYEUX. See *16* and note.

        ROBERT MALET'S MOTHER. See 6,76-77 note.

7,1-2   OCCOLD. Cf. 6,193.

7,1   BRICTERE. From OE *Beorhthere*; PNDB 194.

7,3   BEDINGFIELD ... 40 ACRES. Cf. 75,5.

        IN THE ABOVE-MENTIONED MANNER. Translating *sup(ra)dicto m(odo)*.

7,4   ASPALL. Cf. 6,201 and 16,48.

        THURSTAN. One of the free men belonging to the Holding held by Peter from Abbot Baldwin of St. Edmund's after 1066, see FD xci and no. 168.

        MARCULF. Either ODan *Markulf* or OG *Marculf*; PNDB 325.

        GUNNULF. LDB *Grunulf(us)*, from ON *Gúnnulfr*, ODan, OSw *Gunnulf*, see PNDB 278. He also belonged to the same Holding as Thurstan, above.

        WILLIAM MALET. Robert Malet's father.

        HUBERT OF PORT. One of the King's officials, see 16,34 and note.

        ODIHAM. A royal manor in Hampshire (1,1) and the centre of a Hundred there. It is within 5 miles of Mapledurwell (Hampshire 24,1), the main holding of Hubert of Port, see preceding note.

OLO-   THIS SURVEY ... THE OTHERS. Written in red ink at the end of the text of LDB, which
HON   included the Domesday Survey for Essex, Norfolk and Suffolk, the three counties referred to here. See further, MDB 180-185.

C1-

C2   EXNING. In Cambridgeshire until the 12th century (VCH Cambridgeshire i. 340, n.3).

C2   WYMARC. Count Alan's steward (*dapifer*), ICC (4).

E1   HARKSTEAD. See 1,96 above.

E2   WITH ALL THE ABOVE. Referring to several Freemen described in Essex 23,16-26.

E3   MANOR IN SUFFOLK. Probably either Churchford (36,1) or Stutton (36,2). Both were held in succession by Scalpi and William *de Alno*, the latter from Robert Gernon.

Nf4   EARL R(ALPH). Wader, see above 1,61-95 note.

THE HUNDREDS AND HALF-HUNDREDS

Most of the twenty-five Suffolk Hundreds and Half-Hundreds named in 1086 survived without much change into the 19th century. Some are termed alternatively 'Hundred' or 'Half-Hundred' in DB and later medieval records and there appears to have been little actual difference in legal status between the two terms in the post-Conquest period – a small Hundred might occasion ally be called a Half-Hundred , that was all. In the same way, the Hundred and a Half of Samford was sometimes termed just a Hundred (see 3,67. 39,17. 40,6. etc.). The double Hundred of Babergh is rather more consistently described as two Hundreds, but not always (in 6,1 it is treated as a single Hundred, for example) . All were centres of the same type of Hundredal jurisdiction, whatever their physical size or fiscal capacity.

There is no evidence that the double Hundred of Babergh was formed by the union of two originally separate smaller Hundreds. Several such fusions of Hundreds or Half-Hundreds did occur in Suffolk, however, in the medieval period. The Hundreds of Blackbourn and Bradmere were already intermingled by 1086 and had become the double Hundred of Blackbourn by 1182. Bosmere and Claydon Hundreds were joined together after 1086; later on, by the 13th century, a third part of Claydon Hundred became the separate Half-Hundred of Thredling (the name itself meaning 'third part', from OE *thridling*). The Half-Hundred of Parham was subsumed into the Hundred of Plomesgate after 1086, and the latter was termed a Hundred and a Half by 1240. Even as late as 1763, the two Half-Hundred s of Mutford (called Lothing in 1086) and Lothingland were united to form a single Hundred .

Other changes to the list of Suffolk Hundreds made after 1086 include the name-change of Bishop's Hundred to Hoxne Hundred (by 1191); and the addition of the Half-Hundred of Exning (by 1199), after the transference of the parish from Cambridgeshire.

Some of the Hundreds or Half-Hundreds included detached parts in 1086. Claydon Hundred was then in three separate sections (hence Thredling Half-Hundred, mention ed above), while Parham was in two parts. Sudbury was a detached part of Thingoe Hundred. Kelsale (and probably Aldringham and part of Carlton, see 6,69-70 notes) was an outlier of Bishop's Hundred. Kenton, Woodbridge, Butley, and Gedgrave were outliers of the Hundred of Loes.

The unit known as a Ferthing (from OE *feorthing* 'a fourth part') is mentioned twice in LDB Suffolk, in connection with those of Aldham (14,112) and South Elmham (18,4), see 14,112 note.

A group of eight and a half Hundreds in the west of the county formed the Liberty of the Abbey Bury St. Edmunds in the medieval period. Although it is reputed to have been granted by Edward the Confessor, it is not specifically mentioned in the Domesday Survey. The Liberty included the Hundreds of Blackbourn, Bradmere, Lackford, Risbridge, Thedwestry, and Thingoe; the double Hundred of Babergh; and the Half-Hundred of Cosford. A further five and a half Hundreds in the south-east of the county belonged to the Abbey of Ely. These were the Hundreds of Carlford, Colneis, Loes, Plomesgate, and Wilford; and the Half-Hundred of Parham.

There is no absolute consistency in the order in which the Hundredal units occur within chapter in LDB Suffolk. The following series occur in more than one chapter, however: (i) Thedwestry, Thingoe, Lackford, Babergh, Stow, Ipswich, Bosmere, Claydon, Samford; (ii) Risbridge, Cosford, Bishop's, Blything, Colneis, Carlford, Wilford, Loes; (iii) Parham, Plomesgate, Hartismere; (iv) Wangford, Lothing, Lothingland. Only the last of these makes obvious geographical sense. The others probably reflect an order in which their material was copied into LDB or into a previous draft, rather than any conventional ordering of the Suffolk Hundredal units. Some Hundredal rubrics m have been omitted from chapter 6 (see 6,207-208 notes). Such omissions are rare in the Suffolk folios but others do occur (before 50,1 and 61,1 for example) .

For further information about, and medieval references to, the Suffolk Hundreds and Half-Hundreds, see O. S. Anderson, *The English Hundred-Names* (Lund 1934) 83-98.

THE COUNTY BOUNDARY

The county of Suffolk has its origin as the southern division (or *folc*) of the Kingdom of the East Angles, divided from the northern division (Norfolk) by the rivers of the Little Ouse and the Waveney. To the south it is divided from Essex by the River Stour. Its western boundary against Cambridgeshire was formerly the River Kennet, but part of it was moved westwards to include Exning in the 12th century. There is evidence in the Domesday Survey of some tenurial associatio with estates in Norfolk (Alburgh, Diss, Gillingham, Gorleston, Hardwick, Kenninghall, Mundhan Redenhall, and Yarmouth); Cambridgeshire (Weston Colville); and Essex (Ardleigh, Brightlingse Bures [Essex 23,16 note], Castle Hedingham, Great and Little Henny, Moze, and Nayland [Essex 24,57 note]).

The parish of Ballingdon cum Brundon was transferred from Essex to the Borough of Sudbury i Suffolk in 1832 and 1835 (*The Place-Names of Essex* ed. P. H. Reaney, *English Place-Name Society* xii, Cambridge 1935, 407n.); for its Domesday entries see the Essex volume.

APPENDIX I

THE ELY INQUIRY
Inquisitio Eliensis (IE)

The Ely Inquiry, usually referred to as IE, is a collection of material relating to holdings of Ely Abbey in Cambridgeshire, Essex, Hertfordshire, Huntingdonshire, Norfolk, and Suffolk whose source appears to have been drafts (now lost) of the returns for three different circuits of the DB Survey. It was put together, for the benefit of Ely Abbey, very soon after 1086, but survives only in three manuscripts written in the second half of the 12th century — British Library, Cotton Tiberius A.vi, folios 38-70 (MS A; this manuscript also contains the sole surviving text of the *Inquisitio Comitatus Cantabrigiensis*, ICC, for an account of which, see the Cambridgeshire volume, Introduction); Trinity College Cambridge 0.2.41, pages 161-274 (MS B) and 0.2.1, folios 177v-213 (MS C). Of these three manuscripts, B and C are derived from a common source, while A is a copy of B. Although B is now thought to be the most reliable of them, IE was reproduced in record type in 1816 by Sir Henry Ellis from A (see DB 4, pp. 495-528). N.E.S.A. Hamilton also used A as the base text for his edition of IE in 1876 (pages 97-168 of his *Inquisitio Comitatus Cantabrigiensis*), but also gave variant readings from B and C in footnotes.[1] Footnotes to the Victoria County History translation of LDB Suffolk also supply items of extra information from IE, translated from Hamilton's edition (*The Victoria History of the County of Suffolk*, i (1911), 419-582).

For Suffolk, IE (Hamilton 141-166; and summaries at 122) supplies details of the Ely Abbey holdings in the county (cf. above, Chapter 21) and of other pieces of land and rights claimed by the Abbey. The order of entries is largely on a Hundredal basis but is not always the same as that in LDB. The IE text does not include all the information to be found in LDB, nor are its statistics always identical, but it does have some material not to be found in LDB. Hamilton also edited some other documents, subsidiary to IE, which are dependent on, or relevant to, the DB Survey. The *Inquisitio Eliensis* Breviate (IEBrev; Hamilton 168-173) gives summaries of the numbers of ploughs and people in each of the Abbey's holdings, and the *Nomina Villarum* (IENV; Hamilton 174-175) lists the numbers of ploughs held by the villagers therein. These are followed by lists of holdings alienated from the Abbey's possession (IEAL; Hamilton 175-189) and an account of an inquiry into the Abbey's losses held between 1071 and 1075 (Hamilton 192-195). In the notes to the present volume, quotations from IE and its related documents have only been given where information occurs which is different from, or extra to, that in LDB.

For further comments on IE, see R. Welldon Finn, 'The Inquisitio Eliensis Reconsidered', *English Historical Review* lxxv (1960), 385-409. For the Ely Abbey claims, see E. Miller, 'The Ely land pleas in the reign of William I', *English Historical Review* lxii (1947), 438-456 and *Liber Eliensis*, ed. E. O. Blake, 426-432. See also the Introduction to the Cambridgeshire volume for a sample of text from IE.

Note that in the Cambridgeshire volume, Introduction, The Ely Inquiry, it is wrongly stated that Ellis and Hamilton edited IE from MS C and that Hamilton collated it to MSS A and B. The true situation is as stated in the present Appendix.

APPENDIX II

THE FEUDAL BOOK OF ABBOT BALDWIN OF [BURY] ST. EDMUNDS (FB)

FB is a survey of holdings in Suffolk, Norfolk, and Essex which belonged to the Abbe of [Bury] St. Edmunds (cf. Chapter *14*, above). The fullest surviving version of it forms part of the late 12th-century section of the Black Book of the Abbey, now Cambridge University Library, Mm. 4.19 (folios 124–143v), but its name associates i origin with the time of Abbot Baldwin (1065–1098). Part of FB is also included in th 14th-century Bury register, now Cambridge University Library, Ee. 3.60 (folios 178v foll.); this part was edited by Lord Francis Hervey in *The Pinchbeck Register* (Brighton, 1925) i, 410 foll. The fullest modern edition of FB is that by D. C. Dougl in FD, *Feudal Documents from the Abbey of Bury St. Edmunds* (London, 1932), 3–44, with an introduction, xlvi–lxvii. If in fact it was the work of Abbot Baldwin, FB dates from between 9 September 1087 and (?)29 December 1097, the respective dates of death of William I (see below) and of Abbot Baldwin.[1] However, R. Lennar in *Rural England: 1086–1135* (Oxford, 1959), 359 has disputed the connection with Abbot Baldwin and has suggested a terminal date of March 1119. FB contains three sections:

FB i; folios 124–131v, FD 3–15. A survey of the Abbey's lordship manors in Norfo and Suffolk and of the lands which the Abbey's tenants held there when King Willia caused 'the survey of the whole of England' to be made and also on the day of his death. Within each Hundred in the Suffolk portion the individual entries are largely given in the same order as in LDB, but the Hundreds themselves are in a different order, those in FB beginning with the eight-and-a-half Hundreds of St. Edmund's in the west of the county. A number of places are omitted from FB and there are frequent differences between the statistics given in FB and in LDB.

FB ii; folios 132–134v, FD 15–24. A survey of the lands of the Abbey's *feudati homines* in Norfolk, Suffolk, and Essex (two entries only), arranged by tenants rathe than by Hundred. In the Suffolk section not all the sub-tenancies given in LDB are included and there are a number of discrepancies.

FB iii; folios 135–143v, FD 25–44. A list of the holdings and rents or tax-liability c named peasants, relating only to thirty-one places in the Suffolk Hundreds of Thedwestry and Blackbourn and the Half-Hundred of Cosford.

In the notes to the present volume, reference to FB has only been made where information occurs which is different from, or extra to, that in LDB.

---

[1] Douglas, FD xlviii–xlix, dates between 7 September 1087 and 4 January 1098. For the date Abbot Baldwin's death, see *The Heads of Religious Houses: England & Wales 940–1216*, edd. D. Knowles, C. N. L. Brooke, V. London (Cambridge, 1972), 32.

INDEX OF PERSONS

Familiar modern spellings are given where they exist. Unfamiliar names are usually given in an approximate late 11th century form, avoiding variants that were already obsolescent or pedantic. Spellings that mislead the modern eye are avoided where possible (thus Leofled, not Leofflaed). While an attempt has been made to differentiate individuals with the same name, there remain several individuals who cannot be so differentiated. Readers are therefore advised that a group of references given under a single name (e.g. Edric) do not necessarily refer to the same individual; where the same name occurs more than once in a single entry and could refer to different individuals, the possible number of different individuals is shown in brackets after the entry reference. In general, notes on either personal names or individuals have been placed under the first reference listed in this index.

References are to persons named in the translation of LDB or to those identified in the notes from additional information contained in IE, FB or FD. All names or name-forms which are supplied from IE, FB or FD are printed in italics; to avoid confusion with this extra material, all unidentified place-names (e.g. Carlewuda) which occur as part of personal-names are printed in this index in roman type although they are in italics in the translation. The chapter-numbers of listed landholders are also here printed in italics, as are references to entries governed by a sub-heading (e.g. 1,61–95; but not those added in the translation of Chapter 76).

Acwulf	12,1. 59,1
Adelelm	35,5;7–8
Adelo	14,36 note
Adelund	14,32;36;58;98
Aedi	6,171
Aelfeva mother of Earl Morcar	16,10
(Aelfeva) mother of Earl Morcar	*1,97–99* and note
Aelfeva	7,36;38–39. 21,50. 84,3
Aelfgyth	54,2
Aelfled	6,38;57;211. 8,31;53;55–56. 33,12. 52,1
Aelfric brother of Edric	76,3
Aelfric father of Withgar, see Aelfric son of Withgar	
Aelfric Kemp	16,41. 28,7. 38,2. 76,4
Aelfric of Hopewella	6,110
Aelfric of Sanford	26,12b
Aelfric of Weinhou, Wenhou	39,17. 46,3
Aelfric son of Bondi	7,37
Aelfric son of Brown	16,11
Aelfric son of Rolf, burgess of Ipswich	74,8–10
Aelfric son of (? Edwin) the smith in Carlewuda	6,110
Aelfric son (and father) of Withgar	25,1;60
Aelfric son of Wulfgeat	16,2–3. 68,1
Aelfric Starling	25,71
Aelfric Stickstag	7,77
Aelfric the deacon	38,22
Aelfric the priest	2,17. 3,64;74–78. 16,30. 74,14
Aelfric the reeve of the Abbot (of St. Edmund's)	*14,152*
Aelfric the reeve	1,17;30 and note;60 note;103
Aelfric Wand	*1,100–106*
Aelfric, a thane of King (Edward's)	3,88
Aelfric	1,102. 2,20. 3,66;94;100. 4,11;13;19;21;40. 5,7. 6,40;57;90;110;116;191–192;309–310. 7,40;48–49;66;75;79;104;108;118;121;134; 137. 8,6;55. 9,1–2. 14,41;44;49. 16,15–16; 20(×2);35;38;41(×2);42. 19,18. 21,23;63. 23,2–3. 25,60(×2);64–65. 26,13–14. 31,20; 56. 36,5;12–13. 38,11;20. 43,5;7. 51,1. 56,5. 64,1. 67,6. 74,13(×4). ENf4
Aelfric	notes to 8,12;81

Aelfwin brother of Goda	7,37
Bishop Aelmer (of Elmham)	2,3-5. 3,96. 6,311. 7,4. 8,42. 18,1;4;6. 19,11; 14-16;18;20. 64,3. 75,4
(Bishop) Aelmer (of Elmham)	19,1-3;9;13-14;17
Aelmer the King's reeve	8,60
Aelmer the priest	1,56
Aelmer	1,73-74. 3,95. 4,42. 6,9;92;209;239. 7,79; 80(X2);83;101;104;121. 8,61. 13,3. 16,20. 21,90. 32,23. 38,6. 41,4;6.
Aelmer	21,100 note
Aeschere	1,123f
Aescman	58,1
Aethelgyth	33,1;13. ENf5
Aethelric of Burgh	8,6;9. 32,23;28. 67,23
Aethelric (of Burgh)	26,16
Aethelric	1,18. 6,112. 14,38. 16,18;26;31. 26,17;18;20. 67,10
Aethelric, wife of	14,38
Aethelsi	1,19
Aethelstan	1,19;55. 4,1;18. 16,7;26. 74,13
Aethelward son of Bell	25,20
Aethelward the King's reeve	7,18;36
Aethelward	7,5
Aethelwin	8,65
Aethelwold the priest	3,31
Aethelwold	6,123
Aethelwy of Thetford (?Sheriff of Norfolk)	7,1 and note
Aethelwy	6,46
Aethelwy, see Stanhard	
Agenet	14,13
Ailbern	16,18. 25,68;85
Ailbold the priest	14,13 note;39
Ainuar	25,89
Aitard	7,4
Aki	6,57;85. 66,1-4;13-14;16
Akile Suffering	7,37
Count Alan (of Brittany)	*3* and note. 1,123f. 4,13. 13,3. 26,12a;12d;15. 76,17. EC2. ENf2;4. Also folio 291a
Count Alan (of Brittany)	46,10 note
Count Alan, see Wymarc	
Alan	37,5
Burnt Albert	8,15
Albert	8,13;56-58. 14,11
Albold, a cleric	14,13;39 note
Aldred	5,2
Aldgyth	67,15. 74,6
Aldwin	7,60
Aldwulf	7,80;82;107-109
Alfgeat	1,102. 6,216. 16,35. 25,73. 29,6. 54,3
Alfger	1,111
Alfheah	4,15. 14,43
Alfhere, see Godwin	
Alfnoth	49,1
Alfred	32,4. 36,8
Alfsi	6,191. EC2
Alfwold	16,6 note
Earl Algar	8,33. 12,4. 16,9. 25,58;77. 38,1. 65,1
(Earl) Algar	1,121 and note
Algar the priest	8,75
Algar	6,106;197. 7,18;71;118;124. 8,62. 12,5. 16,36. 19,12. 21,55-56. 27,10. 28,3. 64,3. 66,13
Algar	8,59 note

Algar, see Godwin
Ali   7,19;54
Alnoth   6,32(×2);100;196. 7,36;102. 16,30
Alric the reeve   1,60
Alric   1,44–45. 74,10
Alsi nephew of Earl Ralph   8,50
Alsi nephew of Earl R(alph)   6,216;233
Alsi   5,3. 16,12. 21,28;34. 60,1. 68,5
Alsi, wife of   68,5
Alsi, see Godwin
Alstan   6,191;228. 37,1;4. 67,11. 74,11
Alward   6,202. 61,1
Alwin of Mendlesham   1,77 note. 31,51
Alwin the priest   1,13–14. 16,30
Alwin   1,7;77;110. 3,9. 6,38;48;57;207;211;296.
                                             7,23;85;111;136. 8,8. 16,34;41. 19,14;16.
                                             23,5. 25,73;83–84;90. 33,8. 35,7(×2). 36,5.
                                             38,6;10;27. 40,6. 52,6. 67,11. 74,7;11(×2);13
Alwin, wife of   6,57
Alwold the priest   16,22
Alwold   8,68. 16,45. 69,4. 76,6
Alwulf the priest   1,122d
Alwy   4,22. 12,6. 19,16
Alwynn   6,51
Amund   52,1–2;5;8–9
Anbold   33,7
Andrew   8,11
Ani   67,11
Anselm   14,139
Ansgot   3,67;84
Ansketel the priest, Roger Bigot's chaplain 7,36
Ansketel   7,13. 38,8
Anund the priest   67,11
Anund   1,9. 2,12. 3,32–33;46–48. 7,15. 13,7. 52,11. 53,1
Arkell   6,130
Arnold   8,9. 38,14;16
Arnold, see Roger
Arnulf   8,10. 14,26-27;35;62;115. 27,12
Arnulf   14,52 note
Artald   8,55
Aseret   21,29
Asgar the Constable   25,73. 66,10
Asgar (the Constable)   32,1;3–5;8;19
Asgar   6,217
Askell the priest   4,14
Askell, a guard   67,10
Askell, a villager   68,2
Askell   7,37;109;143. 19,15. 25,53. 30,3. 68,4. 76,14
Aslac   31,28
Asmoth   4,15. 6,91
Asmoth, see Brictmer
Aubrey de Vere   *35*. 1,105. 6,216;227. 68,5. 76,21. EE5
Aubrey, see Humphrey, Walter
Countess of Aumâle   *46*
Auti, a thane   37,6. 40,3
Auti   37,7
Azor   67,20–21;33
Bald, see Leofwin, Richard
Abbot Baldwin (of St. Edmund's)   14,26;167. 18,4
Abbot Baldwin (of St. Edmund's)   notes to 14,5–6;21;28;65;106–107;137–139;151
Abbot Baldwin (of St. Edmund's), see Durand, Frodo
Balki   16,7;26
Barn   3,61

Barthetona, see penultimate entry
Baynard   7,15. 76,20
Baynard, see Ralph, William
Beard, see Brunman
Bedruel, see Hervey
Bell, see Aethelward
Benne, see Leofwin
Beorn   16,3
Berard   14,16;24;57;110–112. 40,5
Berengar   14,38. 76,19
Berengar   14,164 note
Bernard of Alençon   67,15;29
Bernard of London   6,110
Bernard of St. Ouen   47,2
Bernard   7,102. 41,5–6
Berner the crossbowman   21,11
Besi   6,216. 35,7
Bigot of Loges   4,13
Bigot, see Roger
Black, see Brictric
Blackman   6,93–94;112. 7,36;76;99;111;120–121. 16,26
   67,11
Blackman, wife of   6,93
Blackson   6,32. 7,60;146. 16,35
Blackwin   7,60. 25,79. 34,4
Blacun, see Herbert
Blunt, see Gilbert, Robert
Bondi the smith   7,37
Bondi   6,253. 7,29;121. 19,16. 25,56;103. 67,12. 69,
   76,1
Bondi   21,94 note
Bondi, see Aelfric
Bosten   26,8
Boti   2,11. 7,33. 35,7. 38,20
Botild   76,14
Breme   31,50
Count Brian   2,5–6;9
(Count) Brian   2,7;13
Brian, see Ralph
Brict   39,5
Brictere   77,1;3
Brictfled   6,62
Brictman   8,6
Brictmer Bubba   6,226
Brictmer son of Asmoth   4,15
Brictmer the beadle   74,4
Brictmer the reeve of Robert Malet   4,15
Brictmer the reeve of St. Edmund's   62,5
Brictmer   3,65;101. 6,11;173;201;209;215;271. 7,98;1
   121;133;140;145. 8,65. 21,39. 22,2. 32,8.
   35,7. 38,16. 39,5;7–9. 39,2–4;10. 43,6. 61,2.
   67,15;27;31. 74,13
Brictmer, see Queneva
Brictnoth   2,20. 6,46;264. 7,80;120. 8,2. 19,17
Brictnoth   notes to 8,6. 32,29
Brictric Black   25,79. 67,1
Brictric   2,17. 7,80;87;95;106;108;117;137. 8,1;6.
   25,105. 32,28. 39,5. 41,9. 67,12(×2)
Brictric   16,31 note
Brictric, see Wulfric
Brictsi   71,1
Brictwold Muffle   32,28
Brictwold son of Leofmer   notes to 14,5–6;21;28;65;106
Brictwold   6,10;271. 16,16;36. 52,1;3–5;9. 67,3. 74,5

Brictwold	8,23 note
Brother	1,53. 3,89
Brown the reeve of Ipswich	7,63–66
Brown	1,119. 8,8. 16,43. 67,10
Brown, see Aelfric, Leofwin	
Brunard	9,1
Brungar	6,215. 7,62. 16,35. 27,7
Brunloc	14,152
Brunman Beard	7,36
Brunman of Burgh	6,110
Brunman	7,108. 67,32
Brunmer the priest	66,12
Brunmer	2,18. 7,36;109;111
Brunwin	4,15. 16,23. 35,4. 67,14
Bubba, see Brictmer	
Burcard	
Burcard	14,72 note
Burghard of Mendlesham	14,152
Burghard (of Mendlesham)	1,76-77. 14,46 and notes
Burghard	1,83-84;86;95. 4,12;24;26;28-31;33;35;38-39.
	6,215. 7,42-43. 16,15;26. 31,21-24;26-30;
	32-33;35-36
Burghard, see Peter	
Burgric	3,100. 7,79;106. 16,43. 46,7;9. 67,10
Burnin	4,32
Burnin, see Warin	
Burnt, see Albert	
Canute	28,3–4
Ceolric	32,14 note
Ceolwold	25,64
Chipping	6,216
Clarenbold	42,2
Cobbe, see Leofric	
Coleman	6,216. 7,77;80. 14,24. 35,7. 62,2
Corbucion, see Robert	
Crawa	25,78
Croc, see Leofwin	
Culling, a burgess of Ipswich	1,122d
Cus	6,44. 7,37
Cynric	3,57. 4,15. 7,99. 53,3. 77,2–3
Cynwold	67,9
Dering	7,118
Dersi	74,13
Derstan	7,112
Derwulf	21,39. 77,4
Dot	3,100. 29,3
Drogo of Beuvrière	*48*
Drogo	19,12
Durand of Offton	67,23
Durand *the cleric, of St. Edmund's and*	
of Abbot Baldwin	14,119 and note
Durand	6,128. 7,84;111;118;121. 14,77;119. 16,25.
	39,12. 67,12;17–18. 74,3
Dynechaie	6,191
E.	8,11
Countess Edeva	4,17
Edeva the Fair, the Rich	1,61;63;67;73. 3,67. 31,54. 46,4. EC1
Edeva (the Fair, the Rich)	1,64. 3,68–69;71–74;76–77;81;84. 25,104.
	46,5. EC2
Edgar	43,1. 76,20
Edhild	3,91. 7,137
Queen Edith	1,122a-122b. 6,26. 25,56. 37,2. 41,1–2. 52,1.
	76,15
Queen (Edith)	6,112 and note

Edith   1,88–90. 74,13
Edmer, a thane   8,33
Edmer   6,8
King Edmund   14,167
Edmund the priest   47,2–3
Edmund the priest, wife of   47,3
Edmund   3,70–71. 25,67
Ednoth   7,85. 16,37. 36,10
Edred   8,58
Edric Grim   3,21–23;28;34–42;50–52;89;94–95. 8,26. 31, 34,15. 46,10. 67,25
Edric *Grim*   3,24–27;29 and notes
Edric Grim   3,49 note
Edric of Laxfield   1,31. 3,34;39;41. 6,28;58;62;79–80;83–84;1 114;128–129;135;148;260;264; 272-273;29 303–304. 7,23;36. 8,29. 14,68. 16,6;15;25. 19,16. 31,20;27. 64,2. 67,15;28–29;33
Edric (of Laxfield)   6,305-306. 7,114 and notes
Edric son of Ingold   4,15
Edric Spud   25,78
Edric the deacon   76,20
Edric the King's reeve   6,217
Edric   1,50;111;123f. 2,16. 3,45;95;98;101. 4,15; 18(×2). 6,3;5–6;10;11;14–16;32–34;36–37; 44–46;48;57;60–61;64–65;67–69;78–79;82; 87;90;92–95;97(×3);102;106;110–111;115- 118;123;126–127;130;132-133;135-141;149 150;153;156;159;161–162;164–165;170–17 174–180;183–184;187–190;191(×2);192–19 198;201–202;205;236–239;242;245–249;25 253–254;257;261–262;264–271;276–278;28 289;293;296;308;311. 7,13;15;38;56;58;76 77;79(×2);90;98;105;111;121;123;125; 131;142(×2);143;145–146;151. 8,8;25;30. 16,14;16;24;26–30;33;38;43. 21,67;90. 22,9 25,59;87. 26,12a;12d;13;15. 29,4. 30,2. 31,16–18;27. 32,1. 35,7. 38,4;6. 39,5;9. 51,1 64,1. 67,2;5(×2);8;11–12;15–16;20–22;26; 28;30–32. 74,4;11;13. 77,4
E(dric)   6,119-120;122;124;134;143;151-152;154-155; 157;173;197;199–200;203;238;240–241;24 244;252;255–256;290–292. 52,1. 67,10;17
Edric   notes to 8,23. 38,22
Edric, wife of   6,57
Edric, see Aelfric
Edward   4,4. 7,109
Edwin the priest   8,81
Edwin the smith in Carlewuda   6,110
(? Edwin) the smith in Carlewuda, see Aelfric
Edwin   3,72–73;83;86. 7,18. 8,58. 13,2;7. 21,51. 25,7 32,8
Edwold   8,11–12. 39,6
Edwold, wife of   8,11
Edwy   16,41;47
Edwy   8,9 note
Elinant   25,46
Engelric *the priest*   14,101 and note
Engelric   5,3–5. 14,39;107. 39,3
Erchenbald   67,21
Bishop Erfast (of Thetford)   1,119. 25,60. 75,3
(Bishop) Erfast (of Thetford)   19,1–2
Eric   21,22
Erland   3,56;62

mengot	3,67
ngeat	7,83. 61,1
nwulf	6,32
tald	8,22
tmund	1,102
tred	74,13
do son of Nigel	2,16
do (son of Nigel)	2,20
do son of Spirwic	*53*. 6,210
do the Steward	*28*. 16,41. 29,11
en	67,1
unt Eustace	*5*
ount) Eustace	76,16
ir, see Edeva	
lc	14,59. 21,2
rman	7,68. 21,75
rthing, see Robert	
t, see Ralph	
thir	25,24
ermeus	35,3
inn (the Dane)	8,59 and note. 25,19;51-53;56-57;59;61;63; 72;75;77. 35,3
lint	74,11
rani	67,16
rank	48,1
rederick	26,4;9
rewin	7,121
rideb…, a priest	74,16
ridebern	25,82. 32,6
rodo brother of Abbot (Baldwin of St. Edmund's)	*12*. 25,79
rodo *brother of Abbot (Baldwin of St. Edmund's)*	14,21;28;65;106. 21,40 and notes
rodo brother of Abbot (Baldwin of St. Edmund's)	notes to 14,137-139
rodo	1,1. 2,7. 7,56. 14,33;68;86.
ulcard	6,195. 35,7(×2)
ulcher *the Breton*	14,22 and note
ulcher *of Mesnières*	14,11;78;80;89-90;99
ulcher	14,82 note
ulcred	1,10. 6,83;92;95-96;289. 25,9;90
ulcred, see Robert	
ulcric	3,70-71
ulk	30,1;3
amas	14,114
amilo	14,24 note
auti	3,56. 7,15
eoffrey de Mandeville	*32*. 8,4. 61,1. 67,11
(eoffrey) de Mandeville	6,112. 21,58;95
eoffrey son of Hamo	25,86
eoffrey	25,57. 53,5-6. 67,12
erald Marshal	*65*
erald	8,51. 25,105. 38,14;22-23
erald, see Raymond	
erard	40,3
ermund	25,55
ernon, see Robert	
ifard	40,6
iffard, see Walter	
ishop Gilbert of Evreux	*22*
ount Gilbert, see Richard	
ilbert Blunt	6,84-88;105;133;254
(ilbert Blunt)	6,134 and note
ilbert of Coleville	6,127;180;236;272

Gilbert of Wissant	6,30;143;239;244;281;286–287
Gilbert son of Richere	ENf5
Gilbert the crossbowman	68
Gilbert the priest	32,4
Gilbert	6,19–21;29–30;34–37;40;52;83;92;100;279; 283. 25,8;78. 29,8. 31,38
Ginni	8,64
Gladman	67,12
Gleman of Levington	6,110
Goda brother of Aelfwin	7,37
Goda of 'Struostuna'	6,110
Goda	7,22;75;80;82;105;108-109;110(X2);112. 16,29. 25,81
Goda	39,10 note
Godard	25,84
Godfrey of Pierrepont	26,12c;14
Godhere	8,4
Godíng	3,73. 7,89(X2). 16,35. 74,13
Godiva	7,90. 11,4. 25,33. 67,29
Godman, a thane	59,2
Godman	2,17. 3,68. 6,65–66. 7,90;117;119. 8,56. 25,5 29,4. 67,4
Godmer	3,59
Godric Long	7,77
Godric of Peyton	6,238
Godric (of Peyton)	27,13 and note
Godric of Ringshall	29,8
Godric son of Herebold	6,108
Godric the priest	6,128. 7,114
Godric the smith	7,76
Godric the Steward	*13. 1,61–95.* 14,146
G(odric) the Steward	7,9
Godric	1,19;111;123e-123f. 2,17. 3,95. 4,2. 6,36;84 159;176–177;186;191;193;202;234;245. 7,8–9;24;57;77(X3);80(X3);85;91;97–98; 108–109;117–118;120–121;148(X2). 8,3;81 11,1-3. 13,6. 16,23;26;36. 21,52. 25,57;67; 69–70;75. 32,26. 35,7(X2). 39,1;5-6. 45,1. 66,13. 67,10. 68,3–4. 74,13(X2). EC1
Godric	notes to 8,17. 16,8
Godstan	16,43
Godwin of Sutton	6,169
Godwin (of Sutton)	6,165-168
Godwin son of Alfhere	6,1–2;112-114
Godwin son of Algar	7,36
Godwin son of Alsi	6,26–27
Godwin son of Toki	7,22;47–48
Godwin the priest	7,122. 38,11
Godwin, a thane of King Edward's	28,1a
Godwin, a thane	33,3
Godwin	1,49;53. 2,17;19. 3,82. 6,12;116;120; 191;307. 7,14;51;82;92;98. 8,63. 14,164. 16,35;44. 21,39;71. 25,60;79;86. 35,7. 38,8 11. 40,3. 66,13. 67,10-12. 74,12-13
Godwy	16,22;28–29. 25,57. 30,1
Gold, see Hugh	
Gorham, see W.	
Gosbert	8,66;69–70
Goulafre, see William	
Grim	7,56;87;89. 14,123. 36,6–7
Grim, see Edric	
Grimbold	8,8 note
Grimwulf	4,4. 8,12. 52,9
Grip, see Walter	

Ledman 7,15
Ledmer the priest 25,1
Ledmer 5,6. 16,36
Leofcild 7,60;62. 29,2
Leofcwen 35,8
Leofeva 15,3. 16,20;48. 21,70. 32,9. 74,13
Leofgeat 7,76. 25,34;80
Leofled 1,123f. 7,111. 52,1
Leofmer, see Brictwold
Leofred 38,18
Leofric Cobbe 7,36
Leofric Cook 6,107
Leofric Hobbeson 7,59. 29,7. 30,3
Leofric of Hemley 6,110
Leofric Snipe 7,143
Leofric the deacon 7,31
Leofric, a thane 5,1
Leofric 1,11;58. 3,95(×2). 4,15. 6,8;49;58;116;209;
227. 7,15;56;77;80(×2);82;86;94;97–98;101;
108;111;117–118;138–139;143. 8,56(×2);63.
12,4. 14,128. 16,15;24. 21,49;69. 25,70;74;
77;103. 29,8. 34,9. 35,7. 62,4–5. 67,10;12.
74,4;13. 75,5. 76,1
Leofric 16,6 note
Leofsi 6,92;193. 67,12
Leofsi 8,1 note
Leofsidu 14,138
Leofson 7,59;90. 29,1. 38,16
Abbot Leofstan of St. Edmund's 25,1. 68,5
Leofstan of Falkenham 6,110
Leofstan of Loes 29,1
Leofstan the priest 1,122d. 7,40
Leofstan 2,19. 6,111;155;202. 7,41;65;76;87;89;93;98;
110;121. 8,57. 16,26. 25,72. 34,5;8;14. 35,8
Leofwaru 25,84
Young Leofwin 16,30
Young Leofwin 16,4 note
Leofwin Benne 35,7
Leofwin Croc 8,49
Leofwin of Bacton, a thane of King Edward's 6,212;217. 41,10;?11 note
Leofwin (of Bacton) 41,7 and note
Leofwin son of Brown 6,110
Leofwin son of Ringwulf 6,216
Leofwin the Bald 57,1
Leofwin, a thane of King Edward's 8,32
Leofwin, a thane 41,15
Leofwin 6,3;191;209(×2). 7,15;56;76. 8,60. 16,15–16;
24;33;38. 25,103. 26,6. 41,5;17. 74,4;13
Leofwold 8,68
Licteva 21,25. 52,6
Lictwin 8,4
Lisois (of Moutiers) 28,2 and note
Loernic 6,305–306;308;310
Lother 25,87
Lunden 7,80
Lurk 31,13
Lustwin 6,118;184. 7,56. 8,12;66. 52,1
Lustwin, wife of 6,118
Magni 3,101
Male, see Osbern, Osbert
Malet 1,102. 3,86;89. 4,42. 6,11;33;38–39;46–47;49;
57;211;217–218. 7,71;136;140;144–145;148.
16,16;30. 28,6. 45,1

Malet, see Robert, William

Malus Vicinus	76,1
Mann	1,102
Manni Swart	3,1;3
Manni Swart, see Ulf	
Manni	7,19;54. 44,3–4
Manson	7,28;76;84;86
Manstan	7,58
Marculf	16,6. 77,4
Mawa, a free man	36,3
Mawa, a half free woman	32,26 note
Maynard	3,9. 6,169
Menleva	35,7
Mild	35,7
Miles de Belefol	38,25
Miles (de Belefol)	38,6;19-20 and notes
Modgeva of Colcarr	6,110
Modgeva	11,4
Earl Morcar, see Aelfeva	
Morcar	7,77
Moregrim	7,82;89
Morewin	6,247. 21,37;91
Morvant	53,1
Muffle, see Brictwold	
Munding	7,58
Mundret	4,30–31
Munulf the priest	26,5
Munulf	4,15;42
N.	31,13. 39,5
Nardred	3,57
Nicholas	26,3–4;6
Nigel, a servant of Count Robert (of Mortain)'s	2,8
Nigel	2,7
Nigel, see Eudo	
Norigold	33,2
Norman son of Tancred	8,35;46–47;49
Norman the Sheriff	*63*. 6,91;290. 7,36
Norman (the Sheriff)	16,34 and note
Norman, a thane	7,18
Norman	2,19. 3,61. 6,28;84;135;258. 7,3;10–12;28;30 32;37–39;70;76–77;79–80;96;112;114;126– 128;136–143. 8,46;51. 14,1;41. 21,105. 25,2 31,13. 39,9–10. 41,6. 43,3. 74,13. 76,19
N(orman)	7,81–90;92–94;97–101;103–111;113;115;117 121;129;132
Norman, see Hugh	
Odard	14,93
Odard	14,71 note
Odo	3,68. 67,22;30-31
Offa	53,5. 74,13
Ordgar in Kyluertestuna	6,110
Ordgar the reeve of the Abbot (of St. Edmund's)	14,152
Ordmer	12,3. 74,15
Ordric	6,210. 7,92. 31,58. 35,7
Orthi, a thane	20,1
Osbern Male	1,12
Osbern Male, cf. Osbert Male	
Osbern of Wanchy	25,59
Osbern	3,61;97. 6,46. 25,65–66;75;79. 28,5
Osbert Male	34,6
Osbert Male, cf. Osbern Male	
Osbert	7,120-121. 13,3
Osferth	1,31. 6,106. 7,85;91
Osgeat	7,143
Osgot	7,108. 16,17;36

slac, a thane | 31,3
slac | 3,91. 4,7. 6,114
smund | 3,100. 6,186;238. 7,36. 10,1
stula | 3,99
swulf | 7,76. 21,39
theri | 19,19
thulf | 13,3
tti | 7,84
tto the Goldsmith | *1,97–99*
tto (the Goldsmith) | 14,13 and note
udkell, see R.
adda | 7,7
at | 1,111
ayne | 25,81–82;84
eche, see William
eret, see William
esserera | 31,42
eter *brother of Burghard* | 14,17 and note
eter of Palluel | 67,18
eter of Valognes (Sheriff of Essex and Herts.) | *37* and note. *1,96*. 14,78;81–83. 75,2
(eter of Valognes, Sheriff of Essex and Herts.) | EE1 and note
eter *of Valognes, Sheriff of Essex and Herts.* | 14,85;96–97 and notes
eter *the Steward* | 14,53;61;70 and notes
eter, a cleric | 14,13
eter the cleric, see Walter
eter | 14,17;36;53;61. 67,23
everel, see Ranulf
icot (? Sheriff of Cambridgeshire) | *1,120–121*. 28,6 note
inel, see Ralph
irot | 28,6
ueneva mother of Brictmer | 39,8–10
ueneva (mother of Brictmer) | 14,117 and note
Queneva) mother of Brictmer | 39,7 and note
.., see Humphrey
. Oudkell | 66,16
ada | 48,1
adbod | 74,4
adfrid | 14,139 note
ainalm | 32,6
arl Ralph the Constable | 1,101
Earl) Ralph the Constable | 3,15;61;98-100. 4,14. 14,101. 31,53. 46,7
Earl) R(alph) the Constable | 3,10;17–18. 13,6. 32,10
arl Ralph (Wader) | *1,61–95* and note. 1,123f. 3,56. 20,1. 77,4
Earl) Ralph (Wader) | 3,59. 16,33. 25,104. 31,53 and notes
arl R(alph Wader) | 3,40–41. 4,32. 6,169. 7,19;44;133. 16,3. 46,8. 74,8–9. 76,13;17. ENf4 and notes
Earl) R(alph Wader) | 3,57 and note
arl R(alph) | 1,10. 3,1. 46,8
arl Ralph, see Alsi, Hardwin
arl R(alph), see Alsi
alph Baynard | *33*
(alph) Baynard | 4,36
alph Baynard, see William Baynard
alph brother of Robert Blunt | 66,10
alph of Beaufour | *11*
alph of Courbépine | 16,10
alph of Fougères | *50*
alph of Lanquetot | 45,1;3 and note
alph of Limésy | *43*. 8,46. 76,20
alph of Marcy | 5,6
alph of Savenay | 16,4;6–8;13;23–24;30;34–35;48. 21,39. 34,7; 10;12;17
alph of Tourleville | 7,73;86;98
(alph of Tourleville) | 7,99–101

Ralph Pinel	*61*. 39,3. 73,1
Ralph son of Brian	34,8
Ralph son of (Earl) Ralph the Constable (= Earl Ralph Wader)	31,53
Ralph Tallboys	35,3
Ralph the crossbowman	*69*
Ralph *the Fat*	14,35 and note
Ralph the Fat	14,37 note
Ralph	3,79. 4,32. 6,177–178. 7,145–148. 14,3;35;5 25,88. 31,42. 38,16;23
Ranulf brother of Ilger	*39*
R(anulf) brother of Ilger	67,15
Ranulf nephew of William of Warenne	26,13
Ranulf Peverel	*34*. 6,11. 7,64–65. 16,20–22;26;33. 25,56. 7 EE4
R(anulf) Peverel	21,39. 25,112.
(Ranulf) Peverel	16,23;30. 38,11
Ranulf son of Walter	7,20;124
R(anulf) son of Walter	7,21
Ranulf	6,39. 7,71–72. 33,6. 67,4;20
Raven	6,193. 7,100–101
Raymond Gerald	8,51 note;55;63
Regifer	7,110
Reginald brother of Hubert the Breton	14,68 note
Reginald the Breton	*70*. 14,68 note
Reginald	67,2;16
Reginald, see William	
Rich, see Edeva	
Richard *Houerel*	14,151 and note
Richard of Clare, son of Count Gilbert	*25*. 16,15. 21,44. 33,1. 67,1. 76,1–7. EE2
Richard (of Clare), son of C(ount) G(ilbert)	8,63
Richard (of Clare, son of Count Gilbert)	8,35;47;59. 29,1 and notes
Richard of Saint-Clair	11,4
Richard *the Bald*	14,54 and note
Richard	6,304. 14,151. 31,42. 40,1. 57,1. 75,2
Richere	33,2
Richere, see Gilbert, Walter	
Rictan	74,13
Ringwulf	6,216
Ringwulf, see Leofwin	
Count Robert of Mortain	2
Count Robert (of Mortain)	1,1 and note
Count (Robert) of Mortain	21,1. 31,48. 76,16 and notes
Count Robert (of Mortain), see Nigel	
Robert Blunt	*66*. 6,57. 14,92;100–101;123. 25,22. 75,1–2
Robert Blunt, see Ralph	
Robert Farthing	14,146
Robert Gernon	*36*. EE3
Robert Malet, Sheriff of Suffolk, son of William Malet	*6*. 1,103;105. 3,94–95. 4,15. 7,11;15–16;138 140;143. 8,42. 16,14–15;29. 19,9. 20,31. 21,16;45–46;75. 26,12d;13–14. 31,15. 32,1 34,12. 38,6. 43,5. 51,1–2. 64,1. 67,2–4;10; 19;27. 75,4–5. 76,23. 77,2. ENf3
Ro(bert) Malet (as above)	21,71;79;85;100. 39,12
R(obert) Malet (as above)	1,10;14. 2,17–18;20. 3,28;41. 7,6;13;17;21; 26;30;33;36;75;79. 8,8. 16,26. 21,48;65;74 88. 32,28. 34,15. 52,1. 53,6. 67,5;15. 77,4
(Robert) Malet (as above)	3,98–102. 6,177. 7,144. 16,25;33 and note; 38 and note
Robert (Malet, as above)	18,1 and note
Robert Malet (as above)	notes to 21,92;94
Robert Malet (as above), mother of	*77*. *6*,76–77. 6,8;11;156;161;176;191;193– 195;199–201;209;216;229 and note;230; 232;251;253;271;311. 34,13, 75,5

Tallboys, see Ivo, Ralph	
Tancred, see Norman	
Teit	6,217
Tela	36,11
Tepekin	29,11;14. 40,4
Teri	41,11
Theobald *the cleric*	14,14 and note
Theodoric brother of Walter the deacon	41,4;5 note;10–11
Theodoric	7,111. 8,56
Thorbern the priest	38,11
Thorbern	6,22. 7,96;101
Thorbert	67,11
Thored	3,54. 4,36. 13,5. 33,4;6–7;9–11
Thorgar	1,51
Thorgils	35,3
Thorild	7,103
Thorkell of Wrentham	26,12d
Thorkell, a thane	34,7
Thorkell	1,123f. 6,116;223;264. 7,36. 21,29–30;62.
	26,12a. 74,13
Thorkell	notes to 22,2. 39,10
Thormar	16,16
Thormod of Parham	1,93
Thormod	1,75. 22,1;3
Thorold	7,97. 31,41. 34,15. EE4
Thorvold	7,123
Thurgot	16,46
Thuri of Kyluertestuna	6,110
Thuri, a thane of King Edward's	25,61;63
Thuri	16,30. 25,67. 71,2
Thurstan son of Guy	7,122;125;133. 76,15
Thurstan	1,107. 3,74–78. 41,4–5. 77,4
Tigier	6,23;127;271
Tihel of Helléan	42. 16,9
Tihel	16,1
Toki	7,80. 26,4;9;11. 35,3
Toki, see Godwin	
Toli the Sheriff (of Suffolk)	4,15. 7,31;67. 31,53
Toli	6,106. 7,29;36. 27,11. 51,1
Topi	32,30
Tosti	55,1
Tovi, a free man	29,9
Tovi, a thane	29,12
Tovild	74,13
Trumwin	30,1. 36,9
Tulf	7,148
Tumbi	1,122d
Tuneman	16,40
Tutfled	3,101
Uhtred	3,96. 43,1;3
Ulf of Mutford	7,41
Ulf son of Manni Swart	6,109
Ulf the priest	4,13
Ulf, a thane	19,2. 44,1–2
Ulf	1,19;48;55. 3,93;98;103. 7,15;27;37;136;141.
	8,34;42. 32,5. 69,3
Ulfketel the King's reeve	ENf4
Ulfketel	1,53. 4,19. 6,272;274–275. 7,25;27;41;119
Unfrid son of Robert	6,112;122 and note;172 note
Uva, see Ketel	
Viking	7,108. 16,22;26
W. de More	16,3
W. son of Gorham	67,7
W. the Constable	4,32

Wacra	3,102
Wader, see Earl Ralph	
Wailolf	4,3. 7,67
Waldwin	25,60. 29,7
Waleran	32,16
Waleran, see John (×2)	
Walter de Risboil/Risbou	6,28;284–285
Walter Giffard	*45*
Walter *nephew of Peter the cleric*	14,87 and note
Walter of Caen	4,15. 6,5;7;67 note;90;98-99;103;143;191; 245;247;301;316. 25,61
W(alter) of Caen	6,93;162;165;264;265 note
Walter (of Caen)·	6,168–170
Walter of Dol	4,15. 6,212;215. 14,146. 16,34. 31,34
Walter of Douai	31,34 note
Walter of St. Valéry	*51*. 76,22
Walter son of Aubrey	6,2;32;80;183;292
W(alter) son of Aubrey	6,189
Walter son of Grip	6,132 and note;308;311;317–318
Walter son of Richere	6,94
Walter the crossbowman	6,191;238
Walter the deacon	*41*. 25,24
Walter *the deacon*	21,35 and note
Walter the deacon, see Theodoric	
Walter	6,12; 44–45;81;90;129;173;191;202–204;305 306;308;311;314. 14,23;87. 21,35. 33,2
Walter, see Ranulf	
Wand, see Aelfric	
Warengar	3,59. 7,63–65;66 note;67–68. 16,12;38–39. 38,5;21
War(engar)	16,16–17
Warin son of Burnin	4,20-21;29 and note. 6,296
Warin	6,64;304. 14,15;66. 34,4
Warner	67,5–6;8
Wenelincg, Weneling	67,22 note
Werno of Poix	14,68
White	7,117
Widard	25,104
Wigmer	26,10
Wigulf	7,67–68. 8,56. 38,4
Wihtmer	2,7. 7,84;106–107;108(×3);109–110;112–114
Wihtred the priest	1,52
Wihtric of Carlewuda	6,110
Wihtric	1,102. 7,61;76;83;119–120. 16,20
Wilard	25,84
Wilgrip	29,4
Bishop William of Thetford	*18*
Bishop W(illiam of Thetford)	14,101;121
William Baynard, nephew of Ralph Baynard	33,10
William de Alno	36,1–7;16–17
William *de Alno*	EE3 and note
William Goulafre	6,10–11;14;25;65–66;138–141;206
W(illiam) Goulafre	6,271;293
William Hurant	25,7
William Malet, father of Robert Malet	3,94–95;100. 4,42. 6,11. 7,8;15–16;36;138– 140;143;148. 16,6;30. 19,6. 26,14. 28,6. 31,20. 45,2. 52,1. 67,2;4;19;28;30. 75,4. 77
W(illiam) Malet (as above)	3,39–40. 6,93;159. 7,26;33;131;133. 8,42. 18 67,15–16;31
William (Malet, as above)	3,99;144;146. 38,6. 67,29
(William Malet, as above)	notes to 3,98;101. 7,17. 16,15. 51,2. Also 67, 20-21
William of Arques	*47*. 6,192. 31,20
William of Auberville, brother of Roger of Auberville	*30*. 29,8. 76,14

William of Bosc	7,115-116;134. 16,3 note. 39,5
W(illiam) of Bosc	39,11
William of Bourneville	7,56-59;117;121 and note. 76,15
W(illiam) of Bourneville	1,11. 7,119 and note. 62,7
William of Bouville, son of Saxwalo of Bouville	16,11. 32,1-2;19;31 and note
W(illiam) of Bouville (as above)	21,95. 32,13
W(illiam) of Ecouis	21,27
William (of Bouville, as above)	32,15 and note
William of Çaen	6,67
William of Écouis	9. 21,21
William of Émalleville	6,30;33
William of Noyers	1,107-119. 19,17
William of Parthenay	76,8-12
William of Vatteville	54
(William of) Vatteville	70,1
William of Warenne	26. 8,55. 76,18
W(illiam) of Warenne	7,25. 21,1
William of Warenne, see Ranulf	
William Peche	25,6;91
William Peret	25,89
William Shield	6,63. 7,75
William son of Gross	31,50
William son of Reginald	26,12b;15
William the Chamberlain	1,97-99
William	3,57. 4,19. 6,250;265. 19,16. 29,7;9. 41,11. 53,2. 66,3
Withgar son of Aelfric	25,1;60
Withgar	25,78-102. 7,121. 8,35;46-47;59;63;66. 16,11; 38. 25,2-3;17 note;19;25;27-35;37-38;40-49; 52;55-56. 29,1. 32,1. 43,4. 67,1. 72,1. 76,2-5
Withgar, see Aelfric	
Woodbrown	6,271. 16,14;32
Wulfbold	7,65;79;111. 29,10
Wulfbold, see Wulfheah	
Wulfeva	3,102. 6,209;212-216;218;222-225;227-230; 232. 7,3. 39,4
Wulfeva, son of	6,212
Wulfgar	25,48
Wulfgeat	6,13;15;125. 16,35. 21,48. 35,7
Wulfgeat, see Aelfric	
Wulfhard	7,121
Wulfheah father of Wulfbold	7,76(×2);79;99-100
Wulfhere	2,17
Wulfled	25,78
Wulfmer the (King's) reeve	73 note. 1,7. 74,4;7. 76,13-14
Wulfmer the priest	6,110
Wulfmer, a thane	8,44;48;55
Wulfmer	73. 1,110. 2,11. 3,59;95(×2). 6,49;64;211. 7,16;26;61;76-77;85;89;98. 8,20-24. 13,3. 16,35. 21,58. 25,10;58;60;77;84. 35,7-8. 67,2; 11-12. 74,4
Wulfmèr, father of	73,1
Wulfnoth	1,55;102. 2,6;9-10;13. 6,121. 7,71;76;140. 53,6
Wulfred	8,55
Abbot Wulfric of Ely, brother of Guthmund	31,60
Wulfric brother of Wulfsi	1,110
Wulfric Hagni	53,6
Wulfric son of Brictric	55,1
Wulfric son of Hugh	28,6 and note
Wulfric the deacon	7,36
Wulfric, a thane of King Edward's	8,46. 39,16. 46,1-2
Wulfric, a thane	8,36-37;55

Wulfric, a villager	68,2
Wulfric	2,16. 3,53;64;92. 6,81;130;191(×2);210;214 7,58;73;76;79;88;104(×2);111;113;117;14 8,7;19;29. 9,3. 14,43;150. 15,4. 16,20;22;40 25,19;59. 26,12a. 28,6. 30,1. 31,57. 32,11. 38,2. 41,14. 67,9;11. 74,4;11;13(×2);15. 76,13
Wulfric	16,8 note
Wulfsi brother of Wulfric	1,110
Wulfsi	1,16;19;23;36;46;60;111. 4,20–23. 7,6;15;24 50;52. 31,33. 36,9. 50,1
Wulfsi, two brothers of	7,24
Wulfstan	3,81
Wulfward	7,98;118. 8,47. 14,12;19;39. 29,5. 39,5. 42,1
Wulfward	14,20 note
Wulfwaru	5,8. 35,7
Wulfwin the priest	1,122d. 6,124;181. 46,7
Wulfwin, a thane of King Edward's	35,1-2. 68,5 note
Wulfwin	2,17. 6,211;216;227. 7,92;96. 8,55. 16,41. 25,103. 35,5–6. 62,2. 67,10;13. 74,13. 76,1(×2);21. EE4–EE5
Wulfwy, man-at-arms of St. Edmund's	14,69
Wulfwy	7,121. 16,18
Wymarc, *Count Alan's steward*	EC2 and note
Wymarc, see Robert	
Wynning	67,30
Wynstan	6,193
Yric	4,4. 25,59
... of Barthetona	41,11
... of Houdain	7,2

CHURCHES AND CLERGY

Alnesbourn (St. Andrew's)	8,13
Bayeux, Bishop	*16. 77.* 1,6. 75,5. Also folio 372a
Bernai, Abbot	*23*
Blyford	13,2 and note
Blythburgh	7,5
[**Bury**] **St. Edmund's**	*14. 25,78–102.* 1,62;115. 2,1;3–5;15. 3,2;46. 4,10. 6,62;209.299-302. 7,1;2. 8,32;35;45-47. 9,2. 10,1. 11,4. 12,1-2;4;6. 15,3. 16,1;33. 18,4. 19,12. 20,1. 21,2;9;40-41. 25,17;19;22 25;27;33-34;40;103;111-112. 26,2-4. 27,1;? 7. 28,1b;4. 29,12-13. 31,2;40. 33,1-3;12-13. 34,1;14. 35,6-7. 37,6 and note. 38,2. 40,1-2; 5. 41,10. 43,3. 46,1. 49,1. 53,1;6-7. 54,2-3. 59,2. 61,2. 66,1;6;9;11. 73,1. 75,2. 76,1;4-5; 9-12;19;21
Abbot	1,77;88. 6,57;210-211;214-215. 8,55. 9,2. 12,6. 14,1-4;8;11-12;14-19;22-24;27;32-33 36-39;41-46;49;52-54;59;61-64;66;68-70; 72-73;77-78;82;90;96-101;104;106;117; 119-120;122-123;125-128;130;132;133 note 134;136-137;139;143;146;148;153;167. 15,· 16,16. 27,7. 30,1. 40,5. 43,9. 62,5. 66,13. 75,1 and note. 76,12 and note. See also Baldwin, Leofstan
Abbot	21,4 note
cleric	see Durand
monks	14,163;167
reeves	see Aelfric, Brictmer, Brictric, Ordgar
Archbishop	see Lanfranc, Stigand

Canterbury (Holy Trinity) *15*. 34,5
    monks *15*
Chatteris (St. Mary's) *24*
Clare (St. John's) 25,1
Combs 2,10
Coutances, Bishop 21,17 note
Debenham (St. Andrew's) 6,18. 16,28
    (St. Mary's) 6,18. 16,28. 34,12
Elmham, Bishop see Aelmer and 18,1 note
Ely (St. Etheldreda's) *21*. 2,1–2;16;20. 3,27;31;34;36. 4,42. 5,2. 6, 114;116–118;148–149;239;247;251; 258;265. 7,55;122 and note;133. 8,1–2;4–6;8–10;12;17; 20;25;27;46. 12,2. 14,40. 16,3–4;6;8;13;28. 22,2–3. 25,59. 26,1;3;5. 28,2. 31,12–13;15–19; 40. 32,14;26;29–30;31 and note. 34,4;15. 38,22. 39,5;8;10. 41,18. 45,1–3. 46,8. 47,2–3. 52,4. 53,1. 67,9;11–12;15;22;29–30. 74,10

(*St. Etheldreda's*) notes to 3,32-33;46;98;100. 6,33-34;164-165; 271. 8,1;21. 16,5;31. 46,10

Abbot 1,75. 3,57;62;86;89;92–95;97–103. 4,1;3–4;6; 8 and note. 6,11-12;14-15;17;19-20;21-22 and note;23;25;28–30;32–37;39;41;43–49;51–56. 7,15;56;58;61;67;71–72;136–146;148;151. 8,56–57;59;63;66;68;80–82. 16,3;6;20;22; 27;29–34;38–39;48. 21,12;16–19;21–22;25– 31;36–37;40;45–46;49–52;64–65;75;79–80; 82–85. 25,53 and note;112. 28,6. 29,9. 32,1. 34,12;16. 38,3;22. 39,5. 52,10. 53,7. 67,3–6; 30. 77,4. See also Wulfric

Evreux, Bishop *22*. See also Gilbert
Eye (St. Peter's) 6,191
Flixton (St. Michael's) 19,21
Grestain (St. Mary's) 2,9–10
Ipswich (Holy Trinity) 1,122d
    (St. Augustine's) 1,122d. 31,56
    (St. George's) 38,3
    (St. Julian's) 74,9
    (St. Laurence's) 1,122f
    (St. Mary's) 1,122d
    (St. Michael's) 1,122d
    (St. Peter's) 1,122f. 25,52;54 note;60;62
    (St. Stephen's) 1,122f
Ramsey (St. Benedict's) *17*. 36,4
Rochester, Bishop *20*
Rumburgh 3,14 note;105
St. Lô, Bishop 21,17. 29,9
Stowmarket 2,8. 34,6
Sudbury (St. Gregory) 1,97
Thetford, Bishop *18–19*. 6,70–72;76–77;308;311. 8,42. 31,3;5–6. 44,2. 64,3. See also Erfast, William, and folio 372a
Thurleston (St. Botolph's) 1,122e
Tuddenham 38,15
Winchester, Bishop see Stigand
chaplain, to Roger Bigot Ansketel the priest
cleric Albold, Durand, Peter, Theobald
deacon Aelfric, Edric, Leofric, Walter, Wulfric

priest   Aelfric, Aelmer, Aethelwold, Ailbold, Algar, Alwin, Alwold, Alwulf, Ansketel, Anund, Askell, Brunmer, Edmund, Edwin, Engelric, Frideb..., Gilbert, Godric, Godwin, Judicael, Ledmer, Leofstan, Munulf, Snaring, Thorberi, Ulf, Wihtred, Wulfmer, Wulfwin

SECULAR TITLES AND OCCUPATIONAL NAMES

Beadle (*bedel*) ... Brictmer. **Burgess** (*burgensis*), of Ipswich ... Aelfric son of Rolf, Culling. **Chamberlain** (*cambararius, camerarius*) ... Gundwin, Humphrey, William. **Constable** (*cunestabla, stalra, stalre*) ... Asgar, Earl Ralph, W. **Cook** (*cocē*) ... Leofric. **Count** (*comes*) ... Alan, Brian, Eustace, Gilbert, Robert. **Countess** (*comitissa*) ... Aumâle, Edeva. **Crossbowman** (*arbalastarius, balastarius, balistarius*) ... Berner, Gilbert, Ralph, Robert, Walter. **Earl** (*comes*) ... Algar, Gyrth, Harold, Hugh, Morcar, Ralph the Constable, Ralph Wader. **free men** ... in the King's hand (*liberi homines ... in manu regis*) ... 75. **Goldsmith** (*aurifex*) ... Otto. **Guard** (*huscarlus*) ... Askell, Ingulf. **King's reeve** (*prepositus regis*) ... Aelmer, Aethelward, Edric, Ulfketel, Wulfmer. **Man-at-arms** (*miles*) ... Wulfwy. **Marshal** (*mareschalchus*) ... Gerald. **Queen** (*regina*) ... Edith, and 6, 76-77;209;229 and note;230. 7,14-15;63. 41,13. 52,5;9. 54,3. 77,1. **Reeve of Ipswich** (*prepositus de Gypeswiz*) ... Brown. **Reeve** (*prepositus*) ... Aelfric (X2), Alric, Brictmer (X2), Brictric, Ordgar. **Servant** (*seruiens*) ... Nigel, and 35,3 note. **Sheriff** (*vicecomes*) ... Aethelwy of Thetford (?), Norman, Peter of Valognes, Picot (?) Robert Malet, Robert son of Wymarc, Roger Bigot, Swein, Toli. **Smith** (*faber*) ... Bondi, Edwin, Godric. **Steward** (*dapifer*) ... Eudo, Godric, Peter, Wymarc. **Thane of King Edward's** ... Aelfric, Godwin, Ketel, Leofwin of Bacton, Leofwin, Skuli, Thuri, Wulfric, Wulfwin. **Thane** (*tegnus, teignus, teinnus, teinus, tennus, tenus*) ... Auti, Edmer, Godman, Godwin, Guthmund, Ingvar, Ketel, Leofric, Leofwin, Norman, Orthi, Oslac, Scalpi, Siward of Maldon, Thorkell, Tovi, Ulf, Wulfmer, Wulfric. **Vavassors** (*vavasores*) ... 74. **Villager** (*villanus*) ... Askell, Wulfric. **Young** (*cilt*) ... Leofwin.

INDEX OF PLACES

The name of each place is followed by (i) the abbreviated name of its Hundred and its location on the Map in this volume (Suffolk places only); (ii) its National Grid reference; (iii) chapter and section references in LDB Suffolk, or a reference to a note in the present volume which identifies the place. Bracketed chapter and section references denote mention in sections dealing with a different place. Unless otherwise stated, the identifications of DG and the spellings of the Ordnance Survey are followed for places in Suffolk; of OEB for places abroad. Inverted commas denote lost places (that is, those whose former site is known); italic print denotes unidentifiable places. Places whose names have changed since 1086 are entered under their present name. The National Grid reference system is explained on all Ordnance Survey maps, and in the Automobile Association Handbooks; the figures reading from left to right are given before those reading from bottom to top of the map. Places whose grid references are shown within round brackets do not appear on 1-inch or 1:50,000 maps. Where LDB does not differentiate between what are now two or more distinct settlements (e.g. Creeting All Saints, St. Mary, and St. Olave), separate sets of Grid references are given, but the chapter and section references are combined. The Suffolk Hundreds and Half-Hundreds are Babergh (Ba), Bishop's (Bi), Blackbourn and Bradmere (BB denotes places assigned to both Hundreds; *BB those always assigned to Blackbourn Hundred; †BB those always assigned to Bradmere Hundred), Blything (Bly), Bosmere (Bo), Carlford (Ca), Claydon (Cd), Colneis (Cn), Cosford (Co), Hartismere (H), Ipswich (I), Lackford (La), Loes (Ls), Lothing (Lt), Lothingland (Ltl), Parham (Pa), Plomesgate (Pl), Risbridge (R), Samford (Sa), Stow (St), Thedwestry (Td), Thingoe (Tg), Wangford (Wa), Wilford (Wi); the town of Bury St. Edmunds is marked by the letter B. The places in each Hundred or Half-Hundred are listed after the present index, immediately before the Map. References to Ballingdon cum Brundon, in Suffolk only since 1832 and 1835, should be sought in the Essex volume.

	Map	Grid	Text
Acton	Ba	TL 89 45	34,2
Akenham	Cd	TM 14 48	1,117. 8,68;71. 38,11. 14,5;16
Akethorpe	Ltl	(TM 54 93)	1,56
Alburgh (Norfolk)	–	TM 27 87	ENf2
Aldeburgh	Pl	TM 46 56	6,130. 21,105
Alderton	Wi	TM 34 41	6,152;159;162;164;240. 21,77
Aldham	Co	TM 04 44	14,112. 35,6. (1,105)
Aldringham	Bi	TM 44 60	6,70;74
Alfildestuna	Sa	unidentified	16,45. 36,5
Alnesbourn	Ca	TM 19 40	8,13
Alneterne	Bly	unidentified	21,47
Alston'	Cn	(TM 26 34)	2,19. 7,96;101;113
Aluredestuna	Ca	unidentified	39,12
Ampton	Td	TL 86 71	14,64
Ardleigh (Essex)	–	TM 05 29	EE3
Ash	Ls	TM 33 55	6,282;290
Ashbocking	Bo	TM 16 54	1,73. 21,25. 25,59. 52,6
Ashfield	Cd	TM 21 62	3,65. 4,6. 6,20;22. 16,29; 34. 21,32. 52,10. 67,4
Great Ashfield	BB	TL 99 67	14,93. 66,3;17. 14,*92 note*
Ash Street	Co	TM 01 46	2,14
Aspall	H	TM 16 64	6,201;206;221. 16,48. 34,18. 77,4
Assington	Ba	TL 93 38	34,3
Aveley	Ba	TL 94 39	27,7
Bacton	H	TM 05 67	41,7. (41,8)
Bacton, see also Leofwin			
Badingham	Bi	TM 30 68	6,306. (6,55)
Badley	Bo	TM 06 55	1,70. 21,20. 25,53
Badmondisfield	R	TL 74 57	1,121. (65,1)

	Map	Grid	Text
Bardwell	*BB	TL 94 73	14,72 note;82. 25,21. 76,10–12
Barham	Cd	TM 13 50	6,10. 8,66;78;81 note; 21, 26;27 note. (21,22 note;
Barkestone	Ca	TM 27 46	40,4
Barking	Bo	TM 07 53	21,16;18. (21,14;20. 25,5. note)
Barnby	Lt	TM 47 89	1,30. 4,39
Barnham	BB	TL 86 79	4,10. 7,1. 14,89. 26,8. 31,
Barningham	BB	TL 96 76	10,1. 14,81. 37,4
Barrow	Tg	TL 76 64	1,120
Barsham	Wa	TM 39 89	6,296. 7,40;45. 18,5. 19,1
Barthetona, see Persons Index, penultimate entry			
Great Barton	Td	TL 86 67	14,48
Barton Mills	La	TL 71 73	25,33;38. 54,3
Battisford	Bo	TM 05 54	7,57. 31,56. 53,3. 74,3. (2,11)
Bawdsey	Wi	TM 34 40	6,154;157;161. 11,1. 21,7 79 note;80
Baylham	Bo	TM 10 51	7,58;61;63;65. 76,15. (7,5
Great Bealings	Ca	TM 23 48	6,121. 67,11. (67,15)
Little Bealings	Ca	TM 22 48	3,33 note. 16,3. 21,59. 31, 67,12
Beccles	Wa	TM 42 90	1,39;40;43. 14,120
Becclinga	Pl	unidentified	7,72
Bechetuna, see *Beketuna*			
Bedfield	Bi	TM 22 66	6,307
Bedingfield	Bi	TM 17 68	6,68;75–77;232;319. 14,1 19,10. 31,5–6. 43,5. 75,5. 77,3. (6,12)
Beketuna, Bechetuna	Lt	unidentified	1,29. 31,26
Belenei	Sa	unidentified	16,43
Belstead	Sa	TM 12 41	6,26. 16,42. 32,5. 35,3. 46, 71,2
Belton	Ltl	TG 48 02	1,35;59
Benacre	Bly	TM 51 84	14,165
Benhall	Pl	TM 37 61	3,101. 6,47;53–54. 7,140; 149–150
Bentley	Sa	TM 11 38	1,101;103–104. 3,71;75
East Bergholt	Sa	TM 07 34	1,100;102 note;103-105. (1,101;119. 3,68;70;80– 82. 5,6-8. 16,35-37;41;46- 47. 25,65-67;69-70;72-73 75;77. 28,5. 32,5;8. 35,3– 38,21. 40,3-4. 58,1. 61,1. 71,1-2)
Beria	Sa	unidentified	3,69
Bermesdena	Cd	unidentified	52,11
Beuerda, see Hugh			
Beversham	Pa	TM 35 58	67,6
Beyton	Td	TL 93 62	31,54
Bildeston	Co	TL 99 49	41,1
Billingford (Norfolk)	—	TG 01 20	(56,6)
Bing	Wi	TM 28 53	6,187;245
Bixley	Ca	TM 20 44	3,17. 21,68. 31,14
Great Blakenham	Bo	TM 11 50	1,3;67. 8,57. 9,1
Little Blakenham	Bo	TM 10 48	29,5. (21,21)
Blaxhall	Pa	TM 35 56	3,87;89;92. 6,29;33–34;37 39;41. 7,136. 8,80. 16,6 note. 21,36. 45,1
Blundeston	Ltl	TM 51 97	3,54. 7,54
Blyford	Bly	TM 42 76	13,2
Blythburgh	Bly	TM 45 75	1,12. (1,10. 6,82;89b–89c. 7,5. 26,12a. 33,10)

	Map	Grid	Text
Blythburgh, see also Robert			
Bosmere	Bo	TM 09 54	21,47. (21,*16 note*)
Boulge	Wi	TM 25 52	3,33. 6,181;244. 8,18. 26,17. 32,11. 39,15. 46,11. 67,25
Boxted	Ba	TL 82 50	8,46
Boynton	Sa	TM 09 37	3,81. 16,44. 25,72. 71,1
Boyton	Pl	TM 37 47	6,132;134;138;140
Boyton	R	TL 71 44	25,16;88–89
Boyton	Wi	TM 37 47	6,172
Bradfield [Combust, St. Clare, and St. George]	Td	(TL 89 57 (TL 90 57 (TL 90 59	2,3. 14,52;59
[Great and Little] Bradley	R	(TL 67 53 (TL 68 52	14,157. 25,92;103. 44,1. 76,1
Braiseworth	H	TM 13 71	6,198;205;225–226;228
Bramfield	Bly	TM 39 73	3,3. (3,4;3,*7 note*)
Bramford	Bo	TM 12 46	1,2;119. 25,52. (1,7. 74,7)
Brampton	Bly	TM 43 81	1,107. 7,7. 33,4
Brandeston	Ba	TL 91 46	16,10
Brandeston	Ls	TM 24 60	21,96. 47,3
Brandon	La	TL 78 86	21,5. 28,2
Brantham	Sa	TM 11 34	3,73;82;85. 6,27. 16,43. 36,3;7;11. 39,17. (3,*83 note*)
Bredfield	Wi	TM 26 52	3,27;31. 6,169;182;246;258. 7,129. 21,75;79;84–85;87. 25,23. 26,20. 67,19;23
Brettenham	Co	TL 96 53	2,13. 14,115. 25,109
[Great and Little] Bricett	Bo	(TM 03 50 (TM 05 49	25,56. 29,8. 30,3. 34,8. 38,8. 76,14
Bricticeshaga	Bo	unidentified	52,8
Bridge	Bly	TM 47 70	7,6. (7,52)
Brightlingsea (Essex)	—	TM 07 18	EE1. (1,96)
Brightwell	Ca	TM 24 43	21,54
Brihtoluestuna	Cn	unidentified	31,9. (31,14)
Brockford	H	TM 12 65	14,47
Brockley	R	TL 72 47	25,14
Brockley	Tg	TL 82 55	8,45. 14,14. 40,1
Brodertuna	Ls	unidentified	3,41. 6,278
Brome	H	TM 14 76	1,9. 6,63–64;203. 7,75. 11,5. 14,141. 19,20
Bromeswell	Wi	TM 30 50	3,23;53. 6,168;180;185;190. 6,235;249. 21,74;83;86;88
Browston	Ltl	TG 49 01	1,53
Bruisyard	Pl	TM 32 66	3,98. 7,73;145
Bruntuna	Cd	unidentified	41,15
Brutge	Pa	unidentified	6,28. 67,5
Bucklesham	Cn	TM 24 42	2,16. 21,61
Bulcamp	Bly	TM 43 76	7,19. 13,5
Bungay	Wa	TM 33 89	1,110–111. 4,19;25. (1,108 and note)
Burch	Pl	unidentified	6,145
Bures	Ba	TL 90 34	14,30. 25,42. 38,1. 55,1
Burgate	Cn	TM 29 36	7,77;108
Burgate	H	TM 08 75	35,5;7
Burgesgata	Pl	unidentified	6,144
Burgh	Ca	TM 23 51	3,20. 4,17. 6,119;123–124. 8,10. 21,67. 26,16. 31,15. 32,22;28. 46,8. 52,4
Burgh	Cn	TM 29 34	7,80. 39,1
Burgh, see also Aethelric, Brunman			
Burgh Castle	Ltl	TG 47 04	69,1
Burstall	Sa	TM 09 44	16,18;35. 25,71;77. 34,7

	Map	Grid	Text
Bury St. Edmund's	B	TL 85 64	14,167
Butley	Ls	TM 36 51	3,40;50. 6,292. 8,25
Buxhall	St	TM 00 57	5,5. 7,55. 8,49. 12,7. 21,1● 26,5
Caisne(i)d (IE)	–	unidentified	34,*15 note*
Caldecota(n), -coten, Kaldecotes	H	unidentified	6,212. 14,136;149. 31,37 41,8
Caldecott	Ltl	TG 47 01	69,2
Campsey Ash	Ls	TM 32 55	3,*21 note*;38. 6,279;288. 22,2. 67,28
Canap(p)etuna, Canepetuna	Sa	unidentified	1,106. 3,80. 35,4
Candlet	Cn	TM 29 36	7,95
Capel St. Andrew	Wi	TM 37 48	3,21. 6,150;166;183. 7,1● 21,72;79
Carlewuda, see Aelfric son of (?Edwin) the smith, Edwin the smith, Wihtric			
Carlton	Pl	TM 38 64	3,94. 6,69. (3,49;*50 note*)●
Carlton Colville	Lt	TM 51 90	4,38. 31,32
Catesfella	Wa	unidentified	8,29
Cavendish	Ba	TL 80 46	25,47. 43,2. 76,3;6–7;20. (8,46)
Cavenham	La	TL 76 69	25,35. 28,4
Chadacre	Ba	TL 85 52	46,2
Chamberlain's Hall	La	TL 74 77	28,1b
Charsfield	Ls	TM 25 56	3,26;28 'Little';36. 6,179. 7,133. 16,6. 21,78;104. 31,18–19. 32,9. 46,12. (1●
Chattisham	Sa	TM 09 42	1,106
Chedburgh	R	TL 79 57	21,40
Chediston	Bly	TM 35 77	3,13. 7,14–15. 68,2–3
Cheletuna, see *Keletuna*			
Chelsworth	Co	TL 98 47	14,109
Chevington	Tg	TL 78 60	14,5
Chickering	Bi	TM 20 76	6,318. 8,40. 19,7;9
Chilbourne	R	(TL 72 48)	1,91. 25,86
Chiletuna, see *Keletuna*			
Chillesford	Pl	TM 38 52	3,93
Chilton	Ba	TL 88 42	6,2
Chilton	St	TM 04 59	21,12. 31,49
Chippenhall	Bi	TM 28 75	6,311. 14,105;145. 67,7
Churchford	Sa	TM 08 38	36,1. (36,16)
Clachestorp	Ls	unidentified	6,274;284
Clare	R	TL 76 45	25,1
Clare, see also Richard			
Claydon	Cd	TM 13 49	74,10. (8,54)
Cle'pham	Pl	unidentified	6,142
Clopton	Ca	TM 22 52	6,127. 8,7. 31,17. 34,15. 46,7;9. 47,2. 52,2. (8,43. 34,16. 46,6. 47,1)
Clopton	R	TL 76 54	21,41. 25,5–5a;80;91. 26,1
Cockfield	Ba	TL 90 54	14,24
Coddenham	Ba	TL 95 39	43,2. 76,22
Coddenham	Bo	TM 13 54	1,74. 3,60. 6,6. 7,67;69. 8,63;77. 16,20. 21,24. 34,● 38,5;10;17;20. 53,4. 56,2;● 5–6. 74,16
Colcarr, see Modgeva			
Colston	Bi	TM 31 67	67,8
Combs	St	TM 04 56	2,6. (2,8)
Coney Weston	*BB	TL 95 77	14,76. (14,78;80–81;84)
Cookley	Bly	TM 34 75	7,24. 9,3
Coresfella	Ba	unidentified	25,44
[Great and Little] Cornard	Ba	(TL 88 40 (TL 90 39	1,98. 14,29. 25,43. 43,4. 76,4. (1,99)

	Map	Grid	Text
Corton	Ltl	TM 54 97	1,45. 69,3
Cotton	H	TM 07 66	1,77;79;84;95. 6,61;217. 14,135;148. 25,24. 31,35
South Cove	Bly	TM 49 80	3,12. 6,97
Covehithe [formerly 'North Hales']	Bly	TM 52 81	1,108. 3,16. 7,12;25. 26,15. 32,20. (76,14)
Cowlinge	R	TL 71 54	3,1
Cranley	H	TM 16 72	43,7
Cransford	Pl	TM 31 64	3,103. 6,44;52;55;128;137. 7,142. 67,33. (67,8)
Cratfield	Bly	TM 31 74	33,10
Creeting [All Saints, St. Mary, and St. Olave]	Bo	(TM 08 56 (TM 09 56 (TM 09 57	2,10. 6,5. 16,17. 23,2;4. 26,7. 51,2. 74,6. (23,1)
Creeting St. Peter	St	TM 08 57	2,9. 6,3. 8,53. 16,11. 23,1. 32,1. 51,1. (8,52. 51,2)
Cretingham	Ls	TM 22 60	3,47. 4,18. 16,7. 21,98. 31,20. 52,5. (52,8)
Croscroft	Wa	unidentified	4,31
Crowfield	Bo	TM 14 57	16,14. 38,4
'Culeslea'	Wi	(TM 33 43)	6,156
Culford	†BB	TL 83 70	14,70. (14,*53 note*;88)
Culpho	Ca	TM 21 49	8,1;3;5. 32,29
Culuerdestuna, see *Kul-, Kyluertestuna*			
Dagworth	St	TM 04 61	31,43-44;50;52. 41,11
Dalham	R	TL 72 61	25,6
Dallinghoo	Ls	TM 26 54	3,42;48. 6,265;291. 8,26. 21,99;101. 67,32
Darmsden	Bo	TM 09 53	1,71. 3,57. 21,17. 31,57
Darsham	Bly	TM 42 69	1,13. 3,7. 6,78;94–95;101. 7,36;50
Debach	Wi	TM 24 54	3,30. 7,125. 8,19. 16,5. 26,18. 32,10. 34,16. 46,10
Debenham	Cd	TM 17 63	6,11;15–16;18;28;31. 21,31. 34,12. (16,33;48)
Denham	Bi	TM 18 74	1,114. 6,71. 7,4. 19,3
Denham	R	TL 75 61	25,7
Dennington	Bi	TM 28 66	6,303. (6,137;255;257;264; 266–269;*270 note*;289)
Denston	R	TL 76 52	25,4;5a. 65,1
Depden	R	TL 77 56	25,79. 26,9
Derneford	Ca	unidentified	67,17
Desning	R	TL 73 63	25,3. (25,35–36;39–41)
Diss (Norfolk)	H	TM 11 80	1,8. (1,11)
Dodnash	Sa	TM 10 36	3,72
Santon Downham	La	TL 81 87	14,21. 21,8
Drinkstone	Td	TL 95 61	2,1. 14,56. 21,3
Dunningworth	Pl	TM 38 57	7,149
Dunwich	Bly	TM 47 70	6,84;89. 7,6;26. 21,47
Easton	Ls	TM 28 58	6,270. 8,23
Easton Bavents	Bly	TM 51 78	1,10. 68,1;4. (68,3)
Eduinestuna	Sa	unidentified	25,69. 36,14
Eduluestuna	Ca	unidentified	39,14
Edwardstone	Ba	TL 94 42	6,1
[Brent and Monks] Eleigh	Ba	(TL 94 48 (TL 96 47	14,27. 15,5. 16,9. 25,45. 42,1
Ella	Bo	unidentified	29,6
Ellough	Wa	TM 44 86	1,37. 7,44;46
South Elmham [All Saints, St. Cross, St. James, St. Margaret,	Wa	(TM 34 82 (TM 29 84 (TM 32 81	3,105. 6,298. 13,6. 19,14;16. (18,4)

	Map	Grid	Text
South Elmham (cont'd.)			
St. Michael, St. Nicholas,		(TM 31 83	
and St. Peter]	Wa	(TM 34 83	
		(TM 32 82	
		(TM 33 84	
Elmsett	Co	TM 05 46	29,12
Elmswell	*BB	TL 98 63	14,73
Elveden	La	TL 82 79	5,3. 14,20. 25,34. 26,3
Ely (Cambridgeshire)	–	TL 54 80	(25,36)
Eriswell	La	TL 72 78	28,1
Eruestuna	St	unidentified	31,46
Erwarton	Sa	TM 22 34	25,63;68
Ethereg	?Ls	unidentified	4,42
Euston	*BB	TL 89 78	14,98. (68,5)
Exning (formerly Cambridgeshire)	–	TL 62 65	EC1–EC2
Eye	H	TM 14 73	6,191. 76,23. ENf3. (6,71; 204. 18,1)
Eynsford Hundred (Norfolk)	–	–	(56,6)
Facheduna	Bo	unidentified	25,58. 74,2
Great Fakenham	BB	TL 89 76	14,96. 37,1
Little Fakenham	*BB	TL 91 76	14,97
Falkenham	Cn	TM 29 39	7,76;86;98. 39,3
Falkenham, see also Leofstan			
Farley	R	TL 73 53	25,13
Farnham	Pl	TM 36 59	6,50;135. 7,139
Felsham	Td	TL 94 57	14,58
Fenstead	Ba	TL 80 50	43,1
[Great and Little] Finborough	St	(TM 01 57	1,64. 5,4. 21,14. 29,1. 76,1
		(TM 01 54	
'Finesford(a)', 'Finlesford(a)'	Ca	(TM 18 49)	21,70. 29,14. 32,31. 38,24. 41,18
Finningham	H	TM 06 69	6,59;209;231. 14,131;135. 66,15
Flempton	Tg	TL 81 69	14,12
Flixton	Ltl	TM 51 95	1,47;50. 19,21
Flixton	Wa	TM 31 87	19,15;17. 53,5
Flowton	Bo	TM 08 46	7,62. 25,55. 29,4
Fordley	Bly	TM 42 66	6,79;88;106. 7,30;34
Fornham All Saints	Td	TL 83 67	14,9
Fornham St. Genevieve	Td	TL 83 68	14,53
Fornham St. Martin	Tg	TL 85 66	14,50
Foxhall	Ca	TM 22 43	21,60
Framlingham	Ls	TM 28 63	4,42. 6,264; 266;289. 19,11 43,6. (4,12)
Framsden	Cd	TM 20 59	4,1
Freckenham	La	TL 66 71	20,1
Fressingfield	Bi	TM 26 77	6,207 and note
Freston	Sa	TM 17 39	25,76. 27,12
Fritton	Ltl	TG 47 00	1,49;58
Frostenden	Bly	TM 47 81	33,6
Gapton	Ltl	TG 51 05	1,36;55
Gedding	Td	TL 95 58	14,60. 26,2
Gedgrave	Ls	TM 40 48	3,49;51. 6,275;286. 7,132
Gillingham (Norfolk)	–	TM 41 92	1,38
Gisleham	Lt	TM 51 88	4,37. 31,30. (1,23)
Gislingham	H	TM 07 71	1,11;87. 6,194;216;233. 14,44. 31,38. 35,7–8. 66,1 68,5
Great Glemham	Pl	TM 33 61	3,95;102. 6,45;49–51;56. 7,144;151. 8,82. 14,41. 28,6. 45,2
Little Glemham	Pl	TM 34 58	3,96
Glemsford	Ba	TL 83 48	21,10. 34,4
Glevering	Ls	TM 29 57	67,31

	Map	Grid	Text
Gorleston (Norfolk)	Ltl	TG 52 04	1,32;42;54. (1,41)
Grenewic	Ca	unidentified	8,14
Grimston Hall	Cn	TM 26 36	2,20. 7,99
Groton	Ba	TL 95 41	1,99. 14,25. 25,50. 76,2
Grundisburgh	Ca	TM 22 51	4,16. 6,122. 8,2;6. 21,55–56. 32,23. 38,23. 67,10
Gulpher	Cn	TM 30 36	7,81
Guluesteham (IE)	–	–	32,26 *note*
Gusford	Sa	TM 14 42	46,5
'Guthestuna'	Cn	(TM 29 40)	7,89
Hacheston	Ls	TM 31 58	1,94. 3,37. 6,267;283. 14,118
Hadleigh	Co	TM 02 42	15,2
'North Hales', see Covehithe			
Halesworth	Bly	TM 38 77	3,11. 4,13. 7,17
'Halgestou'	Wi	(TM 31 43)	6,176
Hanchet	R	TL 64 45	25,83
Hardwick (Norfolk)	–	TM 22 90	ENf3
Hargrave	Tg	TL 76 60	54,2
Harkstead	Sa	TM 19 35	1,96. 36,13. 46,4. EE1
Harleston	St	TM 03 60	14,36
Harpole	Wi	TM 29 56	3,32;44. 6,251;253;259. 7,124. 21,92;94. 67,22;26
Hartest	Ba	TL 83 52	21,11. 25,48
Hasketon	Ca	TM 25 50	6,118;126. 8,8;12. 21,57. 32,24
Haspley	Ca	(TM 28 41)	14,117. 39,9;13
Hastings (Sussex)	–	TQ 80 09	(31,50)
Hatheburgfelda, Hetheburgafella	Wa	unidentified	4,33. 31,24
Haughley	St	TM 02 62	31,42
Haverhill	R	TL 67 45	14,160. 16,1. 25,82;95;102. 42,2
Hawkedon	R	TL 79 52	8,34. 25,8–9;90;101
Hawstead	Tg	TL 85 59	14,3 *note*;13. 25,30
Castle Hedingham (Essex)	–	TL 78 35	EE5
Helmingham	Cd	TM 19 57	2,12. 4,8. 8,74. 16,25–26. 25,61. 38,18. 52,9
Hemingstone	Bo	TM 14 53	1,7. 3,58. 6,8. 7,68. 8,59–60; 65;67. 16,23. 21,21–22. 56,4. 62,3–4. 67,2. 74,1;5;7. (3,62. 62,6)
Hemley	Cn	TM 28 42	7,91. 8,43. 39,5. 46,6. 47,1. (39,13)
Hemley, see also Leofric			
Hengrave	Tg	TL 82 68	14,8. (14,12)
Henham	Bly	TM 44 78	33,8
Henley	Cd	TM 15 51	6,17. 8,72;79. 21,33. 29,11. 41,14. 62,6
[Great and Little] Henny (Essex)	–	(TL 86 37 (TL 86 38	EE4;EE6
Henstead	Bly	TM 48 86	26,12c
Hepworth	BB	TL 98 74	14,78;79 *note*. 66,7
Herringfleet	Ltl	TM 47 97	1,60
Herringswell	La	TL 71 69	14,18. 25,40. 26,4
Hessett	Td	TL 93 61	12,2. 14,57
Hestley	H	TM 14 68	43,8
Hetheburgafella, see *Hatheburgfella*			
Heveningham	Bly	TM 33 72	7,13;27
Higham	Sa	TM 03 35	5,6. 16,43. 25,75. 38,21. 58,1
Hinderclay	*BB	TM 02 76	14,74
Hintlesham	Sa	TM 08 43	1,118. 3,79;80 *note*
Hinton	Bly	TM 43 72	7,5
Hitcham	Co	TL 98 51	21,42;44. 25,20;106

	Map	Grid	Text
Hobbestuna, see *Hopestuna*			
Holbrook	Sa	TM 17 36	3,68
Hollesley	Wi	TM 35 44	6,148;160. (6,149;154 and note;156–157; 256;294)
Holton	Bly	TM 40 77	6,102. 7,9;23. 13,3
Holton St. Mary	Sa	TM 05 36	32,3
Homersfield	Wa	TM 28 85	18,4. 19,13
Honilega	Ba	unidentified	34,2
Honington	*BB	TL 91 74	14,85
Hoo	Ls	TM 25 59	21,95
Hoo	Wi	TM 29 49	6,158. 21,81
Hopestuna, Hobbestuna	Ca	unidentified	6,117. 32,30
Hopewella, see Aelfric			
Hoppetuna, Opituna	Bly	unidentified	6,100. 7,29
Hopton	*BB	TL 99 79	14,80
Hopton	Ltl	TG 52 00	1,51
Horham	Bi	TM 21 72	6,309;316–317. 14,161. 15 6. 31,4. 64,2. 75,3. (7,4)
Hornes	Lt	unidentified	31,31
Horringer	Tg	TL 82 62	14,2;*17 note*. 25,29
Horswold	Bo	TM 14 56	21,19. 29,9
Houghton	Ba	TL 78 46	43,1
Hoxne	Bi	TM 18 77	18,1. (1,92;114. 6,70;308; 311–313. 8,36–37;42. 14,161. 18,6. 21,45–46. 44,2. 64,3. 75,3;5)
Huggingehale (FB)	–	–	14,*164 note*
'Hundesthoft', -'tuf'	Wi	(TM 32 48)	6,250. 21,82
Hundon	R	TL 73 48	25,2;12
Hunston	*BB	TL 97 68	1,89. 14,95
Huntingfield	Bly	TM 33 74	6,80;82
Icheburna	Wa	unidentified	6,297
Icklingham	La	TL 77 72	1,115. 34,1. 53,1
Ickworth	Tg	TL 81 61	14,10
Ilketshall [St. Andrew, St. John, St. Lawrence, and St. Margaret]	Wa	(TM 37 87 (TM 36 87 (TM 36 86 (TM 34 85	4,20;22–24;26;28;32. 13,7
Ingham	†BB	TL 85 70	8,32. 14,69. (14,64)
Ingoluestuna	Ca	unidentified	21,65. 32,26. 67,18
Ingoluestuna	Pl	unidentified	6,146
Instead	Bi	TM 23 80	75,4
Ipswich	I	TM 16 44	1,116;122a–122d;122f–12: 3,55. 6,4. 16,47. 25,52. 2 31,55. 32,7. 38,3. 39,12. 41,13. 63,1. 74,9. (3,63. 25,60;62. 74,11)
Ipswich, see also Aelfric son of Rolf, Brown, Culling			
Isleton	Ca	TM 21 43	21,66. 32,27
Isteuertona	Cn	unidentified	31,12
Ixworth	BB	TL 93 70	14,100. 66,1;9–10. 75,2
Kaldecotes, see *Caldecota(n)*			
Kalletuna	Co	unidentified	21,64
Kalweton	Sa	TM 24 34	3,78
Kedington	R	TL 70 47	14,158. 25,15;94. 33,1
Keletuna, Cheletuna, Chiletuna	Pl	unidentified	6,42. (6,41;*43 note*;288)
Kelsale	Bi	TM 38 65	6,73. 7,3. (6,69. 7,34–36;7 74;132)
Kembroke	Cn	TM 26 41	7,92;121. 21,52. 67,9
Kenninghall (Norfolk)	–	TM 04 85	ENf1
Kenton	Ls	TM 19 65	6,271. 14,119. 16,8. (6,11)
Kentwell	Ba	TL 86 47	12,5

	Map	Grid	Text
Kersey	Co	TM 00 43	24,1. 25,108
Kesgrave	Ca	TM 21 45	6,114
Kessingland	Lt	TM 52 86	1,31. 4,35. 31,27
Kettlebaston	Co	TL 96 50	14,114
Kettleburgh	Ls	TM 26 60	3,34. 6,261;269. 8,21;22-23 notes. (3,31 and note; 45 note;52 and note;53 note;95)
?Kilverstone (Norfolk), see Kul-, Kyluertestuna			
Kingsland	Ca	TM 23 54	39,11
Kingston	Ca	TM 26 47	21,53. (8,6 note)
Kirkley	Lt	TM 52 91	1,28. 31,33. (1,23)
Kirkton	Sa	TM 23 35	25,67
Kirton	Cn	TM 28 39	7,87;114. 38,26
Kislea	Lt	unidentified	1,25
Knettishall	*BB	TL 97 80	6,208. 14,99. 76,9. ENf1
Knodishall	Bly	TM 42 61	7,21;33;71
Kul-, Kyluertestuna, Culuerdestuna	Cn	?Kilverstone (Norfolk)	7,118. 31,11
Kul-, Kyluertestuna, see also Ordgar, Thuri			
Lackford	Tg	TL 79 70	14,7. (14,12;71)
Lafham	R	unidentified	73,1
Lakenheath	La	TL 71 82	21,6. 25,36. 28,2. (21,7)
'Laneburc', '-burh'	Wi	(TM 32 46)	6,151;173-174
Langer	Cn	TM 28 32	7,100;102
Langham	BB	TL 98 69	14,94. 66,6
Lang(h)edana, -dena	Bo	unidentified	1,68. 7,66. 8,62;64. 29,10. 38,9
Lavenham	Ba	TL 91 49	12,6. 35,1. 76,21
Lawshall	Ba	TL 86 54	17,1
Laxfield	Bi	TM 29 72	6,305
Laxfield, see also Edric			
Layham	Co	TM 03 40	1,109. 14,110. 28,7. 36,15. 49,1. 61,2
Leiston	Bly	TM 43 62	6,83. (6,69-70;106;136)
'Leofstanestuna'	Cn	(TM 25 39)	7,93;106;111
Letheringham	Ls	TM 26 58	8,24. 21,97. 32,14
Levington	Cn	TM 23 39	7,94;117. 31,10
Levington, see also Gleman			
Lewes (Sussex)	–	TQ 41 10	(26,3;5)
Lidgate	R	TL 72 58	54,1. 70,1
Linburne	Wa	TM 28 84	14,121
Lindsey	Co	TL 97 44	14,113. 25,107
Linhou	Ba	unidentified	38,2
Linstead [Magna and Parva]	Bly	(TM 31 76 (TM 33 77	6,81;104. (6,82 note)
Littlecross	Wi	TM 29 46	6,163
Great Livermere	Td	TL 88 71	14,22;68. 21,9. 31,40
Little Livermere	*BB	TL 87 72	14,87
Loes, see Leofstan			
London, see Bernard			
Loose	Co	TM 00 53	34,5. (25,112)
Loudham	Wi	TM 30 54	3,25. 6,188-189;237;247; 257. 7,123;127. 21,91. 22,3. 67,24
Lound	Ltl	TM 50 98	1,34;44;46
Lowestoft	Ltl	TM 55 93	1,33
'Maistana'	Cn	(TM 31 37)	7,79
Maldon (Essex), see Siward			
Manesfort	Sa	unidentified	36,4
Man(e)uuic, Manewic	Cd	unidentified	4,2-3. 6,19. 16,32
Manston	Tg	TL 83 56	14,15. 25,31. 27,2
Manton	Co	TL 97 53	14,114. 34,2

	Map	Grid	Text
Marlesford	Ls	TM 32 58	1,93–94. 3,43. 6,276. 14,
Martlesham	Ca	TM 26 46	39,6
Martley	Ls	TM 28 58	3,35;52. 6,293. 8,28. 67,2
Long Melford	Ba	TL 86 46	14,23
Mellis	H	TM 10 74	6,195;227. 14,140. 35,7
Mells	Bly	TM 40 76	44,3
Melton	Wi	TM 28 50	3,24. 6,175. 8,17. 21,80;
			83 note;93. 32,13
Mendham	Bi	TM 26 82	6,72;313. 8,37;42. 13,1.
			14,106. 19,2
Mendlesham	H	TM 10 65	1,65;76. (1,66;77–80;82;
			87. 8,55. 14,146)
Mendlesham, see also Alwin, Burghard			
Mettingham	Wa	TM 36 89	4,21;23
Mickfield	Bo	TM 13 61	14,38. 34,10
Middleton	Bly	TM 43 67	3,6. 4,15. 6,86. 7,31;39.
			26,13
Milden	Ba	TL 95 46	14,34. 41,10
Mildenhall	La	TL 71 74	1,115. 25,39. ENf5
Minsmere	Bly	TM 46 65	6,107. 7,32
Monewden	Ls	TM 23 58	6,262. 8,20;22;28. 21,104
			46,12
Morston	Cn	TM 25 38	2,17. 7,90;115. 21,48. 39,
Moulton	R	TL 69 64	15,1
Moze (Essex)	–	TM 20 26	(32,7)
Mundham (Norfolk)	–	TM 32 98	ENf4
Mutford	Lt	TM 48 88	1,23;24. (7,46)
Mutford, see also Ulf			
'Mycelegata'	Cn	(TM 26 38)	6,111. 7,110
Nacton	Cn	TM 21 39	31,8;13a. (31,55)
Nayland	Ba	TL 97 34	27,6
Nec(c)hemara, Neckemara	Ca	unidentified	6,113. 32,25. 67,13
Nedging	Co	TL 99 48	21,43
Nettlestead	Bo	TM 08 49	3,56. (3,*59 note*;62. 76,13
Newbourn	Ca	TM 27 43	8,15. 14,117. 39,10. (21,5-
Newton	Ba	TL 91 41	14,32. 43,3
Newton	Cd	TM 19 51	38,16. (38,23–24)
'Newton'	Ltl	(TM 54 98)	1,57
Old Newton	St	TM 05 62	8,50. 16,12. 23,3;5. 31,51.
			(31,35)
Niuetuna	Pa	unidentified	6,32
Nordberia	Pl	unidentified	8,81
Normandy	–	–	(56,1)
Norton	*BB	TL 96 66	1,88. (1,61–64;67;73)
Norton	Cn	TM 25 38	7,84;107;122
Nowton	Tg	TL 86 60	14,4
Oakley	H	TM 15 77	6,65. 7,75. 14,129;137–13
			19,12
Occold	H	TM 15 70	1,82. 6,193;224. 14,144.
			31,60. 43,9. 77,1–2. (31,6
Odiham (Hampshire)	–	SU 74 51	(77,4)
Offton	Bo	TM 06 49	1,69. 7,60. 29,7. 62,1
Offton, see also Durand			
'Olden'	Bo	(TM 12 56)	1,5. 6,7. 8,61. 16,16;21.
			21,23. 23,6. 51,2. 53,2.
			56,3. 74,4
Onehouse	St	TM 01 59	2,7. 14,37. 34,6. 56,1
Opituna, see *Hoppetuna*			
Otley	Ca	TM 20 54	8,11. 38,25. 41,19. 52,1;3;
			(52,9)
Ousden	R	TL 73 59	5,1. 72,1
'Oxelanda'	Cn	(TM 32 36)	7,120

	Map	Grid	Text
Pachetuna	Bo	unidentified	16,19
Pakefield	Lt	TM 53 88	1,27. 4,41. (1,23)
Pakenham	Td	TL 92 67	14,49
Palgrave	H	TM 11 78	14,45
Pannington	Sa	TM 14 40	3,76. 27,10
Parham	Pa	TM 30 60	1,75. 3,88;90. 4,9. 6,32;35. (1,94)
Parham, see Thormod			
Peasenhall	Bly	TM 35 69	6,92;103. 7,10;20;72. (7,12)
Pettaugh	Cd	TM 16 59	16,39. 21,30. 67,3
Peyton	Wi	TM 31 41	27,13
Peyton, see also Godric			
Pileberga	Bo	unidentified	29,3
Playford	Ca	TM 21 48	6,112
'Plumgeard'	Cn	(TM 28 36)	7,85. 21,51
Polstead	Ba	TL 98 38	27,5
Poslingford	R	TL 76 48	14,154. 25,87;98. 33,2
Possefelda	Ls	unidentified	6,277
Potsford	Ls	TM 29 57	67,30
Prestetuna	Pl	unidentified	6,147
Preston	Ba	TL 94 50	8,47. 14,26
Preston	Ca	TM 24 46	8,*1 note*. 39,8
Purtepyt	Sa	unidentified	25,66
Ramsholt	Wi	⌐M 30 42	6,177. 11,3
Rattlesden	Td	ℸL 97 59	2,2. 5,2. 14,61. 21,1-2. 25,26. 26,1
Raydon	Sa	TM 04 38	5,8. 16,37;41. 25,74. 28,5. 32,4;8. 61,1
Rede	Tg	TL 80 55	14,16. 21,4. 25,32. 27,1
Redenhall (Norfolk)	—	TM 26 84	(1,92)
Redgrave	H	TM 05 78	14,42
Redisham	Wa	TM 40 84	7,51
Redles	Co	unidentified	62,7
Redlingfield	H	TM 18 70	6,192
Rendham	Pl	TM 34 64	3,99. 6,43. 7,135;141;146; 148
Rendlesham	Ls	TM 32 52	3,39. 6,268;270;272;281. 7,131. 21,102. 67,29
Reydon	Bly	TM 49 78	33,4
Rickinghall Inferior	*BB	TM 03 75	6,302. 14,75. (14,79)
Rickinghall Superior	H	TM 04 75	6,62. 14,46. 35,7. (14,136 and note)
Rigneseta	Bo	unidentified	25,57
Ringsfield	Wa	TM 40 88	1,16;20. 4,29. 7,41. (1,17)
Ringshall	Bo	TM 04 52	2,11. 7,56. 30,1-2
Ringshall, see also Godric			
Risby	Tg	TL 80 66	8,44. 14,1. (14,12)
Riseburc	?Bly	unidentified	1,12
Rishangles	H	TM 16 68	6,222
Rodeham	St	unidentified	16,13
Rodenhala	Lt	unidentified	4,36. 31,28
Rougham	Td	TL 91 62	14,51. (14,57;67)
Rumburgh	Bly	TM 34 81	ENf2;ENf4. (3,2;105)
Rushbrooke	Co	TL 94 52	14,115. 25,110
Rushbrooke	Td	TL 89 61	14,67
Rushford	†BB	TL 92 81	37,6
Rushmere	Lt	TM 49 87	1,23;26. 4,40. 31,34. (1,24)
Rushmere	Pl	TM 42 59	6,139
Rushmere St. Andrew	Ca	TM 19 46	1,15. 3,17;19. 6,116;125. 8,16. 21,62;69. 67,14. (6,13)
Saibamus	Ba	unidentified	76,5
Sanford, see Aelfric			
Sapiston	BB	TL 92 74	14,83. 37,3. 59,2. 66,5
[Great and Little] Saxham	Tg	(TL 78 62 (TL 79 63	1,63. 14,6;11. 25,28

	Map	Grid	Text
Saxmundham	Pl	TM 38 62	7,70–71;74. (7,20–21)
Saxtead	Bi	TM 26 65	4,12
Seckford	Ca	TM 25 48	16,2
Semer	Co	TL 99 46	14,108
Shadingfield	Wa	TM 43 83	1,112. 7,47;52. 32,16. 33,11
Sharpstone	Cd	(TM 12 51)	1,72. 3,62. 16,24;27. 21,27;9
Shelland	St	TL 99 59	25,51
Shelley	Sa	TM 03 38	1,100;104
Shimpling	Ba	TL 85 51	33,13. 46,1
Shipmeadow	Wa	TM 38 89	4,23;27. 7,48
Shotley	Sa	TM 23 36	1,102–104. 25,64
Shottisham	Wi	TM 32 44	6,167;186;238. 21,73;89
Sibton	Bly	TM 36 69	3,9. 6,90;93
Snape	Pl	TM 39 59	6,129;133
Sogenhoe	Wi	TM 28 52	6,242
Earl Soham	Ls	TM 23 63	3,46. 6,285. 31,59. (3,20;33 and note;48 and note)
Monk Soham	Bi	TM 21 65	14,102. 21,46. 31,3
Somerleyton	Ltl	TM 49 97	1,41;48;52. 69,4
Somersham	Bo	TM 09 48	1,4. 7,59. 29,2. 62,2. 76,13. (29,6)
Somerton	Ba	TL 81 53	14,28;33. 40,2
Sotherton	Bly	TM 44 79	48,1
Sotterley	Wa	TM 45 85	4,30–31
Southwold	Bly	TM 50 76	14,162–163
Stanfelda	Sa	unidentified	5,7. (5,8 note)
Stanningfield	Td	TL 87 56	2,5. 14,66. 33,12
Stansfield	R	TL 78 52	14,155. 25,11;78
Stanstead	Ba	TL 84 49	31,41
Stanton	*BB	TL 96 73	6,301. 14,72. 76,8. (14,78)
Staverton	Ls	TM 35 50	6,260;273;280. (6,31;187; 235)
Sternfield	Pl	TM 39 61	3,97. 6,131;141. 7,138;143
Stoke	I	TM 16 43	21,15
Stoke Ash	H	TM 11 70	1,86. 6,213;220. 14,122;125 146
Stoke by Clare	R	TL 74 43	25,17;97
Stoke by Nayland	Ba	TL 98 36	27,3
Stokerland	Wi	TM 32 48	6,236
Stone Street	Bly	TM 38 82	3,2
Stone Street	Co	TM 01 43	25,112
[Earl and Little] Stonham	Bo	(TM 10 58 (TM 11 60	1,6;66. 3,59. 6,9. 7,64. 8,52; 55;63. 14,39. 16,15;22. 25,54. 34,11. 64,1–2. (7,63. 8,54)
Stonham Aspal	Bo	TM 13 59	38,6–7;19. (38,25)
Stoven	Bly	TM 44 81	7,22. 31,7
West Stow	†BB	TL 81 70	14,71
Stowlangtoft	*BB	TL 95 68	14,77. 25,22
Stowmarket	St	TM 04 58	2,8. (34,6)
Stradbroke	Bi	TM 23 73	6,308. 8,39
Stradishall	R	TL 74 52	25,100
Stratford, see Robert			
Stratford St. Andrew	Pl	TM 35 60	6,48. 45,3
Stratford St. Mary	Sa	TM 05 34	27,9
Stratton	Cn	TM 24 38	6,110. 7,119
Strickland	Bly	TM 38 69	1,14. 6,87;98. 7,35;37
'Struestuna', 'Struustuna'	Cn	(TM 25 40)	7,88;103;105
'Struostuna', see Goda			
Stuston	H	TM 13 77	14,137. 50,1
Stutton	Sa	TM 16 34	3,83. 32,6. 36,2;10
Sudbourne	Pl	TM 41 53	6,143. 21,38. (8,25. 21,37; 82 note)

	Map	Grid	Text
Sudbury	Tg	TL 87 41	1,97. EE2;EE4–EE6
Sutton	Wi	TM 30 46	3,22. 6,149;155;165;170; 178;184;248;252;254. 21,71. 67,21
Sutton, see also Godwin			
Swefling	Pl	TM 34 63	3,100;104. 6,46. 7,147
Swilland	Cd	TM 18 52	41,2
Syleham	Bi	TM 20 78	19,1. 44,2
Tannington	Bi	TM 24 67	6,304
Tattingstone	Sa	TM 13 37	16,46. 36,9;12
Theberton	Bly	TM 43 65	6,109
Thelnetham	*BB	TM 01 78	6,300. 12,1. 14,90
Thetford, see Aethelwy			
Thicchebrom	Wa	unidentified	6,295
Thistleton	Ca	TM 23 52	8,9. 21,58. 67,16
Thorington	Bly	TM 42 74	3,5. 7,38. 26,14. 32,19
Thorington	Sa	TM 01 35	40,6
Thorndon	H	TM 14 69	6,223. 14,128;143
Thorney	St	(TM 05 58)	1,1. 8,51;54. 31,53. 67,1. (1,65. 29,1. 31,44;49)
Thornham Magna	H	TM 10 71	1,81. 6,200;214–215. 14,127; 130;147. 35,7. 62,5
Thornham Parva	H	TM 10 72	6,199;218
Thorpe	Cn	TM 25 37	2,18. 7,104;116
Thorpe	Bly	(TM 34 73)	3,8. 7,16;26
Thorpe	Ca	(TM 27 55)	32,21
Thorpe	Pl	(TM 45 60)	6,136
Thorpe Hall	Cd	TM 20 62	4,6–7. 6,12;21;23;25. 14,40. 21,34
Thorpe Morieux	Co	TL 94 53	8,35. 14,115–116
Ixworth Thorpe	BB	TL 91 72	9,2. 14,91;101. 37,2. 59,1. 75,1
Thorpe, cf. also *Torp, Torpe*			
'Thorstanestuna', see 'Turstanestuna'			
Thrandeston	H	TM 11 76	6,66–67;202;204. 8,30. 14,139;150. 18,6. 19,19. 35,7. 50,2
Thurleston	Cd	TM 15 48	1,122e. 3,64;66. 8,69–70;75. 9,4. 25,60;62. 41,3. 74,8; 12;15
[Great and Little] Thurlow	R	(TL 68 50 (TL 67 51	1,90. 14,156. 25,93;104
'Thurstanestuna', see 'Turstanestuna'			
Thurston	R	TL 79 51	8,33
Thurston	Td	TL 92 65	1,62. 14,54
Timworth	Td	TL 86 69	14,63. 25,25
Toft	Sa	unidentified	16,47. 25,73
Toppesfield	Co	TM 02 41	15,3–4
Torp	Sa	unidentified	25,65
Torpe	St	unidentified	31,47
'Torstanestuna', see 'Turstanestuna'			
Torstuna	St	unidentified	31,49
Tostock	Td	TL 96 63	1,61. 14,65
Trimley [St. Martin, and St. Mary]	Cn	TM 27 37	7,97;112. 21,49. 39,1
Troston	*BB	TL 90 72	14,86
Tuddenham	Ca	TM 19 48	3,18. 6,120. 8,4. 21,63. 38,13; 22. 67,15. (38,15)
Tuddenham	La	TL 73 71	12,4. 25,37. 28,3
Tunstall	Bo	TM 08 49	8,58. 26,6. (8,55)
Tunstall	Pa	TM 36 55	6,36
Turchetlestuna	Sa	unidentified	36,6
'Turstanestuna'	Cn	(TM 28 38)	7,83

	Map	Grid	Text
'Turstanestuna', 'Thor-', 'Thur-', 'Tor-'	Wi	(TM 30 50)	6,153. 11,2. 26,19
Tusemera	H	unidentified	34,17
Ubbeston	Bly	TM 32 72	33,9
'Udeham'	Wi	(TM 30 44)	22,1
Ufford	Wi	TM 29 52	6,239;243;255. 7,127. 14,166. 21,90
Uggeshall	Bly	TM 45 80	4,14. 7,8. 14,164. 68,2. 76,19
Ultuna	St	unidentified	31,48
Ulverston	Cd	TM 14 63	16,29–30;38. 34,13. (34,10; 18)
Undley	La	TL 69 81	21,7
Wadgate	Cn	TM 29 33	7,82;109
[Great and Little] Waldingfield	Ba	(TL 91 43 (TL 92 45	8,48. 14,31. 25,46;49. 34,2. 35,2. 39,16
Waldringfield	Ca	TM 28 44	6,115. 14,117. 39,7
Walpole	Bly	TM 36 74	3,4
Walsham le Willows	BB	TL 99 71	6,299. 14,92. 66,2. (66,13;15)
Walton	Cn	TM 29 39	7,76. 21,50. 31,13. (7,81;122)
Wangford	Bly	TM 46 79	33,7
Wangford	La	TL 75 83	14,19. 21,*5 note;9 note*. 25,41
Wantisden	Pa	TM 36 53	3,86;91. 6,30–31;38;40. 7,137. 8,80. 21,37
Warabetuna, see *Wrabetuna*			
UUarle	Bly	unidentified	13,4
Wattisfield	BB	TM 01 74	4,11. 14,79. 31,2
Wattisham	Co	TM 00 51	25,19. 53,7
Weinhou, see Aelfric			
Weledana	St	unidentified	41,11
[Great and Little] Welnetham	Td	(TL 87 59 (TL 88 60	2,4. 14,62
[Great and Little] Wenham	Sa	(TM 07 38 (TM 08 39	3,67;84. 16,36;40. 40,3–4
Wenhaston	Bly	TM 42 75	3,5
Wenhou, see Aelfric			
Westerfield	Cd	TM 17 47	3,61;63–64. 6,13;24. 8,73;76. 21,29. 31,58. 32,2. 38,12;14. 14,4;6. 74,11;14
Westhorpe	H	TM 04 69	6,58;60;210. 14,132;142. 37,7. 41,9. 53,6. 66,14. (6,*59 note*)
Westleton	Bly	TM 44 69	6,85;96;105. 66,12
Westley	Tg	TL 82 64	14,17. 25,27
Weston	Wa	TM 42 87	1,18;21;113. 7,43;49. 31,22. 32,17. (7,53)
Weston Colville (Cambridgeshire)	—	TL 61 53	(3,1)
Market Weston	*BB	TL 99 78	9,2. 14,84. 60,1
Wetherden	St	TM 00 62	14,35. 31,45. 41,12
Wetheringsett	H	TM 12 66	1,80. 6,234. 14,124;153. 21,39
Weybread	Bi	TM 24 80	1,92. 6,312;314–315. 8,37–38;41. 14,107. 18,2
Whatfield	Co	TM 02 46	2,15. 7,2. 14,111–112. 25,111. 29,13. 34,14. 40,5. 66,11
Whepstead	Tg	TL 83 58	14,3
Wherstead	Sa	TM 16 40	3,70;77. 27,11
Whittingham	Bi	TM 27 78	8,36
Whitton	Cd	TM 13 47	74,13
Wichedis	Wa	unidentified	32,18
Wickham Market	Wi	TM 30 55	3,29. 6,241;251. 7,130. 16,4. 22,2 *note*. 32,12. 67,20
Wickham Skeith	H	TM 09 69	1,78;85. 6,230. 8,31. 14,126; 152

	Map	Grid	Text
Wickhambrook	R	TL 75 54	25,99
Wilby	Bi	TM 24 72	6,310. 18,3. 19,5;7
Wilford	Wi	TM 29 50	6,171;256. 7,128
Willingham	Wa	TM 45 86	1,37. 7,42. 31,21;23. (7,43)
Willisham	Bo	TM 07 50	8,56
UUilmundestun (FB)	—	unidentified	14,*16 note*
Wimundahala	Lt	unidentified	7,53. 31,29
Wimundestuna	R	unidentified	14,*16 note*. 25,18;105
Wingfield	Bi	TM 22 76	6,308. 19,8. 21,45
Winston	Cd	TM 18 61	4,4–5. 6,14. 16,33. 21,28
Wissett	Bly	TM 36 79	3,10;*13 note*;14. 76,17.
			(3,16)
Withermarsh	Ba	TM 00 37	27,4
Withersdale	Bi	TM 28 80	(6,104)
Withersfield	R	TL 65 47	25,84;96. 26,10
Witnesham	Ca	TM 17 50	41,17
Wixoe	R	TL 71 42	33,3
Woodbridge	Ls	TM 27 49	3,45. 6,263;287;294. 7,134.
			8,27. 21,100;103. 32,15.
			38,27
Woolpit	Td	TL 97 62	14,55
Woolverstone	Sa	TM 18 38	3,74. 36,8
Wordwell	*BB	TL 82 72	14,88
Worlingham	Wa	TM 44 89	1,19;22. 4,34. 14,121. 31,25
Worlington	La	TL 69 73	12,3
Worlingworth	Bi	TM 23 68	14,103
Wortham	H	TM 08 77	6,197;219. 11,4. 14,43. 35,7.
			(11,5)
Wrabetuna, Warabetuna,	Bly	unidentified	3,15. 6,91;99;108. 7,11;28
UUrab(r)etuna, Wrabbatuna			
[Great and Little] Wratting	R	(TL 68 48	14,159. 25,10;81;85
		(TL 69 47	
Wrentham	Bly	TM 48 82	26,12
Wrentham, see also Thorkell			
Wyken	†BB	TL 96 71	37,5. 66,4;8
Wyverstone	H	TM 04 67	1,83. 6,57;211. 14,123;134;
			151. 31,36. 57,1. 66,16
Yarmouth (Norfolk)	—	TG 52 07	(1,32. 14,162)
Yaxley	H	TM 12 73	6,196;229. 18,6;19
Yoxford	Bly	TM 39 68	7,18. 44,4

Places not named

7,78. 25,70. 36,15;17. 38,15. EE3

Places not in Suffolk

References are to entries in the Indices of Persons and Places. The names of Churches and Clergy are starred.

Elsewhere in Britain

CAMBRIDGESHIRE ... Chatteris*. Ely*, and Places Index. Exning. ?Sheriff, see Picot. Weston Colville. ESSEX ... Ardleigh. Brightlingsea. Castle Hedingham. Great and Little Henny. Maldon, see Siward. Moze. Sheriff, see Peter of Valognes, Robert son of Wymarc, Swein of Essex. HAMPSHIRE ... Odiham. Winchester*. HERTFORDSHIRE ... Sheriff, see Peter of Valognes. HUNTINGDONSHIRE ... Ramsey*. KENT ... Canterbury*. Rochester*. LONDON ... see Bernard. NORFOLK ... Alburgh. Billingford. Diss. Eynsford Hundred. Gillingham. Gorleston. Hardwick. Kenninghall. ?Kilverstone. Mundham. Redenhall. Thetford*, and see Aethelwy. Yarmouth. SUSSEX ... Hastings. Lewes.

Outside Britain

More precise details as to location are given in the Notes.

Abenon ... Roger. Alençon ... Bernard. Alno ... William. Arques ... William. Auberville ... Roger, William. Aumâle ... Countess. Bayeux*. Beaufour ... Ralph. Belefol ... Miles. Bernai* Berry ... Hervey. Beuvrière ... Drogo. Bosc ... William. Bourges ... Hervey. Bourneville ... William. Bouville ... Saxwalo, William. Brittany ... Count Alan, Fulcher the Breton, Hubert the Breton, Reginald the Breton. Caen ... Walter, William. Candos ... Roger. Claville ... Robert. Coleville ... Gilbert. Corbon ... Hugh. Courbepine ... Ralph. Courson ... Robert. Coutances*. Dol ... Walter. Douai ... Walter. Ecouis ... William. Emalleville ... William. Evreux*. Ferrers ... Hermer. Fougeres ... Ralph. Glanville ... Robert. Grandmesnil ... Hugh. Grestain*. Hellean ... Tihel. Houdain ... Hugh, see also final entry in Persons Index. Lanquetot ... Ralph. Limesy ... Ralph. Loges ... Bigot. Mandeville ... Geoffrey. Marcy ... Ralph. Mesnieres ... Fulcher. Mont-Canisy ... Hubert. Montfort ... Hugh. More ... W. Mortain ... Count Robert. Moutiers ... Lisois. Normandy ... 56,1. Noyers ... William. Orbec ... Roger. Palluel ... Peter. Parthenay ... William. Pierrepont ... Godfrey, Robert. Poitou ... Roger. Poix ... Werno. Port ... Hubert. Rames ... Roger. Risboil, Risbou ... Walter. St. Bertin's ... Humphrey. Saint-Clair ... Hamo, Richard. St. Germain ... Roger. St. Lo. St. Ouen ... Bernard. St. Valery ... Walter. Savenay ... Ralph. Tosny ... Robert. Tourleville ... Ralph. Valognes ... Hamo, Peter. Vatteville ... William Vaux ... Robert. Vere ... Aubrey. Vernon ... Huard. ?Wader ... Ralph. Wanchy ... Hugh, Osbern. Warenne ... William. Wissant ... Gilbert.

MAPS AND MAP KEYS

The County Boundary is marked by thick lines, dotted for the modern boundary; Hundred boundaries are marked by thin lines, broken where uncertain.

The letters of National Grid 10-kilometre squares are shown on the map border. Each four-figure square covers one square kilometre (5/8ths of a square mile).

SUFFOLK HUNDREDS AND HALF-HUNDREDS (WEST)

Babergh (Ba)
20 Acton
29 Assington
27 Ayeley
8 Boxted
18 Brandeston
33 Bures
16 Cavendish
4 Chadacre
22 Chilton
2 Cockfield
28 Coddenham
   Coresfella
26 Great and Little Cornard
23 Edwardstone
13 Brent and Monks Eleigh
7 Fenstead
12 Glemsford
25 Groton
5 Hartest
   Honilega
15 Houghton
14 Kentwell
11 Lavenham
1 Lawshall
   Linhou
17 Long Melford
19 Milden
34 Nayland
24 Newton
30 Polstead
9 Preston
   Saibamus
6 Shimpling
3 Somerton
10 Stanstead
32 Stoke by Nayland
21 Great and Little
   Waldingfield
31 Withermarsh

Blackbourn and Bradmere
(BB: in both Hundreds.
*BB: in Blackbourn.
†BB: in Bradmere)
33 Great Ashfield
18 *Bardwell
3 Barnham
11 Barningham
8 *Coney Weston
27 †Culford
35 *Elmswell

5 *Euston
9 Great Fakenham
10 *Little Fakenham
16 Hepworth
12 *Hinderclay
14 *Honington
4 *Hopton
32 *Hunston
28 †Ingham
29 Ixworth
2 *Knettishall
30 Langham
21 *Little Livermere
34 *Norton
13 *Rickinghall Inferior
1 †Rushford
15 Sapiston
19 *Stanton
26 †West Stow
31 *Stowlangtoft
7 *Thelnetham
23 Ixworth Thorpe
22 *Troston
25 Walsham le Willows
17 Wattisfield
6 *Market Weston
20 *Wordwell
24 †Wyken

Bury (B)
B Bury St. Edmund's

Cosford (Co)
17 Aldham
13 Ash Street
9 Bildeston
2 Brettenham
11 Chelsworth
15 Elmsett
20 Hadleigh
6 Hitcham
   Kalletuna
18 Kersey
8 Kettlebaston
22 Layham
16 Lindsey
4 Loose
3 Manton
10 Nedging
   Redles
5 Rushbrooke
12 Semer

19 Stone Street
1 Thorpe Morieux
21 Toppesfield
7 Wattisham
14 Whatfield

Lackford (La)
12 Barton Mills
2 Brandon
6 Cavenham
9 Chamberlain's Hall
1 Santon Downham
7 Elveden
8 Eriswell
15 Freckenham
16 Herringswell
13 Icklingham
4 Lakenheath
10 Mildenhall
14 Tuddenham
5 Undley
3 Wangford
11 Worlington

Risbridge (R)
7 Badmondisfield
31 Boyton
13 Great and Little Bradley
27 Brockley
8 Chedburgh
22 Chilbourne
30 Clare
12 Clopton
10 Cowlinge
3 Dalham
4 Denham
16 Denston
9 Depden
2 Desning
14 Farley
28 Hanchet
29 Haverhill
18 Hawkedon
23 Hundon
26 Kedington
   Lafham
6 Lidgate
1 Moulton
5 Ousden
24 Poslingford
17 Stansfield
32 Stoke by Clare
15 Stradishall

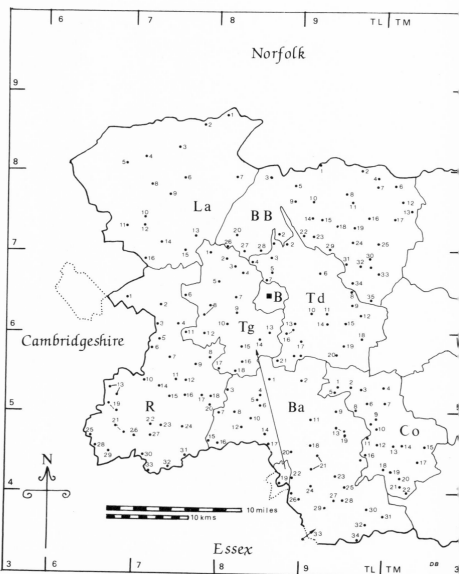

Norfolk

Cambridgeshire

Essex

N

10 miles
10 kms

HUNDREDS AND HALF-HUNDREDS (WEST)

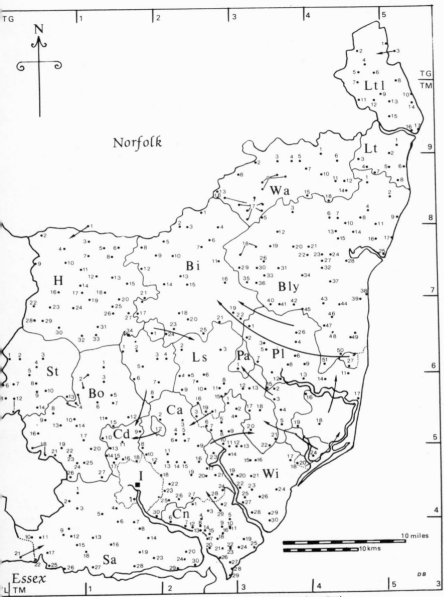

HUNDREDS AND HALF-HUNDREDS (EAST)

19 Great and Little Thurlow
20 Thurston
11 Wickhambrook
Wimundestuna
25 Withersfield
33 Wixoe
21 Great and Little Wratting

Thedwestry (Td)
1 Ampton
5 Great Barton
11 Beyton
17 Bradfield Combust,
 St. Clare, and St. George
15 Drinkstone
20 Felsham
4 Fornham St. Genevieve
7 Fornham St. Martin

19 Gedding
14 Hessett
2 Great Livermere
6 Pakenham
18 Rattlesden
10 Rougham
13 Rushbrooke
21 Stanningfield
8 Thurston
3 Timworth
9 Tostock
16 Great and Little Welnetham
12 Woolpit

Thingoe (Tg)
6 Barrow
18 Brockley

12 Chevington
2 Flempton
4 Fornham All Saints
11 Hargrave
14 Hawstead
3 Hengrave
9 Horringer
10 Ickworth
1 Lackford
16 Manston
13 Nowton
17 Rede
5 Risby
8 Great and Little Saxham
19 Sudbury
7 Westley
15 Whepstead

SUFFOLK HUNDREDS AND HALF-HUNDREDS (EAST)

Bishop's (Bi)
27 Aldringham
19 Badingham
23 Bedfield
17 Bedingfield
9 Chickering
11 Chippenhall
22 Colston
12 Denham
21 Dennington
7 Fressingfield
14 Horham
8 Hoxne
2 Instead
26 Kelsale
16 Laxfield
1 Mendham
25 Saxtead
24 Monk Soham
13 Stradbroke
5 Syleham
20 Tannington
3 Weybread
6 Whittingham
15 Wilby
10 Wingfield
4 Withersdale
18 Worlingworth

Blything (Bly)
Alneterne
2 Benacre
23 Blyford
28 Blythburgh
34 Bramfield
6 Brampton
39 Bridge
24 Bulcamp
19 Chediston
26 Cookley
11 South Cove
9 Covehithe

29 Cratfield
43 Darsham
38 Dunwich
17 Easton Bavents
47 Fordley
8 Frostenden
20 Halesworth
15 Henham
1 Henstead
36 Heveningham
37 Hinton
21 Holton
Hoppetuna, Opituna
30 Huntingfield
51 Knodishall
50 Leiston
18 Linstead Magna and Parva
22 Mells
46 Middleton
49 Minsmere
40 Peasenhall
16 Reydon
?Riseburc
5 Rumburgh
41 Sibton
13 Sotherton
25 Southwold
3 Stone Street
7 Stoven
42 Strickland
48 Theberton
32 Thorington
33 'Thorpe'
35 Ubbeston
10 Uggeshall
31 Walpole
14 Wangford
UUarle
27 Wenhaston
44 Westleton
12 Wissett

Wrabetuna, Warabetuna
 UUrab(r)etuna,
 Wrabbatuna
4 Wrentham
45 Yoxford

Bosmere (Bo)
12 Ashbocking
8 Badley
13 Barking
9 Battisford
17 Baylham
20 Great Blakenham
25 Little Blakenham
10 Bosmere
27 Bramford
18 Great and Little Bricett
Bricticeshaga
11 Coddenham
4 Creeting All Saints,
 St. Mary, and St. Olave
5 Crowfield
14 Darmsden
Ella
Facheduna
26 Flowton
15 Hemingstone
7 Horswold
Lang(h)edana, -dena
1 Mickfield
21 Nettlestead
23 Offton
6 'Olden'
Pachetuna
Pileberga
Rigneseta
16 Ringshall
24 Somersham
2 Earl and Little Stonham
3 Stonham Aspal
22 Tunstall
19 Willisham

Carlford (Ca)
30 Alnesbourn
   Aluredestuna
21 Barkestone
15 Great Bealings
14 Little Bealings
23 Bixley
27 Brightwell
7 Burgh
4 Clopton
11 Culpho
   Derneford
   Eduluestuna
10 'Finesford(a)',
   'Finlesford(a)'
26 Foxhall
   Grenewic
6 Grundisburgh
9 Hasketon
29 Haspley
   Hopestuna, Hobbestuna
   Ingoluestuna
25 Isleton
22 Kesgrave
3 Kingsland
17 Kingston
20 Martlesham
   Nec(c)hemara, Neckemara
28 Newbourn
2 Otley
13 Playford
19 Preston
18 Rushmere St. Andrew
16 Seckford
5 Thistleton
1 'Thorpe'
12 Tuddenham
24 Waldringfield
8 Witnesham

Claydon (Cd)
15 Akenham
4 Ashfield
13 Barham
   Bermesdena
   Bruntuna
14 Claydon
2 Debenham
7 Framsden
8 Helmingham
10 Henley
   Man(e)uuic, Manewic
11 Newton
6 Pettaugh
12 Sharpstone
9 Swilland
3 Thorpe Hall
16 Thurleston
1 Ulverston
17 Westerfield
18 Whitton
5 Winston

Colneis (Cn)
26 'Alston'
   Brihtoluestuna
1 Bucklesham
22 Burgate
27 Burgh
23 Candlet
10 Falkenham
20 Grimston Hall
24 Gulpher
5 'Guthestuna'
2 Hemley
   Isteuertona
3 Kembroke
9 Kirton
   Kul-, Kyluertestuna,
   Culuerdestuna
29 Langer
8 'Leofstanestuna'
7 Levington
19 'Maistana'
14 Morston
15 'Mycelegata'
6 Nacton
13 Norton
25 'Oxelanda'
21 'Plumgeard'
12 Stratton
4 'Struestuna', 'Struustuna'
17 Thorpe
18 Trimley St. Martin and
   St. Mary
16 'Turstanestuna'
28 Wadgate
11 Walton

Hartismere (H)
34 Aspall
29 Bacton
18 Braiseworth
33 Brockford
8 Brome
10 Burgate
   Caldecota(n), -coten,
   Kaldecotes
30 Cotton
15 Cranley
1 Diss (Norfolk)
13 Eye
23 Finningham
16 Gislingham
26 Hestley
11 Mellis
32 Mendlesham
6 Oakley
20 Occold
3 Palgrave
2 Redgrave
21 Redlingfield
9 Rickinghall Superior
27 Rishangles
19 Stoke Ash
5 Stuston

25 Thorndon
17 Thornham Magna
14 Thornham Parva
7 Thrandeston
   Tusemera
22 Westhorpe
31 Wetheringsett
24 Wickham Skeith
4 Wortham
28 Wyverstone
12 Yaxley

Ipswich (I)
I Ipswich
1 Stoke

Loes (Ls)
18 Ash
5 Brandeston
   Brodertuna
21 Butley
17 Campsey Ash
16 Charsfield
   Clachestorp
4 Cretingham
19 Dallinghoo
11 Easton
   ?*Ethereg*
3 Framlingham
24 Gedgrave
14 Glevering
12 Hacheston
7 Hoo
1 Kenton
6 Kettleburgh
10 Letheringham
13 Marlesford
8 Martley
9 Monewdon
   Possefelda
15 Potsford
20 Rendlesham
2 Earl Soham
22 Staverton
23 Woodbridge

Lothing (Lt)
3 Barnby
   Beketuna, Bechetuna
2 Carlton Colville
5 Gisleham
   Hornes
8 Kessingland
1 Kirkley
   Kislea
4 Mutford
6 Pakefield
   Rodenhala
7 Rushmere
   Wimundahala

Lothingland (Ltl)
16 Akethorpe
4 Belton
13 Blundeston
6 Browston
2 Burgh Castle
5 Caldecott
14 Corton
15 Flixton
7 Fritton
1 Gapton
3 Gorleston (Norfolk)
11 Herringfleet
8 Hopton
9 Lound
17 Lowestoft
10 'Newton'
12 Somerleyton

Parham (Pa)
2 Beversham
3 Blaxhall
Brutge
Niuetuna
1 Parham
4 Tunstall
5 Wantisden

Plomesgate (Pl)
17 Aldeburgh
Becclinga
8 Benhall
20 Boyton
1 Bruisyard
Burch
Burgesgata
4 Carlton
19 Chillesford
Cle'pham
2 Cransford
16 Dunningworth
12 Farnham
7 Great Glemham
15 Little Glemham
Ingoluestuna
Keletuna, Cheletuna,
Chiletuna
Nordberia
Prestetuna
3 Rendham
14 Rushmere
6 Saxmundham
13 Snape
9 Sternfield
10 Stratford St. Andrew
18 Sudbourne
5 Swefling
11 'Thorpe'

Samford (Sa)
Alfildestuna
Belenei
5 Belstead
13 Bentley
26 East Bergholt
Beria
15 Boynton
27 Brantham
1 Burstall
Canap(p)etuna,
Canepetuna
3 Chattisham
12 Churchford
18 Dodnash
Eduinestuna
29 Erwarton
8 Freston
4 Gusford
23 Harkstead
22 Higham
2 Hintlesham
19 Holbrook
17 Holton St. Mary
30 Kalweton
24 Kirkton
Manesfort
6 Pannington
Purtepyt
11 Raydon
10 Shelley
20 Shotley
Stanfelda
25 Stratford St. Mary
28 Stutton
16 Tattingstone
21 Thorington
Toft
Torp
Turchetlestuna
9 Great and Little Wenham
7 Wherstead
14 Woolverstone

Stow (St)
11 Buxhall
8 Chilton
14 Combs
13 Creeting St. Peter
4 Dagworth
Eruestuna
12 Great and Little Finborough
5 Harleston
2 Haughley
3 Old Newton
7 Onehouse
Rodeham
6 Shelland
9 Stowmarket
10 Thorney
Torpe
Torstuna
Ultuna
Weledana
1 Wetherden

Wangford (Wa)
5 Barsham
1 Beccles
2 Bungay
Catesfella
Croscroft
11 Ellough
17 South Elmham All Sain
   St. Cross, St. James,
   St. Margaret, St. Mich
   St. Nicholas, and St. I
8 Flixton
Hatheburgfelda, Hetheb
13 Homersfield
Icheburna
9 Ilketshall St. Andrew,
   St. John, St. Lawrenc
   and St. Margaret
15 Linburne
3 Mettingham
16 Redisham
7 Ringsfield
18 Shadingfield
4 Shipmeadow
14 Sotterley
Thicchebrom
10 Weston
Wichedis
12 Willingham
6 Worlingham

Wilford (Wi)
29 Alderton
30 Bawdsey
5 Bing
6 Boulge
18 Boyton
7 Bredfield
12 Bromeswell
17 Capel St. Andrew
26 'Culeslea'
3 Debach
25 'Halgestou'
1 Harpole
24 Hollesley
14 Hoo
15 'Hundesthoft' -'tuf'
21 'Laneburc', -'burh'
19 Littlecross
4 Loudham
10 Melton
28 Peyton
27 Ramsholt
23 Shottisham
8 Sogenhoe
16 Stokerland
20 Sutton
13 'Turstanestuna', 'Thor-',
   'Thur-', 'Tor-'
22 'Udeham'
9 Ufford
2 Wickham Market
11 Wilford

SYSTEMS OF REFERENCE TO THE TWO VOLUMES OF DOMESDAY BOOK

The manuscript of the larger volume (here referred to as DB) is divided into numbered chapters, and the chapters into sections, usually marked by large initials and red ink. Farley did not number the sections and later historians, using his edition, have referred to the text of DB by folio numbers, which cannot be closer than an entire page or column. Moreover, several different ways of referring to the same column have been devised. In 1816 Ellis used three separate systems in his indices: (i) on pages i–cvii, 435–518, 537–570; (ii) on pages 1–144; (iii) on pages 145–433 and 519–535. Other systems have since come into use, notably that used by Vinogradoff, here followed. The present edition numbers the sections, the normal practicable form of close reference; but since all discussion of DB for two hundred years has been obliged to refer to folio or column, a comparative table will help to locate references given. The five columns below give Vinogradoff's notation, Ellis's three systems, and that used by Welldon Finn and others. Maitland, Stenton, Darby, and others have usually followed Ellis (i).

Vinogradoff	Ellis (i)	Ellis (ii)	Ellis (iii)	Finn
152a	152	152a	152	152ai
152b	152	152a	152.2	152a2
152c	152b	152b	152b	152bi
152d	152b	152b	152b2	152b2

The manuscript of Little Domesday Book (here referred to as LDB), in which the text of the Suffolk survey is preserved, has one column per page but is again divided into numbered chapters and the chapters into sections, usually distinguished by paragraph-marks. Modern users of LDB have referred to its text by folio number, e.g. 152(a) 152b. Farley's edition presents both *recto* and *verso* of a folio on one printed page. In Suffolk, the relation between the column notation and the chapters and sections is:

281a	Landholders			308a,b	6,44	– 6,52	338a,b	7,65	– 7,72
b	1,1	– 1,5		309a,b	6,52	– 6,62	339a,b	7,72	– 7,79
282a,b	1,5	– 1,20		310a,b	6,62	– 6,79	340a,b	7,79	– 7,92
283a,b	1,20	– 1,47		311a,b	6,79	– 6,84	341a,b	7,92	– 7,105
284a,b	1,47	– 1,62		312a,b	6,84	– 6,92	342a,b	7,105	– 7,119
285a,b	1,63	– 1,82		313a,b	6,92	– 6,100	343a,b	7,119	– 7,133
286a,b	1,82	– 1,98		314a,b	6,101	– 6,112	344a,b	7,133	– 7,143
287a,b	1,98	– 1,106		315a,b	6,112	– 6,127	345a,b	7,143	– 7,151
288a,b	1,107	– 1,115		316a,b	6,128	– 6,143	346a,b	8,1	– 8,9
289a,b	1,115	– 1,121		317a,b	6,143	– 6,162	347a,b	8,9	– 8,23
290a,b	1,121	– 1,122g		318a,b	6,162	– 6,177	348a,b	8,23	– 8,35
291a,b	2,1	– 2,13		319a,b	6,177	– 6,191	349a,b	8,35	– 8,46
292a	2,14	– 2,20		320a,b	6,191	– 6,202	350a,b	8,46	– 8,55
292b	Landholders			321a,b	6,202	– 6,214	351a,b	8,55	– 8,59
292b	3,1	3,9		322a,b	6,215	– 6,221	352a,b	8,59	– 8,78
293a,b	3,9	– 3,39		323a,b	6,221	– 6,232	353a,b	8,78	– 9,3
294a,b	3,39	– 3,61		324a,b	6,232	– 6,251	354a,b	9,3	– 12,1
295a,b	3,61	– 3,79		325a,b	6,251	– 6,267	355a,b	12,1	– 13,3
296a,b	3,79	– 3,94		326a,b	6,267	– 6,283	356a,b	13,3	– 14,3
297a,b	3,94	– 3,101		327a,b	6,283	– 6,301	357a,b	14,3	– 14,12
298a,b	3,101	– 4,6		328a,b	6,301	– 6,308	358a,b	14,12	– 14,20
299a,b	4,6	– 4,15		329a,b	6,308	– 6,317	359a,b	14,21	– 14,28
300a,b	4,16	– 4,22		330a,b	6,317	– 7,3	360a,b	14,28	– 14,42
301a,b	4,22	– 4,35		331a,b	7,3	– 7,10	361a,b	14,42	– 14,50
302a,b	4,35	– 4,42		332a,b	7,10	– 7,15	362a,b	14,50	– 14,59
303a,b	5,1	– 5,8		333a,b	7,16	– 7,26	363a,b	14,59	– 14,68
304a,b	6,1	– 6,8		334a,b	7,26	– 7,37	364a,b	14,69	– 14,75
305a,b	6,8	– 6,19		335a,b	7,37	– 7,49	365a,b	14,75	– 14,81
306a,b	6,20	– 6,32		336a,b	7,49	– 7,58	366a,b	14,81	– 14,90
307a,b	6,33	– 6,44		337a,b	7,58	– 7,65			

367a,b	14,90	—	14,101	394a,b	25,57	—	25,66	423a,b	38,12	—	3
368a,b	14,102	—	14,110	395a,b	25,66	—	25,78	424a,b	39,3	—	3
369a,b	14,111	—	14,120	396a,b	25,78	—	25,92	425a,b	39,10	—	4
370a,b	14,120	—	14,138	397a,b	25,93	—	25,112	426a,b	40,4	—	4
371a,b	14,138	—	14,166	398a,b	26,1	—	26,10	427a,b	41,10	—	4
372a	14,167			399a,b	26,10	—	26,12d	428a,b	42,2	—	4
	Landholders			400a,b	26,12d	—	26,20	429a,b	43,5	—	4
372b	15,1	—	15,4	401a,b	27,1	—	27,7	430a,b	45,1	—	4
373a,b	15,5	—	16,10	402a,b	27,7	—	28,1b	431a,b	46,4	—	4
374a,b	16,10	—	16,17	403a,b	28,1b	—	29,1	432a,b	48,1	—	5
375a,b	16,17	—	16,25	404a,b	29,1	—	29,11	433a,b	52,1	—	5
376a,b	16,25	—	16,31	405a,b	29,12	—	31,3	434a,b	52,10	—	5
377a,b	16,32	—	16,40	406a,b	31,3	—	31,20	435a,b	53,6	—	5
378a,b	16,40	—	17,1	407a,b	31,20	—	31,34	436a,b	56,1	—	5
379a,b	18,1	—	19,10	408a,b	31,35	—	31,44	437a,b	59,2	—	6
380a,b	19,11	—	19,18	409a,b	31,44	—	31,53	438a,b	62,6	—	6
381a,b	19,18	—	21,5	410a,b	31,53	—	31,60	439a,b	66,1	—	6
382a,b	21,5	—	21,16	411a,b	32,1	—	32,11	440a,b	66,10	—	6
383a,b	21,16	—	21,29	412a,b	32,11	—	32,23	441a,b	67,3	—	6
384a,b	21,29	—	21,42	413a,b	32,23	—	33,2	442a,b	67,11	—	6
385a,b	21,42	—	21,52	414a,b	33,2	—	33,8	443a,b	67,19	—	6
386a,b	21,53	—	21,69	415a,b	33,8	—	33,13	444a,b	67,30	—	68
387a,b	21,69	—	21,86	416a,b	34,1	—	34,6	445a,b	69,1	—	7
388a,b	21,87	—	22,3	417a,b	34,6	—	34,16	446a,b	74,1	—	74
389a,b	23,1	—	25,2	418a,b	34,16	—	35,5	447a,b	74,16	—	76
390a,b	25,2	—	25,17	419a,b	35,5	—	36,4	448a,b	76,3	—	76
391a,b	25,17	—	25,35	420a,b	36,5	—	37,1	449a,b	76,16	—	76
392a,b	25,35	—	25,52	421a,b	37,1	—	38,4	450a	77,1-4		
393a,b	25,52	—	25,57	422a,b	38,5	—	38,12		Colophon		